The Greenwood Encyclopedia of
African American Civil Rights

The Greenwood Encyclopedia of African American Civil Rights

From Emancipation to the
Twenty-First Century
Volume I
A–R

CHARLES D. LOWERY AND
JOHN F. MARSZALEK, EDITORS
THOMAS ADAMS UPCHURCH, ASSOCIATE EDITOR

FOREWORD BY DAVID J. GARROW

Greenwood Press

Westport, Connecticut • London

Library of Congress Cataloging-in-Publication Data

The Greenwood encyclopedia of African American civil rights : from emancipation to the twenty-first century / Charles D. Lowery and John F. Marszalek, editors ; Thomas Adams Upchurch, associate editor ; foreword by David J. Garrow.—2nd ed.

    p. cm.

    Rev. ed. of: Encyclopedia of African-American civil rights. New York : Greenwood Press, 1992.

    Includes bibliographical references and index.

    ISBN 0–313–32171–X (set : alk. paper)—ISBN 0–313–32766–1 (v. 1 : alk. paper)—ISBN 0–313–32767–X (v. 2 : alk. paper)

    1. African Americans—Civil rights—History—Encyclopedias. 2. Civil rights movements—United States—History—Encyclopedias. 3. United States—Race relations—Encyclopedias. I. Lowery, Charles D., 1937– II. Marszalek, John F., 1939– III. Upchurch, Thomas Adams. IV. Encyclopedia of African-American civil rights.
E185.61.E54   2003
323.1′196073′003—dc21   2003040837

British Library Cataloguing in Publication Data is available.

Library of Congress Catalog Card Number: 2003040837
ISBN: 0–313–32171–X (set code)
         0–313–32766–1 (Vol. I)
         0–313–32767–X (Vol. II)

First published in 2003

Greenwood Press, 88 Post Road West, Westport, CT 06881
An imprint of Greenwood Publishing Group, Inc.
www.greenwood.com

Printed in the United States of America

The paper used in this book complies with the Permanent Paper Standard issued by the National Information Standards Organization (Z39.48–1984).

10 9 8 7 6 5 4 3 2 1

In Memory of Those Who Died
So Others Might Be Free

CONTENTS

FOREWORD TO THE SECOND EDITION

David J. Garrow

The updating and expansion of this wonderfully rich research aid is a most welcome event. Ten years ago, reviewing the original manuscript for this volume, I was deeply impressed with how many leads for more extensive future research a large number of these short essays called to mind.

Disappointingly, however, this past decade has unfortunately not witnessed anywhere near as much of a progression in African American civil rights and freedom struggle historiography as there ideally should have been. A number of landmark volumes have appeared, such as Charles Payne's *I've Got the Light of Freedom* (1995) on Mississippi and Adam Fairclough's *Race and Democracy* (1995) on Louisiana, but the overall breadth and scale of "movement" scholarship still falls far short of what one might optimistically have imagined 15 or 20 years ago. When one looks at the tremendous explosions of scholarly energy that in recent years have marked the fields of labor history, women's history, and gay and lesbian history, black freedom struggle scholarship is still waiting for a similar burst of activity. Younger scholars such as Timothy Minchin (*Hiring the Black Worker*, 1999 and *The Color of Work*, 2001) are showing just how many available avenues there are for creatively original research, but presently there are not as many young scholars proceeding down these paths as there should be. That need is all the more pressing as the ongoing passage of time gets to the point where more and more surviving veterans of 1950s and 1960s activism reach the ages where their future time with us threatens to draw to a close.

Undergraduate or graduate students perusing this volume should keep those thoughts in mind, for an expanded pipeline of younger people who are interested in preserving and telling the movement's story in all of the multifaceted local richness that it merits is crucial if freedom struggle historiography is to grow. The range of contributions to this encyclopedia suggests just how many possible paths there are, many of them in areas that are more "cultural" than the political and economic developments that are oftentimes most intriguing to those of us who are traditional historians. And while many topics from the 1950s and 1960s still merit further attention, scholars have been relatively slow to turn their gaze toward post-1968 developments in black America. As a new and younger generation of black elected officials begins to succeed more experienced representatives who in many instances were firsthand veterans of the movement, the political agenda of black America reflects more and more change, with new issues such as black communities' interest in school vouchers being added to more traditional and painful concerns such as racial profiling and police brutality.

But this emerging generation of prospectively "postracial" African American elected officials is only one of a plethora of subjects that ought to interest students and young scholars. The opportunities for new and important work of African American civil rights are almost limitless, and I hope deeply that this new and expanded edition of this rich encyclopedia will stimulate a significant number of young people to take up that task.

FOREWORD TO THE FIRST EDITION

David J. Garrow

This *Encyclopedia of African American Civil Rights* is a valuable and informative reference volume, but it is also so rich a source of important sketches and instructive bibliographical references that it deserves—and encourages—a fairly thorough reading even by knowledgeable senior scholars.

The range and breadth of entries is oftentimes as impressive as it is informative. Most importantly, any thoughtful perusal of the volume—whether thorough or cursory—will quickly bring home to any reader what a large number of individuals, organizations, and events there are from these last ten decades of Afro-American history which deserve greater and more extensive historical research and study than has yet been the case.

As many scholars now recognize, current and future research in Afro-American history will increasingly treat a wider and wider range of participants and events. To date a disproportionate amount of historical attention has been focused on nationally prominent individuals and on organizations that received significant contemporaneous news coverage, but there is widespread appreciation that increased attention to "grass roots" individuals and organizations is our future direction, just as there also is a growing appreciation of the importance of "local" history and events. Less and less will Afro-American history look at the black experience in America largely through a prism of national news and/or national politics.

No one can peruse this volume without thinking again and again about otherwise obscure and/or often unremembered individuals, protests, and court cases that merit a greater presence in secondary sources and textbook surveys than is presently the case. Probably every contributor hopes that this encyclopedia's publication will further stimulate and encourage such a broadening of secondary historical coverage, and such a hope is quite likely to be fulfilled, While many contributors to this encyclopedia are relatively senior scholars such as John Kirby, Steven Lawson, Jo Ann O. Robinson, Hans Trefousse, and Jerry Ward, many of the most thorough and impressive contributions come from promising junior scholars such as Cheryl Greenberg, Patricia Behlar, Peter Wallenstein, Francille Wilson, Lillie Johnson Edwards, and Glenn T. Eskew.

One very important and as yet largely unmined resource for an expanded and enriched Afro-American history since the late nineteenth century, which a number of significant entries highlight or touch upon, is black newspapers. Although many issues of a number of significant publications most tragically seem to have not been preserved, both national papers such as the *Pittsburgh Courier* and more regionally or locally oriented papers such as the *Birmingham World* can be exceptionally rich and instructive sources for future historical studies. Few scholars enjoy spending hundreds upon hundreds of hours reading microfilm, but there is no escaping the fact that far more use can and will be made of black newspapers as a significant historical source than has yet been the case.

The historical importance of black newspapers is just one notable research path that this rich and valuable volume suggests. Notwithstanding the thoroughness of many of this encyclopedia's more than eight hundred articles, hardly any scholar or student will be able to peruse the useful bibliographies that follow each entry without recognizing a significant number of subjects and individuals who undeniably deserve further or greatly increased research attention. If this volume's publication can stimulate even a modest number of such new research interests, it will have provided a significant scholarly service in addition to the very notable long-term reference value that it will offer to innumerable scholars and students. Such a goal is one which undeniably deserves to be fulfilled.

INTRODUCTION TO THE SECOND EDITION

More than a decade has elapsed since we introduced the first edition of this encyclopedia in 1992. During that time there have been many significant developments in the ongoing struggle for African American civil rights. The unending march of history thus compels us to bring our work up-to-date.

Over the past ten years, notable progress has been made in some areas of American race relations, which offers hope that the worst is behind us and that better days lie ahead. For example, blacks can now be found not merely working at the highest levels of government, business, entertainment, sports, and the professions, but excelling in their positions. At the same time, however, devastating setbacks have occurred in other areas, revealing that much remains to be done to make this country truly a land of liberty and justice for all people. Shocking cases of hate crimes, lynchings, police brutality, racial profiling, and race riots have served to remind us that to be black in America—even at the end of the twentieth century and the beginning of the twenty-first—is still to be different. Provocative debates over reparations for slavery, affirmative action, and reverse discrimination, among other issues, have likewise shown us just how complex the racial issues are that this generation of Americans faces. Appallingly high negative demographic statistics— the black male incarceration rate, the percentage of black teen pregnancies and unmarried mothers, the proportion of black families living in poverty or well below the national average, and the prevalence of drug addiction in black communities—continue to demonstrate that African Americans, as a whole, do not yet share fully in the American Dream.

The generation now coming of age has only scant knowledge of the history of the civil rights struggle. Young Americans find it difficult in 2003 to believe that racial segregation was once considered normal and necessary in some parts of the United States. Indeed, separate public schools, movie theaters, restaurants, bus seats, and water fountains seem incredible to the current generation, while spectacle lynchings, church bombings, assassinations of civil rights leaders, acquittals of white murderers of blacks by all-white juries, and government approbation of such injustices seem utterly inexplicable. Ignorance of past racial tragedies, sadly, retard continued progress in race relations.

It is, therefore, important for all people to understand the history of the struggle for civil rights. It is not a matter of having arcane information or memorizing trivia, but rather of realizing that some courageous and noble human beings endured insults, braved dangers, risked their careers, and even sacrificed their very lives so that those who followed after them could enjoy a greater degree of freedom, equality, and opportunity.

This encyclopedia, in the 10 years of its existence, has served students and teachers, average Americans and professional historians alike, as a convenient source for information on the history of the black civil rights struggle. The book has become a standard reference in a wide variety of public and academic libraries, providing essential information and offering bibliographical references for further information. The editors are pleased that this book, in its first edition, received such an enthusiastic reception, and they are happy to provide this revised second edition.

In this edition we have tried to ensure that the essays and bibliographies present the civil rights story as up-to-date to September 2003 as possible. We contacted, or attempted to contact, all the authors of the original essays and bibliographies, asking each to evaluate his or her original contributions carefully and make revisions as appropriate. We also asked for suggestions for new entries. We then invited new authors to write essays dealing with issues and events of the 1990s. We also asked new authors to add a section of primary documents and to update and expand the chronology. Similarly, we updated the bibliography and index. Whenever possible, we also provided in the individual bibliographies accompanying each entry a World Wide Web (WWW) site for readers who wish to use the Internet for further research.

Despite our exhaustive efforts to do so, it proved impossible to contact about one-third of the original contributors. Some had moved without leaving a forwarding address; some did not respond to several letters and e-mails; a few said they did not wish to revise their essays; and a number had passed away over the past decade. The list of contributors, therefore, contains the present affiliation of most authors, but those authors who could not be located are listed in the past tense at their institution of record when they composed their essays 10 years ago. If an author is deceased, that fact is so noted.

The editors have carefully edited all the original essays, whenever possible with the assistance of the original authors. We also added approximately 60 new essays and deleted approximately 15 entries from the first edition because we did not believe them relevant any longer. Each completed essay in the second edition, therefore, has received a thorough reevaluation. In some cases, the decision was to leave an essay exactly as it appeared in the first edition; in most cases, however, changes were made in the text and the bibliography to bring both up-to-date to September 2003.

The result of this effort is a second edition that reflects the philosophy and direction of the first yet is significantly different in content. The editors hope that this new edition will serve the reading public as well as did the first one. African American civil rights remains a subject of immense importance, and we hope that our effort will play a role in educating the public about it.

In order to expeditiously complete the revision of this encyclopedia, we invited a former student to join us as associate editor. We are pleased to welcome Thomas Adams Upchurch, a promising young historian of American race relations, to our team. He has brought to this project energy, efficiency, and insight. His scholarly contributions in the revisions and in the selection of documents have expedited the project.

Many others also made important contributions to the timely completion of this work. Mississippi State University student assistant Lindley Carruth Shedd's organizational abilities kept the editors, publisher, and authors moving forward together. It was her dedicated efficiency that allowed the editors to concentrate on the historical details, because we knew she had everything else under control.

We also thank Patsy Humphrey and Lonna Reinecke of the Mississippi State University History Department for their word-processing skills; Peggy Bonner of that same department for all that she has done to expedite this book and all the past projects of the editors; Horace Nash, Sara Morris, Mike Butler, Marvin Thomas, and David Canton for assisting with revisions; Buck Foster for his producing the index and Tony Iacono for his expansion of the chronology; Cynthia Harris of Greenwood Press for her constant encouragement and ready answers to any questions we posed to her; and finally, our wives, Susie, Jeanne, and Linda, for their loving support over the years.

AN AID TO USING THE ENCYCLOPEDIA

The entries on individuals, organizations, books, events, concepts, and court cases that constitute this encyclopedia are arranged in alphabetical order. The entries are cross-referenced through the use of boldface; that is, any person, group, occurrence, or court case mentioned in an entry that has its own entry is set in boldface. A detailed index provides a convenient way to locate desired information. Each entry includes a brief bibliographical list to guide the reader to other printed sources that contain valuable data on the subject in question.

Judicial citations conform to standard practice. Supreme Court decisions are officially published in *United States Reports* and are cited by volume and page number. The *Plessy v. Ferguson* opinion, for example, cited as 163 U.S. 537, is found in volume 163 of *United States Reports* at page 537. Recent opinions of the federal appeals courts are in *Federal Reporter, 2d Series*. Thus, the appellate decision in *Collins v. Walker*, cited as 339 F.2d 100, is in volume 339 of *Federal Register, 2d Series* at page 100. Federal district court opinions appear in *Federal Supplement* (F. Supp.), also cited by volume and page number.

INTRODUCTION TO THE FIRST EDITION

The African American's struggle for freedom and equality is one of the truly heroic episodes in American history. From earliest colonial days to the present, that enduring struggle, in all its myriad forms, has been as relentless as it has been inevitable. Regardless of when they lived, black Americans have shared with white Americans—and all people everywhere—the innate, timeless, indomitable desire to be free. It is a cruel irony that a people who could so boldly assert as self-evident truth that "all men are created equal" and are "endowed by their Creator" with such "inalienable rights" as "life, liberty, and the pursuit of happiness," could at the same time so resolutely deny to blacks the exercise of these rights. In failing to remain faithful to their own creed, white Americans underscored the hypocrisy and deception, the contradiction of purpose and spirit, that characterized their relationship to blacks.

From the earliest time tragedy has marked race relations in America. The institution of slavery dominated the country's early years until a bloody Civil War opened the possibility for a new racial relationship. The coming of "Jubilee" contained more promise than reality, however, and slavery was soon replaced by segregation, at first through custom and then more firmly by law. Slave codes became Black Codes and then Jim Crow state constitutions and laws. Freed people saw their emancipation turn into the new prison of segregation. The United States Supreme Court in the landmark *Plessy v. Ferguson* case of 1896 legitimated this "separate but equal" Jim Crowism. The law of the land allowed segregation and enforced "separate" conditions for African American citizens in all aspects of their lives, but the "equal" side of the equation was conveniently ignored.

For most of the twentieth century, the average black American's citizenship was a cruel hoax. Even when the Supreme Court in the momentous 1954 *Brown v. Board of Education* decision eliminated the constitutional justification for segregation, the battle was not won. Several more decades of struggle were required to achieve even minimal integration.

At the same time, though, there existed another dimension of race relations. There were blacks and whites who found slavery and segregation to be intolerable, and they battled it as best they could. The African who committed suicide rather than board a slave ship; the plantation slave who broke tools or nurtured aspects of the African past; the black and white abolitionists who served as national conscience; the free blacks who met in conventions of protest; and the politicians who finally took a stand, led the nation through a war of emancipation, and passed the Thirteenth Amendment—all these and many more individuals fought to eliminate the peculiar institutions.

Once slavery was abolished, those who believed that the battle was over withdrew from the fray. Others, both blacks and whites, saw that the nation had much to do if the former slaves were ever really to be free. Theirs was a long, lonely, and often dangerous battle to try to eliminate pervasive racism and provide full citizenship to America's black population.

The battle seemed unending, and it had many fronts. These included the right to vote and hold public office; the chance for a good job and promotion; the opportunity for an education from kindergarten to professional school; access to decent medical treatment; the opportunity to eat in restaurants or at lunch counters, go to theaters, sleep in motels, use public restrooms and waiting areas, worship in churches; the chance to join the military, appear in films or on the stage, participate on amateur and professional athletic teams, have articles and books published, argue cases in court or serve on juries or testify as a witness; live in a decent home in a pleasant neighborhood; live without fear; and enjoy respect, courtesy, and acceptance. From 1865 through the twentieth century the term "civil rights" came to mean the freedom and opportunity to enjoy, unimpeded, this whole complex of American citizenship rights. The civil rights movement, especially in its intensification in the 1950s and 1960s, was the long struggle to bring African Americans into the promise of the American Dream.

Throughout this period, historical writing reflected the bias that the dominant American white society felt against black people. Assumptions of white superiority and black inferiority were as deeply embedded in the history books as they were in society as a whole. When blacks were mentioned in the texts, if they were, it was in the most depreciative language. Favorable books or articles, when they saw print, were patronizingly or forcefully suppressed.

During the years of the modern civil rights struggle, workers in the movement have labored first and foremost to liberate black people, but they also have tried to liberate America's history. A torrent of literature on all aspects of the black-white experience poured forth when the dam of literary discrimination was breached. This literature has both influenced the civil rights struggle and been influenced by it. In the important body of books on race relations, however, there is a conspicuous void. There is no reference book that presents under a single cover an overview of the century-long struggle for civil rights. Excellent books and articles exist on all aspects of this subject, but there is no one convenient, accurate reference source.

This *Encyclopedia of African American Civil Rights* was prepared to fill this void. It contains over eight hundred short articles on a wide variety of individuals, organizations, events, and court cases focusing on the period since emancipation. Librarians of all types of libraries, from the largest reference to the smallest public, will find it a convenient source for information on this topic. The bibliographical references with each article will also provide ready entry into the vast literature in the field.

In organizing and completing this volume, the editors faced several difficult decisions. The topic is broad and the available pages necessarily limited. The editors decided to include, for the most part, only that which, in their judgment, made a significant positive contribution to the advancement of black civil rights. Every state and community had its share of brave, resourceful individuals, influential organizations, and locally significant events and court cases. Unfortunately, all could not be included here, not because they were not important, but because there simply is not space enough for all of them. In order to include as many subjects as possible and be consistent with the purpose of an encyclopedia, the editors have kept the articles brief.

Another difficult decision concerned whether to include those who opposed the civil rights movement. Individuals such as Eugene "Bull" Connor, Ross Barnett, Orval Faubus, and George C. Wallace, and groups such as the Ku Klux Klan, the White Citizens' Council, and the State Sovereignty Commissions, were legion, outnumbering in the South, certainly, those people and organizations championing racial equality. In a perverse way the opponents of black civil rights, because of the depth of their racism and the brutish violence of their opposition, promoted the cause of freedom. But it would require another book to deal with them, and rather than include some and neglect others, we did not include any.

Similarly, we did not include presidents of the United States or every congressman, Supreme Court justice, black novelist, playwright, newspaperperson, soldier, sports figure, or "first black" whose activities contributed to the movement. We are acutely aware of how much we have omitted, but we also think that we have included a representative cross-section of the most significant people, organizations, events, and court cases of the black civil rights movement.

We were fortunate to be able to work with an outstanding group of conscientious and talented authors. They include some of the foremost scholars in the field as well as individuals just beginning their professional careers. We naturally appreciate the support of the former, but we particularly want to express our gratitude to the latter. Their willingness to undertake a wide variety of assignments enabled us to carry the project forward. All editors have horror stories to tell about working on a book such as this, and we have ours, too. Fortunately, our happy experiences far outnumber the unpleasant ones.

We are deeply indebted to a number of other people who have been instrumental in bringing this project to fruition. Undergraduate student-helper Marzett Jordan undertook a wide variety of clerical and research tasks and accomplished them in his usual quietly efficient manner. Graduate Assistant James Stennett was similarly productive, and Research Assistant Danny Blair Moore provided valuable assistance during the last stages of the project. Jean Whitehead and Karen Groce typed goodly portions of the manuscript. Peggy Y. Bonner and Lonna Reinecke not only typed the manuscript and letters to the authors, but provided invaluable assistance in other ways as well. Their organizational skills and their ability to remember where everything was filed saved us from a host of editorial problems. To say that this book could not have been completed without them is no exaggeration. To Professors David J. Garrow and Willard B. Gatewood, Jr., who read the manuscript and offered many discerning suggestions and criticisms, we are especially indebted. Our friend and colleague Allen Dennis not only authored entries for the *Encyclopedia*, but he also compiled the index for the volume. He has long experience as a professional indexer, and the finished product attests to his skill. We thank him for his help. At Greenwood Press, Executive Editor Cynthia Harris has provided, from the outset, guidance and encouragement, for which we are deeply grateful. Production editor Penny Sippel has skillfully managed the editorial responsibilities of bringing the volume into production. Finally, to our wives, Susie and Jeanne, we are most indebted, not just for the freedom they gave us to complete this project, but for their support, love, and companionship in all things.

CONTRIBUTORS

Cassandra August is Assistant Professor of Family and Consumer Sciences at Baldwin-Wallace College.

Dorothy A. Autrey is Associate Professor of History at Alabama State University.

James L. Baggett was a graduate student in history at the University of Mississippi.

Michael B. Ballard is Professor and Coordinator of Congressional and Political Research Center at Mississippi State University.

Larry T. Balsamo is Professor of History at Western Illinois University.

Charles T. Pete Banner-Haley is Associate Professor of History at Colgate University.

Alwyn Barr is Professor of History at Texas Tech University.

Able A. Bartley is Associate Professor of History, University of Akron.

Jennifer J. Beaumont was a graduate student in history at the University of Maryland, Baltimore.

Patricia A. Behlar is Assistant Professor of Political Science at Pittsburgh State University.

Robert A. Bellinger is Assistant Professor of History at Suffolk University.

Manfred Berg is a faculty member in the John F. Kennedy Institute for North American Studies, Free University of Berlin, Germany.

Amos J. Beyan is Associate Professor of History at Western Michigan University.

Monroe Billington is Emeritus Professor of History at New Mexico State University.

Thomas E. Blantz is Professor of History at the University of Notre Dame.

Robert Bonazzi was Editorial Director of *Latitudes*.

James Borchert is Professor of History at Cleveland State University.

Joseph Boskin is Professor of History at Boston University.

Dorsey Oles Boyle was a graduate student in history at the University of Maryland, Baltimore.

Ray Branch is a doctoral graduate of the Department of History, Mississippi State University.

Jeff Broadwater was Director of the John C. Stennis Oral History Project at Mississippi State University.

Brenda M. Brock was a graduate student in English at the State University of New York at Buffalo.

Lisa Brock is Assistant Professor of Liberal Arts at The School of the Art Institute of Chicago.

Lester S. Brooks is Professor of History at Anne Arundel Community College in Maryland.

Michael Butler is Assistant Professor of History at South Georgia College.

Joe Louis Caldwell is Associate Professor of History at the University of New Orleans.

Robert A. Calvert, now deceased, was Professor of History at Texas A&M University.

David Canton is Assistant Professor of History at Georgia Southern University.

Dominic J. Capeci, Jr., is Distinguished Professor of History at Southwest Missouri State University.

JoAnn D. Carpenter is Professor of History at Florida Community College.

Jessie M. Carter is Lecturer in African American Studies at the State University of New York at Buffalo.

William Cash is Emeritus Professor of History at Delta State University.

Joan E. Cashin is Professor of History at Ohio State University.

Suzanne Ellery Green Chapelle is Professor of History and Geography at Morgan State University.

Lawrence O. Christensen is Distinguished Teaching Professor of History and Political Science at the University of Missouri-Rolla.

James R. Chumney is Associate Professor of History at Memphis State University.

Eric C. Clark is a holder of a doctorate in history and the Secretary of State of Mississippi.

Thomas D. Cockrell is Professor and Chair of the Social Sciences Division at Blue Mountain College.

Willi Coleman is Associate Professor of History at the University of Vermont.

Edwin L. Combs III is a history doctoral student at the University of Alabama, Tuscaloosa.

W. Lance Conn lives in London.

Norlisha Crawford is Assistant Professor of English at Bucknell University.

Stephen Cresswell is Professor of History at West Virginia Wesleyan College.

Jeffrey J. Crow is Adjunct Associate Professor of History at North Carolina State University.

Charles Crowe, now deceased, was Professor of History at the University of Georgia.

Lorenzo Crowell is Associate Professor of History at Mississippi State University.

Donald Cunnigen is Associate Professor of Sociology at the University of Rhode Island.

Robert Cvornyek is Associate Professor of History and Secondary Education at Rhode Island College.

Richard V. Damms is Associate Professor of History at Mississippi State University.

Marsha J. Tyson Darling is Professor of History and Director of the African American and Ethnic Studies Program at Adelphi University.

Jack E. Davis is Associate Professor of History at the University of Alabama at Birmingham.

Thomas J. Davis is Professor at Arizona State University College of Law.

Allen Dennis is Professor of History and Chair at Troy State University.

Vincent P. DeSantis is Emeritus Professor of History at the University of Notre Dame.

Kenneth DeVille was a law student at the University of Texas.

Nancy Diamond was a graduate student in history at the University of Maryland, Baltimore.

Bruce J. Dierenfield is Professor of History at Canisius College.

Bernard Donahoe is Professor of History at Saint Mary's College, Indiana.

Michael S. Downs was Staff Historian, U.S. Air Force Space Command at Peterson Air Force Base, Colorado.

W. Marvin Dulaney is Professor and Chair of History at the University of Charleston.

Aingred G. Dunston is Associate Professor of History at Eastern Kentucky University.

Brenda M. Eagles was Research Librarian and Bibliographer at the Center for the Study of Southern Culture at the University of Mississippi.

Charles W. Eagles is Professor of History at the University of Mississippi.

Lillie Johnson Edwards is Associate Professor of History at Drew University.

David P. Eldridge is Instructor of History at Florence-Darlington Technical College.

Glenn T. Eskew is Associate Professor of History at Georgia State University.

Robert Fikes, Jr., is Librarian at San Diego State University.

Nancy E. Fitch was Assistant Professor of History at Lynchburg College.

Marvin E. Fletcher is Professor of History at Ohio University.

Linda G. Ford was Assistant Professor of History at Keene State College and is now in private business.

Tony A. Freyer is University Research Professor of History and Law at the University of Alabama.

David J. Garrow is Professor of Political Science, Emory University.

Phillip A. Gibbs is Associate Professor of History at Middle Georgia College.

Bruce A. Glasrud is Dean of Arts and Sciences and Professor of History at Sul Ross State University.

Ira Glunts was Head of Technical Services at the American International College Library.

Kenneth W. Goings is Professor and Chair of African American Studies at Ohio State University.

Daniel Gomes was a graduate student in history at the University of Maryland, Baltimore.

Hugh Davis Graham, now deceased, was Holland McTyeire Professor of History at Vanderbilt University.

Barbara L. Green is Assistant Professor of History at Wright State University.

George N. Green is Professor of History at the University of Texas at Arlington.

Cheryl Greenberg is Professor of History at Trinity College.

Bernice F. Guillaume was Associate Professor of History at St. Louis University.

Michele M. Hall was a graduate student in history at the University of Maryland, Baltimore.

David A. Harmon is affiliated with Alabama Public Television.

Alferdteen Harrison is Professor of History and Director of the Margaret Walker Alexander National Research Center for the Study of the Twentieth-Century African American at Jackson State University.

Merrill M. Hawkins, Jr., is Assistant Professor of Religion, Carson-Newman College.

Wanda A. Hendricks is Associate Professor of Women's Studies, University of South Carolina.

Clarence Hooker is Associate Professor of American Thought and Language at Michigan State University.

Leonne M. Hudson is Associate Professor of History, Kent State University.

Gary J. Hunter is Professor of History at Rowan College.

Marshall Hyatt was Director of the Center for Afro-American Studies at Wesleyan University.

Anthony J. Iacono is a historian and assistant dean at Indian River Community College.

Jacquelyn Jackson is Associate Professor of English at Middle Tennessee State University.

Robert L. Jenkins is Associate Professor of History at Mississippi State University.

Lavaree Jones was a Community Organizer for the Child Development Group of Mississippi.

Maxine D. Jones is Professor of History at Florida State University.

Maghan Keita is Associate Professor of History at Villanova University.

Judith N. Kerr, now deceased, was Assistant Professor of History at Towson State University.

Amm Saifuddin Khaled is Professor and Chair of History at the University of Chittagong, Bangladesh.

Wali Rashash Kharif is Professor of History at Tennessee Technological University.

Allen Kifer is Emeritus Associate Professor of History at Skidmore College.

Elizabeth Kight was a graduate student in history at the University of Maryland, Baltimore.

John B. Kirby is Emeritus Professor of History at Denison University.

Stephen P. Labash was a graduate student in history at the University of Maryland, Baltimore.

Jane F. Lancaster is a doctoral graduate of the Department of History at Mississippi State University.

Steven F. Lawson is Professor of History at Rutgers University.

Janice M. Leone is Professor of History at Middle Tennessee State University.

Eric Love is Assistant Professor of History, University of Colorado, Boulder.

Charles D. Lowery is Emeritus Professor of History at Mississippi State University.

Andrew M. Manis is on the Social Sciences faculty at Macon State College, Georgia.

John F. Marszalek is W. L. Giles Distinguished Emeritus Professor of History at Mississippi State University.

James Marten is Professor of History at Marquette University.

Robert F. Martin is Professor of History at the University of Northern Iowa.

Michael S. Mayer is Associate Professor of History at the University of Montana.

Contributors

Earlean M. McCarrick was Associate Professor of Government and Politics at the University of Maryland.

Phillip McGuire, now deceased, was Dean of Arts and Sciences at Fayetteville State University.

Neil R. McMillen is Emeritus Professor of History at the University of Southern Mississippi.

Tennant S. McWilliams is Dean of the School of Social and Behavioral Sciences at the University of Alabama at Birmingham.

Mark E. Medina was a student at the Yale University Law School.

Stephen Middleton is Assistant Professor of History at North Carolina State University.

Gary B. Mills, now deceased, was Professor of History at the University of Alabama.

Dennis J. Mitchell is Professor of History, Mississippi State University, Meridian.

Gregory Mixon is Assistant Professor of History at the University of North Carolina at Charlotte.

Christopher Mobley is Assistant Professor of Political Science at DePaul University.

Danny Blair Moore is Associate Professor and Chair of History at Chowan College.

Betsy Sakariassen Nash is a school administrator in San Antonio, Texas.

Horace D. Nash teaches history at Alamo Community College District.

William A. Paquette is Professor of History at Tidewater Community College.

Randall L. Patton is Associate Professor of History at Kennesaw State University.

Glenn O. Phillips is Associate Professor and Chair of History at Morgan State University.

Betty L. Plummer was Assistant Professor of History at the University of Tennessee.

James B. Potts is Associate Professor of History at the University of Wisconsin-LaCrosse.

Steve Rea was a graduate student in history at the University of Mississippi.

Linda Reed is Associate Professor of History at the University of Houston.

Richard W. Resh, now deceased, was Associate Professor of History at the University of Missouri at St. Louis.

Charles A. Risher is Professor of History and Political Science at Montreat College.

Edward J. Robinson is a history graduate of Mississippi State University.

Jo Ann O. Robinson is Professor of History and Geography at Morgan State University.

William "Brother" Rogers is Assistant Director of the Stennis

xxvi

Center for Public Service, Starkville, Mississippi.

William Warren Rogers, Jr., is Associate Professor of History at Gainesville College.

Steve Sadowsky was a graduate student in history at Middle Tennessee State University.

Jeffrey Sainsbury resides in France.

Loren Schweninger is Professor of History at University of North Carolina at Greensboro.

James E. Sefton is Professor of History at California State University, Northridge.

Lindley Carruth Shedd is a student at Mississippi State University.

Carole Shelton was Assistant Professor of History at Middle Tennessee State University.

Malik Simba is Professor and Chair of History at California State University, Fresno.

Frederick G. Slabach was Associate Dean of the Mississippi College School of Law.

James G. Smart is Emeritus Professor of History at Keene State College.

Elizabeth M. Smith is Assistant Professor of History, Kent State University.

Gerald L. Smith is Professor of History at the University of Kentucky.

Thaddeus M. Smith is Professor and Chair of History at Middle Tennessee State University.

Allan H. Spear is Emeritus Associate Professor of History at the University of Minnesota.

James W. Stennett is an executive with a professional baseball team.

Arvarh E. Strickland is Emeritus Professor of History at the University of Missouri.

Quintard Taylor is Scott & Dorothy Bullitt Professor of American History at the University of Washington.

Marvin Thomas is Professor of History at Gordon College.

William J. Thompson was Adjunct Professor of History at Essex Community College, Baltimore.

Hans L. Trefousse is Distinguished Professor Emeritus of History at City University of New York.

Thomas Adams Upchurch is Assistant Professor of History, East Georgia College, Statesboro Branch.

Gloria Waite, now deceased, was Assistant Professor of History at Southeastern Massachusetts University (now University of Massachusetts, Dartmouth).

George E. Walker was Associate Professor of History at George Mason University.

Peter Wallenstein is Associate Professor of History at Virginia Polytechnic Institute and State University.

Jerry Ward is Professor of English at Tougaloo College.

Vibert L. White was Assistant Professor of African American Studies at the University of Cincinnati.

Lawrence H. Williams is Professor of African and Afro-American Studies and History at Luther College, Iowa.

Lee E. Williams, II is Professor of History at the University of Alabama in Huntsville.

LeRoy T. Williams is Associate Professor of History at the University of Arkansas in Little Rock.

Carol Wilson is Associate Professor of History at Washington College.

Francille Rusan Wilson is affiliated with University of Maryland, College Park.

Irvin D. S. Winsboro is History Program Director at Florida Gulf Coast University.

Barbara A. Worthy is Associate Professor of History at Southern University in New Orleans.

Bertram Wyatt-Brown is Milbauer Professor of History at the University of Florida.

Paul Yandle was a graduate student in history at Wake Forest University.

Dean K. Yates was a graduate student in history at the University of Maryland, Baltimore.

Alfred Young is Associate Professor of History at Georgia Southern College.

Robert L. Zangrando is Emeritus Professor of History at the University of Akron.

A

Abbott, Robert S. (28 November 1868, St. Simon's Island, Ga.–28 February, 1940, Chicago, Ill.). Known as "A Founding Father of Black Journalism and the Dean of Negro Publishers," Abbott attended Beach Institute in Savannah, Georgia, spent time at Claflin College in Orangeburg, South Carolina, studied printing at and graduated from **Hampton Institute,** and received his LL. B. degree from Chicago's Kent College of Law in 1899. Abbott practiced law briefly in Kansas and Indiana before founding the *Chicago Defender* (the newspaper that revolutionized the black press) in 1905. From its inception, Abbott used the *Defender*'s columns to urge a militant campaign against segregation and the racial injustices heaped upon African Americans. By the time of his death in 1940, he had urged a generation of black southerners "to leave the lynching South."

Selected Bibliography Alan D. DeSantis, "A Forgotten Leader: Robert A. Abbott and the Chicago Defender from 1910–1920," *Journalism History* 23 (No. 2, 1997), 63–71; Robert L. Green, *Robert S. Abbott: Negro Businessman* (1969); Roi Ottley, *The Lonely Warrior: The Life and Times of Robert S. Abbott* (1955); Edgar H. Toppin, *Biographical History of Blacks in America since 1528* (1971); Roland E. Wolseley, *The Black Press, USA* (1971).

Phillip McGuire

Abernathy, Ralph David (11 March 1926, Linden, Ala.–17 April 1990, Atlanta, Ga.). Abernathy was an African American civil rights and religious leader and a top aide to the Reverend Dr. **Martin Luther King, Jr.** He attended Alabama State College, which later became Alabama State University (B.S., 1950), and **Atlanta University** (M.A., Sociology, 1951). He also received numerous honorary degrees. In 1951 he was appointed Dean of Men and sociology instructor at Alabama State College. In the same year, he joined the **National Association for the Advancement of Colored People** and became pastor of the black First Baptist Church in Montgomery (1951–61). In 1955 he helped organize the **Montgomery bus boycott.** Abernathy was a founder of the **Southern Christian Leadership Conference** (SCLC) in 1957, and he became secretary/treasurer in 1961. He was arrested no fewer than 19 times with King during civil rights marches, and in 1965 he was designated King's heir apparent as SCLC president. Following King's death in 1968, Abernathy assumed leadership of SCLC. Increasing SCLC's level of involvement in the civil rights movement, he directed the **Poor People's March on Washington** in May 1968; led a demonstration at the July 1968 Republican National Convention in Miami; helped organize the 1968 Atlanta sanitation workers' strike; was jailed in June 1969 during the successful Charleston, South Carolina, hospital worker's strike; and helped plan the march from Perry, Georgia, to Atlanta in 1970. In 1977 Abernathy resigned leadership of SCLC and ran, unsuccessfully, for the Georgia congressional seat vacated by **Andrew Young.** Afterward he became less influential in the civil rights movement. In 1980, he surprised many by endorsing Republican Ronald Reagan for president. Later, he founded the Foundation for Economic Enterprises Development, a nonprofit organization to improve black economic opportunities. He became more active on the lecture circuit and served as pastor of West Hunter Street Baptist Church in Atlanta until he suffered the first of several strokes in 1983. In 1989 Abernathy published *And the Walls Came Tumbling Down*, an autobiographical account of the civil rights movement, which contained statements regarding King's alleged sexual infidelities. The book was severely criticized, resulting in loss of prestige for the author. Nevertheless, Abernathy was an important actor in the civil rights struggle.

Selected Bibliography Ralph David Abernathy, Sr., *And the Walls Came Tumbling Down* (1989); A. John Adams and Joan Martin Burke, *A CBS News Reference Book: Civil Rights, A Current Guide to the People, Organizations, and Events* (1970); *Jet* 7 (14 May 1990); Harry A. Ploski et al., eds., *The Negro Almanac* (1983).

Wali Rashash Kharif

Abolish Peonage Committee of America   Following the demise of slavery, white landowners searched for ways to limit black laborers' freedom of movement. **Black peonage,** the forced immobility of labor based on indebtedness, was one of the measures implemented. This system of covert coercion began to be effectively challenged only with the growth of southern Progressivism in the early years of the twentieth century. The apogee of the movement came with the Alonzo Bailey decision (see *Bailey v. Alabama*) in 1911 whereby the Supreme Court declared an Alabama contract-labor law unconstitutional because it violated the **Thirteenth Amendment.** Despite the legal victory, peonage remained a prevalent practice and a constant encroachment upon civil rights. In 1939 William Henry Huff, a Chicago lawyer, learned of an attempt by a Georgia planter named Cunningham to extradite four of his indebted laborers back to his Ogelthorpe County farm. Huff intervened on their behalf and, aided by the International Labor Defense, formed the Abolish Peonage Committee of America, the first public organization to combat this practice. The committee at once joined the defense in the suit Huff had initiated. The *Cunningham* case was catapulted into national prominence. Huff and other members of the committee were called on to testify before the Justice Department on the problem of peonage. The four laborers were acquitted, but to the dismay of the committee, the Georgia planter was not indicted. The Abolish Peonage Committee remained active into the war years, but never again was it to achieve such prominence. Huff's resignation in 1942 helped signal the demise of the organization's influence.

Selected Bibliography Herbert Aptheker, "A Few Battles Against Racism," *Black Scholar* 26 (1996), 3–8; Pete Daniels, *The Shadow of Slavery: Peonage in the South 1901–1969* (1972); Daniel Novak, *The Wheel of Servitude: Black Forced Labor after Slavery* (1978).

Steve Rea

Adams, Henry (17 December 1802, Franklin County, Ga.–3 November 1872, Louisville, Ky.). A prominent African American minister and pioneer educator, Henry Adams served the First African (later Fifth Street) Baptist Church in Louisville. Consisting of nine hundred members before the Civil War, it was the largest Baptist church, black or white, in the area. Adams also started the first school for blacks in the city on 7 December 1841. Consisting of slave and free children, it continued to operate until public schools became available in 1870. Subsequently, Adams helped to organize the black public school system in Louisville. His contribution is important because it demonstrates the early connections among the black church, black education, and black social uplift.

Selected Bibliography Ira V. Birdwhistell, *Gathered at the River: A Narrative History of Long Run Baptist Association* (1978); William J. Simmons, *Men of Mark: Eminent, Progressive, and Rising* (1887); Henry C. Weeden, *Weeden's History of the Colored People of Louisville* (1897); Lawrence H. Williams, *Black Higher Education in Kentucky, 1879–1930: The History of Simmons University* (1987); George D. Wilson, "A Century of Negro Education in Louisville, Kentucky" (unpublished manuscript prepared by workers of the Works Progress Administration, 1941).

Lawrence H. Williams

Adarand Constructors, Inc. v. Peña,* 515 U.S. 200 (1995)** Reflecting the Court's rightward drift following the appointment of conservative justices by Presidents Ronald Reagan and George Bush, a divided Supreme Court seriously undermined legislation encouraging affirmative action by federal contractors. In ***Fullilove v. Klutznick (1980) the Court had upheld similar legislation. Justice Sandra Day O'Conner's plurality opinion on *Adarand* stated that strict scrutiny, the most demanding form of judicial review, had to be applied to all race-based programs, regardless of which race benefitted, and regardless of whether Congress or a state created the program. The relevant governmental entity had to show that it was pursuing a compelling government interest.

Selected Bibliography Elizabeth Drew, *Showdown: The Struggle between the Gingrich Congress and the Clinton White House* (1996); Frank S. Ravitch, "Creating Chaos in the Name of Consistency: Affirmative Action and the Odd Legacy of Adarand Constructors, Inc. v. Peña," *Dickenson Law Review* 101 (1997), 281–324.

Patricia A. Behlar

Adderly v. Florida, 385 U.S. 39 (1966) In September 1963, 107 Florida Agricultural and Mechanical University students were arrested for protesting outside the Tallahassee, Florida, Leon County Jail. The students were convicted of "trespass with a malicious and mischievous intent." Harriet Adderly and 31 others appealed their convictions to the Supreme Court, having failed in the Florida District Court and in the District Court of Appeals. Attorneys Richard Felder and Tobias Simon argued on 18 October 1966 that the students had been deprived of their "rights of free speech, assembly, petition, due process of law and equal protection of the laws under the **Fourteenth Amendment.**" Speaking for the majority, Justice Hugo Black ruled that "the state, no less than a private owner of property, has power to preserve the property under its control for the use to which it is lawfully dedicated." In the dissenting opinion, Justice William O. Douglas claimed that the Court had done "violence to the First Amendment" by permitting "this 'petition for redress of grievances' to be turned into a trespass action."

Selected Bibliography Henry J. Abraham and Barbara A. Perry, *Freedom and the Court: Civil Rights and Liberties in the United States* (1994); Richard Bardolph, ed., *The Civil Rights Record: Black Americans and the Law, 1849–1970* (1970); Glenda A. Rabby, *The Pain and the Promise: The Struggle for Civil Rights in Tallahassee, Florida* (1999).

Maxine D. Jones

Affirmative Action Such concepts as "systemic discrimination" and "unearned privilege" undergird arguments regarding affirmative action for minorities, women, and other historically oppressed groups. Believing that the inequalities and injustices experienced by these groups are so deeply imbedded in American society that extraordinary efforts are required to uproot them, advocates of affirmative action call for proactive initiatives in both the public and the private sectors to assure access to education, employment, advancement, and involvement in all areas of society. The legal foundation on which affirmative action rests includes the Equal Protection Clause of the **Fourteenth Amendment,** Titles VI and VII of the **Civil Rights Act of 1964,** and President Lyndon B. Johnson's **Executive Order 11246.** Opponents associate affirmative action with "quotas" and what they consider to be preferential treatment. They invoke the notion of a so-called color-blind Constitution and insist that race and gender consciousness promotes "discrimination in reverse" and undermines the tradition of success based upon merit. Affirmative action has taken many forms, including rulings, guidelines, decrees, and voluntary plans overseen by a variety of departments and agencies, public and private. Its results are equally varied and widely debated. In light of such variability, some scholars have argued that "affirmative action can-

Reverend Jesse Jackson speaks at the University of Michigan, accompanied by members of the Coalition to Defend Affirmative Action By Any Means Necessary (BAMN), May 14, 2002. © AP/Wide World Photos.

not be deemed either good or bad. It all depends on the goals sought and the means chosen."

Selected Bibliography Herman Belz, *Equality Transformed* (1994); Hugh Davis Graham, *Civil Rights and the Presidency* (1992); John Higham, ed., *Civil Rights and Social Wrongs* (1999); Charles R. Lawrence and Mari J. Matsuda, *We Won't Go Back* (1997); Paul D. Moreno, *From Direct Action to Affirmative Action* (1997); Phil A. Rubino, *A History of Affirmative Action 1619–2000* (2001); Jo Ann O. Robinson, *Affirmative Action: A Documentary History* (2001).

Jo Ann O. Robinson

African Blood Brotherhood Founded in 1917 as a nationalist, revolutionary, Pan-African movement by Cyril Briggs (1888–1966), the short-lived African Blood Brotherhood for African Liberation and Redemption (ABB) sought to ally racial consciousness to the goals of class consciousness. This paramilitary organization, catapulted into national attention by the Tulsa race riot (1921), which destroyed that city's African American community, proposed worldwide federation of all African groups and armed defense of all African American communities. Its reported zenith "enlistment" was five thousand, mostly ex-servicemen, in 56 "posts." The ABB, prefigured by the Hamitic League of the World, became the first African American auxiliary of the American Communist Party in 1925.

Selected Bibliography Robert L. Allen, *Reluctant Reformers* (1974); Scott Ellsworth, *Death in a Promised Land: The Tulsa Race Riot of 1921*, 2nd ed. (1992); Robert A. Hill, ed., *The Crusader*

(1987); Mary E. Parrish, *Race Riot of 1921: Events of the Tulsa Disaster* (1998); Mark I. Solomon, *The Cry Was Unity: Communists and African-Americans, 1917–1936* (1998); *The Crusader* 4 (July 1921), 5–24.

Aingred G. Dunston

Afro-American   Founded by John Murphy, Sr., in 1892, the *Baltimore Afro-American* (and its editions in other cities) was a leader in the fight for civil rights. The newspaper campaigned against the inequities of Baltimore's and other segregated school systems, against **Jim Crow** laws, and against attempts to disenfranchise black voters in the early twentieth century. It led to the revival of the Baltimore chapter of the **National Association for the Advancement of Colored People** in 1935 under the strong leadership of Lillie May Carroll Jackson. The *Afro-American* supported Democrat Franklin Roosevelt in 1936, liberal Republican mayoral candidate Theodore McKeldin in 1943, and black candidates, mostly Democrats, who won election to local and state offices beginning in the 1950s. It gave wide coverage to local and national racial abuses and civil rights protests of the 1950s, 1960s, and later decades. Despite greater coverage of African Americans in the mainstream press, the *Afro-American* has continued into the twenty-first century to be a leading source of news and features on black Americans.

   Selected Bibliography Robert J. Brugger, *Maryland: A Middle Temperament, 1634–1980* (1988); George H. Callcott, *Maryland and America, 1940–1980* (1985); Hayward Farrar, *The Baltimore Afro-American, 1892–1950* (1998).

Suzanne Ellery Greene Chapelle

Afro-American Council   In 1898 **Timothy Thomas Fortune** and African Methodist Episcopal Bishop **Alexander Walters** revived the defunct **Afro-American League** under this new name. Initially, the council adopted its predecessor's aggressive policies. Gradually, however, the moderate **Booker T. Washington** and his supporters came to dominate it. The council attempted to censure Washington in 1899 for his apologetic tone in an appeal to southern white officials regarding lynching of accused black rapists. Washington's supporters blocked the censure, and by the turn of the century the council reflected his conciliatory position. Continuing white attacks on African Americans, plus the growing influence of the combative **W.E.B. Du Bois's Niagara Movement,** undermined the influence of the council, which died out in 1908. Its brief history demonstrated the divisive philosophies of African American leadership during the era of **Jim Crow**.

   Selected Bibliography Louis R. Harlan, *Booker T. Washington: The Making of a Black Leader, 1856–1901* (1972); Louis R. Harlan, *Booker T. Washington: The Wizard of Tuskegee, 1901–1915* (1983); August Meier, *Negro Thought in America, 1880–1915: Racial Ideologies in the Age of Booker T. Washington* (1963).

Michael B. Ballard

Afro-American League   In 1887 **Timothy Thomas Fortune,** the editor of the *New York Age,* conceived the idea of a protective league for African Americans.

From this concept, the Afro-American League emerged in 1890. Under Fortune's leadership, the league espoused agitation and revolution as legitimate means of securing black rights. The league further emphasized black solidarity and proposed an economic program that included an Afro-American bank, the promotion of industrial education, cooperative enterprises, job training, nonpartisan politics, an immigration bureau to help scatter blacks more equitably around the states, self-solutions to black problems, and preservation of black cultural values. At one time or another the league counted as members most prominent black leaders. Internal friction and rivalry with the American Citizens' Equal Rights Association, however, soon caused the league to lapse into inactivity. By 1893 the national body and most of its local branches had ceased to function. The league did help keep alive black hopes for full and equal citizenship, and in 1898 it was revived under a new name, the **Afro-American Council**.

Selected Bibliography Herbert Aptheker, ed., *A Documentary History of the Negro People in the United States*, vol. 1 (1951); Louis R. Harlan, *Booker T. Washington: The Making of a Black Leader, 1856–1901* (1972); August Meier, *Negro Thought in American, 1880–1915: Racial Ideologies in the Age of Booker T. Washington* (1963).

Michael B. Ballard

Alabama Christian Movement for Human Rights   On 5 June 1956, more than one thousand people overflowed the Sardis Baptist Church in Birmingham, Alabama, to join the Reverends **Fred L. Shuttlesworth,** Edward Gardner, R. L. Alford, and N. H. Smith in organizing the Alabama Christian Movement for Human Rights (ACMHR). Formed in response to the state attorney general's ban on the **National Association for the Advancement of Colored People,** the ACMHR quickly became the leading civil rights organization in Birmingham. Using **direct action,** the ACMHR challenged bus segregation in December 1956 and again in October 1958, attempted the integration of schools and the railroad station in 1957, and supported the student sit-ins in 1960 and the **Freedom Riders** in 1961. This dedicated group of militant Christian activists elected Shuttlesworth president, and his association with the **Southern Christian Leadership Conference** led to the **Birmingham Confrontation** of spring 1963. When Shuttlesworth stepped down as president in 1969, Gardner, the longtime first vice president, assumed leadership and held it into the 1990s. The ACMHR endorsed Richard Arrington for the Birmingham City Council in 1971 and worked to get him elected as the first African American mayor of the city in 1979. The organization no longer exists.

Selected Bibliography Jimmie Lewis Franklin, *Back to Birmingham* (1989); David J. Garrow, ed., *Birmingham, Alabama, 1956–1963* (1989); Howell Raines, *My Soul Is Rested* (1977); Marjorie L. White, *A Walk to Freedom: The Reverend Fred Shuttlesworth and the Alabama Christian Movement for Human Rights, 1956–1964* (1998).

Glenn T. Eskew

Alabama Council on Human Relations   Founded in 1954 to promote racial harmony and goodwill, the council was the successor to the Alabama

7

Commission on Interracial Cooperation. It was a state branch of the **Southern Regional Council** organized by an integrated group who believed that the racial tensions of the times could be eased through dialogue and education. During the 1950s and 1960s, operating through its state headquarters and through its branches in major Alabama cities, the council sought to improve race relations. One of its most important roles was that of mediator in racial conflicts such as the **Montgomery bus boycott** of 1955–56 and the **Birmingham Confrontation** of 1963. In 1965 the council shifted its focus from race relations to social programs to benefit the poor. Although hampered by a small membership and limited funding, the council was a positive force in Alabama for building a spirit of understanding and cooperation between the races. In 1996, for example, it opened a new building to provide a **Head Start** program for a rural Alabama county.

Selected Bibliography Taylor Branch, *Parting the Waters: America in the King Years, 1954–63* (1988); Virginia Foster Durr, *Outside the Magic Circle: The Autobiography of Virginia Foster Durr* (1985); David J. Garrow, *Bearing the Cross: Martin Luther King and the Southern Christian Leadership Conference* (1986); Benjamin Muse, *The American Negro Revolution: From Nonviolence to Black Power, 1963–1967* (1968); Jan Gregory Thompson, "The History of the Alabama Council of Human Relations from Roots to Redirection, 1920–1968" (Ph.D. diss., Auburn University, 1983).

Dorothy A. Autrey

Albany, Georgia, Sit-In On Thanksgiving weekend 1961, African American activists decided to test a recent Interstate Commerce Commission ruling on desegregation by using the whites-only facilities at the Trailways bus station in Albany, Georgia. Their actions catapulted this southwest Georgia community of fifty-six thousand, 40 percent of whom were black, into national prominence. Albany quickly became, in the early 1960s, both a catalyst for similar student-initiated actions, particularly those by the **Student Nonviolent Coordinating Committee** (SNCC), and a symbol of organizational factionalism, especially regarding the role of Dr. **Martin Luther King, Jr.,** in the ensuing Albany Movement. On 22 November 1961, SNCC workers Charles Sherrod and Cordell Reagon, along with a group of black students from Albany State College and the local **NAACP** Youth Council, sat down in the whites-only section of the Trailways terminal and refused to leave. Following their expulsion by authorities, a coalition of local black organizations and student leaders began a coordinated attack on Albany's strict color line. Internecine squabbling among the participants prompted King to make an appearance in Albany, but he left without achieving the real or symbolic victories that earlier had won him national acclaim. The mass protest continued in Albany for another six years. Although King would call Albany his most glaring defeat, the actions there galvanized SNCC workers into a stronger commitment to **direct action** campaigns (e.g., the **Freedom Summer of 1964** struggles) and ushered in a new era in civil rights in which black spir-

Black protestors in Albany, Georgia, and elsewhere, encountered the intimidating presence of the Ku Klux Klan. © Carl and Ann Braden Collection, Wisconsin Historical Society.

ituals, such as "Ain't Gonna Let Nobody Turn Me Around," were sung defiantly in the face of white oppression.

Selected Bibliography Clayborne Carson, *In Struggle: SNCC and the Black Awakening of the 1960s* (1981); James A. DeVinney and Callie Crossley, *No Easy Walk* (videocassette, 1986); Cheryl Lynn Greenberg, ed., *A Circle of Trust: Remembering SNCC* (1998); Fred Powledge, *Free at Last?: The Civil Rights Movement and the People Who Made It* (1992); Emily Stoper, *The Student Nonviolent Coordinating Committee: The Growth of Radicalism in a Civil Rights Organization* (1989).

Irvin D. S. Winsboro

***Aldridge v. United States*, 283 U.S. 308 (1931)**   Although the trial judge in this case allowed the plaintiff's attorney to ask questions of prospective jurors regarding their knowledge of the facts in the case, their acquaintance with either the African American defendant or the dead white policeman, and their reaction to circumstantial evidence and capital punishment, he refused to allow them to be questioned regarding their racial prejudices. Aldridge was convicted of murder, and the judge's decision was sustained by the District of Columbia Court of Appeals, which ruled that such questions, proper elsewhere, were not appropriate in the nation's capital. The U.S. Supreme Court in its reversal recognized the propriety of such inquiries. Chief Justice Charles Evans Hughes ruled that the right to examine jurors on their voir dire regarding a disqualifying state of mind had been upheld in cases involving other races, "religious and other prejudices of a serious character." He maintained that the question of racial prejudice was not geared to the matter of civil rights but to the presence of bias in a particular juror. If prejudice of any kind would prevent a juror from "rendering a fair verdict, a gross injustice would be perpetrated in allowing him to sit."

Selected Bibliography Richard Bardolph, ed., *The Civil Rights Record: Black Americans and the Law 1849–1970* (1970); Derrick A. Bell, Jr., *Race, Racism, and American Law* (1980); Alfred H. Kelly and Winfred A. Harbison, *American Constitution: Origins and Development* (1970).

Aingred G. Dunston

Alexander, Clifford L., Jr. (21 September 1933, New York, N.Y.–). The first African American chairman of the **Equal Employment Opportunity Commission** (EEOC) (1967–69), Alexander brought elite credentials to the commission at a turbulent time. A native of New York City with a Harvard B.A. (1955) and a Yale law degree (1958), Alexander served a National Guard tour in 1958, then worked in New York City in the district attorney's office, in Harlem youth work, and in private law practice. In 1963 he joined the National Security Council staff under McGeorge Bundy, and in 1964 he became a presidential assistant to Lyndon B. Johnson. In 1967 the EEOC, created by the **Civil Rights Act of 1964,** faced a troubled environment that included widespread urban violence, feminist demands for stronger enforcement of gender equality, administrative confusion within the agency, and a vacant chairmanship for the third time. Johnson appointed Alexander, who held a series of regional hearings to emphasize employment discrimination outside the South, especially in white-collar jobs. Alexander accelerated the agency's controversial shift from an equal-treatment model of nondiscrimination toward an equal-results model of **affirmative action** that stressed proportional representation of minorities and women in the workforce. In 1969 Senate minority leader Everett Dirksen attacked Alexander for harassing employers and for requiring racial quotas in employment. In May 1969 President Richard Nixon replaced Alexander as chairman with a black Republican, William A. Brown III. The EEOC continued its affirmative action program, but Alexander resigned from the commission in August 1969 to enter private law practice in Washington, D.C. In 1977 he was appointed secretary of the army by President Jimmy Carter and served until 1980.

Selected Bibliography *Contemporary Black Biography,* vol. 26 (2001); Hugh Davis Graham, *The Civil Rights Era* (1990); Elaine Welles, "Alexander, A Man Destined for Greatness," Philadelphia *Tribune,* 12 February 2002.

Hugh Davis Graham

Alexander, John Hanks (6 January 1864, Helena, Ark.–26 March 1894, Springfield, Ohio). The son of slave parents, Alexander attended Oberlin

College for one year until he scored higher on a test than the son of Ohio's chief justice and received an appointment to the United States Military Academy in 1883. Despite white ostracism, he did well in all his courses, particularly those in the languages, and in 1887 became the second black graduate in the history of West Point, ranking 32nd out of a class of 64. After graduation, he reported to the all-black Ninth Cavalry Regiment (see **Buffalo Soldiers**), where he served for the next seven years and compiled an excellent record. **Booker T. Washington** and other black leaders tried to get him assigned as an instructor of military science at **Tuskegee Institute** or some other black college, but they were not successful until January 1894 when, through the efforts of the president of Ohio's Wilberforce College, he was assigned there. He had just begun his tour of duty when he died of a heart attack. Had he lived he might very well have become the ranking black officer in World War I; he outranked the later famous **Charles Young** by two years. During that war, the War Department named a Virginia stevedore encampment Camp Alexander after him.

Selected Bibliography Willard B. Gatewood, Jr., "John Hanks Alexander of Arkansas: Second Black Graduate of West Point," *Arkansas Historical Quarterly* 41 (Summer 1982), 103–28; Rayford W. Logan and Michael R. Winston, eds., *Dictionary of American Negro Biography* (1982); Reverdy C. Ransom, *The Pilgrimage of Harriet Ransom's Son* (n.d.); William S. Scarborough, *A Tribute to Colonel Charles Young* (n.d.).

John F. Marszalek

Alexander, Margaret Walker   (7 July 1915, Birmingham, Ala.–30 November 1998, Jackson, Miss.). Daughter of a middle-class academic family who taught at various southern colleges during her childhood, Margaret Walker graduated from Northwestern University during the Great Depression and went to work for the Works Progress Administration (WPA) in Chicago. She became friends with a group of writers on the South Side that included **Richard Wright.** During that period, Walker wrote most of the poems later published in *For My People* (1942). When the WPA work ended, Walker went to Iowa for her master's degree in English and then taught at a series of black colleges. She married Firnist James Alexander in North Carolina and moved to Jackson, Mississippi, with three children in 1949.

Margaret Walker Alexander's relationship with Jackson State University proved stormy. She felt that the male administration discriminated against her because she was a woman; nevertheless, she worked hard and students considered her a demanding, master teacher who erased disciplinary lines seeking insight and understanding. In addition to continuing her writing, Alexander wrote grants, conducted workshops, and established the Institute for the Study of the Life, History, and Culture of Black People, one of the first academic organizations in the South devoted to black studies.

Alexander has said that her teaching and writing are her contributions to the civil rights movement. She completed her Ph.D. at the University of Iowa and published her dissertation in 1966, which, as *Jubilee*, became a highly successful, popular novel, which describes the black debate in the 1870s in a manner relevant to the 1960s and 1970s. The main character, Vyry, a mulatto daughter of her master, remains faithful to her Christianity and refuses to hate despite the beatings and abuse heaped on her by whites. By contrast, the main male character is pure black and espouses the black nationalist point of view. In her novel and in her life, Alexander made many people uncomfortable because she lived Vyry's strong commitment to a Christian family while uncompromisingly condemning white racism and sympathizing with the black nationalist.

Alexander wrote 10 books during her teaching career and in retirement worked full-time on her writing. She published *Richard Wright: Daemonic Genius* in 1988. A book of poetry entitled *This Is My Century* and two essay collections followed. At the time of her death, she had been writing her autobiography telling the story of the black, southern middle class since Reconstruction.

Selected Bibliography Maryemma Graham, ed., *How I Wrote Jubilee and Other Essays on Life and Literature* (1990); Margaret Walker, *Jubilee* (1966); Margaret Walker, *On Being Female, Black, and Free: Essay by Margaret Walker* (1997); Margaret Walker Alexander Papers, Jackson State University Library, Jackson, Mississippi.

Dennis J. Mitchell

Alexander v. Holmes County Board of Education, 396 U.S. 1218 (1969)

On 29 October 1969, the U.S. Supreme Court unanimously declared that public school desegregation at "all **deliberate speed**," as allowed in the second ***Brown v. Board of Education*** case in 1955, was no longer constitutionally permissible. Instead, the Court ordered that the dual school systems in Mississippi's 33 school districts had to be eliminated and "unitary" school systems established "at once." District officials had argued that massive midterm integration would cause unjustified disruption in the schools. Serving as a precedent, *Alexander* was a major step away from the federal courts' post-*Brown* deliberate approach. It ensured wide-scale school integration across the South within the succeeding 12 months. *Alexander* also marked a milestone in changing federal policy from "desegregation," eliminating barriers to blacks and whites attending school together, to "integration," requiring blacks and whites to attend the same schools. The Justice Department and the Department of Health, Education and Welfare argued for the Mississippi school districts' position. Prior to this case, the Justice Department and the **NAACP Legal Defense and Educational Fund,** the lawyers for the plaintiffs, were uniformly in agreement. Observers commonly saw President Richard Nixon's "Southern Strategy" to win southern votes as the cause for this change. Warren Burger, Nixon's newly appointed chief justice, concurred with his fellow justices.

Selected Bibliography "'Desegregate Now'—But How to Do It? " *U.S. News and World Report* (10 November 1969), 45–46; Paul R. Dimond, *Beyond Busing: Inside the Challenge to Urban Segregation* (1985); Alfred H. Kelly, Winfred A. Harbison, and Herman Belz, *The American Constitution: Its Origins and Development*, 6th ed. (1983); "The Supreme Court: Integration Now," *Time* (7 November 1969), 19–20; J. Harvie Wilkinson III, *The Supreme Court and School Segregation: 1954–1978* (1979).

Eric C. Clark

Alexander, Will W. (15 July 1884, Morrisville, Mo.–13 January 1956, Chapel Hill, N.C.). Born and raised in Missouri and ordained a Methodist minister, Alexander received a divinity degree from Vanderbilt University in Nashville, where he first came in contact with southern poverty and racial segregation. In response to the racial violence of 1919, the resurgence of the Ku Klux Klan, and racial lynching, he founded the Atlanta-based **Commission on Interracial Cooperation** (CIC), which he headed until the mid-1930s. Working within an isolated and racially hostile southern environment, Alexander did not directly challenge Jim Crowism (see **Jim Crow**) but sought social and economic opportunities for blacks while encouraging a more enlightened racial perspective among white religious, business, and civic groups. When Franklin D. Roosevelt took office in 1933, Alexander became a key adviser on racial matters to the New Deal and especially to individuals such as **Eleanor Roosevelt.** He was also close to black leaders such as **Walter Francis White** of the **NAACP** and sociologist **Charles S. Johnson.** In 1935 he left the CIC to become an assistant in the Resettlement Administration and, shortly thereafter, head of the Farm Security Administration (FSA). Under Alexander, the FSA appointed blacks to national and state positions, and black farmers were included in various FSA programs, such as farm loans. During World War II, Alexander and black economist **Robert C. Weaver** worked to secure defense jobs for black workers, and in the late 1940s and early 1950s Alexander supported the interracial efforts of the **Southern Regional Council** and the **Southern Conference for Human Welfare.** Although he died prior to the southern civil rights struggles of the late 1950s and early 1960s, Alexander's long commitment to racial toleration and the rights of black people contributed to some of the later achievements won by blacks in the South.

    Selected Bibliography Sidney Baldwin, *Poverty and Politics: The Rise and Decline of the Farm Security Administration* (1968); Wilma Dykeman and James Stokley, *Seeds of Southern Change: The Life of Will Alexander* (1966); John B. Kirby, *Black Americans in the Roosevelt Era* (1980); Harvard Sitkoff, *A New Deal for Blacks* (1978).

John B. Kirby

Allen, Ivan, Jr. (15 March 1911, Atlanta, Ga.–2 July 2003, Atlanta, Ga.). Allen entered Atlanta's business community in 1933 when he joined his father's office supply company upon graduation from the Georgia Institute of Technology. He became active in politics following World War II, serving two years as executive secretary to liberal Georgia Governor Ellis Arnall. After a failed attempt in the governor's race in 1954, Allen ran for mayor of Atlanta in 1961. Changing from his earlier defense of segregation to a liberal viewpoint that advocated economic growth and community development, he defeated segregationist Lester Maddox. His two terms as mayor saw public facilities and schools integrated and a basis laid for the economic transformation of Atlanta's commercial community. He was the only major southern white politician to support President John F. Kennedy's legislation to desegregate public accommodations. Remaining active in civil rights causes, Allen celebrated his 92nd birthday in March 2003, just 4 months before his death.

Selected Bibliography Ivan Allen, Jr., *Mayor: Notes on the Sixties* (1971); "Atlanta: Voice of Confidence," *Newsweek*, 20 October 1969; Nelson Lichtenstein, ed., *Political Profiles: The Johnson Years* (1976).

Thomas D. Cockrell

Allen v. State Board of Elections, **393 U.S. 544 (1968)** As a result of the **Voting Rights Act of 1965,** African Americans gained access to the polls, but they continued to encounter obstacles to the effective use of the ballot. To dilute the political power of the newly enfranchised blacks, white southern politicians changed electoral laws and practices by establishing multiseat electoral districts and at-large elections, all with the intent of reducing the effect of the black vote. It was not clear that the Voting Rights Act of 1965 prohibited such electoral manipulations. Southern conservatives predictably argued that the act simply prohibited restrictions limiting the right to register and vote but did not pertain to changes that might be made in the electoral process. In *Allen v. State Board of Elections,* a suit brought by the **Legal Defense and Educational Fund** of the **NAACP,** the Supreme Court swept aside a Mississippi statute that permitted a change from district to at-large elections of certain county officials. Because the statute had the effect of diluting black voting power and thereby nullifying or curtailing their ability to elect candidates of their choice, the Mississippi law violated the Voting Rights Act.

Selected Bibliography Derrick A. Bell, Jr., *Race, Racism, and American Law* (1980); Thomas I. Emerson, David Haber, and Norman Dorsen, *Political and Civil Rights in the United States* (1967); Steven F. Lawson, *Black Ballots: Voting Rights in the South, 1944–1969* (1976); Donald G. Nieman, *Promises to Keep: African-Americans and the Constitutional Order 1776 to the Present* (1991); Roland Young, ed., "Review of Recent Supreme Court Decisions," *American Bar Association Journal* 55 (1969), 580–81.

Charles D. Lowery

Alston v. Board of Education of the City of Norfolk, **112 F.2d 992 (4th Cir., 1940)** Public education in the South in the era of "separate but equal" was anything but equal. In the late 1930s and the 1940s, the legal strategy of the **NAACP** called for litigation that would produce greater racial equality, within a segregated public school environment, beginning with teachers' pay. Melvin O. Alston, a teacher at Booker T. Washington High School in Norfolk, Virginia, agreed in 1939 to bring suit against the city's school board. In federal district court, Alston lost, but, on appeal to the Fourth Circuit Court of Appeals, he won. That court ruled that racial discrimination in salary schedules for public schoolteachers violated the "due process" and "equal protection" clauses of the **Fourteenth Amendment.** In turn, the city appealed, but the U.S. Supreme Court let the decision stand (311 U.S. 693 [1940]). The case was a good one, in the view of NAACP attorneys, in that it originated in the largest city of a border state, but, having won, they found that it took continued pressure for several years to approach equal salaries across Virginia. All such efforts—including suits for equal busing to black schools, equal physical facilities, and equal curricula—constituted a prelude to the direct assault, after 1950, on segregation itself.

Selected Bibliography Richard Kluger, *Simple Justice: The History of Brown v. Board of Education and Black America's Struggle for Equality* (1976); Mark V. Tushnet, *The NAACP's Legal Strategy against Segregated Education, 1925–1950* (1987); Peter Wallenstein, *These New and Strange Beings: Conflict, Law, and Change in the Twentieth-Century Virginia* (2003).

Peter Wallenstein

American Civil Liberties Union A national, nonprofit, nonpartisan legal organization dedicated to upholding the constitutional rights of Americans, the American Civil Liberties Union (ACLU) was founded in 1920 by Roger Baldwin—its president for 30 years—and others who opposed the government's treatment of World War I dissidents. Since its founding, the ACLU has worked mainly through the courts to safeguard the Bill of Rights for a large number of individuals and groups, including labor agitators, socialists and communists, religious nonconformists, political radicals, and antiwar protestors. In the matter of civil rights for minorities, it has helped to secure voting rights for blacks, has worked to desegregate public schools, and has defended blacks accused of a crime because of their race. The organization maintains a headquarters in New York City and has state and local offices throughout the nation.

A volunteer from the ACLU explains to Anthony Flowers, an ex-felon, how to apply for restoration of his civil rights. © AP/Wide World Photos.

Selected Bibliography *American Civil Liberties Union: The Roger Baldwin Years, 1917–1950* (microfilm, 1996); Ken Crowder, "The ACLU Defends Everybody," *Smithsonian* 28 (No. 10, 1998), 86–97; Robert Justin Goldstein, *Political Repression in Modern America: From 1870 to the Present* (1978); Barbara Habenstreit, *Eternal Vigilance: The American Civil Liberties Union in Action* (1971); Peggy Lamson, *Roger Baldwin—Founder of the American Civil Liberties Union* (1977); Charles Lam Markmann, *The Noblest Cry: A History of the American Civil Liberties Union* (1965); Samuel E. Walker, *In Defense of American Liberties: A History of the ACLU* (1990); Web site: www.aclu.org.

Dorothy A. Autrey

An American Dilemma   The Carnegie Foundation provided funds for this study of black-white relations and selected the Swedish economist Gunnar Myrdal to direct it. Myrdal came to the United States in 1938 and selected a group of black and white scholars to help him conduct the study. Many of them wrote monographs on specific aspects of race relations, and Myrdal used these in writing the final document. Myrdal concluded that black Americans were prevented from fully participating in American society. This posed a dilemma for Americans because this denial of equality violated the American democratic creed. Myrdal was optimistic that Americans would resolve the dilemma. When it was first published in 1944, the study received a welcome reception from white liberals, but it was strongly condemned by southerners. Blacks were ambivalent. By the 1950s, however, Myrdal's study was the authoritative work on race relations. Lawyers cited it in arguing the civil rights cases of the 1950s and 1960s. By 1965, however, scholars were questioning Myrdal's optimistic prediction that racial equality would come within a decade. Moreover, the rise of the **Black Power** movement caused black Americans to reconsider their favorable opinions of Myrdal's assimilationist views.

Selected Bibliography Obie Clayton, Jr., ed. *An American Dilemma Revisited: Race Relations in a Changing World* (1996); Gunnar Myrdal, *An American Dilemma: The Negro Problem and Modern Democracy* (1944); David W. Southern, *Gunnar Myrdal and Black-White Relations: The Use and Abuse of An American Dilemma, 1944–1969* (1987).

Arvarh E. Strickland

American Friends Service Committee   Started in 1917 by Quakers as a pacifist organization, the American Friends Service Committee (AFSC) soon extended its interest to benevolence and domestic reform. The committee followed the traditional belief of the Friends that there was no difference between idealism and practice, an emphasis that led it to join the struggle for civil rights. An important contribution by the AFSC was its espousal of merit employment, fair housing, and school desegregation after World War II. The migration of southern blacks to northern and western cities had disrupted normal patterns and had led to white resentment and discrimination. The AFSC exerted particular influence in Chicago with its merit employment drives in department stores and banks. It established the Housing Opportunities Program to work with white and black families in creating an open housing market in the area. In 1967 it issued a nationally important report on the difficulties blacks were experiencing in the suburban housing market. Although active in more renowned events like the activities of the **Freedom Riders** and the **Little Rock desegregation crisis,** the AFSC contributed significantly to public awareness of the less dramatic but no less real civil rights violations in housing and employment. It still exists today, working mainly for world peace and performing humanitarian works in war-ravaged countries.

Selected Bibliography J. William Frost, "Our Deeds Carry Our Message: The Early History of the American Friends Service Committee," *Quaker History* 81 (1992), 1–51; Gerald Jonas, *On Doing Good* (1971); Mary H. Jones, *Swords into Ploughshares: An Account of the American Friends Service Committee 1917–1937* (1971); Daisy Newman, *A Procession of Friends* (1972); Web site: www.afsc.org.

Steve Rea

American Missionary Association Born out of the *Amistad* case, which sought and secured freedom for a group of Africans intended for slavery, the American Missionary Association (AMA) was founded on 3 September 1846 in Syracuse, New York, through an antislavery coalition of the Union Missionary Society, the Committee for West Indian Missions, and the Western Evangelical Missionary Society. In 1847 it established relief services for slaves escaping to Canada, but its principal goal was the nonviolent overthrow of slavery. The AMA's commitment to education began in 1859 when John G. Fee founded Berea College in Kentucky. Built on land donated by the ardent abolitionist, Cassius M. Clay, Berea was open to blacks and whites alike. Unfortunately, the college was closed shortly after opening because of growing fears among local whites after John Brown's raid at Harper's Ferry. As Union armies advanced across the South after 1862, the AMA followed behind, providing needed relief to the ever-growing contraband camps of former slaves. At Fortress Monroe in Virginia, the first AMA school for freedmen was established under the direction of Mary S. Peaks. Out of this school grew a network of educational facilities for freedmen across the South. The AMA also established five hundred colleges and normal schools in the southern states, which were eventually absorbed into the public school system. Of the fifteen thousand black teachers in the South in 1870, seven thousand were AMA graduates. Since 1900, the AMA has established services for Native Americans, Chinese, and migrant workers. During the Great Depression, the AMA was a leader in the education of tenant farmers across the South, and the civil rights movement had several leaders who were graduates of AMA schools.

Selected Bibliography Augustus Field Beard, *A Crusade of Brotherhood* (1972); Clara M. DeBoer, *His Truth is Marching On: African Americans Who Taught the Freedmen for the American Missionary Association, 1861–1827* (1995); Clara M. DeBoer, *Be Jubilant My Feet: African American Abolitionists in the American Missionary Association, 1839–1861* (1994); Richard B. Drake, *American Missionary Association and the Southern Negro, 1861–1888* (1969); Joe M. Richardson, *Christian Reconstruction* (1986); Web site: www.tulane.edu/'amistad/digital.htm.

James W. Stennett, revised by Marvin Thomas

American Negro Academy   Existing from 1897 to 1928, the American Negro Academy (ANA) was the first major black learned society in the United States. A small, select organization of authors, scholars, and artists, the ANA promoted the publication of scholarly work dealing with African American culture and history. Several prominent scholars, including **Alexander Crummell, W.E.B. Du Bois, Archibald H. Grimke,** John W. Cromwell, and Arthur Schomberg, served terms as president of the academy. The ANA went out of existence in 1928 because the scholarly elitist tradition embodied by ANA founders became difficult to defend during a decade when African American leaders emphasized the courage, wisdom, beauty, and strength of the African American masses.

Selected Bibliography Leon Litwack and August Meier, eds., *Black Leaders of the Nineteenth Century* (1988); Alfred A. Moss, Jr., *The American Negro Academy: Voice of the Talented Tenth* (1981).

Janice M. Leone

American Negro Labor Congress   The American **Communist Party** created this organization at a meeting held in Chicago in October 1925. Delegates representing black labor, fraternal, farmers', and benefit organizations attended. Lovett Fort-Whiteman, who had only recently returned from the Soviet Union, served as national organizer. He made it clear that the organization would have a distinct Marxist orientation. The American Negro Labor Congress (ANLC) was to be more than a labor movement, however. "The idea of the American Negro Labor Congress," according to the group's call to action, "is to bring together the most potent elements of the Negro race for deliberation and action upon those most irritating and oppressive social problems affecting the life of the race in general and the Negro working class in particular." Even so, the American Communist Party faced a dilemma in sponsoring an organization for black workers. The Communists declared that the problems faced by black Americans stemmed solely from class differences and that solutions to these problems required worker solidarity, not separation. Although the ANLC helped to call attention to the plight of black workers, it did not attract wide support, and it gradually faded from the scene.

Selected Bibliography Herbert Aptheker, ed., *A Documentary History of the Negro People in the United States 1910–1932* (1973); William H. Harris, *Keeping the Faith: A. Philip Randolph, Milton P. Webster, and the Brotherhood of Sleeping Car Porters, 1925–37* (1977); Sterling D. Spero and Abram L. Harris, *The Black Worker: The Negro and the Labor Movement* (1968).

Arvarh E. Strickland

American Student Union   A Communist student group that grew out of the Communist National Student League and the Socialist Student League for Industrial Democracy, the American Student Union (ASU) was one of several such Communist "front" organizations (the American League for Peace and Democracy and the **American Youth Congress** were others) that sought control of U.S. public opinion during the socially turbulent 1930s. Like the

American Youth Congress, ASU championed black interests and challenged **Jim Crow.** Its principal journal, the *Student Advocate*, repeatedly called for an end to racial segregation in southern colleges and universities, intercollegiate athletics, and in ROTC units throughout the country. It called for the development of college studies in black history and culture, urged the hiring of African American professors at white colleges and universities, and equated black civil rights with the universal struggle for freedom. Although short-lived, ASU served on many college campuses during the 1930s to focus attention on the grave injustices African Americans suffered.

Selected Bibliography William E. Leuchtenburg, *Franklin D. Roosevelt and the New Deal* (1963); Arthur B. Link and William B. Catton, *American Epoch, A History of the United States since the 1890s* (1963); Harvard Sitkoff, *A New Deal for Blacks: The Emergence of Civil Rights as a National Issue, The Depression Decade* (1978).

Charles D. Lowery

American Youth Congress   Founded in 1934 as one of several Communist "front" organizations, the American Youth Congress (AYC) pretended to speak for five million young people across the country who decried racism in every form. It joined hands with the **Southern Negro Youth Congress** and the **American Student Union** during the Depression decade to champion social, political, and economic equality for African Americans. At its periodic congresses, the AYC passed numerous resolutions, supporting such things as the enfranchisement of southern blacks, the abolition of **Jim Crow** laws; and efforts of the Southern Negro Youth Congress to unionize black workers. It spoke out in defense of the "boys" in the **Scottsboro Trials** and called for the implementation of black studies courses in public schools and universities. The AYC enjoyed the public endorsement of **Aubrey Williams,** the director of the New Deal National Youth Administration, and the support of **Eleanor Roosevelt.** Its Communist ties led to its demise after World War II.

Selected Bibliography Philip S. Foner, *Organized Labor and the Black Worker, 1619–1973* (1974); Note, *Journal of Negro Education* 5 (October, 1936), 651–52; George Philip Rawick, *The New Deal and Youth: The Civilian Conservation Corps, the National Youth Administration, and the American Youth Congress* (1957); Harvard Sitkoff, *A New Deal for Blacks: The Emergence of Civil Rights as a National Issue, The Depression Decade* (1978).

Charles D. Lowery

Americans for Democratic Action   In 1947 **Eleanor Roosevelt,** Reinhold Niebuhr, Chester Bowles, **Walter Reuther,** Marquis Childs, David Dubinsky, and others led by James Loeb, Jr., founded the Americans for Democratic Action (ADA) as a political organization to support the advance of liberal causes. From the beginning, the ADA excluded Communists from membership although conservatives have often accused it of being, at best, a Communist front. The ADA rates the voting records of members of Congress to identify each one's degree of liberalness. The ADA is nonpartisan in its endorsements but usually supports Democrats. In 1948 the ADA selected civil rights as the issue to use to assert liberal influence in national politics. With

Hubert Horatio Humphrey, Jr., leading on the floor, the ADA and other civil rights groups won a fight to include a strong civil rights plank in the Democratic party platform, which caused southern Democrats to walk out of the convention and run Strom Thurmond as the Dixiecrat candidate for president. ADA membership peaked at approximately seventy-five thousand in the early 1970s. In 2003, it continues to provide rankings of the members of Congress, although its overall influence in the political spectrum is less important than it once was.

Selected Bibliography Clifton Brock, *Americans for Democratic Action: Its Role in National Politics* (1962); Steven M. Gillon, *Politics and Vision: The ADA and American Liberalism, 1947–1985* (1987); Peter J. Kellog, "The Americans for Democratic Action and Civil Rights in 1948: Conscience in Politics or Politics in Conscience," *Midwest Quarterly* 20 (Autumn 1978), 49–63; Web site: www.adaction.org.

Lorenzo Crowell

Amsterdam News   This weekly New York City African American newspaper was established by James H. Anderson in December 1909. Armed with only "six sheets of blank paper, a lead pencil and a dress-maker's table," Anderson laid the foundation for one of the nation's oldest black newspapers. In 1936, physicians Philip Savory and Clelan B. Powell purchased the problem-plagued paper and chose not to crusade, but to feature instead "the accomplishments and progress of the Negro." It both praised and criticized public figures, editorially castigating its former columnist, **Adam Clayton Powell, Jr.,** for example, and benefitted from his frequent inclusion of its activities into the *Congressional Record.* By the 1960s it was read by more blacks than any black newspaper in the nation. It was the only source for New York's large African American population to get the black perspective of the news. It has continued to be a voice for black people in the nation's largest city.

Selected Bibliography *The Crisis Magazine* 45 (April 1938), 105–6; Frederick Detweiler, *The Negro Press in the United States* (1968); J. Kirk Sale, "The Amsterdam News," *New York Times Magazine* (9 February 1969); Ronald E. Wolseley, *The Black Press, U.S.A.* (1990).

Maxine D. Jones

Anderson, Charles W., Jr.   (26 May 1907, Louisville, Ky.–14 June 1960, Louisville, Ky.). After graduating from Wilberforce University and **Howard University** Law School, Anderson returned to his hometown, Louisville, Kentucky, and served as a distinguished politician, trial lawyer, and civil rights leader. In 1935 he became the first African American since Reconstruction to be elected to a southern state legislature. He successfully opposed a bill that advocated the use of glass partitions to segregate blacks and whites on buses. He also sought to expand educational opportunities for black Kentuckians. In 1936 he cosponsored the Anderson-Mayer State Aid Act, which appropriated funds for the out-of-state education of blacks pursuing undergraduate work or advanced degrees in fields not taught at the state's black college. The following year Anderson convinced the legislature to pass a bill requiring Kentucky counties to support high school education for black students in rural areas. In 1944 Anderson presented a bill to amend the 1904 segregation law. It passed in the House but failed in the Senate. In 1959 President Dwight D. Eisenhower nominated Anderson as an alternate delegate to the United Nations.

Selected Bibliography *Kentucky's Black Heritage* (1971); *The Louisville Defender*, 27 August, 19 September, 1959, 16 June, 1960; Gerald L. Smith, "'Mr. Kentucky State': A Biography of Rufus Ballard Atwood" (Ph.D. diss., University of Kentucky, 1988); John C. Smith, *Emancipation: The Making of the Black Lawyer, 1844–1944* (1993).

Gerald L. Smith

Anderson, Marian (17 February 1902, Philadelphia, Pa.–8 April 1993, Portland, Oreg.). As a child chorister at the Union Baptist Church of Philadelphia, this renowned opera singer's untutored voice so impressed the church members that they set up a trust fund to ensure that she could study with the great music and voice teacher, Giuseppe Boghetti. This education allowed her to launch a musical career in 1924; in one year's time she won first prize at New York's Lewisohn Stadium, defeating two hundred contestants in the competition sponsored by the New York Philharmonic Symphony. In the next four years she sang a debut recital in Berlin that was followed by even more successful concerts, usually consisting of a repertoire of Bach, Beethoven, and African American spirituals. In 1939 the Daughters of the American

Marian Anderson. © Library of Congress.

Revolution (DAR) refused her permission to perform in Constitution Hall in Washington, D.C. The outraged First Lady **Eleanor Roosevelt** immediately resigned her membership in the DAR. Anderson became a symbolic rallying point around whom others in agreement with Eleanor Roosevelt's position on racial equality could show their distaste for racial discrimination. Anderson accepted an offer to perform at the Lincoln Memorial on Easter Sunday. An integrated audience of seventy-five thousand people, including members of the Supreme Court, Congress, and President Franklin Roosevelt's cabinet, came to hear her sing. In 1955, she became the first black person to appear on stage at the Metropolitan Opera House. That same year she served as an American delegate to the United Nations. In 1965 she gave a farewell recital at Carnegie Hall. She received honorary degrees from 23 American educational institutions and from a Korean institution, as well as decorations from numerous states and cities and from Sweden, the Philippines, Haiti, Liberia, France, and Japan. She spent most of her retirement on a farm in Danbury, Connecticut, until moving in with her nephew, James DePriest, the director of the Oregon Symphony. She is buried in Philadelphia, Pennsylvania.

Selected Bibliography Marian Anderson, *My Lord, What a Morning: An Autobiography* (1956); Marianna W. Davis, ed., *Contributions of Black Women to America, vol. 1: The Arts, Media, Business, Law, Sports* (1982); Allan Keiler, *Marion Anderson: A Singer's Journey* (2000); Charles Patterson, *Marion Anderson* (2000).

Linda Reed

Angelou, Maya (4 April 1928, St. Louis, Mo.–). Originally named Marguerite Johnson, Angelou's first autobiographical work, *I Know Why the Caged Bird Sings* (1970), achieved both critical and popular success. Although now primarily known as a poet, she is a social activist who has written several autobiographies. Over the course of her long and varied work life, she was the editor of an English-language magazine in Egypt, the features editor for the *African Review* in Ghana, and a television and file director and producer. In 1960, after seeing the Reverend **Martin Luther King, Jr.,** speak at a Harlem church rally, she and actor Godfrey Cambridge wrote a play titled "Cabaret for Freedom," a musical revue that both highlighted issues related to the struggle for racial equality and helped raise money in support of King and the **Southern Christian Leadership Conference** (SCLC). From 1960 to 1961, at King's request, she worked with the SCLC as its northern coordinator. She has authored a wide variety of literary works, including multivolumes of verses. In 1993, she became even more well known when, during the inauguration of President Bill Clinton, she read her poem "On the Pulse of Morning," which called upon the nation for renewal and rejuvenation.

Selected Bibliography Harold Bloom, ed., *Maya Angelou* (2002); *Current Biography* (1994); Stuart Kallen, *Maya Angelou: Woman of Words, Deeds, and Dreams* (1993); Elaine Slivinski Lisandrelli, *Maya Angelou: More than a Poet* (1996); Mary Jane Lupton, *Maya Angelou: A Critical Companion* (1998); Miles Shapiro, with introduction by Coretta Scott King, *Maya Angelou* (1994); Mary E. Williams, ed., *Readings on Maya Angelou* (1997).

Norlisha Crawford

Anna T. Jeanes Fund.   See Jeanes (Anna T.) Fund.

Anthony v. Marshall County Board of Education, **409 F.2d 1287 (5th Cir., 1969)**   In the wake of the U.S. Supreme Court's desegregation decision in *Green v. County School Board of New Kent County, Virginia,* a group of black Mississippi school children, represented by their parents, brought a class action suit against the Holly Springs and Marshall County school districts. The U.S. District Court for the Northern District of Mississippi concluded that the only viable plan of desegregation for the two school districts was to continue under the existing "freedom of choice" plan, and the plaintiffs appealed. In view of the evidence that, during the 1967–68 school year, only 21 of 1,868 black children in one district and only 22 of 3,606 in the other district attended white schools, along with the fact that no white students in either district had ever attended a black school, the **United States Fifth Circuit Court of Appeals** ruled that the school districts remained dual systems. The court also said that "freedom of choice" plans had not been effective in eliminating dual systems and that the burden thus was on the two school boards to produce realistic and workable plans for realizing unified nondiscriminatory systems.

Selected Bibliography Richard Bardolph, ed., *The Civil Rights Record, Black Americans and the Law, 1849–1970* (1970); *Race Relations Law Survey* 1 (1969), 68, 167, 203; Francis B. Stevens and John L. Maxer, "Representing the Under-represented: A Decennial Report of Public Interest Litigation in Mississippi," *Mississippi Law Journal* 44 (1973), 298–314.

W. Lance Conn

Anti-Defamation League of B'nai B'rith   This organization was established in 1913 within the Independent Order of B'nai B'rith, a Jewish fraternal organization. Its founders saw its two goals as inextricably linked: to "stop . . . the defamation of the Jewish people" and to "secure justice and fair treatment to all citizens alike." From its inception, therefore, the Anti-Defamation League (ADL) concerned itself not only with anti-Semitism but also with racism and racial discrimination, and it was active in the modern civil rights movement. From its founding until the present, the ADL has monitored racist and anti-Semitic incidents and white supremacist organizations (including the Ku Klux Klan and the Skinheads), and it takes action against them whenever possible. It also works proactively, promoting civil rights and defending civil liberties through the courts, the legislature, the press, and through school and workplace education programs.

Selected Bibliography Nathan Belth, "Not the Work of A Day: The Story of the Anti-Defamation League of B'nai B'rith," Anti-Defamation League pamphlet (1965); Oscar Cohen and Stanley Wexler, eds., *Not the Work of a Day: Anti-Defamation League of B'nai B'rith Oral Memoirs,* 6 vols. (1987–89); Arnold Forster, *Square One* (1988); Murray Friedman, "One Episode in Southern Jewry's Response to Desegregation," *American Jewish Archives* 33 (November 1981); 170–83; Jill Donnie Snyder and Eric Goodman, *Friend of the Court 1947–1982: To Secure Justice and Fair Treatment for All* (1983); Web site: www.adl.org.

Cheryl Greenberg

A flag announcing a lynching, flown from the window of the NAACP headquarters in New York City, 1936. © Library of Congress.

Antilynching Crusaders   This group organized the first mass interracial attempt to stop lynching. When Congressman L. C. Dyer proposed a federal antilynching bill in 1922, the Crusaders were organized by the **NAACP** to mobilize women. These women, headed by Mary B. Talbert of the **National Association of Colored Women,** had their own collective consciousness of sexual victimization and wanted to fight that, along with the myth of the black male rapist. Crusader volunteers tried stop lynching with mass publicity. They mobilized black and white support and raised money for the Dyer Bill's passage. Unable to reach their goal of one million dollars, they did raise national consciousness and laid the groundwork for future antilynching activism.

Selected Bibliography   Antilynching Crusaders Minutes, NAACP Papers, Library of Congress; Donald B. Grant, *The Anti-Lynching Movement, 1883–1932* (1975); Gerda Lerner, *Black Women in White America: A Documentary History* (1973); NAACP, *The AntiLynching Crusaders: A Million Women United to Suppress Lynching* (1922).

Linda G. Ford

***Arnold v. North Carolina*, 376 U.S. 773 (1964)**   Two black men, Jesse James Arnold and George Dixon, were found guilty of murder in state court in North Carolina. On appeal to the state supreme court, Arnold and Dixon argued that their convictions should be set aside under the equal protection clause of the **Fourteenth Amendment** because local officials had routinely excluded blacks from grand jury service. According to evidence they presented in the state proceedings, county tax rolls listed 12,250 whites and 4,819 blacks. Although roughly a quarter of the local taxpayers were black, the clerk of the state trial court testified that during his 24 years in office, he could remember only one black ever serving on a grand jury. The North Carolina Supreme Court ruled that this was not sufficient evidence of the systematic exclusion of blacks. In a per curiam opinion, the U.S. Supreme Court reversed the state court. Comparing the case to its earlier decision in *Eubanks v. Louisiana*, 356 U.S. 584 (1958), the court determined that the testimony of the defendants had established a prima facie case of the denial of equal protection.

Selected Bibliography Marvin E. Frankel and Gary P. Naftalis, *The Grand Jury* (1975); Richard D. Younger, *The People's Panel: The Grand Jury in the United States, 1634–1941* (1963).

Jeff Broadwater

Ashmore, Harry Scott (27 July 1916, Greenville, S.C.–20 January 1998, Santa Barbara, Calif.). A 1937 Clemson College graduate, Ashmore first worked for Greenville newspapers. He was a Nieman Fellow at Harvard (1941–42) before he served in World War II. After working as an editor for the Charlotte *News*, he became in 1947 the executive editor of the Little Rock *Arkansas Gazette*. A southern liberal, he opposed the Dixiecrats in 1948 and campaigned with Adlai Stevenson in 1952 and 1956. In 1953–54 he directed the Fund for the Advancement of Education's major study of the South's biracial educational system, which was published the day before the 1954 **Brown v. Board of Education** decision as *The Negro and the Schools*. During the 1957–58 **Little Rock desegregation crisis,** Ashmore editorially opposed Governor Orval Faubus and the segregationists. In 1958 he received the Pulitzer Prize for editorial writing, and the *Arkansas Gazette* won the Pulitzer Prize for meritorious public service. Praising Ashmore, Roy Reed once called his former editor "the laughing liberal" because of "his ability to see the absurdity in racial politics." In 1959 Ashmore joined the Fund for the Republic's new Center for the Study of Democratic Institutions in California. He wrote *The Other Side of Jordan* (1960) about northern blacks and also served as editor of the *Encyclopedia Britannica*. As a critic of the war in Vietnam, he twice traveled to North Vietnam. In retirement, Ashmore wrote two personal histories of American race relations, *Hearts and Minds: The Anatomy of Racism from Roosevelt to Reagan* (1982) and *Civil Rights and Wrongs: A Memoir of Race and Politics , 1944–1994* (1994).

Selected Bibliography Harry Ashmore, *Hearts and Minds* (1982); Harry Ashmore, *Civil Rights and Wrongs: A Memoir of Race and Politics, 1944–1994* (1994); *New York Times*, 22 January 1998, 3 January 1999; *Who's Who in America*.

Brenda M. Eagles

Associated Negro Press Established by **Chicago Defender** reporter Claude Barnett in 1919 to provide black newspapers with national and international news, the Associated Negro Press (ANP) thrived during the next three decades, the heyday of the black press. Only the **Pittsburgh Courier** and the *Chicago Defender* did not subscribe to it in 1919, but later they also signed on. The ANP successfully met its aim of providing news of interest to black readers. In 1945, after the failure to merge with the ANP, the National Negro Press Association formed the NNPA News Service. Most black newspapers continued to use the ANP and by the late 1950s over seventy African papers were also subscribers. American black newspapers went into decline during these years, however, which hurt the ANP. It went out of business in 1964.

Selected Bibliography Richard L. Beard and Cyril E. Zoerner II, "Associated Negro Press: Its Founding, Ascendancy, and Demise," *Journalism Quarterly* 46 (Spring 1969), 47–52; Linda J. Evans, "Claude Barnett and the Associated Negro Press," *Chicago History* 12 (Spring 1983), 44–56; Lawrence D. Hogan, A *Black National News Service, The Associated Press and Claude Barnett, 1919–1945* (1984).

John F. Marszalek

Association for the Study of Afro-American Life and History Founded as the Association for the Study of Negro Life and History in Chicago on 9 September 1915, the Association's purposes were the promotion of black history, the preservation of historical manuscripts, and the publication of books about black life and history. The cofounders were **Carter Godwin Woodson,** George Cleveland Hall, W. B. Hartgrove, Alexander L. Jackson, and James E. Stamps. George C. Hall served as its first president. In its early years, the association received grants from the Carnegie Corporation, the Laura Spelman Memorial, and the Rockefeller Foundation. Such foundation support was withdrawn in the 1920s, however, mainly due to some personal animosity for Woodson, whom opponents called a "propagandist." Woodson decided that the future of the association depended on securing support from blacks, and he actively launched a campaign for that purpose. For several years, the association suffered from lack of funds but by 1944 it was financially stable. In 1926 Woodson began a drive through the association to promote Black History Week, and the effort eventually resulted in the celebration of February as Black History Month. The association has also been responsible for the publication of the *Journal of Negro History* and the **Negro History Bulletin;** a mail campaign directed at home, club, and school study; and the publication of black history textbooks for colleges and secondary schools. Since 1915 the association has both sponsored and encouraged hundreds of young men and women to enter the field of historical research. Financial and personnel difficulties in the 1980s led to a reduction in the effectiveness of the organization and saw a reduction in active membership to only 3,500 in 1985. As of 2003, it had 46 branches throughout the nation, and it is headquartered in Silver Springs, Maryland.

Selected Bibliography Editorial, *Negro History Bulletin* 46 (July–September 1983), 74–77; Walter B. Hill, Jr., "The Association For the Study of African American Life and History: An Inside Perspective," Washington *Afro-American*, 12 March 1999, A5; *Jet* 67 (11 March 1985), 39; Rayford W. Logan and Michael R. Winston, eds., *Dictionary of American Negro Biography* (1982); Obituary of Carter G. Woodson, *The Journal of Negro History* 35 (July 1950), 344–48; Web site: www.asalh.com.

Thomas D. Cockrell

Association of Southern Women to Prevent Lynching   The Association of Southern Women to Prevent Lynching, organized in Atlanta in 1930 under the auspices of the **Commission on Interracial Cooperation** (formed in 1919), existed for the express purpose of combating the idea that lynching was needed "to protect Southern womanhood." Led by Jessie Daniel Ames of Palestine, Texas, the group collected thousands of signatures on antilynching petitions, worked to change public opinion and educate children away from racism, and "assisted" southern officials to uphold the law. Although the women suffered hostility and threats, they persisted and repeatedly succeeded in stopping lynchings and moving the public away from mob violence.

Selected Bibliography Jessie Daniel Ames, *The Changing Character of Lynching, 1931–41* (1973); Mary J. Brown, *Eradicating this Evil: Women in the American Anti-Lynching Movement, 1892–1940* (2000); Jacquelyn Dowd Hall, *The Revolt Against Chivalry: Jessie Daniel Ames and the Women's Campaign Against Lynching* (1979); Kathleen A. Miller, "The Ladies and the Lynchers: A Look at the Association of Southern Women to Prevent Lynching," *Southern Studies* 2 (1991), 261–80.

Linda G. Ford

Atlanta [Daily] World   Founded in 1928 by W.A. Scott II as a weekly newspaper, the *Atlanta World* became a daily in 1932, and changed its name to the *Atlanta Daily World*. It also then became part of the Scott Newspaper Syndicate, which by 1941 reached a peak of 29 affiliates. It gained early notoriety by giving wide support to the accused black men in the **Scottsboro Trials.** It was a consistent opponent of segregation, but when the sit-ins of the 1960s targeted some of the newspaper's biggest advertisers, it opposed the protesters. It survived this crisis, however, and remained staunchly Republican, but supported the moderates over the Goldwaterites. At its peak it was one of the nation's only black daily newspapers and had an influence far beyond its city limits.

Selected Bibliography Alton Hornby, Jr., "Georgia," in Henry Lewis Suggs, ed., *The Black Press in the South, 1865–1979* (1983); Vishnu K. Oak, *The Negro Newspaper* (1948).

John F. Marszalek

Atlanta Exposition Speech   On 18 September 1895, **Booker T. Washington** delivered a speech at the Cotton States and International Exposition in Atlanta, Georgia. This Atlanta Exposition Speech has endured as his philosophical contribution to southern race relations. In his address, Washington, first principal of Alabama's **Tuskegee Institute** and one dedicated to the concept and practical application of industrial education, appealed to whites to work with and accept blacks as mutual partners in southern economic progress. He also called upon blacks to be patient and to accommodate themselves to the social system that had emerged in the post-Reconstruction South. The reaction to Washington's speech was overwhelmingly enthusiastic. From President Grover Cleveland to the white press, unstinting praise was bestowed upon Washington. Because the speech did not challenge white supremacy,

Washington was lauded by white America as the spokesperson for the black race. A majority of black Americans concurred. Over time, some blacks, mainly the well-educated, came to disagree with Washington's philosophy and his approach to black economic and social progress. **W.E.B. Du Bois** represented their thinking. The leader of this "Talented Tenth" group, he dubbed Washington's speech the "Atlanta Compromise." Du Bois accused Washington of compromising the human rights of black Americans by accepting their alleged inferiority and asking them to accommodate themselves to the racial injustices perpetuated against them. Washington's supporters have argued that his philosophy and formula for black success was correct in light of the sociopolitical, judicial, and economic climate of the times. His critics have maintained that Washington's speech and brand of racial politics retarded black progress and, perhaps, further contributed to the segregationist and discriminatory mindset of the white South.

Selected Bibliography W.E.B. Du Bois, *The Souls of Black Folk* (1903); Leslie Fishel, Jr., and Benjamin Quarles, *The Black American: A Documentary History* (1970); John Hope Franklin and Alfred A. Moss, Jr., *From Slavery to Freedom: A History of Negro Americans*, 8th ed. (2000); Louis R. Harlan, *The Booker T. Washington Papers*, 13 vols. (1972–83); Louis R. Harlan, *Booker T. Washington: The Making of a Black Leader, 1856–1901* (1972); Bruce Harvey and Lynn Watson-Powers, "The Eyes of the World Are upon Us: A Look at the Cotton States and International Exposition of 1895," *Atlanta History* 39 (No. 3–4, 1995), 5–11; Booker T. Washington, *Up from Slavery: An Autobiography* (1900).

Phillip McGuire

Atlanta Race Riot (1906)   Turn-of-the-century massacres of blacks by urban mobs with the connivance of local authorities in Wilmington, Delaware (1898) and Atlanta, Georgia, and in the **New Orleans race riot** (1900) and elsewhere can be described as American pogroms. Although these bloody episodes were generally followed by new disenfranchisement laws, blacks already lived in subjugation, and the new laws and programs sprang largely from the expressive politics of white supremacy, a rage for more effective caste dominance. In Georgia violence was preceded by an eighteen-month ultraracist Hoke Smith–Clark Howell Democratic gubernatorial primary, a lurid Atlanta "crusade" against "vice" in black neighborhoods, and the increasingly hysterical yellow journalism of the city's highly competitive five dailies on a bogus "rape epidemic" in August and September. Between 22 and 27 September white mobs of several dozen to five thousand persons ranged the central city attacking blacks and black-owned or black-used property. The mobs left 25 persons dead, several hundred injured, and over a thousand in flight.

Selected Bibliography Dominic J. Capeci and Jack C. Knight, "Reckoning with Violence: W.E.B. Du Bois and the 1906 Atlanta Race Riot," *Journal of Southern History* 62 (1996), 727–66; Charles Crowe, "Racial Massacre in Atlanta, Sept. 22, 1906," *Journal of Negro History* 54 (April 1969), 150–73; Charles Crowe, "Racial Violence and Social Reform: Origins of the Atlanta Riot of 1906," *Journal of Negro History* 53 (July 1968), 234–56; Mark Bauerlein, *Negrophobia: A Race Riot in Atlanta, 1906* (2001); Paul S. Hudson, "Immovable Folkways: Thornwell Jacobs's *The Law of the White Circle* and the Atlanta Race Riot of 1906," *Georgia Historical Quarterly* 83

Race riots in the streets of Atlanta, Georgia. © Leonard de Selva/CORBIS.

(1999), 293–313; Gregory L. Mixon, "The Atlanta Race Riot of 1906" (Ph.D. diss., University of Cincinnati, 1989).

Charles Crowe

Atlanta Race Riot (1967)   Atlanta and its racially moderate mayor, **Ivan Allen, Jr.,** were proud of the progress the city had made in race relations. Still there were wide economic, social, and political disparities between whites and blacks, and racial tension was evident in the existence of both civil rights and segregationist organizations. On Saturday, 17 June 1967, a black patron and a black security guard scuffled outside a tavern in the Dixie Hills Shopping Center, and a crowd gathered. The following night an even larger crowd appeared and began to discuss neighborhood grievances. **Stokely Carmichael** arrived and was arrested after a heated discussion with police. The next day, police wounded a young black man during a disagreement in the same shopping center. A protest meeting that evening heard Carmichael urge those present "to take to the streets." Soon a crowd of one thousand people had formed.

Rocks and bottles were thrown at police cars. Police reinforcements quickly put down the melee, and the next day work began on a long-delayed city playground for the community. Despite the opposition of the **Student Nonviolent Coordinating Committee,** a youth patrol was established to help to maintain calm that summer. A brief outburst of violence resulting in one death and a serious injury occurred on Tuesday, 20 June, but calm was maintained. State Senator Leroy Johnson and other black leaders circulated a petition, signed by one thousand people, calling on Carmichael to leave the neighborhood and allow it to work out its own problems.

Selected Bibliography *Atlanta Constitution,* June, 1967; *Atlanta Inquirer,* June, July 1967; *New York Times,* June 1967; *Report of the National Advisory Commission on Civil Disorders* (1968).

John F. Marszalek

Atlanta University Chartered in 1867 under the auspices of the **American Missionary Association** (AMA), Atlanta University matriculated its first 89 students in October 1869. Available to all people regardless of race, color, or creed, the school was nevertheless intended primarily to train African American teachers to educate freedmen following the Civil War. Severing its ties with the AMA in 1892, Atlanta University developed as an undergraduate institution, offering both liberal arts and vocational training programs. In 1929 the university joined with **Morehouse College** and Spelman College in Atlanta to form the Atlanta University Center, with Atlanta University offering only graduate and professional training. All three schools shared a common library funded by the **General Education Board.** In 1988, the school merged with Clark University to form the comprehensive Clark Atlanta University.

Selected Bibliography Clarence A. Bacote, *The Story of Atlanta University* (1969); Florence Matilda Read, *The Story of Spelman College* (1961); Web site: www.cau.edu.

Janice M. Leone

Atlanta University Conference for the Study of Negro Problems This conference, which convened annually during the period from 1896 to 1917, was the first systematic effort to examine black urban social and economic conditions. Its format of an annual research study, spring meeting, and publication series was initiated in 1895 by R. R. Wright Sr., trustees, and alumni as an alternative to conferences held at **Tuskegee Institute** and **Hampton Institute.** Under the direction of **W.E.B. Du Bois** (1898–1914) a 10-year repeating cycle of comprehensive studies was implemented. Du Bois's research methods and results were widely accepted by contemporary social scientists and became the foundation for the serious study of black life. Du Bois's intent was "not only to make the Truth clear but to present it in such shape as will encourage and help social reform." The 20 conference monographs provided the first objective analysis of political and socioeconomic causes of black poverty, crime, and disease as well as an analysis of such black social institutions as the family, the church, clubs, and businesses. The well-attended conferences also reported on and sparked regional efforts by black women's organizations to improve living conditions and to establish kindergartens and settlement houses. Black and white reformers and academics such as Lucy Laney, **John Hope,** Jane Addams, and Franz Boas participated. In 1995 Eugene Rivers, an activist minister, called on black intellectuals to revive the Atlanta University model of annual thematic studies of black communities.

Selected Bibliography Clarence A. Bacote, *The Story of Atlanta University* (1969); W.E.B. Du Bois, *Autobiography* (1968); Tera Hunter, *To Joy My Freedom: Southern Black Women's Lives and Labors after the Civil War* (1997); Ernest Kaiser, introduction, *Atlanta University Conference Publications* (1968); David Levering Lewis, *W.E.B. Du Bois: Biography of a Race, 1868–1919* (1993); Eugene F. Rivers III, "Beyond the Nationalism of Fools: Toward an Agenda for Black Intellectuals," *Boston Review* (Summer 1995), 16–18.

Francille Rusan Wilson

Attaway, William (19 November 1911, Greenville, Miss.–17 June 1986, Los Angeles, Calif.). William Attaway moved with his family to Chicago where he attended public schools and graduated from the University of Chicago. His career as a novelist began while he was involved in the Illinois Federal Writers' Project during the Great Depression. Publishing two novels, *Let Me Breathe Thunder* (1939) and ***Blood on the Forge*** (1941), Attaway is primarily known for his second novel, which concerns the **Great Migration** and the effects of massive industrialization on poor laborers. He reveals that, for blacks, the northward movement was an exchange of "one master for another." In the 1960s, Attaway continued his involvement with the civil rights movement and later gained a considerable reputation as a radio, motion picture, and television scriptwriter, specializing in black scripts.

Selected Bibliography Robert Bone, *The Negro Novel* (1966); Robert Felgar, "William Attaway's Unaccommodated Protagonist," *Studies in Black Literature* 4 (Spring 1973), 1–3; Moody Simms, Jr., "In The Shadow of Richard Wright: William Attaway," *Notes on Mississippi Writers* 8 (Spring 1975), 13–18; Philip Vaughn, "From Pastoralism to Industrial Antipathy, in William Attaway's *Blood on the Forge*," *Phylon* 36 (December 1975), 422–25; Edward Waldron, "William Attaway's *Blood on the Forge*: The Death of the Blues," *Negro American Literature Forum* 10 (Summer 1976), 58–60.

Jacquelyn Jackson

The Autobiography of an Ex-Colored Man This novel by **James Weldon Johnson** (printed anonymously in 1912 and reprinted with author acknowledgment in 1927), describes the wanderings, geographical and mental, of a light-skinned black person who at first believed he was white, but learned during elementary school that he was black. After graduation, the protagonist travels to the South, Europe, and the North in search of himself and his heritage. After witnessing a lynching in the South, he decides to "let the world take me for what it would." He divulges his "secret" to his wife and then he must decide how to raise his children. For him there was really no choice. Given the way black people were treated in America, he decided to continue "passing" and to raise his children as white. In a very poignant conclusion, the

Ex-Colored Man does recognize that by remaining "an ordinary successful white man" he opted to discard his history and his race, and he concludes, "I cannot repress the thought that, after all I have chosen the lesser part, that I have sold my birthright for a mess of pottage."

Selected Bibliography Nathan Irving Huggins, *Harlem Renaissance* (1971); James Weldon Johnson, *The Autobiography of an Ex-Colored Man* (1927); Eugene Levy, *James Weldon Johnson: Black Leader, Black Voice* (1973).

Kenneth W. Goings

Avery v. Georgia, **345 U.S. 559 (1953)** This U.S. Supreme Court case helped clarify the issue of what constituted racial discrimination in a state's jury-selection process as proscribed under the "equal protection" clause of the **Fourteenth Amendment.** James Avery, a black, was tried and convicted of rape in the Superior Court of Fulton County, Georgia in 1952. He appealed on the grounds that racial discrimination in the selection of the trial jury had deprived him of the equal protection of the law. On 25 May 1953, the Supreme Court upheld his appeal, ruling that although the petitioner might be unable to identify particular acts of discrimination, the jury-selection process itself, in which prospective white jurors' names were handled on white tickets and prospective black jurors' names on yellow tickets, so lent itself to abuse of the sort alleged as to constitute "prima facie evidence of discrimination." The burden of proof in such instances falls upon the state, and, in the absence of countervailing evidence of blacks actually serving on juries, convictions obtained before juries so selected had to be reversed.

Selected Bibliography Richard Bardolph, ed., *The Civil Rights Record, Black Americans and the Law, 1849–1970* (1970); Marvin E. Frankel and Gary P. Naftalis, *The Grand Jury* (1975); Jack Greenberg, *Race Relations and American Law* (1959); *New York Times*, 26 May 1953; *United States Supreme Court Reports*, vol. 73, 891–94, and vol. 97, 1244–50.

Robert A. Calvert

Ayers Case, 112 S. Ct. 2727 (1992) An ongoing federal district court and U.S. Supreme Court case brought in 1975 by Jake Ayers, Sr., of Glen Allen, Mississippi, with the support of the NAACP, on behalf of his son, Jake Ayers, Jr., and other black Mississippi students against the state of Mississippi. Ayers charged that the state discriminated against Mississippi's historically black universities (Jackson State, Alcorn State, and Mississippi Valley State) by funding the state's historically white universities at a disproportionately higher level. This underfunding for the black universities, the suit claimed, violated the civil rights of the students at those universities by lowering the quality of education they received compared to what students at the white universities received, thus reducing their economic opportunities after graduation. After 12 years of investigation, the case first came to trial in 1987 under the title *Ayers v. Allain* in the federal district court for North Mississippi. The ruling established that the state of Mississippi and its Board of Trustees for Institutions of Higher Learning had discriminated against black students and black colleges: it provided no training schools for black teachers between 1904 and 1940, it provided no graduate programs at any of the black public colleges until 1951, it made no efforts to help secure accreditation for the black public colleges until 1961, it still allowed none of the black universities to offer professional degrees, it set the standard for admission to the black universities considerably lower than at the white universities, and it otherwise made no efforts to elevate the black universities to equal status with the white universities. The U.S. Supreme Court upheld the ruling in *United States v. Fordice* (1992) ordering the state to develop a plan to remedy the problem with all due speed, and the Court remanded the case to its original district court. The state responded by proposing to merge one of its three black public universities with a white public university and to do away with one of the universities by turning it into a facility to relieve overcrowding in the state's penal system. Many African Americans protested this proposition, saying they wanted to preserve their historically black universities in their traditional capacities but with equal funding. The plan was presented to Federal District Court Judge Neal Biggers, who ruled in 1995 that the state must commit more money to upgrade the black public universities, ordered the white universities to make greater efforts to attract black students, and likewise ordered black universities to make greater efforts to attract white students. The state complied. In 2000, however, Judge Biggers rescinded his order, stating that Alcorn State and Mississippi Valley State had misappropriated their funds and had not shown any substantial improvements in white enrollment. Biggers specifically ordered the black universities to earmark a large portion of their funds for scholarships for white students. In February 2002 Biggers declared a "Final Judgment," but appeals from the Ayers lawyers have continued.

Selected Bibliography *Ayers v. Fordice* briefs, in Ayers Case Vertical File, Mitchell Memorial Library Special Collections, Mississippi State University; *Daily Mississippian Online*, 10 July 2000; Dannye Holley and L. Darnell Weeden, "*United States v. Fordice* (112 S. Ct. 2727, 1992): The Mississippi Aftermath," *New England Law Review* 31 (1997), 769–829; Elizabeth Martinez, "'On Time' in Mississippi: 1964–1996," *Z Magazine*, September 1994, www.zmag.org; Memorandum Opinion of Judge Neal Biggers on *Ayers v. Fordice*, 6 July 2000 and final judgments, www.ca5.uscourts.gov. Other Fifth Circuit Links, Mississippi Northern District Court.

Thomas Adams Upchurch

B

Bailey v. Alabama, 219 U.S. 219 (1911) This case was one of a series of Supreme Court rulings between 1905 and 1914 that struck at **black peonage,** a form of involuntary servitude for debt that developed in the South after Reconstruction and enslaved many impoverished blacks desperate for work. Alonzo Bailey, an illiterate Alabama black, received a small advance from an employer with whom he had entered into a 12-month labor contract. When he walked off the job before the year had expired still owing the advance, he was promptly arrested and brought to trial. He was charged with having violated an Alabama statute that stipulated that a worker who accepted an advance from an employer and left before repaying it would be presumed to have taken the money with intent to defraud and would be liable to criminal action. Bailey's attorneys lost their case in state court and appealed to the Supreme Court in 1908. The plaintiff maintained that the Alabama statute contravened the **Thirteenth Amendment** as well as certain congressional antipeonage statutes. In the first hearing, the Supreme Court remanded the case to the lower courts, but three years later, in 1911, it struck down the Alabama statute. Because the law prohibited Bailey from testifying that his intent was not to defraud his employer, he "stood stripped by the statute of the presumption of innocence, and exposed to conviction for fraud upon evidence only of breach of contract and failure to pay." The court went on to say that "the essence of peonage is compulsory service in payment of a debt." Although this decision did not completely end the new slavery, it did rule with finality that the state statutes that created a presumption of guilt from the mere signing of a contract and failing to carry out the agreement to work offended both the Thirteenth Amendment and federal antipeonage laws.

Selected Bibliography Pete Daniel, *The Shadow of Slavery: Peonage in the South, 1909–1969* (1972); Loren Miller, *The Petitioners: The Story of the Supreme Court of the United States and the Negro* (1966); Donald G. Nieman, *Promises to Keep: African-Americans and the Constitutional Order, 1776 to the Present* (1991); Benno C. Schmidt, Jr., "Principle and Prejudice: The Supreme Court and Race in the Progressive Era: Part 2: The Peonage Cases," *Columbia Law Review* 82 (1982), 646–717.

Charles D. Lowery

Baker, Ella Jo (1903, Norfolk, Va.–18 December 1986, New York, N.Y.). During most of her life, Ella Baker was active in civil rights and peace causes. When she came to the South in the 1960s to help in the **Southern Christian Leadership Conference** of **Martin Luther King, Jr.,** she had years of experience behind her. After the student sit-ins began, Baker organized a conference for students at her alma mater, Shaw University, in North Carolina. One hundred and fifty students came from nine states; the group became the **Student Nonviolent Coordinating Committee** (SNCC). Baker fought for the students' autonomy from SCLC. Although her talk at the Shaw Conference, "More than a Hamburger," was not very well received, many credited her with starting the organization and providing the initial vision. For this she had the enduring admiration of early SNCC members. Although she left the Southern Christian Leadership Conference, Ella Baker continued to provide counsel to SNCC. Ella Baker was clearly a living symbol of the "Beloved Community." She died in New York City well remembered and well loved.

Selected Bibliography Taylor Branch, *Parting the Waters: America During The King Years, 1954–63* (1989); obituary, *New York Times,* 17 December 1986; Robert Weisbrot, *Freedom Bound: A History of America's Civil Rights Movement* (1990).

Charles T. Pete Banner-Haley

Baker, George (Father Divine) (1877, Hutchinson Island, Ga.–10 September 1965, Philadelphia, Pa.). The name George Baker is thought to be the given name of Father Divine. He was one of the most important social reformers and advocates of racial justice and equality in the twentieth century. During the Great Depression, he founded the Interracial Peace Mission, which was headquartered in Harlem and had branches throughout the United States and abroad. It was the largest movement of its kind during the Depression. Thousands of people received free meals at Peace Mission centers. Hundreds more were housed in properties owned by the mission or found work through the business cooperatives organized by the mission in urban and rural areas. Racial harmony and integration at Peace Mission centers were unprecedented. White members broke residential color barriers in several northern communities by purchasing property for use by the Peace Mission. Father Divine's followers also participated in the campaign for a federal antilynching law, which was a burning issue at the time. Prior to Father Divine, few black preachers were politically active or socially conscious. His Peace Mission was also the first large scale interracial civil rights movement in the twentieth century.

Selected Bibliography Arthur Huff Fauset, *Black Gods of the Metropolis: Negro Religious Cults in the Urban North* (1944); Jill Watts, *God, Harlem U.S.A.: The Father Divine Story* (1992); Robert Weisbrot, *Father Divine and the Struggle for Racial Equality* (1983).

Gloria Waite

Baldwin, James (2 August 1924, New York, N.Y.–1 December 1987, Harlem, N.Y.). James Baldwin was an expatriate writer in Paris, France, when the civil rights movement began. His writings had a significant impact on students, intellectuals, and those in the movement. He emphasized in his books, especially in *The Fire Next Time,* the urgent need for the civil rights movement to succeed. Born to a father who was an Alabama minister, James Baldwin grew up in Harlem. Early in his youth he became a boy preacher. As a young adult, he went to Greenwich Village where he worked at being a writer. His first novel, the semiautobiographical *Go Tell It on the Mountain,* recounted his early years and his wrestling with religion. It was this black spirituality that provided Baldwin with a keen sensitivity and perspective onto the black urban condition. He felt stifled in this country because of its overwhelming racism and went to France where he lived for almost ten years. Although he returned to America and participated in the civil rights movement, he displayed impatience with the Kennedy administration for its slowness in dealing with southern segregation. This impatience showed itself during an intense meeting of several famous African American writers and performers called by Kennedy. Baldwin continued to write about the movement and blacks, often becoming very pessimistic. In the end, however, he retained some hope that the racial situation in this country could be resolved.

James Baldwin; portrait by Max Petrus, 1979. © Library of Congress.

Selected Bibliography James Baldwin, *The Fire Next Time* (1963); Taylor Branch, *Parting The Waters: America during the King Years, 1954–1963* (1989); David Leeming, *James Baldwin A Biography* (1994); Carol Polsgrove, *Divided Minds: Intellectuals and the Civil Rights Movement* (2001); William Weatherby, *James Baldwin: Portrait of a Writer* (1989).

Charles T. Pete Banner-Haley

Barnett, Ida Wells (16 July 1862, Holly Springs, Miss.–25 March 1931, Chicago, Ill.). From an early age, Ida Wells Barnett demonstrated the courage and persistence that were to become trademarks of her later life. In 1878 when a yellow fever epidemic left her and her siblings orphaned, she managed with her father's savings and assistance from the Prince Hall Masons, guardians for the Wells children, to keep the family together. Despite difficulties, she received an education at Rust College in Mississippi and became a teacher in Memphis, Tennessee.

When she was forced to give up her first-class seat on the Chesapeake and Ohio Railroad in 1884, she sued the company and became the first southern black to appeal to a state court since the U.S. Supreme Court's **Civil Rights Cases** in 1883. The lower court ruled in Wells Barnett's favor, but the decision was reversed by the Tennessee Supreme Court in 1887. Recounting the story of the lawsuit, she launched a career in journalism in a black church weekly, *The Living Way*. She had established her prominence in Memphis literary circles by 1887 and was made secretary of the Afro-American Press Association; she was the first woman representative to attend the conclave. She became part owner of *Memphis Free Speech* in charge of editorial operations. When her criticism of the racist school system in Memphis caused her to lose her teaching job, she devoted more time and energy to speaking out forcefully for racial equality. She began a crusade against lynching, which caused a white mob to destroy *Free Speech*. **Timothy Thomas Fortune** hired Wells to work at his **New York Age,** where she continued her antilynching campaign.

Wells Barnett organized the Woman's Loyal Union in Brooklyn, New York, the first black women's antilynching club and established similar antilynching clubs in Boston, Massachusetts, Washington, D.C., and other cities. She toured Europe and was correspondent for the *Inter-Ocean*, later known as the *Chicago Herald Examiner*. She organized the first black women's suffrage group and in 1909 she was among the prominent blacks and whites who formed the **NAACP.** In the years thereafter, according to **Langston Hughes,** "[h]er activities in the field of social work laid the groundwork for the **Urban League.**"

Selected Bibliography Marianna W. Davis, ed., *Contributions of Black Women to America, vol. 1: The Arts, Media, Business, Law, Sports* (1982); Alfreda M. Duster, ed., *Crusade for Justice: The Autobiography of Ida B. Wells* (1970); Margaret L. Dwight and George A. Sewell, *Mississippi Black History Makers* (1984); John Hope Franklin and August Meier, eds., *Black Leaders of the Twentieth Century* (1982); Linda O. McMurry, *To Keep the Waters Troubled: The Life of Ida B. Wells* (1998); Patricia A. Schechter, *Ida B. Wells-Barnett and American Reform, 1880–1930* (2001).

Linda Reed

Barrows v. Jackson, 346 U.S. 249 (1953)   Restrictions placed in property deeds by developers or neighborhood organizations served as a key legal device that whites used to segregate their neighborhoods from African Americans and others. While ***Shelley v. Kraemer*** (1948) prohibited public enforcement of racially restrictive covenants, it did not bar damage suits against white sellers by their white neighbors in areas covered by restrictive covenants. In *Barrows,* Mrs. Leola Jackson, a white Los Angeles property owner, faced suit for damages from neighbors for selling deed restricted property to an African American. Although both parties were white and no discrimination was directly involved, Loren Miller of the **NAACP** defended Jackson with support from many governmental and private organizations. White property owners' associations supported Barrows. When California courts refused to award damages, Barrows appealed to the U.S. Supreme Court. Justice Sherman Minton's majority opinion concluded that a damage award would cause "a prospective seller of restricted land . . . either [to] refuse to sell to non-Caucasians or . . . require non-Caucasians to pay a higher price to meet the damage which the seller may incur," thus denying the third party's right to equal protection guaranteed by the **Fourteenth Amendment.** Whites continued to use violence to segregate their neighborhoods from African Americans and others.

Selected Bibliography Charles Abrams, *Forbidden Neighbors: A Study of Prejudice in Housing* (1955); Arnold R. Hirsch, *Making the Second Ghetto: Race and Housing in Chicago, 1940–1960* (1983); Kenneth T. Jackson, *Crabgrass Frontier: The Suburbanization of the United States* (1985); B. T. McGraw and George B. Nesbitt, "Aftermath of *Shelley v. Kraemer* on Residential Restrictions by Race," *Land Economics* 29 (August 1953), 280–87; Stephen Grant Meyer, *As Long As They Don't Move Next Door: Segregation and Racial Conflict in American Neighborhoods* (2000); C. Herman Pritchett, *Civil Liberties and the Vinson Court* (1954); Clement E. Vose, *Caucasians Only: The Supreme Court, the NAACP, and the Restrictive Covenant Cases* (1959).

James Borchert

Barry, Marion S.   (6 March 1936, Itta Bena, Miss.–). Longtime mayor of the District of Columbia from 1979 to 1991 and from 1995 to 1999, Barry received his B.S. from Le Moyne College in Memphis, Tennessee, and a master's from **Fisk University** in Nashville, Tennessee. Barry also pursued doctoral studies at the University of Kansas and the University of Tennessee. In 1960 he became actively involved in the civil rights movement when he participated in the **Nashville sit-ins,** which included demonstrations at lunch counters. When college students met in April 1960 at Shaw University to form the **Student Nonviolent Coordinating Committee** (SNCC), they chose Barry as the first national chairman. After a few months in this position, however, he began his doctoral studies in chemistry, and had to abandon his full-time commitment to the movement. However, while in Tennessee, he worked part-time, conducting workshops on nonviolence, raising funds, and registering voters. In 1964 Barry dropped out of graduate school to work full-time for civil rights. He planned demonstrations and boycotts and was frequently jailed. SNCC headquarters sent him to New York City to open an office. From there he moved to Washington, D.C., and became the Washington director of SNCC. Eventually, Barry started his own "wildcat" movement, where he staged boycotts and struck out against police brutality and harassment. In 1990 while mayor of Washington, he was sentenced to six months in prison for his conviction on a drug charge, but was once again elected Washington's mayor in 1994. Barry's 16 years as Washington, D.C., mayor ended in 1999 when he chose not to seek another term.

Selected Bibliography Jonathan Agronski, *Marion Barry: The Politics of Race* (1991); Jonetta R. Barras, *The Last of the Black Emperors: The Hollow Comeback of Marion Barry in a New Age of Black Leaders* (1998); William C. Matney, ed., *Who's Who Among Black Americans* (1988); George A. Sewell and Margaret L. Dwight, *Mississippi Black History Makers*, rev. ed. (1984); Emily Stoper, *The Student Nonviolent Coordinating Committee* (1989); *Washington Post Magazine*, 16 December 1979, 26 April 1987.

Betty L. Plummer

Bassett, Ebenezer Don Carlos (16 October 1833, Litchfield, Conn.–13 November 1908, Philadelphia, Pa.). The first African American diplomat to represent the United States government abroad, Ebenezer D. Bassett rose to prominence as a scholar and teacher. Immediately after his inauguration in 1869, President Ulysses Grant appointed Bassett as minister-resident to Haiti, a position he held with honor and distinction from 1869 to 1877. At the time of his appointment, he was principal of the Institute for Colored Youth, a Quaker school in Philadelphia. He had been educated at Wesley Academy in Wilbraham, Massachusetts, and at the Connecticut State Normal School.

Bassett served the United States in Haiti during a period of tense relations with Santo Domingo. He managed to ease the strong anti-American feeling there. When he completed his assignment in 1877, the Haitians expressed their confidence in his integrity by appointing him as their consul general to the United States for 10 years. Upon his retirement, he returned to live as a private citizen in Haiti. He published his *Handbook of Haiti*—a valuable contribution to the geographical knowledge of the island—in French, English, and Spanish.

Selected Bibliography Nancy Gordon Heinl, "America's First Black Diplomat," *Foreign Service Journal*, 50 (August 1973), 20–22; Michael L. Krenn, *Black Diplomacy: African Americans and the State Department, 1945–1965* (1999); Rayford W. Logan, *The Diplomatic Relations of the United States with Haiti, 1776–1891* (1941).

George E. Walker

***Bates v. Little Rock*, 361 U.S. 516 (1960)** In 1957 Little Rock, Arkansas, amended its license tax ordinance to require any organization operating within the municipality to supply the city clerk upon request: (1) its official name; (2) its headquarters or regular meeting place; (3) the names and salaries of officers, agents, servants, employees, or representatives; (4) its purpose; (5) its dues, assessments, and contributions paid (by whom and when), together with a statement reflecting the disposition of the funds and the total net income;

(6) an affidavit stating whether the organization was subordinate to a parent organization and, if so, the latter's name. Daisey Bates, the records custodian of the local **NAACP,** was convicted of violating the ordinance even though she supplied all the information required by ordinance except the names of the members and contributors, which she withheld due to the "anti-NAACP climate in this state." The Arkansas Supreme Court upheld the conviction, concluding that "compulsory disclosure of the membership list was not an unconstitutional invasion of the freedoms guaranteed." The U.S. Supreme Court reversed the conviction, ruling that compulsory disclosure of the membership lists would work unjustified interference with the members' freedom of association, a right protected by the due process clause of the **Fourteenth Amendment.**

Selected Bibliography Daisey Bates, *The Long Shadow of Little Rock: A Memoir* (1962); Loren Miller, *The Petitioners, The Story of the Supreme Court of the United States and the Negro* (1966); George Rossman, ed., "Review of Recent Supreme Court Decisions," *American Bar Association Journal* 46 (1960), 420–21; Roy Wilkins, *Standing Fast: The Autobiography of Roy Wilkins* (1982).

Michael S. Downs

Battle of September 14th (or Canal Street) 1874 During Reconstruction, politically inspired violence was commonplace in Louisiana. The ultimate erosion of Republican strength in the state was tied directly to the existence of well-organized white paramilitary groups. The most violent and reactionary of this lot was the White League. Founded in Louisiana in April 1874, it had nearly blanketed the state by late summer. By September, the White League had overturned or neutralized the Republican governments of at least eight parishes. Emboldened by these triumphs and federal timidity, the New Orleans White League planned to force the resignation of the Republican Governor, William Pitt Kellogg, and thereby gain control of state government. They asked for his resignation in the early afternoon of 14 September 1874. When he refused to resign, fighting commenced. The might of the White League was opposed by the five-hundred-man Metropolitan Police, an integrated unit that was the most professional force New Orleans had prior to the twentieth century, and by about three thousand black militiamen led by General James Longstreet. White Leaguers outflanked and vanquished the Metropolitan Police and the militia. Battlefield casualties were light on both sides; the Metropolitan Police force lost 11 men and 60 were wounded. Sixteen White Leaguers lost their lives and 45 were wounded. The toppled state government was restored on 17 September by federal troops. To commemorate the event, conservative whites later erected a monument that became an embarrassment to city officials and an affront to the black community.

Selected Bibliography Stuart Omer Landry, *The Battle of Liberty Place: The Overthrow of Carpet-Bag Rule in New Orleans. September 14, 1874* (1955); Oscar H. Lestage, Jr., "The White League in Louisiana and its Participation in Reconstruction Riots," *The Louisiana Historical Quarterly* 18 (July, 1935), 617–95; Lawrence Powell, "A Concrete Symbol," *Southern Exposure* 18 (Spring 1990), 40–43; Dennis Charles Rousey, "The New Orleans Police, 1805–1889: A

Social History" (Ph.D. diss., Cornell University, 1978); Ted Tunnell, *Crucible of Reconstruction: War, Radicalism, and Race in Louisiana, 1862–1877* (1984); Bennett H. Wall, ed., *Louisiana: A History* (1984).

Joe Louis Caldwell

Beecher, John (22 January 1904, New York, N.Y.–11 May 1980, San Francisco, Calif.). A great-great-nephew of abolitionists, Henry Ward Beecher and Harriet Beecher Stowe, John Beecher was born in New York City, but reared in Birmingham, Alabama. After receiving an undergraduate degree from the University of Alabama (1926) and a graduate degree from the University of Wisconsin (1930), Beecher worked as an English instructor at both Dartmouth College and the University of Wisconsin until 1933. During the Great Depression, Beecher, for eight years, administered New Deal programs in the South, which aided African Americans discriminated against in employment. His interaction with black southerners impacted his poetry, which often reflected biracial themes. In World War II, Beecher served as a Marine officer aboard an integrated navy vessel, the *S.S. Booker T. Washington*, and subsequently wrote a book, *All Brave Soldiers* (1945), which illustrated the brotherhood of all men. Because he refused to sign the Levering Act, a McCarthy loyalty oath to the U.S. government, Beecher lost his teaching post at San Francisco State College in 1950, took up ranching, and opened his publishing company, "Morning Star Press" in Sebastopol, California. A prolific author, Beecher composed many poems, which reflected his interest in civil rights and egalitarianism. His poem "Report to the Stockholders" captures the unpleasant experiences of laborers and their need to unionize. "In Egypt Land" he describes the revolt of African American farmers and their efforts to create their own unions. Beecher held a variety of positions, serving as lecturer in English at Arizona State University, Tempe and poet-in-residence at the University of Santa Clara, North Shore Community College, Berverly, Massachusetts, and St. John's University, Collegeville, Minnesota. In his later years, Beecher, while working for the *San Francisco Chronicle*, reported on the civil rights movement and held visiting professorships at Miles College, Birmingham, Alabama, and Duke University.

Selected Bibliography *Atlanta Constitution,* 26 August 1945; John Beecher, *All Brave Soldiers* (1945); John Beecher, *To Live and Die in Dixie and Other Poems* (1966).

Edward J. Robinson

Bell v. Maryland, **378 U.S. 226 (1964)** The last sit-in case decided before the public accommodations provision of the **Civil Rights Act of 1964** took effect, this was one of four such cases the Supreme Court adjudicated that year. The case involved 12 black students who were convicted of criminal trespass for their 1960 attempt to desegregate Hooper's Restaurant in Baltimore. The court reversed the convictions and returned the case to the Maryland court for further clarification because the city of Baltimore had passed a public accommodations law after the sit-ins occurred. Thus the Supreme Court avoided settling the constitutional issue of whether the **Fourteenth Amendment** provided the right to service in public accommodations. Six justices, however, did issue statements on this question. In an opinion joined by William O. Douglas and Chief Justice Earl Warren, Arthur J. Goldberg discussed the history of the Fourteenth Amendment, explaining that its intent was to prohibit racial discrimination in public places. Hugo L. Black, joined by **John Marshall Harlan** and Byron R. White, took the opposite position, stating that the amendment had not been designed to cover private businesses. If the Fourteenth Amendment was intended to prohibit segregation, he added, Congress would have had no reason to enact civil rights legislation.

Selected Bibliography Albert P. Blaustein and Robert L. Zangrando, eds., *Civil Rights and the Black American: A Documentary History*, 2nd ed. (1991); Leon Friedman and Fred L. Israel, eds., *The Justices of the Supreme Court, 1789–1976* (1980); *New York Times*, 23 June 1964; George Rossman, ed., "Recent Supreme Court Decisions" *American Bar Association Journal* 51 (1965), 78–79; Bernard Schwartz, *Super Chief: Earl Warren and His Supreme Court: A Judicial Biography* (1983).

Carol Wilson

Benson, William E. (1876, Elmore County, Ala.–14 October, 1915, Tallapoosa County, Ala.). A graduate of **Howard University,** William E. Benson attempted to establish a stable community of landowning African American farmers. The nucleus of the enterprise was the **Kowaliga Industrial Community,** which he founded in 1897 or 1898. By 1915, Benson had organized the Dixie Industrial Company, which owned ten thousand acres of land, a cottonseed-oil mill, a timber operation, a general store, a turpentine plant and 15 miles of railroad that linked the community to the larger society. The ideology of self-help was put into practice as African Americans built their own farms and the buildings that housed the community's businesses.

Selected Bibliography James D. Anderson, *Education of Blacks in the South: 1860–1935* (1988); August Meier, *Negro Thought in America: 1880–1915: Racial Ideologies in the Age of Booker T. Washington* (1971); W.E.B. Du Bois, ed., *Economic Co-Operation among Negro Americans: Report of a Study Made by Atlanta University, under the Patronage of the Carniegie Institution of Washington, D.C., together with the Proceedings of the 12th Conference for the Study of the Negro Problems* 1907), http://docsouth.unc.edu/authors.html#D; Elliot Rudwick, W.E.B. Du Bois (1969); U.S. Department of Interior, Bureau of Education, *Negro Education Bulletin* 39 (1917).

Aingred G. Dunston

Berea College v. Kentucky, 211 U.S. 26 (1908)   In this decision, the U.S. Supreme Court upheld the Kentucky legislature's passage of the 1904 Day Law, making it unlawful to teach white and black students in the same institution. After approximately 42 years of integrated education, Berea was forced to segregate. Moreover, the Supreme Court had upheld the 1896 *Plessy v. Ferguson* decision making the **separate-but-equal** philosophy the official law of the land. Yet there remained the question of whether a state legislature could compel a private institution to segregate. The Court responded by upholding the legality of the Day Law. Earlier the Court had allowed each state to resolve the question on an individual basis.

Selected Bibliography Jacqueline G. Burnside, "Suspicion Versus Faith: Negro Criticisms of Berea College in the Nineteenth Century," *Register of Kentucky Historical Society* 83 (Summer 1985), 237–66; Jack Greenberg, *Race Relations and American Law* (1959); Richard Allen Heckman and Betty Jean Hall, "Berea College and the Day Law," *Register of Kentucky Historical Society* 66 (1968), 35–52; James M. McPherson, *The Abolitionist Legacy: From Reconstruction to the NAACP* (1975); George C. Wright, "The Founding of Lincoln Institute," *Filson Club History Quarterly* 49 (1975), 57–70.

Lawrence H. Williams

Berry, Mary Frances (17 February 1938, Nashville, Tenn.–). Distinguished historian and attorney, she earned her B.A. and M.A. from **Howard University** and the Ph.D. and J.D. from the University of Michigan. As an undergraduate, she wanted to leave school and plunge into the civil rights movement, but a professor persuaded her to remain, arguing that some must earn degrees and become leaders. She followed this advice. In 1976 she was the first black woman appointed chancellor at a major white institution—the University of Colorado, in Boulder. In 1977 President Jimmy Carter appointed her as Assistant Secretary of Education, in the Department of Health, Education, and Welfare. In 1980 he named her to the **Civil Rights Commission,** where she took positions for which President Ronald Reagan tried to have her removed. Nevertheless, Berry retained her position into the new century and led criticism of **racial profiling** by police officers and the 2000 election disparities in Florida.

Selected Bibliography Joan Barthel, "Mary Frances Berry," *MS* 15 (January, 1987), 68–70, 95; Mary Frances Berry, *The Pig Farmer's Daughter and Other Tales of American Justice: Episodes of Racism and Sexism in the Courts from 1865 to the Present* (2000); Marianna W. Davis, ed., *Contributions of Black Women to America*, vol. 1: *The Arts, Media, Business, Law, Sports* (1982); William C. Matney, ed., *Who's Who among Black Americans* (1988).

Betty L. Plummer

Bethune, Mary McLeod (10 July 1875, Mayesville, S.C.–18 May 1955, Daytona Beach, Fla.). Distinguished orator, executive, and educator, she was founder and president of Bethune-Cookman College. As early as 1914 a trustee at the then Daytona Normal and Industrial School for Negro Girls recommended her for a place on Vice President Thomas R. Marshall's Red Cross panel. During the administrations of Presidents Calvin Coolidge and Herbert Hoover, Bethune was the lone African American invited to participate in child welfare conferences. **Eleanor Roosevelt** entertained Bethune at a 1934 luncheon for representative women leaders and often worked with her afterward, sometimes helping Bethune raise funds for her college and occasionally giving White House benefits for that purpose.

All of her adult life, Bethune remained active with national civil rights organizations, especially the **NAACP** and the **National Urban League.** The

Mary McLeod Bethune seated in her office, 1943. © Library of Congress.

NAACP awarded her its **Spingarn Medal** for distinguished services in 1935. She was vice president of the **Commission on Interracial Cooperation** and the National Urban League; president of the **National Association of Colored Women,** and founder and president of the **National Council of Negro Women,** all while simultaneously maintaining the presidency of Bethune-Cookman College. She was also one of the founders of the **Southern Conference for Human Welfare** (SCHW) in Birmingham, Alabama, in 1938 and remained active in that organization until it ceased operations in 1948. By then SCHW had set up the Southern Conference Educational Fund, with which Bethune worked until her death in 1955. She was particularly noted as a counselor to Franklin D. Roosevelt on black affairs and the divisional director of the National Youth Administration. By 1940 she was cited as "among the fifty most distinguished American women." In 1974 the Mary McLeod Bethune Memorial, the first monument to a black person, or to a woman, erected on public land in the nation's capitol, was unveiled in Lincoln Park.

Selected Bibliography Carolyn L. Bennett, *An Annotated Bibliography of Mary McLeod Bethune's Chicago Defender Columns* (2001); Audrey T. McCluskey and Elaine M. Smith, eds., *Mary McLeod Bethune: Building a Better World: Essays and Selected Documents* (1999); Clarence Genu Newsome, "Mary McLeod Bethune in Religious Perspective: A Seminal Essay" (Ph.D. diss., Duke University, 1982); Linda Reed, "The Southern Conference for Human Welfare and the Southern Conference Education Fund, 1938–1963" (Ph.D. diss., Indiana University, 1986); *Who's Who in America* (1899–); *Who's Who in Colored America* (1940).

Linda Reed

Bevel, James   (19 October 1936, Itta Bena, Miss.–). An African American minister educated in Mississippi and at the American Baptist Theological Seminary in Nashville, Tennessee, Bevel was a member of the **Student Nonviolent Coordinating Committee** (SNCC), the **Southern Christian Leadership Conference** (SCLC), and other civil rights organizations. At **Highlander Folk School** he came into contact with other civil rights activists who shared and reinforced his own commitment to the cause of freedom. In the early 1960s he helped to organize and lead protest movements in Nashville, Tennessee, Jackson, Mississippi, and Birmingham, Alabama.

Sixteenth Street Baptist Church in Birmingham, shown here after it was bombed by white racists in 1963. James Bevel led children marchers during the Birmingham Confrontation. Courtesy of Birmingham Public Library, Department of Archives and Manuscripts, Birmingham, Alabama.

During the **Birmingham Confrontation** of 1963 he organized and coordinated the children's marches. Having urged the Birmingham police in advance to eschew force in dealing with the young protesters, he led the children in a series of marches during the month of May from the Sixteenth Street Baptist Church. These marches infused new life into the Birmingham demonstrations and contributed significantly to the final victory. Parents who had previously remained on the sidelines joined their children in the city's streets and jails. Soon after the Birmingham demonstrations Bevel and his wife, Diane Nash, proposed the **Selma to Montgomery March.** He was with **Martin Luther King, Jr.,** in Memphis, Tennessee on 4 April 1968 when King was assassinated. He later called for a new trial for King assassin James Earl Ray. In 1992, he was vice-presidential candidate with Lyndon LaRouche. In 2001, he was a Republican and supporter of **Louis Farrakhan.**

Selected Bibliography Taylor Branch, *Parting the Waters: America in the King Years, 1954–1963* (1989); James Forman, *The Making of Black Revolutionaries* (1972); David J. Garrow, *Bearing the Cross: Martin Luther King, Jr., and the Southern Christian Leadership Conference* (1986); William Kunstler, *Deep in My Heart* (1966); Aldon D. Morris, *The Origins of the Civil Rights Movement: Black Communities Organizing for Change* (1984); *(Nashville) Tennessee Tribune*, 22 January 1998; *(New York) Tri State Defender*, 25 September 1996; *Philadelphia Tribune*, 29 September 1992.

LeRoy T. Williams

Birmingham Bus Boycott   When the U.S. Supreme Court outlawed segregated seating on buses in Montgomery, Alabama, in 1956, the **Reverend Fred L. Shuttlesworth,** president of the **Alabama Christian Movement for Human Rights** (ACMHR), notified the Birmingham City Commission that segregation was unconstitutional. Klansmen dynamited Shuttlesworth's house on Christmas night, but the next day he led an integration attempt on the city buses. When the subsequent appeal of the 21 blacks convicted of violating Birmingham's segregation ordinance reached federal court, the commission repealed the law on 14 October 1958 and passed a new one that authorized the Birmingham Transit Company to enforce segregated seating. The ACMHR challenged the new ordinance on 20 October 1958, and T. Eugene "Bull" Connor arrested 14 blacks including Shuttlesworth. Charging them with vagrancy, Connor also arrested three members of the **Montgomery Improvement Association**—the Reverends A. W. Wilson, H. H. Hubbard, and S. S. Seay—who had arrived in the city in support of the jailed protestors. This abuse of the law united the ACMHR with the Jefferson County Betterment Association headed by the Reverend J. L. Ware, in a boycott of the city's buses that began on 31 October 1958. The total dependence of Birmingham's black community on the city transit system combined with the successful use of police intimidation and a press blackout caused the boycott to fail by the end of 1958. A federal court ruling on 14 December 1959 finally desegregated seating on Birmingham's buses.

Selected Bibliography *Birmingham News*, 18, 25 November; 13 December 1958; Glenn T. Eskew, "The Alabama Christian Movement for Human Rights and the Birmingham Struggle for

Civil Rights, 1956–1963," in David J. Garrow, ed., *Birmingham, Alabama, 1956–1963* (1989); Andrew M. Manis, *A Fire You Can't Put Out: The Civil Rights Life of Birmingham's Reverend Fred Shuttlesworth* (1999); *Montgomery Advertiser*, 28, 29 October 1958.

Glenn T. Eskew

Birmingham Confrontation The Reverend **Fred L. Shuttlesworth,** president of the **Alabama Christian Movement for Human Rights,** invited the **Southern Christian Leadership Conference** (SCLC) to Birmingham, Alabama, to lead demonstrations against segregation. Code-named "Project C" for "confrontation," the protests began on 3 April 1963 with sit-ins conducted by a few college students. On 7 April 1963, Public Safety Commissioner T. Eugene "Bull" Connor set police attack dogs on the marchers, gaining national attention for the fledgling campaign. Violating a state court injunction against further protest marches, the Reverends **Martin Luther King, Jr.,** and **Ralph David Abernathy,** among others, were arrested and jailed on Good Friday, 12 April 1963. While incarcerated, King wrote the **"Letter from Birmingham Jail,"** which eloquently defended **direct action.** President John F. Kennedy called **Coretta Scott King** and expressed his concern for her jailed husband—foreshadowing the federal commitment to civil rights achieved by the Birmingham campaign. On 26 April 1963, King and the other 10 defendants were convicted of criminal contempt and released on appeal, initiating the court case *Walker v. City of Birmingham.* **James Bevel** of the SCLC suggested using school children to regain press attention, and the first student demonstrations began on 2 May 1963. As hundreds of youth marched on 3 May 1963, Connor turned the fire hoses on at pressures that tore the bark off trees in Kelly Ingram Park. Black spectators responded by throwing bricks and rocks at firemen. Kennedy sent Assistant Attorney General for Civil Rights **Burke Marshall** to help negotiate a settlement that was announced on 10 May 1963. Despite the failure of Birmingham whites ever to

Firemen hose marchers, 17 May 1963. Copyright. Photo by *The Birmingham News*, 2003. All rights reserved. Reprinted with permission.

implement the full accord, the action precipitated the Civil Rights Bill of 1963. On 11 May 1963, Klansmen bombed the A. G. Gaston Motel and the house of the Reverend **A. D. King.** The first of the decade's riots began as black residents burned cars and buildings. Colonel Al Lingo directed the Alabama state troopers in the brutal suppression of the disorders. The climax of the civil rights movement occurred in Birmingham in 1963 inasmuch as the original goals of the movement were achieved with the passage of the **Civil Rights Act of 1964.**

Selected Bibliography Glenn T. Eskew, "The Alabama Christian Movement for Human Rights and the Birmingham Struggle for Civil Rights, 1956–1963," in David J. Garrow, ed., *Birmingham, Alabama, 1956–1963* (1989); Adam Fairclough, *To Redeem the Soul of America: The Southern Christian Leadership Conference and Martin Luther King, Jr.* (1987); David J. Garrow, *Bearing the Cross: Martin Luther King and the Southern Christian Leadership* Conference (1986); Andrew M. Manis, *A Fire You Can't Put Out: The Civil Rights Life of Birmingham's Reverend Fred Shuttlesworth* (1999); Marjorie L. White, *A Walk to Freedom: The Reverend Fred Shuttlesworth and the Alabama Christian Movement for Human Rights, 1954–64* (1998).

Glenn T. Eskew

Black Boy Among African American autobiographies, *Black Boy* (1945) by **Richard Wright** is a classic example of the genre. Its achievement resides in Wright's yoking the pattern of slave narrative with perceptive social analysis, rendering his life story symbolic for a generation of black males who came of age in the South during the early twentieth century. In vivid often painful detail, *Black Boy* documents the process of maturation in a racist society. As a record of hostility, alienation, violence, and the psychology of race, the autobiography illustrates why many blacks fled the South and why long-repressed black anger eventually burst forth in demonstrations to achieve civil rights and to dismantle the system of segregation. *Black Boy*, which covers the period from 1912 to 1927, emphasizes the limitations of a brutal environment and the impact of racism on the sensibility of a black youth. Race riots, lynchings, the degrading social norms blacks were expected to observe in the presence of whites, discrimination in schooling and employment, and exclusion from public libraries were crucial elements in Wright's socialization and that of his peers. His autobiography is a powerful metaphor for one stage of the black struggle toward full citizenship in America. Regularly the stark realism of the book causes movements to ban it from the schools, as for example in Jacksonville, Florida, in 1997.

Selected Bibliography Stephen Butterfield, *Black Autobiography in America* (1974); Charles T. Davis, "From Experience to Eloquence: Richard Wright's *Black Boy*," in Michael S. Harper and Robert B. Stepto, eds., *Chant of Saints* (1979); Ralph Ellison, "Richard Wright's Blues," *Antioch Review*, 5 (Summer 1945), 198–211; Madison D. Lacy, director, producer *Black Boy* (video, 1994); Los Angeles *Sentinel*, 28 May 1997, p. A3.

Jerry Ward

Black Cabinet Given their already marginal status in American society prior to 1929, black Americans found themselves in particularly desperate circumstances in the 1930s depression. A key factor in the New Deal's ability to respond to black concerns was the appointment of prominent blacks to race relations advisory positions within federal departments and newly established federal agencies. A number of black advisers formed an informal network in 1936 that came to be known as the Black Cabinet, Black Brain Trust, or Federal Council on Negro Affairs. Prominent figures included **Mary McLeod Bethune,** head of the Negro Division of the National Youth Administration; **Robert C. Weaver,** adviser to **Harold L. Ickes** in the Department of the Interior and later the U.S. Housing Authority; **Lawrence Augustus Oxley,** Department of Labor; **William Johnson Trent, Jr.,** Interior and Federal Works Agency; **Eugene Kinckle Jones,** Department of Commerce; and Frank S. Horne, who served in various federal housing programs. This Black Brain Trust, or Black Cabinet, was never a formal organization nor did its members meet on any regular basis. Rather it consisted of a group of black advisers who came together on their own initiative, often at the urging of their most powerful members, Bethune and Weaver, to assess programs and develop strategies to assure black participation in administration measures. The cabinet served also as an opportunity for many to share their personal problems in government, formulate common goals, and develop tactics to enhance the black perspective. In directly affecting policy, most black advisers had limited impact, and a number left the Roosevelt administration in frustration. But the cabinet was important because of its symbolic role in giving recognition to blacks within the federal government, educating white New Dealers to racial issues, and establishing a precedent within both the national government and the Democratic party for future black participation.

Selected Bibliography Thomas Lee Green, "Black Cabinet Members in the Franklin Delano Roosevelt Administration" (Ph.D. diss., University of Colorado, 1981); John B. Kirby, *Black Americans in the Roosevelt Era* (1980); Jane R. Motz, "The Black Cabinet: Negroes in the Administration of Franklin D. Roosevelt" (M.A. thesis, University of Delaware, 1964); B. Joyce Ross, "Mary McLeod Bethune and the National Youth Administration: A Case Study of Power Relationships in the Black Cabinet of Franklin D. Roosevelt," *Journal of Negro History* 60 (January 1975), 1–28.

John B. Kirby

Black Capitalism   This term refers to the accumulation of capital by individual African American entrepreneurs, strategies designed to maintain African American control over the African American consumer market in the United States, and collective programs that are designed to improve the overall position of African Americans. Black capitalism has undergone two primary periods of development. **Booker T. Washington,** through the **National Negro Business League,** and **Marcus Garvey,** through the **Universal Negro Improvement Association,** created the idea of concentrating on establishing entrepreneurial success via the African American consumer market. "Buy Black" campaigns became popular in the 1920s and 1930s as a result of their efforts. In the contemporary period, beginning in the 1960s, the development of African American participation in the corporate sector has constituted the primary emphasis of activities. One notable black entrepreneur around the turn of the twentieth century was **Madame C. J. Walker**, whose hair- and skin-care products earned her a fortune. Major developments in black capitalism around the turn of the twenty-first century include the FUBU apparel company, **Black Entertainment Television** (BET), and the incredible success of many black athletes and music/movie/television stars. These notable developments have created a small, but growing, class of black millionaires in America.

Selected Bibliography George Davis and Glegg Watson, *Black Life in Corporate America* (1982); Manning Marable, *How Capitalism Underdeveloped Black America* (1983); Juliet E. K. Walker, *The History of Black Business in America: Capitalism, Race, and Entrepreneurship* (1998).

Christopher Mobley

Black Codes During 1865 and 1866, all the southern states except North Carolina passed a number of laws designed as substitutes for the old slave codes. The main purpose of these so-called Black Codes was to insure an immobile dependent black labor force for each state's agricultural interest. They were designed to immobilize penniless, unemployed, and powerless black laborers. If charged with being vagrants, such individuals had to post a bond or offer the required security. Failure to adhere to these stipulations resulted in arrest and being hired out for a period not to exceed one year. An antienticement provision made it a misdemeanor to lure an employee under contract away from his employer. While most Black Codes made no distinction based on race, they were worded in such a way as to exempt white workers. Moreover, a few counties and towns passed ordinances that were blatantly discriminatory against blacks. When Presidential Reconstruction came to a close, the Black Codes were made illegal. The maintenance of such southern practices as the convict lease system, **black peonage,** and contract labor laws, well into the twentieth century, however, ensured continuing forms of forced labor in the South.

Selected Bibliography Berry A. Crouch, "'All the Vile Passions': The Texas Black Code of 1866," *Southwestern Historical Quarterly* 97 (No. 1, 1993), 12–34; Eric Foner, *Nothing But Freedom: Emancipation and Its Legacy* (1983); Idus A. Newby, *The South: A History* (1978); W. C. Nunn, *Texas Under the Carpet Baggers* (1962); Charles Vincent, *Black Legislators in Louisiana During Reconstruction* (1976); Michael Wayne, *The Reshaping of Plantation Society: The Natchez District* (1983); Vernon Lane Wharton, *The Negro in Mississippi: 1865–1890* (1947); Theodore Brantner Wilson, *The Black Codes of the South* (1965).

Joe Louis Caldwell

Black Conventions Although state and national conventions of African Americans began in the 1830s, the primary focus of the conventions changed after the Civil War from antislavery, economic development, and some nationalism to voting, legal rights, and schools. These meetings debated the contradiction between being all-black and their goal of greater participation in society. As political roles of African Americans declined at the end of Reconstruction, the sporadic conventions returned to an emphasis on economic improvement. In the 1880s, the conventions expanded their concerns to include education, lynching, and various forms of discrimination. They ceased in the 1890s with the formation of ongoing civil rights groups.

Selected Bibliography Philip S. Foner and George E. Walker, eds., *Proceedings of the Black National and State Conventions, 1865–1900* (1986); August Meier, *Negro Thought in America, 1880–1915: Radical Ideologies in the Age of Booker T. Washington* (1963).

Alwyn Barr

Black Economic Development Conference   This organization began as a conference held by the Interreligious Foundation for Community Organization (IFCO) at Wayne State University, Detroit, Michigan, in April 1969. At the meeting, former **Student Nonviolent Coordinating Committee** director **James Forman** presented and led the adoption of the "Black Manifesto," which called for, among other things, reparations from American white churches and synagogues of $500 million. Although by 1970 only about $300,000 had been received, this action did result in the formation and funding of many black organizations within various major denominations. Disassociated from IFCO, the Black Economic Development Conference invested most of its funds in a revolutionary publishing house, Black Star Publications.

Selected Bibliography James Forman, *The Making of Black Revolutionaries* (1985); Jerry K. Frye, " The Black Manifesto and the Tactics of Objectification," *Journal of Black Studies* 5 (no 1, 1974), 65–76; C. Eric Lincoln, *Race, Religion, and the Continuing American Dilemma* (1984); Merle Longwood, "Justice and Reparation: The Black Manifesto Reconsidered," *Lutheran Quarterly* 27 (No. 3, 1975), 203–19; *New York Times*, 4, 5 May 1969.

Ray Branch

Black Entertainment Television (BET)   Founded in 1980, BET was the first television network aimed strictly at an African American audience. By 1991 BET had thirty million subscribers within the United States and revenues of about $60 million. BET Holdings Inc., the parent company of BET, had controlling power in three magazines, *Emerge*, *YSB*, and *Heart and Soul* as well as a number of other entrepreneurial endorsements including additional television channels and a radio station. That same year, it became the first African American controlled business to be traded on the New York Stock Exchange. In 1998, however, the company removed itself from stock trading, returning to private status. *Business Week*, in 1993, named BET as one of the hundred best small corporations in the nation. The founder of BET, Robert Johnson, has received numerous awards, including the NAACP's Image Award (1982) and the Turner Broadcasting Trumpet Award (1993). In November 2000, he sold BET to the media company Viacom. This sale made Robert Johnson one of the first African American billionaires. BET continues to appeal to the African American community, but it is no longer owned by African Americans.

Selected Bibliography *Contemporary Black Biography*, vol. 3 (1993); *Current Biography* (1994); *Sacramento Observer* 22 November 2000; *Who's Who in America* (1994).

Lindley Carruth Shedd

"Black Is Beautiful"   Coming into vogue around 1966, the slogan "Black Is Beautiful" signaled a mood of black racial pride and a rejection of white values of style and appearance. It was particularly popular with young black people, who expressed this attitude by foregoing the skin lighteners and hair straighteners used by their parents' generation and by adopting Afro hairstyles, and such African forms of dress as dashikis. Along with the political concept of **Black Power** and the increasing interest in African American and African history and culture, the slogan was a manifestation of black nationalism in the period after 1965.

Selected Bibliography Stokely Carmichael and Charles V. Hamilton, *Black Power: The Politics of Liberation in America* (1967); August Meier and Elliott M. Rudwick, *From Plantation to Ghetto: An Interpretive History of American Negroes* (1970).

Carol Wilson

Black Muslims   This term, coined by writer C. Eric Lincoln, refers to members of the Nation of Islam, a black nationalist and religious organization founded in Detroit, Michigan, in or around 1930 by W. D. Fard. Fard taught that blacks could obtain success through discipline, racial pride, knowledge of God, and physical separation from white society. In June 1934, Fard mysteriously disappeared and was succeeded by Elijah Muhammad (born **Elijah Poole**). Muhammad proclaimed that Fard was Allah (God) and that he had selected him as his messenger. Muhammad moved the organization's headquarters to Chicago. The Black Muslims promoted integrity, honor, and cleanliness; they practiced abstinence from intoxicants and all controlled substances; they published their own newspaper; they purchased thousands of acres of southern farmland; they invested in business ventures; and they negotiated independently with foreign governments. The Nation of Islam also had its own educational system and a paramilitary force—Fruit of Islam. The most effective spokesman for the Black Muslims was **Malcolm X** (El Hajj Malik al-Shabazz, born Malcolm Little). From the late 1950s to 1963 he served as Muhammad's national representative, and the Nation of Islam gained national attention and a strong following. In 1963, Malcolm X lost favor with Elijah Muhammad and in 1964 he resigned from the Nation of Islam to form the Muslim Mosques, Inc., and the **Organization of Afro-American Unity.** In 1965 Malcolm X was assassinated, allegedly by Black Muslims. When Elijah Muhammad died in 1975, the Nation of Islam split. The American Muslim Mission, later called the Muslim American Community, is headed by Muhammad's son Imam (Reverend) Warith Deen Muhammad. Warith introduced his followers to internationally accepted practices of the Islamic religion. Those refusing to deviate from Elijah Muhammad's teachings comprise a smaller sect, retain the name Nation of Islam, and follow **Louis Farrakhan** (born Louis Eugene Walcott). Farrakhan became prominent when he replaced Malcolm X as Muhammad's national representative. His highpoint occurred in October 1995 with a successful **Million Man March** in the nation's capital.

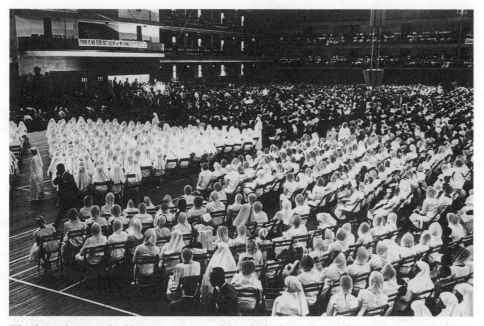

Elijah Muhammad addressing an assembly of Black Muslim followers, 1964. © Library of Congress.

The march brought together diverse groups in the black community in a sense of unity. There have also been attempts by Farrakhan in recent years to cooperate with the other groups.

Selected Bibliography A. John Adams and Joan Martin Burke, *A CBS News Reference Book: Civil Rights, A Current Guide to the People, Organizations and Events* (1970); Martha F. Lee, *The Nation of Islam An American Millenarian Movement* (1984); C. Eric Lincoln, *The Black Muslims in America* (1973); Louis E. Lomax, *The Negro Revolt* (1963); Clifton E. Marsh, *From Black Muslims to Muslims: The Transition From Separatism to Islam, 1930–1980* (1984); Barbara Ann Norman, "The Black Muslims: A Rhetorical Analysis" (Ph.D. diss., University of Oklahoma, 1985); Harry A. Ploski, et al., eds., *The Negro Almanac* (1983).

Wali Rashash Kharif

Black Panthers   The Black Panther party was organized in October 1966 in Oakland, California, by **Bobby Seale** and **Huey P. Newton.** Dedicated to the principle of self-defense in the face of racist aggression and police brutality, the Panthers captured instant media attention by combining militant rhetoric with overt brandishing of automatic weapons as they trailed Oakland police to monitor their dealings with the African American community. The party was founded on the Ten Point Program, which took its inspiration from the Algerian freedom fighter, Frantz Fanon. Subscribing to the belief that African Americans constituted an oppressed black colony within a white mother country, the Panthers worked to liberate that colony. The party's platform demanded that African Americans be given freedom to decide their own destiny, control of their own communities, decent housing and education, exemption from military service, justice, and liberation from control by the white power structure. The party allied itself with the Weather Underground faction of Students for a Democratic Society, specifically because both groups sought to free themselves from American oppression. Panther workers organized many community-based programs, including a highly successful free breakfast program for school children.

Selected Bibliography Curtis J. Austin, "The Role of Violence in the Creation, Sustenance, and Destruction of the Black Panther Party, 1966–1972" (Ph.D. diss., Mississippi State University, 1999); Eldridge Cleaver, *Soul On Ice* (1968); Kathleen Cleaver and George Katsiaficas, eds., *Liberation, Imagination, and the Black Panther Party: A New Look at the Black Panthers and their Legacy* (2001); Theodore Draper, *The Rediscovery of Black Nationalism* (1970); Philip S. Foner, ed., *The Black Panthers Speak* (1970); Gene Marine, *The Black Panthers* (1969); Gilbert Moore, *A Special Rage* (1971); Bobby Seale, *Seize the Time: The Story of the Black Panther Party and Huey P. Newton* (1968).

Marshall Hyatt

Black Peonage   Following the Civil War many southern blacks became victims of peonage, a form of involuntary servitude akin to slavery. The system developed because southern planters needed a cheap and stable labor force and because the recently freed slaves, lacking land and capital of their own, needed employment. Frequently employing deception, coercion, or intimidation, landowners entered into exploitative contractual labor arrangements with impoverished blacks. Because the labor contracts and other devices employed by whites to impose peonage were sanctioned by state laws, blacks were often victimized for years by the system. The sharecropping system so widely employed in the South after 1865 was itself a means sometimes used to convert Negro workers into peons. Indebtedness was the perpetual condition of sharecroppers, who went ever deeper into debt to the landowners whose land they farmed. Because the white landlord advanced the goods the sharecropper needed and kept the account ledgers himself, it was difficult if not impossible for the cropper to extricate himself from debt and get free from the oppressive system. The widespread practice of imposing fines for petty crimes and then allowing white employers to pay the fines for impecunious blacks in exchange for their labor was another easy avenue to peonage. Although the Peonage Abolition Act of 1867 was passed by Congress to end the practice, peonage persisted. Forced labor because of debt enjoyed legal sanction in the South until 1911, when in the decision **Bailey v. Alabama** the Supreme Court declared unconstitutional a state law that made peonage possible. Even then, peonage did not completely disappear. During the 1920s and 1930s the **NAACP,** the Communist-backed **Abolish Peonage Committee of America,** and other civil rights groups pressured the Justice Department to bring action against southern peonage bosses. In 1941 the Supreme Court in **Taylor v. Georgia** again struck down a state statute permitting coerced labor. After that time a sharp drop in peonage occurred, although peonage prosecutions were still being filed by the Justice Department as late as the 1950s.

Selected Bibliography Pete Daniel, *The Shadow of Slavery: Peonage in the South, 1901–1969* (1972); Daniel A. Novak, *The Wheel of Servitude, Black Forced Labor After Slavery* (1978); C. Vann Woodward, *Origins of the New South, 1877–1913* (1951).

Charles D. Lowery

Black Power

On 17 June 1966, **Stokely Carmichael,** the chairman of the **Student Nonviolent Coordinating Committee** (SNCC), spoke at a rally in Greenwood, Mississippi, and called for Black Power. The speech split the civil rights movement and angered many of its supporters. Although the press interpreted Black Power as black violence against whites, Carmichael defined it as "a call for black people in this country to unite, to recognize their heritage, [and] to build a sense of community." He also defined Black Power as a call for African Americans to define their own goals, to lead their own organizations, and to reject the racist institutions and values of American society. While the press and conservative civil rights organizations such as the **NAACP** and **Southern Christian Leadership Conference** rejected and condemned Black Power as black racism, many of the young people in the civil rights movement adopted the slogan as a rallying cry for more aggressive action in the African American liberation struggle.

Selected Bibliography Stokely Carmichael, "What We Want," *New York Review of Books* (22 September 1966), 5–8; Stokely Carmichael and Charles V. Hamilton, *Black Power: The Politics of Liberation in America* (1967); Christopher Lasch, "The Trouble with Black Power," *New York Review of Books* (29 February 1968), 4–5, 8–14; Alvin Poussaint, "How the White Problem Spawned Black Power," *Ebony* (August 1967); Charles J. Stewart, "The Evolution of a Revolution: Stokely Carmichael and the Rhetoric of Black Power," *Quarterly Journal of Speech* 83 (1997), 429–40.

W. Marvin Dulaney

Black Star Steamship Line

Marcus Garvey and his **Universal Negro Improvement Association** operated a black-owned steamship line between 1919 and 1922. Stocks were sold inexpensively and widely within the black community. This corporation was established to foster black trade by linking black enterprises into a worldwide economic network, and to provide transportation to Africa. The plan enjoyed widespread support among African Americans, suggesting as it did self-reliance and racial pride. Grave financial problems forced the closing of the Black Star Line, and it was replaced by the Black Cross Navigation and Training Company in 1924. This too failed. Garvey was convicted of mail fraud in connection with the Black Star Line, found guilty, and deported from the United States in 1927.

Selected Bibliography John Clarke, *Marcus Garvey and the Vision of Africa* (1974); Robert Hill, ed., *The Marcus Garvey and UNIA Papers*, vols. 1–6 (1983–89); Tony Martin, *Race First* (1986); Judith Stein, *The World of Marcus Garvey* (1986).

Cheryl Greenberg

Black Suffragettes

By the end of the Civil War, African American women in both the North and South had begun to demonstrate an interest in acquiring the right to vote. Viewing the ballot as a vehicle that could advance women as well as secure civil and social rights for blacks, they formed all-black organizations and also attempted to work within integrated groups. Throughout the country black women's involvement in various forms of suffrage agitation and education continued until the passage of the Nineteenth Amendment.

Selected Bibliography Adele L. Alexander, "How I Discovered My Grandmother . . . and the Truth bout Black Women and the Suffrage Movement," in Darlene C. Hine, ed., *Black Women in United States History*, vol. 1 (1990); Angela Davis, "Working Women, Black Women and the History of the Suffrage Movement," *Women, Race, & Class* (1983); Paula Giddings, "The Quest for Woman Suffrage," *When and Where I Enter: The Impact of Black Women on Race and Sex in America* (1984); Ann D. Gordon, Bettye Collier-Thomas, John H. Bracey, Arlene Voski Avakian, Joyce Berkman, *African American Women and the Vote, 1837–1965* (1997).

Willi Coleman

Blair Education Bill A U.S. bill first introduced in 1882 by Republican Henry W. Blair of New Hampshire that called for the creation of a national system of education paid for and supervised by the federal government. The bill appropriated $77 million in federal aid over a period of eight years to be distributed among the states according to their needs. It was designed primarily to help educate the South's black population, and African Americans were almost unanimous in their support of the bill. The measure passed the Senate in 1884, 1886, and 1888, each time to be tabled by Democrats in the House of Representatives. In 1890, the Blair Bill died in the Senate, and was never brought up again. The bill marked the last notable attempt by the federal government to help ensure equal educational opportunities for African Americans before the civil rights movement more than half a century later.

Selected Bibliography Daniel W. Crofts, "The Black Response to the Blair Education Bill," *Journal of Southern History* 37 (1971), 41–65; Allen J. Goings, "The South and the Blair Education Bill," *Mississippi Valley Historical Society* 44 (1957), 276–90; Thomas Adams Upchurch, "The Billion Dollar Congress and Black America: Debating the Race Problem on the Eve of Jim Crow" (Ph.D. diss., Mississippi State University, 2001).

Thomas Adams Upchurch

Blake, Eugene Carson (7 November 1906, St. Louis, Mo.–31 July 1985, Stamford, Conn.). An influential white clergyman, scholar and author, Blake attended Princeton (A.B., 1928), Princeton Theological Seminary (Th.B., 1932), and Occidental College (D.D., 1941). He received 20 honorary degrees. Blake headed the United Presbyterian Church and the National Council of Churches, and, after the 1963 Birmingham violence, challenged white clergymen: "Some time or other, we are all going to have to stand and be on the receiving end of a fire hose." Active in the civil rights movement, he was arrested in a Baltimore, Maryland, march. He was a principal organizer of the 1963 **March on Washington.** Blake supported nonviolence and opposed militancy in the civil rights movement.

Selected Bibliography Taylor Branch, *Parting the Waters: America in the King Years, 1954–63* (1988); Ebony, *Ebony Pictorial History of Black America*, vol. 3 (1971); John Hope Franklin and

Alfred A. Moss, Jr., *From Slavery to Freedom: A History of Negro Americans*, 8th ed. (2000); William Loren Katz, *Eyewitness: The Negro in American History* (1968); *Who's Who in America, 1980–1981* (1981).

Wali Rashash Kharif

Bland, James W. B. (1838, Prince Edward County, Va.–1870, Richmond, Va.). Born free, Bland was taught how to read and write by his mother's enslaver, and later enrolled in a school run by the **American Missionary Association** (AMA) in the early 1860s. Following his studies in 1864, Bland wanted to establish a school for blacks, but his attempt was stopped by the AMA on the grounds that he was morally unqualified. Consequently he became a domestic worker, and then a substitute teacher. Bland was selected to represent Prince Edward and Appomattox counties in the constitutional convention of 1869–70, and served in the Virginia Senate from 1869 to 1870. He also worked as a tax assessor for the national government. During the convention, Bland called for railroad companies to provide equal accommodations for all convention delegates. He introduced a proposal designed to give every individual the right to study in public schools without discrimination. Bland also wrote to Republican congressman Elihu Washburne of Illinois, protesting against the attempts undertaken by other Republican leaders in 1869 to increase the political influence of the former Confederates. In the Virginia Senate, Bland proposed a bill that incorporated Hampton Institute, a black college established after the Civil War. Bland was among the 60 people who died in 1870 when the second floor of Virginia's capitol building collapsed.

Selected Bibliography *The Debates and Proceedings of the Constitutional Convention of the State of Virginia* (1868); Eric Foner, *Freedom's Lawmakers: A Dictionary of Black Officeholders during Reconstruction* (1993); Luther P. Jackson, *Negro Office-Holders in Virginia, 1865–1895* (1945); Richard Lowe, *Republicans and Reconstruction in Virginia, 1856–70* (1991); Robert C. Morris, *Reading, Writing, and Reconstruction: The Education of the Freemen in the South, 1861–1870* (1981).

Amos J. Beyan

Blood on the Forge Published in 1941 by African American novelist **William Attaway,** this novel, like *12 Million Black Voices* by **Richard Wright,** which appeared in the same year, deals with the harsh and disillusioning realities of northern working-class life faced by black southerners who participated in the **Great Migration** (1910–20). Attaway's story is set in rural Kentucky and in a steel town outside Pittsburgh, Pennsylvania, where his protagonists, the sharecropping Moss brothers, flee to escape racial and economic oppression. *Blood on the Forge* was one of the first examples of African American proletariat fiction.

Selected Bibliography Phyllis R. Klotman, "An Examination of Whiteness in William Attaway, *Blood on the Forge*," *CLA Journal* 15 (June 1972), 459–64; Nicholas Lemann, "In Introduction" in William Attaway, *Blood on the Forge* (1992); Philip H. Vaughn, "From Pastoralism to Industrial Antipathy in William Attaway, *Blood on the Forge*," *Phylon* 36

(December 1975), 422–25; Edward R. Waldon, "The Death of the Blues, in William Attaway, *Blood on the Forge*," *Negro American Literature Forum* 10 (Summer 1976), 58–60; Richard Yarborough, afterword to William Attaway, *Blood on the Forge* (1941; reprint, 1987).

Judith N. Kerr

Blues Perhaps the best definition of the blues came from the Classic Blueswomen. These black women in the 1920s recorded the first blues discs for commercial distribution. Bessie Smith stated in 1924 that the blues were not funny songs. "Of course," she said, "the modern songs are greatly modified, but the original blues songs are deep, emotional melodies, bespeaking of a troubled heart." Two years later, the *Chicago Defender* featured a statement by Ethel Waters in which she claimed that one must feel the blues, not just sing them. Waters stated: "The blues are our own and they originated not from religious hymns as many people think, but from the feeling of sorrow and oppression born with the darky. Any religious Negro can sing a spiritual, but it takes a good one to sing blues." Although Ma Rainey, Bessie Smith, Alberta Hunter, Mamie Smith, and other blues singers often expressed personal pain, they also sang about the black poor. Songs such as these represented social protest and reflected the response in music to the oppressive racial injustices blacks experienced in America. Mamie Smith's success paved the way for other blues and black music artists to enter the world of professional entertainment. Thus began the "race record" industry that ended black exclusion from the commercial record industry. This was a civil rights milestone for black America. Although many African American blues artists were exploited and experienced segregation and racial discrimination in recording, promoting, and performing the blues, eventually they were recognized as a significant aspect of

Portrait of Bessie Smith by Carl van Vechten, 1936. © Library of Congress.

American musical culture and, later, as a major force in the recording and performing industries. As with other genres of black music, the blues genre has been adopted and propagated by countless white performers since the 1950s.

Selected Bibliography William Barlow, *"Looking Up at Down": The Emergence of Blues Culture* (1989); *Chicago Defender,* 25 December 1926; Daphne Duval Harrison, *Black Pearls: Blues Queens of the 1920s* (1988); LeRoi Jones, *Blues People* (1961); Gerhard Kubik, *Africa and the Blues* (1999); *Living Blues* magazine (1970–); Phillip McGuire, "Black Music Critics and the Classic Blues Singers," *The Black Perspective in Music* 14 (Spring 1986); Jeffrey P. Melnick, *A Right to Sing the Blues: African Americans, Jews, and American Popular Song* (1999); Hirem Nall, "From Down South to Up South: An Examination of Geography in the Blues," *Midwest Quarterly* (2001), 306–19; Paul Oliver, *The Story of the Blues* (1969).

Phillip McGuire

Bob Jones University v. United States, **461 U.S. 574 (1983)** Until 1970 the Internal Revenue Service (IRS) granted tax-exempt status to private schools regardless of their racial admissions policies. In 1971 the District Court for the District of Columbia ruled in *Green v. Connally* that racially discriminatory private schools were not entitled to exemption under the Internal Revenue Code. Bob Jones University, a nonprofit corporation in Greenville, South Carolina, had excluded blacks until 1970 and, from 1971 to 1975, accepted only blacks married within their race. After May 1975 the university enrolled unmarried blacks but prohibited interracial dating and marriage. On 16 January 1976, the IRS revoked the university's tax-exempt status, effective 1 December 1970, because of its racially discriminatory policy. The university filed suit to recover $21 it had paid in 1975 unemployment taxes, and the government counterclaimed for unpaid unemployment taxes for the years 1971–75, totaling almost half a million dollars. The federal district court in South Carolina found in favor of the plaintiff, ruling that the IRS had exceeded its delegated powers in revoking the university's tax-exempt status. The Fourth Circuit Court of Appeals rejected the lower court's arguments and reversed the decision. The Supreme Court, on appeal, affirmed the decision of the appellate court.

Selected Bibliography Richard Nathan, "Reflections on Pragmatic Jurisprudence: A Case Study of Bob Jones University v. United States," *American Business Law Journal* 22 (1984), 227–48; Donald G. Nieman, *Promise to Keep: Afro-Americans and the Constitutional Order, 1776 to the Present* (1991); J. Harvie Wilkinson III, *From Brown to Bakke: The Supreme Court and School Integration, 1954–1978* (1979).

Michael S. Downs

Bob-Lo Excursion Co. v. Michigan, **333 U.S. 28 (1948)** When this case reached the U.S. Supreme Court, constitutional doctrine held that state laws based upon race affecting passengers in interstate commerce infringed upon the power of Congress to regulate interstate and foreign commerce. The effect of that doctrine in *Morgan v. Virginia* (1945) had been to protect black travelers on interstate buses from Virginia segregation law. Application of the doctrine to the *Bob-Lo* case, however, would have had the effect of permitting racial discrimination, which the Court was unwilling to allow. Bob-Lo Excursion Company operated an amusement park on an island in Canadian waters and used steamships to carry its customers there. It refused to serve blacks, and, when a group of 13 young women, one of whom was black, boarded a Bob-Lo ship, the company required the black to leave. She brought charges against the company, which the state successfully prosecuted under its civil rights law. The company appealed. Rather than follow doctrine and hold the state civil rights act unconstitutional, the Court distinguished the *Bob-Lo* case, noting that the only access to the island was from Detroit, Michigan, and that most of the customers lived there, making the matter primarily local, rather than foreign, commerce. The state law did not infringe upon Congress's commerce power.

Selected Bibliography Note, "Discrimination and the Commerce Clause: Application of State Civil Rights Acts in Interstate and Foreign Commerce," *Yale Law Journal* 58 (1949), 329–34; C. Herman Pritchett, *The American Constitution* (1977).

Patricia A. Behlar

Boley, Oklahoma   This was the most celebrated of the black towns established in Oklahoma as a result of black migration. When Congress created the Oklahoma Territory in 1889 and opened it for settlement, southern blacks moved in and claimed homesteads. The migrants brought with them dreams of a better life. They hoped to own land and to enjoy freedom and independence. Edwin P. McCabe, founder of the black town of Langston, thought it possible to carve an all-black state out of the Indian Territory. This dream soon faded, but it was still thought possible to gain control of Okfuskee County and have Boley named the county seat. Boley was founded in 1903 at the urging of W. H. Boley, president of the Fort Smith & Western Railroad, for whom it was named. By 1905, there were over two thousand people in the area and economic, social, and cultural institutions were flourishing. On the eve of statehood, the white-dominated constitutional convention passed over Boley for the county seat. By gerrymandering Okfuskee County, white Oklahomans neutralized the black vote. Then, in 1910 black Oklahomans were disfranchised. This ended the dream of political power, and the cotton depression of 1913 ended Boley's economic prosperity. Soon, the town began losing population to northern industrial cities.

Selected Bibliography William E. Bittle and Gilbert L. Geis, "Racial Self-Fulfillment and the Rise of an All-Negro Community in Oklahoma," *Phylon* 18 (3rd quarter, 1957), 247–60; Jimmie Lewis Franklin, *Journey Toward Hope: A History of Blacks in Oklahoma* (1982); Kent Ruth, *Oklahoma: A Guide to the Sooner State* (1958).

Arvarh E. Strickland

Bolling v. Sharpe*, 347 U.S. 497 (1954)**   On 17 May 1954, in ***Brown v. Board of Education, the Supreme Court ruled that school segregation violated the equal protection clause of the **Fourteenth Amendment.** *Bolling v. Sharpe*, which dealt with the same issue in Washington, D.C., was decided separately because the Fourteenth Amendment specifically prohibited states from deny-ing citizens the equal protection of the laws; it did not, however, apply to the federal government. The Court ruled in *Bolling* that discrimination could be "so unjustifiable as to be violative of due process" and that segregation in Washington's schools fell into that category and therefore violated the Fifth Amendment's guarantee of due process. If the legal reasoning seemed some-what less than irrefutable, the Court concluded by stating the real rationale behind its decision: "In view of our decision that the Constitution prohibits the states from maintaining racially segregated public schools, it would be unthinkable that the same Constitution would impose a lesser duty on the Federal Government."

Selected Bibliography Daniel M. Berman, *It Is So Ordered* (1966); David Chang, "The Bus Stops Here: Defining the Constitutional Right of Equal Education Opportunity and an Appropriate Remedial Process," *Boston University Law Review* 83 (1983), 1–58; Richard Kluger, *Simple Justice: The History of Brown v. Board of Education and Black America's Struggle for Equality* (1976).

Michael S. Mayer

Bond, Horace Julian (14 January 1940, Nashville, Tenn.–). Bond was exposed at a young age to the importance of education and social activism by his father, Horace Mann Bond, the first president of Georgia's Fort Valley State University and first black president of Lincoln University. In 1957 Julian Bond entered Morehouse College and joined civil rights activities in Atlanta. In 1960 he helped form the **Student Nonviolent Coordinating Committee** (SNCC) and became its director of communications. Bond dropped out of school the next year to devote more time to the movement and organized voter registration drives in Georgia, Alabama, Mississippi, and Arkansas. In 1965 he was elected to the Georgia House of Representatives, but its members refused to seat him because of his vocal opposition to the Vietnam War. The U.S. Supreme Court later ruled that the legislature's actions violated Bond's civil rights and he served four terms in the House. At the 1968 Democratic Convention, Bond became the first black person nominated for the vice pres-idency, but he withdrew from the race because he was too young to serve. Three years later, he received his B.A. in English from Morehouse. In 1974, Bond was elected to the Georgia Senate and served until 1987, the longest tenure of any black official in Georgia history. In 2003 Bond remained an active civil rights lecturer, teacher, writer, and activist. He has received numerous honorary degrees, has taught at universities such as Pennsylvania, Harvard and Virginia, was President Emeritus of the **Southern Poverty Law Center,** and was elected chairman of the **NAACP** in 1998, a post he retained into the twenty-first century.

Selected Bibliography Julian Bond, *A Time to Speak, A Time to Act: The Movement in Politics* (1972); Thomas E. Bell, *Julian Bond vs John Lewis* (1988); John Neary, *Julian Bond: Black Rebel* (1971); Thomas Rose and John Greenya, *Black Leaders, Then and Now: A Personal History of Students Who Led the Civil Rights Movement in the 1960's—And What Happened to Them* (1984); Roger M. Williams, *The Bonds: An American Family* (1971).

Michael Butler

Bontemps, Arna Wendell   (13 October 1902, Alexandria, La.–4 June 1973, Nashville, Tenn.). Bontemps was part of his home state's long tradition of producing outstanding nonwhite politicians, artists, educators, musicians, writers, and businessmen. He received his B.A. from Union Pacific College (1923) and his M.A. from the University of Chicago (1943), and his career included teaching and administration as well as writing. Among his various educational posts were positions at Oakwood School in Huntsville, Alabama (1930–32); the University of Illinois (1966); Yale University (1969–72); and **Fisk University** (1943–65 and 1972–73). Scholarly recognition of his contributions is evidenced by his receipt of Guggenheim and Rosenwald Fellowships; his awards for writing include two Alexander Pushkin Prizes for poetry and *Crisis* magazine's Poetry Prize. Bontemps was a novelist, historian, biographer, and playwright as well as a poet. Among his numerous works are *God Sends Sunday* (1931), *You Can't Pet a Possum* (1934), *Black Thunder* (1936), *Drums at Dusk* (1939), *Golden Slippers: An Anthology of Negro Poetry for Young People* (1941), *Story of the Negro* (1948), *George Washington Carver* (1950), *Frederick Douglass: Slave, Fighter, Freeman* (1959), *American Negro Poetry* (1963), *Famous Negro Athletes* (1964), and *The Harlem Renaissance Remembered* (1972). This productivity made him one of the outstanding figures of the **Harlem Renaissance;** however, his novel *Black Thunder,* depicting a slave insurrection amid the French Revolution, led to accusations that he was encouraging violent revolution. Arna Bontemps spent his last years as writer-in-residence at Fisk University, preparing his autobiography.

   Selected Bibliography Bruce Kellner, *The Harlem Renaissance: A Historical Dictionary for the Era* (1984); Charles H, Nichols, ed., *Arna Bontemps–Langston Hughes Letters, 1925–1967* (1967); John O'Brien, ed., *Interviews with Black Writers* (1973); Wilhelmena S. Robinson, *Historical Negro Biographies* (1969); Douglas Wixson, "Black Writes and White! Jack Conroy, Arna Bontemps, and International Collaboration in the 1930s," *Prospects* 23 (1998), 401–30.

Gary B. Mills

Boston Guardian   This African American protest newspaper was established in 1901 by the militant **(William) Monroe Trotter** and George W. Forbes. The first issue pledged "to voice intelligently the needs and aspirations of the colored American." As managing editor, Trotter used the *Guardian* to demand full citizenship and equality for African Americans. The *Guardian's* editorials attacked **Booker T. Washington** and his philosophy of accommodation. Trotter effectively used the *Guardian* as a forum not only to denounce Washington's policies, but also to fight increasing racism and to keep the protest tradition operative. The *Guardian* experienced a decline in the 1920s, but continued in circulation even after Trotter's death in 1934.

   Selected Bibliography The *Boston Guardian*, 1901–57; Stephen R. Fox, *The Guardian of Boston: William Monroe Trotter* (1970); Louis R. Harlan, *Booker T. Washington: The Wizard of Tuskegee, 1901–1915* (1983); Charles W. Puttkammer and Ruth Worthy, "William Monroe Trotter, 1872–1934," *Journal of Negro History* 43 (October 1958), 298–316.

Maxine D. Jones

Boston Riot (1903)   Appalled at the influence of **Booker T. Washington**'s doctrine of accommodation, **(William) Monroe Trotter** and George W. Forbes of the *Boston Guardian* sought to challenge Washington's leadership directly. Drafting a series of probing questions on Washington's racial philosophy, Trotter and Forbes organized a group of about thirty people to interrupt Washington's speech to Boston's Negro Business League at the African Methodist Episcopal (A.M.E.) church on 30 July 1903. Trotter and his followers' attempts to ask questions disrupted the meeting, caused him to be arrested, fined 50 dollars, and sentenced to 30 days in prison. The incident, sensationalized and exaggerated in the local press as "the Boston Riot," made the militant Trotter a martyr to other Negro radicals and he became a rallying point for the anti-Washington forces. Later, Trotter and **W.E.B. Du Bois** formed the **Niagara Movement,** the first national organization of militant blacks, which favored direct political and social protest over Washington's accommodationist stance.

Selected Bibliography Robert H. Brisbane, *The Black Vanguard: Origins of the Negro Social Revolution, 1900–1960* (1970); W.E.B. Du Bois, "William Monroe Trotter," *Crisis* (May 1934); Stephen R. Fox, *The Guardian of Boston: William Monroe Trotter* (1970); Charles W. Puttkammer and Ruth Worthy, "William Monroe Trotter 1872–1934," *Journal of Negro History,* 43 (1958), 298–316; Booker T. Washington, *My Larger Education: Being Chapters from My Experience* (1911).

Thaddeus M. Smith

Boswell Amendment   The Boswell Amendment was representative of the system of legislative hurdles and literacy tests designed to exclude black voters from the polls in the post-Reconstruction period through the late 1960s. Authored by Alabama State Senator E.C. "Bud" Boswell in 1946, the amendment was offered especially "as a device for eliminating Negro applicants." The amendment was struck down along with other literacy restrictions by the federal courts in the 1949 litigation ***Davis et al. v. Schnell et al.***

Selected Bibliography Loren Miller, *The Petitioners, The Story of the Supreme Court of the United States and the Negro* (1966); Mabel M. Smythe, ed., *The Black American Reference Book* (1976).

Maghan Keita

Bouey, Harrison N.   (1849, Augusta, Ga.–1909, Monrovia, Liberia). A teacher, minister, judge, and emigrationist, Bouey taught in Augusta, Georgia, and later moved to Edgefield County, South Carolina where he served as a Baptist minister and principal of a secular school in 1873. Although he was threatened with death, Bouey won the probate judge election in 1874. He was victorious in the election for sheriff, but was defrauded of his victory in 1876. Like Henry M. Turner, Bouey became a leading spokesperson for black civil rights and a supporter of black emigration to Liberia, a country that had been established in West Africa by the American Colonization Society in 1822. He informed Turner that America was too racist to extend full citizenship to blacks, and that the best thing for them to do was to emigrate to Liberia where they would be truly free. He sailed to Liberia together with a number of black families on the vessel *Azor* in 1878. He returned to America and continued to serve as a Baptist minister among blacks when again he sailed to Liberia, where he died in 1909.

Selected Bibliography Amos J. Beyan, *The American Colonization Society and the Creation of the Liberia State, 1822–1900* (1991); Eric Foner, *Freedom's Lawmakers: A Dictionary of Black Officeholders During Reconstruction* (1993); Alfred B. Williams, *Hampton and His Red Shirts* (1935).

Amos J. Beyan

Boynton v. Virginia, 364 U.S. 454 (1960)   This case extended the prohibition against segregation in interstate travel to cover accommodations in terminals. The Supreme Court held that racial segregation practiced by a privately operated restaurant in an interstate bus terminal in Richmond, Virginia, violated the Interstate Commerce Act. Writing for the majority, Justice Hugo Black ruled that, if a bus company "has volunteered to make terminal and restaurant facilities . . . available to its interstate passengers as a regular part of their transportation," then the "terminal and restaurant stand in place of the bus company in the performance of its transportation obligations," and they "must perform these services without discriminations prohibited by the [Motor Carrier] Act." In spite of this decision and **Morgan v. Virginia** (1945), which had prohibited segregation on buses engaged in interstate travel, blacks who tried to sit in the front seat of buses or who tried to use terminal facilities other than those assigned to them were usually ejected or arrested. The **Congress of Racial Equality** decided to test the *Boynton* decision with **Freedom Riders.**

Selected Bibliography Catherine A. Barnes, *Journey from Jim Crow: The Desegregation of Southern Transit* (1983); James Farmer, *Lay Bare the Heart* (1985); Donald G. Nieman, *Promises to Keep, African-Americans and the Constitutional Order, 1776 to the Present* (1991).

Michael S. Mayer

Bradley, Thomas   (29 December 1917, Calvert, Tex.–29 September 1998, Los Angeles, Calif.). Bradley's family moved to Los Angeles when he was seven. A temporary police department job in 1940 turned into a career of 21 years, during which time he rose to the rank of lieutenant, studied law, received the LL.B. at Southwestern University in 1956, and was admitted to the California bar. He became the first black man elected to the Los Angeles City Council in 1963, and he ran unopposed in 1967 and 1971 in a racially mixed district. A Democrat, he won 56 percent of the vote on 1 July 1973, in a city with a 15 percent black electorate to defeat incumbent Sam Yorty to become the first black mayor of a predominantly white American city. He served until 1993. He proudly called his city one of hope and opportunity saying, "I am a living example of that."

Selected Bibliography *Current Biography* (1973, 1992, 1999); *New York Times*, 30 September 1998; "How Blacks are Faring as Government Leaders," *U.S. News and World Report*, 5 March 1984; "Los Angeles: A Black Mayor," *Newsweek*, 11 June 1973; *Roundtable* (1986); *Who's Who among Black Americans* (1988).

Thomas D. Cockrell

William Stanley Braithwaite, c. 1910–1920. © Library of Congress.

Braithwaite, William Stanley Beaumont (6 December 1878, Boston, Mass.–8 June 1962, Boston, Mass.). The son of William Smith and Emma DeWolf Braithwaite, he was self-educated. As a youth, he became an apprentice type-setter at Ginn and Company. During his career, Braithwaite was literary editor and columnist for the *Boston Evening Transcript*, publisher of the *Poetic Journal of Boston* (1912–14), editor of the *Poetry Review* (1916–17), founder and editor of B. J. Brimmer Publishing Co. (1921–27), and a member of the editorial board of **Phylon.** His works include collections of poetry (the first, *Lyrics of Life and Love*, appeared in 1904), essays, novels, a Brontë biography—*The Bewitched Parsonage: The Story of the Brontës* (1950)—and an autobiography, *The House under Arcturus*, serialized in *Phylon* 1941–42. He also contributed articles, essays, verse, and book reviews to periodicals. Braithwaite's poetry is classified as Romantic, but because it neither addressed social and political issues nor was identifiably African American, some colleagues accused him of being ashamed of his race. Braithwaite chose to emphasize the aesthetic qualities of literature. Even so, as the editor of anthologies, he published the works of many black writers who otherwise might not have attained public recognition. This was his contribution to the **Harlem Renaissance.** In 1918, William Braithwaite was the first winner of the **NAACP Spingarn Medal** for literary achievement. He also received honorary degrees from **Atlanta University** and Talladega College.

Selected Bibliography Benjamin Brawley, *The Negro in Art and Literature* (1918); Phillip Butcher, "William Stanley Braithwaite's Southern Exposure: Resume and Revelation," *Southern Literary Journal* 3 (Spring 1971), 49–61; Trudier Harris, ed., *Afro-American Writers Before the Harlem Renaissance* (1986); Peter Quartermain, ed., *American Poets, 1880–1945*, 3rd ser. (1987); William H. Robinson, *Black New England Letters* (1977).

Judith N. Kerr

Braun, Carol Moseley (16 August 1947, Chicago, Ill.–). Born in Chicago, she graduated from the University of Illinois in 1969, and earned a law degree from the University of Chicago in 1972. In 1992, she defeated incumbent Alan Dixon in the Democratic primary to become only the second African American in the twentieth century, and the first African American woman ever elected to the U.S. Senate. She has spent her political career defending black interests. She was defeated for reelection in 1998 and later served as ambassador to New Zealand. In 2003, she was one of 10 Democratic candidates vying for the 2004 presidential nomination.

Selected Bibliography Laverne McCain Gill, *African American Women in Congress: Forming and Transforming History* (1997); John Hope Franklin and Alfred E. Moss, Jr., *From Slavery to Freedom: A History of African Americans*, 8th ed. (2000).

Thomas Adams Upchurch

Senator Carol Moseley Braun with then first lady Hillary Rodham Clinton and others at a women's issues rally in Chicago, 1988. © AP/Wide World Photos.

Breedlove v. Suttles, **302 U.S. 277 (1937)** The **poll tax,** usually retroactive and cumulative, had the effect of disfranchising all indigent voters and on the surface was not aimed specifically at the African American. However, the **Southern Conference for Human Welfare** condemned it as "patently a device for disfranchising Negroes." In 1937 a white, 28-year-old male challenged the Georgia poll tax as offensive to the rule of equality because it required a one dollar annual payment from all inhabitants between the ages of 21 and 60 as a prerequisite for voting in all elections. The U.S. Supreme Court ruled that the tax, properly administered, did not violate any protection or privilege guaranteed by the **Fourteenth, Fifteenth,** or **Nineteenth Amendment**s and was, therefore, constitutional. Justice Butler stated that it was reasonable to exclude those under 21 years of age because the burden of payment would rest on their parents or guardians and those over 60 years because they were exempt from jury duty and military service. The final destruction of the poll tax occurred with the ratification of the Twenty-fourth Amendment (1964), the passage of the **Civil Rights Act of 1964** and the **Voting Rights Act of 1965,** and the Supreme Court decision reached in *Harper v. Virginia Board of Elections* (1966).

Selected Bibliography Richard Bardolph, ed., *The Civil Rights Record: Black Americans and the Law, 1849–1970* (1970); Federal Legal Information through Electronics, *Supreme Court Decisions, 1937–1975,* http://www.fedworld.gov/supcourt; Paul Freund et al., *Constitutional Law: Cases and Other Problems* (1961); Jack Greenburg, *Race Relations and American Law* (1959); Alfred H. Kelly and Winfred A. Harbison, *American Constitution: Origins and Development* (1970).

Aingred G. Dunston

Briggs v. Elliot, **132 F. Supp. 776 (E.D. S.C., 1955)** This case originally came before a federal appeals court in 1951 and then was added to a group of four other cases that went before the U.S. Supreme Court under the nomenclature of **Brown v. Board of Education.** The *Briggs* case concerned Harry Briggs, a black parent, who brought suit with other black parents against R. W. Elliot, school board chairman of Clarendon County, South Carolina. The parents were represented by a team of **NAACP** lawyers headed by **Thurgood Marshall.** Marshall, arguing for the plaintiff, charged that the county schools provided for black children were unequal and inferior and that segregation was unconstitutional and detrimental to black children. Marshall's case relied heavily upon the testimony of psychologist Kenneth Clark whose "doll" studies demonstrated the effects of segregation. The attorney general of South Carolina did not even try to defend the unequal nature of the schools; he said that the state assembly was working to pass a bond issue that would rectify the NAACP's first argument. As for the second point, the attorney general stood on the *Plessy v. Ferguson* decision, which upheld **separate-but-equal** facilities. The Fourth Circuit Court of Appeals found for South Carolina. The case was then appealed by the NAACP to the U.S. Supreme Court.

Selected Bibliography Daniel Berman, *It is So Ordered: The Supreme Court Rules on School Segregation* (1966); Richard Kluger, *Simple Justice: The History of Brown versus Board of Education and America's Struggle for Equality* (1976); George Rossman, ed., "Review of Recent Supreme Court Cases," *American Bar Association Journal* 40 (1954), 618–19.

Kenneth W. Goings

Brimmer, Andrew Fenton (13 September 1926, Newellton, La.–). An African American economist and public servant, Andrew Brimmer attended the University of Washington, where he earned bachelor's and master's degrees in economics. His master's thesis concerned economic aspects of fair employment. Noted for research on international monetary issues, he was appointed a Governor of the Federal Reserve Board in 1966. Brimmer also researches and writes about the economic status of black Americans. He presented expert testimony on discrimination in interstate commerce for hearings on the **Civil Rights Act of 1964** and initiated a study of the skewed income levels of blacks and whites after the 1968 **Watts race riot.** President Bill Clinton appointed Brimmer to the Federal Reserve Board in 1995, a position he held for one term. He also chaired a financial reform board for Washington, D.C., which successfully balanced that city's budget in the late 1990s.

Selected Bibliography Andrew F. Brimmer, *Trends, Prospects, and Strategies for Black Economic Progress* (1985); Andrew F. Brimmer, "Long Term Trends and Prospects for Black-Owned Businesses," *Review of Black Political Economy* 26 (Summer 1998), 19–37; Andrew F. Brimmer, "Economic Cost of Discrimination," *Black Enterprise* 24 (November 1993), 27; *Current Biography* (1968).

Nancy E. Fitch

Brooke, Edward William (26 October 1919, Washington, D.C.–). Elected from Massachusetts in 1966, the liberal Republican Edward W. Brooke, the first African American to serve in the U.S. Senate after Reconstruction, became a symbol of civil rights advances through moderate means. Educated at **Howard University** (B.S., 1941) and Boston University (LL.B., 1948; LL.M., 1949), Brooke established a national reputation as an articulate and thoughtful spokesman for equality under the law while serving as Massachusetts attorney general (1963–66). He pushed particularly hard for desegregated housing and, while a member of the Senate Banking, Housing, and Urban Affairs Committee, advocated open, private housing and low- and moderate-income public housing projects. Losing his bid in 1978 for a third term in the Senate, Brooke became chair of the National Low-Income Housing Coalition in 1979 and resumed the practice of law. In 2000, the state courthouse in Boston was named in his honor.

Selected Bibliography Edward W. Brooke, *The Challenge of Change* (1966); Edward W. Brooke, *United States Foreign Assistance for Haiti* (1974); Los Angeles *Sentinel*, 5 July 2000; *Washington Post*, 8, 10 November 1978.

Thomas J. Davis

Brooks, Gwendolyn (7 June 1917, Topeka, Kans.–3 December 2000, Chicago, Ill.). Nine years after graduation from Wilson Junior College (1936) in her native Chicago, Brooks published *Street in Bronzeville* (1945), which received an award from the American Academy of Arts and Letters. Her second volume *Annie Allen* (1949) won the 1950 Pulitzer Prize for Poetry. In 1960 Brooks published *The Bean Eaters* and was named Poet Laureate of Illinois in 1968. Marked by technical accomplishment and subtlety, Brooks's early poetry focuses on the lives of black Americans, particularly on the plight of urban existence, racial discrimination, and the special problems of women. After 1967 her poetry became more overtly political. The watershed volume *In the Mecca* (1968) contains poems on the assassinations of **Medgar W. Evers** and **Malcolm X,** the militant turn of the civil rights movement, and urban unrest as evidenced by Chicago street gangs. In *Riot* (1969), *Aloneness* (1971), the first volume of her autobiography *Report from Part One* (1972), *Beckonings* (1975), and *A Primer for Blacks* (1980), Brooks demonstrated her deepened commitment to the problems of racial injustice, empowerment, and independence. In recognition of her distinguished achievements as a poet and black American intellectual, Brooks was chosen Poetry Consultant to the Library of Congress for 1985–86.

Selected Bibliography Chicago *Defender*, 26 May 2001, 40; Mari Evans, ed., *Black Women Writers (1950–1980): A Critical Evaluation* (1983); Timothy J. Gelfoyle, "A Chicago School of Literature–Gwendolyn Brooks and Studs Terkel," *Chicago History* 26 (No. 1, 1997), 62–72; George E. Kent, *A Life of Gwendolyn Brooks* (1900); D. H. Melhem, *Gwendolyn Brooks: Prophecy and Poetic Process* (1986); Maria K. Mootry and Gary Smith, eds., *A Life Distilled: Critical Essays on Gwendolyn Brooks* (1987); Claudia Tate, ed., *Black Women Writers at Work* (1983).

Jerry Ward

Brooks v. Board of Education of the City of Moberly, Missouri, 3 R.R.L.R. 660 (E.D. Mo., 1958) When the Board of Education in Moberly, Missouri, desegregated its schools in 1955 in compliance with *Brown v. Board of Education,* they did not rehire African American teachers who had worked in its segregated school system. Naomi Brooks and seven other teachers filed a class action suit against them, arguing that race and color were the only criteria used in their dismissal. Such discrimination, they argued, violated the equal protection clause in the **Fourteenth Amendment.** The defendant argued that they needed fewer teachers after the consolidation of white and black schools. They also pointed out that four white teachers had been relieved for the same reason. The trial court ruled against the plaintiffs on the grounds that they presented insufficient proof that race was a factor in their dismissal. The court of appeals affirmed the decision, holding that Missouri law allowed the school board to use its discretion in renewing contracts. In later cases **NAACP** lawyers argued that a school with an all-white staff amounted to a segregated institution.

Selected Bibliography *Brooks v. School District of City of Moberly,* Missouri 267 F.2d 733, 1959; Jack Greenberg, *Race Relations and American Law* (1959); Leon Jones II, *From Brown to Boston, 1954–1974* (1979).

Stephen Middleton

Brotherhood of Sleeping Car Porters and Maids This union's founding and struggle for recognition was a dramatic episode in the history of black workers. From its beginning in 1867, the Pullman Company employed black workers as porters and maids. Through the years these workers became increasingly dissatisfied with their wages and working conditions. In 1925 a small group in

Group portrait of members of the Brotherhood of Sleeping Car Porters taken at a national board meeting. © Library of Congress.

New York City invited **A. Philip Randolph** to lead their cause. Randolph formally organized the Brotherhood of Sleeping Car Porters and Maids (BSCP) on 25 August 1925. The Pullman Company refused to recognize the fledgling union and continued to deal with the porters through a company union. The BSCP leaders hoped to get federal help against the company under the provisions of the Watson-Parker Act of 1926, but this help did not come. Continued failure to receive company recognition caused the union to lose most of its members. New Deal labor legislation strengthened the BSCP's hand and finally led to its recognition by the Pullman Company on 25 August 1937. In the meantime, Randolph had been carrying on a struggle for acceptance of the BSCP by the American Federation of Labor (AFL). In 1935 the AFL granted the BSCP an international charter, and Randolph carried on a fight against discrimination and on behalf of black workers from within the AFL and, after 1955, the AFL-CIO.

Selected Bibliography Jervis Anderson, A. *Philip Randolph: A Biographical Portrait* (1972); Bralisford R. Brazeal, *The Brotherhood of Sleeping Car Porters: Its Origin and Development* (1946); William H. Harris, *Keeping the Faith: A. Philip Randolph, Milton P. Webster, and the Brotherhood of Sleeping Car Porters, 1925–1937* (1977); Sterling D. Spero and Abram L. Harris, *The Black Worker: The Negro and the Labor Movement* (1968).

Arvarh E. Strickland

Browder v. Gayle, 142 F. Supp. 707 (M.D. Ala., 1956)   A landmark in the demise of segregated public transportation, this case was filed by the **Montgomery Improvement Association** (MIA) on behalf of five local black women. The MIA had intended to challenge **Jim Crow** buses following the incident involving **Rosa Parks** in December 1955 but feared endless delays in Alabama tribunals. By filing *Browder* in the federal district court in Montgomery, on which Judge **Frank Minis Johnson** sat, they had a much better chance of success. **NAACP** attorneys argued that segregated buses were unconstitutional and that Jim Crow laws should be struck down. The three federal judges who heard testimony, including Johnson and Fifth Circuit Judge **Richard Taylor Rives,** ruled that statutes requiring segregated seating violated the due process and equal protection clauses of the **Fourteenth Amendment.** *Plessy v. Ferguson* had by implication been overruled by recent Supreme Court decisions, said Judge Rives, and there remained "no rational basis upon which the **separate-but-equal** doctrine can be validly applied to public transportation." City and state officials appealed the decision, but the Supreme Court unanimously upheld the lower court's ruling in *Gayle v. Browder,* 352 U.S. 903 (1956). Thus was repudiated the momentous 1896 decision that had been the basis of the separate-but-equal doctrine and the mainstay of Jim Crow laws for more than half a century.

Selected Bibliography Richard Bardolph, ed., *The Civil Rights Record: Black Americans and the Law, 1849–1970* (1970); Catherine A. Barnes, *Journey from Jim Crow: the Desegregation of Southern Transit* (1983); Jack Bass, *Unlikely Heroes* (1981), Roberta Hughes Wright, *The Birth of the Montgomery Bus Boycott* (1991).

Charles D. Lowery

Brown, Edgar G.   (2 March 1898, Sandoval, Ill.–10 April 1954, Washington Park, Ill.). Publisher and editor of the *St. Louis Standard News* and president of the National Lawn Tennis Association, Brown also was the founder and president of the United Government Employees, which sought and won pay increases for the lowest ranks of government workers. A member of Franklin D. Roosevelt's **Black Cabinet,** Brown served as director of public relations for the Negro press with the Civilian Conservation Corps. Later, as president of the National Negro Council, he was instrumental in instigating the U.S. Senate's investigation of Theodore Bilbo's win in the 1946 Mississippi primary election.

Selected Bibliography Ralph J. Bunche, *The Political Status of the Negro in the Age of FDR* (1973); John Kirby, ed., *New Deal Agencies and Black America in the 1930s* (1984); *Negro Year Book, 1937–1938; New York Times,* May 19, September 7, 1946; *Who's Who in Colored America* (1940).

Ray Branch

Brown, Hubert Gerold "Rapp" (Jamil Abdullah Al-Amin)   (4 October 1943, Baton Rouge, La.–). Brown attended Southern University between 1960 and 1964, during which time he became involved in such youth-oriented civil rights organizations as the Nonviolent Action Group (NAG) and the **Student Nonviolent Coordinating Committee** (SNCC). He rose quickly in these organizations, becoming director of the NAG in 1964, Alabama project director for SNCC in 1966, and national director of SNCC in May 1967 when he replaced **Stokely Carmichael,** who had called Brown "a bad man." He also held office in the **Black Panthers** in the late 1960s. His increasingly radical stance on black separatism and black power led him to turn away from—and to alienate—white liberal support for SNCC. The radical philosophy that became his trademark (symbolized by the phrase "Burn, Baby, Burn") is evident in his 1969 book *Die Nigger Die!* and in his speeches. He advocated black "self defense" and economic and political control of ghettoes, and he agitated against the draft. Riots after some of his speeches; a disastrous fire in Cambridge, Maryland; and the importation of a weapon into Louisiana, led to charges against him of inciting to riot, arson, and violating the Federal Firearms Act. His attorney, William Kunstler, attempted to brand Brown's troubles as harassment and to portray him as a political prisoner, but he gained little support from an unsympathetic public. In and out of trouble and jail from 1967 to 1970, Brown dropped out of sight until he eventually was shot and captured by New York City police during a robbery. He was sentenced to New York's Attica Prison in 1973 for a term of from 5 to 15 years. He was paroled in 1976 after converting to Islam and changing his name to Jamil Abdullah al-Amin. For the next several decades he lived a relatively quiet life as a Muslim spiritual leader in the West End area of Atlanta. He occasionally made public appearances such as when he addressed the United Nations about the slaughter of Muslims in Bosnia, but he spent most of his time trying to raise $47 million to build an Islamic center in rural Alabama. Charged in May of 1999 with theft by receiving stolen property, he was arrested in March of 2000 for the murder of a sheriff's deputy sent to arrest him and the wounding of another officer. Two years later a jury found him guilty of murder and he was sentenced to life in prison. Brown's perception of history sparked a philosophy that only violent revolution could bring about change. In that sense, he and his followers presented an extreme and unacceptable alternative to the inertia of the white power structure—the spectre of a violent race war. The incessant pressure of Brown and fellow radicals on the mainstream moderates did perhaps quicken changes. Had his radicalism gone unchecked, however, and had he secured adequate support from the masses, he could have been a serious impediment to progress in race relations.

Selected Bibliography Joan Martin Burke, *Civil Rights: A Current Guide to the People, Organizations, and Events* (1974); "Civil Rights: The Man From SNCC," *Newsweek,* 22 May 1967; John D'Emilio, *The Civil Rights Struggle: Leaders in Profile* (1979); Herbert H. Haines, *Black Radicals and the Civil Rights Movement, 1954–1970* (1988); *New York Times,* 25 January 1975, 22 October 1976; Vern E. Smith, "Ministers or Murderers, *Emerge* 11 (30 June 2000), 34; Edward Vernoff and Rima Shore, *The International Dictionary of 20th Century Biography* (1987); "Where Have All the Soldiers Gone?" *Saturday Review* (28 April 1979).

Gary B. Mills

Brown, John Robert (10 December 1909, Funk, Neb.–22 January 1993, Houston, Tex.). Educated at the University of Nebraska (A.B., 1930) and the University of Michigan (J.D., 1933; LL.D., 1939), Brown was admitted to the Texas bar in 1932 He joined a Houston and Galveston law firm that specialized in admiralty law. In 1955 he was appointed to the **U.S. Court of Appeals for the Fifth Judicial Circuit,** which he served as chief judge from 1968 to 1980. An active Presbyterian churchman, he believed strongly in the concept of brotherhood, which was evident in his decisions from the bench. On the Fifth Circuit Court he was an effective champion of minority rights. Together with fellow Fifth Circuit judges **Elbert Parr Tuttle, Richard Taylor Rives,** and **John Minor Wisdom,** he helped assure the success of the civil rights movement by making the federal courts, and especially the Fifth Circuit Court, whose heavy caseload made it the major battleground of the civil rights movement, a powerful vehicle for political and social change. As a regular member of three-judge panels that usually included Rives and Wisdom, he helped implement the *Brown v. Board of Education* decision desegregating public education. He also helped to expand *Brown* mandate for equality beyond education to include landmark decisions that swept away racial discrimination in jury selection, employment, and voting.

Selected Bibliography Jack Bass, *Unlikely Heroes* (1981); Harvey C. Couch, *A History of the Fifth Circuit, 1891–1981* (1984); J. W. Peltason, *Fifty-eight Lonely Men, The Federal Judges and School Desegregation* (1961); Frank T. Read and Lucy S. McGough, *Let Them Be Judged: The Judicial Integration of the Deep South* (1978).

Charles D. Lowery

Brown, Richard Jess, Sr. (2 September 1912, Muskogee, Okla.–31 December 1989, Jackson, Miss.). An African American Mississippi lawyer educated at Illinois State University, Indiana University, and Texas Southern University Law School, Brown filed Mississippi's first civil rights lawsuit in the 1950s. In 1948, while a public school teacher, Brown joined Gladys Noel Baker in seeking equal salaries for black teachers in Jackson at a time when few blacks dared challenge white supremacy. In the 1960s, he filed lawsuits to desegregate school systems and transportation in Mississippi. Brown was coattorney for **James Howard Meredith** when Meredith successfully enrolled at the University of Mississippi in 1962. He also defended Mack Charles Parker (accused of rape and subsequently lynched) and raised the issue of jury discrimination.

Selected Bibliography Alexander M. Bickel, "Impeach Judge Cox," *The New Republic*, 4 September 1965; *Jackson Clarion-Ledger*, 2 and 3 January 1990; *Martindale-Hubell Law Directory* (1984); *New York Times*, 3 January 1990; *Who's Who among Black Americans*, 5th ed., 1988.

Wali Rashash Kharif

Brown, Ronald H. (1 August 1941, Washington, D.C.–3 April 1996, Croatia). Brown was born in Washington, D.C., graduated from Middlebury College in Vermont in 1962 and St. John's Law School in 1970. In 1988, he ran Jesse Jackson's unsuccessful presidential campaign. From 1988 to 1993,

Brown became the first African American to serve as chairman of the Democratic National Committee. He was influential in getting Bill Clinton elected president in 1992, and Clinton rewarded him with the post of Secretary of Commerce, which he held until his untimely death in 1996, in a plane crash over Croatia. Before his death, the Office of the Independent Counsel investigated Brown for accepting illegal contributions from companies seeking favors from the Department of Commerce. Although the investigation revealed that Brown had indeed received over a half-million dollars, all charges against him were dropped postmortem.

Selected Bibliography Jack W. Germond and Jules Witcover, *Mad As Hell: Revolt at the Ballot Box, 1992* (1993); Shirelle Phelps, ed., *Who's Who Among African Americans*, 10th ed. (1999); Mark J. Rozelle and Clyde Wilcox, *The Clinton Scandal and the Future of American Government* (2000).

Thomas Adams Upchurch

Brown v. Board of Education, 347 U.S. 483 (1954) This decision removed the most important constitutional obstacle to equal rights for blacks. During Reconstruction, Congress inserted the equal protection clause into the **Fourteenth Amendment** so that black as well as white Americans would be equal before the law. After Reconstruction, however, the willingness of the federal government and the states to enforce the clause in race cases abated. In 1896 the Supreme Court held in **Plessy v. Ferguson** that as long as transportation facilities were theoretically equal, separation based on race was lawful under the equal protection clause. Shortly thereafter, amid the triumph of white supremacy throughout the South, the Court extended the separate but equal doctrine to educational facilities. Over the next half century the educational facilities provided blacks by southern and a few border states were always separate but never equal.

During the 1930s the **Legal Defense and Educational Fund** of the **NAACP** began to challenge the *Plessy* doctrine in federal court. Lawyers for the Legal Defense and Educational Fund argued that education was indispensable to the legal equality and economic opportunity of black Americans. After World War II, **Thurgood Marshall** and other Defense Fund lawyers won victories in the Supreme Court that opened graduate and law schools to blacks. The Court accepted Marshall's argument that because of various intangible factors associated with the need to mix with peers in an academic setting, racial discrimination in education was inherently unequal.

Encouraged by these decisions the Defense Fund attacked the *Plessy* doctrine in grade schools. Seeking to demonstrate the broad-based character of racial injustice, Marshall and the NAACP initiated suits simultaneously in South Carolina, Virginia, Delaware, Kansas, and Washington, D.C. The cases reached the Supreme Court in December 1952. The Court consolidated the four state suits under the style of the Kansas litigation, *Brown v. Board of Education,* while treating separately the federal questions raised in the Washington appeal.

White students protest the *Brown v. Board of Education* decision. Copyright. Photo by *The Birmingham News*, 2003. All rights reserved. Reprinted with permission.

Because the number of students involved was comparatively small, the Court had decided the graduate school cases unanimously. *Brown*, however, raised the larger issue of desegregating grade schools, touching virtually all southern families and the fundamental emotions underlying white supremacy. On this problem the Court was "severely divided." Not until Earl Warren became chief justice in 1953 was the Court able to agree on the constitutional status of grade schools under the equal protection clause and the *Plessy* doctrine. In 1954 the Court concurred unanimously in Warren's reversal of *Plessy*, holding that "in the field of public education the doctrine of **'separate but equal'** has no place." As a result, the black children in the four state suits, "by reason of the segregation complained of," had been deprived of the equal protection of the laws guaranteed by the Fourteenth Amendment. Separate facilities based on race were therefore "inherently unequal."

A year later in the decision pertaining to the enforcement of *Brown*, the Court invited delay and massive resistance, declaring that state compliance with the desegregation could proceed "with all **deliberate speed**." Nevertheless, the 1954 *Brown* decision set in motion the most important social transformation of twentieth-century America, the impact of which is still felt today and is still hotly debated.

Selected Bibliography Derrick A. Bell, "*Brown v. Board of Education*: Forty-five Years after the Fact," *Ohio Northern University Law Review* 26 (2000), 171–81; Tony Freyer, *Hugo L. Black and the Dilemma of American Liberalism* (1990); William H. Harbaugh, et al., "*Brown v. Board of Education*: an Exercise in Advocacy," *Mercer Law Review* 52 (2001), 549–629; Richard Kluger, *Simple Justice: The History of Brown v. Board of Education and Black America's Struggle for Equality* (1977); Waldo E. Martin, *Brown v. Board of Education: A Brief History with Documents* (1998); James T. Patterson, *Brown v. Board of Education: A Civil Rights Milestone and Its Troubled Legacy* (2001).

Tony A. Freyer

Brown v. Board of Education*, 349 U.S. 294 (1955)**   A year after its landmark 1954 ***Brown v. Board of Education decision declaring that separate educational systems were inherently unequal, the Supreme Court handed down a second *Brown* decision, commonly called *Brown II*, which addresses the difficult question of implementation. In its 1954 decision the Court, hoping to defuse southern white resistance, had postponed answering the question of how the legal principle it had articulated was to be translated into practice. In *Brown II* the court declared that implementation would be gradual and would be influenced by local conditions. School desegregation cases would be returned to the courts where they had been tried. There federal district judges, who were familiar with local conditions, would be responsible for implementing *Brown I*. School officials were expected to "make a prompt and reasonable start" toward compliance, but the lower court judges might interpret the phrase "with all **deliberate speed**" loosely when complex local problems and difficulties called for delays. In *Brown I* the Supreme Court had held unequivocally that segregated education deprived black children of "the equal protection of the laws guaranteed by the **Fourteenth Amendment**." It also had affirmed that constitutional rights are always "personal and present;" in other words, petitioners challenging segregated schools could expect immediate relief. *Brown II* disappointed this expectation. Black victims of segregated education could be required to defer the exercise of their constitutional rights. *Brown II*, in the words of one prominent lawyer-historian, was "a great mistake." It invited white southerners to resist implementation, and gave conservative federal judges, many of whom shared the social and political conservatism of their neighbors, power to postpone integration.

Selected Bibliography Derrick A. Bell, "*Brown v. Board of Education*: Forty-five Years after the Fact," *Ohio Northern University Law Review* 26 (2000), 171–81; Harvey C. Couch, *A History of the Fifth Circuit, 1891–1981* (1984); William H. Harbaugh, et al., "*Brown v. Board of Education*: An Exercise in Advocacy," *Mercer Law Review* 52 (2001), 549–629; Richard Kluger, *Simple Justice: The History of Brown v. Board of Education and Black America's Struggle for Equality* (1976); Waldo E. Martin, *Brown v. Board of Education: A Brief History With Documents* (1998);

Loren Miller, *The Petitioners: The Story of the Supreme Court of the United States and the Negro* (1961); Donald G. Nieman, *Promises to Keep: African-Americans and the Constitutional Order, 1776 to the Present* (1991); James T. Patterson, *Brown v. Board of Education: A Civil Rights Milestone and Its Troubled Legacy* (2001).

Charles D. Lowery

***Brown v. Mississippi*, 297 U.S. 278 (1936)**   In 1934 Ed Brown and two other African Americans were convicted of murder in Mississippi based solely upon their confessions. Brown challenged the sufficiency of his confession, contending that it had been obtained through violent means. During Brown's trial, the deputy sheriff admitted that he had hung Brown from a tree and had whipped the other defendants to procure their confessions. Despite these admissions, Brown and the others were convicted. The U.S. Supreme Court reversed the convictions, stating that a confession obtained by force violated the due process clause of the **Fourteenth Amendment.** The Court compared Brown's ordeal to medieval torture practices and found his trial and conviction to be an embarrassment to American justice. The *Brown* case is a milestone in the protection of individuals against police abuse, the use of involuntary confessions, and the complicity of prosecutors and judges. Following soon after the **Scottsboro Trials,** affirming the right of a defendant to adequate legal counsel and time to prepare a proper defense, *Brown* enlarged federal supervision of civil rights by declaring the use of coerced confessions to be a denial of due process.

Selected Bibliography Richard Bardolph, ed., *The Civil Rights Record, Black Americans and the Law, 1849–1970* (1970); Derrick Bell, Jr., *Race, Racism and American Law* (1980); Morgan Cloud, "Torture and Truth," *Texas Law Review* 74 (May 1996), 1211–15; Richard C. Cortner, A *"Scottsboro" Case in Mississippi: The Supreme Court and Brown v. Mississippi* (1986); Loren Miller, *The Petitioners: The Story of the Supreme Court of the United States and the Negro* (1966).

Steve Sadowsky

Brownsville, Texas, Affray   (1906). Despite local protests, in July 1906 three companies of the 25th Infantry, an African American regiment, arrived at Fort Brown in the city of Brownsville. During the night of 13 August, some unknown men went on a rampage—shooting at buildings, wounding a policeman, and killing a bartender. Immediately the townspeople accused members of the garrison. Most Army officers accepted this conclusion. The soldiers' refusal to admit guilt was taken as evidence of a conspiracy of silence. In November 1906 President Theodore Roosevelt responded with an order discharging 167 of them. This miscarriage of justice greatly disturbed the African American community, but **Booker T. Washington** remained publicly silent. Despite a congressional investigation and an army court of inquiry, 14 men were exonerated and offered a chance to rejoin the service. Although their guilt was never proven, the others lost everything including their pensions. In 1971 Representative Augustus F. Hawkins began an effort to have the conviction overturned and restitution made to the survivors. Eventually one soldier received some money and the discharges were changed to honorable. This travesty of justice indicated the powerlessness of African Americans in the Progressive era.

Selected Bibliography Marvin E. Fletcher, *The Black Soldier and Officer in the United States Army* (1974); Ann J. Lane, *The Brownsville Affair* (1971); John D. Weaver, *The Brownsville Raid* (1972).

Marvin E. Fletcher

Bruce, Blanche K. (1 March 1841, Farmville, Va.–17 March 1898, Washington, D.C.). Born and reared a slave, he admittedly suffered few hardships under bondage. The tutor of his master's son provided him with the rudiments of an education. During the Civil War Bruce emancipated himself. He briefly attended Ohio's Oberlin College before migrating in 1869 to Bolivar County, Mississippi, a delta region seemingly unlimited in its political opportunities for intelligent and ambitious freedmen. Fellow Republicans soon recognized his talents and he rose to prominence rapidly. Numerous local and appointive posts preceded his election in 1875 to a full term in the U.S. Senate. Although he spoke infrequently in the Senate, Bruce was a fine orator and had a wide range of interests. A strong advocate of minority rights, he criticized the government's treatment of Indians and Congress's effort to restrict Chinese immigration into the country. Affected most by the plight of his own people, he appealed eloquently and emotionally for greater justice for southern blacks. He urged full compensation for black depositors of the failed **Freedman's Bank** and sought to end segregated army units. He argued valiantly, but unsuccessfully, for federal assistance to Mississippi Republicans following the conservatives' violent overthrow of the Reconstruction government. Bruce seldom achieved the results he desired. Nevertheless, the Senate became an important forum for him to articulate his concerns for political justice, minority rights, and improved conditions for his race.

Selected Bibliography Henry C. Bruce, *The New Man: Twenty-nine Years a Slave, Twenty-nine Years a Free Man* (1969); Maurine Christopher, *America's Black Congressmen* (1976); William Harris, *Day of the Carpetbagger: Republican Reconstruction in Mississippi* (1979); Howard Rabinowitz, "Three Reconstruction Leaders: Blanche K. Bruce, Robert Brown Elliott, and Holland Thompson," in Leon Litwack and August Meier, eds., *Black Leaders of the Nineteenth Century* (1988); Melvin Urofsky, "Blanche K. Bruce, United States Senator 1875–1881," *Journal of Mississippi History*, 29 (February 1967), 118–41.

Robert L. Jenkins

Bryan v. Austin, 354 **U.S. 935 (1957)** In the mid-1950s, as the **NAACP** began to make legal inroads to secure the civil rights of African Americans, several southern states reacted by denouncing the organization as destructive to the relations between the races. They made it illegal for state and school district employees to be members of the organization. In South Carolina the legislature required school district employees to sign an oath that they were not members of the NAACP. When 17 African American schoolteachers in Orangeburg County refused to complete the section of the oath concerning their membership in the NAACP and their views on school segregation, they were forced to resign. The schoolteachers filed suit in the federal district court in Charleston, seeking a ruling that the South Carolina law was unconstitutional and violated their rights to free speech and free assembly under the First

Amendment. The federal district court refused to rule on the case, justifying its action on the ground that the South Carolina Supreme Court had not ruled on the constitutionality of the statute. The schoolteachers appealed this decision to the U.S. Supreme Court, but in the meantime, the South Carolina legislature repealed the statute and the case had become moot. This case showed the power of African Americans to influence the repeal of oppressive state legislation by suing for their constitutional rights.

Selected Bibliography Thomas I. Emerson, David Haber, and Norman Dorsen, *Political and Civil Rights in the United States* (1967); Aldon D. Morris, *The Origins of the Civil Rights Movement* (1984).

Steve Sadowsky

Buchanan v. Warley, 245 U.S. 60 (1917)   This landmark civil rights case declared residential segregation ordinances—first passed in 1910 in Baltimore, Maryland—unconstitutional. These laws represented efforts by urban whites in southern and border states to legalize **Jim Crow;** whites also used violence to establish residential segregation. *Buchanan* tested a 1914 Louisville, Kentucky, racial residential zoning ordinance that restricted black and white residences to separate districts. William Warley, an African American and local **NAACP** president, offered to buy a lot in a white neighborhood from a white real estate agent, Charles Buchanan, contingent on Warley's ability to occupy the property. As arranged, Buchanan accepted the offer, then sued for contract breech when Warley refused payment because the ordinance prohibited his residence on the land. When Kentucky courts upheld the local law, the NAACP with national president **Moorfield Storey** joining the case, appealed to the U.S. Supreme Court. The unanimous Court found that the ordinances "destroyed the right of the individual to acquire, enjoy and dispose of his property," a right protected by the **Fourteenth Amendment**'s due process clause. *Buchanan's* precedent against residential segregation represented a major NAACP victory, although southern and border cities passed new racial zoning ordinances for several decades, while racially restrictive covenants legalized segregation until *Shelley v. Kraemer* (1948).

Selected Bibliography Barbara J. Flint, "Zoning and Residential Segregation: A Social and Physical History, 1910–1940" (Ph.D. diss., University of Chicago, 1977); Daniel T. Kelleher, "St. Louis' 1916 Residential Segregation Ordinance," *The Bulletin* [Missouri Historical Society] 26 (April 1970), 239–48; Stephen Grant Mayer, *As Long as They Don't Move Next Door: Segregation and Racial Conflict in American Neighborhoods* (2000); Roger L. Rice, "Residential Segregation by Law, 1910–1917," *Journal of Southern History* 34 (May 1968), 179–99; Christopher Silver, "The Racial Origins of Zoning: Southern Cities from 1910–40," *Planning Perspectives* 6 (1991), 189–205; George C. Wright, *Life Behind a Veil: Blacks in Louisville, Kentucky, 1865–1930* (1985).

James Borchert

Buffalo Soldiers   Shortly after the Civil War, Congress established six regular army regiments consisting of black enlisted men and white officers. Two of these units were cavalry regiments (9th and 10th) and four were infantry regiments (38th, 39th, 40th, and 41st). In 1869, an army reorganization bill consolidated the four infantry regiments into two: the 24th and 25th Infantries. For over two decades, these black regiments of cavalry and infantry played prominent roles in settling the West, serving at diverse locations such as the Texas frontier, Indian Territory, New Mexico, Arizona, and the Dakota Territory.

Indians called them "buffalo soldiers" because the texture of their hair resembled the fur of the buffalo. A term of respect, the name was first applied to members of the cavalry; however, it soon became a term that also referred to the black infantrymen. These units served with distinction in campaigns against the Indians. During this period, 14 black soldiers won the Congressional Medal of Honor. Despite inferior equipment and horses, their desertion rates soon came to be the lowest in the army.

In addition to facing hostile Indians, the buffalo soldiers often faced discrimination and resentment in many civilian communities where they served, sometimes resulting in racial clashes. For the black male in the 1870s and 1880s, the army, although not the epitome of democracy and equality, did provide as fair an opportunity as was available. For many black citizens of that time, these soldiers were symbols of pride and a hope for a better future.

All four black regiments took part in the fighting of the Spanish-American War period, serving in Cuba and later the Philippines. Many African Americans had hoped that the participation of black regulars and volunteers would improve the plight of their race in the United States. Instead, racism intensified in the post–frontier period, especially in the South where some of these units were stationed. Tension between soldiers and the local civilian communities heightened. When black soldiers objected to indignities inflicted on them by local whites, violent racial outbreaks occurred—in Tampa, Florida, in 1898; **Brownsville, Texas,** in 1906; and **Houston, Texas,** in 1917. In some cases harsh punishment was meted out to some of the soldiers. After having served in the Mexican Punitive Expedition in 1916–17 and along the U.S.-Mexico border during the Mexican Revolution, these units suffered from post–World War I military cuts. During and after service in World War II, they were either disbanded or merged into the integrated armed forces.

Selected Bibliography Marvin E. Fletcher, *The Black Soldier and Officer in the United States Army, 1891–1917* (1974); Arlen L. Fowler, *The Black Infantry in the West, 1869–1891* (1971); William H. Leckie, *The Buffalo Soldiers: A Narrative of the Negro Cavalry in the West* (1976); Monroe L. Billington, *New Mexico's Buffalo Soldiers, 1866–1900* (1991); Willard B. Gatewood, Jr., *Black Americans and the White Man's Burden, 1898–1903* (1975); John F. Marszalek and Horace D. Nash, "African Americans in the Military of the United States"; Arvarh E. Strickland and Robert E. Weems, Jr., eds., *The African-American Experience: An Historiographical and Bibliographical Guide* (2001).

Horace D. Nash

Bunche, Ralph Johnson (7 August 1904, Detroit, Mich.–9 December 1971, New York, N.Y.). The son of Fred and Olive Johnson Bunch[e], this scholar and diplomat spent his childhood in the Midwest and the South before graduating *summa cum laude* in 1927 from the University of California at Los Angeles. An

Ralph Bunche, second from right, arriving in Los Angeles to receive the Spingarn medal, 1949. © Library of Congress.

M.A. in political science (1928) and a Ph.D. (1934) in government and international relations, both from Harvard University, were achieved while Bunche taught at Howard University. He received Julius Rosenwald and Social Science Research Council fellowships in 1932 and 1936, respectively. Early in his career he displayed an analytical approach to studying the origins and results of racial discrimination. His energies found domestic focus by helping found the **National Negro Congress** in 1936. In 1941 Bunche was a senior social sciences analyst in the Africa and Far East Section of the Office of the Coordinator of Information. By the time he won appointment as adviser to the U.S. delegation at the San Francisco conference that drafted the United Nations (UN) Charter, he was regarded as a brilliant mediator and an authority on peoples of color. Subsequent international achievements included Acting Mediator of the UN Special Committee on Palestine 1948; successfully negotiating an armistice agreement between Egypt and Israel in 1949 (and thereby establishing a precedent for similar agreements elsewhere in the Middle East); receiving the Nobel Peace Prize in 1950; and appointment as undersecretary-general (without portfolio) of the United Nations, 1954. Bunche received over 69 honorary degrees, was a trustee of the Rockefeller Foundation, 1955–71, and was awarded the **Spingarn Medal** of the **NAACP** in 1949. He participated in the **Selma to Montgomery March** of

1965. Bunche produced over 40 published monographs and articles, including *A World View of Race* (1936); *Ideologies, Tactics, and Achievements of Negro Betterment and Interracial Organizations* (1940); *The Political Status of the Negro in the Age of FDR* (1973); and *The Atlantic Charter and Africa* (1942).

Selected Bibliography Souad Halila, *The Intellectual Development and Diplomatic Career of Ralph J. Bunche* (Ph.D. diss., University of Southern California, 1988); Charles P. Henry, *Ralph Bunche: Model Negro or American Other?* (1999); Peggy Mann, *Ralph Bunche: UN Peacemaker* (1975); Babatunde Williams, *Makers of Peace: Dr. Ralph Bunche and Chief Albert John Luthuli* (1965); Brian Urquhart, *Ralph Bunche: An American Life* (1993).

Bernice F. Guillaume

Burke, Yvonne Brathwaite   (5 October 1932, Los Angeles, Calif.–). An attorney, Yvonne Brathwaite Burke became the first black woman elected to the California Assembly and the first black congresswoman from California. The talented Burke worked for the McCone Commission's investigation of the **Watts race riot,** chaired the California assembly's Committee on Urban Development and Housing, was vice chair of the 1972 Democratic convention, chaired the **Congressional Black Caucus,** campaigned unsuccessfully for state attorney general, and became a Los Angeles County supervisor. A civil rights advocate, she supported busing, voted to extend the **Voting Rights Act of 1965,** vigorously backed the Equal Rights Amendment, and authored the 1975 Burke Amendment, which provided equal opportunity for women and minorities on the Alaska pipeline. Since 1992 Burke has served continuously on the Los Angeles County Board of Supervisors (elected chair in 2002), practiced law, participated in numerous public and private boards, and received many noteworthy honors and awards.

Selected Bibliography *Current Biography*, 36 (1975), 59–62; Jeffrey M. Elliot, "An Interview with Yvonne Brathwaite Burke," *Negro History Bulletin* 40 (1977), 650–52; Darlene Clark Hine, Elsa Barkley Brown, and Rosalyn Terborg-Penn, eds., *Black Women in America: An Historical Encyclopedia* (1993); Los Angeles *Sentinel*, 18 December 2002; Dorothy C. Salem, *African American Women* (1993); *Who's Who among Black Americans*, 6th ed. (1990); *Who's Who in America*, 45th ed. (1989); "Women Lawmakers on the Move," *Ebony* 27 (1972), 49–52.

Bruce A. Glasrud

Burton v. Wilmington Parking Authority, 365 U.S. 715 (1961)   In the **Civil Rights Cases** of 1883, the Supreme Court held that there was a distinction between public and private action. However, the mixing of state and private activities in modern society made this distinction difficult to apply. In this case, the Eagle Coffee Shoppe, a private business located in a parking garage, refused service to blacks. Burton, the plaintiff, brought suit against the owner and operator of the garage, the Wilmington Parking Authority. According to Burton, the leasing arrangement between the garage and the coffee shop made the state a party to discrimination. The Supreme Court agreed, concluding that the coffee shop's policy was state action. Wilmington Parking Authority, an agency of the state of Delaware, leased space and services to the coffee shop. In return, the agency received rental fees that enabled it to sustain the garage. The interdependent nature of their relationship, said the Court, made the Eagle Coffee Shoppe and the garage a joint venture. Although the Court warned that no universal truth could be drawn from the case, its decision did broaden the scope of the equal protection clause of the **Fourteenth Amendment.** In future cases, private racial segregation and discrimination would not be deemed private if the authority of the state loomed in the background.

Selected Bibliography Richard Bardolph, ed., *The Civil Rights Record: Black Americans and the Law, 1849–1970* (1970); Derrick A. Bell, Jr., *Race, Racism, and the Law* (1980); Thomas I. Emerson, David Haber, and Norman Dorsen, eds., *Political and Civil Rights in the United States* (1967); Alfred H. Kelly and Winfred A. Harbison, *The American Constitution: Its Origins and Development,* 5th ed. (1976).

Phillip A. Gibbs

Bush v. Orleans Parish School Board, 364 U.S. 500 (1960) This Supreme Court action was part of a prolonged constitutional controversy over the desegregation of New Orleans public schools, which had been ordered by **J. Skelly Wright,** Federal District Judge for the Eastern District of Louisiana, as he sought to implement the requirements of *Brown v. Board of Education.* The order to desegregate met resistance from state officials. In defiance of the desegregation order, in regular session and in special sessions called by Governor Jimmie Davis, the state legislature enacted numerous segregation laws, including an Interposition Act, in which the state of Louisiana claimed to interpose itself between the federal court and the people. The federal district court held the Louisiana legislature's enactments unconstitutional and enjoined the legislature, the governor, and several other officials from enforcing them. In December 1960, the Supreme Court, in the case cited above, refused to stay the injunctions pending appeal. In early 1961, in a one-sentence per curiam opinion, the Court affirmed the actions of the district court. (*Orleans Parish School Board v. Bush,* 365 U.S. 569). This prolonged controversy illustrated the extreme difficulty of the task placed by the Supreme Court upon the shoulders of southern federal judges in the 1955 *Brown v. Board of Education* decision.

Selected Bibliography Liva Baker, *The Second Battle of New Orleans: The Hundred Year Battle to Integrate the Schools* (1996); Jack Bass, *Unlikely Heroes* (1981); Earlean M. McCarrick, "Desegregation and the Judiciary: The Role of the Federal District Court in Educational Desegregation in Louisiana," *Journal of Public Law* 16 (1967), 107–27; Arthur Selwyn Miller, *A "Capacity for Outrage": The Judicial Odyssey of J. Skelly Wright* (1984); J. W. Peltason, *Fifty-eight Lonely Men: Southern Federal Judges and School Desegregation* (1961).

Patricia A. Behlar

Butler, Benjamin Franklin (4 November 1818, Deerfield, N.H.–11 January 1893, Washington, D.C.). A prominent Massachusetts lawyer and politician, Butler enlisted in the Union Army in 1861 and was appointed general by President Abraham Lincoln. While commanding Fortress Monroe, Virginia, he refused to return fugitive slaves to their masters, labeling them confiscated enemy property or "contrabands of war." On 6 August 1861 Congress incorporated this principle into law in the **Confiscation Acts** authorizing the seizure of all property, including slaves, used in "aiding the rebellion." In April 1862, General Butler was named commander of the occupational forces in New Orleans where, on 22 August, he issued a general order authorizing the enlistment of free blacks. On 27 September, the First Regiment Louisiana Native Guards became the first unit of black soldiers mustered into the U.S. Army during the Civil War. Butler, concerned with educational aid to free blacks, supported many freedmen's relief associations. In December 1864 he consolidated 37 black regiments to form the 25th Corps and ordered regimental chaplains to teach the troops to read. By 1865 approximately twenty thousand black soldiers were literate. After resigning his commission, Butler served in the U.S. House of Representatives from 1866 to 1874 where he promoted the **Civil Rights Act of 1875.**

Selected Bibliography Chester G. Hearn, *When the Devil Came Down to Dixie: Ben Butler in New Orleans* (1997); James M. McPherson, *The Negro's Civil War: How American Negroes Felt and Acted during the War for the Union* (1965); Benjamin Quarles, *The Negro in the Civil War* (1953); William Preston Vaughn, *Schools for All: The Blacks and Public Education in the South, 1865–1877* (1974); Richard S. West, Jr., *Lincoln's Scapegoat General: A Life of Benjamin F. Butler, 1818–1893* (1965).

Betsy Sakariassen Nash

Byrd, James, Jr.   (2 May 1949, Jasper, Tex.–7 June 1998, Jasper, Tex.). On 7 June, 1998, near Jasper, Texas, James Byrd, Jr., a 49-year-old black, divorced father of three, was apparently offered a ride by three white men. The men beat Byrd severely, then chained him to a truck and dragged him through Jasper, eventually ripping his right arm and head from his body. Byrd's body was then dumped outside a black cemetery. The Justice Department's civil rights division, the FBI, the local attorney's office, and local law enforcement and prosecutors charged the three men, who had previously served time for burglary and other nonviolent crimes, with racially motivated capital murder. Mostly white juries in Jasper and Bryan, Texas, convicted and then sentenced John William "Bill" King, 25, and Russell Brewer, 32, to death. An all-white jury, in Jasper, sentenced Shawn Berry to life in prison, eligible for parole after 40 years. According to testimony, King's and Brewer's bodies were decorated with racist tattoos; they had been members of a Ku Klux Klan–affiliated white supremacist group while serving together in a Texas prison. They apparently killed Byrd as the initiation rite to their own chapter of this Klan-style group. The case attracted international attention and created a national outrage. It dredged up memories of the violent history of the race-motivated **lynchings** of the **Jim Crow** era. As a result of this incident, in May 2001, the Texas legislature passed and the governor signed the James Byrd Jr. Hate Crime Act. The bill strengthened penalties for crimes motivated by hate against people because of their race, ancestry, national origin, sexual orientation, disability, age, or gender.

Selected Bibliography Houston *Chronicle*, 9, 10, 12 June 1998, 29 September, 11, 12, 17, 19, 20 November 1999, 22 June, 22, 24 July 2000, 31 January, 13 May 2001; *Newsweek*, 22 June 1998, 17 February, 8 March 1999; *New York Times*, 11, 14, 28 June 1998, 26 January, 17, 24, 26 February, 18, 21 September 1999; San Antonio *Express News*, 12 May 2001.

Horace D. Nash

C

Cable, George Washington   (12 October 1844, New Orleans, La.–1 January 1925, St. Petersburg, Fla.). A late-nineteenth- and early-twentieth-century southern novelist and advocate of freedmen civil rights, he was born into a slaveholding family and served in the Confederate army. After the Civil War he became an occasional columnist for the *New Orleans Picayune*. His writing interests included short stories and novels focusing on themes of local color and southern black-white relationships. Subtle criticism of southern race relations in his novels angered his white reading audience, but his open and public attacks enraged them the most. His first public views were expressed in 1875 when he condemned New Orleans's efforts to reinstitute a segregated public school system. During the mid-1880s and 1890s his stand on the race question became uncompromising. Through speeches and essays he denounced segregation and black disfranchisement as unnecessary, unconstitutional, and oppressive. He dismissed as absurd the arguments of white supremacists that full black civil and political rights would lead to social equality. "We may reach the moon some day," he wrote, but "not social equality." His periodic appeals to the "Silent South" to support racial justice found little audience. Essentially a lone white voice in the South, Cable's views jeopardized his career and forced him into exile in New England where he continued to oppose bigotry and racial injustice and to battle for what he believed.

Selected Bibliography Christopher Benfey, *Degas in New Orleans: Encounters in the Creole World of Kate Choin and George Washington Cable* (1997); George Cable, *The Silent South* (1885); Barbara Ladd, *Nationalism and the Color Line in George W. Cable, Mark Twain, and William Faulkner* (1996); Louis D. Rubin, Jr., *George W. Cable, The Life and Times of a Southern Heretic* (1969); Arlin Turner, *George W. Cable; A Biography* (1956).

Robert L. Jenkins

Cain, Richard Harvey (12 April 1825, Greenbrier County, Va.–18 January 1887, Washington, D.C.). Richard Harvey Cain stands as an outstanding example of an African American who combined the roles of gospel minister and political leader. At the age of six Cain moved to Cincinnati, Ohio, where he attended public schools and then worked several years on Mississippi River steamboats as porter and handyman. At nineteen, he joined the Methodist Episcopal Church and was licensed to preach, but, owing to racial discrimination, he cut short his affiliation and joined the African Methodist Episcopal (A.M.E.) Church. Ordained an elder in 1860, he pastored a church in Brooklyn but received an assignment to Charleston, South Carolina after the victory there by Union troops. Almost immediately active in politics, Rev. Cain served successively as a delegate to the state constitutional convention, a member of the legislature, and as one of the most prominent advisers to Republican Governor Franklin J. Moses, Jr., a native white. In 1872 he was elected congressman-at-large by a tremendous majority. He served creditably in Congress, giving strong support to a civil rights bill and to public education. After leaving Congress in 1878, Cain continued his religious work, and in 1880 he was elected bishop of the A.M.E. Church for Louisiana and Texas. At Waco, Texas, he founded Paul Quinn College and became its first president while continuing in the duties of the episcopacy.

Selected Bibliography Maurine Christopher, *America's Black Congressmen* (1971); W.E.B. Du Bois, *Black Reconstruction in America* (1935); Peggy Lamson, *The Glorious Failure, Black Congressman Robert Brown Elliott and the Reconstruction of South Carolina* (1973).

George E. Walker

Calhoun v. Latimer, **377 U.S. 263 (1963)** Vivian Calhoun initiated a law suit in Atlanta to bring city schools into compliance with **Brown v. Board of Education.** The court ruled in her favor, stating that the school board had violated the **Fourteenth Amendment** by maintaining segregation. It ordered desegregation of city schools. Officials in Atlanta pursued a number of tactics to delay compliance, including the "grade-a-year-plan." Under this scheme, the school board proposed to transfer black children to a "white school," beginning at the twelfth grade, at a rate of one grade per year. This plan would take more than a decade to reach the first grade. African American parents, counseled by the **NAACP,** challenged the plan, arguing that compliance with *Brown* meant reorganization of the school district on a nonracial basis. They complained that the Atlanta plan stalled desegregation. Ultimately, the Court approved a plan designed to achieve integration by 1970. Desegregation moved slowly in Atlanta in spite of the *Calhoun* case. NAACP lawyers also urged the Court to apply *Brown* to school personnel, arguing that a school with a one-race staff was a one-race school. This contention produced few changes in school personnel, however.

Selected Bibliography Leon Jones II, *From Brown to Boston: Desegregation in Education* (1979); Stephen L. Wasby, *Desegregation from Brown to Alexander: An Exploration of Supreme Court Strategies* (1977).

Stephen Middleton

Cambridge, Maryland, Demonstrations   The Cambridge, Maryland, demonstrations during the spring of 1963 marked a turning point in the civil rights movement from nonviolent demonstrations against legal segregation to violent protests that originated in the poverty and anger of the black community. African Americans, approximately one-third of the population of eleven thousand in Cambridge, suffered from unemployment. Some town facilities remained segregated in January 1963 when college students from Baltimore, Pennsylvania, and New York began sit-ins. Cambridge resident Gloria Richardson, a recent graduate of **Howard University,** emerged as a leader. She emphasized militance and black pride as students and local working-class residents joined in boycotts, sit-ins, pickets, and parades. Militance led to opposition by town police and angry whites. Fighting and arrests mounted. On 11 June windows of white-owned stores were smashed and shooting began. Martial law was declared. When Gloria Richardson refused to meet with state officials, U.S. Attorney General Robert Kennedy entered negotiations and promised open accommodations, a biracial commission to deal with unemployment, a new public housing program, and school integration at every grade level. Emotions remained high and troops stayed until May 1965. In July 1967 the National States' Rights party, a racist organization, held a rally in Cambridge. Gloria Richardson replied in a radio special. Then on 24 July, **Hubert Gerold "Rapp" Brown** came to town, urged local blacks to take control, and said, "It's time for Cambridge to explode." A shooting occurred, then fires broke out in the black district. Two blocks burned to the ground. White firemen refused to enter the area without protection. Governor Spiro Agnew ordered the Maryland National Guard to Cambridge, and the rioting ended.

Selected Bibliography   Robert J. Brugger, *Maryland: A Middle Temperament, 1634–1980* (1988); George H. Callcott, *Maryland and America, 1940–1980* (1985); *Cambridge Daily Banner,* January–July, 1963; Peter B. Levy, "Civil War on Race Street: The Black Freedom Struggle and White Resistance in Cambridge, Maryland, 1960–1964," *Maryland Historical Magazine* 89 (No 3, 1994), 290–318; *Washington Post,* January–July 1963, July 1967.

Suzanne Ellery Greene Chapelle

Campbell, Will D.   (24 July 1924, Amite County, Miss.–). A Baptist minister by profession, Will D. Campbell became one of the first white Mississippians to advocate desegregation following the 1954 ***Brown v. Board of Education*** landmark case. Campbell held the position of Director of Religious Life at the University of Mississippi when he chose to use the annual Religious Emphasis Week as a forum for bringing in nationally known speakers to address the court decision. Working closely with **James W. Silver,** a history professor and social progressive, and P. D. East, an iconoclastic newspaper publisher, Campbell challenged the social mores of the state and called, in particular, on the white religious community to embrace integration. Campbell's work allowed him to be the only white person at the organizational meeting of **Martin Luther King, Jr.**'s **Southern Christian Leadership Conference.**

After growing up in the East Fork community of Amite County, Campbell graduated from the Southwest Junior College in Summit and enrolled in Louisiana College, drawn to the Baptist college by his interest in becoming a minister. Following service in the military, which broadened his horizons, he completed his undergraduate degree at Wake Forest University in North Carolina. After a year of graduate study in philosophy at Tulane University, Campbell enrolled in Yale Divinity School and earned a degree in theology. With several other southern divinity students from Yale, Campbell returned to the South committed to working on "the race question." A brief, uneventful, and unfulfilling pastorate in Taylor, Louisiana, pushed Campbell to take the position at the University of Mississippi. After losing his position at the university, Campbell became a field representative for the National Council of Churches in 1956. Campbell left that position in 1963 for multiple reasons, including his sense that the ecumenical organization was replacing its theological rationale for integration with legal rationale. Since 1963, he has been an author and, by his own description, a "bootleg preacher." His sense that many of the poor whites who populated the Ku Klux Klan were victims of poverty and class discrimination caused him to develop personal relationships with members of the group. Despite this controversial act, he remains committed to social justice for African Americans, guided by King's theology of the "beloved community."

Selected Bibliography Will D. Campbell, *Brother to a Dragonfly* (1977); Thomas L. Connelly, *Will Campbell and the Soul of the South* (1982); Merrill M. Hawkins, Jr., *Will Campbell: Radical Prophet of the South* (1997).

Merrill M. Hawkins, Jr.

***Canty v. Alabama,* 309 U.S. 629 (1940)** Dave Canty, a 23-year-old Montgomery, Alabama, black man, was arrested and later convicted and sentenced to death on the charge of murdering a white woman, Eunice Ward, a county health nurse, on 21 March 1938. In his appeal to the U.S. Supreme Court, Canty's lawyers maintained that Alabama authorities had denied him due process of law. They argued that the lone witness had not positively identified him either before or during the trial. But the primary basis of their appeal was that Canty had been subjected to "persistent and prolonged" torture to extract a confession. Citing the precedent of **Brown v. Mississippi** (1936), attorneys for the petitioner reminded the Court that "the use of confessions obtained by coercion, brutality and violence constituted a denial of due process." The lawyers also pointed out that several witnesses supported Canty's alibi. In 1940, the Supreme Court reversed the murder conviction without comment. The Alabama court retried Canty, again convicted him, and sentenced him to life imprisonment.

Selected Bibliography Dorothy A. Autrey, "The National Association for the Advancement of Colored People, 1913–1953" (Ph.D. diss., University of Notre Dame, 1985); "Brief in Support of the Petition for Writ of Certiorari in Supreme Court of the United States, October Term, 1939," NAACP Files, Library of Congress, Washington D.C.; *Montgomery Advertiser*, 21, 23, 24, 25 March 1938, 6, 18 June 1942.

Dorothy A. Autrey

Capon Springs Conference (21–23 June, 1899). In Capon Springs, West Virginia about forty educators and businessmen adopted a platform calling for increased industrial education and the establishment of a universal system of secondary schools in the South. Presided over by H. B. Frissell of **Hampton Institute** and including Presidents W. L. Wilson of Washington and Lee, Frank G. Woodworth of **Tougaloo College,** and Dr. J.L.M. Curry of the **Peabody Education Fund** and **Slater Fund,** the conference agreed to set up a committee to supervise the channeling of northern funds into worthwhile southern black schools. In its general philosophy of self-help, this conference was very similar to the **Lake Mohonk Conference,** the **Hampton Conference,** and other such conferences that took place in the 1890s.

Selected Bibliography James D. Anderson, *The Education of Blacks in the South, 1860–1935* (1990); August Meier, *Negro Thought in America, 1880–1915: Racial Ideologies in the Age of Booker T. Washington* (1963); *New York Times,* 22–25 July 1899.

Ray Branch

Cardozo, Francis L. (1 February 1836, Charleston, S.C.–22 July 1903, Washington, D.C.). A free black man, Cardozo received enough education to make him one of the best-educated men in his state and probably one of the best-qualified persons to hold office during Reconstruction. After four years at the University of Glasgow, he continued his studies at seminaries in Scotland and England before returning to the United States in 1864. Serving briefly as a pastor in New Haven, Connecticut, he accepted a post as head of an **American Missionary Association** school in Charleston, South Carolina, in 1865. His later service to education included a position teaching Latin at **Howard University.** It was in politics, rather than in education or religion, that Cardozo made his most noted contributions. Active in the Republican party and president of the **Union League** in South Carolina, he was selected a delegate to the state's 1868 constitutional convention and was elected secretary of state—a term cut short by his tenure at Howard University. He won election as South Carolina's secretary of the treasury in 1872 and 1876. After Reconstruction, he continued in public service in the U.S. Treasury Department from 1878 to 1884. His remaining active years were spent as principal of a black secondary school in Washington, D.C., until 1896. His honesty, coupled with his intelligence and efficiency, made him one of South Carolina's most respected politicians. The *Abbeville Press* commended him as being "an able officer of undoubted integrity."

Selected Bibliography Thomas Holt, *Black over White: Negro Political Leadership in South Carolina During Reconstruction* (1977); Joe M. Richardson, "Francis L. Cordozo: Black Educator During Reconstruction," *Journal of Negro Education* 48 (No. 1, 1979), 73–83; Wilhelmena S. Robinson, *Historical Negro Biographies* (1969); Francis B. Simkins and Robert H. Woody, *South Carolina During Reconstruction* (1932, 1966); Alrutheus A. Taylor, *The Negro in South Carolina During Reconstruction* (1924,1969).

Gary B. Mills

Carmichael, Stokely (Toure, Kwame) (29 June 1941, Port-of-Spain, Trinidad–15 November 1998, Conarky, Guinea). A native of Trinidad who emigrated to the United States in 1952, Carmichael became one of the most dynamic leaders of the civil rights and the **Black Power** movements. He attended Bronx High School of Science in New York City and then earned his bachelor's degree from **Howard University** in 1964. While a student at Howard, he became active in the civil rights movement. In 1960 he participated in demonstrations, sit-ins, and picketing in the Washington, D.C., area. He participated in numerous activities sponsored by the **Congress of Racial Equality** (CORE), the **Nonviolent Action Committee** (NAC) and the **Southern Nonviolent Coordinating Committee** (SNCC) in many southern states. During one **Freedom Ride** in 1961, he was arrested and served seven weeks in Mississippi's Parchman Penitentiary. His brave and outspoken manner, compelling speeches, and determination propelled him to the forefront of the student civil rights leadership. He became deeply involved in black voter registration drives in many southern states, including **Freedom Summer** in Mississippi. The Second Congressional District, which he coordinated, was the

best run of SNCC's five districts in Mississippi. As early as 1963, however, he began to disagree with some members of SNCC and other civil rights leaders over the value of peaceful demonstrations. He promoted self-defense against the racist violence and urged African Americans to use political process to control their own communities and their own destinies. He repeatedly called for the expulsion of whites from SNCC. In March 1965, he went to Lowndes County, Alabama, where along with his successful registration activities, he founded the **Lowndes County Freedom Organization** (LCFO). In 1966 LCFO challenged the Democratic party regulars in county elections but failed. In 1966 he was elected chairman of SNCC and made his

Stokely Carmichael addressing an audience, 1966. © Library of Congress.

famous **"Black Power"** speech in Greenwood, Mississippi. This marked the movement of some black Americans from nonviolence and integration to self-defense and black nationalism. His name change came after Sekou Toure, one of the pioneering African political independence movement leaders, who led the Republic of Guinea to independence from France, invited him to travel and observe conditions in Africa. Carmichael (Toure) returned to the United States a strong Pan-Africanist. He became head of the All African Peoples Revolutionary party. He authored two books, *Black Power* (1976) with Charles Hamilton, and *Stokely Speaks* (1971). He was twice married, first to Miriam Mekeba, a famous South African singer, and then to Maryiatou Barry, a leading Guinean physician. He died in his adopted homeland and was given a hero's burial.

Selected Bibliography Stokely S. Carmichael and Charles V. Hamilton, *Black Power: The Politics of Liberation in America* (1967); Stokely Carmichael, *Stokely Speaks: Black Power Back to Pan-Africanism* (1971); Cleveland Sellers with Robert Terrell, *The River of No Return: The Autobiography of A Black Militant and the Life and Death of SNCC* (1973); Scott Peacock, ed., *Contemporary Authors* (1999); Clifford Thompson, ed., *Current Biography Year Book* (1999).

W. Marvin Dulaney and Glenn O. Phillips

Carnegie Hall Meeting (6–8 January 1904). This closed meeting of black intellectuals selected by **Booker T. Washington** and **W.E.B. Du Bois** attempted to articulate a common strategy toward racial uplift. Its most concrete outcome was the creation of the Committee of Twelve for the advancement of the Negro Race, which was effectively controlled by Washington and secretly funded by Andrew Carnegie. Du Bois was offended by Washington's manipulation of the new organization and soon resigned, effectively limiting both its credibility and long term significance. Ironically, Du Bois's prominent role at the Carnegie Hall meeting helped to propel him to the forefront of the anti-Bookerites. The meeting marked a last and lost opportunity for the two men to compromise before Du Bois founded the militant **Niagara Movement** in 1905. **Archibald Grimke** and **Richard R. Wright, Jr.,** were among the anti-accommodationists who participated in the Committee of Twelve for several years before joining the Niagara Movement.

Selected Bibliography W.E.B. Du Bois, *Autobiography* (1968); The W.E.B. Du Bois Papers, University of Massachusetts, Amherst; Louis R. Harlan, *Booker T. Washington: The Wizard of Tuskegee, 1901–1915* (1983); Louis R. Harlan and Raymond Smock, eds., *The Booker T. Washington Papers* (1972); David Levering Lewis, *W.E.B. Du Bois: Biography of a Race 1868–1919* (1993).

Francille Rusan Wilson

Carter, Hodding, II (3 February 1907, Hammond, La.–4 April 1972, Greenville, Miss.). Louisiana native Hodding Carter made his mark on the twentieth-century civil rights revolution through editorials in the Greenville, Mississippi, *Greenville Delta Democrat-Times,* which he purchased in 1938. In 1946 Carter won a Pulitzer Prize for a series of editorials that dealt primarily with racial issues. He criticized the racism of Mississippi senators James

Eastland and Theodore Bilbo and called for equal public service facilities, such as playgrounds and hospitals, for the state's black citizens. By later standards a racial conservative, Carter called for gradualist solutions to southern racial problems. Opposing rapid change that might exacerbate race relations, Carter opposed such measures as the public accommodations provision of the **Civil Rights Act of 1964.** Yet he never wavered in his contention that blacks should have equal rights. Carter denounced the segregationist white power structure in Mississippi. At one point he described the Citizens' Councils as "uptown" chapters of the Ku Klux Klan. An outraged Mississippi House of Representatives reacted by voting 89–19 to brand the Delta editor a liar. Carter responded that, by a "vote of 1 to 0, . . . there are 89 liars in the State Legislature." Furthermore, "those 89 character mobbers can go to hell, collectively or singly, and wait there until I back down. They needn't plan on returning." Such was typical of the biting, humorous, controversial style of Hodding Carter, a courageous voice for reason and justice during a turbulent era.

Selected Bibliography *Biloxi-Gulfport Sun-Herald*, 11 February 1979; Biographical Sketches and Publication Series, Hodding and Betty Werlein Carter Papers, Manuscripts Division, Special Collections Department, Mississippi State University Library; Hodding Carter [II], "The Civil Rights Issue as Seen in the South," *New York Times Magazine* (21 March 1948), pp. 15, 52–54; *Greenville Delta Democrat-Times*, 5 April 1972; Ann Waldron, *Hodding Carter: The Reconstruction of a Racist* (1993).

Michael B. Ballard

Carter v. Texas, 177 U.S. 442 (1899) During the post-Reconstruction era, both legal and extralegal measures were utilized to diminish the recently acquired civil rights of African Americans. Throughout the South new laws separated the races in virtually every aspect of life. The U.S. Supreme Court reflected the mood of much of the nation as it affirmed **"separate but equal"** as the law of the land. The Court also adhered to a strict interpretation of the provisions of both the **Fourteenth** and **Fifteenth Amendments** to the federal Constitution by ruling against "state action" to deprive blacks of certain rights while ignoring such violations engaged in by individual or private citizens. It would be decades before the Supreme Court broadened its interpretation, and new laws would be enacted to include "individual action" against another's civil rights. In *Carter* the Court continued to hold against "state action" to deprive or deny individual rights and ruled that Seth Carter, a black resident of Galveston, Texas, had to be given a new trial on the charge of murder because the "state" had purposefully excluded blacks from jury service at the time of his conviction.

Selected Bibliography Richard Bardolph, ed., *The Civil Rights Record, Black Americans, and the Law, 1849–1970* (1970); Joseph Tussman, ed., *The Supreme Court on Racial Discrimination* (1963).

LeRoy T. Williams

Catholic Interracial Council The Catholic Interracial Council was started in New York City in 1934 by the Catholic Layman's Union, a group of black professional and businessmen organized by Father John La Farge. The organization soon grew to 60 branches throughout the United States, and has survived into the twenty-first century. It seeks to perpetuate understanding and goodwill among people of different races and ethnic groups through the teachings of the Catholic Church. Local branches collect statistics on black employment, urge employers to hire black workers, and encourage Catholic colleges' admittance of black Catholics. From 1934 to 1971, the council also published a monthly newsletter, the *Interracial Review.*

Selected Bibliography Thomas J. Harte, *Catholic Organizations Promoting Negro-White Relations in the United States* (1947); *Interracial Review,* 1932–71; John La Farge, *The Race Question and the Negro: A Study of Catholic Doctrine on Interracial Justice* (1943).

Carol Wilson

Cayton, Horace Roscoe (12 April 1903, Seattle, Wash.–22 January 1970, Paris, France). A sociologist and writer, Cayton was an insightful commentator on black labor and urban life. During the New Deal, Cayton was a special assistant to Secretary of the Interior **Harold L. Ickes,** then directed a Works Progress Administration research unit studying black life in Chicago. Cayton's most important work was the award winning *Black Metropolis* (1945), coauthored with **St. Clair Drake.** Director of Parkway Community Center in Chicago (1940–49) and longtime columnist for the *Pittsburgh Courier,* Cayton worked in his later years as a researcher and university lecturer. His autobiography, *Long Old Road* (1965), is a revealing account of the often turbulent life of the grandson of Reconstruction Senator **Hiram R. Revels.**

Selected Bibliography Horace R. Cayton, "Ideological Forces in the Work of Negro Writers," in Herbert Hill, ed., *Anger and Beyond* (1966); Horace R. Cayton and George S. Mitchell, *Black Workers and the New Unions* (1939); Horace R. Cayton interview with Studs Terkel in *Hard Times* (1970); Horace R. Cayton Papers, Harsh Research Collection, Chicago Public Library; Jack B. Moore, "Horace Roscoe Cayton" in *Dictionary of American Biography,* 8 (1988).

Francille Rusan Wilson

***Chambers v. Florida,* 309 U.S. 227 (1940)** In *Chambers v. Florida* the U.S. Supreme Court ruled that the due process clause of the **Fourteenth Amendment** prohibited the introduction of forced confessions as evidence in criminal trials. The case had originated in 1933 when four black men were convicted of murder in Broward County, Florida. The defendants were migratory farm workers who had been arrested for the crime, held without a warrant, and deprived of legal counsel. Interrogated relentlessly for a week, they had little opportunity to sleep or eat and were threatened and beaten. Finally, three of them confessed and also incriminated their companion, Isiah (Izell) Chambers. They were tried, convicted, and sentenced to death. Through appeals, the case dragged on in state courts for six years and resulted in guilty verdicts on three separate occasions. After the state's highest tribunal sustained the last conviction in 1939, the Supreme Court reversed it a year later. On 12 February 1940, Justice Hugo L. Black threw out the confessions because they had been obtained under duress. His opinion constituted a milestone in assisting those most vulnerable to harsh police interrogation: the poor, the uneducated, the unpopular, and the powerless. Without the admissibility of the tainted confessions, the case against the accused men collapsed, and they were set free.

Selected Bibliography Reed T. Phalen, "Comments," *Michigan Law Review* 39 (1940), 270–83; Otis H. Stephens, *The Supreme Court and Confessions of Guilt* (1973); Rocco J. Tresolini, *Justice and the Supreme Court* (1963).

Steven F. Lawson

Chaney, James Earl (30 May 1943, Meridian, Miss.–21 June 1964, Philadelphia, Miss.). An African American plasterer and civil rights field worker who attended Harris Junior College, Chaney worked diligently with the **Congress of Racial Equality** (CORE) and the **Council of Federated Organizations** (COFO) recruiting workers, and organizing freedom schools and voter registration activities. On 21 June 1964, on the eve of the launching of the **Freedom Summer of 1964** in Mississippi, Chaney, along with **Andrew Goodman** and **Michael Schwerner,** was arrested in Philadelphia, Mississippi, released from jail, abducted by Klansmen, beaten with chains, and shot. Their bodies were found on 4 August 1964 and retrieved from an earthen dam. James Chaney was buried on 7 August 1964 in Memorial Park Cemetery atop Mount Barton in Meridian, Mississippi.

Selected Bibliography Seth Cagin and Philip Dray, *We Are Not Afraid: The Story of Goodman, Schwerner and Chaney and the Civil Rights Campaign for Mississippi* (1988); William Bradford Huie, *Three Lives for Mississippi* (1964); *New York Times*, 6 August 1964; Juan Williams, *Eyes on the Prize: America's Civil Rights Years, 1954–1965* (1987).

Barbara L. Green

A picture of civil rights worker James Chaney that was distributed by the FBI after his disappearance, 1964. © AP/Wide World Photos.

Charleston Race Riot (1919) Economic, social and historical causes of interracial maladjustment, compounded by years of physical and psychological abuses, combined to produce the Charleston, South Carolina, riot. White sailors from the nearby naval yard and white civilians attacked black civilians after a black man was accused of shooting a white sailor. Fighting commenced near Market and West streets and spread through the city, on Saturday night, 10 May, and continued into Sunday morning, 11 May, during which time more than one thousand sailors participated. Provost guards, marines, and city and county police were employed to quell the rioting. Four persons died and more than 60 sustained injuries. A naval board of inquiry indicted three white sailors for riot related offenses; however, one was acquitted and the other two received one year's imprisonment at the Parris Island, South Carolina, Naval Prison with the possibility of parole after four months, at which time they were dishonorably discharged.

Selected Bibliography Arthus I. Waskow, *From Race Riot to Sit-In, 1919 and the 1960's: A Study in the Connections Between Conflict and Violence* (1966); L. E. Williams, II, "The Charleston, South Carolina, Riot of 1919," in Frank A. Dennis, ed., *Southern Miscellany: Essays in Honor of Glover Moore* (1981).

Lee E. Williams, II

Charlotte, North Carolina, Sit-In Approximately one hundred African American students, primarily from Johnson C. Smith University, staged sit-ins at five different downtown Charlotte segregated lunch counters on 9 February 1960. The demonstration forced the closing of four of these counters and hurt business in the other store. Strongly supported by many African American and white organizations, the students continued sporadic sit-down protests at lunch counters for several months. The nonviolent protests were successful. On 9 July 1960 nearly one hundred African Americans in Charlotte exercised their civil rights by eating at desegregated lunch counters. This grassroots demonstration was a catalyst to the forceful integration of other public facilities in the area and to the demand for social, economic, and political equality.

Selected Bibliography *The Charlotte News*, 1960; *The Charlotte Observer*, 1960; Charlotte-Mecklenburg Community Relations Committee Papers, J. Murrey Atkins Library, University of North Carolina at Charlotte; Aldon D. Morris, *The Origins of the Modern Civil Rights Movement: Black Communities Organized for Change* (1984); Martin Oppenheimer, *The Sit-In Movement of 1960* (1989).

Wanda A. Hendricks

Chase, W. Calvin (2 February 1854, Washington, D.C.–3 January 1921, Washington, D.C.). Born a free man, he was admitted to the Virginia and District of Columbia bar in 1889 and was a practicing attorney for the rest of his life. In 1882, he became editor of the *Washington Bee*, an important black newspaper. In the *Bee*, Chase forthrightly attacked lynchings and race riots, utilizing cartoons after 1914 to make his argument. He pointedly criticized the federal government for the continued existence of American racism. He opposed the biased treatment of black soldiers in the Spanish American War and World War I and the widening segregation of black civilians in government offices. Chase helped found the **Afro-American League** and the **Afro-American Council,** but feuded with fellow journalist **Timothy Thomas Fortune** and criticized **W.E.B. Du Bois.** He was also critical of **Booker T. Washington** until the *Bee* ran into financial difficulties and needed Washington's help. Chase was a lifelong Republican, but he battled the increasing encroachment of lily-whitism into party thinking.

Selected Bibliography Hal S. Chase, "Honey for Friends, Stings for Enemies: William Calvin Chase and the Washington Bee, 1882–1921" (Ph.D. diss., University of Pennsylvania, 1973); Rayford W. Logan and Michael R. Winston, eds., *Dictionary of American Negro Biography* (1982). I. Garland Penn, *The Afro-American Press and Its Editors* (1891, reprint, 1969); David Howard-Pitney, "Calvin Chase's Washington Bee and Black Middle Class Ideology, 1882–1900," *Journalism Quarterly* 63 (Spring 1986), 89–97.

John F. Marszalek

Chattanooga Freedom Walk   White Baltimore postman William L. Moore began an individual "freedom walk" from Chattanooga, Tennessee, to Jackson, Mississippi, on 21 April 1963 to deliver a message to Mississippi Governor Ross Barnett protesting southern segregation. Wearing a sign reading "Equal Rights for All—Mississippi or Bust," Moore was murdered two days later near Gadsden, Alabama. On 1 May 1963 an interracial group of Student National Coordinating Committee and **Congress of Racial Equality** members left Chattanooga to complete Moore's pilgrimage. Physically assaulted, the freedom walkers were arrested after crossing into Alabama. Moore's death and subsequent Chattanooga Freedom Walks focused national attention on the social and economic grievances of African Americans.

Selected Bibliography The *Chattanooga Times,* 21 April–16 May 1963; Murray Kempton, "Pilgrimage To Jackson," *New Republic* 148 (11 May 1963), 14–16; *Nashville Tennessean,* 21 April–7 May 1963; *Newsweek,* 6, 13 May 1963; Harvard Sitkoff, *The Struggle for Black Equality, 1954–1980* (1981).

Thaddeus M. Smith

Chesnutt, Charles Waddell   (20 June 1858, Cleveland, Ohio–15 November 1932, Cleveland, Ohio). Chesnutt was the first African American to be recognized as an indisputable member of the American literati. His works, which pioneered realistic portrayals of African Americans, endowed black dialect characters with dignity. Chesnutt also poignantly described the effects of **Jim Crow** and caste distinctions on black America's middle class. After an adolescence in Fayetteville, North Carolina, Chesnutt became a teacher and principal at its normal school. Following his marriage to Susan W. Perry in 1878, Chesnutt moved to New York City and then to Cleveland, Ohio. He passed the Ohio bar exam in 1887 with highest honors and became a legal stenographer. His professional debut into fiction was the short story, "Uncle Peter's House," which appeared in the *Cleveland News and Herald* in 1885. Subsequent works include *The Conjure Woman, The Wife of His Youth,* and *Frederick Douglass,* all published in 1899, *The House Behind the Cedars,* 1900,

The Marrow of Tradition, 1901, and *The Colonel's Dream*, 1905. The acceptance of Chesnutt's works by Houghton Mifflin, and his collegiality with William Dean Howells and **George Washington Cable,** mark significant departures from the social and intellectual patterns of the "nadir" period. Chesnutt's civic activities included newspaper articles, memberships on the General Committee of the **NAACP** and the Cleveland Chamber of Commerce, and testimony before a Senate Committee against the Shipstead Anti-Injunction Bill. Additionally, he helped found the Playhouse Settlement of Cleveland (Karamu House). Chesnutt was awarded the L.L.D. degree by Wilberforce University in 1913, and he received the **Spingarn Medal** of the NAACP in 1928.

Selected Bibliography William L. Andrews, *The Literary Career of Charles W. Chesnutt* (1980); Helen M. Chesnutt, *Charles Waddell Chesnutt, Pioneer of the Color Line* (1952); J. Noel Heermance, *Charles W. Chesnutt: America's First Great Black Novelist* (1974); Frances R. Keller, *An American Crusade: The Life of Charles Waddell Chesnutt* (1977); Cynthia L. Lehman, "The Social and Political Views of Charles Chesnutt; Reflections on His Major Writings," *Journal of Black Studies* 26 (1996), 274–86; Sylvia L. Render, *Charles W. Chesnutt* (1980).

Bernice F. Guillaume

Chester, Thomas Morris (11 May 1834, Harrisburg, Pa.–13 September 1892, Harrisburg, Pa.). Following his studies at Allegheny Institute, a school not far from Pittsburgh, Chester became an active abolitionist, involved with the American Colonization Society (ACS), an organization that had established Liberia in 1822 on the West African coast for the settlement of black Americans. In fact, Chester sailed to Liberia in 1853, but returned to America in 1854 to continue his studies at Thetford Academy, a school run by the ACS in Vermont. Chester again sailed to Liberia where he directed a public school and edited a newspaper called, the *Star of Liberia*. He returned to America in 1859, and between that year and the eve of the American Civil War, Chester told blacks in Pennsylvania to emigrate to Liberia, because he believed that their poor social, economic, and political conditions could never improve in America. With President Abraham Lincoln's Emancipation Proclamation in 1863, Chester became hopeful, however, that there were prospects for blacks in America. Indeed, he helped to recruit blacks in Pennsylvania for the Union army, and traveled to Britain where he gave speeches that chastised the Confederate states. Near the end of the Civil War as a reporter for the Philadelphia *Press*, he described the Union capture of Richmond, while seated, it was said, in Confederate President Jefferson Davis's chair. He was then among the blacks who appealed to President Andrew Johnson and O. O. Howard of the Freedmen's Bureau in 1865 to protect the newly stipulated black civil rights. Chester returned to Britain in 1866 to raise funds for the newly freed blacks. Although he worked occasionally for state and national governments in capacities that had nothing to do with blacks, Chester continued to fight for the rights of black people until his death in 1892.

Selected Bibliography Amos J. Beyan, *The American Colonization Society and the Creation of the Liberian State, 1822–1900* (1991); R.J.M. Blackett, *Thomas Morris Chester: Black Civil War Correspondent* (1989); D. Elwood Dunn, Amos J. Beyan, and Patrick Burrowes, eds., *The Historical Dictionary of Liberia,* 2nd ed. (2001); Eric Foner, *Freedom's Lawmakers: A Dictionary of Black Officeholders during Reconstruction* (1993); Howard N. Rabinowitz, ed,. *Southern Black Leaders of the Reconstruction Era* (1982).

Amos J. Beyan

Chicago Black Belt   Evolving between 1873 and the 1940s, the Chicago Black Belt was probably the most prominent black community after New York's Harlem. This narrow section of Chicago's South Side, seven miles long by one and one-half miles wide, grew in population from five thousand to over three hundred thousand residents. Political leaders such as **Oscar DePriest,** elected to Congress in 1928, and William Dawson, leader of Chicago's black political community from the 1940s until the 1960s, were elected from this area, which contained 90 percent of Chicago's black population.

Selected Bibliography James L. Cooper, "South Side Boss," *Chicago History* 19 (No 3–4, 1990–91), 66–81; St. Clair Drake and Horace R. Cayton, *Black Metropolis* (1962); Wanda A. Hendricks, "Vote for the Advantage of Ourselves and Our Race: The Election of the First Black Alderman in Chicago," *Illinois Historical Journal* 87 (No. 3, 1994), 171–84; Dempsey J. Travis, *An Autobiography of Black Chicago* (1981); Dempsey J. Travis, *An Autobiography of Black Politics* (1987); James Q. Wilson, *Negro Politics* (1960).

Christopher Mobley

Chicago Commission on Race Relations   Established by Illinois Governor Frank Lowden to study the causes of the violent five day **Chicago race riot** of 27 July 1919 and composed of an equal number of blacks and whites, the Commission examined the complex set of factors that led to 38 deaths and over 520 injuries. The commission based its 59 recommendations on the examination of discrimination in the areas of housing, employment, public accommodations, and the reluctance of police and courts to protect blacks from white violence. The commission recommended that laws prohibiting discrimination be strictly enforced.

Selected Bibliography C. K. Doreski, "Chicago Race and the Rhetoric of the 1919 Riot," *Prospects* 18 (1993), 283–309; Chicago Commission of Race Relations, *The Negro in Chicago: A Study of Race Relations and a Race Riot* (1922); Allen Spear, *Black Chicago: The Making of a Negro Ghetto, 1890–1920* (1967); William Tuttle, *Race Riot: Chicago in the Red Summer of 1919* (1970).

Malik Simba

Chicago Conservator   Chicago's first black newspaper, the *Conservator,* was founded in 1878 by attorney and civic leader Ferdinand L. Barnett. Reflecting the values of the city's black professional and business elite, the paper reported social and organizational activities within the black community and stressed the importance of education, self-improvement, and cultural refinement. After 1900, the *Conservator* became a pawn in the struggle between **Booker T. Washington** and his more militant critics for the support of black Chicagoans.

Editors and owners changed frequently, and editorial policy veered sharply from one position to another. The *Conservator* ceased publication in 1910; only a few scattered issues are extant.

Selected Bibliography *Chicago Conservator* (scattered issues) 1882, 1883, 1886, *Miscellaneous Negro Newspapers* (microfilm); Ralph N. Davis, "Negro Newspapers in Chicago" (M.A. thesis, University of Chicago, 1939).

Allan H. Spear

Chicago Defender Begun by **Robert S. Abbott** as a 4-page weekly with a press run of 300 copies in 1905, it grew into a 32-page newspaper with a national circulation of 180,000 in the early 1920s. Proclaiming itself "The World's Greatest Weekly," the *Defender* combined sensationalistic reporting with hard-hitting racial protest to become the country's leading black newspaper and the first to employ an integrated staff. The paper made Abbott into a millionaire and one of the country's leading African American businessmen. Abbott's nephew, **John H. Sengstacke,** took over the paper in 1940 and in 1956 converted it to a daily, making it the flagship of the nation's largest black newspaper chain. In the 1910s, the *Defender*, which was smuggled into the South by Pullman porters and black entertainers, urged southern blacks to escape from racism. Letters from successful migrants and reports of plentiful jobs and southern cruelty encouraged the **Great Migration** of 1916 to 1919. From 1942 to 1962, the poet Langston Hughes wrote a column for the paper. Although the *Daily Defender* is still published, financial problems brought about partly by the terms of John H. Sengstacke's will forced the newspaper to be auctioned off. Committed largely to community news, the *Defender's* daily circulation at the beginning of the twenty-first century was 17,600.

Selected Bibliography Frederick G. Detweiler, *The Negro Press in the United States* (1922); Roi Ottley, *The Lonely Warrior: The Life and Times of Robert S. Abbott* (1955); Alan Douglas DeSantis, "Selling the American Dream: The *Chicago Defender* and the Great Migration of 1915–1919" (Ph.D. diss., Indiana University, 1993).

James Marten

Chicago Freedom Movement The movement was a coalition of the Coordinating Council of Community Organizations and the **Southern Christian Leadership Conference** led by **Martin Luther King, Jr.** These organizations sought to create a desegregated "Open City." King felt that Chicago's impoverished slums existed because someone profited from keeping Negroes poorly housed, educated, and employed. As the campaign progressed, dissension developed among the various organizations due to ideological differences heightened by Mayor Richard J. Daley's manipulative intransigence, by the deeply divisive race riot in March 1966, and by King's ill-fated march in Cicero during late August 1966. These strains doomed the movement.

Selected Bibliography Alan B. Anderson and George W. Pickering, *Confronting the Color Line: The Broken Promise of the Civil Rights Movement in Chicago* (1986); Mike Royko, *Boss: Richard J. Daley of Chicago* (1971); Lori G. Waite, "Overcoming Challenges and Obstacles to

Social Movement Mobilization: The Case of the Chicago Freedom Movement" (Ph.D. diss., Northwestern University, 1998).

Malik Simba

Chicago Race Riot (1919)   The worst of the series of racial confrontations that swept America in the "red summer" of 1919, the Chicago race riot came in the wake of the World War I black migration from the South. Between 1916 and 1919, Chicago's black population doubled, and white Chicagoans reacted with hostility, often violence, to the newcomers. This racial tension came to a climax on 27 July 1919, when a black teenager, floating on a raft near a racially contested beach, was stoned by a white man and drowned. Fighting on the beach spread to nearby neighborhoods, and for the next five days, rioting raged throughout the city. White mobs assaulted black workers leaving the stockyards, dragged black passengers from streetcars, and fired shots into black homes from automobiles. Whites were, for the most part, the aggressors, but unlike in earlier riots, blacks fought back. The riot left 38 dead, 537 wounded, and hundreds homeless. Although Chicagoans of both races deplored the violence, the riot led to no real changes in the city's race relations. Segregation in housing and jobs continued, and racial discrimination was evident in the disproportionate number of blacks who were brought to trial for participation in the riot. The one constructive reaction to the riot was the appointment of a biracial commission on race relations that published a comprehensive report on the causes of the riot (see **Chicago Commission on Race Relations**). Historians have emphasized three factors in explaining the riot: the large influx of black migrants into a rigidly segregated housing market led to bitter competition for residential space; white fear of black job competition exacerbated labor tension, particularly in the stockyards; and whites resented the growing political influence of black voters, which had been demonstrated in the 1919 mayoral election. The riot should also be viewed within the context of the worldwide racial, ethnic, and political tensions that followed World War I.

Selected Bibliography Chicago Commission on Race Relations, *The Negro in Chicago: A Study of Race Relations and a Race Riot* (1922); James R. Grossman, *Land of Hope: Chicago, Black Southerners, and the Great Migration* (1989); Allan H. Spear, *Black Chicago: The Making of a Negro Ghetto* (1967); William M. Tuttle, Jr., *Race Riot: Chicago in the Red Summer of 1919* (1970).

Allan H. Spear

Chicago Race Riot (1965)   On Friday, 13 August 1965, violence erupted in Chicago's West Garfield Park neighborhood when people gathered to hold a protest meeting near the site where a fire truck had accidentally swerved into and killed a black woman. Police were soon called to the scene to stop a bottle-throwing incident. The fire station had been a focal point of discontent in the area all summer as civil rights groups had sought repeatedly to have African American firemen assigned to the station in this 85 percent black neighborhood. More than three hundred persons gathered at the protest meeting and clashed with police until shortly before dawn. By then, 104 persons

National Guardsmen search men on the streets of Chicago during the riots. © Bettmann/CORBIS.

had been arrested and 60, including 18 policemen, were hospitalized. The outbreak was characterized as "Chicago's worst racial rioting in thirteen years." The upheaval came in the midst of the Chicago civil rights movement and Dr. **Martin Luther King, Jr.**'s launching of the Chicago Campaign (1965–66), an unsuccessful attempt to secure significant changes in **de facto segregation,** ghetto housing, and massive black unemployment. The **Chicago** and **Watts race riots** that weekend brought the country's attention to the national issues of *de facto* segregation and other persistent dilemmas of democratic social change.

Selected Bibliography Alan B. Anderson and George W. Pickering, *Confronting the Color Line: The Broken Promise of the Civil Rights Movement in Chicago* (1986); David Garrow, *Chicago 1966: Open Housing, Marches, Summit Negotiations, and Operation BreadBasket* (1989); *New York Times*, 15 August 1965.

Barbara L. Green

Childers, James Saxon (19 April 1899, Birmingham, Ala.–17 July 1965, Atlanta, Ga.). After his education in the Birmingham public schools, Childers graduated from Oberlin College, served in World War I, and became a Rhodes Scholar. For four decades he was a journalist, serving first as a columnist for *The Birmingham News* and later as an associate editor of *The Atlanta Journal*. Among Childers's numerous publications, none attracted more attention than his novel of racial liberalism, *A Novel about a Black Man and a White Man in the Deep South*, published in 1936. The book reflects an extreme form of southern white liberalism of the day. The key characters, Gordon Nicholson, a young white, and Dave Parker, a young black, struggle to have friendship and normal, middle-class social exchange in Birmingham, Alabama in the 1930s. Although Childers's personal experience suggests that such interracial friendship could, on occasion, exist in Birmingham, these characters ultimately are defeated by the racial tensions of their environment. In telling this story, Childers provides, at times, a brilliant depiction of the terrains of the human heart sometimes overlooked in the broader story of American race relations. When Childers arrived in Atlanta, Georgia, in 1951, he found his racial liberalism at odds with the corporate community. He remained generally silent on racial matters. His staff writers wanted to cover the civil rights stories, however, and Childers was fired in 1956. In some ways Childers provides an example of the 1930s southern white liberal who did not turn the corner into the civil rights movement of the 1950s and 1960s. His later silence was not without torment.

Selected Bibliography Tennant S. McWilliams, "James Saxon Childers and Southern White Liberalism in the 1930s," in James Saxon Childers, *A Novel about a White Man and a Black Man in the Deep South* (reissue, 1988); Obituary, *Birmingham News*, 19 July 1965; Obituary, *New York Times*, 18 July 1965.

Tennant S. McWilliams

Chisholm, Shirley Anita St. Hill (30 November 1924, New York, N.Y.–). Born to a Barbadian seamstress and a Guyanese factory worker in New York City's second most infamous ghetto, Brooklyn's Bedford-Stuyvesant, Shirley Chisholm received much of her early education in Barbados while living with her maternal grandmother. She attended Brooklyn College on a scholarship and graduated with a bachelor's degree magna cum laude. She soon earned her master's degree in education from Columbia University. She became a school-teacher, a director of a child care center, and an educational consultant with New York's Day Care Division. Gradually, community activities brought her into Democratic party work in New York.

In 1964 Bedford-Stuyvesant sent Chisholm to the state assembly in Albany where she became only the state's second black female member. Her constituents liked her work so well that they reseated her three times. As an assemblywoman, Chisholm supported three significant measures—day care centers, unemployment insurance for domestic workers, and the Search for Elevation, Education, Knowledge (SEEK) college students program, a program that helps place talented underprivileged students in college.

Shirley Chisholm. © Library of Congress.

In 1968 Chisholm relinquished the assembly seat to seek a congressional seat in a revamped Twelfth Congressional District where she found **James Farmer,** the former director of the **Congress of Racial Equality,** her major opponent. The astute Chisholm made her decision to run upon learning that her district included a large number of registered female voters. Her victory was secured, however, because she was a native to the area whereas Farmer resided in Manhattan. As U.S. Representative, she served on the Veterans Affairs Committee (her first appointment after she upset the traditional seniority rule in Congress), the House Education and Labor Committee, and the Select Education, General Education and Agricultural Labor Subcommittees. She was also a member of the **Congressional Black Caucus,** before resigning from Capital Hill in 1983. Wishing to be a catalyst for change, Chisholm made a bid for the presidency of the United States in 1972, the first woman or black to do so. Unsuccessful in her candidacy, she now spends much of her time lecturing at various colleges and universities about the unfortunate rise of racism in these institutions. In 2001, the House of Representatives unanimously passed a resolution lauding her accomplishments and contributions.

Selected Bibliography Shirley Chisholm, *The Good Fight* (1973); Shirley Chisholm, *Unbought and Unbossed* (1970); *Who's Who among Black Americans* (1976).

Linda Reed

Cincinnati Race Riot (1967) The death sentence of a black man for the murder of a white woman and the almost simultaneous suspended sentence for a white man convicted of the death of his girl friend convinced the black community, once again, that justice in Cincinnati, Ohio, was racially biased. On 11 June 1967, a black man was arrested for soliciting money for a legal appeal of the death sentence. These events highlighted other social and economic wrongs inflicted on the city's blacks, grievances they felt powerless to enunciate. A protest meeting on the heels of an incident in which a police officer allegedly used the expression "young nigger punks" was followed by sporadic black youth violence on 12 June and a municipal judge's threat to mete out maximum punishment for any riot activity. The next night, the Avondale district of the city exploded. Fires were set, and responding firefighters were attacked. Automobiles were stoned, and gunshots rang out. The mayor asked for the National Guard, and, although the violence continued for three more nights and **Hubert Gerold "Rapp" Brown** arrived in the city to present demands, the rioting ended, leaving behind the conditions that had spawned the upheaval in the first place.

Selected Bibliography *Cincinnati Enquirer*, June 1967; *Cincinnati Herald*, June, July 1967; *New York Times*, June 1967; *Report of the National Advisory Commission on Civil Disorders* (1968).

John F. Marszalek

Citizens' League for Fair Play   Harlem citizens organized during the Great Depression to win clerical jobs for blacks in local white-owned businesses. The league, a coalition of 62 political, religious, fraternal, and social groups, picketed white-owned stores in 1934 and requested that Harlemites boycott discriminatory establishments. Several other groups worked alongside the coalition. Despite white resistance, the coalition's efforts brought some victories, but the **"Don't Buy Where You Can't Work"** movement derailed over internal divisions, and competition between the league and other groups. The league disbanded late in 1934 after a state court ruled that racially motivated picketing was illegal. In 1938 the Supreme Court ruled such picketing was in fact legal, and the League reformed as the Greater New York Coordinating Committee for Employment. Much larger, the committee soon won a crucial victory with the Harlem Merchants Association guaranteeing no discrimination in hiring. It then turned its focus to the city as a whole, and fought to expand black employment opportunities in public utilities and private industry.

Selected Bibliography Cheryl Greenberg, *"Or Does It Explode?" Black Harlem in the Great Depression* (1991); Charles Hamilton, *Adam Clayton Powell, Jr.: The Political Biography of an American Dilemma* (1991); Gary Hunter, "'Don't Buy From Where You Can't Work': Black Urban Boycott Movements during the Depression, 1929–41" (Ph.D. diss., University of Michigan, 1977); Mark Naison, *Communists in Harlem During the Depression* (1983); *New York Age*, 26 May, 9, 16, 23, 30 June, 7, 16, 21, 28 July, 4 August 1934; Adam Clayton Powell, Jr., *Marching Blacks: An Interpretive History of the Rise of the Black Common Man* (1945).

Cheryl Greenberg

Citizenship Schools   When Tennessee authorities closed down citizenship education at the **Highlander Folk School** in 1960, the **Southern Christian Leadership Conference** adopted the program. The Citizenship Education Program gave poorly educated, rural blacks a crash course in American government, focusing on overcoming obstacles to voting, such as teaching people how to fill out registration forms. Supervised first by black minister **Andrew Young** and later by Dorothy Cotton, classes resumed in the summer of 1961 in Dorchester, Georgia. Septima P. Clark, a founder of the Highlander program, trained about thirty people a month; they returned home to teach classes.

Selected Bibliography Adam Fairclough, *To Redeem the Soul of America: The Southern Christian Leadership Conference and Martin Luther King, Jr.* (1987); David J. Garrow, *Bearing the Cross: Martin Luther King, Jr., and the Southern Christian Leadership Conference* (1986).

Carol Wilson

City of Mobile v. Bolden, **446 U.S. 55 (1980)** After passage of the **Voting Rights Act of 1965,** suffrage disputes shifted from restoring the right to vote to increasing the power of the ballot. *City of Mobile v. Bolden* involved the question of whether the at-large election of city commissioners unfairly reduced the voting strength of blacks in violation of the **Fourteenth** and **Fifteenth Amendments.** Blacks constituted about 35 percent of Mobile, Alabama's, population, but none had ever won election in the city commission. Wiley L. Bolden charged that citywide elections diluted black votes, particularly within a racially polarized electorate. The lower federal courts agreed and ordered the replacement of the commission form of government with a mayor and council elected from single-member districts. On 22 April 1980, the Supreme Court reversed the judgment. Speaking for a majority of six, Justice Potter Stewart held that official bias could not be inferred from its impact; rather, discrimination had to be intentionally motivated. Despite this stringent constitutional standard of proof, upon retrial in the district court Bolden's attorneys exhibited the necessary evidence to win their suit. In 1982, Congress amended the Voting Rights Act to allow litigants to prove vote dilution based on the effect of discrimination, rather than its intent.

Selected Bibliography Chandler Davidson, ed., *Minority Vote Dilution* (1984); Steven F. Lawson, *In Pursuit of Power: Southern Blacks and Electoral Politics, 1965–1982* (1985); Abigail M. Thernstrom, *Whose Votes Count?: Affirmative Action and Minority Voting Rights* (1987).

Steven F. Lawson

City of Richmond v. Deans, **37 F.2d 712 (1930)** The city of Richmond, Virginia, adopted an ordinance in 1911 that restricted people of either race, white or black, from taking up residence on a block where a majority of the homes were occupied by people of the other race. In *Buchanan v. Warley* (1917), the U.S. Supreme Court ruled that such ordinances violated the **Fourteenth Amendment,** but cities continued to enact them. In 1929, the Richmond City Council replaced its old ordinance with one that placed a similar restriction on people who, under state law, could not marry members of the other group. J. B. Deans, a black resident of Richmond, forced a judicial ruling by buying a house in a white neighborhood and seeking an injunction from the federal district court against enforcement of the ordinance. When that court ruled in his favor, the city appealed, as attorneys for Deans and the city argued the relative merits of the Fourteenth Amendment and the state's police powers. The U.S. Supreme Court (273 U.S. 668 [1930]) let stand rulings of the district and appeals courts. Given the fact that the city's ordinance rested on state law that, in turn, rested on racial distinctions, the latest ordinance in no material way differed from the original, and it no better met the test of constitutionality. The concerns of the **NAACP** moved on to restrictive covenants, the tool adopted by exclusionary groups to replace ordinances.

Selected Bibliography Richard Bardolph, ed., *The Civil Rights Record: Black Americans and the Law, 1849–1970* (1970); NAACP Papers, Library of Congress; *Richmond Times-Dispatch*, 20 May 1930; Christopher Silver, *Twentieth-Century Richmond: Planning, Politics, and Race* (1984); John Douglas Smith, "Managing White Supremacy: Politics and Culture in Virginia 1919–1939" (Ph.D. diss., University of Virginia, 1998).

Peter Wallenstein

Civil Rights Act of 1866   Enacted on 9 April 1866 by an increasingly radical Congress over President Andrew Johnson's veto, the act declared that all persons (except Indians not taxed) born in the United States were now citizens, without regard to race, color, or previous condition. As citizens, they could make and enforce contracts, sue and be sued, give evidence in court, and inherit, purchase, lease, sell, hold, and convey real and personal property.

Outside the galleries of the House of Representatives during the passage of the Civil Rights Bill. *Harper's Weekly*, April 28, 1866. © Library of Congress.

Persons who denied these rights to former slaves were guilty of a misdemeanor and upon conviction faced a fine not exceeding $1,000, or imprisonment not exceeding one year, or both. Authority for prosecuting cases was given to United States district attorneys, marshals, and deputy marshals, who were instructed to submit indictments to United States district and circuit courts. The law did not mention the rights of blacks with regard to public education or public accommodations. Some of its language, however—that all persons born in the United States were citizens of the United States and that citizens of one state had the same rights and privileges as citizens of another—became part of the **Fourteenth Amendment,** but in the midst of racial violence, intimidation, the Ku Klux Klan, and political turmoil, the law failed to protect the civil rights of freedmen.

Selected Bibliography Richard Bardolph, *The Civil Rights Record: Black Americans and the Law, 1849–1970* (1970); John and LaWanda Cox, *Politics, Principles and Prejudices, 1865–1866* (1963).

Loren Schweninger

Civil Rights Act of 1875   Introduced by Massachusetts Senator **Charles Sumner** in 1870, the bill did not become law until 1 March 1875, a year after Sumner's death. It promised that all persons, regardless of race, color, or previous condition, were entitled to full and equal enjoyment of accommodations in "inns, public conveyances on land or water, theaters, and others places of public amusement." Nor could any citizen be denied the right to serve on grand or petit juries. Responsibility for enforcement fell to the federal district and circuit courts; those convicted faced a fine of between $500 and $1,000 for each offense as well as a forfeiture of $500 to the aggrieved individual. Excluded from the law was a section concerning equal enjoyment of public education. Supporters of the bill argued that it was necessary to protect the rights of all citizens against class and race prejudice; opponents, including a number of prominent Republicans, deemed it an unconstitutional attempt to legislate "social equality" between the races. Although blacks asserted their rights under the law, federal officials were often indifferent to their claims of discrimination. In 1883, the Supreme Court struck down the law by declaring that Congress did not have the power to regulate the conduct and transactions of individuals.

Selected Bibliography David Donald, *Charles Sumner and the Rights of Man* (1970); John Hope Franklin, *Race and History* (1988).

Loren Schweninger

Civil Rights Act of 1957   This act provided for the establishment of the **Civil Rights Section, Justice Department,** empowered federal prosecutors to obtain court injunctions against interference with the right to vote, and established a federal **Civil Rights Commission** with authority to investigate discriminatory conditions and to recommend corrective measures. Its chief importance, however, lay in providing a psychological lift for the black race; it was the first civil rights law Congress had passed since Reconstruction. Black Americans reasoned that, with additional pressure, further effective legislation might also be passed. They were correct.

Selected Bibliography John W. Anderson, *Eisenhower, Brownell, and the Congress: The Tangled Origins of the Civil Rights Bill of 1956–1957* (1964); Robert Fredrick Burk, *The Eisenhower Administration and Black Civil Rights* (1984); Congressional Quarterly Service, *Congress and the Nation, 1945–1964: A Review of Government and Politics in the Postwar Years*, vol. 1 (1965).

Monroe Billington

Civil Rights Act of 1960   This act made unlawful flight to avoid prosecution for bombing offenses and interference with court orders regarding school desegregation. Federal judges were empowered to appoint referees to hear persons claiming that state election officials had denied them the right to register and vote. The law was difficult to enforce because, before a finding could be made and referee machinery started, the Justice Department had to bring forth specific cases to prove that qualified citizens had been denied the vote because of race or color.

Selected Bibliography Daniel M. Berman, *A Bill Becomes a Law: The Civil Rights Act of 1960* (1962); Robert Fredrick Burk, *The Eisenhower Administration and Black Civil Rights* (1984); Congressional Quarterly Service, *Congress and the Nation, 1945–1964: A Review of Government and Politics in the Postwar Years*, vol. 1 (1965).

Monroe Billington

Civil Rights Act of 1964   During the civil rights struggle of the 1960s, Congress passed this landmark piece of comprehensive legislation. The most important provisions of this act banned discrimination by businesses offering food, lodging, gasoline, or entertainment to the public; forbade discrimination by employers or labor unions when hiring, promoting, dismissing, or making job referrals; authorized government agencies to withhold federal money from any program permitting discrimination; authorized the attorney general to file suit to force desegregation of schools, playgrounds, parks, libraries, and swimming pools; tightened provisions to prevent denial of black voting rights in federal elections by declaring that any person with a sixth grade education was presumed literate and that state literacy tests were not to be applied to him or her; established a federal agency to assist local communities in settling racial disputes; and granted additional powers to the **Civil Rights Commission.** Congressional opponents, some of whom had participated in a three-and-a-half month Senate filibuster, had directed most of their attention to the public accommodations section of this act, the most controversial section. Under threat of prosecution, most businesses generally accepted the fact that the issue of separate public accommodations for the races was settled permanently. Desegregated public facilities became the norm throughout the nation. No other act of Congress more directly affected the appearance of American society. The voting section of this act promised more than it could deliver, and this weakness in the law stimulated black demonstrations, a large factor in the passage of the effective **Voting Rights Act of 1965.**

Selected Bibliography Civil Rights Files, Lyndon B. Johnson Library, Austin, Texas; Congressional Quarterly Service, *Congress and the Nation, 1945–1964: A Review of Government and Politics in the Postwar Years,* vol. 1 (1965); Lyndon Baines Johnson, *The Vantage Point: Perspectives of the Presidency, 1963–1969* (1971); Charles and Barbara Whalen, *The Longest Debate: A Legislative History of the 1964 Civil Rights Act* (1985).

Monroe Billington

Civil Rights Act of 1968   Stalled in Congress for two years, it was not until the heightened racial tension following the assassination of **Martin Luther King, Jr.,** threatened to erupt into widespread rioting that the Civil Rights Act of 1968 gained the necessary support for passage. Its most important section prohibited discrimination in the rental or sale of housing. Fair housing was one of the most sensitive areas of civil rights legislation, which made it the last major area on which Congress took action. Not since 1866, indeed, had Congress passed any open housing legislation. (See **Open Housing Act** of 1968 for a full discussion of the open housing provision.)

Apart from open housing, the act contained several important provisions protecting civil rights and upholding civil obedience. It provided criminal penalties for anyone who interfered with or injured a person for exercising certain specified rights, such as voting, using public accommodations, serving on a jury, attending school or college, and the like. Civil rights workers who encouraged citizens to exercise the above and other fundamental rights were similarly protected. An antiriot provision provided criminal penalties for persons utilizing interstate commerce facilities, including the mails, telephone, radio, and television, with the intent to incite, organize, or take part in a riot. The act also provided federal penalties for persons who manufacture or teach the use of a firearm or explosive for use in a riot or public disturbance.

Selected Bibliography Raymond J. Celada, *The Civil Rights Act of 1968: Background and Title-by-Title Analysis* (1968); Hugh Davis Graham, *The Civil Rights Era* (1990); Donald G. Nieman, *Promises to Keep: African-Americans and the Constitutional Order, 1776 to the Present* (1991); Robert G. Schwemm, *The Fair Housing Act after Twenty Years* (1988).

Charles D. Lowery

Civil Rights Act of 1990, 1991   During his presidency, Ronald Reagan managed to roll back many of the hard-won civil rights gains of the 1970s. His political and judicial appointees were, for the most part, conservatives who shared his opposition to busing, affirmative action, quotas in hiring and promotion, and other similar measures that had been utilized with some success in the 1970s to redress the effects of racial discrimination. His appointees to the Supreme Court formed a new conservative majority that succeeded in the late 1980s in shifting the Court's direction on civil rights. In 1989, for example, it handed down no fewer than five separate rulings that weakened civil rights protections.

These controversial Supreme Court decisions spurred a coalition of civil rights and women's rights groups to pressure Congress in 1990 for legislation to reverse the most damaging rulings, primarily those relating to discrimination in the hiring and promotion of minorities and women. Senator Edward Kennedy and Representative Augustus Hawkins responded by sponsoring the desired legislation. The Kennedy-Hawkins Bill strengthened Title VII of the **Civil Rights Act of 1964** by providing stronger guarantees against discrimination in employment. Anyone suffering from job discrimination because of race, religion, national origin, or gender was empowered to bring suit against the employer, not just for job reinstatement and back pay, as provided for in the 1964 legislation, but for punitive damages as well. Despite strong opposition from business interests fearful of a flood of job discrimination litigation, the bill passed Congress in October. President George Bush vetoed the measure because, he said, it introduced "the destructive force of quotas into our national employment system." Since the early days of Ronald Reagan's administration the White House's civil rights strategy had been to link almost every progressive measure affecting blacks to despised quotas. In vetoing the bill, Bush joined Reagan as one of only two presidents since the modern civil rights era began in the early 1950s to veto civil rights legislation. The Senate failed by two votes to override Bush's veto. In February 1991 House Democrats revived the bill and succeeded in gaining its passage. The Civil Rights Act of 1991 strengthened Title VII of the **Civil Rights Act of 1964** by authorizing compensation and punitive damages to victims of intentional discrimination in the workplace.

Selected Bibliography Julian Bond, "Color Blinders," *Nation* 251 (13 August 1990), 152–53; Diana R. Gordon, "A Civil Rights Bill for Workers," *Nation* 251 (9 July 1990), 44–46; Daniel F. Piar, "The Uncertain Future of Title VII Class Actions After the Civil Rights Act of 1991," *Brigham Young University Law Review* (2001); *New York Times*, 23, 25 October 1990; Donald G. Nieman, *Promises to Keep: African-Americans and the Constitutional Order, 1776 to the Present* (1991); "A Quota vs. Voters Dilemma," *Time*, 29 October 1990.

Charles D. Lowery

***Civil Rights Cases,* 109 U.S. 3 (1883)** The **Civil Rights Act of 1875** sought to combat private discrimination against blacks by punishing the denial of equal access or privileges on grounds of race in common carriers, hotels, and places of entertainment. For purposes of review, the Supreme Court consolidated five separate complaints, one on a railroad and the others at sites ranging from Maguire's Theater in San Francisco to the Grand Opera House in New York. Justice Joseph Bradley's majority opinion struck down the act's key provisions. The **Fourteenth Amendment** gave Congress no power to prevent private wrongs, but only to supersede state laws that were discriminatory. Bradley observed that at some point the black person had to take "the rank of a mere citizen" and cease being "the special favorite of the laws." The "state action" interpretation, based on the strict wording of the amendment, made it difficult to legislate against the traditional forms of social and economic discrimination. A vigorous dissent by Justice **John Marshall Harlan** insisted that inns, amusement places, and conveyances were not private persons, but because of licensing and other regulatory laws they were public services operating with state permission and thus subject to public control. This philosophy has been central to federal civil rights legislation since 1964 and presents a continuing need to judicially interpret state action.

Selected Bibliography Charles Fairman, *Reconstruction and Reunion, 1864–1888* (1987); Robert M. Goldman, *Reconstruction and Black Sufferage: Losing the Vote in Reese and Cruikshank* (2001); Milton Konvitz, *A Century of Civil Rights* (1961); Donald G. Nieman, *Promises to Keep: African-Americans and the Constitutional Order, 1776 to the Present* (1991); Alan Westin, "John Marshall Harlan and the Constitutional Rights of Negroes: The Transformation of a Southerner," *Yale Law Journal* 66 (1975), 637–710.

James E. Sefton

Civil Rights Commission   See United States Commission on Civil Rights.

Civil Rights Section, Justice Department   On 3 February 1939, Attorney General Frank Murphy established a Civil Liberties Unit within the Criminal Division of the Department of Justice. The Unit increased its activity in the 1940s and 1950s and came to be known as the Civil Rights Section. The **Civil Rights Act of 1957** elevated the Civil Rights Section to the status of a division of the Justice Department headed by an assistant attorney general. The creation of a separate Civil Rights Division also reflected the Eisenhower administration's desire to have access to civil as well as criminal remedies in civil rights cases.

Selected Bibliography Michael R. Belknap, *Federal Law and Southern Order: Racial Violence and Constitutional Conflict in the Post-Brown South* (1987); John T. Elliff, "The United States Department of Justice and Individual Rights, 1937–1962" (Ph.D. diss., Harvard University, 1967); Steven F. Lawson, *Black Ballots: Voting Rights in the South, 1944–1969* (1976); Web site: www.usdoj.gov.

Michael S. Mayer

Clark, Kenneth Bancroft   (24 July 1914, Panama Canal Zone–). An African American educator and psychologist, Clark's research on the development of black children within segregated schools was used by the **NAACP** as part of its strategy in winning *Brown v. Board of Education* (1954). A decade earlier, he had worked as a researcher on Gunnar Myrdal's landmark and controversial, *An American Dilemma*(1944). Clark's "behavorialist" testimony before the Supreme Court introduced social science research into legal and constitutional issues, especially those relating to racial discrimination. Its use and validity generated debate then and continues to do so even decades later. In the 1950s, Clark also investigated the effects of segregated schools in the North, particularly in New York City, where he found de facto discrimination as effective as any southern law. One consequence he found was that segregated schools led to segregated neighborhoods. Clark earned bachelor's and master's degrees from **Howard University** and his doctorate in experimental psychology from Columbia University. In 1967, he founded the Metropolitan Applied Research Center, a social research organization.

Kenneth B. Clark. © Library of Congress.

Believing that the increasing numbers of black public officials would require research and technical assistance, he was instrumental in establishing the Joint Center for Political Studies, the nation's only black think tank, which is located in Washington, D.C.

Selected Bibliography Kenneth B. Clark, *Dark Ghetto* (1965); Kenneth B. Clark, *The Black Man in American Politics* (1969); Kenneth B. Clark, "Separate is Never Equal" *New York Times*, 1 April 1995, p19; Harold Cruse, *Plural But Equal. A Critical Study of Blacks and Minorities and America's Plural Society* (1987); *Current Biography* (1964); Ben Keppel, *The Work of Democracy: Ralph Bunche, Kenneth B. Clark, Lorraine Hansberry, and the Cultural Politics of Race* (1995); Sam Roberts, "Conversations With Kenneth B. Clark: An Integrationist to This Day, Believing All Else Had Failed," *New York Times*, 7 May 1995; David W. Southern, *Gunnar Myrdal and Black-White Relations: The Use and Abuse of "An American Dilemma," 1944–1969* (1987).

Nancy E. Fitch

Clark, Peter Humphries (1829, Cincinnati, Ohio–21 June 1925, St. Louis, Mo.). A freeborn African American, Clark attended high school in Cincinnati and taught there for more than 30 years. As a youth, he helped slaves escape, served as national secretary of the Colored Convention in Rochester, New York, in 1853, and wrote the constitution for the **National Equal Rights League.** During the Civil War, he organized a fighting unit that he memorialized in the book *The Black Brigade of Cincinnati.* A sometime Republican and a consistent race man, Clark became the first black socialist, and then a Democrat. He moved to St. Louis in 1887, where he taught at

Sumner High School and engaged in politics. He retired in 1908, remaining in St. Louis until his death.

Selected Bibliography Lawrence O. Christensen, "Peter Humphries Clark," *Missouri Historical Review* 88 (January 1994), 145–56; Lawrence O. Christensen, "Clark, Peter Humphries (1829–1925)," *Dictionary of Missouri Biography* (1999), 189–90; Lawrence Grossman, "In His Veins Coursed No Bootlicking Blood: The Career of Peter H. Clark," *Ohio History* 86 (January 1977), 79–94; Herbert Gutman, "Peter H. Clark: Pioneer Negro Socialist, 1877," *The Journal of Negro Education* 34 (Fall 1965), 413–15.

Lawrence O. Christensen

Cleaver, Eldridge (31 August 1935, Wabbaseka, Ark.–1 May 1998, Pomona, Calif.). One of the most radical and articulate public spokesmen and revolutionary writers of the 1960s, Cleaver grew up in Watts, Los Angeles. Frequently in trouble with the law during his teens, he spent many of his early years in reformatories and prisons where he received most of his education. Cleaver turned to writing as a means of self preservation and in 1968 his first book, *Soul on Ice*, highly influential and widely read, became a best seller, "a classic contemporary black militant expression." Rising to national prominence as a writer for *Ramparts* and as the Minister of Information and major formulator of the **Black Panther** party's ideology, Cleaver served as a symbol of growing black urban unrest and disillusionment and its bitter opposition to white America's oppression. Moreover, his pronouncement of "total liberty for black people or total destruction for America" signaled a new voice and a unique vision of the civil rights movement. Calling for a new assessment of the black condition and new strategies, Eldridge Cleaver helped raise the struggle for civil rights to a more militant level. Later in his life he disavowed many of his earlier radical views.

Selected Bibliography Jervis Anderson, "Race Rage and Eldridge Cleaver," *Commentary* 46 (December 1968), 63–69; Stokely Carmichael and Charles Hamilton, *Black Power: The Politics of Liberation in America* (1967); M. Karenga, *The Roots of the US/Panther Conflict* (1976); Manning Marable, *Race, Reform and Rebellion: The Second Reconstruction in Black America, 1945–1982* (1984); Joyce Nower, "Cleaver's Vision of America and the New White Radical: A Legacy of Malcolm X," *Negro American Literature Forum* 4 (March 1970), 12–21; Kenneth O'Reilly, *"Racial Matters": The FBI's Secret File on Black America, 1960–1972* (1989); Stanley Pacion, "Soul Still on Ice? The Talents and Troubles of Eldridge Cleaver," *Dissent* 16 (July–August 1969), 310–16; Harvey Suados, "Old Con, Black Panther, Brilliant Writer and Quintessential American," *New York Times Magazine* (7 September 1969), 38–39, 139–54.

Jacquelyn Jackson

Cleveland Gazette Under the editorial direction of Harry C. Smith, this leading black weekly newspaper in Cleveland, Ohio, forcefully protested discrimination nationwide. During Neval Thomas's 1924–28 Washington, D.C.–based campaign against governmental mandated segregation in the federal civil service, the *Gazette* provided Thomas with a forum for disseminating information on his activities. Smith also utilized the paper as a vehicle to express his own civil rights convictions, including a controversial call for

African Americans in Cleveland to buy guns for their self-defense during the Red Summer of 1919.

Selected Bibliography Larry Cuban, "A Strategy for Racial Peace: Negro Leadership in Cleveland, 1900–1919," *Phylon* 28 (Fall 1967), 299–311; Russell H. Davis, *Memorable Negroes in Cleveland's Past* (1969); Felicia G. Jones-Ross, "Preserving the Community: Cleveland Black Papers' Response to the Great Migration," *Journalism Quarterly* 71 (1994), 531–39; Kenneth Kusmer, *A Ghetto Takes Shape: Black Cleveland 1870–1930* (1976); Summer E. Stevens and Owen V. Johnson, "From Black Politics to Black Community: Harry C. Smith and the *Cleveland Gazette,*" *Journalism Quarterly* 67 (1990), 1090–1102.

Marshall Hyatt

Clinton Advisory Board to the President's Initiative on Race (1997). On 14 June 1997, President Bill Clinton announced "One America in the 21st Century: The President's Initiative on Race," his administration's formalized effort to educate the American public about race, encourage racial reconciliation through national dialogue on race, identify policies that could expand opportunities for racial and ethnic minorities, and coordinate the work of the White House and federal agencies to improve race relations. A seven-member presidential advisory board, led by historian **John Hope Franklin**, also consisted of Linda Chavez-Thompson, Executive Vice President of the AFL-CIO; Susan D. Johnson Cook, senior pastor of the Bronx Christian Fellowship; Thomas H. Kean, former Republican governor of New Jersey; Angela E. Oh, attorney and lecturer on race relations; Bob Thomas, business executive; and William Winter, former Democratic governor of Mississippi. They conducted a series of open meetings across America over the next year. On 18 September 1998 the advisory board concluded its work and presented its final recommendations. Its report outlined the commission's observations on what they saw and heard about race and its impact upon communities throughout the country. The report also offered recommendations on specific steps that should be taken to eliminate racial disparities experienced by people of color. In addition, the initiative identified and published a list of successful community efforts on racial reconciliation, and it distributed a dialogue guide to promote discussions about race in neighborhoods, schools, and places of worship. It received criticism from conservative circles for ignoring conservative opinion, especially on affirmative action. As President Clinton left office in January 2001, he left a list of priorities for his successor and Congress entitled, "The Unfinished Work of Building One America."

Selected Bibliography "One America in the 21st Century: Forging a New Future, The Advisory Board's Report to the President"; "Pathways to One America in the 21st Century: Promising Practices for Racial Reconciliation"; "Message to Congress from President William J. Clinton: The Unfinished Work of Building One America," 15 January 2001; http://clinton5.nara.gov/library/hot_releases/January_15_2001_8.html; http://clinton2.nara.gov/Initiatives/OneAmerica/america.html; http://www.pbs.org/newshour/bb/race_relations/OneAmerica/links.html; http://jointcenter.org/nabre/; *Boston Globe,* 12 June 2000; *Washington Post,* 17 December 1998.

William "Brother" Rogers

Clinton, Tennessee, School Integration Crisis Building upon litigation precedents established by the **NAACP,** the East Tennessee African American community of Clinton filed suit in Knoxville's federal district court in 1951 seeking the integration of Clinton High School. District Judge Robert L. Taylor denied the plea, and Clinton's black students continued to be bused 18 miles to Knoxville's segregated high school. After the 1954 *Brown v. Board of Education* ruling, Taylor directed Clinton school authorities to desegregate. Local citizens organized to delay integration, and racist agitator Frederick John Kasper of New Jersey successfully inflamed the area's antiblack sentiments until Governor Frank G. Clement sent troops to maintain order for the first nine days when integrated schools opened in August 1956.

Selected Bibliography Lester C. Lamon, *Blacks in Tennessee, 1791–1970* (1981); Neil R. McMillen, "Organized Resistance To School Desegregation in Tennessee," *Tennessee Historical Quarterly* 30 (Fall 1971), 314–28.

Thaddeus M. Smith

"Close Ranks" This editorial, written by **W.E.B. Du Bois,** appeared in the July 1918 issue of the *Crisis*, the organ of the **NAACP**, after the United States had declared war against Germany. "We of the colored race," Du Bois wrote, "have no ordinary interest in the outcome. . . . Let us not hesitate. Let us, while the war lasts, forget our special grievances and close our ranks shoulder to shoulder with our own white fellow citizens and the other nations that are fighting for democracy." For Du Bois, as for many Progressives, the war represented an opportunity to battle militarism; unlike most whites, he also saw it as a struggle against racism. Over 2.2 million African Americans registered for the draft; 367,000 were called into service, and 50,000 went overseas. Taunted by *The Messenger* for supporting the war and stunned at army discrimination, Du Bois later repudiated his position: "We killed Faith and Hope." But in 1942, amidst the struggle against the Axis powers, he again endorsed the principles of "Close Ranks."

Selected Bibliography Mark Ellis, "Closing Ranks and Seeking Honors: W.E.B. Du Bois in World War II," *Journal of American History* 79 (1992), 96–124; David L. Lewis, ed., *W.E.B. Du Bois: A Reader* (1994); W. Manning Marable, *W.E.B. Du Bois* (1986); Elliott M. Rudwick, *W.E.B. Du Bois: Propagandist of the Negro Protest* (1960).

Richard W. Resh

***Clyatt v. United States,* 197 U.S. 207 (1905)** Samuel Clyatt was accused of holding two black Georgians, Will Gordon and Mose Ridley, in **black peonage** as a repayment of debt. Clyatt was convicted by a jury and was sentenced to four years of confinement. He appealed his sentence, contending that the **Thirteenth Amendment** pertained to actions of a state and not to an individual. Justice David Brewer in the initial point of law stated for the majority that the **Fourteenth** and **Fifteenth Amendments** were state prohibitions, but that Congress held the authority to enforce the Thirteenth Amendment and had applied its laws to an individual. In a second point of law, Brewer distinguished between peonage and voluntary actions in repayment of a debt, and he observed that Gordon and Ridley were forced to return to Georgia. In a more narrow ruling, Brewer stated that the specific charge against Clyatt was "returning" the two men to peonage, and no evidence had been presented as to prior conditions of peonage. Thus, the lower court decision was reversed and remanded for a new trial. Justice **John Marshall Harlan** dissented in the latter opinion. He argued that the men were returned to Georgia by force and against their will. He observed that Clyatt admitted the blacks owed him and did not object to a jury trial. Harlan held that the evidence "reflects barbarities of the worst kind against these negroes."

Selected Bibliography Richard Bardolph, ed., *The Civil Rights Record: Black Americans and the Law, 1849–1970* (1970); Pete Daniel, *The Shadows of Slavery: Peonage in the South, 1901–1969* (1972); Loren Miller, *The Petitioners: The Story of the Supreme Court of the United States and the Negro* (1966).

William Cash

Coalition of Black Trade Unionists Angered by the decision of the American Federation of Labor and Congress of Industrial Organizations (AFL-CIO) to remain neutral in the 1972 presidential election, nearly twelve hundred African Americans representing 37 unions convened in Chicago, Illinois, on 23–24 September of that year, and established the Coalition of Black Trade Unionists (CBTU). Since 1972, the Coalition has grown to represent more than 50 national and international unions. Founded on the principle that a progressive trade union movement depends on black participation at all levels of the decision-making process, the Coalition functions as a pressure group within the AFL-CIO to identify and help realize the needs and aspirations of African American workers. Continuing in the tradition of its founding members, labor and civil rights activists including William Lucy, Charles Hayes, Nelson "Jack" Edwards, Cleveland Robinson, and William Simons, the CBTU functions as an independent voice to enhance the power and influence of black workers in the United States and around the world. The CBTU was the first labor organization to oppose white minority rule in South Africa and actively to support human rights and labor reform in Africa and the Caribbean.

Selected Bibliography *Coalition of Black Trade Unionists National Constitution and Bill of Rights, as Amended at the 17th Annual Convention, Washington, D.C., May 20, 1988;* "Coalition of Black Trade Unionists: The Awakening Giant," *Bulletin* 3 (April 1974), 3; Philip S. Foner, Ronald L. Lewis, and Robert Cvornyek, eds., *The Black Worker: A Documentary History from Colonial Times to the Present,* vol. 8: *The Black Worker since the AFL-CIO Merger, 1955–1980* (1984); Coalition of Black Trade Unionists Collection, 1972–88, Schomburg Center for Research in Black Culture.

Robert Cvornyek

***Coke v. City of Atlanta,* 184 F. Supp. 579 (N.D. Ga., 1960)** On 23 December 1958 D. H. Coke, a Birmingham, Alabama, insurance executive, filed suit in district court attacking the segregated eating facilities at the

Atlanta Municipal Airport in Atlanta, Georgia. Dobbs House Inc., operator of the airport terminal restaurant, segregated its customers on the basis of race by seating African Americans behind a screen. Because Dobbs House was a lessee of the city of Atlanta, the central issue of this case was whether the restaurant's policy of segregation constituted private conduct or state action. Previous legal opinion held that only discriminatory conduct on the part of the state violated the **Fourteenth Amendment.** The city of Atlanta and Dobbs House contended that the restaurant was a private organization. Because Dobbs House did not receive any instructions from the city regarding its operations, attorneys for the company maintained that its policy of segregation was "private conduct" and was not inhibited by the Fourteenth Amendment. On 5 January 1960 the court held that the conduct of Dobbs House was "state action" and that its policy of segregating customers on the basis of race violated the Fourteenth Amendment. This decision narrowed the definition of what constituted state and private action in regard to racial discrimination and it defined the legal conduct of lessees of government property.

Selected Bibliography Henry J. Abraham and Barbara A. Perry, *Freedom and the Court, Civil Rights and Liberties on the United States* (1994); *Atlanta Constitution,* (6 January 1960), 138–42; Richard Bardolph, ed., *The Civil Rights Record, Black Americans and the Law, 1849–1970* (1970); Ronald H. Bayor, *Race and the Shaping of Twentieth-Century Atlanta* (1996); David Andrew Harmon, *Beneath the Image of the Civil Rights Movement and Race Relations: Atlanta, Georgia 1946–1981* (1996).

David A. Harmon

Collins, Cardiss Robertson (24 September 1931, St. Louis Mo.–). A graduate of Northwestern University in Evanston, Illinois, Collins became Illinois's first black congresswoman when she won the Seventh Congressional District seat vacated by the death of her husband, George Collins, in 1973. She won 87 percent of the vote in a district that was 55 percent black. Previously she had been a secretary, accountant, and revenue auditor with the Illinois Department of Revenue. She became the first African American to serve as majority whip-at-large, was chairman of the **Congressional Black Caucus,** and chairman of the Manpower and Housing Committee. She retired from the House of Representatives in 1996. A post office in Chicago was named after her in 2000.

Selected Bibliography *Chicago Defender,* 8 July 2000; *Who's Who of American Women,* 1989–90.

Ray Branch

Collins, Leroy (10 March 1909, Tallahassee, Fla.–12 March 1991, Tallahassee, Fla.). Governor of Florida from 1955 to 1961, Thomas LeRoy Collins guided the Sunshine State along a course of racial moderation. Following the ruling in **Brown v. Board of Education,** he supported a pupil assignment program, based on criteria other than race, that allowed Florida to obey the law with a minimum of desegregation and racial confrontation. In this way, Collins averted school shutdowns and other forms of massive resistance that were popular throughout the South. By 1960, Collins had begun to bend with the moral force of the civil rights struggle. In response to the sit-in movement, he established a biracial committee to assist in desegregating lunch counters in stores where blacks shopped. A few years after leaving office, he was appointed by President Lyndon B. Johnson to head the Community Relations Service, a mediation agency created by the **Civil Rights Act of 1964.** In this capacity in 1965, he went to Selma, Alabama, and worked out an arrangement with Dr. **Martin Luther King, Jr.,** and local officials that prevented bloodshed during a voting demonstration. As Collins became more closely identified with the civil rights cause, he suffered politically at home. In 1968 he was defeated in his race for U.S. Senator by Edward Gurney, a Republican who used the race issue against him.

Selected Bibliography David R. Colburn and Richard K. Scher, *Florida's Gubernatorial Politics in the Twentieth Century* (1980); Tom R. Wagy, *Governor LeRoy Collins of Florida: Spokesman of the New South* (1985).

Steven F. Lawson

Collins v. Walker, 339 F.2d 100 (5th Cir., 1964)   Like the famous case of the **Scottsboro Trials** in the 1930s, numerous legal decisions involving black defendants were challenged in the twentieth century because of the exclusion of blacks from juries. In an interesting twist on the theme of jury selection, the case of *Collins v. Walker* dealt with discrimination against the defendant, not because blacks had been excluded from his jury, but rather because they had been purposely included. Woodman J. Collins, a black man, had been convicted and sentenced to death for the aggravated rape of a white woman. This decision was upheld by the Louisiana Supreme Court in 1962. Collins appealed to the U.S. Circuit Court on three grounds. His attorneys claimed that Collins was mentally incompetent and unable to stand trial, and that his confession had been coerced. They also argued that Collins had been discriminated against because blacks had been intentionally placed on the jury for his case only. The grand jury that indicted Collins was composed of five blacks and seven whites. The judges agreed that the five black jurors had been deliberately added to the jury because the defendant was black; therefore, he had been discriminated against. The case was remanded to a new jury.

Selected Bibliography Derrick A. Bell, Jr., *Race, Racism and American Law* (1980); Thomas I. Emerson, David Haber, and Norman Dorsen, *Political and Civil Rights in the United States* (1967); Landman Teller, Jr., "Constitutional Law: Discrimination by Systematic Inclusion of Negroes on Grand Jury," *Mississippi Law Journal* 36 (1965), 243–45.

Carol Wilson

Colored Farmers' National Alliance and Cooperative Union   Founded in Houston County, Texas, in December, 1886, the Colored Farmers' Alliance was an appendage to the post-bellum southern white Farmers' Alliance movement. Organized to educate black farmers in the agricultural sciences and to promote brotherhood, black rights, and communal support for black farm families, the Alliance suffered from white paternalistic leadership and negative public reaction to its labor protests and other political activities. The Alliance's general superintendent, R. M. Humphrey, and several of its state presidents who were white, attempted to restrain the assertiveness of the black farmers. But the alliance established its own official newspaper, the *National Alliance*, set up a network of cooperatives, and pressured Humphrey to support Alliance strikes and other forms of protest. White resistance to Alliance activism grew rapidly. In 1891, a strike by cotton pickers in an Arkansas county led to several deaths, including the lynching of some of the instigators. By 1892 the white backlash had destroyed the Alliance. Significant as an expression of agrarian protest and as an experiment in black self-determination, the Alliance fell victim to the racist **Jim Crow** milieu of the late-nineteenth-century South.

Selected Bibliography Jack Abramowitz, "The Negro in the Agrarian Revolt," *Agriculture History* 24 (April 1950), 89–98; N. A. Dunning, ed., *The Farmers' Alliance History and Agricultural Digest* (1891); William F. Holmes, "The Arkansas Cotton Pickers Strike of 1891 and the Demise of the Colored Farmers' Alliance," *Arkansas Historical Quarterly* 32 (1973), 107–19; Floyd J. Miller, "Black Protest and White Leadership: A Note on the Colored Farmers' Alliance," *Phylon* 33 (1972), 169–74.

Michael B. Ballard

Colored Merchants' Association   Organized by Albon L. Holsey, of **Booker T. Washington's National Negro Business League,** the Colored Merchants' Association established black-owned grocery stores, which purchased merchandise cooperatively from selected dealers. The purpose was to stimulate black business, provide jobs for blacks, and pass on cost reductions to black consumers. The first CMA store opened in Montgomery, Alabama, in 1928; the concept soon spread to 18 other cities. Despite initial enthusiasm and support from many black organizations, CMA stores failed within a few years because of the Great Depression. Few businesses joined, and consumers continued to buy national brands from white-owned chains, rather than chance the untested brands carried by the CMA.

Selected Bibliography E. Franklin Frazier, "Negro Business: A Social Myth," in Ronald W. Bailey, ed., *Black Business Enterprise: Historical and Contemporary Perspectives* (1971); Albon L. Holsey, "Business Points the Way," *Crisis* (July 1931); Albon L. Holsey, "The CMA Stores Face the Chains," *Opportunity* (July 1929).

Carol Wilson

Commission on Interracial Cooperation   This organization was an interracial body of prominent blacks and whites who wished to address the social, political, and economic problems facing African Americans. Founded in December 1918 and incorporated 11 years later in Georgia, the Commission consisted of state and local committees throughout the South. In 1920 a Department of Women's Work was created within the organization enabling black and white women to meet and discuss the problems they shared. The

119

director of the organization was **Will W. Alexander,** a white Methodist minister who devoted 25 years of service to the organization. Throughout its existence the Commission used research and education to ameliorate race relations. It held conferences and published literature that espoused equal treatment. It endorsed various worthy causes including boy scout troops for African American boys and training homes for delinquent girls. It called for the abolishment of the **poll tax** and **white primaries.** The organization was especially concerned about racial violence. In the early 1930s the Commission engaged in a research project on lynching designed to give the public more information on the brutality of this crime. By the 1940s the organization was experiencing financial difficulties as support from northern philanthropists declined. The organization was dissolved on 16 February 1944 and succeeded by the **Southern Regional Council.**

Selected Bibliography Edward F. Burrows, "The Commission on Interracial Cooperation" (Ph.D. diss., University of Wisconsin, 1954); Wilma Dykeman and James Stokely, *Seeds of Southern Change: The Life of Will Alexander* (1962); John Hope Franklin and Alfred A. Moss, Jr., *From Slavery to Freedom: A History of Negro Americans,* 8th ed. (2000); Julia A. McDonough, "Men and Women of Good Will: A History of the Commission on Interracial Cooperation and the Southern Regional Council, 1919–1954" (Ph.D. diss., University of Virginia, 1993); Cynthia Neverdon-Morton, *Afro-American Women of the South and the Advancement of the Race, 1895–1925* (1989).

Gerald L. Smith

***Commonwealth of Pennsylvania v. Brown,* 270 F. Supp. 782 (E.D. Pa., 1967)** Stephen Girard, a wealthy merchant and banker, established Philadelphia's Girard College in 1848. His will specified that this secondary school's enrollment was to be restricted to "poor, white, male orphans." Charged with administrating the school, the city of Philadelphia established a board of trustees that strictly enforced the will's terms. In 1957 the Supreme Court held that the board's refusal to admit blacks constituted governmental discrimination. In response, Philadelphia dissolved the board of trustees and appointed private persons to administer the school. Ten years later, seven black male orphans, together with the Commonwealth of Pennsylvania, its attorney general, and the city of Philadelphia, brought a class action suit against the private trustees in a federal district court to prevent the further denial of admission to blacks. Based on *Evans v. Newton,* a 1966 Supreme Court case that involved a privately endowed park, the court ruled that the college had associated itself with the state in such a way as to suggest to the community that the institution's policy was approved by public authority. While Girard College was not accessible to the general public, said the court, it had always been an "institution whose benefits are available to any needy, fatherless boy—as long as he is 'white.'" In this way, the college was similar to a public boarding school or orphanage that practiced racial restriction. In addition, by requiring the trustees of the school to make periodic reports, Pennsylvania had become actively involved in overseeing the instruction and upbringing of Girard's students. The Court concluded that Girard's racial policy was "so afflicted with State action" that it violated the equal protection clause of the **Fourteenth Amendment.**

Selected Bibliography Richard Bardolph, ed., *The Civil Rights Record: Black Americans and the Law, 1849–1970* (1970); Derrick A. Bell, Jr., *Race, Racism, and the Law* (1980).

Phillip A. Gibbs

Communist Party The largest impact the American Communist Party (ACP) had on African Americans occurred during the Great Depression when the party sought to organize this most oppressed sector of America. The ACP offered equality in the party's organization, attacked social and economic discrimination, and promoted legal efforts at ending American racial injustice. In 1931 the International Labor Defense and **NAACP** battled to handle the appeal of the **Scottsboro Trials,** the focal point of the party's southern initiative. Also during the 1930s, the ACP, through the **National Negro Congress,** attempted to join with other black organizations for a United Front Against Fascism and eventually to expand its political base. The party promoted expanded educational opportunities for black youth and black cultural enterprises that attracted such notables as **Richard Wright** and **Paul Robeson.** Politically, the ACP was an active force in Harlem political life during the period, and James Ford, recruited via the **American Negro Labor Congress** in 1926, became the special organizer in Harlem in 1931 and ran as the party's vice-presidential candidate in 1932, 1936, and 1940. The ACP's significance in the African American community declined because of its failure to attract the aspiring black middle class firmly dedicated to the capitalist system.

Selected Bibliography Dan T. Carter, *Scottsboro: A Tragedy of the American South* (1969); Harvey Klehr, *Communist Cadre: The Social Background of the American Communist Party Elite* (1978); Harvey Klehr, *The Heyday of American Communism: The Depression Decade* (1984); Mark Naison, *Communist in the Harlem during the Depression* (1983); Wilson Record, *The Negro and the Communist Party* (1951); Web site: www.cpusa.org (American Communist Party).

Thaddeus M. Smith

Compromise of 1877 When the vote was counted in the presidential election of 7 November 1876, neither the Republican Rutherford B. Hayes nor the Democrat Samuel J. Tilden had won the necessary majority of the electoral vote. Although Tilden had the majority of the popular vote (4,282,020 to 4,036,572), the electoral count was 184 to 165; the disputed votes of Florida, Louisiana, South Carolina, and Oregon had not been counted. Both candidates claimed the presidency. Tilden needed 1 vote and Hayes needed 20 to achieve the necessary majority. Rival canvassing boards and state governments pressed their claims and contrived a variety of "deals," but the deadlock remained. Because there was no constitutional provision for resolving the dilemma, on 29 January 1877 the House and Senate created an Electoral Commission consisting of five members each from the House, Senate, and Supreme Court. The commission voted 8 to 7 in favor of Hayes. It is generally agreed that behind-the-scenes negotiating actually ensured congressional approval. The main parts of the so called Compromise of 1877 consisted of a promise to end Reconstruction, to appoint a Southerner to the cabinet, and to support the building of southern railroads. The actual result of the compromise was the Republican party's abandonment of black people to southern native whites.

Selected Bibliography Allan Peskin, "Was There a Compromise of 1877?" *Journal of American History* 60 (June 1973), 63–73; Keith I. Polakoff, *The Politics of Inertia* (1973); George C. Rable, "Southern Interests and the Election of 1876: A Reappraisal," *Civil War History* 26 (December 1980), 357–61; C. Van Woodward, *Reunion and Reaction: The Compromise of 1877 and The End of Reconstruction* (1951); C. Vann Woodward, "Yes, There Was a Compromise of 1877," *Journal of American History* 60 (June 1973), 215–23.

Clarence Hooker

Confiscation Acts   (1861, 1862). The First Confiscation Act approved on 6 August 1861 empowered the federal government to confiscate the property, including slaves, of disloyal Southerners who used such property in direct support of the Confederate war effort. The Second Confiscation Act, the product of intense and lengthy debate and complex parliamentary maneuvering, became law on 17 July 1862 only after Congress took the unusual step of attaching to the legislation an explanatory joint resolution that prevented a threatened veto by President Abraham Lincoln. The act gave disloyal Southerners 60 days to cease rebellious activity. At the close of that grace period, the government was authorized to confiscate the slaves and other property of rebellious Southerners. Such confiscated slaves were to be freed. In most cases confiscation took place after legal process in federal courts. However, slaves abandoned by disloyal masters or slaves who escaped to Union lines were immediately freed. Other provisions of this law authorized the president to enlist freed slaves into the Union military and appropriated $500,000 for colonization of ex-slaves out of the country. Both acts were cautiously enforced by the Lincoln administration and were overshadowed by the **Emancipation Proclamation.**

Selected Bibliography Roy P. Basler, ed., *The Collected Works of Abraham Lincoln*, vol. 5 (1953); Leonard P. Curry, *Blueprint for Modern America: Nonmilitary Legislation of the First Civil War Congress* (1968); James G. Randall, *Constitutional Problems under Lincoln* (1951).

Larry T. Balsamo

Congress of Racial Equality   In 1942 George Houser and other pacifists affiliated with the **Fellowship of Reconciliation** (FOR) formed a Committee of Racial Equality in Chicago, Illinois. Following a "Brotherhood Mobilization Plan" written by **James Farmer,** they practiced **nonviolent resistance** to public segregation. As Farmer and **Bayard Rustin,** both FOR field secretaries, spread the concept to other cities, committees multiplied, and a national organization was formed with the name, Congress of Racial Equality (CORE).

After declining in the 1950s, CORE emerged as a major civil rights force in the 1960s. Among the first to respond to the 1960s sit-ins, which began at a

CORE picketers protest slum housing in New York City. © Library of Congress.

Woolworth's lunch counter in North Carolina, CORE leaders initiated picket lines and boycotts of northern Woolworth stores. In 1961 CORE **Freedom Riders** tested a Supreme Court ban on segregated interstate transportation. Prevailing over vicious resistance in the Deep South, this strategy broke the back of **Jim Crow.**

In 1962 CORE's emphasis shifted from **direct action** to voter registration. Part of the **Council of Federated Organizations,** CORE contributed leadership and resources to the **Freedom Summer of 1964,** the **Mississippi Freedom Democratic Party** (MFDP), and the MFDP's challenge of party regulars at the 1964 Democratic National Convention. Meanwhile, northern CORE workers immersed themselves in "community organization" battles against poverty and racism in urban ghettos.

James Farmer, CORE's first national chairman and national director after 1961, retired in 1966. **Floyd B. McKissick,** elected in his stead, was succeeded two years later by Roy Innis. Changes in leadership reflected changes in philosophy and tactics, and nonviolence and interracialism were eclipsed by the **Black Power** movement.

While CORE veered toward separatism, historians began to assess its earlier strategies. Crediting the organization with contributing substantially to desegregation and landmark civil rights laws, they suggested that the record numbers of African Americans who attained public office in the 1970s were direct beneficiaries of the efforts of CORE.

Selected Bibliography Inge Powell Bell, *CORE and the Strategy of Nonviolence* (1968); James Farmer, *Lay Bare the Heart, an Autobiography of the Civil Rights Movement* (1985); George M. Houser, *CORE: A Brief History* (1949); August Meier and Elliot Rudwick, *CORE: A Study in the Civil Rights Movement* (1973); James Peck, *Cracking the Color Line: Nonviolent Direct Action Methods of Eliminating Racial Discrimination* (1962); Web site: www.core-online.org.

Jo Ann O. Robinson

Congressional Black Caucus   In 1969, when the number of black congressmen grew from six to nine, informal discussions of the group on matters primarily affecting the well-being of African Americans began. Chaired by Representative **Charles Diggs** (D-Mich.), the meeting of informal groups led to the founding of the official Congressional Black Caucus (CBC) in January 1971. It quickly gained press attention when its members boycotted President Richard Nixon's State of the Union address, citing his failure to grant them an audience, a stance he soon reversed. With a less than sympathetic ear in the Oval Office and a conservative political trend in the nation, caucus members focused their energies on gaining seniority, acquiring political clout through important congressional committee assignments, and mobilizing constituencies in support of caucus objectives ranging from minority set-aside legislation to voter registration. CBC members sponsored and were instrumental in the passage of such measures as the Anti-Apartheid Act of 1986, the establishment of a national holiday in honor of **Martin Luther King, Jr.,** in 1982; and the Humphrey-Hawkins Full Employment and Balanced Growth Act and the Public Works Employment Act in 1977. In order to maximize its effectiveness, caucus members have voted as a bloc on legislation of common concern, maintained ties with black elected officials and organizations across the nation, formed coalitions with other special-interest groups, and disseminated information outlining its goals and activities through its periodic publications and seminars. Each year the CBC publicizes its agenda reflecting national priorities it supports. In 1976, the Congressional Black Congress Foundation was set up to fund research, scholarships, internships, and sponsor an annual legislative conference. By 1990, membership in the caucus had grown to 24, and a decade later to 37.

Selected Bibliography Frank Dexter Brown, "The CBC: Past. Present, and Future," *Black Enterprise* (September 1990), 25–26; William L. Clay, *Just Permanent Interests: Black Americans in Congress. 1870–1992* (1993); Lynn Norment, "Congressional Black Caucus: Our Team on Capital Hill," *Ebony* (August 1984), 40, 42, 44, 46; Robert Singh, *The Congressional Black Caucus: Racial Politics in the U.S. Congress* (1997); Carol M. Swain, *Black Faces, Black Interests: The Representation of African Americans in Congress* (1993); Michael W. Williams, ed., *The African American Encyclopedia*, vol. 15 (1993); Web site: www.house.gov/ebjohnson/cbcmain.htm.

Robert Fikes, Jr.

Cooper v. Aaron, 358 U.S. 1 (1958)   After the 1954 **Brown v. Board of Education** decision, the city of Little Rock, Arkansas, drew up a plan for the gradual desegregation of its public schools (see **Little Rock Desegregation Crisis**). The parents of several black children, represented by the **NAACP,** challenged the plan, contending that it provided for the continued operation of segregated schools. A federal district judge upheld the board's plan. Governor Orval Faubus declared the white schools off limits to blacks, but Judge Ronald Davies ordered the board to proceed with the plan forthwith. After the Arkansas National Guard turned away black students attempting to enter Central High School, the board filed a petition for a temporary suspension of the plan. Davies denied the petition and issued a preliminary injunction prohibiting the governor and officers of the National Guard from interfering with black students entering Central High. Faubus withdrew the National Guard, and on 23 September 1957 black students again entered the school. A large and threatening crowd prompted authorities to remove the black children from the school, and Mayor Woodrow Wilson Mann requested aid from President Dwight Eisenhower, who nationalized the guard and sent one thousand troops from the 101st Airborne Division to escort the black students into Central High. On 23 June 1958, District Judge Harry J. Lemley granted a request by the school board to delay implementing the desegregation plan until 1961. The Eighth Circuit Court of Appeals reversed Lemley's decision. Sitting in special session, the Supreme Court affirmed the decision of the Eighth Circuit on 12 September 1958.

Selected Bibliography Tony Freyer, *The Little Rock Crisis: A Constitutional Interpretation* (1984); George Rossman, ed., "Review of Recent Supreme Court Decisions," *American Bar Association Journal* 44 (1958), 1178–79; Robert G. Webb, "Constitutional Law: Little Rock Litigation," *North Carolina Law Review* 37 (1959), 177–84.

Michael S. Mayer

Corrigan v. Buckley, **271 U.S. 323 (1926)** In the early twentieth century, it was common for white urban homeowners to enter into agreements that excluded certain groups from owning property in their neighborhood. The agreements, directed most often against African Americans and Jews, bound not only the signatories to the agreement but also any future purchasers of the property.

In 1921, Irene Corrigan, a homeowner in Washington, D.C., entered into an agreement with her neighbors to exclude African Americans from purchasing, leasing, or otherwise occupying any property in her neighborhood. A year later, Corrigan attempted to sell her property to an African American woman in violation of the neighborhood agreement. Corrigan's neighbors filed suit to stop her. The U.S. Supreme Court decided that it had no jurisdiction in this case, stating that the provisions of the Fifth Amendment and the **Fourteenth Amendment** relating to equal protection under the laws applied only to governmental actions, not to private contracts such as the one Corrigan had signed. In so ruling, the Supreme Court inferred that although restrictive covenants were instruments of racial discrimination, they were not unconstitutional because no governmental action was involved.

Selected Bibliography Richard Bardolph, ed., *The Civil Rights Record, Black Americans, and the Law, 1849–1970* (1970); Loren Miller, *The Petitioners: The Story of the Supreme Court of the United States and the Negro* (1966); Gilbert Osofsky, *Harlem: The Making of a Ghetto* (1971); Clement E. Vose, *Caucasians Only: The Supreme Court, the NAACP, and the Restrictive Covenant Cases* (1959).

Steve Sadowsky

Costigan-Wagner Antilynching Bill   In 1934 the **NAACP** led the fight to obtain from Congress an antilynching measure designed to give equal protection of the law to African Americans, to challenge the complacent acceptance of mob murder, and to make lynching a punishable crime in every state. Senate Democrats Edward Costigan (Colorado) and Robert Wagner (New York) sponsored the NAACP measure. The Costigan-Wagner Bill was aimed at state and local law enforcement officials who permitted lynching. The bill also proposed a $10,000 fine on the county in which the lynching occurred. The NAACP maintained that the bill would pressure local authorities and that federal jurisdiction would protect judges, juries, attorneys, and witnesses against reprisals. Although President Franklin D. Roosevelt reportedly favored the measure, he refused to publicly endorse it and risk a congressional battle at the expense of other national reform measures. The NAACP was not successful in the Senate, but the bill did pass in the House of Representatives and progress was made toward gaining broad based congressional support for a national antilynching law. Likewise, the NAACP secured its position as a major lobbying voice in Congress for African Americans for the next two decades.

Selected Bibliography Joseph Huthmacher, *Senator Robert F. Wagner and the Rise of Urban Liberalism* (1968); James R. McGovern, *Anatomy of a Lynching: The Killing of Claude Neal* (1982); George C. Rable, "The South and the Politics of Antilynching Legislation, 1920–1940," *Journal of Southern History* 51 (May 1985), 201–20; Robert L. Zangrando, *The NAACP Crusade Against Lynching, 1909–1950* (1980).

Thaddeus M. Smith

Council of Federated Organizations   In 1962 **Robert Moses** of the **Student Nonviolent Coordinating Committee** (SNCC) and **David Dennis** of the **Congress of Racial Equality** led in the formation of this statewide coalition of civil rights organizations in Mississippi. Moses served as director, Dennis as assistant director, and **Aaron Henry** of the **NAACP** as president. During 1962 and 1963, the Council of Federated Organizations (COFO) conducted a voter registration campaign, which was supported by funds from the Voter Education Project. White Mississippians responded to the campaign by harassing and terrorizing COFO workers and would-be black voters, with the result that few blacks were registered. Recognizing the need for new tactics, in August 1963 COFO mobilized about a thousand black voters to cast protest votes in the August Democratic primary. As a next step, COFO leaders wanted to show the desire and willingness of black Mississippians to vote. The "freedom vote" campaign provided a way to do this without having voters face intimidation at the regular polling places and by giving them the opportunity to vote for candidates of their own choosing. COFO members selected Aaron Henry of the NAACP and **R. Edwin King, Jr.,** a white minister at **Tougaloo College,** as candidates for governor and lieutenant governor. About a hundred northern white students came to Mississippi to help with the campaign. This experiment with white volunteers led to the **Freedom Summer of 1964** in Mississippi. Moses and Dennis decided that the only way to get the country to respond to what was going on in Mississippi was to involve white college students. The National Council of Churches provided support. In spite of opposition to white participation from some SNCC staff members, COFO undertook the project. Northern students responded with enthusiasm to the invitation to come help in the all-out campaign in Mississippi. In addition to working in voter-registration campaigns, the summer workers set up schools to teach reading and writing and voting procedures. The numerous reports of murders, beatings, arrests, church burnings, and home bombings attest to the response of white Mississippians. The killing of **James Earl Chaney, Andrew Goodman,** and **Michael Henry Schwerner** in Neshoba County was the most tragic event that occurred that summer. The most spectacular result of the project was the organization of the **Mississippi Freedom Democratic Party** and the challenge this group made to the seating of the regular Democratic delegates to the National Democratic Convention in 1964. COFO disbanded soon after the summer project ended.

Selected Bibliography Clayborne Carson, *In Struggle: SNCC and the Black Awakening of the 1960s* (1981); John Dittmer, *Local People: The Struggle for Civil Rights in Mississippi* (1994); Aaron Henry, with Constance Curry, *Aaron Henry: The Fire Ever Burning* (2000); August Meier and Elliot Rudwick, *CORE: A Study in the Civil Rights Movement, 1942–1968* (1973); Benjamin Muse, *The American Negro Revolution: From Nonviolence to Black Power, 1963–1967* (1968); Howell Raines, *My Soul Is Rested: Movement Days in the Deep South Remembered* (1977).

Arvarh E. Strickland

Cox v. Louisiana, **379 U.S. 559 (1965)** This U.S. Supreme Court case helped define the limits of state regulation of First Amendment rights. B. Elton Cox was conducting an officially sanctioned student demonstration in Baton Rouge when he was arrested for violating a Louisiana law prohibiting protests near courthouses. His subsequent conviction in district court in East Baton Rouge Parish was upheld by the Louisiana Supreme Court. The U.S. Supreme Court reversed Cox's conviction. It noted that the Louisiana statute prohibiting demonstrations near courthouses was not itself unconstitutional; the state's interest in safeguarding its judicial system renders such picketing and protesting subject to regulation. Yet in this case, where the defendant had in effect received permission from officials of the city government to demonstrate in a specified area across the street from the courthouse, the application of the regulation violated **Fourteenth Amendment** due process guarantees. Prosecution of the defendant once he had received official permission to conduct a peaceful protest was tantamount to entrapment. Citizens had to know the restrictions on peaceful protest, otherwise the breadth of regulatory power would stifle First Amendment freedoms, which "need breathing space to survive."

Selected Bibliography Derrick A. Bell, *Race, Racism, and American Law* (1980); Morroe Berger, *Equality by Statute: The Revolution in Civil Rights* (1968); Thomas I. Emerson et al., *Political and Civil Rights in the United States* (1967); Peter Irons and Stephanie Guitton, eds., *May It Please the Court: The Most Significant Arguments Made before the Supreme Court since 1955* (1994); *New York Times*, 19 January 1965.

Robert A. Calvert

Crisis The journal of the **NAACP**, the *Crisis* was first published in November, 1910. Its founder and first editor was **W.E.B. Du Bois,** who served in that office until 1934 when he resigned over differences with NAACP leadership. The *Crisis* set out to be "A Record of the Darker Races." It has served as a vehicle for the dissemination of information by and about African Americans, "to set forth those facts and arguments which show the danger of race prejudice." Throughout its history, regular columns, including "Along the Color Line" and, later, "Along the NAACP Battlefront," have documented developments relating to race or racism as well as the activities of the NAACP. The art work, poetry, stories, and photographs of both prominent and newly emerging black artists are highlighted in its pages. Every important issue of interest to the black community has been discussed both in its editorials and feature articles including nationalism, integration, voluntary segregation, protest strategies, the black press, education, and examples of racism. The journal also covers events or individuals of interest to the community and reviews new music and literature. It is published monthly.

Selected Bibliography Kenneth Jones, "Seventy-five Years on the Cutting Edge," *Crisis* 92 (December 1985), 16–28, 30, 34, 62; NAACP Papers, Manuscript Division, Library of Congress; Elliot M. Rudwick, *W.E.B. Du Bois, Propagandist of the Negro Protest* (1968); Sandra Kathryn Wilson, ed., *In Search of Democracy: The NAACP Writings of James Weldon Johnson, Walter White, and Roy Wilkins* (1999); Sandra Kathryn Wilson, ed., *The Crisis Reader* (1999); Web site: www.thecrisismagazine.com.

Cheryl Greenberg

Crummell, Alexander (c. 1819, New York, N.Y.–10 September 1898, Point Pleasant, N.J.). A religious leader, intellectual, nationalist, Pan-Africanist, and integrationist, Crummell received his secondary education in New York and New Hampshire. Having been denied admission to the General Technological Seminary of the Episcopal Church in 1839 because he was black, Crummell decided to attend Queen's College in England, where he earned his A.B. degree in 1853. Following his graduation, Crummell went to Liberia, West Africa, where he served as a missionary for 20 years. Crummell's return to the land of his ancestors was a manifestation of the **Pan-African movement.** But Crummell was not only a Pan-Africanist, he was also an African American nationalist. After his return to America in 1873, he told blacks that they would be treated with respect if they improved their spiritual and material well being. Crummell founded the American Negro Academy in

1897; its primary goal was to help blacks acquire mainstream American values that would win them respectability. In this sense, Crummell was also an integrationist like most of his contemporaries.

Selected Bibliography Alexander Crummell, *Africa and America, Addresses and Discourses* (1891); Floyd Miller, *The Search for a Nationality: Black Emigration and Colonization, 1787–1863* (1975); Wilson J. Moses, *Alexander Crummell: A Study of Civilization and Discontent* (1989); Wilson J. Moses, *The Golden Age of Black Nationalism 1850–1925* (1978).

Amos J. Beyan

The Crusader Launched in 1918, by Cyril Briggs (1888–1966), this Pan-Africanist New York based monthly magazine called for a separate African American nation within the United States, an "Africa for Africans," and the defeat of the imperialistic League of Nations. The publication, supported by African American socialists, journalists, businessmen and entertainers, operated as the publicity organ of the Hamitic League of the World (1919–20) and the **African Blood Brotherhood** (1920–21). It ceased to exist in 1922. If one of the most significant features of post–World War I revolution was the emergence of African American radicalism, then one of the most important documents of the phenomenon was *The Crusader*.

Selected Bibliography Robert L. Allen, *Reluctant Reformers* (1974); Walter C. Daniel, *Black Journals of the United States* (1982); Philip S. Foner and James Allen, eds., *American Communism and Black Americans* (1986); Robert A. Hill, ed., *The Crusader* (1987); Mark I. Solomon, *The Cry Was Unity: Communists and African Americans, 1917–1936* (1998).

Aingred G. Dunston

Cullen, Countee (30 May 1903, Louisville, Ky.–9 January 1946, New York, N.Y.). Like many of his contemporaries, Cullen was preoccupied more with the problems of art than sociopolitical issues. Cullen believed that success in art would dispel notions about black inferiority and would thus ameliorate the American dilemma. Cullen possessed what **W.E.B. Du Bois** called the "double consciousness" of being at once American and something apart. This ambivalence about identity led him to write in the foreword to his anthology *Caroling Dusk* (1927) that "Negro poets, dependent as they are on the English language, may have more to gain from the rich background of English and American poetry than from any nebulous atavistic yearnings toward an African inheritance." Cullen had gained recognition as a talented poet before be graduated Phi Beta Kappa from New York University in 1925. The following year he earned an M.A. degree from Harvard University. His first collection of poems, *Color* (1925), secured his place as a leading poet of the **Harlem Renaissance.** He served as assistant editor of **Opportunity,** the official journal of the **National Urban League** (1926–28) and he won a Guggenheim Fellowship in 1928. He published two books of poetry in 1927, *Copper Sun* and *The Ballad of the Brown Girl*. These were followed by *The Black Christ and Other Poems* (1929), the novel *One Way to Heaven* (1932), *The Medea and Some Poems* (1935), two children's books *The Lost Zoo* (1940) and *My Lives*

Countee Cullen in Central Park, New York, 1941. © Library of Congress.

and How I Lost Them (1942), and the posthumously published selection of his best poems *On These I Stand* (1947).

Selected Bibliography Houston A Baker, Jr., *A Many-Colored Coat of Dreams: The Poetry of Countee Cullen* (1974); Blanche E. Ferguson, *Countee Cullen and the Negro Renaissance* (1966); Margaret Perry, *A Bio-Bibliography of Countee Cullen* (1971); Peter Powers, "The Singing Man Who Must Be Reckoned With: Private Desire and Public Responsibility in the Poetry of Countee Cullen," *African American Review* 34 (No. 4, 2000), 661–78; Alan R. Shucard, *Countee Cullen* (1984).

Jerry Ward

Cumming v. Richmond County Board of Education, 175 U.S. 528 (1899)

Cumming was the first case to apply the separate-but-equal doctrine to education, and it demonstrated that separation would be enforced more vigorously than equality. Richmond County, Georgia, maintained separate high schools for whites and blacks. Enrollments in the black primary schools exceeded their capacity. The school board addressed the problem by converting the black high school into an elementary school, thus leaving 60 black high school students without a school to attend. Several black parents went to court seeking a prohibition against operating the white high schools until secondary education was made available to blacks as well. The trial court granted their request but suspended the order until the Georgia Supreme Court could hear the case. The Georgia Supreme Court reversed the decision, and the black parents appealed to the U.S. Supreme Court. A unanimous Supreme Court, speaking through Justice **John Marshall Harlan,** the lone dissenter in **Plessy v. Ferguson,** accepted the county's argument that it could not afford to maintain a high school for black students and rejected the sought-after remedy. Not providing any high school, ruled the Court, was not appropriate because the black students would not benefit. Richmond County continued to provide high schools for whites but not for blacks.

Selected Bibliography Richard Bardolph, ed., *The Civil Rights Record: Black Americans and the Law, 1849–1970* (1970); "Recent Cases," *Yale Law Review* 9 (1900), 235; Mark V. Tushnet, *The NAACP's Legal Strategy Against Segregated Education, 1925–1950* (1987).

Michael S. Mayer

Cuney, Norris Wright (1846, Sunnyside Plantation, near Hempstead, Tex.–1896, Galveston, Tex.). One of the most powerful African American politicians of the post-Reconstruction era, Cuney was one of eight children born to white planter Colonel Philip Cuney and his slave Adeline Stuart. In 1856, Colonel Cuney sent Norris and two brothers to Wylie Street School in Pittsburgh, Pennsylvania. They might have attended Oberlin College, but the Civil War disrupted their financial support. After the war, Norris Cuney settled in Galveston, Texas, where he became interested in politics. In 1870 black carpetbagger George T. Ruby helped secure his appointment as first assistant to the Texas legislature's sergeant-at-arms. Subsequently, Cuney became affiliated with the E.J. Davis wing of the Republican party. His career advanced steadily after that. He was Inspector of Customs, 1872–77; Collector of Customs, 1889–93; Secretary of the Republican State Executive Committee, 1874; delegate to the Republican National Convention, 1896; and Alderman in Galveston, 1881–83. Cuney's rise to power reflected the strength of the black vote, which he was said to control by 1884. Conversely, the lily-white political movement in Texas contributed to his decline.

Selected Bibliography Maud Cuney-Hare, *Norris Wright Cuney: A Tribune of the Black People* (1913, revised 1995); Virginia Neal Hinze, "Norris Wright Cuney" (M.A. thesis, Rice University, 1965); Lawrence Rice, *The Negro in Texas, 1874–1900* (1971).

Judith N. Kerr

Cuney, William Waring (6 May 1906, Washington, D.C.–30 June 1976, Washington, D.C.). This **Harlem Renaissance** poet was the son of Norris Cuney II and Madge Baker Cuney. He attended **Howard University** and Lincoln University, where he became a friend of **Langston Hughes.** He studied music at the New England Conservatory of Music, in Boston, Massachusetts, and at the Conservatory, in Rome, Italy. In 1926, *Opportunity* awarded him first prize for "No Images," a poem capturing the militancy of the Harlem Renaissance. Reflecting the rhythm of urban life, it is his most anthologized work. Cuney authored several poetry collections—*Chain Gang* (1930), *Puzzles* (1960), and *Storefront Church* (1973)—a number of broadsides, and songs. "Southern Exposure" and "Hard Times Blues," for example, were created for balladeer and protest singer Josh White.

Selected Bibliography *Black World* 20 (November 1970), 20–36, 52–58; Arna Bontemps, *The Harlem Renaissance Remembered* (1972); Thudier Harris, ed., *Afro-American Writers from the Harlem Renaissance to 1940* vol. 51 (1986); Linda Metzger et al., *Black Writers: A Selection of Sketches from Contemporary Authors* (1988).

Judith N. Kerr

D

Dahmer, Vernon Ferdinand (10 March 1908, Hattiesburg, Miss.–10 January 1966, Hattiesburg, Miss.). Vernon Dahmer, merchant, farmer, and sawmill owner, was a leading member of the black community in Hattiesburg, Mississippi. By the mid 1960s, commensurate with his local status, Dahmer was taking an active role locally in the civil rights drive. Passage of the **Voting Rights Act of 1965** precipitated problems in previously quiet Forrest County. Dahmer urged blacks to vote; he even offered to pay their **poll taxes.** Not long thereafter, early on the morning of 10 January 1966, Klansmen fire-bombed his home. Family members escaped the blaze that consumed his residence and nearby store while Dahmer fired on the assailants. The 58-year-old Dahmer suffering from facial burns and smoke inhalation, was rushed to the local hospital where he soon died. Speaking from his hospital bed, Dahmer reasoned, "I figure a man needs to do his own thinking." The *Hattiesburg American* condemned the act as "a revolting, cowardly crime." President Lyndon B. Johnson telegraphed his condolences and ordered a federal investigation that resulted in the arrest of 14 Klansmen who were charged with arson and the murder of Vernon Dahmer. In 1998, a Mississippi jury found one of the Klansmen guilty of murder and arson, and he was sentenced to life imprisonment.

Selected Bibliography *Hattiesburg American,* January 10–12, 1966; *Jackson Clarion-Ledger,* January 11, 1966; Sara Bullard, ed., *Free At Last* (1989).

William Warren Rogers, Jr.

Daniel and Kyles v. Paul, **395 U.S. 298 (1969)** The **Civil Rights Act of 1964** banned racial discrimination in a wide range of areas. Under its authority to regulate interstate commerce, Congress, in Title II of the act, specifically prohibited racial bias in public accommodations. Many white businesses, however, sought to evade the act's restrictions by claiming status as private clubs. The Lake Nixon Club, a privately owned recreation center with swimming, boating, dancing, and a snack bar near Little Rock, Arkansas, routinely admitted whites but excluded blacks. The Pauls, the owners of the club, claimed that their establishment was not a public accommodation covered under Title II of the act. The plaintiffs, Daniel and Kyles, maintained that the snack bar that was located on the club's premises brought the recreation center within the coverage of Title II. The Supreme Court agreed with Daniel and Kyles. The fact that the snack bar served both interstate travelers and sold food and drink that had moved in interstate commerce brought the entire Lake Nixon facility within the provisions of Title II. The Court's ruling, consequently, extended the power of the federal government to prevent private discrimination.

Selected Bibliography Derrick Bell, *Race, Racism and American Law* (1980); Alfred H. Kelly and Winfred A. Harbison, *The American Constitution: Its Origins and Development*, 5th ed. (1976).

Phillip A. Gibbs

Daniels, Jonathan Myrick (20 March 1939, Keene, N.H.–20 August 1965, Hayneville, Ala.). After graduating from the Virginia Military Institute in 1961 and studying English for a year at Harvard University on a Woodrow Wilson Fellowship, Jon Daniels entered the Episcopal Theological School in Cambridge, Massachusetts. He joined a dozen others from the theological school who responded to **Martin Luther King, Jr.**'s call for clergy to join a voter registration drive in Selma, Alabama. After the **Selma to Montgomery March,** Daniels continued his Christian witness in Selma under the auspices of the **Episcopal Society for Cultural and Racial Unity.** He lived in the black community, worked in voter registration, integrated the local Episcopal church, and publicized the social services available to blacks. In August Daniels began working with the **Student Nonviolent Coordinating Committee** in adjacent Lowndes County. He was one of two whites arrested with two dozen blacks on 14 August for demonstrating in Fort Deposit. After six days in jail in Hayneville, they were all suddenly released. When Daniels, the Rev. Richard Morrisroe (a white Catholic from Chicago), and two young black women approached a store to buy soft drinks, Tom L. Coleman ordered them away. When Daniels questioned the middle-aged local white man, Coleman shot and killed Daniels instantly, then wounded Morrisroe. Six weeks later an all-white Lowndes jury found Coleman not guilty for reason of self-defense. In 1979 Daniels was honored as one of the 12 representative martyrs listed in Canterbury Cathedral's Chapel of Saints and Martyrs of Our Own Time.

Selected Bibliography Charles W. Eagles, *Outside Agitator: Jon Daniels and the Civil Rights Movement in Alabama* (1993); Marshall Frady, "A Death in Lowndes County," *Southerners: A Journalist's Odyssey* (1980). Jack Mendelsohn, *The Martyrs: Sixteen Who Gave Their Lives for Racial Justice* (1966); William J. Schneider, ed., *The John Daniels Story, with His Letters and Papers* (1967).

Charles W. Eagles

Daniels, Jonathan Worth (26 April 1902, Raleigh, N.C.–6 November 1981, Raleigh, N.C.). Writer and newspaperman, he edited the family paper, the Raleigh *News and Observer* from 1933 to the mid-1960s, except for 1941–48, when his father, Josephus Daniels, resumed control. Partly because of his racial views, Daniels became known as a southern liberal. In the 1930s he advocated equal treatment for blacks but he did not challenge segregation. By the late 1930s he called for equal treatment without regard to race. During World War II, he served as President Franklin D. Roosevelt's assistant in charge of monitoring domestic race relations. In the late 1940s Daniels supported many of President Harry Truman's racial policies, opposed the Dixiecrats, and served on the United Nations Subcommission for the Prevention of Discrimination and the Protection of Minorities. After the ***Brown v. Board of Education*** decision, Daniels advocated compliance through voluntary segregation or "free choice schools," but he also condemned proposals to close the public schools, denounced interposition and massive resistance, and criticized white supremacist groups. Although he opposed **poll taxes,** unequal protection of the law, and discriminatory health care and housing, he preferred moderate, informal compromises instead of disruptive confrontations and demonstrations. He endorsed the **Civil Rights Act of 1964** and the **Voting Rights Act of 1965** but he maintained that economic advancement remained the key to black progress.

Selected Bibliography Jonathan Daniels Papers, Southern Historical Collection, University of North Carolina, Chapel Hill; Charles W. Eagles, *Jonathan Daniels and Race Relations: The Evolution of a Southern Liberal* (1982).

Charles W. Eagles

Davis, Angela (26 January 1944, Birmingham, Ala.–). She was born in a city particularly known for steel and racial violence, in a segregated middle-class neighborhood called "Dynamite Hill," Davis graduated magna cum laude from Brandeis University in 1965 and received her master's and doctoral degrees from the University of California at San Diego several years later. In California she worked with the **Student Nonviolent Coordinating Committee,** the **Black Panthers,** and the **Communist party,** which she joined in 1968.

While completing her dissertation, Davis served as an instructor at the University of California at Los Angeles. The California board of regents declined to renew her contract, and she was dropped from the staff when Federal Bureau of Investigation leaks identified her as a member of the Communist party. UCLA objected to her speeches in support of the Soledad Brothers. In 1970 Davis became involved in an alleged kidnapping attempt of three San Quentin prisoners from the Marin County Civic Center. Accused of planning the incident and supplying the gun that killed four people during the incident, Davis was charged with murder, kidnapping, and conspiracy and eventually was incarcerated. In 1972, however, after 16 months in jail, she was acquitted of the charges, after only 13 hours of deliberations by the jurors.

Davis has since spent much of her time traveling to the Soviet Union and several other Communist countries. In the United States, she lectures on long-range goals that affect blacks and all working people. In 2003 she was a professor at University of California at Santa Cruz.

Selected Bibliography Bettina Aptheker, *The Morning Breaks: The Trial of Angela Davis* (1999); Angela Davis, *Angela Davis: An Autobiography* (1974); *Journal of Blacks in Higher Education* 38 (31 January 2003): 120; Joy James, *The Angela Y. Davis Reader* (1998); Regina Nadelson, *Who Is Angela Davis? The Biography of a Revolutionary* (1972); J. A. Parker, *Angela Davis: The Making of a Revolutionary* (1973).

Linda Reed

Davis, Benjamin O., Sr.   (28 May 1880, Washington, D.C.–26 November 1970, Chicago, Ill.). In 1898 Davis joined the Army and in 1940 he became the first African American promoted to the rank of brigadier general. As a member of the Inspector General's Office during World War II, he grappled with the problems in the United States and Europe caused by segregation and discrimination. Despite Davis's abhorrence of racial separation, his low-key approach led some blacks to charge that he was ineffective and too conciliatory. One of his accomplishments was the partial integration of combat units in Germany and France. Until his retirement in 1948, he continued to act as a military adviser on race relations.

Captain Benjamin O. Davis, Jr., leader of the Tuskegee Airmen, during training at Tuskegee, Alabama, 1942. © Library of Congress.

Selected Bibliography Marvin E. Fletcher, *America's First Black General* (1989); Ulysses Lee, *The Employment of Negro Troops* (1966).

Marvin E. Fletcher

Davis, Benjamin O., Jr. (18 December 1912, Washington, D.C.–4 July 2002, Washington, D.C.). Best known as commanding officer of the famed **Tuskegee Airmen** of World War II, Davis was also the first black West Point graduate of the twentieth century (1936), one of the first four black U.S. military pilots (1942), the first black Air War College graduate (1949), and the first black Air Force general (1954). In 1941 President Roosevelt ordered the Army Air Corps to create an all-black flying unit, of which Davis commanded the 99th Fighter Squadron and later the 332nd Fighter Group. Davis flew combat missions over North Africa, Italy, Romania, the Balkans, France, and Germany. His most important sortie came on 24 March 1945, when the 332nd shot down three jet aircraft during a 1,600-mile round-trip escort mission to Berlin. As squadron and base commander of Lockbourne Army Air Base (Ohio) after World War II, he supported white flying units and supervised hundreds of white civil servants without incident, proving that whites could work under black supervisors. Davis earned his first star in 1954 while director of operations and training for the Far East Air Forces. Davis's most significant postwar position was vice commander, 13th Air Force, where he helped create an air force for the Republic of China. In 1967, after tours in Germany, the Pentagon, and Korea, he commanded the 55,000-strong 13th Air Force headquartered in the Philippines. In 1970, after 33 years of service, Lieutenant-General Davis retired from the U.S. Air Force. Thereafter, as a civilian, he served as director of public safety for the city of Cleveland, Ohio, and later as U.S. director of civil aviation security. In the last position of his extraordinary career, Davis served as assistant secretary for the U.S. Department of Transportation, where he reduced the number of skyjackings from 34 to 0 in two years.

Selected Bibliography Benjamin O. Davis, Jr., *Benjamin O. Davis, Jr., American: An Autobiography* (1991); Alan L. Gropman, "Benjamin Davis, American," *Air Force Magazine* 80 (No. 8, 1997), 70–74; Alan L. Gropman, "General Benjamin O. Davis, Jr.: American Hero," *Air Power History* 46 (No. 2, 1999), 4–15; Alan L. Gropman, "Tuskegee Airmen," *Air Force Magazine* 79 (No. 3, 1996), 52–56; Bernard C. Nalty, *Strength for the Fight: A History of Black Americans in the Military* (1986); National Archives and Record Administration, "WWII Role for Minorities," http://www.nara.gov/exhall/people/newroles.html, Key word search: 99 Fighter Squadron.

David P. Eldridge

***Davis et al. v. Schnell et al.,* 81 F. Supp. 872 (S.D. Ala., 1949)** *Davis v. Schnell* struck down the **Boswell Amendment** to the Alabama state constitution. The 1944 Supreme Court ruling outlawing the **white primary** alarmed many of Alabama's conservative white Democrats. To prevent increased black voter registration, state representative E. C. Boswell in 1946 sponsored a state constitutional amendment to require that voter applicants be able to "understand and explain" any article of the U.S. Constitution. Hunter Davis and other black Mobile residents who had been refused voter registration filed a federal suit against the Mobile County Board of Registrars, including Milton Schnell. The decision in *Davis v. Schnell,* written by District Judge Clarence Mullins, found that the Boswell Amendment gave local boards "arbitrary power to accept or reject any prospective elector." The Mobile registrars had routinely rejected black applicants who could not fulfill the requirements of the Boswell Amendment, but the same requirement was not made of most white applicants. E. J. Gonzales, one of the Mobile registrars, had confirmed this in testimony before the court. The court held that this practice violated the **Fifteenth Amendment,** and it also cited Democratic party propaganda and newspapers editorials published before the general election as proof that the amendment's sponsors, and the voters of Alabama, understood that the purpose of the Boswell Amendment was to limit black suffrage.

Selected Bibliography William D. Barnard, *Dixiecrats and Democrats: Alabama Politics, 1942–1950* (1974); Steven F. Lawson, *Black Ballots: Voting Rights in the South, 1944–1969* (1976); "Recent Cases," *Vanderbilt Law Review* 2 (1949), 696–98.

James L. Baggett

Davis, John P. (1905–12 September 1973, New York, N.Y.). Trained at Harvard Law school, where he knew **Robert C. Weaver, William Henry Hastie,** and **Ralph Johnson Bunche,** Davis was a major spokesperson for black civil rights and black and white working-class alliances during the 1930s and early 1940s. With Weaver, Davis established the Negro Industrial League in 1933 to argue the cause of black workers and farmers before congressional hearings then debating proposed New Deal reform and recovery measures. With financial backing from the **NAACP** and the **Rosenwald Fund,** Davis and Weaver established an umbrella organization of black rights groups called the **Joint Committee on National Recovery,** which sought support for black needs within and outside the Roosevelt administration. After Weaver joined the New Deal, Davis became the joint committee's chief organizer, researcher, and spokesperson.

After the joint committee lost the support of the NAACP and Rosenwald, Davis turned to a grass roots black movement allied with progressive white and labor groups. Following the **Howard University** conference of 1935, organized with Ralph Bunche, which critically assessed the New Deal's impact on the black American, a **National Negro Congress** (NNC) was formed with **A. Philip Randolph** as president and Davis as executive secretary. By constructing a coalition of national and local black groups, left-wing political parties, and organized labor, the NNC hoped to build an independent movement and to force greater social and economic reforms from the New Deal. Davis was never successful in his efforts because the NNC was later dominated by the **Communist party** and certain Congress of Industrial Organization unions and lost the support of both Bunche and Randolph. In the early 1940s, Davis left the NNC and became a political writer for the ***Pittsburgh Courier.*** A tireless organizer, Davis's efforts to build an independent political base for black protest in the 1930s provided an important precedent for the later civil rights struggles.

Selected Bibliography Hilmar Ludvig Jensen, "The Rise of African-American Left: John P. Davis and the National Negro Congress" (Ph.D. diss., Cornell University, 1997); John B. Kirby, *Black Americans in the Roosevelt Era* (1980); John Baxter Streater, "The National Negro Congress" (Ph.D. diss., University of Cincinnati, 1981); Raymond Wolters, *Negroes and the Great Depression* (1970).

John B. Kirby

Davis, [William] Allison (14 October 1902, Washington, D.C.–21 November 1983, Chicago, Ill.). A social anthropologist and psychologist, Davis's most influential work, *Deep South* (1941) was the first comprehensive analysis of caste, class, and race relations in a southern town. A graduate of Williams College and Harvard University, Davis received a Ph.D. from the University of Chicago in 1942, where he was a member of the Department of Education from 1939 until his death. One of the first blacks to become a tenured professor at the university, Davis was named John Dewey Distinguished Service Professor in 1970. Davis was an early critic of the cultural and class biases of IQ tests, arguing that their misinterpretation unfairly limited the educational opportunities for low-income children. He also studied the psychological effects of segregation on blacks. He was a member of the president's **Civil Rights Commission,** 1966–67. A U.S. postage stamp honoring Davis was issued in 1993.

Selected Bibliography Allison Davis, *Leadership, Love, and Aggression* (1983); Allison Davis, *Social-Class Influences upon Learning* (1948); Allison Davis and John Dollard, *The Children of Bondage: The Personality Development of Negro Youth in the Urban South* (1940); St. Clair Drake, "In the Mirror of Black Scholarship: W. Allison Davis and *Deep South,*" *Harvard Educational Review* 2 (1974), 42–54.

Francille Rusan Wilson

Deacons for Defense and Justice Based in Louisiana, the Deacons for Defense advocated self-defense in the face of white supremacist aggression and violence. Over the vehement objections of **Martin Luther King, Jr.,** the Deacons were an armed presence during the 1966 **James Meredith March.** At the invitation of the **Student Nonviolent Coordinating Committee** and the **Congress of Racial Equality,** armed Deacons patrolled the sides of the highway along which demonstrators were to pass, making certain that no snipers were in hiding. Fashioned as a vigilante organization, the Deacons sought to protect themselves and other African Americans because they believed that southern law enforcement neither could nor would do that on their behalf.

Selected Bibliography Clayborne Carson, *In Struggle: SNCC and the Black Awakening in the 1960s* (1981); Lance E. Hill, "The Deacons for Defense and Justice: Armed Self-Defense and the Civil Rights Movement" (Ph.D. diss., Tulane University, 1997); Gray L. LaSimba, *The Deacons for Defense and Justice: Defenders for the African American Community in Bogolusa, Louisiana during the 1960's* (2000); Christopher B. Strain, "We Walked Like Men: The Deacons for Defense and Justice," *Louisiana History* 38 (1997), 43–62.

Marshall Hyatt

Dees, Morris Seligman, Jr.   (16 December 1936, Shorter, Ala.–). Born and raised in Shorter, Alabama, Morris Dees, Jr., was the son of a farmer, who according to Dees shaped his desire for justice. He gained his undergraduate and law degrees from the University of Alabama. While Dees was in college, he started a successful mail order business, and in 1966, he was named one of the Ten Outstanding Men in America. Dees became a major civil rights attorney in 1968, victorious in the *Smith v. Montgomery YMCA* case in 1969. This case desegregated the Montgomery YMCAs. Two years later, Dees and attorney Joseph Levin, Jr., created the **Southern Poverty Law Center** (SPLC), a nonprofit organization committed to justice and eradicating race, class, and gender bias in the American justice system. Dees founded Klanwatch to monitor Klan activity and filed law suits against Klan members who violated an individual's civil rights. In 1987, Dees obtained a life sentence verdict for Klansman Frank Cox's brutal 1983 lynching of Michael Donald, and there was monetary compensation for the victim's family, thus bankrupting the Klan.

Selected Bibliography Morris Dees, Jr., with Steve Fiffer, *A Season for Justice: The Life and Times of Civil Rights Lawyer Morris Dees* (1991); Southern Poverty Law Center Web site: www.splcenter.org.

David Canton

De Facto Segregation   This term refers to segregation that existed without the sanction of law. Constitutional provisions and laws in the South required segregation, and this legal segregation was called de jure segregation. In the North, segregation existed even though there were no laws requiring it and often in spite of civil rights laws prohibiting discrimination and inequality of treatment. De facto segregation resulted from custom, policies of real estate firms, actions of school officials and school boards, governmental policies, and the actions of private persons and groups. Civil rights organizations often found it more difficult to fight segregation in the North than in the South. The **Congress of Racial Equality** began as a movement to end segregation in the North. Long legal battles led to court decisions outlawing racially restrictive covenants in housing, and civil rights groups urged changes in those federal housing policies that promoted segregated housing developments. The most bitter struggle was the continuing one to end de facto segregation in schools. This campaign received stimulation from the 1961 ruling of a federal district court in a case involving segregation in the schools of New Rochelle, New York. The judge held that segregation resulting from the action of school boards was as unconstitutional as that resulting from laws creating a dual school system.

Selected Bibliography Richard Bardolph, ed. *The Civil Rights Record: Black Americans and the Law, 1849–1970* (1970); John Hope Franklin and Alfred A. Moss, Jr., eds., *From Slavery to Freedom: A History of Negro Americans*, 8th ed. (2000); Gunnar Myrdal, *An American Dilemma: The Negro Problem and Modern Democracy* (1944).

Arvarh E. Strickland

Delany, Martin Robinson   (6 May 1812, Charles Town, Va.–January 1885, Wilberforce, Ohio). Born in what is now West Virginia, Martin R. Delany became an advocate for black self-reliance and uplift through education, skilled labor, property ownership, and entrepreneurship. He championed the cause of black freedom and equality as an abolitionist, a journalist, a Union Army major and recruiter of black troops during the Civil War, and as an important member of the Republican party in South Carolina Reconstruction politics. Best known for his claim that African Americans constituted "a nation within a nation," he advocated the establishment of an African American nation in Africa as the cornerstone for the freedom and elevation of black people. Although the masses of black people never adopted his elitist ideas for racial uplift and his campaign for African immigration, future generations used Delany's philosophies as the foundation for the contemporary black nationalist ideology.

Selected Bibliography Tunde Adeleke, "Black Biography in the Service of a Revolution: Martin R. Delany in Afro-American Historiography" *Biography* 17 (No. 3, 1994), 248–67; Martin R. Delany, *The Condition, Elevation, Emigration, and Destiny of the Colored People of the United States* (1852); Cyril E. Griffith, *The African Dream: Martin R. Delany and the Emergence of Pan-African Thought* (1975); Robert S. Levine, *Martin Delany, Frederick Douglass, and the Politics of Representative Identity* (1997); Floyd J. Miller, *The Search for a Black Nationality: Black Emigration and Colonization, 1787–1863* (1975); Wilson J. Moses, *The Golden Age of Black Nationalism 1850–1925* (1978); Nell Irvin Painter, "Martin R. Delany: Elitism and Black Nationalism," in Leon Litwack and August Meier, eds., *Black Leaders of the Nineteenth Century*, (1988); Frank A. Rollin, *Life and Public Services of Martin R. Delany* (1883); Victor Ullman, *Martin R. Delany: The Beginnings of Black Nationalism* (1971).

Lillie Johnson Edwards

"Deliberate Speed"   When the Supreme Court ruled segregation unconstitutional in **Brown v. Board of Education** on 17 May 1954, it did not order immediate relief. On 31 May 1955, the Court handed down its ruling on implementation, known as **Brown II.** In that decision, the Supreme Court remanded the cases to the lower courts with instructions that school districts "make a prompt and reasonable start toward full compliance with our May 17, 1954 ruling" and that the lower courts "enter such orders and decrees consistent with this opinion as are necessary and proper to admit to public schools on a racially nondiscriminatory basis with all deliberate speed the parties to these cases." The phrase *all deliberate speed* was added at Felix Frankfurter's suggestion; its origin remains obscure. Southerners took the phrase as an invitation to obstruction, and it became the basis for a generation of litigation.

Selected Bibliography Daniel M. Berman, *It Is So Ordered* (1966); Alexander Bickel, "Integration, the Second Year in Perspective," *New Republic*, 8 October 1956; Jack Greenberg, *Race Relations and American Law* (1959); Dennis J. Hutchinson, "Unanimity and Desegregation: Decision Making and the Supreme Court, 1948–1958," *Georgetown Law Journal* 68 (1979), 1; Richard Kluger, *Simple Justice: The History of Brown versus Board of Education and America's Struggle for Equality* (1976).

Michael S. Mayer

Delta Ministry An outgrowth of the National Council of Churches' involvement in the **Freedom Summer of 1964** in Mississippi, the Delta Ministry was organized in September 1964 with the dual goals of reconciling the black and white communities and ameliorating economic, health, and social conditions among Mississippi blacks. The Delta Ministry established community centers for day care, recreation, and education; provided health education in hygiene, nutrition, first-aid, and other areas through local health committees; created programs for literacy, vocational training, and liberal arts studies; instituted workshops to teach basic constitutional rights and to train black political candidates; and organized community **Head Start** programs and government surplus food distributions despite state government opposition. The Ministry supported striking plantation workers, organized picketers against companies guilty of job discrimination, and filed allegations of non-compliance with antidiscrimination clauses against plants with government contracts. An object of controversy during its 20-year existence, the Delta Ministry is an example of the mobilization of the liberal church in support of civil rights; it was the first civil rights or church project in the United States to receive funds from foreign countries as a foreign mission.

Selected Bibliography Eric D. Blanchard, "The Delta Ministry," *The Christian Century* (17 March 1965), 337–38; Bruce Hilton, *The Delta Ministry* (1969); Henry J. Pratt, *The Liberalization of American Protestantism: A Case Study in Complex Organizations* (1972); Mary Aickin Rothschild, *A Case of Black and White: Northern Volunteers and the Southern Freedom Summers, 1964–65* (1982); Wilmina Rowland, "How It Is in Mississippi," *The Christian Century* (17 March 1965), 340–42.

Carole Shelton

Dennis, David (17 October 1940, Omega, La.–). A sharecropper's son, Dennis joined the New Orleans **Congress of Racial Equality** (CORE) in 1960 while attending Dillard University. He immediately began to organize new CORE chapters and projects in Louisiana. As CORE representative in Mississippi, he was instrumental in the founding of the **Council of Federated Organizations** (COFO), along with **Aaron Henry** of the Mississippi **NAACP, James Forman** of the Student Nonviolent Coordinating Committee (SNCC) national office, and **Robert Moses** of the Mississippi SNCC. Setting up a CORE chapter in Canton, Mississippi, Dennis worked to organize demonstrations there and to help launch the Mississippi Freedom Democratic Party's challenge to the regular state Democrats in 1964. In September 1964, he became CORE's Southern Regional Office program director. In 2002, he participated in the American Civil Rights Educational Services, Inc. (ACRES) travel study expedition for students to Civil Rights sites in the South.

Selected Bibliography Taylor Branch, *Parting the Waters: America in the King Years, 1954–1963* (1988); James Forman, *The Making of Black Revolutionaries* (1985); August Meier and Elliott Rudwick, *CORE: A Study in the Civil Rights Movement, 1942–1968* (1973); New York *Amsterdam News*, 25 September 2002; Web site: http://core-online.org.

Ray Branch

Department of Racial and Cultural Relations, National Council of Churches Organized in 1949 as the Council's successor to its Commission on Race Relations, the Department of Racial and Cultural Relations under director J. Oscar Lee was primarily involved in mobilization for civil rights legislation. In January 1963, working with Catholic and Jewish organizations, it helped to sponsor the National Conference on Religion and Race, which issued the "Appeal to the Conscience of the American People" on the eradication of racism. When its educational philosophy proved to be too slow to deal with political events, it gave way in strategy to the Commission on Religion and Race, which eventually superseded it and went on to develop such projects as the **Delta Ministry.**

Selected Bibliography James F. Findlay, Jr., *Church People in the Struggle: The National Council of Churches and the Black Freedom Movement, 1950–1970* (1993); Henry J. Pratt, *The Liberalization of American Protestantism* (1972); Mark Silk, *Spiritual Politics: Religion and America since World War II* (1988).

Ray Branch

DePriest, Oscar Stanton (9 March 1871, Florence, Ala.–12 May 1951, Chicago, Ill.). The first African American elected to Congress during the twentieth century and the first ever elected from outside the South, Oscar De Priest championed equal protection of law, especially in employment. Like many he represented, De Priest made his way from southern rural poverty to northern urban opportunity during the **Great Migration.** His parents moved from his native Florence, Alabama, to Salina, Kansas, when he was seven years old. He attended public schools and completed a business curriculum at the Salina Normal School. At 17 he moved to Dayton, Ohio, and then to Chicago, Illinois, where he worked his way up to become a successful real estate agent and a controversial, longtime Republican party ward boss. He served as Cook County commissioner (1904–8) and in 1915 he became Chicago's first black member of the city council, where he served until 1917 and again from 1943 to 1947. In 1929 he entered the U.S. House of Representatives, where he pressed for blacks to have their share of federal jobs, appointed blacks to the U.S. Military Academy at West Point and the U.S. Naval Academy at Annapolis, and pushed for a federal antilynching bill. He was unseated by black Democrat **Arthur W. Mitchell** in 1934.

Selected Bibliography *Biographical Directory of the American Congress, 1774–1971* (1971); Maurine Christopher, *America's Black Congressmen* (1971); Thomas J. Davis, "Oscar Stanton De Priest" *Encyclopedia USA* (1991); Harold F. Gosnell, *Negro Politicians: The Rise of Negro Politics in Chicago* (1935); Rayford W. Logan and Michael F. Winston, eds., *Dictionary of American Negro Biography* (1982); Obituary, *New York Times*, 13 May 1951.

Thomas J. Davis

Derrington v. Plummer, 240 F.2d 922 (5th Cir 1957) After the **Civil Rights Cases** of 1883, and before the **Civil Rights Act of 1964,** the equal protection clause of the **Fourteenth Amendment** provided limited protection against the discriminatory acts of private individuals. In *Derrington* the **United**

States Court of Appeals for the Fifth Judicial Circuit provided reasoning that allowed the invocation of constitutional protections in cases where the state and the private discriminator were engaged in close mutually beneficial relationships.

Harris County, Texas, had built a court with a basement specifically designed for use as a cafeteria. The county leased the cafeteria to Derrington, who agreed to keep the facilities open whenever the courthouse was open, paid the county a percentage of his gross sales, and promised to give county employees a discount on their food. Derrington routinely refused to serve blacks in the cafeteria "solely because they were negroes." A group of blacks sued in federal court, claiming that they had been denied equal protection of the law. The county and Derrington argued that the Fourteenth Amendment only prohibited discrimination that arose from state action and that the cafeteria restrictions constituted permissible, individual action.

The court of appeals ruled that Derrington could not constitutionally discriminate against blacks; the majority opinion reasoned that the cafeteria had been built with county funds and therefore was serving county purposes. When state purposes are served through the "instrumentality of a lessee," the court explained, the lessee "stands in the place of the County." As a result, "[h]is conduct is as much state action as would be the conduct of the County itself." The *Derrington* rationale provided constitutional protection in those situations in which an individual and the state maintained a close symbiotic relationship and in which the private individual was acting in the interest of the state.

Selected Bibliography Charles Black, "Forward: 'State Action,' Equal Protection, and California's Proposition 14," *Harvard Law Review* 80 (1967), 69–109; William W. Van Alstyne, "Mr. Justice Black, Constitutional Review and the Talisman of State Action," *Duke Law Journal* (1965), 219–47.

Kenneth DeVille

Detroit Race Riot (1943)　　The worst riot to take place during World War II began in Detroit, Michigan, on June 20 and raged for 48 hours; its toll in lives and property set national records. The Detroit outbreak manifested black-white strains wrought by historical, perennial, and, most significant, wartime circumstances. A heritage of interracial violence plagued the city, as did employment discrimination and slum conditions that confined most blacks to the eastside ghetto, known as Paradise Valley. Two hundred thousand immigrants of both races, particularly from the South, compounded the usual antagonisms. The competition and rising expectations clashed several times, primarily in the spring of 1943 when thirty-five thousand black newcomers joined black natives in their "Double V" protest for democratic victories at home and abroad.

The riot began on Belle Isle, spread quickly to the ghetto, and then reached the city's major thoroughfare, Woodward Avenue. At Belle Isle Park, black youth harassed white picnickers who, with the aid of numerous sailors, fought back. Rumors of the fight incited Paradise Valley residents to attack white bypassers and policemen and loot white-owned stores. Soon whites along Woodward Avenue began to beat black citizens and laid siege to the black community (which police repulsed). The Belle Isle and Woodward Avenue clashes were typical of interracial combat or communal riots of earlier eras. Whites fought with police support to uphold the very system challenged by blacks; indeed, Detroit police killed 17 blacks but no whites. The Paradise Valley destruction resulted from the anger and frustration of blacks, who struck at the symbols of their degradation and whites who lived beyond the riot zone. Both races employed violence as protest.

Signaling the decline of communal racial outbursts and the emergence of commodity uprisings, the Detroit riot pointed to shifting patterns of racial disorder and future conflicts whenever whites seemed to block opportunities and blacks sensed the failure of nonviolent strategies. It also resulted in the creation of the Mayor's Interracial Committee, which evolved into the first permanent municipal body designed to ease tensions and promote civil rights. Unfortunately, these efforts fell short in Detroit—and elsewhere—and large-scale rioting recurred in the 1960s.

Selected Bibliography Dominic J. Capeci, Jr., and Martha Wilkerson, *Layered Violence: The Detroit Rioters of 1943* (1991); Dominic J. Capeci, Jr., *Race Relations in Wartime Detroit: The Sojourner Truth Housing Controversy of 1942* (1984); Robert Shogan and Thomas Craig, *The Detroit Race Riot: A Study in Violence* (1964, 1976); Alfred M. Lee and Norman D. Humphrey, *Race Riot* (1943, 1968); Harvard Sitkoff, "The Detroit Race Riot of 1943," *Michigan History* 53 (Fall 1969), 183–206; Marilynn S. Johnson, "Gender, Race and Rumors: Reexamining the 1943 Race Riots," *Gender and History* 10 (August 1998), 252–77.

Dominic J. Capeci, Jr.

Detroit Race Riot (1967)   On 23 July 1967, the Detroit, Michigan, police raided an afterhours club on Twelfth Street in the center of the African American ghetto. The club was crowded with celebrants, and it took the police longer than usual to clear the premises of the revelers and to arrest them. Onlookers threw bottles and broke out the windows of the police vehicle. The riot that erupted that Sunday morning lasted until the following Thursday. Of the 59 urban riots that occurred in 1967, the one in Detroit took the most lives, 43 people, mostly blacks shot by the National Guard, and caused the most property damage. Most white Americans were shocked by the Detroit riot. Mayor Jerome P. Cavanagh, a Democrat, had instituted model programs in urban renewal and in poverty programs. Nevertheless, tensions between the black community and the police had been increasing, exacerbated by a recall petition led by conservatives to remove Cavanagh from office for his alleged failure to fight crime. When the tensions exploded into a riot, Republican Governor George Romney sent in the National Guard, but the 700 guards, 200 state police, and 600 Detroit police could not restore order. President Lyndon B. Johnson reluctantly ordered into Detroit, on July 25, 4,700 troops of the elite 82nd and 101st Airborne units. Some Republicans

Gutted buildings and a burning service station attest to the destruction caused by two days of rioting in Detroit's West Side, 1967. © Bettmann/CORBIS.

criticized Johnson, asserting that he had delayed sending in troops to embarrass Romney, a potential Republican nominee for the presidency. Republicans, including Barry Goldwater, Ronald Reagan, and Richard M. Nixon, cited the riot as an example not only of the lawlessness sweeping the nation because of the refusal of Democrats to be tough on crime but also of a planned insurrection caused by radicals. Johnson denied vehemently all charges. His position has been supported by most historians and by the **Kerner Commission** (National Advisory Commission on Civil Disorders), which blamed "white racism" and emphasized needed social reform as the alternative to violence.

Selected Bibliography Sidney Fine, *Violence in the Model City: The Cavanagh Administration, Race Relations, and the Detroit Riot of 1967* (1989); Godfrey Hodgson, *America in Our Time* (1976); *New York Times*, 24, 25, 30 July 1967; Harvard Sitkoff, *The Struggle for Black Equality, 1954–1980* (1981).

Robert A. Calvert

Diallo, Amadou   (2 September 1975–4 February 1999, New York, N.Y.). Amadou Diallo was a young West African immigrant who worked as a street vendor in lower Manhattan. On 4 February 1999, four plainclothes New York City police officers, members of a special crime unit established to reduce violent crimes, approached Diallo for questioning as he stood in the entrance to his Bronx apartment building. Thinking he was reaching for a gun, the officers shot 41 bullets at Diallo, hitting him 19 times. He actually had been reaching for his wallet. The officers testified that Diallo fit the general description of a serial rapist who had been active in the neighborhood a year earlier. In early

2000, the policemen were brought to trial in Albany and cleared of all charges by a jury of four blacks and eight whites. The U.S. Justice Department reviewed the shootings and concluded that federal civil rights charges against the four officers were not warranted. The incident reinforced already existing perceptions that the New York Police Department's aggressive police tactics violated basic rights. Many residents remembered the recent police assault on Abner Louima, an innocent Haitian immigrant who had been sexually tortured with a broom handle by a city police officer. The killing of Diallo led to antipolice demonstrations and ultimately to the reorganization of the street crime unit. Throughout the country, a number of similar high-profile incidents had damaged relations between police departments and the mostly minority communities that they serve. Civil rights leaders complained that police officers conducting traffic stops were unfairly singling out blacks and Hispanics. In June 1999, in response to the growing concerns over such **racial profiling,** President Clinton ordered federal law enforcement agencies to gather statistics from their arrests and detentions as a means of tracking the practice, but he rejected calls for a ban on it.

Selected Bibliography Attorney General Eric H. Holder, Statement Regarding the Closing of the Amadou Diallo Case, 31 January 2001, www.usdoj.gov; *Houston Chronicle,* 5 April 1999, 6 October 2000, 9 February 2001; *New York Times,* 13, 14, 15, 23 February, 9, 30 March, 10, 28 June 1999, 26, 27 February 2000, 12, 13, 14, 16, 18 April, 8 May, 27 September 2001; *Newsweek,* 5 April, 7 June 1999, 13 March 2000; *Washington Post,* 13, 16 February, 16, 23, 25, 26, 30 March 1999, 31 January, 26 February, 25 March, 17 June 27 August 2000, 1 February 2000.

Horace D. Nash

Diggs, Charles C., Jr. (2 December 1922, Detroit, Mich.–24 August 1998, Washington, D.C.). The youngest member of the Michigan State Senate from 1951 to 1954, he became the first African American elected to represent Michigan in the U.S. Congress. Elected 12 times in Detroit's 13th Congressional District, he became a powerful and respected congressman. He and 12 others founded the **Congressional Black Caucus** in 1971; he became chairman of the House Committee on the District of Columbia in 1973; he was instrumental in winning home rule for the capital city; and he rose to the chairmanship of the House of Representatives' Subcommittee on African Affairs. After 30 years in public office, his career was interrupted in 1978 when a federal grand jury charged him with using taxpayers' money for personal, business, and office expenses. Censured by the House in July 1979, he resigned in 1980. He later opened a funeral home in Maryland, returning to his original career. He is buried in Detroit, Michigan.

Selected Bibliography Lenore Cooley, *Ralph Nader Congress Project Citizens Look at Congress: Charles Diggs Jr.* (1972); *Detroit Free Press,* 16 May 1976; *The Detroit News Magazine,* 22 July 1979; Carolyn P. Du Bois, *The Untold Story of Charles Diggs: The Public Figure, the Private Man* (1999).

Clarence Hooker

Direct Action Ordinarily associated with the nonviolent ideology espoused by **Martin Luther King, Jr.,** direct action actually predated his rise to civil rights leadership. Early protests against segregation in the federal civil service, the **"Don't Buy Where You Can't Work"** movement in the depression decade, and the **Congress of Racial Equality**'s desegregation activities in the 1940s all utilized direct action. The sit-ins of 1960, modeled after similar protests by industrial workers in the 1930s, also employed nonviolent, public demonstration tactics and initiated many new and creative ways of combatting segregation and discrimination. It was King, however, who strove to adapt direct action protest to the changing realities of American racism and eventually fashioned that philosophy into creative tension.

Selected Bibliography Kenneth B. Clark, "The Civil Rights Movement: Momentum and Organization," in Talcott Parsons and Kenneth B. Clark, eds., *The Negro American* (1966); Adam Fairclough, *To Redeem the Soul of America: The Southern Christian Leadership Conference and Martin Luther King, Jr.* (1987); James Farmer, *Lay Bare the Heart: The Autobiography of the Civil Rights Movement* (1985); David J. Garrow, *Bearing the Cross: Martin Luther King, Jr., and the Southern Christian Leadership Conference* (1986); Martin Luther King, Jr., *Stride toward Freedom: The Montgomery Story* (1958); Martin Luther King, Jr., *Why We Can't Wait* (1963).

Marshall Hyatt

District of Columbia v. John R. Thompson Co., 346 U.S. 100 (1953) This case upheld the validity of Washington, D.C.'s "lost" antidiscrimination laws that were passed during Reconstruction. Although they had not been enforced for years, these laws required that restaurants, bars, and similar establishments serve all "respectable, well-behaved" persons and sell to them "at their usual prices." In 1950, Washington's Board of Commissioners brought suit against a segregated cafeteria owned by the John R. Thompson Restaurant Company. Municipal Judge Frank Myers decided that the laws had been repealed "by implication" and quashed the case. The following year, the Municipal Court of Appeals reversed Myers's ruling on the law regarding prices but upheld his position on the law requiring service. The U.S. Court of Appeals for the District of Columbia voted to overturn the Municipal Court of Appeals and affirm Myers's decision. Throughout the course of the case, President Harry Truman's attorneys general had declined to become involved. With the case pending before the Supreme Court, the Eisenhower administration filed an amicus brief arguing for the validity of the so-called lost laws. Attorney General Herbert Brownell argued the case himself. On 8 June 1953, the Supreme Court unanimously sustained the validity of both Reconstruction era ordinances.

Selected Bibliography Robert Frederick Burk, *The Eisenhower Administration and Black Civil Rights* (1984); Constance McLaughlin Green, *The Secret City* (1967); Michael S. Mayer, "The Eisenhower Administration and the Desegregation of Washington, D.C.," *Journal of Policy History* 3 (January 1991), 24–41.

Michael S. Mayer

Doar, John M. (3 December 1921, Minneapolis, Minn.–). A Republican and a graduate of Princeton University and the law school at the University of California, Berkeley, in 1960 Doar became an attorney and in 1965 assistant attorney general in the **Civil Rights Section, Justice Department**. He gained the respect of civil rights protesters as a trial lawyer and troubleshooter in the South. Following the murder of **Medgar W. Evers** in Jackson, Mississippi, in 1963, Doar helped calm a tense confrontation between angry blacks and hostile whites at the funeral of the civil rights leader. Despite his close association with civil rights workers, Doar maintained that the federal government lacked the constitutional authority to protect them from racist intimidation. He preferred to rely on negotiation and cooperation with state and local officials to obtain compliance with federal law. However, in the face of violent, criminal wrongdoing, he brought federal prosecutions against the murderers of civil rights activists in Mississippi and Alabama. Combining conciliation with pressure, he helped enforce the **Voting Rights Act of 1965,** which enfranchised a majority of southern blacks. From 1967 to 1973, he served as Director of the Bedford-Stuyvesant Development and Service Corporation in Brooklyn. From 1973 through 1974, Doar served as Special Counsel to the U.S. House of Representatives Judiciary Committee during the Richard Nixon Watergate deliberation. In 1979, he founded the law firm of Doar Pieck and Mark in New York City in which he remained in practice in 2003.

Selected Bibliography Michal Belknap, *Federal Law and Southern Order: Racial Violence and Constitutional Conflict in the Post-Brown South* (1987); John Doar, "Civil Rights and Self-Government," in Dona Baron, ed., *The National Purpose Reconsidered* (1978); Steven F. Lawson, *In Pursuit of Power: Southern Blacks and Electoral Politics, 1965–1982* (1985); Victor Navasky, *Kennedy Justice* (1971).

Steven F. Lawson

"Don't Buy Where You Can't Work" Movement Prominent in the black political revival of the 1930s were numerous organized boycotts and picketing of any white owned businesses within black communities that had refused to hire black employees. By the early 1930s, what became known as "Don't Buy Where You Can't Work" campaigns existed in many cities. First begun in Chicago, Illinois, in late 1929, the Chicago "Don't Buy" movement had the support of the black newspaper, the *Chicago Whip*, the local **NAACP,** and black church groups. Successful in breaking the color line in a number of local industries and securing white collar jobs for some blacks, the Chicago campaign spread during the early 1930s to New York, Washington, D.C., Cleveland, and Los Angeles, as well as to smaller communities like Evansville, Indiana, and Alliance, Ohio. By the time the movement died out during the war, some thirty-five cities had experienced it. Despite their mixed impact, the "Don't Buy Where You Can't Work" movements sharpened black political consciousness and reflected the ability of blacks to build indigenous grass roots organizations seeking economic and social equality. Many of the struggles of the 1940s and later drew from the efforts of these campaigns.

Selected Bibliography Ralph J. Bunche, "The Programs, Ideologies, Tactics, and Achievements of Negro Betterment and Interracial Organizations," (unpublished ms. for Carnegie-Myrdal Study, 1940); Cheryl Lynn Greenburg, *Or Does It Explode? Black Harlem in the Great Depression* (1991);

The boycotts of the 1960s and 1970s were inspired by the same spirit of the earlier "Don't Buy Where You Can't Work" Movement. © Charles H. Ramberg Collection; Courtesy of Mississippi Department of Archives and History.

Larry Greene, "Harlem in the Great Depression: 1928–1936" (Ph.D. diss., Columbia University, 1979); Gary Hunter, "'Don't Buy Where You Can't Work': Black Urban Boycott Movements During the Depression, 1919–1941" (Ph.D. diss., University of Michigan, 1977).

John B. Kirby

Douglas, Aaron (26 May 1898, Topeka, Kans.–2 February 1979, Nashville, Tenn.). The murals of Aaron Douglas, one of the best known painters of the **Harlem Renaissance,** revealed an awakened interest in black life. Following his graduation from the University of Kansas, he came under the tutelage of Winold Reiss, who influenced many black painters of the period. Douglas painted murals for the New York Public Library and **Fisk University,** where he later served on the faculty. He became well known for his illustrations in black periodicals and magazines in addition to his work for such black authors as **James Weldon Johnson, Langston Hughes,** and **Alain Leroy Locke.**

Selected Bibliography Richard Bardolph, *The Negro Vanguard* (1958); Bruce Keller, ed. *The Harlem Renaissance* (1984); Amy H. Kirsch, *Aaron Douglas: Art, Race, and the Harlem Renaissance* (1995).

Michael S. Downs

Douglass, Frederick (February 1818, Tuckahoe, Md.–20 February 1895, Anacostia, Washington, D.C.). Born a slave, probably of white paternity, Douglass learned to read and write as a hired ship's caulker in Baltimore, Maryland. He escaped to the North in 1838 and settled in New Bedford, Massachusetts, where he became an agent and orator for the Massachusetts Anti-Slavery Society. During the 1840s, he published his *Narrative of the Life of Frederick Douglass* (the first of three autobiographies), spoke at numerous abolitionist rallies, and traveled to England. In 1847, he moved to Rochester, New York, and brought out the *North Star*, wielding his pen, as he put it, against the evils of slavery. His remarkable abilities as an orator and writer pushed him to the forefront among reform leaders during the antebellum period. He favored women's rights, temperance, better working conditions, and the abolition of slavery. Following the passage of the Fugitive Slave Act of 1850 (giving slave catchers the authority to journey north and secure fugitives), Douglass wrote that the best remedy for the law was a "good revolver, a steady hand, and a determination to shoot down any man attempting to kidnap." In 1852 he gave his support to the Free Soil party, and four years later,

Frederick Douglass, lithograph. © Library of Congress.

to the newly formed Republican party. Although espousing standard middle-class values—industry, thrift, honesty, and sobriety—Douglass, called "the father of the civil rights movement," opposed unceasingly all forms of racial discrimination. Following the Civil War, he urged President Andrew Johnson to extend the franchise to freedmen, advocated equal rights as the editor of the *New National Era,* a weekly newspaper, and spoke against convict lease, the crop-lien system, the practice of lynching, and anti-Negro rulings of the Supreme Court. After moving to Washington, D.C., in 1872, he continued his strong support for the Republican party and served in patronage positions both as marshal (1877–81) and recorder of deeds (1881–86) for the District of Columbia. Later, he served as minister-resident and consul-general to the Republic of Haiti, and charge d'affaires for the Dominican Republic. During the 1870s and 1880s, he continued to speak out and write on the issues of the day, but he was criticized by some blacks when, in 1884, two years after the death of his wife, he married a white woman, Helen Pitts. While some of his postwar stances might be considered conservative—supporting a proposed annexation of Santo Domingo in 1871 and opposing the black "Exodus" from the South in 1879—Douglass never vacillated from his belief that black Americans should be accorded equal civil and political rights. Only then, he said, would America begin to solve its "color problem."

Selected Bibliography John W. Blassingame, ed., *The Frederick Douglass Papers* (1979); Eric Foner, *Frederick Douglass* (1964); Frederic Holland, *Frederick Douglass: The Orator* (1891); William S. McFeely, *Frederick Douglass* (1991); Waldo E. Martin, Jr., *The Mind of Frederick Douglass* (1984); Michael Meyer, ed., *Frederick Douglass: The Narrative and Selected Writings* (1984); Benjamin Quarles, *Frederick Douglass* (1948).

Loren Schweninger

Dowell v. School Board of Oklahoma City Public Schools, 244 F. Supp. 971 (W.D. Okla., 1965)

Dowell v. School Board of Oklahoma City Public Schools, a class action suit, was filed in federal district court in 1963 by A. L. Dowell on behalf of his son Robert L. Dowell and other black Oklahoma City school children. It challenged the school board's policy of allowing white students to transfer from schools that were predominantly black to schools that were predominantly white. The U.S. District Court ruled in July 1963 that the student transfer policy was unconstitutional and ordered the school board to submit an integration plan within 90 days.

Before ruling on the school board's new integration plan in January 1964, the court appointed three educational experts to study the Oklahoma City schools. Based on this panel's report, the court ordered the school board to submit another integration plan by 30 October 1965. The court ruled that the system of "neighborhood" schools proposed by the board would perpetuate racial segregation, and it outlined measures that the new plan must include. Certain segregated schools within the city were to be combined and teachers transferred to achieve faculty integration. The student transfer policy had to be standardized and revised so that black students could transfer from predominantly black to predominantly white schools. The court retained jurisdiction to issue "additional orders which may become necessary" to "complete desegregation."

Selected Bibliography Richard Bardolph, ed., *The Civil Rights Record: Black Americans and the Law, 1849–1970* (1970); Thomas I. Emerson, David Haber, and Norman Dorsen, *Political and Civil Rights in the United States* (1967); Leon Jones II, *From Brown to Boston: Desegregation in Education* (1979).

James L. Baggett

Drake, St. Clair (2 January 1911, Suffolk, Va.–14 June 1990, Palo Alto, Calif.). A distinguished scholar and author of several books and articles in professional journals on topics in African and Pan-African studies, urban anthropology, and race relations theory, Drake received numerous honors and honorary degrees, awards, and fellowships, including being named an Honorary Fellow of the Royal Anthropological Society of Great Britain and Ireland. He taught at Dillard University in New Orleans, Louisiana (1935–36), Roosevelt University in Chicago, Illinois (1946–68), the University of Liberia (1954), the University of Ghana (1958–61), and Stanford University (1969–76). An activist for interracial harmony and economic justice, Drake advocated nonviolent approaches to social change and he refused to serve in the segregated armed forces during World War II.

Selected Bibliography George Clement Bond, "A Social Portrait of John Gibbs St. Clair Drake: An American Anthropologist," *American Ethnologist* 15 (November 1988), 762–81; St. Clair Drake, *Black Folk Here and There: An Essay in History and Anthropology* (1987); St. Clair Drake, *The Redemption of Africa and Black Religion* (1970); St. Clair Drake, "Value Systems, Social Structure and Race Relations in the British Isles" (Ph.D. diss., University of Chicago, 1954); St. Clair Drake and Horace R. Clayton, *Black Metropolis: A Study of Negro Life in a Northern City* (1945); St. Clair Drake (with George Shepperson), "The Fifth Pan-African Conference, 1945, and the All African Peoples Congress, 1958," *Contributions in Black Studies: A Journal of African and Afro-American Studies* 8 (1986–87), 35–66; *New York Times*, 21 June 1990.

Gloria Waite

Drew, Charles Richard (3 June 1904, Washington, D.C.–1 April 1950, Haw River, N.C.). Charles R. Drew, a researcher in the use of blood plasma, was educated at Amherst College (B.A., 1926), McGill Medical College (M.D., 1933), and Columbia University Medical School (M.D.Sc., 1940). He was the first black person in the United States to earn the Doctor of Science degree. His professional positions included assistant professor of surgery, **Howard University** School of Medicine (1940), medical director of "Blood for Britain Project" (1940), director of the American Red Cross Blood Bank (1941), assistant director of blood procurement for the National Research Council (1941), professor and chairman, Department of Surgery, Howard University School of Medicine (1941–50), and medical director, Freedman's Hospital (1944–50). Believing that excellence of performance would transcend racial bias, Dr. Drew focused his energies on training and educating black medical students, interns and residents in general surgery. He was honored for his work with the **Spingarn Medal** (1944), a fellowship in the International College of Surgeons (1946), and two honorary Doctor of Science degrees (1945 from Virginia State College and 1947 from Amherst College).

Selected Bibliography Claude H. Organ, Jr., and Margaret M. Kosiba, *A Century of Black Surgeons: The U.S.A. Experience*, vol. 1 (1987); Spencie Love, *One Blood: The Death and Resurrection of Charles R. Drew* (1996); Harold Wade, Jr., *Black Men of Amherst* (1976); Charles E. Wynes, *Charles Richard Drew: The Man and the Myth* (1988).

Robert A. Bellinger

Du Bois, William Edward Burghardt (23 February 1868, Great Barrington, Mass.–27 August 1963, Accra, Ghana). W.E.B. Du Bois dedicated his life to the struggle for race advancement by using research and scholarship as tools of propaganda to elevate the African American's political status. His writings were a brilliant articulation of black protest in the twentieth century. Educated in the public schools of Great Barrington, Massachusetts, he received baccalaureate degrees from **Fisk University** and Harvard University and, in 1896, a doctorate from Harvard. After teaching at Wilberforce University in Ohio from 1894 to 1896, Du Bois became an instructor at the University of Pennsylvania where he produced the first sociological study of an African American community. Du Bois spent 13 years conducting similar research at Atlanta University and produced a series of 16 monographs. In 1903 Du Bois compiled 14 essays into a book entitled *The Souls of Black Folk.* In a prophetic voice, he defined "the color line" as the problem of the twentieth century and he created the metaphors of the "veil" and "double consciousness" to describe the political and cultural dilemma of being black in America. Du Bois promoted a black nationalist platform of racial unity, leadership by the black elite, which he called "The Talented Tenth," and full participation of African Americans in American society. In one particular essay Du Bois courageously challenged **Booker T. Washington**'s accommodationist strategies and his platform of vocational education. He told blacks that, in order to achieve social justice, they must demand their rights insistently and continuously, using a college education to gain the wisdom and knowledge to serve the race. Having alienated Washington, Du Bois left Atlanta University in order to protect the institution from Washington's retaliation. In 1909, Du Bois became one of the founders of the **National Association for the Advancement of Colored People** (NAACP). From 1910 to 1934 he served as editor of the *Crisis,* the official publication of the NAACP. *Crisis* gave him a national audience to campaign for the rights of African Americans and to protest against racial discrimination in the United States and throughout the colonial worlds of Africa, Asia, and South America. Du Bois's message was not only political, it was also cultural. In *Crisis* and in the children's publication *The Brownies' Book,* Du Bois educated the public about African culture, promoted African American artists, and proclaimed that **"Black Is Beautiful."** In 1934, Du Bois resigned from *Crisis* and the NAACP to chair the Department of Sociology at

W.E.B. Du Bois in the 1920s. © Library of Congress.

Atlanta University for the next 11 years. After a brief return to the NAACP as a consultant from 1945 to 1948, Du Bois left the organization for the last time. His perception of the world had changed. In his search for the most appropriate political philosophy for the liberation of African American people and all other oppressed peoples, Du Bois came into conflict with many of the policies of the NAACP. An early prophet of the **Pan-African movement,** Du Bois helped to organize five Pan-African Congresses from 1919 to 1945. Though he demanded full participation of blacks in American society, Du Bois also called for racial unity. In 1911 he had joined the Socialist party and in 1961 he joined the **Communist Party.** In a final act of Pan-Africanism and black nationalism, Du Bois emigrated to Ghana, where he died in 1963 at the age of 95. Having championed social justice for seven decades, Du Bois, by the time of his death, had incorporated into his thinking, the full range of black political and social thought and strategies.

Selected Bibliography Francis L. Broderick, *W.E.B. Du Bois: Negro Leader in Time of Crisis* (1959); W.E.B. Du Bois, *The Autobiography of W.E.B. Du Bois,* (1968); W.E.B. Du Bois, *Black Reconstruction* (1935); W.E.B. Du Bois, *Darkwater* (1920); W.E.B. Du Bois, *Dusk of Dawn,* (1940); W.E.B. Du Bois, *The Philadelphia Negro* (1899);W.E.B. Du Bois, *The Souls of Black Folk* (1903); W.E.B. Du Bois, *The Suppression of the Slave Trade to the United States of America* (1896); David Levering Lewis, *W.E.B. Du Bois: Biography of a Race 1868–1919* (1993); David Levering Lewis, *W.E.B. Du Bois: The Fight for Equality and the American Century* (2000); W. Manning Marable, *W.E.B. Du Bois* (1986); Arnold Rampersad, *The Art and Imagination of W.E.B. Du Bois*

(1976); Elliott M. Rudwick, *W.E.B. Du Bois: A Study in Minority Group Leadership* (1960); Elliott M. Rudwick, *W.E.B. Du Bois: Propagandist of the Negro Protest* (1969).

Lillie Johnson Edwards

Dunbar, Paul Laurence   (27 June 1872, Dayton, Ohio–9 February 1906, Dayton, Ohio). An African American poet, novelist, and journalist, Dunbar was the son of ex-slaves. Born in Dayton, Ohio, in 1827, he was educated in the city's public schools. Dunbar's service as editor-in-chief of the *High School Times*, as president of the literary society, and as the class poet early indicated his literary interest. Publication of his first poem in the *Dayton Herald* when he was just 16 years old formally signaled the beginning of a prolific literary career. In 1893 *Oak and Ivy*, Dunbar's first full length volume of poetry, was published. An 1896 review of Dunbar's *Majors and Minors* written by William Dean Howells praised Dunbar's gift for writing dialect and brought him to the attention of American literati. Dunbar's *Lyrics of a Lowly Life* (1898), published in New York and England brought him international fame. In 1898 his first novel, *The Uncalled*, appeared in *Lippincott's* and in book form. While highly praised for his poetry, Dunbar also published four novels and numerous articles in his later years. **Booker T. Washington** called him "The Poet Laureate of the Negro People." His legacy to American literature is a rich body of prose and poetry that reflect the African American experience in American culture.

Selected Bibliography Addison Gayle, *Oak and Ivy: A Biography of Paul Lawrence Dunbar* (1971); Jay Martin, ed., *Centenary Conference on Paul Laurence Dunbar* (1972); Jay Martin and Gossie H. Hudson, eds., *The Paul Laurence Dunbar Reader: A Selection of the Best of Paul Laurence Dunbar's Poetry and Prose* (1975).

Brenda M. Brock

Durham, North Carolina, Sit-Ins   (1957–64). North Carolina's introduction to the sit-in technique came in Durham in August 1957 when the Reverend Douglas E. Moore of Asbury Temple, accompanied by a few students from North Carolina College, asked for service at the white section of the Royal Ice Cream Company store. The group sat down and was arrested for trespassing. No further attempts were made until 1960 when the **NAACP** chapter at North Carolina College, led by Lacy Streeter, Callis Brown, and other students from Durham Business College, Bull City Barber College, DeShazor's Beauty College, and Hillside High School, moved against segregated lunch counters, movie theaters, recreational facilities, and the bus station. Inspired by visits from **Martin Luther King, Jr., Ralph David Abernathy,** and **Roy Wilkins,** and with the support of the Ministerial Alliance and of students and professors from other local colleges, the sit-ins made progress toward integrating retail services in Durham. By 1962 a local chapter of the **Congress of Racial Equality** (CORE), organized by longtime participant and advisor **Floyd B. McKissick,** joined in the effort. Additional visits by Roy Wilkins, **James Farmer,** and Jim Peck served to rally the cause. In one sit-in on 12 August

1962, four thousand people participated, seven hundred of whom were arrested. On the night of Mayor Wense Grabarek's election on 18 May, 1963, protesters held a rally followed by a march through the city and sit-ins at six eating places. The NAACP and CORE announced that 30 days of mass demonstrations would begin on 20 May. Mayor Grabarek met with the protesters at Saint Joseph A.M.E. Church and set up the Durham Interim Committee (DIC). Two of its 11 members were black. Grabarek met repeatedly with McKissick, the students, and the restaurant owners, and the combined efforts were productive. Although sit-ins would continue in a few places until 1964, relative peace was achieved. The DIC was later replaced by the biracial Committee on Community Relations. Grievances and racial confrontations continued to the end of the decade, but bolder and more strident attention-getting methods replaced the sit-ins.

Selected Bibliography Jean Bradley Anderson, *A History of Durham County, North Carolina* (1990); *Durham Morning Herald,* 5, 17, 23 February, 1 March, 7, 12 May 1960, 2, 17 January, 1961, 15 March, 10, 19 April, 31 July, 13, 20 August 1962, 19, 20, 22, 24 May, 5, 9 June 1963.

Charles A. Risher

Durr, Clifford J. (2 March 1899, Montgomery, Ala.–12 May 1975, Montgomery, Ala.). Educated at the University of Alabama and Oxford University, where he was a Rhodes Scholar, Durr earned a degree in jurisprudence from Oxford in 1922 and returned to his native Montgomery to practice law. In 1933 he went to Washington, D.C., to assume the position of assistant general counsel of the Reconstruction Finance Corporation. For almost two decades he continued in government service, holding a number of positions in New Deal agencies, including a stint as the Federal Communications Commissioner. An able administrator of liberal political persuasion who was related by marriage to Supreme Court Justice Hugo Black, he was an outspoken champion of civil liberties. He declined reappointment to the Federal Communications Commission in 1948 because he would not support President Harry Truman's Cold War loyalty program, some of whose early victims he represented. His defense of these innocent people during the McCarthy era isolated him from mainstream politics, and he returned in 1951 to Montgomery to resume his private practice of the law.

He soon found himself again isolated from mainstream politics, ostracized by Montgomery's white society because of his defense of another group of hapless citizens victimized by unjust laws and oppressive political authority—the black community. In the early 1950s Montgomery's long-suffering black citizens were, unwittingly, about to launch the civil rights revolution. When **Rosa Parks** challenged segregation on the city's buses and precipitated the 1955–56 **Montgomery bus boycott** that thrust **Martin Luther King, Jr.,** onto the national stage, Clifford Durr and his wife, **Virginia Foster Durr,** were among a mere handful of white Alabama liberals who stood unflinchingly with the blacks in their struggle for freedom. Durr was confidante and counsel to

Montgomery's black leaders, especially **Edgar Daniel Nixon;** and he quietly worked with a young black attorney, Fred Gray, to prepare a solid legal challenge to segregated public transportation. Success came in late 1956 with the *Browder v. Gayle* decision that ended segregated busing. His championship of civil rights cost Durr most of his white Montgomery clients, but he never reckoned personal cost when human dignity, individual rights, and equal justice under the law were at issue.

Selected Bibliography Taylor Branch, *Parting the Waters, America in the King Years, 1954–1963* (1988); Sarah Hart Brown, *Standing Against Dragons: Three Southern Lawyers in an Era of Fear* (1998); Virginia Foster Durr, *Outside the Magic Circle: The Autobiography of Virginia Foster Durr,* ed. Hollinger F. Barnard with a foreword by Studs Terkel (1985); Obituary, *New York Times,* 13 May 1975; John A. Salmond, *Conscience of a Lawyer: Clifford J. Durr and American Civil Liberties, 1899–1975* (1990); Harvard Sitkoff, *The Struggle for Black Equality, 1954–1980* (1981); J. Mills Thornton III, "Challenge and Response in the Montgomery Bus Boycott of 1955–1956," *The Alabama Review* 33 (July 1980), 163–235.

Charles D. Lowery

Durr, Virginia Foster   (6 August 1903, Birmingham, Ala.–24 February 1999, Carlisle, Pa.). A civil rights activist for many years, Virginia Foster Durr did relief work during the Great Depression. After her husband, **Clifford J. Durr,** accepted a job with the Roosevelt administration, she lobbied in Washington, D.C., against the **poll tax** and later took part in Henry Wallace's presidential campaign. In 1951 the family moved to Montgomery, Alabama, where she worked with integrated women's groups and the **Southern Regional Council,** while Clifford Durr practiced law. The Durrs became friends with **Edgar Daniel Nixon, Ralph David Abernathy,** and **Rosa Parks;** Nixon and Clifford Durr secured Parks's release from jail after she was arrested in 1955. Virginia Durr supported the **Montgomery bus boycott** by organizing car pools for black workers. The Durrs were scorned and ostracized by many other whites, yet they continued to support the civil rights movement after the boycott ended. Virginia Durr's memoir, *Outside the Magic Circle,* which recounts these experiences in rich detail, is filled with insights on family, gender, and southern culture.

Selected Bibliography Virginia Foster Durr, *Outside the Magic Circle: The Autobiography of Virginia Foster Durr,* ed. Hollinger F. Barnard with a foreword by Studs Terkel (1985); David J. Garrow, ed., *The Montgomery Bus Boycott and the Women Who Started It: The Memoir of Jo Ann Gibson Robinson* (1987); J. Mills Thornton III, "Challenge and Response in the Montgomery Bus Boycott of 1955–1956," *The Alabama Review* 33 (July 1980), 163–235.

Joan E. Cashin

Dyer Antilynching Bill   A humanitarian measure introduced in the House of Representatives in 1919 by Republican Leonidas D. Dyer of Missouri to stop mob **lynchings** in the United States, most of which were committed in the South against African Americans. The bill called for the levying of harsh penalties against state and local government officials who willfully refused to protect the accused from mob violence. The bill garnered the support of the **NAACP** and sparked the emergence of the **Antilynching Crusaders,** headed by Mary B. Talbert. The Crusaders launched a campaign to raise $1 million to fund prosecutions of lynchers, but managed to raise only $70,000. The bill passed the House of Representatives only to be defeated in 1922 in the Senate by a southern filibuster. Despite its failure, the Dyer Bill influenced later anti-lynching legislation, and thus played an important role in raising awareness about the need for federal enforcement of African American civil rights.

Selected Bibliography W. Fitzhugh Brundage, *Under Sentence of Death: Lynching in the South* (1997); Donald L. Grant *The Anti-Lynching Movement, 1883–1932* (1975); Robert Zangrando, *The NAACP Crusade against Lynching, 1909–1950* (1980).

Thomas Adams Upchurch

E

East St. Louis Race Riot (1917). East St. Louis, Illinois, an industrial satellite of St. Louis, was, in 1917, a city of about seventy-five thousand with a long history of labor strife, inept political leadership, poor living conditions, and widespread corruption. The World War I **Great Migration** from the South brought migrants to the city in search of jobs and created a climate of fear and prejudice among white residents, especially industrial workers. On 1 July, two police detectives were killed, probably by blacks who mistook them for marauders who had been shooting into black homes. Convinced that black "armies" were mobilizing for a race war, white mobs formed the next morning and rampaged through the city, indiscriminately beating and killing black residents on the streets and in their homes. Police and militiamen did little to stop the carnage. The official death toll of 39 blacks and 9 whites made East St. Louis the deadliest urban race riot of the twentieth century. Only a few white rioters were prosecuted or convicted and city officials did little to correct the conditions that had led to the riot. Nationally, there were numerous protests, and a congressional committee conducted an investigation. Historians attribute the riot to the economic insecurity of the city's white workers, which led to exaggerated fears of black competition for jobs, and to the political corruption and mismanagement that had bred disrespect for the law.

Selected Bibliography Elliot Rudwick, *Race Riot at East St. Louis: July 2, 1917* (1964); U.S. House of Representatives, "Report of the Special Committee Authorized by Congress to Investigate the East St. Louis Riots" (1918).

Allan H. Spear

Ebony   *Ebony* magazine was founded by the young black entrepreneur, John H. Johnson, just after World War II. Johnson wanted a magazine that would reflect the unknown contributions and achievements of African Americans. The magazine, although it had a decidedly middle-class bent and was in many ways modeled after *Life* magazine, was a major source of information about the civil rights movement. One feature was its annual August special issue devoted to a theme of particular interest to the black community at that moment. One such issue of the early 1960s focused on the civil rights movement. *Ebony* continues to explore various facets of that movement and has remained a major black publication.

   Selected Bibliography Taylor Branch, *Parting the Waters: America during the King Years, 1954–63* (1989); *Ebony* (August 1963); John H. Johnson, *Succeeding against the Odds* (1989); Web site: www.ebony.com.

Charles T. Pete Banner-Haley

Edwards, Harry   (22 November 1924, St. Louis, Mo.–). An African American sociologist and sports activist who had conducted seminal research on black participation in American sports, Harry Edwards is best known as the force behind an attempted boycott by black track and field athletes in the 1968 Olympic Games in Mexico because of South Africa's participation. It was during these games that two African American medal winners gave the **Black Power** salute while the national anthem was being played. Edwards saw the "revolt of black athletes [as] the newest phase of the black liberation movement in America." Edwards has served as the chairman of the Olympic Committee for Human Rights and an advisor to Major League Baseball. Longtime professor of sociology at the University of California at Berkeley, in 2000 Edwards became Director of Parks and Recreation for the City of Oakland.

   Selected Bibliography Joan Martin Burke, *A CBS News Reference Book: Civil Rights, A Current Guide to the People, Organizations, and Events* (1974); Harry Edwards, *The Revolt of the Black Athlete* (1969); Harry Edwards, "The Athlete as a Role Model," *Sport,* 1 November 1994; Oakland *Post,* 17 May 2000; *Who's Who among Black Americans 1990–1991* (1990).

Nancy E. Fitch

Edwards v. South Carolina, 372 U.S. 229 (1963)   In the spring of 1961, James Edwards, Jr., along with almost two hundred other African American high school and college students, marched to the South Carolina State House in Columbia to protest against segregation and racial discrimination. The protesters carried placards to publicize their grievances and marched in an orderly fashion on the public sidewalks surrounding the State House. When a crowd of onlookers gathered to watch, the police ordered the protesters to disperse. The students responded by singing patriotic and religious songs, clapping their hands and stomping their feet. They were arrested and convicted of breaching the peace in violation of South Carolina law.

   The U.S. Supreme Court overturned the protesters' convictions, finding that the students were within their First Amendment rights of free speech, free assembly, and freedom to petition against grievances in their peaceful demonstration. The Supreme Court did not find any evidence that would support

Edwards's conviction and declared that the states could not subvert the principles of liberty found in the First Amendment by criminally prosecuting individuals peacefully expressing their political views.

Selected Bibliography Richard Bardolph, ed., *The Civil Rights Record, Black Americans and the Law, 1849–1970* (1970); Derrick A. Bell, Jr., *Race, Racism and American Law* (1980); Loren Miller, *The Petitioners, the Story of the Supreme Court of the United States and the Negro* (1966); George Rossman, ed., "Review of Recent Supreme Court Decisions," *American Bar Association Journal* 49 (1963), 1494–95.

Steve Sadowsky

Elaine, Arkansas, Race Riot (1919)   Blacks protesting the traditional pattern of economic exploitation by white landlords organized tenant cotton farmers into The Organization of the Progressive Farmers' and Household Union of America. This occurrence led to rumors in Elaine that blacks were plotting an uprising to slaughter a large number of whites in the county. Allegations concerning the planning of the presumed uprising brought sheriff's deputies to investigate proceedings at a Union meeting at Hoop Spur on the night of 1 October 1919. Gunfire erupted and fighting spread to a 50-mile radius. At least 2 persons died and many were injured. An investigation ordered by the governor incorrectly found "a mature plan of insurrection" by the Union and 21 white men marked for death. In a kangaroo-court-like atmosphere, some 50 blacks were found guilty of second degree murder and 10 received 21-year terms in the state penitentiary. Eleven blacks received 1-year terms for night-riding, and 12 were sentenced to die. These sentences were overturned by the Supreme Court in 1924.

Selected Bibliography Robert H. Brisbane, *The Black Vanguard: Origins of the Negro Social Revolution, 1900–1960* (1970); J. W. Butts and Dorothy James, "The Underlying Causes of the Elaine Riot of 1919," *Arkansas Historical Quarterly* 20 (Spring 1961), 95–104; Richard C. Cortner, *A Mob Intent on Death: The NAACP and the Arkansas Riot Cases* (1988); Ralph H. Desmarais, "Military Intelligence Reports on Arkansas Riots: 1919–1920," *Arkansas Historical Quarterly* 33 (Summer 1974), 175–91; O. A. Rogers, Jr., "The Elaine Race Riots of 1919," *Arkansas Historical Quarterly* 19 (Summer 1960), 142–50; Lee E. Williams II and Lee E. Williams, Sr., *Anatomy of Four Race Riots* (1972).

Lee E. Williams, II

Ellison, Ralph   (1 March 1914, Oklahoma City, Okla.–16 April 1994, New York, N.Y.). In his fiction, essays, and reviews, Ellison insists upon the necessity of coming to grips with the multiethnic composition of American society and seeking to be tolerant of differences in a highly diversified culture. "Our pluralistic democracy," Ellison said in a 1979 address at Brown University, "is a difficult system under which to live, our guarantees of freedom notwithstanding. Socially and politically we have yet to feel at ease with our principles, and on the level of culture no one group has managed to create the definitive American style." After completing high school in Oklahoma where one of his teachers was the former black West Point cadet, **Johnson C. Whittaker,** Ellison studied music for three years (1933–36) at **Tuskegee Institute,** a model for the college portrayed in his novel *Invisible Man*. He then moved to New York with the intention of becoming a musician. There he met **Richard Wright** and **Langston Hughes,** both of whom encouraged Ellison to develop his writing talents. After 1937, Ellison wrote reviews and short stories for such magazines as *New Masses, Tomorrow, Partisan Review,* and *Common Ground.* He worked on the Federal Writers Project from 1938 to 1942. Ellison received a Rosenwald Fellowship in 1945 and published *Invisible Man* in 1952. This book, now recognized as the most distinguished novel published between 1945 and 1965, won the National Book Award (1953), the Russwurm Award, and the National Newspaper Publishers' Award. In it Ellison deals with the phenomenon of invisibility, the failure of the dominant American society to see or to understand the humanity of black Americans. Through the adventures of the nameless hero, Ellison sketches the racial rituals of American civilization in tragicomic detail: education about the Negro's "place" in the South, the duplicity involved in accommodationist postures, militant rebellion and black nationalism, and Marxist attempts to create a black proletarian advance guard in the class struggle. Indeed, *Invisible Man* might be considered a fictional companion to Gunnar Myrdal's classic study of race problems, **An American Dilemma** (1944). In his two collections of essays, *Shadow and Act* (1964) and *Going to the Territory* (1988), Ellison has written brilliantly about literature, music, and American culture. His ideas about race and civil rights are succinctly summarized in the closing of his essay "Perspective of Literature" (1976): "The great writers of the nineteenth century and the best of the twentieth have always reminded us that the business of being an American is an arduous task, as Henry James said, and it requires constant attention to our consciousness and to our conscientiousness. The law ensures the conditions, the stage upon which we act; the rest of it is up to the individual." After his death Ellison's widow arranged to have material taken from a two-thousand-page manuscript for the 1999 publication of another novel, *Juneteenth*.

Selected Bibliography Mark Busby, *Ralph Ellison* (1991); Ralph Ellison, *Juneteenth* (1999); John Hersey, ed., *Ralph Ellison: A Collection of Critical Essays* (1974); Richard H. King, "The Uncreated Conscience of My Race/The Uncreated Features of His Face: The Strange Career of Ralph Ellison," *Journal of American Studies* [Great Britain] 34 (2000), 303–10; Robert List, *Daedalus in Harlem: The Joyce-Ellison Connection* (1982); Robert O'Meally, *The Craft of Ralph Ellison* (1980); Albert Murray, John F. Callahan, and Ralph Waldo Ellison, *Trading Twelves : The Selected Letters of Ralph Ellison and Albert Murray* (2000); John Reilly, ed., *Twentieth Century Interpretations of Invisible Man* (1970); Philip M. Richards, "Juneteenth and Ralph Ellison's Impact on American Literature," *Journal of Blacks in Higher Education* 25 (31 October 1999), 129; Gregory Stephen, *On Racial Frontiers: The New Culture of Frederick Douglass, Ralph Ellison, and Bob Marley* (1999); Jerry Gafio Watts, *Heroism and the Black Intellectual: Ralph Ellison, Politics, and Afro-American Intellectual Life* (1994).

Jerry Ward

Emancipation Proclamation   Issued by President Abraham Lincoln on 1 January 1863, the Emancipation Proclamation freed all slaves in areas still in rebellion. The proclamation, promulgated after considerable pressure by radicals and designed to make foreign recognition of the Confederacy difficult, was the President's way of dealing with a formidable problem. A minority executive personally committed to freedom but held back by constitutional limitations and the necessity of keeping the border states loyal, he also had to consider the

The first reading of the Emancipation Proclamation by Abraham Lincoln before his cabinet c. 1866. Mezzotint after a painting. © Library of Congress.

Democrats' opposition to abolition. He solved the dilemma by giving the insurgents a chance to return to their proper allegiance before freeing the slaves only in rebellious territory. In June and July 1862 Lincoln, who, while signing two **Confiscation Acts** and the bill freeing the blacks in the District of Columbia, had vetoed individual generals' attempts at emancipation, wrote his proclamation of freedom. He presented the document to the Cabinet on 22 July, but upon William H. Seward's advice, he delayed its publication pending some Union victory. The Battle of Antietam provided him with the success he needed, and on 22 September Lincoln issued the Preliminary Emancipation Proclamation announcing his intention of freeing all slaves in places that had not returned to their allegiance within the following three months. In spite of pressure to desist, he promulgated the final document on 1 January 1863. Clearly indicating that he was acting in his capacity as commander-in-chief of the army in times of actual armed rebellion and ending with a felicitous conclusion suggested by Salmon P. Chase, the president declared free all slaves in areas still in rebellion and invited blacks to enlist in the armed forces. Tennessee and part of Louisiana and Virginia were specifically exempted, so that on the day of issue only a few slaves in the Department of the South were legally affected by the document. As time went on, however, and as more and more territory fell to the Union, the proclamation became effective in the rest of the Confederacy. Although it was not the sweeping measure advocated by the radicals, it nevertheless signaled the end of slavery in the United States.

Selected Bibliography John Hope Franklin, *The Emancipation Proclamation* (1963); Howard Jones, *Abraham Lincoln and a New Birth of Freedom: The Union and Slavery in the Diplomacy of the Civil War* (1999); Hans L. Trefousse, *Lincoln's Decision for Emancipation* (1975).

Hans L. Trefousse

Enforcement Acts In order to protect black rights under the **Fourteenth** and **Fifteenth Amendments,** and more specifically to break up the Ku Klux Klan, Congress passed a series of three Enforcement Acts. The acts of 31 May 1870 and 20 April 1871 were quite similar; they define a number of crimes and provide punishments for these crimes. Among the crimes defined are intimidating or hindering voters, failing to do one's duty as an election officer, and "going in disguise upon the public highway" with intent to deny a citizen his constitutional rights. Punishments ranged as high as 10 years' imprisonment and a fine of $5,000. The Enforcement Act of 28 February 1871 provided for federal supervision of elections in northern and southern cities with a population of more than 20,000.

Federal prosecutors won some notable victories under the Enforcement Acts. In South Carolina over 1,500 and in northern Mississippi about 1,070 indictments were found. On the other hand, 85 percent of the cases in South Carolina were dismissed before trial. In northern Mississippi, the conviction rate was a respectable 55 percent, yet the federal judge's mild sentencing provided little deterrence to further violations. Overall, these laws led to the breakup of the Ku Klux Klan, but black voting had nevertheless become rare in the South by 1900.

Selected Bibliography Stephen Cresswell, "Enforcing the Enforcement Acts: the Department of Justice in Northern Mississippi, 1870–1890," *Journal of Southern History* 53 (1987), 421–40; Everette Swinney, "Enforcing the Fifteenth Amendment, 1870–1877," *Journal of Southern History* 27 (1962), 202–18.

Stephen Cresswell

Episcopal Society for Cultural and Racial Unity An unofficial church organization founded in 1959 at St. Augustine's College in Raleigh, North Carolina, the Episcopal Society for Cultural and Racial Unity (ESCRU) both participated in the civil rights movement and tried to reform the church. From 1959 to 1967, Rev. John B. Morris served as executive director of ESCRU, which had a membership of about five thousand. In its first year, ESCRU supported the sit-ins and opposed bars to interracial marriage. In September 1961 it staged an interracial Prayer Pilgrimage by bus from New Orleans, Louisiana, to the General Convention in Detroit, Michigan, which led to arrests in Mississippi and demonstrations at the University of the South. ESCRU opposed segregation throughout the country, from a church hospital in Brooklyn, New York, to Lovett School in Atlanta, Georgia, and it participated in the **March on Washington** and the **Selma to Montgomery March.** In 1966 ESCRU charged the Episcopal Church with racism in clergy assignments, education, and investments. Affected by the **Black Power** movement and torn by disagreements between liberals and radicals over its objectives, ESCRU in 1967–68 decided to commit its "primary attention to combating white racism." Internal dissension, declining membership, and a lack of funds led to its demise in November 1970.

Selected Bibliography John L. Kater, Jr., "The Episcopal Society for Cultural and Racial Unity and Its Role in the Episcopal Church, 1959–1970" (Ph.D. diss., McGill University, 1973); Papers of the Episcopal Society for Cultural and Racial Unity, the Martin Luther King, Jr., Center for Nonviolent Social Change, Atlanta, Georgia; Gardiner H. Shattuck, *Episcopalians and Race: Civil War to Civil Rights* (2000); David E. Summer, "The Episcopal Church's Involvement in Civil Rights: 1943–1973" (S.T.M. thesis, University of the South, 1983).

Charles W. Eagles

Equal Employment Opportunity Act of 1972 Passage of the Equal Employment Opportunity Act of 1972 on 8 March 1972 represented both the culmination of a seven-year drive by civil rights groups to provide enforcement powers for the **Equal Employment Opportunity Commission** (EEOC) and a legislative victory for the Nixon administration. The EEOC had been stripped of direct enforcement powers during Senate debate over passage of the **Civil Rights Act of 1964,** and the compromise version of Title VII, which created the new agency, allowed only the attorney general to file pattern-or-practice suits against discriminating employers in cases in which EEOC mediation had failed. Between 1965 and 1968, President Lyndon B. Johnson failed to persuade Congress to grant cease-and-desist authority to the EEOC. In 1969, the Nixon administration countered with its own bill that would deny cease-and-desist authority but would allow the EEOC to file suit against discriminating employers. Committee hearings and debate on EEOC enforcement bills continued in stalemate throughout the period from 1969 to 1971. In 1972 the Republican president and the Democratic Congress compromised on a bill that established a presidentially appointed EEOC counsel authorized to bring suit in federal court and extended Title VII coverage to state and local government and educational institutions. The EEOC subsequently filed class action suits that won large awards for minorities and women in numerical requirements for hiring and promotion, back pay, and damages for past discrimination.

Selected Bibliography Alfred W. Blumrosen, *Black Employment and the Law* (1971); Hugh Davis Graham, *The Civil Rights Era* (1990); U.S. Equal Employment Opportunity Commission, *A History of the Equal Employment Opportunity Commission, 1965–1984* (1984).

Elizabeth Kight

Equal Employment Opportunity Commission The Equal Employment Opportunity Commission (EEOC) was established through Section 705 of the **Civil Rights Act of 1964** and was charged with enforcing the provisions of Title VII of that act. The 1964 law provided for a bipartisan commission composed of five members appointed by the president for staggered five-year terms. The commission is staffed by over three thousand employees in its Washington, D.C., headquarters and regional offices. The EEOC enforces nondiscrimination by private employers, unions, and employment agencies (excluding federal contractors, who are regulated by the **Office of Federal Contract Compliance Programs**). The powers available to the EEOC to accomplish Title VII compliance represent compromises reached after heated battles in Congress and constraints placed upon it by Supreme Court decisions. In its first seven years, the EEOC lacked the authority to compel employers to conform, but instead relied on investigation and conciliation to achieve voluntary compliance with Title VII. Unlike the antidiscrimination commissions that were created by legislation in most of the nonsouthern states following World War II, the EEOC was denied "cease and desist" powers. The **Equal Employment Opportunity Act of 1972** added educational institutions and government agencies to the commission's coverage, and gave the EEOC the authority to bring class action suits. Jurisdiction was further expanded by the Age Discrimination in Employment Act and Amendments (1974, 1978), and the Fair Labor Standards Act Amendments of 1974. In 1978 Chairperson **Eleanor Holmes Norton** executed major reorganization to increase efficiency. Clarence Thomas, who chaired the EEOC during the Reagan administration, criticized the agency for pursuing **affirmative action** quotas. It is still in operation. Its thrust since 1992 has been enforcing the American Disability Act (ADA), although it held hearings on the Florida vote in the disputed 2000 presidential election.

Selected Bibliography Norman C. Amaker, *Civil Rights and the Reagan Administration* (1988); Hugh Davis Graham, *The Civil Rights Era* (1990); Kathanne W. Greene, *Affirmative Action and Principles of Justice* (1989); U.S. Equal Employment Opportunity Commission, *A History of the Equal Employment Opportunity Commission, 1965–1984* (1984); Web site: www.eeoc.gov/.

Michele M. Hall

Espy, Alphonso Michael (30 November 1953, Yazoo City, Miss.–). Mike Espy graduated from Howard University and the University of Santa Clara Law School, and in 1987 became the first African American elected to Congress from Mississippi since Reconstruction. In 1993, he joined President Bill Clinton's cabinet, becoming the first African American to serve as U.S. Secretary of Agriculture. In 1994 the Office of Independent Counsel investigated allegations that Espy had accepted $35 thousand worth of gifts from companies seeking favors from the U.S. Department of Agriculture, resulting in an indictment on 35 counts. In 1998, Espy was acquitted on all counts, but there were 15 other convictions and $11 million in fines for others implicated in the scandal. In 2003, Espy was an attorney in Jackson, Mississippi.

Selected Bibliography *Biographical Directory of the United States Congress, 1789–1989* (1989); John Hope Franklin and Alfred E. Moss, Jr., *From Slavery to Freedom: A History of African Americans*, 8th ed. (2000); Shirelle Phelps, ed., *Who's Who among African Americans*, 10th ed. (1999); Mark Rozelle and Clyde Wilcox, eds., *The Clinton Scandal and the Future of American Government* (2000); *U.S. News Online*, 14 December 1998.

Thomas Adams Upchurch

Europe, James Reese (22 February 1881, Mobile, Ala.–9 May 1919, Boston, Mass.). James Reese Europe was at the center of American music from 1910 to 1919. He formed one of the first black musicians' unions, the Clef Club, in April 1910. The Clef Club bands were among the first black bands to make recordings. From 1913 to 1915 Europe provided the music and many of the dances for Vernon and Irene Castle. As a member of the U.S. Army he was responsible for organizing and conducting the 369th Division "Hellfighters" band. Known as "the best damned brass band in the United States Army," it introduced the music of black Americans to the world. Europe was instrumental in the development of orchestral jazz and was a major force in countering the return of white minstrelsy to the American stage.

Selected Bibliography Reid Badger, "The Conquests of Europe: The Remarkable Career of James Reese Europe," in *Alabama Heritage* 1 (Summer 1986), 34–49; Reid Badger, *Life in Ragtime: A Biography of James Rose Europe* (1995); Robert Kimball and William Bolcom, *Reminiscing with Sissle and Blake* (1973); Eileen Southern, *Biographical Dictionary of Afro-American and African Musicians* (1982); Eileen Southern, *The Music of Black Americans: A History* (1971).

Robert A. Bellinger

***Evans v. Newton,* 382 U.S. 296 (1966)**   Under the terms of the 1911 will of Senator Augustus Bacon, the city of Macon, Georgia, was appointed the trustee of a privately owned park that was to be reserved for whites only. When the city failed to keep the park racially segregated, members of the park's board of managers sued to remove the city as trustee and return the park to private trustees who would enforce racial segregation and exclusion in accordance with Senator Bacon's will. Macon's African American citizens sought to block the return of the park to private trustees who would exclude them.

The U.S. Supreme Court ruled that, although the park was privately owned, the city had operated and managed it in such a way that the equal protection clause of the **Fourteenth Amendment** applied. Under the Fourteenth Amendment, the city could not exclude members of any race from the enjoyment of a public facility, whether it be a park, golf course, or pool. Once the city has taken on the operation of a recreational facility, it must make that facility available to all members of the public, without regard to race.

Selected Bibliography Derrick A. Bell, Jr., *Race, Racism and American Law* (1980); Thomas I. Emerson, David Haber, and Norman Dorsen, *Political and Civil Rights in the United States* (1967); "Recent Cases," *Vanderbilt Law Review* 19 (1966), 939–45.

Steve Sadowsky

Evers, James Charles   (11 September 1922, Decatur, Miss.–). A civil rights leader, businessman, and politician educated at Alcorn A&M College, Evers's life was shaped early by the racism characteristic of Mississippi's "closed society." Acute poverty, rigid segregation, disfranchisement, and mob violence permeated his environment, causing him to lament the misery of growing up black in the Magnolia State. Outspoken and direct in his reaction to prejudice and discrimination, Evers became state chairman of a voter registration campaign in the 1950s, frequently using radio time to encourage blacks to register and vote. His activities antagonized many whites in the area. An abortive assassination attempt by irate segregationists followed by job reprisal forced him to leave Mississippi in 1956 for Chicago where he prospered financially from both legal and illegal pursuits. He kept abreast of the Mississippi situation through his younger brother, **Medgar Evers,** the state's indefatigable civil rights leader.

Medgar's assassination in 1963 shook Charles tremendously, and it brought him back to Mississippi on a permanent basis to continue Medgar's work. Charles succeeded Medgar as **NAACP** field secretary for Mississippi and committed himself to nonviolent racial change. His advocacy of political and economic tactics as keys to eradicating white racism focused on voter registration drives and boycotts. Targeting several key defiant cities, he helped organize economic boycotts and selective buying campaigns in an effort to end discriminatory business practices, and to promote black employment in private and public sector jobs. He was jailed and harassed, but his leadership helped lead to significant cracks in the Mississippi monolith by the 1960s. In 1969 Evers personally tested the extent of the state's racial progress by running for mayor of the biracial town of Fayette. He won that election and three subsequent mayoral contests between 1973 and 1981. He became the first of his race to launch serious, although unsuccessful, statewide campaigns for governor and the U.S. Senate. His efforts have inspired other blacks to seek public office in a state where, until recently, participation in politics had been restricted to "white only." Always controversial, in the early twenty-first century Evers belonged to the Republican party and was out of the mainstream of Mississippi black politics.

Selected Bibliography Jason Berry, *Amazing Grace* (1973); Charles Evers, edited by Grace Halsell, *Evers* (1971); Charles Evers, "Playboy Interview: Charles Evers," *Playboy* (October 1971); Charles Evers and Andrew Szantor, *Have No Fear: The Charles Evers Story* (1997); Walter Rugaber, "The Brothers Evers," *New York Times*, 4 August 1968; George A. Sewell and Margaret Dwight, *Mississippi Black History Makers* (1977).

Robert L. Jenkins

Evers, Medgar W. (2 July 1925, Decatur, Miss.–11 June 1963, Jackson, Miss.). For nearly a decade, Medgar Evers was a central figure in Mississippi's civil rights struggle. Like countless other Deep South blacks of his generation, Evers daily experienced the region's bigotry and racism. In 1946 he returned from World War II determined to work to change what was perhaps the South's most segregated and oppressive state. After graduation from Alcorn A&M College, he sold insurance in the Mississippi delta where black conditions were among the South's most deplorable. There he employed economic boycotts to mobilize blacks against inequality. He joined the largely inactive **NAACP** and helped organize and revitalize branch chapters all over the state, accepting in 1954 the NAACP's offer of full-time work as state field secretary. Much of his new job involved monitoring, collecting, and publicizing data concerning civil rights violations, but he also organized campaigns against racial injustice in Jackson, Mississippi's largest and most densely black populated city. In defiance of the conservative NAACP national leadership, he often pursued a policy of mass **direct action,** which both unified the Jackson black community and antagonized the recalcitrant white power structure. He conducted numerous mass meetings and led and participated in sit-ins and lunch-counter demonstrations. Like many of those who followed his leadership, Evers was frequently beaten and jailed. Although his life was constantly

Medgar Evers, NAACP field secretary, interviewing the widow of a shotgun victim in her Mississippi home, 1955. © Library of Congress.

threatened, Evers never allowed fear to discourage him. In the early morning of 11 June 1963, however, the threats became a reality when he was ambushed in the driveway of his home. His killer was not successfully tried and sentenced until 1994. Although his death left the civil rights movement void of one of its most influential and dedicated leaders, it also greatly enhanced his historical position in African American communities everywhere and he became a major symbol of the struggle to overcome racial bigotry and oppression.

Selected Bibliography Ronald Bailey, *Remembering Medgar Evers . . . For a New Generation* (1988); Jennie Brown, *Medgar Evers* (1994); Cleveland Donald, Jr., "Medgar Wylie Evers: The Civil Rights Leader as Utopianist" in Dean Faulkner Wells and Hunter Cole, eds., *Mississippi Heroes* (1980); Charles Evers, edited by Grace Halsell, *Evers* (1971); (Mrs.) Medgar Evers, with William Peters, *For Us the Living* (1967); Myrlie Evers, "For Us the Living," *Proteus* 15 (1998), 1–3; George R. Metcalf, *Black Profiles* (1968); Willie Morris, *The Ghost of Medgar Evers: A Tale of Race, Murder, Mississippi and Hollywood* (1998); Adam Nossiter, *Of Long Memory: Mississippi and the Murder of Medgar Evers* (1994); John Salter, *Jackson: An American Chronicle of Struggle and Schism* (1979); Maryanne Vollers, *Ghosts of Mississippi: The Murder of Medgar Evers, the Trials of Byron de la Beckwith, and the Haunting of the New South* (1995).

Robert L. Jenkins

***Evers v. Dwyer*, 358 U.S. 202 (1958)**   Plaintiff O. Z. Evers, a black resident of Memphis, Tennessee, boarded a city bus on April 26, 1956, and seated himself in the front. He refused to move to the back of the bus as instructed by the driver and he left the vehicle only when faced with arrest by city police officers. Evers brought a class action suit in federal district court against Memphis city officials, the transportation company and the bus driver. He sought a declaratory judgment as to his claimed constitutional right to travel on buses within the city without being subjected, as required by Tennessee statute, to segregated seating arrangements on account of race. The district court dismissed the complaint on the grounds that no "actual controversy" within the meaning of the Declaratory Judgment Act had been shown because appellant had ridden the bus only on one occasion, had done so for the purpose of instituting litigation, and was not "representative of a class of colored citizens who do use the buses in Memphis as a means of transportation." The Supreme Court reversed the lower court's decision and remanded the case for further adjudication, ruling that evidence in the case had established the existence of an actual controversy. No further judicial action followed.

Selected Bibliography Stewart A. Baker, "A Strict Scrutiny of the Right to Travel," *UCLA Law Review* 22 (1975), 1129–60; James Peck, *Freedom Ride* (1962); George Rossman, ed., "Review of Recent Supreme Court Decisions," *American Bar Association Journal* 45 (1959), 283–84.

Michael S. Downs

Executive Order 8802   In 1941, as billions of dollars flowed into defense industries, African Americans were excluded from all but menial jobs. Protests yielded only weak responses. **A. Philip Randolph,** president of the **Brotherhood of Sleeping Car Porters and Maids,** proposed a 1 July march of from fifty thousand to one hundred thousand African Americans on Washington, D.C., to force President Franklin Roosevelt to issue an executive order abolishing discrimination in all government departments, the armed services, and national defense jobs. To prevent the march, Roosevelt, on 25 June, issued Executive Order 8802 prohibiting discrimination in government departments and defense industries and establishing a **Fair Employment Practices Committee** to enforce the order. Although enforcement was sometimes lax and the armed services remained segregated, the order's impact was widespread. Randolph's threat to march anticipated the **direct action** techniques of the civil rights leaders of the 1950s and 1960s.

Selected Bibliography Jervis B. Anderson, *A. Philip Randolph: A Biographical Portrait* (1990); John H. Bracey, Jr., August Meier, and Elliott Rudwick, ed., *The Afro-Americans: Selected Documents* (1972); William H. Harris, *Keeping the Faith: A. Philip Randolph, Milton P. Webster, and the Brotherhood of Sleeping Car Porters, 1925–37* (1991); Joseph P. Lash, *Eleanor and Franklin* (1971); Kenneth R. Mayer, *With the Stroke of a Pen: Executive Orders and Presidential Power* (2001).

Suzanne Ellery Greene Chapelle

Executive Order 9808   Signed by President Harry S. Truman on 5 December 1946, this order created the President's Committee on Civil Rights. The 15 member committee's task was to determine how existing powers of federal, state, and local governments could be "improved to safeguard the civil rights of the people," to submit a written report, and to make recommendations for the more adequate protection of civil rights. The report published on 29 October 1947, included the following recommendations: (1) establish a permanent **Civil Rights Commission,** a joint Congressional Committee on Civil Rights, and a **Civil Rights Section, Justice Department;** (2) strengthen existing civil rights statutes; (3) provide federal protection against lynching; (4) protect more adequately the right to vote; and (5) establish a Fair Employment Practices Commission (see **Fair Employment Practices Committee**). Although the order resulted in little legislation, it did succeed in dramatizing the civil rights problem.

Selected Bibliography William C. Berman, *The Politics of Civil Rights in the Truman Administration* (1970); Kenneth R. Mayer, *With the Stroke of a Pen: Executive Orders and Presidential Power* (2001); President's Committee on Civil Rights, *To Secure These Rights* (1947).

Clarence Hooker

Executive Order 9981 Moved by political and military expediency and apparently by genuine concern for racial justice, President Harry S. Truman issued an executive order on 26 July 1948 directing the armed forces to provide "equality of treatment and opportunity for all personnel without regard to race, color, religion, or national origin." Truman's directive also established a presidential committee—chaired by Charles Fahy—to make appropriate recommendations to ensure equality of treatment and opportunity. Prodded by the **Fahy Committee,** the U.S. Air Force and U.S. Navy moved toward integration in 1949, the U.S. Army, with far more blacks, grudgingly adopted a gradualist policy the following year. With full integration spurred by the Korean War and nearly complete by the end of 1954, the armed services had become the most completely integrated segment of American society. Desegregation of the military may have been Truman's most significant civil rights accomplishment.

Selected Bibliography Richard M. Dalfiume, *Desegregation of the U.S. Armed Forces: Fighting on Two Fronts, 1939–1953* (1969); Morris J. MacGregor, *Integration of the Armed Forces, 1940–1965* (1981); Kenneth R. Mayer, *With the Stroke of a Pen: Executive Orders and Presidential Power* (2001); Bernard C. Nalty, *Strength for the Fight: A History of Black Americans in the Military* (1986); Lee Nichols, *Breakthrough on the Color Front* (1954).

James B. Potts

Executive Order 10577 In response to recommendations by the Committee on Government Contracts, President Dwight D. Eisenhower issued this order on 3 September 1954. Its purpose was to clarify existing orders obligating contractors and subcontractors not to discriminate against an employee or applicant for employment because of race, creed, color, or national origin. The recommended clarification specified that nondiscrimination applied to "employment, upgrading, demotion or transfer; recruitment or recruitment advertising; layoff or termination, rates of pay or other forms of compensation; and selection of training, including apprenticeship." Contractors were required to post nondiscrimination clauses in conspicuous places. Excluded from the order were contracts to meet special requirements or emergencies, and contracts executed outside the United States for which American workers had not been recruited.

Selected Bibliography Kenneth R. Mayer, *With the Stroke of a Pen: Executive Orders and Presidential Power* (2001); *The Code of Federal Regulations*; Thomas R. Wolanin, *Presidential Advisory Commissions* (1975).

Clarence Hooker

Executive Order 10590   President Dwight D. Eisenhower signed this order on 18 January 1955, establishing the President's Committee on Government Employment Policy and abolishing the Fair Employment Board of the Civil Service Commission. The five-member committee consisted of representatives from the Civil Service Commission, Department of Labor, the Office of Defense Mobilization, and two presidential appointees. The committee's mandate was to ensure that government agencies did not discriminate because of race, color, religion, or national origin in employment or application for employment in the federal government. The order provided for an employment policy officer in each department or agency; empowered the committee to undertake necessary research; and authorized it to advise, make recommendations, and act as a consultant to the president and government agencies.

Selected Bibliography Dwight D. Eisenhower, *Mandate for Change* (1963); Kenneth R. Mayer, *With the Stroke of a Pen: Executive Orders and Presidential Power* (2001); Thomas R. Wolanin, *Presidential Advisory Commissions* (1975).

Clarence Hooker

Executive Order 10925   President John F. Kennedy signed this order that established the President's **Equal Employment Opportunity Commission** on 6 March 1961. The committee, consisting primarily of cabinet officers and chaired by Vice President Lyndon B. Johnson, was charged with eliminating race, creed, color, and national origin as barriers to employment in the government as well as in firms employed on government contracts. Unlike similar efforts made in the Roosevelt, Truman, and Eisenhower administrations, this order demanded **affirmative action** to make the policy effective. The committee was empowered to publish the names of noncomplying contractors and unions, and to recommend that the Justice Department file suits to compel compliance, and institute criminal suits for filing false information.

Selected Bibliography Howard J. Anderson, *Primer of Equal Employment Opportunity* (1978); C. Raymond Barrow, "Martin Luther King and Affirmative Action," *Proteus* 15 (1998), 37–42; Paul Burstein, *Discrimination, Jobs, and Politics* (1985); Kenneth R. Mayer, *With the Stroke of a Pen: Executive Orders and Presidential Power* (2001).

Clarence Hooker

Executive Order 11063   During the presidential campaign of 1960 Senator John F. Kennedy criticized the civil rights record of the Eisenhower administration and promised, if elected, to ban racial discrimination in federally assisted housing "with the stroke of a pen." Kennedy did not redeem that pledge until November 20, 1962, when he issued Executive Order 11063. The order prohibited racial discrimination in federally owned and operated housing, in public housing built with federal assistance, and in new housing funded through Federal Housing Administration and Veterans Administration loans.

This represented approximately 25 percent of all housing; it excluded housing built through commercial mortgages from banks and savings and loan associations. Kennedy omitted commercially funded housing on Justice Department advice that the president lacked the authority to enforce social programs through independent agencies of financial regulation. Kennedy delayed the "penstroke" order for two years because he feared it might jeopardize his plan to create a Department of Housing and Urban Affairs and to appoint **Robert C. Weaver** to head it as the first black member of the cabinet. Kennedy was also urged by northern Democrats in Congress, who feared a white backlash at the polls, not to issue the order until after the 1962 elections. Kennedy's order had little observable effect on housing patterns and was superseded by the **Open Housing Act of 1968,** signed by President Lyndon B. Johnson, which made nondiscrimination in housing a national policy.

Selected Bibliography Carl M. Brauer, *John F. Kennedy and the Second Reconstruction* (1977); Hugh Davis Graham, *The Civil Rights Era* (1990); Kenneth R. Mayer, *With the Stroke of a Pen: Executive Orders and Presidential Power* (2001).

Hugh Davis Graham

Executive Order 11114 Issued by President John F. Kennedy on 22 June 1963, Executive Order 11114 extended Kennedy's fair employment and **"affirmative action"** order of March 1961 **(Executive Order 10925)** to cover federally assisted contracts in the construction industry. The issue was politically difficult for the Kennedy administration because it brought two Democratic constituencies into conflict: minority workers and union members. Hiring decisions in construction were made not by the builders who signed the contracts, but rather by white-dominated craft unions whose collective bargaining agreements gave them hiring-hall authority. To blue-collar union members, the order threatened seniority and labor solidarity. But civil rights leaders pointed to a black unemployment rate that doubled the white rate, and demanded that minority workers help build the tax-subsidized hospitals, highways, schools, and urban renewal projects. The threat of federally enforced minority hiring, like the parallel issue of housing desegregation, split the Democrats' northern constituency in much the same way that the school desegregation issue split the party in the South. Kennedy withheld the construction order until the **Birmingham Confrontation** in the spring of 1963. Then he sent Congress for the first time, on 19 June, a strong civil rights bill. Three days later, on a news-quiet Saturday, Kennedy released Executive Order 11114 without ceremony or comment. Subsequent difficulties in enforcing the order led to the controversy over the **Philadelphia Plan** during the Nixon administration.

Selected Bibliography Hugh Davis Graham, *The Civil Rights Era* (1990); Kenneth R. Mayer, *With the Stroke of a Pen: Executive Orders and Presidential Power* (2001).

Hugh Davis Graham

Executive Order 11246 Signed by President Lyndon B. Johnson on September 24, 1965, Executive Order 11246 distributed authority among federal agencies for enforcing the **Civil Rights Act of 1964.** To enforce Title VI, it established the equal opportunity obligations for federal contractors and sub-contractors by requiring procuring agencies to insert an equal opportunity clause into each contract. Under this clause, contractors were barred from discriminating against employees and applicants on the basis of race, color, religion or national origin (sex discrimination was added in 1967 by Executive Order 11375). Such employers were required to take **affirmative action** (a term first mentioned in 1961 in Kennedy's **Executive Order 10925,** but not defined until the Labor Department issued regulations regarding the program's implementation in May 1968) to employ and advance in employment, all applicants and employees without regard to such factors. Evidence of these nondiscriminatory policies alone did not ensure compliance, however. By 1970 federal officials were requiring contractors to provide minorities and women with a share of jobs that reflected their representation in the labor force or population. The goal of compliance became a form of numerical parity between those minority workers who were available and the percentage who held jobs. Johnson's directive granted responsibility for enforcement to the Secretary of Labor, who was to administer the program through the **Office of Federal Contract Compliance Programs.**

Selected Bibliography Hugh Davis Graham, *The Civil Rights Era* (1990); Kenneth R. Mayer, *With the Stroke of a Pen : Executive Orders and Presidential Power* (2001); Floyd D. Weatherspoon, *Equal Employment Opportunity and Affirmative Action: A Sourcebook* (1985).

Nancy Diamond

Executive Order 11478 Executive Order 11478 was issued by President Richard M. Nixon on 8 August 1969, during the height of the Labor Department's struggle to regulate federal construction contracts as outlined in the revised **Philadelphia Plan.** While the Labor Department was being accused by congressional conservatives and by the General Accounting Office of trying to enforce minority hiring quotas on private contractors, the President in his memorandum announcing Executive Order 11478 to the heads of all federal agencies declared, "Equal employment opportunity must become an integral part of the day-to-day management of Federal agencies and interwoven with every action which has an effect on employees." Under Section II of the order, each agency was required to establish and maintain an **affirmative action** program of equal employment opportunity. Executive Order 11478 proved to be redundant, because it superseded President Lyndon B. Johnson's similar **Executive Order 11246** of 1965 and its amendment of 1967 for gender discrimination. Nixon's requirement of "affirmative programs" in all federal agencies supplanted the Johnson orders as the source of policy for equal employment opportunity in the federal government.

Selected Bibliography *Codification of Presidential Proclamations and Executive Orders, April 13, 1945–January 20, 1989* (1989); Hugh Davis Graham, *The Civil Rights Era* (1990); Kenneth R. Mayer, *With the Stroke of a Pen : Executive Orders and Presidential Power* (2001); *Public Papers of the Presidents of the United States: Richard M. Nixon* (1971).

Dorsey Oles Boyle

Ex parte Virginia,* 100 U.S. 339 (1880)** The **Civil Rights Act of 1875** stated that no person could be disqualified from jury service because of race, and that any officer who disqualified a potential juror because of his or her race was subject to a fine of up to $5,000. In this dramatic case, a Virginia county judge named J. D. Coles was indicted for excluding blacks from juries and was imprisoned by the U.S. marshal. In petitioning for a writ of habeas corpus, Coles argued that he could not be tried by a U.S. court for actions he had taken as a state judge. He argued that although his actions might be over-ruled by a federal court, he could not be punished for these actions. The Supreme Court refused to issue the writ of habeas corpus, declaring that the jury rights provisions of the Civil Rights Act of 1875 were firmly based upon the **Thirteenth** and **Fourteenth Amendments.** The Court's decision also held that in enforcing the Constitution, Congress cannot punish the abstract entity called a state, but must punish individuals—including officials in charge of jury selection. As a civil rights victory, *ex parte Virginia* was effectively watered down by another decision handed down the same day: ***Virginia v. Rives.

Selected Bibliography Stephen Cresswell, "The Case of Taylor Strauder," *West Virginia History* 44 (Spring 1983), 193–211; Benno C. Schmidt, "Juries, Jurisdiction, and Race Discrimination: The Lost Promise of *Strauder v. West Virginia*," *Texas Law Review* (1983), 1402–99; Charles Warren, *The Supreme Court in United States History* (1926).

Stephen Cresswell

***Ex parte Yarbrough,* 110 U.S. 651 (1884)** Jasper Yarbrough and seven accomplices beat Berry Saunders to discourage him from voting in a federal election in Georgia. Indicted under the enforcement legislation for the **Fifteenth Amendment,** which prohibited intimidation of voters and conspiracy to do so, the defendants sought a writ of habeas corpus. They claimed that Congress could not control the actions of private individuals in the guise of regulating elections. The Supreme Court unanimously denied their appeal. Justice Samuel Miller observed that democratic government required free elections, and that free participation in federal elections was a federal right guaranteed by the Constitution without reference to state law. This case was the Court's strongest statement on electoral freedom in the aftermath of Reconstruction. It concluded a 10-year period of vacillation in which the Court took several contradictory positions about the nature of the right to vote, its source, and its relation to the privileges and immunities clause. The *Yarbrough* case raised the Court's contemporary statements on protection of federal elections higher than its positions on most other aspects of civil rights. The doctrine of the *Yarbrough* case remained significant in the voter registration movement of the 1960s and forms part of the philosophical foundation of the constitutional law of all civil rights.

Selected Bibliography Charles Fairman, *Reconstruction and Reunion, 1864–1888,* (1987); William Gillette, "Samuel Miller," in Leon Friedman and Fred Israel, eds., *The Justices of the United States Supreme Court, 1789–1969: Their Lives and Major Opinions* (1969); Robert M. Goldman, *Reconstruction and Black Suffrage: Losing the Vote in Reese and Cruikshank* (2001); Donald G. Neiman, *Promises to Keep: African Americans and the Constitutional Order, 1776 to the Present* (1991).

James E. Sefton

F

Fahy Committee The Committee on Equality of Treatment and Opportunity in the Armed Forces, commonly called the Fahy Committee, after its chairman Charles H. Fahy, was authorized to examine the rules, procedures, and practices in the armed services to determine how these might be altered or improved in order to abolish racial discrimination. Beginning in January 1949, the committee not only investigated the racial practices of the army, navy, and air force but also worked directly with them to bring about desegregation. From the beginning, the air force and the navy cooperated with the committee, making the necessary changes with little difficulty. After first resisting the committee's desegregation suggestions, the army finally accepted the committee's basic recommendations. In less than a year and a half, the committee helped establish nondiscriminatory racial policies in the military services, even though the policies on paper were not always carried out in practice. The Fahy Committee was an important factor in the eventual total desegregation of the armed forces of the United States.

Selected Bibliography Monroe Billington, "Freedom to Serve: The President's Committee on Equality of Treatment and Opportunity in the Armed Forces, 1949–1950," *Journal of Negro History* 51 (October 1966), 262–74; Richard M. Dalfiume, *Desegregation of the U.S. Armed Forces: Fighting on Two Fronts, 1939–1953* (1969); Records of the President's Committee on Equality of Treatment and Opportunity in the Armed Forces, 1949–1950, Harry S. Truman Library, Independence, Mo.

Monroe Billington

Fair Employment Practices Committee In 1941 President Franklin D. Roosevelt declared that racial discrimination in defense industries was a violation of public policy, and he established a temporary Committee on Fair Employment Practices to receive and investigate complaints of discrimination. The committee had no enforcement powers. Following World War II, blacks pressured Congress to establish a permanent Fair Employment Practices Commission to outlaw job discrimination in industries receiving government contracts. Southern members of Congress successfully filibustered against establishing a permanent FEPC, and not until the passage of the **Civil Rights Act of 1964** were many of the objectives of its supporters incorporated into law.

Selected Bibliography FEPC File, Harry S. Truman Library, Independence, Mo.; Louis Coleridge Kesselman, *The Social Politics of FEPC: A Study in Reform Pressure Movements* (1948); President's Committee on Fair Employment Practice File, Franklin D. Roosevelt Library, Hyde Park, N.Y.; Louis Ruchames, *Race, Jobs, and Politics: The Story of FEPC* (1953).

Monroe Billington

Farmer, James (12 January 1920, Marshall, Tex.–9 July 1999, Fredericksburg, Va.). During the civil rights movement of the 1960s, Farmer became one of the nation's most recognizable and influential black leaders. Educated at Wiley College in Marshall, Texas, and **Howard University,** he began his civil rights activism in 1942 when he and several Christian pacifists founded the **Congress of Racial Equality.** The interracial organization's purpose was to apply direct challenges to American racism by using Gandhian tactics of nonviolence. Farmer participated in the organization's pioneering demonstrations in 1947, a campaign of sit-ins that successfully ended two Chicago restaurants' discriminatory service practices against blacks. CORE quickly recognized Farmer's leadership abilities and his influence in the group increased considerably. Articulate, aggressive, and charismatic, he became CORE national director in 1961 and led it to its greatest successes during the decade. It was in the South that he achieved for himself and for CORE national exposure and recognition. In 1961 he initiated the **Freedom Rides** throughout the Deep South. Opposition to the rides highlighted southern intransigence to the U.S. Supreme Court decision prohibiting segregated interstate terminal facilities. Farmer was arrested with the courageous young riders when they tested Mississippi's resistance in the Jackson Trailways Bus Station. When convicted, he and hundreds of other riders chose to serve prison terms in the state penitentiary to focus further national attention on their cause. CORE increased its **direct action** activities as Farmer expanded the organization's branches throughout the nation. While much of the activity involved purely local campaigns of the autonomous chapters, Farmer's leadership was notable in numerous CORE-led projects of voter registration and antisegregation protests, not just in the South but throughout the country. In 1964, for example, he led a CORE demonstration at the New York World's Fair to protest black conditions in that city. In 1966 Farmer resigned as CORE's leader to direct a national adult literacy project. By then both he and CORE were prominent members of the "Big Four" of the civil rights leaders and groups. In 1969 he accepted a minor post in the Department of Health, Education, and Welfare under the conser-

James Farmer making a speech, 1965. © Library of Congress.

vative President Richard M. Nixon. Militant black activists, unimpressed with Nixon's civil rights agenda, criticized him for his decision, but Farmer viewed the appointment as another opportunity to further black causes. He served the administration less than two years, but he succeeded in establishing several programs increasing black employment in the agency. Until 1981 he devoted most of his energy to lecturing, directing the Council on Minority Planning and Strategy, a Washington, D.C.–based black think tank, and administering a public employees labor group. Farmer will be remembered for helping to popularize the nonviolent direct action methods that became synonymous with the civil rights movement and that led to many of the gains of the era. From 1985 to 1998 he taught at Mary Washington College in Virginia.

Selected Bibliography Jacqueline Conciatore, "James Farmer Rests in Peace, but Mary Washington College Still Wrestles with Multicultural Issues," *Black Issues in Higher Education* 17 (2000), 20–21; Inge P. Bell, *CORE and the Strategy of Non-violence* (1968); James Farmer, *Freedom When?* (1965); James Farmer, *Lay Bare the Heart: An Autobiography of the Civil Rights Movement* (1985); James Farmer, "Civil Rights Events in 1963," *Proteus* 15 (1998), 4–6; August Meier and Elliott Rudwick, *CORE: A Study in the Civil Rights Movement, 1942–1968* (1973); Charles Moritz, ed., "James Farmer," *Current Biography Yearbook* (1964).

Robert L. Jenkins

Father Divine.   See Baker, George.

Farrakhan, Louis Abdul   (17 May 1933, Bronx, N.Y.–). Louis Farrakhan, a leader of the **Nation of Islam** with strong ties to the movement's founder, **Elijah Muhammad,** and to **Malcolm X,** was born Louis Eugene Walcott. A devout Episcopalian, Walcott served as an alter boy and carried a strong religious devotion with him as a student at Winston-Salem Teachers College in North Carolina. Shortly after leaving college to become a professional musician, he met Malcolm X and Elijah Muhammad. Converting to the Nation of Islam, he adopted the name Louis X and became a leader in the movement, eventually receiving the name Louis Abdul Farrakhan. Malcolm X's departure from the Nation of Islam opened more opportunities for Farrakhan, and he expected to become the successor to Elijah Muhammad. His expectation turned to disappointment when the son of the movement's founder, **Warith Deen Muhammad,** assumed leadership of the movement and quickly moved it toward orthodox Islam. By 1978, Farrakhan created a new organization, also known as the Nation of Islam, which followed more strictly the original teachings of Elijah Muhammad. Farrakhan at first placed little stress on political involvement. In 1984, though, he came out in support of **Jesse Jackson**'s presidential campaign. Farrakhan organized the **Million Man March**, which brought together up to one million African American men to a mass rally that stretched from the Lincoln Memorial to the Washington Memorial on 16 October 1995. In 2003, he remained a major influence in the African American community.

Selected Bibliography Louis Farrakhan, *A Torchlight for America* (1993); C. Eric Lincoln, *The Black Muslims in America* (1961); Arthur J. Magida, *Prophet of Rage: A Life of Louis Farrakhan and His Nation* (1996); Gardell Mattias, *In the Name of Elijah Muhammad: Louis Farrakhan and the Nation of Islam* (1996).

Merrill M. Hawkins, Jr.

Fauset, Jessie Redmond   (26 April 1882, Camden County, N.J.–30 April 1961, Philadelphia, Pa.). One of the major African American woman writers to come out of the **Harlem Renaissance,** Jessie Redmond Fauset was born in Camden County, New Jersey. She was the only black to be educated in Philadelphia's High School for Girls. After graduating Phi Beta Kappa from Cornell University, she taught French and Latin to middle-class black youth at the M Street High School in Philadelphia (later renamed Dunbar). Jessie completed her education at the Sorbonne in Paris and received an M.A. from the University of Pennsylvania in 1919. She was deeply involved in the Harlem Renaissance as literary editor for the *Crisis,* where she developed a strong working relationship with **W.E.B. Du Bois.** She encouraged the work of many of the leading writers and artists of that period. Her own writing addressed the issues confronting the black middle class. Her political work revolved around helping Du Bois put together the Pan-African Conferences of 1919–21. She was later involved in national politics; her brother Arthur Huff Fauset, an anthropologist, was vice president of the **National Negro Congress.** Jessie married Herbert Harris, a businessman, in 1929. They lived in New

Jersey until his death in 1958 when Jessie moved to Philadelphia where she died in 1961. Her most enduring contributions are her novels: *There Is Confusion* (1924), *Plum Bun* (1929), and *Chinaberry Tree* (1931), which depicted the world of middle-class African Americans.

Selected Bibliography Bruce Kellner, ed., *The Harlem Renaissance: A Historical Dictionary for the Era* (1985); David Levering Lewis, *When Harlem Was in Vogue* (1981).

Charles T. Pete Banner-Haley

Fellowship of Reconciliation Members of this Christian pacifist organization, which originated during World War I, believed that peace meant not simply an absence of war but a spirit of unity and harmony among people of all nationalities, races, and classes. Throughout the 1920s Fellowship of Reconciliation (FOR) members such as **James Weldon Johnson,** Hollingsworth Wood, and **Will W. Alexander,** engaged in pioneering interracial work. From the late 1920s to the late 1930s the Fellowship focused considerable attention upon the South. FOR secretaries **Howard Anderson Kester** and Claude Nelson traveled across the region speaking about economic and social problems before black and white students and organizing interracial Fellowship conferences at which the race problem was an important topic for discussion. Meanwhile, across the nation, Fellowship members labored quietly to defuse tense racial situations, promote integration, and register black voters. During the early 1940s, under the leadership of **Abraham John Muste,** FOR attempted to develop effective nonviolent tactics with which to combat American racism and promote Christian fraternity. Among Fellowship members involved in this endeavor were **James Farmer, Bayard Rustin,** and George Houser. Their efforts led to the establishment of the **Congress of Racial Equality,** which soon disassociated itself from the fellowship. For a time, however, the leadership of the two groups overlapped, and FOR members assisted in CORE fund-raising and organizational work into the early 1950s.

During the 1950s and 1960s Fellowship members either participated in or supported emerging groups such as the **Southern Christian Leadership Conference** and the **Student Nonviolent Coordinating Committee.** As the civil rights movement became more militant in the mid 1960s, the Fellowship continued to endorse peaceful means to achieve just ends but refused to abandon its financial or legal support of those for whom frustration led to violence.

Selected Bibliography Betty Lynn Barton, "The Fellowship of Reconciliation: Pacifism, Labor, and Social Welfare, 1915–1960" (Ph.D. diss., Florida State University, 1974); Fellowship of Reconciliation Papers, Friends Historical Library of Swarthmore College, Swarthmore, Pa.; John N. Sayre, *The Story of the Fellowship of Reconciliation, 1915–1935* (1935).

Robert F. Martin

Fellowship of Southern Churchmen This interracial, interdenominational fellowship was founded in 1934 by neoorothodox Christian social activists who believed that southern Protestantism had failed to bring a prophetic voice to bear upon the economic and social ills plaguing their region. From the mid-

1930s to the early 1960s this little band of a few hundred radical Christians worked quietly but courageously to resolve the problems of the South's industrial workers, impoverished farmers, and disinherited blacks. In the years before the civil rights movement, fellowship members of both races traveled and ate together in violation of law and custom. Whites opened their homes to black travelers denied public accommodations. Whenever racial tensions flared they worked behind the scenes to defuse explosive situations before these erupted into violence. At their periodic conferences and through the pages of their journal, *Prophetic Religion*, fellowship members denounced lynching and all other forms of racial violence, called for the integration of workers within the labor movement, advocated political equality for all races, demanded justice for blacks in the courts, and supported the integration of schools, churches, and other social institutions. During the 1950s the fellowship was eclipsed by other, more dramatically active, groups but for more than a quarter century it was the most radical expression of Christian social consciousness in the South.

Selected Bibliography Don Donahue, "Prophets of a New Social Order: Presbyterians and the Fellowship of Southern Churchmen, 1934–1963," *American Presbyterians* 74 (No. 3, 1996), 209–21; Anthony P. Dunbar, *Against the Grain: Southern Radicals and Prophets, 1929–1959* (1981); Fellowship of Southern Churchmen Papers, Southern Historical Collection, The University of North Carolina at Chapel Hill; Robert F. Martin, "Critique of Southern Society and Vision of a New Order: The Fellowship of Southern Churchmen, 1934–1957," *Church History* 52 (March 1983), 66–80; Robert F. Martin, *Howard Kester and the Struggle for Social Justice in the South, 1904–1977* (1991); John A. Salmond, "The Fellowship of Southern Churchmen and Interracial Change in the South," *North Carolina Historical Review* 69 (No. 2, 1992), 179–99.

Robert F. Martin

Ferris, William H. (20 July 1874, New Haven, Conn.–23 August 1941, New York, N.Y.). An African American intellectual, nationalist, Pan-Africanist, and integrationist, Ferris earned M.A. degrees at Yale and Harvard. He argued that blacks are not naturally inferior as was alleged by the American popular culture, and that their poor conditions had been imposed on them by the American system. Like **W.E.B. Du Bois,** Ferris repudiated **Booker T. Washington**'s vocational educational philosophy. Ferris became a member of the American Negro Academy and later a vice president of the **Universal Negro Improvement Association,** an organization founded by **Marcus Garvey** to send blacks to Africa. Ferris also recognized with pride the achievements of African intellectuals such as Fadumah Orishautukeh and Ka Issaka Seme, who were students in the United States. Despite his Pan-Africanist sentiment, Ferris had strong admiration for Western civilization and was therefore a strong advocate of black assimilation into the dominant American culture.

Selected Bibliography William H. Ferris, *The African Abroad: or, His Evaluation in Western Civilization, Tracing his Development under Caucasian Milieu*, 2 vols. (1913); Wilson J. Moses, *The Golden Age of Black Nationalism, 1850–1925* (1978).

Amos J. Beyan

THE FIFTEENTH AMENDMENT.
CELEBRATED MAY 19ᵗʰ 1870.

Detail from a large commemorative print marking the enactment of the Fifteenth Amendment, March 30, 1870. © Library of Congress.

Fifteenth Amendment The Fifteenth Amendment, ratified by Congress in 1870, enfranchised black males. The amendment states that "the right of citizens of the United States to vote shall not be denied or abridged by the United States or by any State on account of race, color, or previous condition of servitude" and that "Congress shall have power to enforce this article by appropriate legislation." This legislation produced a small cadre of African Americans in southern politics—black legislators, judges, superintendents of education, lieutenant governors and other state officers, members of Congress and two U.S. Senators. Fearful of black political participation, the white southern leadership enforced measures to disenfranchise black voters. The **poll tax,** the **grandfather clause,** literacy tests, confusing election procedures, gerrymandering, and intimidation effectively eliminated black political participation in the South until the passage of the **Voting Rights Act of 1965**.

Selected Bibliography William Gillett, *The Right to Vote: Politics and the Passage of the Fifteenth Amendment* (1965); William Gillett, *Retreat from Reconstruction, 1869–1879* (1979); Thomas Holt, *Black over White: Negro Political Leadership in South Carolina during Reconstruction* (1977); Harold M. Hyman, *A More Perfect Union: The Impact of the Civil War and Reconstruction on the*

Constitution (1973); Stanley I. Kutler, *Judicial Power and Reconstruction Politics* (1968); Michael Perman, *The Road to Redemption: Southern Politics, 1869–1879* (1984); Harold O. Rabinowitz, *Southern Black Leaders of the Reconstruction Era* (1982); Everette Swinney, "Enforcing the Fifteenth Amendment 1870–1877," *Journal of Southern History* 28 (No. 2, 1962), 202–18.

Lillie Johnson Edwards

51st Composite Defense Battalion   Pressure from President Franklin D. Roosevelt and the need for manpower caused the U.S. Marine Corps in February 1942 to enlist 1,000 blacks for general service, ending 167 years of black exclusion. Montford Point Camp, a new facility near Camp Lejeune, North Carolina, provided segregated infantry, armor, and artillery training for these first black marines who formed the 51st Composite Defense Battalion in 1943. Although trained for combat, the 51st remained at Montford Point until 1944, providing reception and specialized training for black marines who followed. In all, some twenty thousand recruits served, mostly in all-black service units; many of them saw combat in Saipan, Iwo Jima, and other Pacific battles. The Marines continued to bar blacks from their main combat divisions, the air arm, and commissions as officers.

Selected Bibliography Jack D. Foner, *Blacks and the Military in American History* (1974); Morris J. MacGregor, *Integration of the Armed Forces, 1940–1965* (1981); Bernard C. Nalty, *Strength for the Fight: A History of Black Americans in the Military* (1986); Henry I. Shaw, Jr., and Ralph W. Donnelly, *Blacks in the Marine Corps* (1973).

James B. Potts

Fikes v. Alabama, 352 U.S. 191 (1957)   In 1953 William Earl Fikes was sentenced to death in Alabama for burglary with intent to commit rape. Fikes's conviction rested on a confession that had been obtained by psychological intimidation in violation of the due process clause of the **Fourteenth Amendment.** Fikes was an Alabama African American of limited mental ability. He had been taken to jail in a distant county where he was confined in isolation except for periods of interrogation, which lasted several hours at a time over the course of five days. He was denied contact with his father and a lawyer who had come to see him. After his extended confinement and interrogation, Fikes confessed to the crime for which he was later sentenced. The U.S. Supreme Court ruled that Fikes's confession had been coerced and could not be used against him. Although no physical brutality had been employed, the circumstances of his interrogation were reminiscent of the Inquisition and had the same effect as physical brutality in forcing his confession. The Supreme Court affirmed that only voluntary confessions were consistent with the Fourteenth Amendment's guarantee of due process and that coercion by physical or psychological means could not be reconciled with this fundamental principle of justice.

Selected Bibliography Robert Frederick Burk, *The Eisenhower Administration and Black Civil Rights* (1984); Loren Miller, *The Petitioners: The Story of the Supreme Court of the United States and the Negro* (1966); George Rossman, ed., "Review of Recent Supreme Court Decisions," *American Bar Association Journal* 43 (1957), 254–55.

Steve Sadowsky

The Fire in the Flint **Walter Francis White**'s first novel was a significant historical landmark in American fiction. Written from within the southern black experience, which White knew so well because of his extensive knowledge and experience as a lynching investigator for the **NAACP,** the 1924 novel exposed the terrible truth about the American South: its double standard of justice and heinous crime of lynching. Realistically portraying the violent, oppressive racial atmosphere, this serious work of fiction was designed to destroy the plantation tradition myth of the innately "happy," "stupid" Negro, to jolt America's social conscience, and to force the nation's attention to the dire need for antilynching legislation. More important, it paved the way for other Negro writers to voice opinions on previously taboo subjects.

Selected Bibliography Arna Bontemps, ed., *The Harlem Renaissance Remembered* (1972); Nathan Irving Huggins, *Harlem Renaissance* (1973); James Weldon Johnson, *Black Manhattan* (1930; reprint, 1969); Amrithit Singhn, *The Novels of the Harlem Renaissance: Twelve Black Writers* (1976); Edward E. Waldron, *Walter White and the Harlem Renaissance* (1978); Cary D. Wintz, *Black Culture and the Harlem Renaissance* (1988).

Jacquelyn Jackson

The Fire Next Time Published for the 100th anniversary of the **Emancipation Proclamation,** *The Fire Next Time* (1962) by **James Baldwin,** expressed a prophetic vision of what would happen if the Negro's grievances were not addressed. In the first of two essays, Baldwin urged his nephew (and all black Americans) to develop a black consciousness so that they could resist the temptation to become socially accepted by becoming "white." In the second essay, "Down at the Cross," Baldwin related his earlier religious experiences, his rejection of white Christianity and his understanding (but not acceptance) of the **Black Muslims**' teachings. He concludes this extremely powerful work with the prophetic words "If we do not now dare everything, the fulfillment of that prophecy, recreated from the Bible in a song by a slave, is upon us: God gave Noah the rainbow sign, no more water, the fire next time."

Selected Bibliography Therman B. O'Daniel, ed., *James Baldwin: A Critical Examination* (1977); Louis H. Pratt, *James Baldwin* (1978); W. V. Weatherby, *James Baldwin: Artist on Fire, A Portrait* (1989).

Kenneth W. Goings

Firefighters v. Stotts, **467 U.S. 561 (1984)** The Department of Justice under President Ronald Reagan attempted to roll back gains blacks had made in the 1970s under **affirmative action** programs. Taking its cue from administration officials who vociferously denounced all "race conscious remedies which require preferential treatment for blacks," the department encouraged whites to challenge affirmative action policies and sometimes filed amicus curiae briefs in affirmative action cases. *Firefighters* was such a case. In it the Justice Department, intervening on behalf of aggrieved white male firefighters, sought to overturn a federal district court ruling that set aside the seniority rights of white firefighters. The trial court had ruled that because blacks had been discriminatorily excluded from the fire department in question until very recently, layoffs based on seniority alone would be discriminatory. To apply the last hired, first-fired rule would have the effect, in this instance, of eliminating only blacks from the force. Therefore, the court decreed that the fire department must develop a work reduction plan that would not reduce the proportion of blacks on the force, even if the plan meant that whites with seniority would have to be laid off in order to retain blacks with less seniority. On appeal, the Supreme Court reversed the lower court. It declared that under federal civil rights statutes courts could not set aside seniority systems in the workplace unless they had been adopted with discriminatory intent. The scope of the *Firefighters* ruling was quite limited, but Reagan officials interpreted it to mean that the courts lacked authority under Title VII of the **Civil Rights Act of 1964** to establish employment goals and quotas.

Selected Bibliography Derrick Bell, *And We Are Not Saved: The Elusive Quest for Racial Justice* (1987); Dawn D. Bennett- Alexander, "The State of Affirmative Action in Employment: A Post-Stotts Retrospective," *American Bar Association Journal* 27 (1990), 565–97; Donald G. Nieman, *Promises to Keep: African-Americans and the Constitutional Order, 1776 to the Present* (1991).

Charles D. Lowery

Fisher v. Hurst,* 333 U.S. 147 (1947)** Oklahoma operated a law school for whites but did not provide one for blacks. A black woman, Ada Sipuel, applied for admission to the University of Oklahoma Law School on the ground that Oklahoma provided no opportunity for black students to receive a legal education. A trial court refused to order Sipuel's admission, and the Oklahoma Supreme Court upheld that decision. The U.S. Supreme Court reversed the decision, ruling that Oklahoma had an obligation to provide Sipuel with equal opportunity for a legal education. Oklahoma responded by creating a black law school; it set aside three rooms in the state capitol and hired three white attorneys to serve as faculty. However, even this flimsy excuse for a law school could not open by the same date as the University of Oklahoma's. Sipuel, who had married and changed her name to Fisher, refused to apply to the newly created black law school. Her attorney asked that the trial court order her admission to the University of Oklahoma Law School. The trial court ruled that Oklahoma could either admit Fisher or refuse to enroll any white students at the University of Oklahoma until the black law school began to operate. The Supreme Court ruled that the trial court's decision met the requirement of the Supreme Court's ruling in ***Sipuel v. Board of Regents of the University of Oklahoma. Justices Wiley Rutledge and Frank Murphy dissented.

Selected Bibliography "Notes and Comments," *Boston University Law* Review 28 (1948), 240–42; *Sipuel v. Board of Regents* 199 Oklahoma 36 (1947); Mark V. Tushnet, *The NAACP's Legal Strategy Against Segregated Education, 1925–1950* (1987).

Michael S. Mayer

Students in the library, Fisk University, 1900. © Library of Congress.

Fisk University   Founded in 1866 in Nashville, Tennessee, by the **American Missionary Association,** the school was incorporated as Fisk University on 22 August 1867. Fisk graduated its first college class in 1872 and became the first black college to receive a class-A rating by the Southern Association of Colleges and Secondary Schools. In spite of poverty and white hostility, Fisk fulfilled the vision of its founders by becoming a leading black educational institution and cultural center. It has and continues to train many educational and civil rights leaders, including **W.E.B. Du Bois,** Henry Hugh Proctor, **John Hope Franklin,** and **Constance Baker Motley.**

Selected Bibliography American Missionary Association Archives, Amistad Research Center, Tulane University, New Orleans, La.; Fiskiana Collection, Fisk University Library, Nashville, Tenn.; Joe M. Richardson, *A History of Fisk University, 1865–1946* (1980); Web site: www.fisk.edu.

Maxine D. Jones

Fletcher, Arthur Allen   (22 December 1924, Phoenix, Ariz.–). Following his graduation from Washburn University of Topeka in Topeka, Kansas, in 1950, Fletcher played professional football with the Baltimore Colts and the Los Angeles Rams. He also worked in public relations for the highway commission in Kansas (1954–57), and became involved in Republican politics in 1960 as a paid staff member of the Nixon-Lodge campaign. After a losing race for lieutenant-governor in Washington State in 1968, he worked as special assistant to Governor Dan Evans (1969). He also served as alternate delegate to the United Nations General Assembly.

Fletcher's most important early position was assistant secretary for wage and labor standards for the U.S. Department of Labor, which made him at the time the highest-ranking black official in the Nixon administration. Working closely with Secretary George Shultz, in 1969 Fletcher supervised the redesign of the **Philadelphia Plan.** During the summer of 1969 Fletcher held hearings in Philadelphia that produced official findings of discrimination by seven different construction trade unions. Based on these findings, the Labor Department required contractors to establish target ranges for minority employment in order to qualify for bidding. When the Nixon administration defeated a congressional attack on the Philadelphia Plan in December 1969, and a federal appeals court upheld it in April 1970, Fletcher pushed its expansion to include all federal contractors. During 1971–72 Fletcher was executive director of the **National Urban League.** In 1989 President Bush appointed Fletcher chairman of the U.S. **Civil Rights Commission,** which he chaired from 1990 to 1993. In 1996 Fletcher ran an unsuccessful presidential campaign and later became an active advocate of the National Black Chamber of Commerce.

Selected Bibliography Hugh Davis Graham, *The Civil Rights Era* (1990); William Safire, *Before the Fall* (1975); Mary Mace Spradling, ed., *In Black and White* (1980).

Daniel Gomes

Flipper, Henry Ossian (21 March 1856, Thomasville, Ga.–3 May 1940, Atlanta, Ga.). The first African American to graduate from the U.S. Military Academy in West Point, New York, Flipper had a brief career in the U.S. Army but achieved much greater success as an engineer. In 1882, seven years after his graduation, Flipper was convicted (under questionable circumstances) of "conduct unbecoming an officer" and dismissed from the service. During the next 30 years, while continually appealing the verdict, he worked as an engineer, surveyor, and translator for the United States and Mexico and a number of corporations. In 1921 Flipper again was in the black vanguard when he became an assistant to the secretary of the interior. In 1976 he was granted an honorable discharge and in 1999 he was pardoned.

Selected Bibliography Paul H. Carlson, *"Pecos Bill": A Military Biography of William R. Shafter* (1989); Bruce J. Dinges, "The Court-Martial of Lieutenant Henry O. Flipper," *The American West* 9 (January 1972), 12–17, 59–61; Henry O. Flipper, *The Colored Cadet at West Point* (1878).

Marvin E. Fletcher

Florida 2000 Presidential Election After months of legal wrangling, Florida's electoral votes were awarded to Republican presidential candidate George W. Bush, and these votes narrowly gave him the presidency over his Democratic opponent, Al Gore. Florida African Americans felt particularly aggravated. In the wake of the tumultuous redistricting battles of the 1990s, they had confronted numerous obstacles to the exercise of their voting rights. Fresh from redistricting litigation battles over majority-minority legislative voting districts in Florida, many African American voters in Florida faced a maze of disenfranchising election procedures and practices on election day. Among the complaints in Florida were alleged voting irregularities and fraud, the wrongful purging of qualified voters from voter lists, the lack of enforcement of the provisions of the National Voter Registration Act, and the lack of translation of ballots into Creole for Haitian voters. Responding to the black community's call for investigation and a proactive response, the United States Commission on Civil Rights convened official hearings in Tallahassee in January, 2001, collecting 30 hours of sworn testimony from more than 100 witnesses. The commission concluded that there had been serious violations of the Voting Rights Act, and its recommendations for election reform were published in June and November 2001. To address the issue of felon disfranchisement, African American plaintiffs and civil rights and voting rights advocacy organizations filed suits to eliminate discriminatory voting practices in Florida's electoral system. Following the election, the controversy remained a major political and race relations issue, with Florida and other states struggling to enact electoral reform to prevent any future such problems.

Selected Bibliography Marsha J. Tyson Darling, ed., *Race, Voting, Redistricting, and the Constitution: Sources and Explorations on the Fifteenth Amendment, Vol. 3: Alternative Redistricting, Registering, and Voting Systems* (2001); Linda Greenhouse, "Divining the Consequences of a Court Divided," *New York Times*, 17 December 2000; Pamela S. Karlan, "The Court Casts Its Vote," *New York Times*, 11 December 2000; *NAACP v. Harris*, Case No. 01-CIV-120-GOLD; Adam Nagourney and David Barstow, "G.O.P.'s Depth Outdid Gore's Team in Florida," *New York Times*, 22 December 2000; *Thomas Johnson et al. v. Jeb Bush et al.*, Case No. 00-3542-Civ-King (S.D. Fla.); United States Commission on Civil Rights, "Appendix: Voting Irregularities in Florida During the 2000 Presidential Election" (June 2001); United States Commission on Civil Rights, "Election Reform: An Analysis of Proposals and the Commission's Recommendation for Improving America's Election Systems," (November 2001); United States Commission on Civil Rights, "Voting Irregularities in Florida during the 2000 Presidential Election," (June 2001).

Marsha J. Tyson Darling

Florida ex rel. Hawkins v. Board of Control of Florida, **347 U.S. 971 (1954), 350 U.S. 413 (1956)** In 1949 Virgil D. Hawkins, a graduate of Pennsylvania's Lincoln University, was denied admittance to the University of Florida Law School in Gainesville. Hawkins turned to the courts for assistance. In August 1952 the Florida Supreme Court upheld the Board of Control's decision and dismissed the case on the grounds that Hawkins could get an adequate legal education at the recently created law school at the all black Florida Agricultural and Mechanical University in Tallahassee. Hawkins appealed the decision to the U.S. Supreme Court, which on 24 May 1954 ordered the state court to reconsider the case in light of the recent *Brown v. Board of Education.* In March 1956 it directed the Board of Control to register Hawkins without further delay. Claiming that violence would result, the state Supreme Court employed stall tactics. The U.S. Supreme Court refused to hear a Hawkins appeal in 1957, but suggested that he "seek relief in an appropriate United States District Court." Federal district court Judge Dozier De Vane on 18 June 1958 ordered the University of Florida graduate schools opened to qualified blacks. The Law School then admitted African American George H. Starke in the fall semester of 1958.

Selected Bibliography Algia R. Cooper, "*Brown v. Board of Education* and Virgil Darnell Hawkins: Twenty-eight Years and Six Petitions to Justice," *Journal of Negro History* 64 (Winter 1979), 1–20; George Rossman, ed., "Recent Supreme Court Decisions," *American Law Association* Journal 42 (1956), 450; Samuel Selkow, "Hawkins, the United States Supreme Court and Justice," *Journal of Negro Education* 31 (Winter 1962), 91–101; Joseph A. Tomberlin, "Florida and the School Desegregation Issue, 1954–59: A Summary Review," *Journal of Negro Education* 43 (Fall 1974), 457–66; Joseph A. Tomberlin, "The Negro and Florida's System of Education: The Aftermath of the Brown Case" (Ph.D. diss., Florida State University, 1967).

Maxine D. Jones

Force Bill   (1890). Properly known as the Federal Elections Bill, Democrats labeled this Republican attempt to enforce the **Fifteenth Amendment** in the South a "force bill" because it authorized military supervision of federal elections. Sometimes called the "Lodge Bill" for its author, Massachusetts Congressman Henry Cabot Lodge, this measure was debated in the 51st, or "Billion Dollar" Congress of 1889–91. It represents the first and last significant federal attempt to ensure the franchise for African Americans between Reconstruction and the **Civil Rights Act of 1957.** The bill passed the House of Representatives in July 1890 on a strict party-line vote, but in one of the longest and bitterest filibusters in American history, Democrats and western Republicans united to defeat it in the Senate in February 1891. Its defeat marked a turning point in the history of the Republican party, as it has never sponsored any notable African American civil rights legislation since.

Selected Bibliography Thomas A. Upchurch, "The Billion Dollar Congress and Black America: Debating the Race Problem in the Eve of Jim Crow, 1889–1891" (Ph.D. diss., Mississippi State University, 2001); Daniel W. Crofts, "The Blair Bill and the Elections Bill: The Congressional Aftermath of Reconstruction" (Ph.D. diss., Yale University, 1968); Stanley P. Hirshson, *Farewell to the Bloody Shirt: Northern Republicans and the Southern Negro, 1877–1893* (1962); Rayford Logan, *The Negro in American Life and Thought: The Nadir, 1877–1901* (1954).

Thomas Adams Upchurch

Ford, James W.   (1893, Pratt City, Ala.–21 June 1957, New York, N.Y.). Son of an Alabama steel worker and a domestic working mother, Ford graduated from **Fisk University** in 1920, earning high marks as an athlete and scholar. During the 1920s, Ford migrated to Chicago where he worked as a parcel post dispatcher, joined the Postal Workers Union, read widely in the trade union movement, and became a member of the **Communist party.** He traveled to the Soviet Union in 1927 and 1928, rose through the ranks of the American Communist Party, and in 1929 became head of the International Trade Union Committee of Negro Workers. In the early Depression years, he left Chicago for New York City where he became chief organizer for the Harlem section of the Communist party and was deeply involved in leftist politics. A consistent supporter of Communist ideology and Marxist class theories, Ford was committed to building alliances between the black and white working classes. Running with William Z. Foster, he was the Communist party's vice presidential candidate in 1932, 1936, and 1940. In 1938 he was an unsuccessful candidate on the Communist ticket for a seat in the U.S. Senate. When party ideology shifted in the mid 1930s to the "united front," Ford gave his support to traditional black rights organizations, progressive unions, and the newly formed **National Negro Congress.** Despite a rather unyielding commitment to party ideology, Ford and Harlem Communists helped to spotlight civil rights issues such as the *Scottsboro* case and worked tirelessly against racial discrimination in public and private employment.

Selected Bibliography Harold Cruse, *Crisis of the Negro Intellectual* (1967); James W. Ford, *The Negro and the Democratic Front* (1938); Mark Naison, *Communists in Harlem During the Depression* (1983); Fraser M. Ottanelli, *The Communist Party of the United States: From the Depression to World War II* (1991); Wilson Record, *The Negro and the Communist Party* (1951).

John B. Kirby

Foreman, Clark H. (19 February 1902, Atlanta, Ga.–15 June 1977, Atlanta, Ga.). Born to a well-known Georgia family whose grandfather owned the *Atlanta Constitution,* Foreman studied at Harvard University, Columbia University, and the London School of Economics. As an undergraduate at the University of Georgia he witnessed the lynching of a black man. He committed himself to the cause of racial justice. In the 1920s, he worked for the **Commission on Interracial Cooperation** and the **Rosenwald Fund.** In 1933, he was chosen by **Harold L. Ickes** to be Special Adviser on Negro Affairs for the Department of Interior and Public Works Administration. Although appointment of a white southerner was initially criticized by many blacks, Foreman's strong support for the inclusion of blacks within New Deal programs and his selection of black economist, **Robert C. Weaver,** (who later replaced him) as his assistant, won over many of his critics. Leaving Interior in 1935, he held a number of other positions within the Roosevelt administration. In 1942 he was dismissed from the Federal Works Administration because of his strong condemnation of the racial conflict that occurred at the Sojourner Truth Housing Project in Detroit, Michigan. From 1942 to 1948, he led the **Southern Conference for Human Welfare,** one of the few organizations within the South during the 1940s and postwar years that continued to work for the improvement of race relations and black justice. At the time of his death, Foreman had long been associated with the Emergency Civil Liberties Committee and the cause of equal rights. He symbolized a small but influential group of white southern racial liberals who helped shape racial thought during the Roosevelt era and provided encouragement to the civil rights struggles of the 1950s and 1960s.

Selected Bibliography John G. Kirby, *Black Americans in the Roosevelt Era* (1980); Thomas A. Krueger, *And Promises to Keep* (1967); Linda Reed, *Simple Decency and Common Sense: The*

Southern Conference Movement, 1938–1963 (1991); Morton Sosna, *In Search of the Silent South* (1977); Patricia Sullivan, *Days of Hope: Race and Democracy in the New Deal Era* (1996).

John B. Kirby

Forman, James (4 October 1928, Chicago, Ill.–). A persistent African American leader, James Forman grew up in a working-class neighborhood in Chicago's southside. After high school, he entered the U.S. Air Force, became a veteran of the Korean War, and graduated from Chicago's Roosevelt University in 1957. On assignment for the *Chicago Defender* in 1958 reporting on the aftermath of the **Little Rock desegregation crisis** in Little Rock, Arkansas, he became active in the civil rights struggle. Later as a leader in Fayette County, Tennessee, he joined the **Student Nonviolent Coordinating Committee** (SNCC). The following year he became SNCC's executive secretary, a post he held for five years (1961–66). Forman's most widely publicized act was the demand for the United States to give reparations to the African American community. Forman first voiced this view in 1969 during a surprise speech at New York City's Riverside Church. He called for $500 million in reparations for the injustices of slavery, racism, and capitalism. Detailed in his 1969 Black Manifesto, the demand effectively raised the consciousness of white America to the enduring socioeconomic disadvantages experienced by African Americans. During the 1970s he continued to speak and work for civil rights causes across the country. He served several terms as president of the Unemployment and Poverty Action Council (UPAC) during the mid-1970s. He pursued educational goals and received his M.A. degree from Cornell University (1980) and his Ph.D. from the Union Institute (1982). In April, 1990 he received the 1990 National Conference of Black Mayors' **Fannie Lou Hamer** Freedom Award. A prolific writer, Dr. Forman has published several books about the civil rights movement, including *Sammy Young, Jr: The First Black College Student to Die in the Black Liberation Movement* (1968); *The Political Thought of James Forman* (1970); *The Makings of Black Revolutionaries* (1972); and *Self Determination: An Examination of the Question and Its Application to the African-American People* (1985). In later years, he worked with others in the struggle for the District of Columbia to gain statehood.

Selected Bibliography Michael Harrington and Arnold S. Kaufman, "Black Reparations: Two Views," *Dissent* 16 (July-August 1969), 317–20; *Afro-American Encyclopedia*, vol. 4 (1974); Robert S. Lecky and H. Elliot Wright, eds., *Black Manifesto* (1969); Derrick Bell, *And We Are Not Saved* (1987); Arnold Schuchter, *Reparations* (1970).

Glenn O. Phillips

Fortune, Timothy Thomas (3 October 1856, Jackson County, Fla.–2 June 1928, New York, N.Y.). Born into slavery, Fortune received limited education, but he did briefly attend a school sponsored by the **Freedmen's Bureau.** He learned the printer's trade in Jacksonville, Florida, where he became an expert compositor, and later moved to Washington, D.C., in the mid-1870s to work on the *People's Advocate*, a black newspaper. In 1879, Fortune moved to New

York City and took part ownership of the *Rumor*, which became the *Globe* in 1881 with Fortune as its editor. Following the failure of the *Globe* in 1884, Fortune became sole owner of the *New York Freeman*, which changed its name to the **New York Age** in 1887. Within a few years the *Age* became the premier black newspaper published in the United States, and Fortune rose to become the dean of African American journalists in America. The program and methods proposed in his contentious editorials in the *New York Age* and other publications anticipated the direction that would be taken by the civil rights movement in the twentieth century. Through the columns of his newspaper Fortune waged a militant struggle against all forms of discrimination and racial repression. He was the prime mover in the formation of the **Afro-American League** in 1890; this organization, although short-lived, later merged with the **Afro-American Council,** organized in 1898 at Rochester, New York. During the early 1920s, Fortune became editor of the **Negro World** the organ of **Marcus Garvey**'s **Universal Negro Improvement Association.**

Selected Bibliography *New York Age*, 27 February, 1886; *New York Amsterdam News*, 13 June, 1928; Emma Lou Thornbrough, *T. Thomas Fortune, Militant Journalist* (1970); Thomas A. Upchurch, "The Billion Dollar Congress and Black America: Debating the Race Problem on the Eve of Jim Crow, 1889–1891" (Ph.D. diss., Mississippi State University, 2001).

George E. Walker

Fourteenth Amendment   The Fourteenth Amendment to the Constitution of the United States was ratified in 1868. Of the Amendment's five sections, two directly punished the former Confederate states by repudiating the Confederate debt, guaranteeing the war debt of the United States, and prohibiting prominent Confederates from political participation. The final section delegated to Congress the power to enforce the provisions of the article.

The first two sections of the Amendment tried to redress the violence and discrimination of the **Black Codes** instituted to resubjugate the freed black population after the end of slavery. It conferred citizenship on African Americans; guaranteed the privileges and immunities of citizenship; prohibited states from depriving "any person of life, liberty, or property, without due process of law"; and guaranteed "equal protection of the laws." In addition, it empowered African Americans to exercise their citizenship and punished Confederate politicians by reducing state representation in Congress in proportion to the number of male voters denied the right to vote.

By 1877 southern politicians overlooked the civil rights guaranteed by the Fourteenth Amendment and, with the complicity of all branches of the federal government, neutralized the black vote and all black political participation. However, when enforced, the civil rights sections of the Amendment were used throughout the twentieth century to guarantee the civil rights of African Americans.

Selected Bibliography Mary Frances Berry, *Military Necessity and Civil Rights Policy: Black Citizenship and the Constitution, 1861–1868* (1977); James E. Bond, *No Easy Walk to Freedom: Reconstruction and the Ratification of the Fourteenth Amendment* (1997); Richard C. Cortner, *The*

Iron Horse and the Constitution: The Railroads and the Transformation of the Fourteenth Amendment (1993); Richard C. Cortner, *The Supreme Court and the Second Bill of Rights: The Fourteenth Amendment and the Nationalization of Civil Liberties* (1981); Michael Kent Curtis, *No State Shall Abridge: The Fourteenth Amendment and the Bill of Rights* (1990); Stephen P. Halbrook, *Freedmen, the Fourteenth Amendment, and the Right to Bear Arms, 1866–1876* (1998); Robert John Kaczorowski, *The Nationalization of Civil Rights: Constitutional Theory and Practice in a Racist Society, 1866–1883* (1972); Hermine Herta Meyer, *The History and Meaning of the Fourteenth Amendment: Judicial Erosion of the Constitution through the Misuse of the Fourteenth Amendment* (1977); Michael J. Perry, *We the People: The Fourteenth Amendment and the Supreme Court* (1999); United States Supreme Court, *The Civil Rights Cases [109 U.S. 3] in the Supreme Court of the United States, October 15, 1883* (1963).

Lillie Johnson Edwards

Franklin, John Hope (2 January 1915, Rentiesville, Okla.–). Graduating magna cum laude from **Fisk University** in Nashville, Tennessee, in 1935, Franklin enrolled at Harvard University where he received his M.A. in 1936. After he spent a year as an instructor at Fisk (1936–37), he returned to Harvard to work for his Ph.D., which he earned in 1941. A teaching position at St. Augustine's College (1939–43) in Raleigh, North Carolina, afforded him access to the sources he needed to complete his dissertation on free blacks in that state. When that work was published in 1943, he went to North Carolina College at Durham; and in 1947, he moved to **Howard University** in Washington, D.C. Brooklyn College invited him to join its faculty in 1956, and in 1964 he became a professor of history at the University of Chicago, where he served as department chair and was named the first John Matthews Manly Distinguished Service Professor of History. After retirement in 1982, he accepted appointment as the James B. Duke Professor of History at Duke University. Prominent among his works are *The Free Negro in North Carolina, 1790–1860* (1943); *From Slavery to Freedom: A History of Negro Americans* (1947; 8th ed., 2000); *The Militant South* (1956); *Reconstruction after the Civil War* (1961); and *A Southern Odyssey; Travellers in the Antebellum North* (1975). He became the first black to read a paper before the Southern Historical Association in 1949, and subsequently he was elected president of five major national scholarly organizations, including the American Studies Association, the American Historical Association, and the Organization of American Historians. His honors include the **Spingarn Medal,** the Presidential Medal of Freedom, more than one hundred honorary degrees, and other honors too numerous to list. He has generously given his professional expertise to public causes. Notable among his contributions was the research he did on the **Fourteenth Amendment** for the plaintiff's case in **Brown v. Board of Education**. In 1997 President Bill Clinton appointed him chair of the White House Initiative on Race and Reconciliations, which engaged in a year-long dialogue about race. In the same year Duke University, and the **Association for the Study of Negro Life and History** sponsored a symposium honoring Franklin and the 50th anniversary of the publication of *From Slavery to Freedom*. In the late 1990s he served as chair of the President Bill **Clinton Advisory Board to the President's Initiative on Race.**

Selected Bibliography William Leuchtenberg, "Tribute to John Hope Franklin," *Duke Law Journal* 42 (March 1993), 1022–27; Frank L. Matthews, "The Genius of John Hope Franklin," *Black Issues in Higher Education* (13 January 1994), 16–22; August Meier and Elliott Rudwick, *Black History and the Historical Profession, 1915–1980* (1986); Jessie Carney Smith, ed., *Notable Black American Men* (1998); Charles V. Willie, *Five Black Scholars: An Analysis of Family Life, Education, and Career* (1986).

Gary B. Mills

***Frasier v. Board of Trustees of the University of North Carolina*, 134 F. Supp. 589 (M.D.N.C., 1955)** Some states continued to enforce segregation in higher education in 1955, despite the Supreme Court rulings in *Sipuel v. Board of Regents of the University of Oklahoma* and *Brown v. Board of Education.* The University of North Carolina (UNC) system pursued such a policy, although it had admitted blacks to graduate and professional programs. Leroy Benjamin Frasier and two other African American students challenged this policy in the spring of 1955. The University declined their application because of their race. The students appealed to the board of trustees without success. In May, the board affirmed its policy: "It is hereby declared to be the policy of the Board of Trustees . . . that applications of Negroes to the undergraduate schools of the three branches of the Consolidated University be not accepted." It assumed that segregated colleges satisfied the terms of the **Fourteenth Amendment.** The students then filed a class action suit in federal courts. Attorneys argued that the policy of the UNC system violated the equal protection of the law clause of the Fourteenth Amendment. The court agreed. That fall, the university enrolled three black students in its undergraduate program.

Selected Bibliography Richard Bardolph, ed., *The Civil Rights Record, Black Americans and the Law, 1849–1970* (1970); U.S. Commission on Civil Rights: *Equal Protection of the Laws in Public Higher Education* (1957).

Stephen Middleton

Frazier, Edward Franklin (24 September 1894, Baltimore, Md.–17 May 1962, Washington, D.C.). After graduating from **Howard University** with honors in 1916, Frazier taught at **Tuskegee Institute** in Alabama; St. Paul's Normal and Industrial School at Lawrenceville, Virginia; and Baltimore High School. Entering graduate school at Clark University in Worcester, Massachusetts, in 1919, he completed his master's degree in sociology in 1920. A Russel Sage Foundation fellowship financed a year's study at the New York School of Social Work; then, aided by an American Scandinavian Foundation Fellowship, he studied another year at the University of Copenhagen. Returning in 1922, he accepted a position at **Atlanta University** as director of its school of social work, but his stay there was terminated in 1927 by white reactions to an article he wrote for *Forum Magazine*, "The Pathology of Race Prejudice." He entered the doctoral program in sociology at the University of Chicago, and his dissertation, "The

Negro Family in Chicago," was completed in 1931 while he was teaching at **Fisk University.** He went to Howard University in 1934, where he served in various capacities until his death. Among his published works were *The Negro Family in Chicago* (1932), *The Negro Family in the United States* (1939), *Black Bourgeoisie* (1957), and *Race and Culture Contacts in the Modern World* (1957). His intellectual achievements won him elective offices in numerous professional organizations—most significantly to the presidency of the American Sociological Society in 1948. He was one of the first blacks to serve as the head of a national professional association in the United States. His major contributions were his studies of the black family and race relations. His analysis of the impact that slavery, sudden freedom, urban migrations, and dislocations had had on the family produced sociological explanations rather than racial or genetic condemnations; thus, Frazier helped find a plausible cause for African American problems that was prerequisite to any cure. He also attacked the theories of **Melville Jean Herskovits** on the survival of Africanisms, for enabling whites to blame black antisocial behavior upon surviving African traits rather than upon societal oppression. Although he argued for equal rights and integration, Frazier nevertheless felt that blacks should not sacrifice their positive cultural identity for the sake of equality. He was not an "assimilationist," as some have asserted.

Selected Bibliography Rayford W. Logan and Michael R. Winston, eds., *Dictionary of American Negro Biography* (1982); August Meier, *Negro Thought in American, 1880–1915: Racial Ideologies in the Age of Booker T. Washington* (1963); August Meier and Elliott Rudwick, *Black History and the Historical Profession, 1915–1980* (1986); Anthony M. Platt, *E. Franklin Frazier* (1991); Vernon J. Williams, Jr., "E. Franklin Frazier and the African American Family in Historical Perspective," *Western Journal of Black Studies* 23 (No. 4, 1999), 246–51.

Gary B. Mills

Free Southern Theater During the fall of 1963, three civil right workers in Mississippi conceived the idea of using drama to communicate the aims of the civil rights movement to masses of black people in the rural South. John O'Neal and Doris Derby of the **Student Nonviolent Coordinating Committee** and Gilbert Moses, a reporter for the *Mississippi Free Press*, established an integrated touring company whose productions were intended to educate southern blacks about the institutional barriers to progress and to encourage people to either join or support the civil rights movement in their local communities. During **Freedom Summer of 1964,** the Free Southern Theater conducted a theater workshop for students from **Tougaloo College** and Jackson State College. After opening with *In White America* in Jackson with an integrated cast drawn from the Mississippi Summer Project volunteers, Free Southern Theater made a 21-town tour of Mississippi, Louisiana, and Tennessee. The successful tour touched audiences in much the way the organizers had envisioned. After the 28 November 1964 performance of *Waiting for Godot*, for example, **Fannie Lou Hamer** is reported to have remarked that the play presented a character "somewhat similar to any person in a suffering condition who just keeps on waiting and nothing happens." Drama of the absurd could intensify the meaning of what the ardent struggle for civil rights entailed. By 1970, Free Southern Theater was less a touring company than a community theater project in New Orleans, Louisiana, where it ceased to be a cultural arm of the civil rights movement.

Selected Bibliography Annemarie Bean, ed., *A Sourcebook of African-American Performance: Plays, People, Movements* (1999); Tom Dent, Gilbert Moses, and Richard Schechner, eds., *The Free Southern Theater by the Free Southern Theater* (1969); Genevieve Fabre, *Drumbeats, Masks, and Metaphor: Contemporary Afro-American Theater* (1983); Larry Neal, "Free Southern Theatre, the Conquest of the South," *The Drama Review* 14 (1970), 169–74; John O'Neal, "Motion in the Ocean: Some Political Dimensions of the Free Southern Theatre," *Drama Review* 12 (Summer 1968), 70–77.

Jerry Ward

Freedman's Bank   The Freedman's Bank chartered by Congress on 3 March 1865 as the Freedman's Savings and Trust Company was "designed to furnish a place of security and profit for the hard earnings of the colored people, especially at the South." It began operations on 4 April 1865. The business of the bank was confined to blacks. Its 34 branches were located in every state of the South as well as in New York City and Philadelphia. Although it was an independent institution, the bank worked closely with the **Freedmen's Bureau** in encouraging blacks to deposit their money in the bank's offices. During the nine years that the bank operated, total deposits amounted to 56 million dollars. The Freedman's Bank was forced to close its doors on 28 June 1874, and its depositors lost their savings. The failure of the bank was partially due to a general business depression in the country; but the major cause was mismanagement of its funds by its officers, many of whom were influential members of the Republican party.

Selected Bibliography George R. Bentley, *A History of the Freedmen's Bureau* (1974); W.E.B. Du Bois, *Black Reconstruction in America* (1935); Walter L. Fleming, *Documentary History of Reconstruction* (1906).

Robert A. Bellinger

Freedmen's Bureau   Many have viewed the Freedmen's Bureau as the original federal civil rights agency for blacks. Congress created the bureau in March 1865 under its official title, the Bureau of Refugees, Freedmen, and Abandoned Lands. It initially fed, clothed, sheltered, and gave medical care to more whites than blacks; it became identified with freedmen only after Congress directed it to promote their general welfare. President Andrew Johnson criticized the Bureau in 1866 and attempted to kill it, charging that it "would not be consistent with the public welfare." Headed by Commissioner **Oliver Otis Howard,** a veteran U.S. Army major general, the bureau supervised freedmen's labor and legal relations. To secure justice in hostile jurisdictions it sometimes conducted court proceedings. Its services reached far, even to establishing a missing persons agency to help reunite families separated by slavery. The bureau had established more than 40 hospitals by 1867 and had

The Misses Cooke's school room, Freedmen's Bureau, Richmond, Virginia, 1866. ©
Library of Congress.

distributed 21 million meals by 1869. By 1870 it had initiated 4,239 schools with 9,307 teachers and 247,333 students. Many of the oldest historically black colleges and universities owe a debt to the bureau. Feeble congressional and national commitment to full and equal citizenship for blacks caused the bureau to die after 1868.

Selected Bibliography George R. Bentley, *A History of the Freedmen's Bureau* (1955); John A. Carpenter, *Sword and Olive Branch: Oliver Otis Howard* (1964); Paul A. Cimbala and Randall M. Miller, eds., *The Freedman's Bureau and Reconstruction: Reconsiderations* (1999); William S. McFeely, *Yankee Stepfather: General O. O. Howard and the Freedmen* (1968); Donald G. Nieman, *To Set the Law in Motion: The Freedmen's Bureau and the Legal Rights of Blacks, 1865–1868* (1979); Donald G. Nieman, ed., *The Freedman's Bureau and Black Freedom* (1994); Donald G. Nieman, "Andrew Johnson, the Freedmen's Bureau, and the Problem of Equal Rights, 1865–1866," *Journal of Southern History* 44(August 1978), 399–420; Claude F. Oubre, *Forty Acres and a Mule: The Freedmen's Bureau and Black Landownership* (1978); Paul S. Pierce, *The Freedmen's Bureau* (1904).

Thomas J. Davis

Freedom Riders   **James Farmer,** national director of the **Congress of Racial Equality** (CORE), planned the first Freedom Ride of the 1960s as a nonviolent direct action test of ***Boynton v. Virginia*** (1960), which had declared segregation in railway and bus terminal accommodations to be unconstitutional. Thirteen persons, including Farmer, left Washington, D.C., on 4 May 1961 for Georgia, Alabama, and Mississippi. In Anniston, Alabama, one bus was destroyed and riders on another were attacked. The interracial Freedom Riders

Freedom Riders met with violence in Anniston, Alabama, and other destinations in the South. Copyright. Photo by *The Birmingham News*, 2003. All rights reserved. Reprinted with permission.

continued the protest throughout the summer. By the time the Interstate Commerce Commission prohibited segregated accommodations in November 1961, over a thousand participants had attempted a Freedom Ride, and CORE's credentials as a militant pacifist organization had been established. Later Freedom Riders met with similar violence but with eventual success.

Selected Bibliography Catherine A. Barnes, *Journey From Jim Crow: The Desegregation of Southern Transit* (1983); R. J. Brisbane, *Black Activism: Racial Revolution in the United States, 1954–1970* (1974); James Farmer, *Lay Bare the Heart: An Autobiography of the Civil Rights Movement* (1985); August Meier and Elliot Rudwick, *CORE: A Study in the Civil Rights Movement: 1942–1968* (1973); August Meier and Elliot Rudwick, "The First Freedom Ride," *Phylon* 30 (Fall 1969), 213–22; Kenneth O'Reilly, "The FBI and the Civil Rights Movement during the Kennedy Years: From the Freedom Rides to Albany," *Journal of Southern History* 54 (May 1988), 201–32.

Thaddeus M. Smith

Freedom Summer of 1964   Approximately one thousand northern, predominantly white, college students joined a cadre of predominantly African

Freedom Summer school class, Mississippi, summer, 1964.
© Staughton Lynd Collection, Wisconsin Historical Society.

American freedom fighters in Mississippi. They registered thousands of black voters and provided health and education services through community centers and Freedom schools. The **Student Nonviolent Coordinating Committee** initiated this project, which was jointly supported through the **Council of Federated Organizations** and directed by **Robert Moses.**

Volunteers received prior training in nonviolence, self-defense, Mississippi mores, and how to behave under arrest. On June 21 three volunteers were reported missing from Neshoba County. The search for **James Earl Chaney,** a local African American, and New York volunteers **Michael Henry Schwerner** and **Andrew Goodman** continued until August 4, when their bodies were unearthed from a dam. (Seven members of the Ku Klux Klan, convicted of the murders in 1967, were later paroled and set free.) Terrorism pervaded the summer. Workers endured at least 80 beatings, 1,000 arrests, and 67 incidents of bombings and arson.

A major focus of the project was building the grassroots **Mississippi Freedom Democratic Party** (MFDP). A MFDP delegation challenged the all-white regulars for their seats at the Democratic National Convention in August 1964. Party chiefs responded with overt compromises and covert sabotage and suppression.

Short-term perceptions of Freedom Summer emphasized disillusionment with liberal politics and increasingly strained relations between African American activists and white volunteers. Later perspectives credited the project with hastening passage of the **Voting Rights Act of 1965** and opening the way for federally funded health clinics and **Head Start** programs. Increasingly, scholarly assessments qualify the importance of the roles played by the volunteers and emphasize the agency and perseverance of local African Americans.

Selected Bibliography Seth Cagin and Philip Dray, *We Are Not Afraid: The Story of Goodman, Schwerner, and Chaney and the Civil Rights Campaign for Mississippi* (1988); John Dittmer, *Local People: The Struggle of Civil Rights in Mississippi* (1994); Sara Evans, *Personal Politics* (1980); Mary King, *Freedom Song: A Personal Story of the 1960s Civil Rights Movement* (1987); Doug McAdam, *Freedom Summer* (1988); Charles M. Payne, *I've Got the Light of Freedom: The Organizing Tradition and the Mississippi Freedom Struggles* (1995); Mary Aiken Rothschild, *A Case of Black and White: Northern Volunteers and the Southern Freedom Summers, 1964–1965* (1982); Elizabeth Sutherland, ed., *Letters From Mississippi* (1965).

Jo Ann O. Robinson

Freedom Vote Campaign In November of 1963, the **Student Nonviolent Coordinating Committee** sponsored a protest vote within the Mississippi African American community. According to Mississippi law, voters who claimed illegal exclusion from registration were permitted to cast ballots that would be set aside until they could appeal their exclusion. With the assistance of Allard Lowenstein and numerous northern white student volunteers, more than eighty thousand African Americans cast ballots in the Freedom Vote Campaign. Because regular polling stations were intimidating, the Freedom

Vote Campaign provided African Americans with an opportunity to vote for civil rights candidates in their own communities.

Selected Bibliography Clayborne Carson, *In Struggle: SNCC and the Black Awakening of the 1960s* (1981); James Forman, *The Making of Black Revolutionaries* (1972); Lawrence Guyot and Mike Thelwell, "The Politics of Necessity and Survival in Mississippi," *Freedomways* (1966); Margaret Long, "The Mississippi Freedom Vote," *New South* (December 1963) 10–13; August Meier and Elliot Rudwick, *CORE: A Study in the Civil Rights Movement, 1942–1968* (1973); Joseph A. Sinsheimer, "The Freedom Vote of 1963: New Strategies of Racial Protest in Mississippi," *Journal of Southern History* 55 (1989), 217–44.

Donald Cunnigen

Freedomways   In an attempt to unite the liberation movements in Africa and the United States, Shirley Graham Du Bois, wife of famed scholar and activist, **W.E.B. Du Bois,** established the journal *Freedomways* in 1961. Designed to uplift all black peoples, *Freedomways* sought to examine and enhance relations of black peoples in Africa, North and South America, and wherever such peoples existed anywhere in the world. A Pan-African journal, *Freedomways* not only highlighted the struggle for freedom shared by blacks worldwide, but it also offered opportunities to veteran and fledging writers to enunciate their views on black liberation. African Americans such as **Martin Luther King, Jr.,** **James Baldwin**, and **Alice Walker** made contributions to the journal. After Mrs. Du Bois's death in 1977, John Henrik Clarke, a staunch Pan-Africanist and prolific author, assumed editorial responsibilities until 1982. Three years later *Freedomways* ceased publication. Despite its brief 24-year existence, *Freedomways* aided and united black peoples globally, by bringing to the fore racial, social, and political inequities.

Selected Bibliography Shirley Graham Du Bois, *His Day is Marching On* (1971); Kathy A. Perkins, "The Unknown Career of Shirley Graham," *Freedomways* 25 (No. 1, 1985), 6–17; Rhonda Stewart, "Anthology Revives the Spirit of *Freedomways*," *Emerge* 11 (28 February 2000), 106.

Edward J. Robinson

Freeman v. Pitts, **503 U.S. 467 (1992)**   School officials in a Georgia county school system, which was once segregated by law, filed a motion in federal court to end judicial supervision over schools in DeKalb County (a suburb of Atlanta). The Supreme Court, in a majority opinion written by Justice Anthony M. Kennedy, held that a federal court in a school desegregation case has the authority and discretion to order partial withdrawal of the court's supervision and control of the school district before full compliance ("unitary status") has been achieved in every area of school operations. In reaching this decision, the Supreme Court confirmed the importance of returning schools to the control of local authorities at the "earliest practicable date." To determine whether a court should partially withdraw its supervision, the Supreme Court ruled that a district court needs to consider three factors: (1) whether there had been full and satisfactory compliance with the decree on those aspects of the system where supervision was to be withdrawn, (2) whether retention of judicial control was necessary or practicable to achieve compliance with the decree in other aspects of the school system, and (3) whether the school district had demonstrated a good faith commitment to complying with the court's decree and the Constitution. The Supreme Court also observed that a district court could consider the factor of quality of education in determining whether a school system had achieved unitary statue. A school district, however, could not be held responsible for subsequent racial imbalances in schools due to independent demographic factors.

Selected Bibliography Henry J. Abraham and Barbara A. Perry, *Freedom and the Court: Civil Rights and Liberties in the United States*, 6th ed. (1994); David J. Armor, *Forced Justice: School Desegregation and the Law* (1995); Wendy Parker, "The Future of School Desegregation," *Northwestern University Law Review* 94 (Summer 2000), 1157–1227.

Elizabeth M. Smith

Friends Association of Philadelphia and Its Vicinity for the Relief of Colored Freedmen Organized in November 1863, this organization (also known as the Friends Freedmen's Relief Association and the Friend's Colored Relief Association of Philadelphia) was one of two Quaker freedmen's aid societies in Philadelphia. Among its officers were Richard Cadbury, Thomas Scattergood, Benjamin Coats, and Charles Rhoads. Its purpose was "to relieve the wants, provide for the instruction and protect the rights of the freedmen." The association did its work mainly in Virginia and North Carolina, where it opened stores. It began with funds of $53,000, some of which was donated by English Quakers. By 1867 the association had spent $210,500 in support of its activities. It went out of existence in 1869.

Selected Bibliography Julius H. Parelee, "Freedmen's Aid Societies, 1861–1871," U.S. Department of the Interior, Office of Education, *Bulletin* 38 (1916), 268–300; Henry Lee Swint, *The Northern Teacher in the South, 1862–1870* (1967).

Judith N. Kerr

Friends of Negro Freedom Founded in Washington, D.C., in May 1920 by **A. Philip Randolph** and Chandler Owen, the Friends of Negro Freedom organized the "Garvey Must Go" campaign to eliminate the **Universal Negro Improvement Association** led by Jamaican-born **Marcus Mosiah Garvey.** The organization, made up of black conservatives, moderates, and radicals all linked by their fear of Garveyism, in January 1923 wrote an open letter to United States Attorney General Harry M. Daugherty, urging Garvey's deportation as an "undesirable alien."

Selected Bibliography Tony Martin, *Race First: The Ideological and Organizational Struggles of Marcus Garvey and the Universal Negro Improvement Association* (1976).

Quintard Taylor

Fuller, Meta Vaux Warrick (9 June 1877, Philadelphia, Pa.–18 March 1968, Framingham, Mass.). One of America's first African American women studio sculptors, Fuller attended Philadelphia public schools and received her art education at J. Liberty Tadd's, the Pennsylvania Museum School (1895–98), and the Pennsylvania Academy of the Fine Arts (1906). Between 1899 and 1902, Fuller studied in Paris, where in 1902 she became a protegee of Auguste Rodin. Although Fuller's work predates the **Harlem Renaissance,** she was active during that period. In 1917 she produced two antilynching sculptures, one of which depicted Mary Turner, whose case **Walter Francis White** investigated for the **NAACP.** Her *Ethiopia Awakening* (1921) was a compelling representation of the Harlem Renaissance's spirit. Meta Fuller was still working at the time of the civil rights movement of the 1960s. She produced sculpture that symbolized that era as well: *The Crucifixion*, her reaction to the murder of four girls in the bombing of the Sixteenth Street Baptist Church in Birmingham, Alabama on 15 September 1963, and *The Good Samaritan*, dedicated to the clergy who had gone south to Alabama to join **Martin Luther King, Jr.**'s march across Selma's Edmund Pettus Bridge on Sunday, 9 March 1965. During a career that spanned more than 60 years, Fuller portrayed the dignity and human rights struggle of African Americans realistically, chronicled historical events, and, occasionally, created a silent protest against racial injustice.

Selected Bibliography *Crisis* (January 1918), 133, (January 1919), 135, (November 1919), 350, (April 1920), 337; Judith N. Kerr, "God-Given Work: The Life and Times of Sculptor Meta Vaux Warrick Fuller, 1877–1968" (Ph.D. diss., University of Massachusetts, 1986); William Francis O'Donnell, "Meta Vaux Warrick, Sculptor of Horrors," *The World Today* 13 (November 1907), 1139–45; James A. Porter, *Modern Negro Art* (1943).

Judith N. Kerr

Fuller, S. Bacon (4 June 1905, Monroe, La.–24 October 1988, Blue Island, Ill.). A Chicago African American businessman, Fuller, in 1935, established Fuller's Products Company with 25 dollars and built a multimillion-dollar national sales corporation by 1960. In spite of having only a sixth-grade education, Fuller was the "Godfather" of many other black businesses. His holdings included the *Pittsburgh Courier* and *New York Age* newspapers, a department store and theater, and farming and beef cattle investments. He was the first black member of the National Association of Manufacturers (NAM). At a December 1963 NAM convention, Fuller infuriated black leaders when he stated that blacks should show more initiative in raising their economic level. In response blacks boycotted his enterprises, which nearly led to his bankruptcy.

Selected Bibliography "S. Bacon Fuller," *Jet*, 7 November 1988; *New York Times*, 7 December 1963, 16 January 1965, 28 October, 7 November 1988; *Who's Who in America*, *1974–1975* (1975).

Wali Rashash Kharif

***Fullilove v. Klutznick*, 448 U.S. 448 (1980)** Race-conscious programs to remedy the effects of past discrimination have been extremely controversial. *Fullilove v. Klutznick* presented the Supreme Court with the congressional application of a race-conscious policy to the granting of contracts for state or local public works projects funded by the Public Works Employment Act of 1977. State or local governments receiving federal construction grants were required to set aside at least 10 percent of the funds to purchase goods or services from minority business enterprises. By a vote of six to three, the Supreme Court upheld the constitutionality of this minority "set-aside." The controversial nature of such programs was evident in that the six justices who voted to uphold the legislation could not produce a majority opinion. Three believed that the legislation was supported by several of Congress's powers. For the other three justices, class-based remedies were justified because discrimination against blacks had been class-based. However, when the city of Richmond, Virginia, adopted a minority set-aside patterned after the one upheld in *Fullilove,* another divided Court held that a city had no such authority. The latter decisions reflected President Ronald Reagan's appointments to the Court. The increasingly conservative Court further undermined *Fullilove* in **Aderand Constructors, Inc. v. Peña** (1995).

Selected Bibliography *Aderand Constructors, Inc. v. Peña,* 115 S Ct. 2097 (1995); *City of Richmond v. J. A. Croson Co.,* 109 U.S. 706 (1989); Comment, "*Fullilove* and the Minority Set Aside: In Search of an Affirmative Action Rationale," *Emory Law Journal* 29 (Fall 1980), 1127–82; Peter Kilgore, "Racial Preferences in the Federal Grant Programs: Is There a Basis for Challenge after Fullilove v. Klutznick?" *Labor Law Journal* 32 (May 1981), 306–14.

Patricia A. Behlar

G

Galamison, Milton A. (25 January 1923, Philadelphia, Pa.–9 March 1988, New York, N.Y.). An African American Presbyterian minister in Brooklyn, New York, Galamison waged a campaign for full school desegregation through the use of black student boycotts and strikes. As chairman of the City Wide Committee for Integrated Schools, Galamison spearheaded the 1964 boycott of New York City schools and played a vital role four years later in a teachers' strike for equity and racial equality. For Galamison, the public school boycott was an effective "form of civil disobedience" against social injustice.

Selected Bibliography Kenneth B. Clark, *Dark Ghetto* (1965); August Meier and Elliott Rudwick, eds., *Black Protest in the Sixties* (1970); Benjamin Muse, *The American Negro Revolution: From Nonviolence to Black Power, 1963–1967* (1968).

LeRoy T. Williams

Garner v. Louisiana, 368 U.S. 157 (1961) In the spring of 1960, several African American college students in Baton Rouge, Louisiana, held a sit-in at drugstore and bus terminal lunch counters that were reserved for white customers. They were arrested and convicted of disturbing the peace. The U.S. Supreme Court overturned the students' convictions, stating that there was no evidence that they had violated Louisiana law by their peaceful sit-in at the lunch counters. The Court found that the students' peaceful protest did not fall within the state's own interpretation of its statute relating to disturbance of the peace and noted that the Louisiana legislature had, after the students' arrest, attempted to modify the statute to fit the actions of the sit-in participants. Garner and the other protesters had violated the custom of segregated lunch counters, but their activities could not be considered to be a violation of Louisiana law. The students' convictions had been a misapplication of the disturbing the peace statute and had deprived them of their right to due process under the **Fourteenth Amendment.** This case struck a blow at the ability of states to prosecute African Americans for violating the custom of segregation and for peacefully protesting for their civil rights.

Selected Bibliography Derrick A. Bell, Jr., *Race, Racism and American Law* (1980); Loren Miller, *The Petitioners, the Story of the Supreme Court of the United States and the Negro* (1966); Aldon D. Morris, *The Origins of the Civil Rights Movement* (1984); George Rossman, ed., "Review of Recent Supreme Court Decisions," *American Bar Association Journal* 48 (1962), 169.

Steve Sadowsky

Garvey, Marcus Mosiah   (17 August 1887, St. Ann's Bay, Jamaica–10 June 1940, London, England). A Pan-African nationalist and founder of the **Universal Negro Improvement Association** (UNIA), Garvey was born in rural Jamaica. After about seven years of schooling, he became an apprentice printer, became disillusioned after participating in an unsuccessful printers' strike that made him skeptical of trade unions, and migrated to England about 1911. Enrolled briefly at Birbeck College, he came into contact with African intellectuals who ignited in him a desire to study and disseminate information about Africa and Africans.

Returning to Jamaica in 1914, he launched the Universal Negro Improvement and Conservation Association and African Communities League. Its main aim was "to draw the peoples of the race together," and one of its earliest goals was to develop a trade school for the poor and unskilled patterned after **Tuskegee Institute** in Alabama.

Garvey arrived in the United States on 23 March 1916 and immediately launched a year-long speaking tour of 38 states. His message was well received, and he organized the first branch of UNIA in the United States in June 1917. He began publishing the **Negro World,** which promoted his African nationalist ideas and made Liberty Hall in New York City the official headquarters of the UNIA.

During 1919, Garvey's popularity soared as he initiated a Back-to-Africa Movement. He presided over a UNIA with dozens of chapters and thousands of followers in the United States and around the world. The UNIA stressed the need for real economic opportunities and the uniting of persons of African descent for their collective betterment. In 1919 Garvey's UNIA purchased three ships and developed the **Black Star Steamship Line.** In August 1920, at a UNIA convention, he was unanimously elected the provisional president of Africa. Garvey sought to work with the Liberian government to settle followers in Africa.

In 1925 Garvey was convicted on a mail fraud charge and sentenced to a five-year prison term. He had served half of the sentence when President Calvin Coolidge commuted the rest of his prison term and had him deported. Garvey returned to Jamaica to a hero's welcome from the Jamaican under classes. He established the Peoples' Political Party and sought to enter Jamaican politics in 1929. The British Colonial authorities discouraged his efforts. He was imprisoned for three and a half months for statements he made at a public meeting. He made his last attempt in the 1930 elections for a seat in the Legislative Council. Beginning in July 1932 he published *The New Jamaican* and *The Black Man's Magazine*. He also launched a development program aimed at raising millions of dollars for new jobs for the poor.

On March 26, 1935, Garvey sailed for England where he resided for the rest of his life. He continued speaking out on civil rights and the ideals of the **Pan-African movement.** He died on 10 June 1940 in London with unfulfilled aspirations, but his ideas and writings inspired many of the leaders and spokespersons of the civil rights era.

Selected Bibliography David E. Cronon, *Black Moses: The Story of Marcus Garvey and the Universal Negro Improvement Association* (1955); Elton C. Fax, *Garvey: The Story of a Pioneer Black Nationalist* (1972); Amy Jacques Garvey, ed., *Philosophy and Opinions of Marcus Garvey* (1969); Robert A. Hill, ed., *The Marcus Garvey and Universal Negro Improvement Association Papers*, 7 vols. (1983–90); Judith Stein, *The World of Marcus Garvey: Race and Class in Modern Society* (1986); Tony Martin, *Race First: The Ideological and Organizational Struggles of Marcus Garvey* (1976).

Glenn O. Phillips

Gaston County v. United States, 395 U.S. 285 (1969)   Among the devices used by southern states to disfranchise blacks was the literacy test. Gaston County, North Carolina, had utilized such a test. When Gaston County came under the coverage of the **Voting Rights Act of 1965,** however, its literacy test, like that of other covered states and subdivisions of states, was suspended. The county, under the terms of the Voting Rights Act, sought to have the ban on its literacy test lifted by obtaining a declaratory judgment from the District Court for the District of Columbia that no "test or device" had been used during the previous five years for the purpose or effect of denying the right to vote based upon race. In an opinion by Judge **J. Skelly Wright,** the district court denied Gaston County's petition on grounds that the majority of its voting-age blacks had attended inferior, segregated schools; therefore, even a fairly administered literacy test would have a discriminatory effect. The Supreme Court affirmed the decision for "substantially the reasons given by the majority of the District Court." The decision meant that the literacy tests of other areas under the Voting Rights Act would remain suspended, since they, too, had had segregated schools.

Selected Bibliography Richard Claude, *The Supreme Court and the Electoral Process* (1970); Owen M. Fiss, "*Gaston County v. United States:* Fruition of the Freezing Principle," *Supreme Court Review* (1969), 379–445; *Washington Post*, 3 June 1969.

Patricia A. Behlar

General Education Board   John D. Rockefeller, with an initial one-million-dollar gift, founded this organization in 1902. By the time of its final grant in 1960, the General Education Board (GEB) had appropriated almost $325 million to aid education. Approximately 20 percent of GEB funds went toward the development of African American industrial and agricultural education in the South. Credited with helping to establish southern high schools through support of African American training schools, the GEB is criticized for following an accommodationist policy that expanded educational programs modeled on the Hampton-Tuskegee industrial training curriculum and thus perpetuated racially segregated and unequal school systems.

Selected Bibliography James D. Anderson, "Northern Foundations and the Shaping of Southern Black Rural Education, 1902–1935," *History of Education Quarterly* (Winter 1978), 371–96; Raymond B. Fosdick, *Adventure in Giving* (1962); Waldemar A. Nielsen, *The Big Foundations* (1972); J. M. Stephen Peeps, "Northern Philanthropy and the Emergence of Black Higher Education: Do-Gooders, Compromise, or Co-conspirators?" *The Journal of Negro Education* 50 (Summer 1981), 251–69.

Janice M. Leone

***Georgia v. McCollum*, 505 U.S. 42 (1992)** The Supreme Court, in a majority opinion written by Justice Harry Blackmun, held that a criminal defendant's racially discriminatory use of peremptory challenges in the process of selecting a jury violates the equal protection clause of the **Fourteenth Amendment.** The Supreme Court determined that a criminal defendant's exercise of peremptory challenges constitutes state action for equal protection purposes, and that a defendant charged with such discrimination could be described as a "state actor." Prohibiting the defendant's discriminatory exercise of peremptory challenges did not violate a criminal defendant's Sixth Amendment right to an impartial jury. The Supreme Court also concluded that a prosecutor had third-party standing to raise the equal protection claim on behalf of excluded jurors.

Selected Bibliography Henry J. Abraham and Barbara A. Perry, *Freedom and the Courts: Civil Rights and Liberties in the United States* (1994); Stephen R. DiPrima, "Note: Selecting a Jury in Federal Criminal Trials after Baston and McCollum," *Columbia Law Review* 95 (May 1995), 888–928; Randall Kennedy, *Race, Crime, and the Law* (1997).

Elizabeth M. Smith

***Gibson v. Florida Legislative Investigation Committee*, 372 U.S. 539 (1963)** Following **Brown v. Board of Education,** the Florida Legislative Investigation Committee attempted to obtain the membership rosters of the state branches of the **NAACP.** At a public hearing in 1958, Father Theodore R. Gibson, president of the Miami chapter, declined to turn over the records for fear of exposing NAACP members to the danger of racist retaliation. The committee claimed that it needed to uncover the identity of NAACP followers as part of its probe into Communist influence on race relations. The Florida Supreme Court ordered Gibson to consult his files before answering questions about the presence of alleged Communists in his group, but it did not require him actually to hand over the lists to the committee. Gibson refused, and in March 1963, the U.S. Supreme Court upheld his decision. Speaking for a majority of five, Justice Arthur Goldberg declared that the investigation committee had not shown a direct connection between the NAACP and subversive activities and could not infringe upon the group's right to privacy and the free association of its members. This opinion stymied further efforts to investigate the NAACP and raised the standard of protection for members of legitimate organizations investigated by legislative committees.

Selected Bibliography Harry Kalven, Jr., *The Negro and the First Amendment* (1965); Steven Lawson, "The Florida Legislative Investigation Committee and the Constitutional Readjustment of Race Relations, 1956–1963," in Kermit L. Hall and James W. Ely, Jr., eds., *An Uncertain Tradition: Constitutionalism and the History of the South* (1989); Paul L. Murphy, *The Constitution in Crisis Times* (1972); Wilson Record, *Race and Radicalism: The NAACP and the Communist Party in Conflict* (1964).

Steven F. Lawson

Giles v. Harris, **189 U.S. 475 (1903)**   Alabama's 1901 constitution embodied various devices including the good character requirement and understanding and literacy tests designed to disenfranchise blacks. Jackson W. Giles, a black citizen of Montgomery, was denied the right to register, so he sought a federal court order compelling local election officials to register qualified blacks. He alleged that various provisions of the state constitution violated the **Fourteenth** and **Fifteen Amendments.** The district court held that it did not have jurisdiction. Upon appeal, the Supreme Court held that federal courts could hear the case. However, on the curious grounds that if, as alleged, Alabama's registration scheme was a fraud upon the Constitution, an order to register Giles would make the Court a party to that fraud by adding another voter to a fraudulent registration list. The Court refused to order Giles's registration. Further, the Court took a narrow view of the judiciary's enforcement power; short of supervising elections in Alabama, the Court could envisage no means of enforcing political rights. It concluded that those suffering from political wrongs should turn to the political branches, not to the judiciary, for relief.

Selected Bibliography Richard Claude, *The Supreme Court and the Electoral Process* (1970); Donald R. Matthews and James Prothro, *Negroes and the New Southern Politics* (1966); Richard H. Pildes, "Democracy, Anti-Democracy, and the Canon," *Constitutional Commentary* 17 (2000), 25–319.

Earlean M. McCarrick

Giles v. Teasley, **193 U.S. 146 (1904)**   After the Supreme Court in 1903 refused in *Giles v. Harris* to order local officials to register Jackson W. Giles, a black citizen of Montgomery, Giles sued voting registrars in state court. He sought monetary damages and a court order compelling his registration, alleging that the state constitution's voting requirements, by design and administration, violated the **Fifteenth Amendment.** The lower state court dismissed his suit. Giles next appealed to the Alabama State Supreme Court. The highest state court avoided the national constitutional question by saying that if the challenged state constitutional provisions were in conflict with the national constitution, they were invalid, and registrars appointed under those provisions were not authorized to register anyone. If, on the other hand, the provisions were valid, the registrars had acted within their authority. Upon appeal, the U.S. Supreme Court held that it had no authority to hear the case. Because it could review only federal questions decided by state courts and because the state court had not ruled on the national constitution issue, the Supreme Court could not review the decision. As in Giles's earlier suit, the Supreme Court afforded no remedy for Fifteenth Amendment violations.

Selected Bibliography Derrick A. Bell, Jr., *Race, Racism, and American Law* (1980); Richard Claude, *The Supreme Court and the Electoral Process* (1970).

Earlean M. McCarrick

Giovanni, Nikki (7 June 1943, Knoxville, Tenn.–). Educated at **Fisk University,** where she was an honors graduate in history, and at the University of Pennsylvania, where she pursued postgraduate studies in social work, Giovanni abandoned plans for a social work career in order to pursue one in writing and teaching. She has taught creative writing and black studies at Rutgers, Queens College of the City University of New York, and elsewhere. She emerged in the late 1960s as one of the most popular of the "New Black Poets" and was a leader of the black oral poetry movement. Her works include *Black Feeling, Black Talk/Black Judgement* (1970), *Re: Creation* (1970), *Gemini: An Extended Autobiograhical Statement on My First Twenty-five Years of Being a Black Poet* (1976), and *My House* (1972). Among her works for children, *Ego Tripping and Other Poems for Young People* (1973) remains popular. Central to Giovanni's poetry is her political activism and militancy. She is a pioneer of the Black Arts movement, an artistic version of the 1960s **Black Power** ideology. Some of her early poems crackle with the intensity of defiance and black pride, others are gently satirical, personal, and introspective. In her later work some of her revolutionary fire fades and she shows a greater concern with the nature of poetry itself. Her collaborative works with **James Baldwin** and **Margaret Walker Alexander,** *A Dialogue* (1972) and *A Poetic Equation* (1974) respectively, received critical acclaim. Her awards include an honorary doctorate from Wilberforce University in Wilberforce, Ohio. She was serving on the faculty of Virginia Polytechnic University as a Distinguished Professor of English when the twenty-first century began.

Selected Bibliography Mari Evans, ed., *Black Women Writers (1950–1980): A Critical Evaluation* (1984); Virginia Fowler, *Nikki Giovanni* (1992); Nikki Giovanni, *The Selected Poems of Nikki Giovanni* (1996); Harry A. Ploski and James Williams, *The Afro-American* (1983); *Time*, 17 January 1972.

Maghan Keita

God's Trombones Acclaimed as "one of the most beautiful volumes of verse ever produced by a black poet," it ranks as one of **James Weldon Johnson**'s greatest and most lasting contributions to African American and American poetry. Breaking out of the confines of the dialect tradition, these seven free-verse renditions authentically captured and preserved the spirit, idiom and rhythm of the Negro folk sermon with powerful folk imagery, beauty, and originality. Johnson's 1927 work was a pioneering effort and a major influence on later **Harlem Renaissance** poets. *God's Trombones* provided a model of excellence for the creation of a new Negro language and poetry.

Selected Bibliography Stephen Bronz, *Roots of Negro Racial Consciousness: The 1920s: Three Harlem Renaissance Authors* (1964); Eugenia W. Collier, "James Weldon Johnson: Mirror of Change," *Phylon* 21 (Winter 1960), 351–59; Robert Fleming, *James Weldon Johnson* (1987); Hugh M. Gloster, "James Weldon Johnson," in *Negro Voices in American Fiction* (1948); Richard Long, "A Weapon of My Song: The Poetry of James Weldon Johnson," *Phylon* 32 (December 1971), 374–82.

Jacquelyn Jackson

Gomillion, Charles G. (1 April 1900, Johnston, S.C.– 4 October 1995, Montgomery, Ala.). After he graduated from Georgia's Paine College in 1928, Gomillion accepted a faculty appointment at **Tuskegee Institute** to teach history. He spent the 1933–34 academic year at **Fisk University** studying sociology under **Edward Franklin Frazier,** after which he returned to Tuskegee and taught sociology. In the 1950s he studied sociology at Ohio State University, where he was awarded the Ph.D. in 1959. During his tenure at Tuskegee Institute he held various administrative leadership positions, including two deanships. Gomillion devoted much time after 1934 working for civic improvement. Tuskegee blacks enjoyed few public services. Frustrated by the unresponsiveness of the local government to black requests for better streets, sanitation, and the whole range of black concerns, Gomillion turned to political action. Believing that the ballot was the ultimate solution to African American problems, he succeeded after some years of effort in registering to vote and he encouraged others of his race to do the same. By the early 1940s enough blacks had registered to influence the outcome of close political contests. In 1941 Gomillion organized the Tuskegee Civic Association to support black interests—such as better public services and equal educational opportunities—and to promote what he called a color-blind civic democracy. His leadership of the Tuskegee Civic Association carried with it leadership of the entire local black community. Employing a gradualist approach, he worked indefatigably over the next quarter of a century to improve the living and working conditions for his race and to establish a solid base for harmonious race relations. He made great strides. In the late 1950s he challenged the state legislature's racial gerrymander of Tuskegee's boundaries, which was a blatant move to dilute the effect of the black vote in the town. He was upheld in the Supreme Court's *Gomillion v. Lightfoot* decision in 1960. This victory notwithstanding, Gomillion came under attack from many younger blacks who were impatient with his gradualist approach and his unwillingness to engage whites in **direct action** confrontations. The younger generation, many of whom were students at Tuskegee, turned to sit-ins, protest marches, and other similar strategies for gaining rights and privileges long denied them. Disappointed in his goal of achieving racial equality and shared political power without confrontation and bloodshed, Gomillion resigned his positions of leadership and retired in the early 1970s to Washington, D.C. The honorary degree of LL.D was conferred on him by Howard University in 1965 and by Ohio State University in 1967.

Selected Bibliography Loren Miller, *The Petitioners: The Story of the Supreme Court of the United States and the Negro* (1966); Robert J. Norrell, *Reaping the Whirlwind: The Civil Rights Movement in Tuskegee* (1985); Bernard Taper, *Gomillion versus Lightfoot: The Tuskegee Gerrymander Case* (1963).

Charles D. Lowery

Gomillion v. Lightfoot, 364 U.S. 339 (1960)   In May 1957 the Alabama legislature redrew the municipal boundaries of Tuskegee to place most of its 400 black voters outside the city limits, assuring political control by the white minority. The action changed the city map from a four-sided figure to one with 28 sides. Disfranchised black residents led by **Charles G. Gomillion** sued Mayor Philip Lightfoot and the city of Tuskegee, contending that the gerrymander sought to deny black citizens their rights guaranteed by the **Fourteenth** and **Fifteenth Amendments.** The lower federal courts would not reverse the legislature, which they held had full power to set municipal boundaries regardless of the motives or consequences. In *Gomillion v. Lightfoot* the Supreme Court reversed the lower courts, holding that the Tuskegee gerrymander was not merely political, but was "solely concerned" with segregating black citizens by "fencing" them from town. The action "despoiled" them exclusively "of their theretofore enjoyed voting rights," for the Fifteenth Amendment banned both "sophisticated" and "simple-minded" discrimination. The Supreme Court ordered review by the trial court, which nullified the offending statute in February 1961. This first instance of federal judicial involvement in state redistricting not only proscribed racial gerrymandering, but was also precedent for later "one man, one vote" decisions that affected legislative apportionment throughout the nation.

Selected Bibliography Paul L. Murphy, *The Constitution in Crisis Times, 1918–1969* (1972); Robert J. Norrell, *Reaping the Whirlwind: The Civil Rights Movement in Tuskegee* (1985); Martin Shapiro, *Law and Politics in the Supreme Court: New Approaches to Political Jurisprudence* (1964); Bernard Taper, *Gomillion versus Lightfoot: The Tuskegee Gerrymander Case* (1962).

James B. Potts

Goodman, Andrew   (23 November 1943, New York City, N.Y.–21 June 1964, near Philadelphia, Miss.). A civil rights activist from a liberal Jewish background, Goodman was a junior at Queens College in New York, majoring in anthropology, when he became a volunteer for the **Council of Federated Organizations'** (COFO) **Freedom Summer of 1964** in Mississippi. He met **James Earl Chaney** and **Michael Henry Schwerner** at the COFO training session for summer volunteers at Western College for Women in Oxford, Ohio. On 21 June 1964, Goodman, along with Chaney and Schwerner, was arrested in Philadelphia, Mississippi, released from jail, abducted by Klansmen, and shot. Their bodies were found on 4 August 1964 and retrieved from an earthen

Civil rights activist Andrew Goodman at an integration training lecture, 1964.
© Library of Congress.

dam. On 9 August 1964, Goodman was buried in Mount Judah Cemetery in Brooklyn, New York.

Selected Bibliography Seth Cagin and Philip Dray, *We Are Not Afraid: The Story of Goodman, Schwerner, and Chaney and the Civil Rights Campaign for Mississippi* (1988); William Bradford Huie, *Three Lives for Mississippi* (1964, 1965, 1968); Jonathan Kaufman, *Broken Alliance: The Turbulent Times between Blacks and Jews in America* (1988); *New York Times*, 6 August 1964; Juan Williams, *Eyes on the Prize: America's Civil Right Years, 1954–1965* (1987).

Barbara L. Green

Goss v. Board of Education of Knoxville*, 373 U.S. 683 (1963)**   In the early 1960s, in response to federal mandates stemming from ***Brown v. Board of Education (1954), the school boards of Knoxville and Davidson County, Tennessee, promulgated desegregation plans that included a provision for a student to transfer from a desegregated school to one in which the student would be in the racial majority. Parents of African American schoolchildren in the affected districts sued to block the implementation of the transfer provisions, charging that the provisions were designed to perpetuate racial segregation by allowing students to transfer from integrated to segregated schools. The Supreme Court found for the plaintiffs and voided the school transfer plans because their effect would be to perpetuate the segregation of the school systems.

Selected Bibliography Richard Bardolph, ed., *The Civil Rights Record, Black Americans, and the Law, 1849–1970* (1970); Loren Miller, *The Petitioners: The Story of the Supreme Court of the*

United States and the Negro (1966); George Rossman, ed., "Review of Recent Supreme Court Decisions," *American Bar Association Journal* 49 (1963), 1123–24; Mark Tushnet, *The NAACP's Legal Strategy against Segregated Education, 1925–1950* (1987).

Steve Sadowsky

Graham, Frank Porter (14 October 1886, Fayetteville, N.C.–16 February 1972, Chapel Hill, N.C.). A history professor, college president, and social activist, Graham received an A.B. degree at the University of North Carolina in 1909 and a M.A. from Columbia University in 1916. Graham also studied at the Brookings Institute, the London School of Economics, and the University of Chicago where he completed courses for the doctorate but chose not to write a dissertation. A recognized leader of southern white liberals, Graham served as the first chairperson of the **Southern Conference for Human Welfare** (1938–48). This University of North Carolina president was one of two southerners appointed by President Harry S. Truman to the first President's Committee on Civil Rights. In 1947 this committee issued the report *To Secure These Rights,* which called for a sweeping transformation of race relations in the United States.

Selected Bibliography Warren Ashby, *Frank Porter Graham: A Southern Liberal* (1980); David R. Goldfield, *Black, White, and Southern: Race Relations and Southern Culture, 1940 to the Present* (1990); Thomas Krueger, *And Promises to Keep: The Southern Conference for Human Welfare, 1938–1948* (1969); Morton Sosna, *In Search of the Silent South: Southern Liberals and the Race Issue* (1977).

Barbara L. Green

Grandfather Clause The grandfather clause was one post-Reconstruction device instituted by southern state legislatures to formalize restrictions on black voting already established through violence and intimidation. Unlike residence requirements, the **poll taxes,** literacy tests, and the **white primary**— all used to deny the vote to blacks—grandfather clauses enabled those whites who would otherwise be disqualified to register and vote. The Louisiana constitution of 1898, for example, provided that males entitled to vote prior to 1867, and their sons and grandsons, were exempt from educational and property restrictions. In 1915 the Supreme Court ruled in *Guinn v. United States* that such clauses were an evasion of the **Fifteenth Amendment.**

Selected Bibliography Scott A. Jones, "Arkansas and the Grandfather Clause Amendment of 1912," *Southern Historian* 17 (1996), 5–16; Alfred H. Kelly and Winfred A. Harbison, *The American Constitution: Its Origins and Development* (1970); V. O. Key, Jr., *Southern Politics in State and Nation* (1949); J. Morgan Kousser, *The Shaping of Southern Politics: Suffrage Restriction and the Establishment of the One-Party South, 1880–1910* (1974); Paul Lewinson, *Race, Class, and Party: A History of Negro Suffrage and White Politics in the South* (1932).

Allen Kifer

Granger, Lester B. (16 September 1896, Newport News, Va.–9 January 1976, New Orleans, La.). Granger's career in the Urban League Movement spanned the difficult years of the Great Depression, World War II, and the

Joseph McCarthy era of the 1950s. He graduated from Dartmouth in 1918 and also attended New York University and the New York School of Social Work. After a tour as a lieutenant of artillery during World War I, Granger took the post of industrial secretary with the Newark League. He left the Urban League Movement in 1922 to become director of extension at the New Jersey State vocational school at Bordentown. Before becoming executive director of the **National Urban League** in 1941, Granger served as educational secretary from 1934 to 1938 and assistant executive secretary from 1940 to 1941. From 1938 to 1940, he worked for the Welfare Council of New York City. By the 1950s, criticism of Granger conservatism was mounting. Nevertheless, he had led the Urban League in pursuing more militant goals in civil rights. The League joined in pressuring the federal government to deny funding to any public or private housing developments that practiced discrimination. Granger played an active role in the desegregation of the armed forces, and he worked to organize black workers and to fight discrimination within the ranks of organized labor.

Selected Bibliography Jesse Thomas Moore, Jr., *A Search for Equality: The National Urban League, 1910–1961* (1981); Guichard Parris and Lester Brooks, *Blacks in the City: A History of the National Urban League* (1971); *Who Was Who in America* (1976).

Arvarh E. Strickland

Gratz v. Bollinger, 123 S.Ct. 2411 (2003) and ***Grutter v. Bollinger*** 123 S.Ct. 2315 (2003)   These U.S. Supreme Court cases resulted in a landmark decision affecting the future of affirmative action. At issue was whether the University of Michigan's affirmative action undergraduate and law school admissions policies should stand. The university based its undergraduate policy on a 150-point system, in which African American, Native American, and Hispanic applicants were awarded 20 extra points for their race, whereas a perfect SAT score counted for only 12 points for students of any race. The law school policy had no point system, but it sometimes admitted minority applicants over white applicants with similar qualifications.

The litigation originated in U. S. District Court in 1997 as two distinct class action lawsuits, one brought by white undergraduate applicants who were denied admission and the other by a white law school applicant denied admission. In *Gratz,* the federal district court ruled in 2000 that the undergraduate admissions policy was constitutional, and in *Grutter*, it ruled that the law school policy was not. Both cases were appealed, and both rulings were overturned in 2002 in federal appeals court. The Supreme Court agreed to hear the cases jointly in 2003.

The plaintiffs complained that the University of Michigan seemed to be trying to fill racial quotas, rather than merely giving equal opportunity to minorities. President of the United States George W. Bush agreed with that assessment and, hoping to influence the decision of the court, issued a public statement to that effect just before the Supreme Court heard the case. His administration also filed a brief with the court itself. The University of

Michigan had the support of several Fortune 500 companies plus the U.S. military, whose spokespersons supported the measures the university had taken to ensure diversity, claiming that adequate diversity in the workforce and in the armed forces is dependent upon minority admissions to major universities such as Michigan. The Court ruled negatively on the undergraduate policy and affirmatively on the law school policy, although in both instances the justices were divided in their opinions.

Proponents of affirmative action, including the administrators of the university and the **NAACP Legal Defense and Educational Fund**, were largely pleased at the verdict of the Court, hailing it as a modern-day *Brown v. Board of Education.* Not surprisingly, opponents found fault with two aspects of the opinion on the law school policy, written by Justice Sandra Day O'Connor: her rationale that the hardships inherent in minorities' life experiences should be a prime consideration in university admissions, and her contention that the need for such racial considerations will likely disappear within another quarter-century. What both sides agreed on is the fact that this ruling would not be the final word on the subject, for the debate over affirmative action will surely continue.

Selected Bibliography "Affirmative Action in College Admissions," in *Documents in the News 1997–2003*, University of Michigan Documents Center Online, http://www.lib.umich.edu/govdocs/affirm.html; Perry Bacon, Jr., "And the Winner Is . . . Affirmative Action," *Time*, 23 June 2003, http://www.time.com/time/nation/article/0,8599,460435,00.html; Terrence J. Pell, "Camouflage for Quotas," *Washington Post*, 30 June 2003; "What Others in the Media are Saying," *Detroit Free Press*, 25 June 2003; "What's New," NAACP–Legal Defense Fund Online: http://www.naacpldf.org/whatsnew/wn_doc_ldf_michigan_compared.html.

Thomas Adams Upchurch

Gray, William H., III (20 August 1941, Baton Rouge, La.–). A Baptist minister, William Gray was elected to Congress in 1978, representing the Second Congressional District of Pennsylvania. His congressional career was a series of successes, including the chairmanship of the House Budget Committee. Budgetary constraints prevented him from supporting the kinds of policies preferred by most African Americans, but he did play a major role in the imposition of sanctions against South Africa in 1988. In 1989, he was elected majority whip, the highest Democratic leadership post ever held by a black person up to that time. In 1991, Gray left Congress to become president of the United Negro College Fund. He streamlined the organization and raised more money than any previous president.

Selected Bibliography Michael Barone and Grant Ujifusa, *The Almanac of American Politics* (1980–92); Janet Hook, "Representative Gray Preaches the Gospel of Party Unity," *Congressional Quarterly Weekly Report* (10 December 1988), 3472–73; Julie L. Nicklin, "No More Business as Usual," *The Chronicle of Higher Education*, 24 November 1993.

Patricia A. Behlar

Great Migration Eighty thousand black Southerners moved to the North, mostly to cities, in the two decades after 1870. The northern movement of blacks quickened significantly, however, as southern repression increased by the

Λ rare photograph of one of the hundreds of thousands of migrating families arriving at Chicago's Illinois Central station. The railroad provided a vital link between North and South. © Library of Congress.

turn of the century. During World War I, the economic boom produced a genuine Great Migration, marked by an exodus of more than five hundred thousand blacks, and in the next decade nearly seven hundred fifty thousand streamed northward. Slowed by the Great Depression, the Great Migration received fresh impetus from World War II and continued in the decades after 1940. The result was dramatic: in 1910, 75 percent of the nation's blacks lived in rural areas, and nine-tenths were in the South; in 1960, more than three-fourths lived in cities, mostly outside the South; blacks had been transformed into a predominantly northern-based proletariat. Several factors precipitated the Great Migration. Racism evidenced in disfranchisement, injustice and segregation, and serious economic problems, including a decline in cotton prices (1913–15) that increased the burdens of sharecropping and tenancy, disposed blacks to flee to the North. Floods in the Mississippi Valley in 1915 and the destructive march of the boll weevil (1914–17) spread destitution. Meanwhile, demands for war material from the Allies and then from American forces coupled with a decline in immigration generated opportunities for skilled and unskilled workers, often underscored by free transportation and wages as high as four dollars a day. Newspaper reports, particularly in the *Chicago Defender,* and letters emphasizing good wages and less severe discrimination in the North were especially attractive to younger blacks. The Great Migration produced competition for jobs and housing with whites that greatly altered northern life for blacks. Dramatic events like the **East St. Louis race riot** in 1917 and the **Chicago race riot** in 1919 punctuated long-term economic trends that reduced blacks to the fringe of the industrial economy. The urban ghetto, attended by slumlords, overcrowding, disease and inadequate education emerged.

Selected Bibliography Florette Henri, *Black Migration: Movement North, 1900–1920* (1975); Thomas N. Maloney, "Migration and Economic Opportunity in the 1910's: New Evidence on African-American Occupational Mobility in the North," *Explorations in Economic History* 38 (2001), 147–65; Stewart E. Tolnay, "The Great Migration and Changes in the Northern Black Family, 1940 to 1990," *Social Forces* 75 (1997), 1213–38; Stewart E. Tolnay et al., "Narrow and Filthy Alleys of the City? The Residential Settlement Patterns of Black Southern Migrant to the North," *Social Forces* 78 (2000), 989–1015.

James B. Potts

Green, Paul Eliot　(17 March 1894, Lillington, N.C.–4 May 1981, Chapel Hill, N.C.). Green attended the University of North Carolina and later taught philosophy there, when he became associated with a group that taught students to produce plays about regions of the South. In the 1920s, Green drew upon his knowledge of southern problems, particularly the plight of oppressed blacks, to champion civil rights, one of the first white playwrights to do so. His plays *White Dresses* (1923) and *In Abraham's Bosom* (1926) depicted failed efforts by southern blacks to better their lot. He wrote seven Broadway plays, collaborated with black novelist **Richard Wright** on **Native Son,** and wrote the 1963 film script *Black Like Me,* the story of a white man who experienced racial prejudice after changing the color of his skin. He is also known for his 15 "symphonic outdoor dramas" of the 1950s and 1960s, which included folksongs, dance, drama, and music of the local community.

Selected Bibliography Stanley Hochman, ed., *McGraw-Hill Encyclopedia of World Drama* (1984); *Newsweek,* 18 May 1981; *New York Times,* 6 May 1981.

Thomas D. Cockrell

***Green v. School Board of New Kent County, Virginia,* 391 U.S. 430 (1968)** New Kent County is a rural county in eastern Virginia, whose population of 4,500 in 1960 was divided evenly between blacks and whites. No distinct pattern of residential segregation existed. The county maintained two schools, a traditionally white one in the eastern part of the county and an all-black school in the west. In 1968 the U.S. Supreme Court took up the question of the constitutionality of the county's freedom-of-choice plan for school desegregation. Of the county's 1,300 school children, 740 were black and 550 were white. In the three years the plan had been in effect, no whites had attended the black school, and although 115 blacks had attended the predominantly white school, 85 percent of the black students still attended the all-black facility. In a unanimous opinion by William J. Brennan, the court rejected the freedom-of-choice plan. Brennan's opinion stressed the local school board's long defiance of the court's **Brown v. Board of Education** decision, the meager results of the freedom-of-choice plan, and the burden it placed on black parents. *Green* represented a milestone among school desegregation cases. The opinion went beyond a simple prohibition of segregation to place a clear duty on local school boards to take affirmative measures to abolish dual school systems.

Selected Bibliography "The Supreme Court, 1967 Term," *Harvard Law Review* 82 (1968), 111–18; J. Harvie Wilkinson III, *From Brown to Bakke: The Supreme Court and School Integration, 1954–1978* (1979); Raymond Wolters, *The Burden of Brown: Thirty Years of School Desegregation* (1984); Rowland Young, "Review of Recent Supreme Court Decisions," *American Bar Association Journal* 54 (1968), 912–13.

Jeff Broadwater

Greene, Percy (7 September 1898, Jackson, Miss.–6 April 1977, Jackson, Miss.). After serving during World War I in England and France and graduation from Jackson State College, Greene studied law, but he was determined to be a journalist. His first publication, *The Colored Veteran* (1927), addressed the problem of denial of blacks to membership in veterans' organizations. He founded the *Jackson Advocate* in 1939 and served as editor until his death in 1977. Greene organized the Mississippi Negro Democrat Association in 1946 in an effort to give blacks a voice in the Democratic party. During the civil rights movement of the 1950s and 1960s, he became something of a paradox, receiving criticism from both white segregationists and the **NAACP.** Although he spoke strongly for black political rights, he also advocated moderation regarding integration, which brought chastisement from the NAACP leadership. His reputation was marred in the 1960s by his acceptance of contributions from Mississippi's segregationist Sovereignty Commission.

Selected Bibliography *Jackson Advocate* (1950–1970); Henry Lewis Suggs, ed., *The Black Press in the South, 1865–1979* (1983); Julius E. Thompson, *The Black Press in Mississippi, 1865–1985* (1993); *Who's Who among Black Americans* (1978).

Thomas D. Cockrell

Greensboro, North Carolina, Sit-in On 1 February 1960, Ezell Blair, Jr., Franklin McCain, Joseph McNeil, and David Richmond, all African American students at North Carolina Agricultural and Technical College, staged a sit-in at the Woolworth Store lunch counter in Greensboro, North Carolina. Although these were not the first sit-ins in North Carolina (there was a network of sit-ins between 1957 and 1960), this was the opening gambit of an unequaled student protest movement that shook the South to its foundations. On the evening of 1 February, 50 students met and created the Student Executive Committee for Justice. On 2 February, the original four protesters were joined by African American students from A&T and Bennett College and by white students from Women's College. Soon more than 300 demonstrators were protesting by sit-ins at all the city's downtown lunch counters. Sixteen hundred students decided at a mass meeting on 5 February to halt all demonstrations when asked by city leaders for time to negotiate the crisis.

The first Woolworth's lunch-counter sit-in, Greensboro, NC, 1960. © Jack Moebes/ CORBIS.

However, when no compromise was reached, the sit-ins resumed on 1 April, and the first arrests of 45 demonstrators occurred on 21 April. Subsequent sit-ins and economic boycotts forced the city's business and political leaders to reopen lunch counters on a desegregated basis by July 1960.

Selected Bibliography William Chafe, *Civilities and Civil Rights* (1980); Aldon D. Morris, *Origins of the Civil Rights Movement* (1984); National Parks Service, *We Shall Overcome:Historic Places of the Civil Rights Movement*, http://www.cr.nps.gov/nr/travel/civilrights/sitelsit.htm; Harvard Sitkoff, *The Struggle for Black Equality: 1954–1980* (1981).

Aingred G. Dunston

Greenville Delta Democrat-Times The Greenville, Mississippi, *Delta Democrat-Times* was established in 1938 by the merger of that city's *Delta Star* and *Daily Democrat-Times*. **Hodding Carter II** editor and publisher of the *Delta Star*, assumed the same duties at the *Delta Democrat-Times*. A Louisianan by birth but educated in Maine and New York, Carter became one of the South's most noted advocates of racial justice. Greenville, in the heart of the overwhelmingly black Mississippi Delta, seemed an unlikely place for such a journalist and newspaper. Yet, the Delta's confidence in the fixity of its caste system combined with the region's affinity for good writing allowed Carter—despite many threats—to produce the virtually unthinkable: a white-edited newspaper in the Deep South that promoted the cause of black civil rights. Carter won a Pulitzer Prize for his editorial writing, and he served as a model of journalistic courage throughout the South. Several editors drew strength from his example, as did other southern whites who sought to promote racial tolerance and goodwill. After Carter's death in 1972, his son Hodding Carter III continued the editorial policies of the *Delta Democrat-Times* before going to Washington, D.C., to work in the Jimmy Carter administration. Subsequent editors of the newspaper have been less activist than the Carters, yet its niche in the cause of civil rights is secure.

Selected Bibliography Hodding Carter II, *So the Heffners Left McComb* (1965); *Greenville Delta Democrat-Times* (1938–2003); Charles Reagan Wilson and William Ferris, eds., *The Encyclopedia of Southern Culture* (1989). Web site: www.ddtonline.com.

Allen Dennis

Gregory, Richard Claxton "Dick" (12 October 1932, St. Louis, Mo.–). From his achievement as an outstanding athlete at Southern Illinois University in 1953 to his inclusion in *Who's Who In America* (1968), Dick Gregory achieved national recognition in the 1960s as a comedian, popular lecturer, and civil rights activist. By the 1970s he was being referred to as a noted political analyst. In the 1980s he became the guru of good health. His electric personality focused national attention on the student efforts to register African American voters in Mississippi **(Freedom Summer of 1964),** and he aided in the food, clothes and book drives that funded the young activists. In June 1964 when three civil rights workers were murdered in Mississippi, Gregory offered a substantial reward for any information that would lead to arrests. He publicly accused the Federal Bureau of Investigation of "lying and hiding" in its attempts to uncover the truth. In his efforts to promote peaceful change, he was shot during the **Watts race riot** in Los Angeles in 1965 and spent several periods in jail, the most publicized of which was in Birmingham, Alabama, in 1963. This National Committee Chair of the United Black Church Appeal (appointed 1980) and continuing activist for both African and Native American issues has authored and coauthored nine books including his autobiography (*Nigger*, 1964) and his view of the assassination of **Martin Luther King, Jr.** (*Code Name Zorro*, 1977).

Selected Bibliography African American Directory, *United Black Church Appeal*, www.philipmorris.com/home/asp; Joanne Grant, ed., *Black Protest* (1968); Stephen B. Oates, *Let the Trumpet Sound: The Life of Martin Luther King, Jr.* (1982); Edward Peeks, *Long Struggle for Black Power* (1971); Harry Ploski and James Williams, eds., *The Negro Almanac: A Reference Work on the African American*, 5th ed. (1989).

Aingred G. Dunston

Griffin, John Howard (16 June 1920, Dallas, Tex.–9 September 1980, Fort Worth, Tex.). A white Texan, Griffin journeyed through the South in 1959 disguised as a black man, and wrote about his experiences in *Black Like Me*, which established a unique double perspective of racism. As the first white to experience the reality of darkened pigment, he lost his personal identity and was transformed into a cultural stereotype. Facing death threats and hate stares, he pursued the ideals of brotherhood and justice. He did not speak for blacks but became a bridge across the racial divide. The integrity of his witness was read by millions worldwide and heard by thousands on his lecture tours during the 1960s and 1970s. Throughout his life he articulated the universal patterns of prejudice he had experienced as a black, as a member of the *Defense Passive* in France during World War II, and during his years of blindness (1946–57). In these diverse contexts, Griffin realized the condition of the other—that individual perceived as intrinsically inferior. He learned to think human and to understand the essential oneness of humankind. His work reveals both a highly refined artistic temperament (as writer, photographer, and musicologist) and a spiritual dimension that transcends politics or sociology.

Selected Bibliography Robert Bonazzi, *Man in the Mirror: John Howard Griffin and the Story of "Black Like Me"* (1997); John Howard Griffin, *Black Like Me* (1961); John Howard Griffin, *A Time to Be Human* (1977).

Robert Bonazzi

Griffin v. Prince Edward School Board, 377 U.S. 218 (1964) This case originated in 1951 as one of the cases eventually decided in **Brown v. Board of Education** (1954 and 1955). Virginia's Prince Edward County's public schools remained open but segregated until 1959, when federal courts ordered the county to proceed with desegregation. In response, the school board ordered the closing of all public schools. State funds, through tuition grants, supported the Prince Edward Academy, a private school newly opened only to white students. After years of continued litigation, the U.S. Supreme Court ruled in 1964 that the school board was in violation of the "equal protection" clause of the **Fourteenth Amendment.** Speaking for the Court, and referring back to the language of the 1955 decision, Justice Hugo Black observed that Prince Edward had displayed "entirely too much deliberation and not enough speed" in moving against segregation in its schools. Under court order, the county resumed taxes for public schools and reopened the schools in 1964, although in the early years of "desegregation," few white students attended.

Selected Bibliography James T. Ely, *The Crisis of Conservative Virginia: The Byrd Organization and the Politics of Massive Resistance* (1976); Bob (Robert Collins) Smith, *They Closed Their Schools: Prince Edward County, Virginia, 1951–1964* (1965); Raymond Wolters, *The Burden of Brown: Thirty Years of Desegregation* (1984).

Peter Wallenstein

Griggs v. Duke Power Company, 401 U.S. 424 (1971) Although the **Civil Rights Act of 1964** opened some new doors of opportunity, many employers found new ways to exclude blacks from better paying jobs. This, contended Willie S. Griggs and his fellow black employees, was the case at Duke Power Company in North Carolina. Requirements for certain jobs included an educational component or standardized general intelligence test for placement or transfer. In a class action, blacks sued the company. They lost in district court but were affirmed in part by the court holding at the appellate level, "that residual discrimination arising from past employment practices was" not "insulated from remedial action." The U.S. Supreme Court unanimously held for the plaintiffs. It affirmed the prohibitions of the Civil Rights Act against requiring "a high school education or passing a standardized general intelligence test as a condition of employment or transfer" when neither could be "shown to be significantly related to successful job performance," when both requirements disqualified blacks at a substantially "higher rate than whites," and when the jobs "in question" had formerly been "filled by whites only due to long standing preference." This decision was a significant gain for civil rights.

Selected Bibliography Derrick A. Bell, Jr., *Race, Racism, and American Law* (1980); Robert L. Gill, "Justice for Black Americans 200 Years after Independence: The Afro-American before the Burger Court, 1969–1976," *Negro Educational Review* 27 (July 1976), 271–317; Rowland L. Young, "Supreme Court Report," *American Bar Association Journal* 57 (1971), 609.

LeRoy T. Williams

Grimké, Angelina Weld (27 February 1880, Boston, Mass.–10 June 1958, New York, N.Y.). Trained as a teacher, Grimké was educated at various schools including Carleton Academy in Northfield, Minnesota; Cushing Academy in Ashburnham, Massachusetts; Girls' Latin School in Boston; and the Boston Normal School of Gymnastics. Her teaching experience included work at Armstrong Manual Training School, 1902, and Dunbar High School, both in Washington, D.C., between 1916 and the 1930s. She wrote the first successful drama created by a black and interpreted on stage by black actors. Produced in 1916 by the Drama Committee of the **NAACP** in Washington, D.C., Grimké's *Rachel*, a play in three acts dealing with the lynching of a girl's father, addressed one of the leading concerns of the NAACP of that time. The program announcement made evident Grimké's and the NAACP's expectation of the play: "This is the first attempt to use the stage for race propaganda in order to enlighten the American people relative to the lamentable condition of ten millions of colored citizens in this free republic." In the 1920s, during the peak of the **Harlem Renaissance,** Grimké contributed poetry and short stories to various magazines.

Selected Bibliography Stephen H. Brown, *Angelina Grimké: Rhetoric, Identity, and the Radical Imagination* (1999); Gloria T. Hull, *Color, Sex, and Poetry: Three Women Writers of the Harlem Renaissance* (1987); Gloria T. Hull, Patricia Bell Scott, and Barbara Smith, eds., *All the Women Are White, All the Blacks Are Men, But Some of Us Are Brave: Black Women's Studies* (1982).

Linda Reed

Grimké, Archibald (17 August 1849 Cane Acre Plantation, S.C.–25 February 1930, Washington, D.C.). One of three sons of Nancy Weston, a slave, and Henry Grimké, a South Carolina planter, Grimké was emancipated from slavery by the Civil War. He graduated in 1870 from Lincoln University in Pennsylvania and in 1874 from Harvard Law School with some financial assistance from his aunts, the abolitionists Sarah Grimké and Angelina Grimké Weld. Coeditor of *The Hub* (1883–86) and a practicing attorney, in the early 1880s, Grimké was a leader of the "Boston radicals," blacks who vigorously opposed racial discrimination. For the next 40 years he fought segregation and disfranchisement with lawsuits, pamphlets, newspaper articles, and petitions to presidents from William McKinley to Warren G. Harding. Grover Cleveland appointed Grimké, a lifelong independent, consul to Santo Domingo (1894–98). After moving to Washington, D.C., in the early 1900s, he played a moderating political role among black leaders, maintaining contacts with **Booker T. Washington** even as he joined the **Niagara Movement** and the **NAACP.** He was president of the **American Negro Academy** (1903–19), which published many of his later essays. While president of the Washington branch of the NAACP (1913–24), he helped prevent the passage of bills designed to segregate the Civil Service. In 1919 Grimké won the NAACP's fifth **Spingarn Medal** "for service to race and country."

Selected Bibliography Dickson D. Bruce, Jr., *Archibald Grimké: Portrait of a Black Independent* (1993); Archibald H. Grimké, "The Shame of America, or the Negro's Case against the Republic," *American Negro Academy* 21 (1924); Archibald H. Grimké Papers, Moorland-Spingarn Research Center, Howard University, Washington, D.C.; Rayford W. Logan and Michael R. Winston, eds., *Dictionary of American Negro Biography* (1982); Rayford W. Logan, *The Betrayal of the Negro* (1965); August Meier, *Negro Thought in America, 1880–1915: Racial Ideologies of Booker T. Washington* (1963).

Francille Rusan Wilson

Undated photo of Rev. Francis J. Grimké. © Library of Congress.

Grimké, Francis James (4 November 1850, Charleston, S.C.–11 October 1937, Washington, D.C.). The son of Nancy Weston, a slave, and her master, Henry Grimké, he graduated from Lincoln University in Pennsylvania in 1870. With the moral and financial support of his famous aunts, the abolitionist sisters Angelina and Sarah Grimké, Francis continued his education at Princeton Theological Seminary, graduating in 1878. In the same year he married the abolitionist, teacher, and writer, Charlotte Forten. For the next two generations he served as minister at Washington's Fifteenth Street Presbyterian Church and he became a leading advocate of civil rights for blacks. Known as the "Black Puritan," Grimké rejected **Booker T.**

Washington's accommodationism and, as a well-known lecturer, essayist, and president of the capital's chapter of the **NAACP,** he urged blacks to look beyond mere economic survival to full social and civil equality.

Selected Bibliography Gerda Lerner, *The Grimké Sisters of South Carolina: Rebels against Slavery* (1967); August Meier, *Negro Thought in America, 1880–1915: Racial Ideologies in the Age of Booker T. Washington* (1963); Carter G. Woodson, ed., *The Works of Francis J. Grimké,* 4 vols. (1942).

James Marten

Grovey v. Townsend, 295 U.S. 45 (1935) In Harris County, Texas, black resident R. R. Grovey attempted to vote in the Democratic party primary in 1934. His vote was refused by white party official Albert Townsend. Grovey filed suit against Townsend, but lost at both the district and appellate levels. The U.S. Supreme Court decided the case on 1 April 1935. The question before the court was whether or not Grovey's rights under the **Fourteenth** and **Fifteenth Amendments** had been violated. The court concluded that the Democratic party was "a private organization" and so, too, was Townsend a private citizen. Therefore, the party and Townsend were "not subject to limitations imposed on state action" under the constitutional amendments in question. "We find no ground," stated the court, "for holding" that discrimination has occurred. It would be almost a decade later before the Supreme Court reversed its view of the political party as a private organization.

Selected Bibliography Richard Bardolph, ed., *The Civil Rights Record: Black Americans and the Law 1849–1970* (1970); Derrick A. Bell, Jr., *Race, Racism, and American Law* (1980); Alfred H. Kelly and Winfred A. Harbison, *The American Constitution* (1970); "Recent Decision," *Columbia Law Review* 35 (1935), 607–8.

LeRoy T. Williams

Guinn v. United States, 238 U.S. 347 (1915) This case involved a **grandfather clause** in Oklahoma. In 1910 the state adopted an amendment to its constitution exempting or "grandfathering" from its literacy test all people "who, on January 1, 1866 or who at that time resided in some foreign nation, and their lineal descendants." The government argued and the Court agreed that this amendment recreated the exact situation the **Fifteenth Amendment** sought to prevent. The **NAACP** filed an amicus curiae brief on behalf of the United States. This case was the first of the long line of successful constitutional cases supported by the NAACP.

Selected Bibliography Charles Flint Kellogg, *NAACP: A History of the National Association for the Advancement of Colored People* (1967); Melvin I. Urofsky, *A March of Liberty: A Constitutional History of the United States* (1987).

Kenneth W. Goings

H

Haas, Francis J. (18 March 1889, Racine, Wis.–29 August 1953, Grand Rapids, Mich.). A Roman Catholic priest of the archdiocese of Milwaukee, Haas received a Ph.D. in sociology from the Catholic University of America in 1922 and, assigned to Washington, D.C., in 1931, served on several of President Franklin D. Roosevelt's labor relations boards and agencies. Appointed by Roosevelt to chair the reconstituted **Fair Employment Practices Committee** (FEPC) in May 1943, he investigated charges of discrimination in various wartime industries, including the nationwide railway system, and spent three days in Detroit, Michigan, to report on the causes of racial violence there. Named bishop of Grand Rapids, Michigan, he resigned from the FEPC after serving only four months. In 1946, he was appointed to President Harry S Truman's Committee on Civil Rights and was a signer of that committee's influential report, *To Secure These Rights,* in 1947.

Selected Bibliography Thomas E. Blantz, "Francis J. Haas: Priest and Government Servant," *Catholic Historical Review* 57 (January 1972), 571–92; Thomas E. Blantz, *A Priest in Public Service: Francis J. Haas and the New Deal* (1982); Franklyn Kennedy, "Bishop Haas," *The Salesianum* 39 (January 1944), 7–14; Constance Randall, "A Bio-Bibliography of Bishop Francis J. Haas" (M.A. thesis, Catholic University of America, 1955).

Thomas E. Blantz

Hale v. Kentucky, 303 U.S. 613 (1938)   The Supreme Court, in a unanimous decision, struck down an earlier murder conviction and death sentence on the grounds that the plaintiff's civil rights had been violated. In an earlier 1936 trial in McCracken County, Joe Hale, an African American, had been convicted by an all-white jury, and his conviction was upheld by the Kentucky

Court of Appeals. Hale argued that blacks were "systematic[ally] and arbitrar[ily] exclud[ed]" from the jury. In a county in which 40,000 whites resided, there also were 8,000 people of "African descent." And at least 7,000 blacks were eligible for jury service. Yet no blacks had been members of any McCracken County jury within the past 50 years. The *Hale* decision was one in a series of cases in which the Supreme Court consistently opposed jury discrimination in the lower courts, the earliest of which was **Strauder v. West Virginia** in 1880 and the most recent of which was **Norris v. Alabama** in 1935. Hale was represented by **NAACP** counsel, including **Charles H. Houston** and **Thurgood Marshall.** This case shows that the NAACP was concerned about jury discrimination before it focused its attention on public school integration in the 1940s and 1950s.

Selected Bibliography John R. Gillespie, "The Constitution and the All-White Jury," *Kentucky Law Journal* 39 (1950–51), 65–78; *Louisville Courier-Journal*, 31 January, 11 April 1938; *New York Times*, 12 August 1938; Harry A. Ploski and James Williams, eds., *The Negro Almanac: A Reference Work on the African American*, 5th ed. (1989).

Lawrence H. Williams

Haley, Alex Palmer (11 August 1921, Ithaca, N.Y.–10 February 1992, Seattle, Wash.). Since 1976 Alex Haley has been one of the most familiar names in contemporary American literature. He studied two years in North Carolina's Elizabeth City Teacher's College preparing to become a teacher before opting for a military career. Upon retiring from the military in 1959, he worked as a freelance writer. His 1962 *Playboy Magazine* interview of **Black Muslim** spokesman **Malcolm X** became the genesis of a book, The *Autobiography of Malcolm X*, which Haley largely wrote. Passionately written, the book familiarized Americans with both men—Malcolm as a committed, but angry race leader, and Alex Haley as an emerging literary talent. Haley's greatest literary achievement was the 1976 publication of a historical novel entitled **Roots:** *The Saga of An American Family*. The book grew out of childhood stories told to Haley by his grandmother of the family's West African beginnings and its history through slavery and freedom in the American South. Despite reviewers' criticisms of the factual errors found in *Roots*, the book quickly became a best seller and achieved even greater acclaim the next year when it was serialized on network television in a remarkably successful miniseries. However transitory their effect, the dramatizations impacted U.S. race relations by raising the consciousness of white America and sensitizing it to the African American historical experience. Perhaps of greater long-term significance, Haley's work unleashed an energy in the black community that helped to "spur black identity and hence black pride." In 1992, the U.S. Coast Guard named a cutter for him. As late as 1997, charges of plagiarism continued to swirl around his *Roots* book.

Selected Bibliography Robert Bain, Joseph M. Flora, and Louis D. Rubin, Jr., eds., *Southern Writers: A Biographical Dictionary* (1979); "Fact or Fiction? Hoax Charges Still Dog *Roots* 20 Years On," *Publishers Weekly* 244 (1997), 16–17; David Gerber, "Haley's *Roots* and Our Own:

An Inquiry into the Nature of a Popular Phenomenon," *Journal of Ethnic Studies* 3 (1977), 87–111; Alex Haley, "Roots: A Black American's Search for His Ancestral African," *Ebony* 31 (August 1976), 100–102, 104, 106–7; Alex Haley, *Roots: The Saga of An American Family* (1976); "Haley First Journalist with Name on Cutter," *Quill* 87 (1999), 7; Jesse T. Moore, Jr., "Alex Haley's *Roots*: Ten Years Later," *Western Journal of Black Studies* 18 (1994), 70–76; Charles Moritz, ed., "Alex Haley" in *Current Biography Yearbook* (1977); "Why *Roots* Hit Home," *Time*, 14 February 1977, 68–72, 75.

Robert L. Jenkins

Hall v. DeCuir, 95 U.S. 485 (1878)   In a Louisiana state court, Josephine DeCuir won a judgment of $1,000 against the master of a steamboat who refused her passage because of her race. An 1869 state law forbade common carriers to discriminate on grounds of race and permitted recovery of damages. The master claimed that the statute was an unconstitutional encroachment upon the federal interstate commerce power, since he operated from New Orleans to Vicksburg and back. Chief Justice Morrison Waite, for the Court, agreed that the law placed a burden on interstate commerce. Steamboats and railroads often crossed state lines, and local regulations that varied from place to place were invalid, a conclusion supported by some pre–Civil War precedents. Waite noted that if the public interest required legislation on such a subject, it would have to be federal legislation, yet the case occurred in a period when the Court was also weakening federal protection for civil rights. The applicability of state antidiscrimination laws to interstate carriers returned to the Court in 1963, this time in relation to the hiring of airline pilots. By then the reasoning in the *DeCuir* case seemed clearly archaic, and the Colorado law in question prevailed.

   Selected Bibliography Charles Fairman, *Reconstruction and Reunion, 1864–1888* (1987); C. Peter Magrath, *Morrison R. Waite: The Triumph of Character* (1963).

James E. Sefton

Hamburg, South Carolina, Race Riot (1876)   On 4 July 1876, Hamburg's Negro militia company, under the command of "Doc" Adams, was marching down the main street of town and failed to permit the passage of the carriage of two local whites. Following a complaint, Adams refused to apologize for the incident or to appear in court on 7 July. The refusal resulted in a demand by General Matthew C. Butler, counsel for the complainants, that the militia give up its weapons. Local whites armed themselves and others from nearby Augusta, Georgia, arrived in Hamburg with a cannon. Adams and his militiamen gathered at their armory. Refusing to surrender the guns stored there, the militia fired from the windows but were finally routed from the armory. Five militiamen were captured, disarmed, and later singly executed by the white mob. A grand jury bound over the accused whites for trial, but the case was postponed at the insistence of the state's attorney-general, who advised Governor Daniel H. Chamberlain that the white community's prevailing sentiments would only lead to further trouble. Chamberlain requested and received federal troops to restore order in Hamburg, but Butler and other whites were never brought to justice.

Selected Bibliography George C. Rable, *But There Was No Peace: The Role of Violence in the Politics of Reconstruction* (1984); Otis A. Singletary, *Negro Militia and Reconstruction* (1957); Alfred B. Williams, *Hampton and His Red Shirts: South Carolina's Deliverance in 1876* (1935; reprint, 1970).
Thaddeus M. Smith

Hamer, Fannie Lou (6 October 1917, Montgomery County, Miss.–14 March 1977, Mound Bayou, Miss.). She became an active member of the **Student Nonviolent Coordinating Committee** (SNCC) in Ruleville, Mississippi, in 1962 and immediately met opposition when she attempted to register to vote. She was fired from her plantation job. In 1963 she became a field secretary for SNCC and a registered voter. Hamer then worked with voter registration drives and with programs designed to assist economically deprived black families in Mississippi. She knew poverty firsthand, being the youngest of 20 siblings whose parents seldom were able to provide adequate food and clothing. In 1963, she was instrumental in starting the **Delta Ministry,** an

Fannie Lou Hamer campaign poster, Mississippi, 1971. © Tougaloo College, L. Zenobia Coleman Library, Archives.

extensive community development program. Next she took part in the founding of the **Mississippi Freedom Democratic Party** and was a chosen member of its delegation to the Democratic National Convention that challenged the seating of the regular all-white Mississippi delegation. She made a famous address to the convention, which television carried to the nation. In 1965 Hamer, Victoria Gray, and Annie Devine unsuccessfully challenged the seating of the regular Mississippi representatives before the U.S. House of Representatives and they became the first three black women ever to sit on the floor of the House. Hamer remained active in civic affairs in Mississippi for the remainder of her life, being selected a delegate to the National Democratic Convention in 1968. She founded the Freedom Farms Corporation (FFC), a nonprofit venture designed to help needy families raise food and livestock. The FFC also provided social services, minority business opportunity, scholarships, and grants for education.

Selected Bibliography Jerry DeMuth, "Tired of Being Sick and Tired," *Nation* 198 (1 June 1964), 548–51; Joyce A. Ladner, "Fannie Lou Hamer: In Memoriam," *Black Enterprise* 7 (May 1977), 56; Chana K. Lee, *For Freedom's Sake: The Life of Fannie Lou Hamer* (1999); Eleanor Holmes Norton, "Woman Who Changed the South: Memory of Fannie Lou Hamer," MS 5 (July 1977), 51.

Linda Reed

***Hamilton v. Alabama*, 376 U.S. 650 (1964)**   In a hearing for a writ of habeas corpus, Mary Hamilton, an African American citizen of Alabama, refused to answer questions on cross examination when she was addressed on a first-name basis. It was not uncommon in Alabama courts for attorneys and judges to address a black witness as "boy" or to refer to the accused as "this nigger." Offended by the demeaning courtroom etiquette, Hamilton refused to respond to questions unless she were addressed by the polite title "Miss Hamilton" rather than the disrespectful "Mary." She was fined and jailed for contempt. Denied a rehearing by the Alabama Supreme Court, she appealed to the U.S. Supreme Court. It responded to her writ of certiorari by reversing the contempt conviction. The decision was a small but significant step forward for blacks in their struggle for equality before the law.

Selected Bibliography A Symposium, "The Justice Hugo L. Black Centennial," *Alabama Law Review* 36 (1985), 789–926; Richard Bardolph, ed., *The Civil Rights Record: Black Americans and the Law, 1849–1970* (1970); Thomas L. Emerson, David Haber, and Norman Dorsen, *Political and Civil Rights in the United States*, vol. 2 (1967); George C. Longshore, "Case Notes," *Alabama Law Review* 14 (1962), 431–38.

Charles D. Lowery

Hampton Conference   The First and Second Hampton Negro Conferences were part of a series of gatherings, commencing in the 1890s and lasting well into the turn of the century, which considered the plight of African Americans in the post-Reconstruction era. The Second Hampton Negro Conference of 1894 proved to be the more important of the two in terms of giving impetus and notoriety to the work of **Booker T. Washington.** The Hampton

Conference, as well as the earlier Tuskegee Conferences, served as inspiration for **W.E.B. Du Bois** and the development of the **Atlanta University Conference for the Study of Negro Problems.**

Selected Bibliography W.E.B. Du Bois, *The Autobiography of W.E.B. Du Bois* (1968); Louis R. Harlan, ed., *The Booker T. Washington Papers* (1972–77); Louis R. Harlan, *Booker T. Washington: The Making of A Black Leader, 1856–1901* (1989); David Levering Lewis, *W.E.B. Du Bois: Biography of a Race, 1868–1919* (1993).

Maghan Keita

Hampton Institute   The Hampton Normal and Agricultural Institute was started on 1 April 1868. Founded by General Samuel C. Armstrong and the **American Missionary Association,** its initial purpose was to train young black students to teach and lead their people. Using a system of "practical education" that combined academic classes with manual labor, it produced hundreds of teachers for the black educational system of the South. The training of these teachers was designed to help blacks adjust to a subordinate role in the politics and economy of the post–Civil War South. The "Hampton Idea," as the school's philosophy was called, was supported by the nation's leading philanthropists, businessmen, and politicians, and was seen as a national solution to

Young men training in blacksmithing, Hampton Institute 1899–1900. © Library of Congress.

231

the "Negro problem." **Booker T. Washington** later helped popularize this idea at **Tuskegee Institute.**

Selected Bibliography James D. Anderson, *The Education of Blacks in the South, 1860–1935* (1988); M. F. Armstrong and Helen W. Ludlow, *Hampton and Its Students* (1874; reprint, 1971); Robert Francis Engs, *Educating the Disfranchised and Disinherited: Samuel Chapman Armstrong and Hampton Institute, 1839–1893* (1993); Thomas Jesse Jones, ed., *Negro Education* (1969); Robert C. Morris, *Reading, 'Riting, and Reconstruction* (1981); Booker T. Washington, *The Story of the Negro: The Rise of the Race from Slavery* (1909; reprint, 1969).

Robert A. Bellinger

Hansberry v. Lee, 311 U.S. 32 (1940)   In 1937 Carl Hansberry, a black real estate agent, purchased a building in the Hyde Park section of Chicago, an area that had always been restricted to whites. Hansberry, the father of Lorraine Hansberry, the author of "Raisin in the Sun," diligently attempted to resist the threats and vandalism from white neighbors who tried to force him to move and sell his property to a white. Finally the Kenwood Improvement Association (KIA) forced Hansberry to seek legal assistance. The KIA relied on a restrictive covenant prohibiting the purchase of any home in the area by African Americans. In 1940 the Hansberry family hired Earl B. Dickerson, a black civil rights lawyer to challenge the restrictive covenant law that barred African Americans from living in certain areas of the city. Dickerson pointed out to the U.S. Supreme Court that the law legalizing restrictive covenants stipulated that 85 percent of the residents in a neighborhood had to agree to exclude people of color. Dickerson found that less than 85 percent of the Hyde Park residents had signed the contract to keep minorities out. Therefore, the contract was not binding. The court concurred—the immediate result being the opening of 30 blocks of Southside Chicago to African American families. Although the case did not argue that restrictive covenants were unlawful, it marked the beginning of their end across the nation.

Selected Bibliography Earl B. Dickerson Papers, Chicago Historical Society, Chicago, Illinois; Edward R. Moran, "Notes and Comments," *Cornell Law Quarterly* 26 (1941); Geraldine R. Segal, *Blacks in the Law* (1983); Vibert L. White, "Developing the 'School' of Civil Rights Lawyers: From the New Deal to the New Frontier" (Ph.D. diss., The Ohio State University, 1988).

Vibert L. White

Harlan, John Marshall   (1 June 1833, Boyle County, Ky.–14 October 1911, Washington, D.C.). Born into a proslavery family, John Marshall Harlan nevertheless became the first Supreme Court justice to take a significant stand against post–Civil War racial discrimination. Joining the Democratic party in the 1850s, Harlan served in the Federal army during the Civil War and opposed Lincoln's reelection in 1864. He converted to the Republican party in the late 1860s, was appointed to the Supreme Court in 1877 by President Rutherford B. Hayes, and served until his death in 1911.

Branded as somewhat eccentric in his lifetime, Harlan has emerged in recent revisionist writing as an articulate spokesman for the most basic rights of citizenship. His eloquent dissent in **Plessy v. Ferguson** (1896), in which he asserted that the Constitution is "color-blind," became a seminal source for desegregation arguments in the 1950s and 1960s. In this famous opinion, Harlan prophetically warned that the court's ruling (upholding the doctrine of **separate but equal**) would "prove to be quite as pernicious as the decision . . . in the *Dred Scott* case."

Harlan wrote more opinions (1,161) than any other justice in the Court's history, and more dissenting opinions than any before him. Combining a belief in a powerful national government with an awareness of human needs, he spoke positively for civil rights in an era when there were few echoes.

Selected Bibliography Loren P. Beth, "Justice Harlan and the Uses of Dissent," *American Political Science Review* 49 (December 1955), 1085–1104; Albert P. Blaustein and Roy M. Mersky, *The First One Hundred Justices: Statistical Studies on the Supreme Court of the United States* (1978); Louis Filler, "John M. Harlan," in Leon Friedman and Fred L. Israel, eds., *The Justices of the United States Supreme Court 1789–1969: Their Lives and Major Opinions*, vol. 2 (1969).

Allen Dennis

Harlem Race Riot (1935) On 19 March 1935, a boy was caught stealing from a Harlem department store. Rumors flew that the police had killed the boy, and several groups protested on the street corner that evening. A rock thrown through the store window began the riot. Thousands eventually joined the crowd, breaking windows and looting. Police arrested 75 people, mostly black, and 57 civilians and 7 policemen were injured that night. Over 600 store windows were broken. The riot arose out of the intense hardship of the Great Depression, intensified in black communities by racial discrimination. Blacks in Harlem were more often unemployed than whites, with far less mobility. Crowding and mortality rates were higher, and both private and public programs routinely served Harlem less well than other city neighborhoods. When the rumor of police brutality spread, Harlemites could well believe it; it fit their perception of race relations. Nor did there seem to be anything they could do to counter this discrimination effectively. Resentment at white racism, and at unrelenting hardship, made Harlemites riot. In the aftermath of the riot, many government programs improved their records on race, and several private organizations took black grievances more seriously.

Selected Bibliography Dominic J. Capeci, Jr., *The Harlem Riot of 1943* (1977); Cheryl Greenberg, *"Or Does It Explode?" Black Harlem in the Great Depression* (1991); Claude McKay, "Harlem Runs Wild," *Nation* 140 (3 April 1935), 382–83; Mayor's Commission on Conditions in Harlem, "The Negro in Harlem: A Report on Social and Economic Conditions Responsible for the Outbreak of March 19, 1935" (Report, 1935), Mayor LaGuardia Papers, box 2550; New York City Police Department, Sixth Division, "Memo to Police Commissioner: Report of the Disorder" (20 March 1935), Mayor LaGuardia Papers, box 41, Municipal Archives, New York City.

Cheryl Greenberg

Harlem Race Riot (1943) On 1 August 1943 Harlem erupted in riot. Before peace returned to New York City's best-known black community 12 hours later, the disorder had officially recorded 6 deaths, 185 injuries, and $225,000 worth of property damage. It came amid war, on the heels of several other racial upheavals and, surprisingly, in the municipality of liberal mayor Fiorello H. La Guardia. Like other major outbreaks in Mobile, Beaumont, Los Angeles and elsewhere, it revealed perennial racial conflict over job discrimination, abject living conditions, and police-community strain. Unlike them, it occurred more for reasons of unfulfilled democratic tenets, black soldier mistreatment, and previous outbursts. Harlemites seethed as city authorities committed several racial affronts, such as permitting segregated Women Accepted for Volunteer Emergency Service units use of public facilities. They were agitated further by white assaults of Harlem recruits at southern military camps and, in late June, the killing of 25 blacks in the **Detroit race riot (1943).** Hence the confrontation between a white patrolman and a black private in Harlem drew together longstanding and war-related grievances, including unsuccessful community efforts at grassroots politics, to spark violence. Rather than interracial combat between large numbers of both races, blacks fought white police and destroyed and looted white-owned stores in a protest that resembled both earlier and later commodity riots; for example, **Harlem** (1935) and **Watts** (1965). And, despite La Guardia's even-handed quelling of the disturbance, it signaled increased black consciousness and future militancy in the face of failed political and civil rights initiatives.

Selected Bibliography Dominic J. Capeci, Jr., *The Harlem Riot of 1943* (1977); Kenneth B. Clark, "Group Violence: A Preliminary Study of the Attitudinal Pattern of Its Acceptance and Rejection: A Study of the 1943 Harlem Riot," *Journal of Social Psychology* 19 (May 1944), 319–37; Kenneth B. Clark and James Barker, "The Zoot Effect in Personality: A Race Riot Participant," *Journal of Abnormal and Social Psychology* 40 (1945), 143–48; Cheryl Greenburg, "The Politics of Disorder: Reexamining Harlem's Riots of 1935 and 1943," *Journal of Urban History* 18 (August 1992), 395–441; Harold Orlansky, *The Harlem Riot: A Study in Mass Frustration* (1943).

Dominic J. Capeci, Jr.

Harlem Race Riot (1964)   When an off-duty policeman shot a 15-year-old black male on 16 July 1964, the long simmering anger in Harlem against what was perceived as police brutality rushed to the surface. The long-held demand for a civilian police review board intensified. A **Congress of Racial Equality** (CORE) protest meeting on July 18 turned into a march on the local police station. Police arrested the leaders and tried to disperse the protestors. Matters quickly escalated, and Central Harlem exploded. Protestors threw firebombs, bricks, and various kinds of other missiles all that night, and the police responded with gun fire. For the next four nights, there was widespread looting and violence. The acting mayor fanned the discord when he blamed the violence on communist instigators. Organizer of the 1963 **March on Washington Bayard Rustin** and CORE national director **James Farmer** were on the scene trying to negotiate a settlement, and **Roy Wilkins** of the **NAACP, A. Philip Randolph,** and President Lyndon B. Johnson, all called for calm. But the established civil rights leaders were helpless in the face of the unleashed black rage over years of discrimination. The Harlem Riot was the first of many such major 1960s disturbances in the urban areas of the North. It began as a protest against unfair police treatment, but its deeper causes were the white-imposed overcrowding and horrible living conditions of ghetto life.

Selected Bibliography "Civil Rights: The White House Meeting," *Newsweek*, 3 August 1964; *New York Times*, July 1964; Fred C. Shapiro and James W. Sullivan, *Race Riots, New York, 1964* (1964); Arthur I. Waskow, *From Race Riot to Sit-In, 1919 and the 1960s: A Study in the Connections between Conflict and Violence* (1966).

John F. Marszalek

Harlem Renaissance   The Harlem Renaissance was a literary movement in Harlem during the 1920s and 1930s when poets, fiction writers, and playwrights expressed pride in the race and in the colorful mosaic of African American life while revealing the hardships visited upon African Americans. After **Jean Toomer**'s *Cane*, which captured southern life, the Renaissance writers aimed largely at capturing the dignity and beauty possessed by a newly urbanized people. Elevator operators, domestic workers, numbers runners, bootleggers, jazz and blues musicians, as well as the emerging small black middle class, were their subjects. **Langston Hughes**'s "Harlem Sweeties" revels in the beauty of black women, while Claude McKay's *Harlem Dancer* describes a prostitute whose "self was not in that strange place." The African Americans' struggle for their heritage was reflected in Hughes's "The Negro Speaks of Rivers" and racist violence in McKay's **"If We Must Die."** Tragedy dramatically unfolded in Hughes's "A Dream Deferred" and through a man's "passing" in **James Weldon Johnson**'s *The Autobiography of an Ex-Colored Man* (1927).

The Harlem Renaissance writers were eclectic. They held differing views and lived diverse lifestyles. McKay and Hughes were socialists, while **Zora Neale Hurston,** Wallace Thurman, and Rudolf Fisher were freewheeling Bohemians. Older than the others, James Weldon Johnson and **Jessie Redmond Fauset** remained fairly middle class in their perspectives. Jean Toomer never wrote a book after *Cane*. Sadly, he became preoccupied with denying his black identity. Hurston was an outspoken woman who challenged domineering patrons as well as some of the conventions established during the Renaissance. Hurston held a deep appreciation for black southern language and folklore. Most Renaissance writers rejected dialect because of past misrepresentations. Hurston's career suffered especially after her publication of *Their Eyes Were Watching God*, which drew on dialect and feminism.

Writers developed strong ties with black and white promoters, patrons and publishers. Some supporters were deeply involved in the movement itself, while some others were not. Critics argue that there was too much dependence on white patrons who unduly influenced the movement. Yet, white publishers would never have published black writers had not there been active advocates and a white market. The openness of the roaring twenties, greater exposure to black culture through vaudeville and minstrel shows, and new anthropological perspectives that defined non-European cultures as "primitive" but not inferior, created greater acceptance for black culture among whites. Problematically, many whites came to Harlem in search of stereotypical images of the "primitive" and the "exotic."

Grounded in the fluidity and contradictions of post–Civil War African American life, the Harlem Renaissance captured what **Alain Leroy Locke** termed the "New Negro." From the crowded segregated cities of the South and the North, dynamic forces breathed life into blues, jazz, and literature. Writers gleaned the diverse experiences of discrimination, racist violence, and poverty, on the one hand, and those associated with urban culture, a burgeoning black intelligentsia, and an increasingly vocal group of political activists, on the other. The Harlem Renaissance provided literary roots for generations of black writers and became the rich cultural reservoir of the civil rights movement.

Selected Bibliography Arna Bontempts, ed., *The Harlem Renaissance Remembered* (1972); Carole Marks and Diana Edkins, *The Power of Pride: Stylemakers and Rulebreakers of the Harlem Renaissance* (1999); David L. Lewis, ed., *The Portable Harlem Renaissance Reader* (1995); Amritjit Singh, William S. Silver, and Stanley Brodwin, eds., *The Harlem Renaissance: Reevaluations* (1989); Jean Wagner, *Black Poets of the United States from Paul Lawrence Dunbar to Langston Hughes* (1973); Cary D. Wintz, *Black Culture and the Harlem Renaissance* (1988).

Lisa Brock

Harlem Suitcase Theatre   One of the independent community-based theaters founded during the Great Depression, this theater was established in 1937 by the noted writer **Langston Hughes** and Louis Thompson under the auspices of the leftist International Workers Order and the New Theatre League. During its brief and turbulent two years of existence, it staged several of Hughes's satirical skits and his well received *Don't You Want to Be Free?*, the Theatre's inaugural stage production and its concluding production two years later.

Selected Bibliography Don Evans, "Langston Hughes, the Poet as Playwright: A Love-Hate Relationship," *Afro-Americans in New York Life and History* 19 (1995), 7–16; James V. Hatch, ed., *Black Theater, U.S.A.: 1847–1974* (1974); Lindsay Patterson, ed., *Anthology of the American Negro in the Theatre* (1967); Arnold Rampersad, *The Life of Langston Hughes, vol. 1: 1920–1941: I, Too, Sing America* (1986).

Malik Simba

Harmon Foundation   The Harmon Foundation was created in 1922 by the noted philanthropist William E. Harmon to promote and honor black achievement in the arts. Under its auspices, black artists and writers, among them **Countee Cullen, Langston Hughes,** and Laura Wheeler Waring, have been recognized since the 1920s. The Harmon Foundation was instrumental in establishing an art gallery at **Howard University** in 1930, and established the Harmon Gallery in New York City for the showing of black art.

Selected Bibliography Peter M. Bergman, *The Chronological History of the Negro in America* (1969); Harry A. Ploski and James Williams, eds., *The Negro Almanac: A Reference Work on the African American*, 5th ed. (1989).

Allen Dennis

Harmon v. Tyler, 273 U.S. 668 (1927)   During the first half of the twenti-eth century it was not uncommon for both northern and southern cities to adopt ordinances that prohibited blacks from residing in predominantly white neighborhoods. In the 1920s the city of New Orleans, Louisiana, adopted a municipal code that forbade public authorities from issuing a building permit for the construction of a residence for black occupancy in a white community without the written consent of a majority of the persons living in the commu-nity. Another section of the code applied the same restrictions to white citi-zens seeking residency in a black community. These provisions, however, did not deter Benjamin Harmon, a black man, from seeking a building permit in a white residential area. After being denied his permit, Harmon brought suit against the city in federal court. The Supreme Court, after hearing the case on appeal, invalidated the New Orleans ordinance. Citing **Buchanan v. Warley,** a 1917 case involving a similar statute, the Court held that the ordinance vio-lated the **Fourteenth Amendment** by denying both whites and blacks the right to acquire and use property. The Court's decision, however, did little or nothing to prevent discrimination in residential housing. Until the landmark case **Shelley v. Kraemer** (1948), state courts enforced restrictive deeds and contracts that prohibited the sale of property to blacks.

Selected Bibliography Derrick A. Bell, Jr., *Race, Racism, and American Law,* 2nd ed. (1980); *New York Times,* 22 May 1927; Joel Williamson, *The Crucible of Race: Black-White Relations in the American South since Emancipation* (1984).

Phillip A. Gibbs

Harper v. Virginia Board of Elections, 383 U.S. 663 (1966)   The Twenty-fourth Amendment (1964) banned **poll taxes** as a condition of voting in fed-eral elections. Annie E. Harper, a retired domestic, was one of many black southerners who brought cases in the federal courts seeking a decision that would apply such a ban on poll taxes in state elections. Harper's case originated in Virginia, where poll taxes had restricted the electorate since 1902. In a six-to-three decision in March 1966 that relied on the **Fourteenth Amendment's** "equal protection" clause, the Supreme Court overruled **Breedlove v. Suttles** (1937) and overturned a lower court decision in striking down a requirement in the Virginia state constitution that prospective voters must have paid the previous three years' poll taxes or forfeit the privilege of voting. In Virginia, whose political leaders preferred to leave controversial initiatives to the federal courts, an effort to undo the poll tax requirement had failed in the previous ses-sion of the legislature. By the time the Court made its ruling, lower federal courts had recently outlawed the poll tax as a requirement for voting in Texas and Alabama, and it had remained in effect only in Mississippi and Virginia. The decision culminated a series of significant changes in the electoral and leg-islative environments in Virginia and other southern states.

Selected Bibliography American Civil Liberties Union Papers, Princeton University, Princeton, N. J.; Philip B. Knight and Gerhard Casper, eds., *Landmark Briefs and Arguments of the Supreme Court of the United States: Constitutional Law* 62 (1975), 833–1087; Peter

Wallenstein, *These New and Strange Beings: Conflict, Law, and Change in Twentieth-Century Virginia* (2003).

Peter Wallenstein

Harris, Abram Lincoln (17 January 1899, Richmond, Va.–16 November 1963, Chicago, Ill.). This African American scholar and activist received his B.S. from Virginia Union University, his M.A. from the University of Pittsburgh, and his Ph.D. in economics at Columbia University. His dissertation was published in 1931 as *The Black Worker* (with Sterling Spero). Except for a brief stint as executive secretary of the Minneapolis Urban League, Harris remained in academe, teaching at West Virginia State College (1924–25), **Howard University** (1927–46), and the University of Chicago (1946–63). He served on the consumer advisory board of the National Recovery Administration and was a fellow of the John Simon Guggenheim Foundation. He was married to Callie McGuinn (1925), then to Phedorah Wynn (1946). In his early years Harris devoted his political and scholarly efforts to developing economic programs based on an interracial working-class alliance and critiquing alternative strategies. After the 1930s he retreated from activism to study different economic philosophies. He eventually embraced the classical liberalism of John Stuart Mill. Throughout his life he was concerned with the problems of race and the political implications of various programs of social reform.

Selected Bibliography *Chicago Tribune*, 17 November 1963; William Darity, Jr., "Abram Harris: An Odyssey from Howard to Chicago," *Review of Black Political Economy* 15 (Winter 1987), 4–40; William Darity, Jr., "Introduction," in William Darity, Jr., ed., *Race, Radicalism, and Reform: Selected Papers of Abram Harris* (1989); Abram Harris, *The Negro as Capitalist* (1936); *New York Times*, 17 November 1963; Rayford W. Logan, and Michael R. Winston, eds., *Dictionary of American Negro Biography* (1982).

Cheryl Greenberg

Harris, Patricia Roberts (31 May 1924, Mattoon, Ill.–23 March 1985, Washington, D.C.). The daughter of a railroad dining car waiter and a teacher, Harris was a graduate of **Howard University** and George Washington University law school, She was appointed ambassador to Luxembourg by President Lyndon B. Johnson, the first black woman to hold such diplomatic rank. Under President Jimmy Carter she became the first black woman to hold a cabinet position, serving as Secretary of both Housing and Urban Development and Health and Human Services. Described as "tough, abrasive and irascible," she was a powerful advocate for minorities and the poor.

Selected Bibliography *Dictionary of Black Culture*; Charles Moritz, ed., *Current Biography Yearbook* (1985); Obituary, *New York Times*, 24 March 1985.

Bernard Donahoe

Hastie, William Henry (17 November 1904, Knoxville, Tenn.–14 April 1976, Philadelphia, Pa.). With the exception of Supreme Court Justice **Thurgood Marshall,** William Henry Hastie was probably the twentieth century's best-known black lawyer. In 1925 he graduated from Amherst College and went on to law school, receiving a bachelor of law degree from Harvard in 1930 and a doctorate in jurisprudence in 1933. After a brief stint practicing law, he joined the faculty of **Howard College**'s law school in 1930 and became its dean in 1939. Hastie quickly became active in the **NAACP** and the **New Negro Alliance**. His involvement in civil rights cases soon earned him a reputation as a talented lawyer even when decisions went against him. Notably he aided the attempt of **Thomas R. Hocutt** to enter the University of North Carolina, argued cases involving salary equalization in North Carolina and Maryland, and fought employment discrimination. His public-service career began in November 1933, when Secretary **Harold L. Ickes** recruited him to work for the Department of the Interior as an assistant solicitor. This, in turn, led to his appointment to the district court of the Virgin Islands in March 1937 and a position in the War Department in 1940. After two years, Hastie resigned the position in protest of the continuation of segregation and discrimination policies in the U.S. military. By 1946 he was back in public service holding the governorship of the Virgin Islands. In 1949 President Harry S Truman elevated him to the U.S. Court of Appeals for the Third Judicial Circuit, a post he held until 1971.

Selected Bibliography Phillip McGuire, *He, Too, Spoke for Democracy: Judge Hastie, World War II, and the Black Soldier* (1988); Gilbert Ware, *William Hastie: Grace under Pressure* (1984); Robert C. Weaver, "William Henry Hastie, 1904–1976," *Crisis* 83 (No. 8, 1976), 267–70; *Who Was Who in America* (1981).

Gary B. Mills

Hastings, Alcee L. (5 September 1936, Altamonte Springs, Fla.–). With a law degree from Florida A&M University, Alcee Hastings practiced law from 1964 to 1977. In 1979, President Jimmy Carter appointed him a federal district judge, the first black federal judge in Florida. In 1981, Hastings was indicted on a bribery charge. Although a jury acquitted him, he was impeached and removed from office. In 1992, Hastings was elected to the U.S. House of Representatives, where he has since had a liberal voting record. In 2000, he criticized Governor Jeb Bush's plan to end **affirmative action** admissions in Florida higher education.

Selected Bibliography Michael Barone, et al., *The Almanac of American Politics: 2002* (2001); William E. Gibson, "Impeached Mr. Hastings Blossoms in Congress," *The National Law Journal* 16 (1994), A1, A26; Mary L. Volcansek, *Judicial Impeachment: None Called for Justice* (1993).

Patricia A. Behlar

Hatcher, Richard Gordon (10 July 1933, Michigan City, Ind.–). An African American lawyer and the first black mayor of a major U.S. city, Hatcher was mayor of Gary, Indiana, from 1967 to 1988. Winning his first election by a slim margin in a campaign marred by racism and a corrupt Democratic machine, Hatcher ran as a reform candidate. His victory symbolized to black America the phrase: "from protest to politics." In 1972 Hatcher cochaired the first National Black Political Convention in Gary. Its purpose was "unification of black people." He served as president of the National Black Political Council, a member of delegate selection and executive committees of the National Democratic Committee, and began teaching at Valparaiso University Law School in 1989.

Selected Bibliography *Current Biography* (1972); Alex Poinsett, *Black Power: Gary Style, The Making of Mayor Richard Gordon Hatcher* (1970); *Who's Who in American Politics, 1989–1990* (1989); *Who's Who among Black Americans, 1990–1991* (1990).

Nancy E. Fitch

Hayden, Robert E. (4 August 1913, Detroit, Mich.–25 February 1980, Detroit, Mich.). Robert Hayden became a consultant in poetry to the Library of Congress in the 1970s. It was a fitting tribute to a man whose poetry, although not often consciously black, nonetheless dealt with major themes in African American life during the 1960s. He is best known for his poems on **Frederick Douglass** and **Malcom X.** Hayden, born in the North, taught at **Fisk University** for 23 years. While there, he influenced a number of black writers, among them **Julius Bernard Lester.** He symbolized the best of the early civil rights movement in his belief that good art spoke from one's experience and should not be tainted with ideological notions of color. Many of the later followers of the Black Aesthetic Movement would reject that belief, viewing black art as political. Hayden, however, held to his views. His best known poetry appeared in the late 1960s and early 1970s. In 1969, he accepted a professorship at the University of Michigan, where he remained until his death in 1980.

Selected Bibliography *New York Times*, 27 February 1980; Robert Hayden, *Words in Mourning Time* (1975); *Commentary*, September 1980.

Charles T. Pete Banner-Haley

Hayes, Roland (3 June 1887, Curryville, Ga.–31 December 1976, Boston, Mass.). An African American tenor of classical and Negro spiritual music, Hayes was noted for his introduction and interpretation of indigenous "Aframerican" religious folk songs to concert-goers around the world. His outstanding talent and perseverance during the 1920s and 1930s provided opportunities for other black concert and operatic artists. Hayes attended **Fisk University**'s preparatory school and studied music privately in this country and Europe. Through his research, he came to the realization that liberty and freedom were realities for American slaves and that "The Negro has his God-given music to bring to the sum total of good in the world."

Selected Bibliography *Current Biography* (1942); John Lovell, Jr., *Black Song: The Forge and the Flame. The Story of How the Afro-American Spiritual Was Hammered Out* (1986); Edgar A. Toppin, *A Biographical History of Blacks in American since 1528* (1971).

Nancy E. Fitch

Haynes, George Edumund (11 May 1880, Pine Bluff, Ark.–8 January 1960, New York, N.Y.). A pioneering sociologist whose writings chronicled the creation of a black industrial working class, Haynes was also an influential social reformer. Like **W.E.B. Du Bois,** an early mentor, Haynes was editor of the

Fisk University *Herald,* and class valedictorian (1903). After receiving an M.A. from Yale University (1905) and studying at the University of Chicago, Haynes became the first black to graduate from the New York School of Philanthropy (1910) and to earn a Ph.D. from Columbia University (1912). In 1910 Haynes and Mrs. William Baldwin, a wealthy philanthropist, cofounded the **National Urban League** and Haynes became its executive secretary from 1910–17. At the same time, Haynes became professor of sociology at Fisk where he established an undergraduate program to train black social workers. Haynes's own academic success convinced Columbia and other major universities to participate in the League's Urban Fellows Program, which granted scholarships to black graduate students. Urban Fellows became executives of Urban League branches, established **Atlanta University**'s and **Howard University**'s schools of social work, and included influential social scientists in their own right, such as **Abram Lincoln Harris,** and **Ira De A. Reid.** In 1918 Haynes was appointed Director of the Division of Negro Economics in the Department of Labor and used a staff of black professionals to coordinate black defense workers during World War I. From 1921 until his retirement in 1947 Haynes was the head of the Department of Race Relations of the Federal Council of Churches. He developed the concept of the Interracial Clinic to deal with post–World War II racial tensions and introduced Race Relations Sunday exchanges between black and white congregations (1923) and National Brotherhood Month (1940). Haynes conducted surveys for the YMCA in Africa in 1930 and 1947 and taught at City College of New York from 1950–59.

Selected Bibliography George E. Haynes, *Africa: Continent of the Future* (1950); George E. Haynes, *The Negro at Work during the World War and Reconstruction* (1921); George E. Haynes, *The Negro at Work in New York City* (1912); George E. Haynes, *The Trend of the Races* (1929); Rayford W. Logan and Michael R. Winston, eds., *Dictionary of American Negro Biography* (1982); Daniel Perlman, "Stirring the White Conscience: The Life of George E. Haynes" (Ph.D. diss., New York University, 1972); Nancy Weiss, *The National Urban League* (1974); Francille Rusan Wilson, *The Segregated Scholars: Black Social Scientists and the Development of Black Labor Studies, 1895–1950* (2002).

Francille Rusan Wilson

Head Start Head Start is a federal preschool compensatory program for economically deprived families. It was developed as a part of the Community Action Program established by the 1964 Economic Opportunity Act that authorized the **War on Poverty** program. The first Head Start program in the summer of 1965 was an eight-week national demonstration project for the 50 states and territories. To help deprived preschool children achieve their potential, Title II of the Economic Opportunity Act was amended in 1966 to include a year-round program in social, educational, mental, and physical health services. The local community provided 10 percent and later 20 percent of program costs while Congress provided the balance. Funds were granted directly to the local nonprofit community group or community action agency from the U.S. Department of Education and later the Department of

Mississippi Head Start children, mid-1960s. © Tougaloo College, L. Zenobia Coleman Library, Archives.

Health and Human Services. Programs were organized to meet the community needs and to involve low-income parents, usually as teacher aids and council members.

The Mississippi civil rights movement and Head Start's integration requirements caused one of the most heated controversies during the early years. Civil rights activists organized the Child Development Group of Mississippi. This group submitted an application through Mary Holmes Junior College on behalf of the low-income families in some of Mississippi's poorest counties. The group was in the news because of the involvement of civil rights workers, unclear guidelines, and fiscal irregularities. The controversy subsided with the organization of the Mississippi Action for Progress as an alternative local Head Start Program in Mississippi.

Nationally, Head Start is representative of the best response to the injustices that Americans tried to alleviate during the civil rights movement. More than any other social program, it has provided the means for upward mobility, encouraged self-advancement and self-help in low-income families. In 2003, the call by the George W. Bush presidential administration to change Head Start created an adverse reaction from its supporters.

Selected Bibliography Polly Greenberg, *The Devil Has Slippery Shoes, A Biased Biography of the Child Development Group of Mississippi* (1969); "Learning from Head Start's Efforts," *Insight* 6 (10 December 1990), 44–46; Maris A. Vinovskis, "Do Federal Compensatory Education Programs Really Work? A Brief Historical Analysis of Title I and Head Start," *American Journal of Education* 107 (1999), 187–209; Edward Zigler and Jeanette Valentine, eds., *Project Head*

Start: A Legacy of the War on Poverty (1979); Edward Zigler and Susan Muenchow, *Head Start: The Inside Story of America's Most Successful Education Experiment* (1992). Web site: www2.acf.dhhs.gov/programs/hsb.

Alferdteen Harrison and Lavaree Jones

Heart of Atlanta Motel, Inc. v. United States, 379 U.S. 241 (1964)

Within hours after the signing of the **Civil Rights Act of 1964,** the manager of the Heart of Atlanta Motel filed suit in federal court attacking the constitutionality of the public accommodations section of this act. Prior to the passage of the Civil Rights Act, this motel, like similar establishments across the South, had refused to rent rooms to African Americans. The suit contended that the Civil Rights Act of 1964 exceeded the powers of Congress to regulate interstate commerce; violated the rights of business owners to choose their customers and operate their businesses as they desired; and subjugated owners to "involuntary servitude." Attorneys for the government countered that the commerce clause in the Constitution allowed Congress to remove restraints on interstate commerce such as the discriminatory policies of motels; that the Fifth Amendment allowed reasonable regulation of property; and that references to "involuntary servitude" were "frivolous." On 14 December 1964 the U.S. Supreme Court upheld the constitutionality of the public accommodations section of the 1964 Civil Rights Act. The decision was based on the commerce clause and the equal protection clause of the **Fourteenth Amendment.** By upholding the constitutionality of the 1964 Civil Rights Act, the Supreme Court legally ensured the desegregation of public accommodations.

    Selected Bibliography *Atlanta Constitution*, 15 December 1964; Ronald H. Bayor, *Race and the Shaping of Twentieth-Century Atlanta* (1996); Derrick A. Bell, Jr., ed., *Civil Rights: Leading Cases* (1980); David Andrew Harmon, *Beneath the Image of the Civil Rights Movement and Race Relations: Atlanta, Georgia 1946–1981* (1996); *Race Relations Law Reporter* 9 (1964), 908–11, 1650–68; George Rossman, ed., "Review of Recent Supreme Court Decisions," *American Bar Association Journal* 51 (1965), 268.

David A. Harmon

Henderson v. U.S. Interstate Commerce Commission and Southern Railway, 339 U.S. 816 (1950)

Although this decision dealt a stinging blow to segregation in interstate transit, its impact proved to be limited because it fell short of overturning the basic tenets of **Plessy v. Ferguson.** Elmer W. Henderson filed his complaint in 1942 after he was repeatedly denied service in the dining car of the Southern Railway. That incident occurred because white passengers continued to occupy the two tables in the black section, which a curtain separated from the rest of the car. After lower courts determined that the railway's revised rules met the separate but equal holding of *Plessy*, Henderson appealed to the Supreme Court. In an unprecedented move, the Justice Department intervened to argue against the constitutionality of *Plessy*. Eschewing that question, a unanimous Court held that Henderson had been denied equal access in violation of the Interstate

Commerce Act, and that the use of partitions, curtains, and signs emphasized "the artificiality of a difference in treatment." In amicus briefs for *McLaurin v. Oklahoma State Regents* and *Sweatt v. Painter,* segregation cases decided the same day as *Henderson,* the Justice Department reiterated its argument against *Plessy.* But in all three decisions, the Court addressed only the question of equality, and avoided the legal issue of racial separation established in *Plessy.*

Selected Bibliography Catherine A. Barnes, *Journey from Jim Crow: The Desegregation of Southern Transit* (1983); Richard Kluger, *Simple Justice: The History of Brown v. Board of Education and Black America's Struggle for Equality* (1976); Laughlin McDonald, *Racial Equality* (1977); Paul L. Murphy, *The Constitution in Crisis Times, 1918–1969* (1972).

Jack E. Davis

Henry, Aaron (2 July 1922, Dublin, Miss.–19 May 1997, Clarksdale, Miss.). A black businessman, civil rights and political leader, who was educated at Xavier University in New Orleans, Louisiana, Henry was at the center of the drive for racial justice for black Mississippians for nearly four decades. Upon graduation from Xavier in 1960, he returned to his hometown of Clarksdale to establish a pharmacy. The racial inequities faced by that Delta town's large black population prompted him and other local leaders to organize the Coahoma County branch of the **NAACP.** The state organization soon recognized his leadership abilities and, in 1960, elected him president of the state branches, an office that he held into the 1990s. A board member of numerous civil and human rights groups and governmental agencies, Henry was clearly one of the country's best and respected civil rights activists. His involvement in the civil rights struggle was active and direct. In 1961 he participated in the violence-plagued activities of the **Freedom Riders.** He was arrested with the riders when they arrived in Jackson to challenge Mississippi's segregated facilities. A close friend of **Martin Luther King, Jr.,** and Mississippi's charismatic leaders, **Medgar W. Evers** and **James Charles Evers,** Henry marched with them in many of their demonstrations.

Henry worked hard to reform his home county of Coahoma, where blacks enjoyed few of the advantages of real citizenship. During the 1960s, Henry launched an aggressive campaign of demonstrations, economic boycotts, and voter registration to help eliminate white intransigence. In response, he was arrested and convicted of spurious moral charges, and his home and business were repeatedly fire-bombed and vandalized. Despite constant threats on his life, he remained committed to nonviolent change of Mississippi's racial order. He also worked for change through the **Council of Federated Organizations** (COFO), a coalition of the nation's four major civil rights groups operating in the state. As its president, he directed the **Freedom Summer of 1964** project when hundreds of mostly white college students came to Mississippi to participate in a massive voter registration drive and educational effort. A founding father of the biracial **Mississippi Freedom Democratic Party,** he served as its chairman when it successfully unseated the regulars at the 1968 Democratic national convention. A member of the Mississippi legislature in the 1990s, he remained until his death an active participant in all aspects of Mississippi life and a living reminder of the turbulent 1960s.

Selected Bibliography T. H. Barker, "Interview with Aaron Henry;" Lyndon Baines Johnson Oral History Collection, University of Texas, Austin; John Ditmer, "Dr. Aaron Henry, Mississippi Freedom Fighters," *Crisis (The New)* 104 (1997), 25–26; Aaron Henry and Constance Curry, *Aaron Henry: The Fire Ever Burning* (2000); George A. Sewell and Margaret L. Dwight, *Mississippi Black History Makers* (1977); James W. Silver, *Mississippi, the Closed Society* (1966); Robert Penn Warren, *Who Speaks for the Negro* (1965).

Robert L. Jenkins

Herndon, Angelo   (6 May 1913, Wyoming, Ohio–). The son of a miner and a domestic servant with a childhood marked by poverty and emotional religion, Herndon entered into the mines at age thirteen on the death of his father. He worked in the **Communist Party** from 1930 for the **Scottsboro Trials,** for unemployed councils for the relief and the unionization of miners (Alabama and Tennessee) and for striking longshoremen (New Orleans). On 30 June 1932, with demands for relief, he led a march of about a thousand unemployed blacks and whites on the Fulton County, Georgia, courthouse. Arrested and tried (like the "Atlanta Six" earlier) for "attempting to incite an insurrection," he became the focal point of a racial cause celebre of the 1930s. Although young white reformers (C. Vann Woodward), "Southern moderates" **(Will W. Alexander),** and major organizations (the **NAACP,** and the **American Civil Liberties Union**) opposed his conviction, the effective defense of both Herndon and the cause of black rights in and out of court came mainly from radical black attorney William L. Patterson, the International Labor Defence, and the Communist Party. In 1937 the U.S. Supreme Court invalidated the Georgia statute (which was nevertheless invoked against **Stokely Carmichael** in 1966). After World War II, Herndon abandoned the Communist Party and public activities for a chosen life of obscurity as a salesman in the Midwest.

Selected Bibliography Charles Crowe, *Slavery, Race, and American Scholarship* (1988); Angelo Herndon, *Let Me Live* (1937); Charles H. Martin, *The Angelo Herndon Case and Southern Justice* (1976); Charles H. Martin, "Communists and Blacks: The ILD and the Angelo Herndon Trial," *Journal of Negro History* 64 (1979), 131–41.

Charles Crowe

Herskovits, Melville Jean   (10 September 1895, Bellfontaine, Ohio–25 February 1963, Evanston, Ill.). A distinguished anthropologist and pioneer in African and African American studies, Melville Herskovits, the son of Jewish immigrants, earned a B.A. degree in history (1920) from the University of Chicago, an M.S. (1921) and Ph.D. (1923) in anthropology from Columbia University. In 1927 Herskovits began a 36-year career at Northwestern University. He played a key role in establishing African and African American studies as acceptable scholarly fields. His landmark work, *The Myth of the Negro Past* (1941) describes a rich African heritage and debunks the myth that

African Americans have no cultural past. Herskovits founded the first university program of African Studies in the United States. In 1970 Northwestern named its Africana library collection for him.

Selected Bibliography Sidney W. Mintz, "Introduction," in Melville J. Herskovits, *The Myth of the Negro Past* (1941); George E. Simpson, *Melville J. Herskovits* (1973); Earl E. Thorpe, *The Central Theme of Black History* (1969).

Barbara L. Green

Hesburgh, Theodore M. (25 May 1917, Syracuse, N.Y.–). President of the University of Notre Dame from 1952–87, and a member of the **United States Commission on Civil Rights** from its creation in 1957 to 1972, and its chairman from 1969–72, Hesburgh was an important influence in the American civil rights movement for these years. Deeply moved by the poignant testimony before the Commission of black Americans being deprived of their right to vote, Hesburgh developed and acted upon the conviction that the Commission was a kind of "national conscience." When President Richard M. Nixon named Hesburgh chairman of the Commission in 1969, some observers thought that he regarded Hesburgh as a "pillar of the establishment, to be used by the White House for its own purposes." If so, this did not happen. Instead, Hesburgh publicly criticized the Nixon administration's civil rights policies, or what he perceived to be a lack of them. Testifying before the House Committee on Education and Labor in 1972, Hesburgh censured Nixon's proposed antibusing legislation in the guise of the Equal Opportunities Educational Act as failing to implement the Supreme Court's 1954 decision on desegregation, of failing to provide equal educational opportunities, and of succeeding to fractionize further the nation along racial lines. Hesburgh's testimony against the proposed legislation aroused the Nixon administration to force his resignation as chairman and as a member of the Commission. Nixon's abrupt dismissal of Hesburgh allowed the President to weaken the Civil Rights Commission's influence with the public and Congress and to remove it from the front pages where Hesburgh had put it for some years.

Selected Bibliography Charlotte A. Ames, Comp., *Theodore M. Hesburgh, A Bio-Bibliography* (1989); Dorothy Gilliam, "The Hesburgh Years: Civil Rights," *Notre Dame Magazine* 1 (June 1972), 23–25; John C. Lungren, *Hesburgh of Notre Dame* (1987).

Vincent P. DeSantis

High Point, North Carolina, Sit-In On Thursday, 11 February 1960, 26 black teenagers from William Penn High School sat down at the downtown High Point Woolworth segregated lunch counter. Unprepared for this direct assault, Woolworth promptly closed the lunch counter and later announced the closing of the store. Fear of similar protests by black youth caused several other stores in the vicinity to close their doors as well. This grassroots movement, strongly encouraged and supported by black adults in the community, set the pace for achieving equality. Despite abusive and violent attempts by whites to curtail the demonstrations, the sit-in movement was a success. By mid-1960, lunch counters were integrated. This victory set the stage for the successful integration of other facilities and was one method blacks used to pursue parity throughout the social, economic, and political arena in High Point.

Selected Bibliography *Charlotte Observer*, 16, 17 February 1960; Wanda A. Hendricks, interview with Attorney Sammie Chess, 1222 Montlieu Avenue, High Point, N.C. 27262 (30 July 1990); *High Point Enterprise*, February 1960, 25 January 1985; Aldon D. Morris, *The Origins of the Modern Civil Rights Movement: Black Communities Organizing for Change* (1984); Martin Oppenheimer, *The Sit-In Movement of 1960* (1989).

Wanda A. Hendricks

Highlander Folk School   Myles Horton and Don West cofounded a school in 1932 in Monteagle, Tennessee, to serve as a community folk school in the Danish tradition. Horton remained as its director until 1970; Septima Clark served as director of education. Until the 1950s the school worked primarily with trade unions; after that time its focus shifted to the civil rights struggle. In the early 1970s Highlander turned to local problems of poverty and political powerlessness. Highlander served as a training center and meeting place for southern union and civil rights leaders, and sought to empower community members to organize on behalf of their own concerns. Its residential workshops, whose agendas were set by the students, included voter education, literacy, racial integration, cooperatives, union organizing, training in nonviolence, and civil rights strategies. Tremendously successful in its goal to develop leadership within oppressed communities, Highlander was frequently harassed by agents of the state and federal government. FBI surveillance, IRS investigations, criticism and investigation by state officials, the revoking of Highlander's charter in 1962, the confiscation of its property (Highlander returned under a new name and moved first to Knoxville, then to New Market, Tennessee in 1971) and occasional attacks of the Ku Klux Klan failed to deter Highlander staff members from continuing their programs.

Selected Bibliography Frank Adams, *Unearthing Seeds of Fire: The Idea of Highlander* (1975); John Glen, *Highlander: No Ordinary School* (1988); Aimee Horton, *The Highlander Folk School: A History of Its Major Programs, 1932–1961* (1989); Myles Horton and Paolo Freire, *We Made the Road by Walking: Conversations on Education and Social Change* (1990); C. Alvin Hughes, "A New Agenda for the South: The Role and Influence of Highlander Folk School 1953–1961," *Phylon* 46 (September 1985), 242–50; Theresa Quinn, "Dream that Keeps on Growing: Myles Horton and Highlander," in William Ayers, Jean Ann Hunt, and Theresa Quinn, eds., *Teaching for Social Justice* (1998); Eliot Wigginton, *Refuse to Stand Silently By: An Oral History of Grass-Roots Activism in America 1921–1964* (1991).

Cheryl Greenberg

Hill, Oliver W.   (1 May 1907, Richmond, Va.–). An African American educated at **Howard University,** Hill was the first black elected to public office in Richmond, Virginia, since the 1890s. His 1948 election resulted from a developing belief among blacks and some whites that the black population of 40 thousand deserved some representation on the city council. In a poll of voters, Hill was voted as the second most effective member of the nine-mem-

Attorney Oliver Hill (right) chief counsel of the Virginia State Conference, NAACP, in court, 1953. © Library of Congress.

ber council. However, in a 1951 reelection bid, he was defeated by 44 votes. He returned to his legal practice and became active in **NAACP** school suits. Furthermore, he defended seven Martinsville, Virginia, blacks who were convicted of rape and electrocuted. Hill was strongly supported for an appointive vacancy on the council, but his refusal to compromise his stance on civil rights resulted in his failure to gain the position. Blacks were angered, and the controversy helped to destroy the improved relationship between the races initiated by Hill's election. Subsequently he served as a member of the President's Commission on Government Contracts, and as an Assistant to the Commissioner of the Federal Housing Authority. Between 1940 and 1961, Hill served as chairman of the Virginia Legal Commission of the NAACP. In 1994, he, along with Supreme Court Justice Lewis Powell, received the first City of Richmond Distinguished Citizen Awards.

Selected Bibliography Oliver W. Hill, *The Big Bang: Brown v. Board of Education and Beyond: The Autobiography of Oliver W. Hill, Sr.* (2000); "Lily White Council," *New Republic* 124 (April 1951), 7; *Who's Who among Black Americans 1975–1976*, vol. 1 (1976), 293.

William Cash

Hill v. Texas, 316 U.S. 400 (1942)   Henry Hill was charged by a Dallas County, Texas, grand jury of rape. His attorneys challenged the indictment on "the grounds that Negroes had been excluded from the jury." Hill was convicted by an all-white jury, and the verdict was sustained by the Texas Court of Criminal Appeals. When the case reached the U.S. Supreme Court, Hill's attorneys presented poll tax receipts to show that there were "duly qualified blacks" in the county for jury service. They also provided evidence of the number of black males aged 25 and over who had formal schooling, including higher education, but were denied participation as jurors. The defense also made use of the testimony of elected officials to contend that "no Negro had been on the grand jury list for sixteen or more years." The Supreme Court reversed the conviction.

Selected Bibliography Derrick A. Bell, Jr., *Race, Racism, and American Law* (1980); Marvin E. Frankel and Gary Naftalis, *The Grand Jury* (1975); Joseph Tussman, ed., *The Supreme Court on Racial Discrimination* (1963).

LeRoy T. Williams

Himes, Chester Bomar (29 July 1909, Jefferson City, Mo.–12 November 1984, Moraira, Spain). An expatriate African American master of quick-action prose packed with social protest and caustic visions of civil rights, Chester Himes flailed out early against the shackles restraining blacks. He went from the Ohio State University (1926–28) to the Ohio State Penitentiary (1928–35) for a $53,000 armed robbery. He depicted raw racism in several early novels: *If He Hollers Let Him Go* (1945) paints prejudice in a Los Angeles shipyard, and *Lonely Crusade* (1947) plumbs a black man's fears in America. He gained popular American notice with his black detective fiction featuring Coffin Ed Johnson and Grave Digger Jones in works such as *Cotton Comes to Harlem* (1965).

Selected Bibliography Chester B. Himes, *My Life of Absurdity: The Later Years; The Autobiography of Chester Himes* (1976); Chester B. Himes, *The Quality of Hurt; The Early Years: The Autobiography of Chester Himes* (1972); Edward Margolies and Michel Fabre, *The Several Lives of Chester Himes* (1997); James Sallis, *Chester Himes: A Life* (2001); Charles L. P. Silet. ed., *The Critical Response to Chester Himes* (1999); Robert E. Skinner, *Two Guns from Harlem: The Detective Fiction of Chester Himes* (1989).

Thomas J. Davis

Hobson v. Hansen, 265 F. Supp. 902 (D.D.C. 1967) This case was part of civil rights activist Julius Hobson's broader attack on **de facto segregation** in the public schools of Washington, D.C. Although Congress would later make the school board elective, a three-judge district court upheld the constitutionality of congressional legislation empowering the judges of the district court to appoint board members. Far more controversial was the next phase of the litigation, determining whether the operation of the public schools, with their system of ability grouping (track system), unconstitutionally discriminated against black children by segregating them into the lower tracks. In *Hobson v. Hansen,* Circuit Judge **J. Skelly Wright,** sitting by designation as a District Judge, concluded that the Board of Education had deprived black children of equal educational opportunity with white children. He did not hold that ability grouping was unconstitutional but rather that the Washington, D.C., track system failed to provide remedial and compensatory education to those in the lowest tracks, many of whom had not had the advantage of kindergarten in their neighborhood schools, which put them at a disadvantage when they were tested for placement. Critics of the decision believed it would result in increased white flight to the suburbs.

Selected Bibliography Alexander M. Bickel, "Skelly Wright's Sweeping Decision," *New Republic* (8 July 1967), 11–12; Robert L. Carter, "The Law and Racial Equality in Education," *Journal of Negro Education* 37 (Summer 1968), 204–11; Aaron Cohodes, "Who Can Perform What the Courts Promise?" *Nation's Schools* 80 (August 1967), 31; John N. Drowatzky, "Tracking and Ability Grouping in Education," *Journal of Law and Education* 10 (January 1981), 43–59; Carl F. Hansen, *Danger in Washington: The Story of My Twenty Years in the Public Schools of the Nation's Capital* (1968); Arthur Selwyn Miller, A *"Capacity for Outrage": The Judicial Odyssey of J. Skelly Wright* (1984).

Patricia A. Behlar

Hocutt, Thomas (dates unavailable). Thomas Hocutt, an African American, applied for admission to the University of North Carolina College of Pharmacy in 1933 but was rejected because of his race. Receiving legal representation from the national **NAACP** in the person of **William Henry Hastie,** he petitioned for admission. His legal appeal failed, however, partly because the president of the North Carolina College for Negroes reportedly would not supply him with necessary credentials supporting his eligibility. Although Hocutt lost, the judge declared that North Carolina had an obligation to provide "substantially equal" educational facilities for black residents. NAACP strategy thereafter was to contest segregation first in the schools.

Selected Bibliography Lerone Bennett, Jr., *Before the Mayflower. A History of the Negro in America, 1619–1964* (1981); John Hope Franklin and Alfred A. Moss, Jr., *From Slavery to Freedom: A History of Negro Americans,* 8th ed. (2000); Harvard Sitkoff, A *New Deal for Blacks: The Emergence of Civil Rights as a National Issue, The Depression Decade* (1978).

Nancy E. Fitch

Hollins v. State of Oklahoma,* 295 U.S. 394 (1935)** This U.S. Supreme Court case involved the reversal of a rape conviction. The reversal was based on the denial of the defendant's equal protection under the law. In 1931, Jess Hollins was convicted by an all-white jury of raping a white woman in Sapulpa, Oklahoma. Before his scheduled execution, the **NAACP's** attorneys appealed on the basis of the exclusion of African American jurors. African Americans were excluded historically from jury duty in the county solely on the basis of their race or color. The reversal was a per curiam decision based on the previous decision in the famous Scottsboro case of ***Norris v. Alabama, 294 U.S. 587 (1935).

Selected Bibliography Mary D. Brite, "Kentucky's Scottsboro Case," *Crisis* (April 1936); Marvin E. Frankel and Gary P. Naftalis, *The Grand Jury* (1975); Richard Kluger, *Simple Justice: The History of Brown v. Board of Education and Black America's Struggle for Equality* (1975).

Donald Cunnigen

Holmes v. Atlanta, **350 U.S. 879 (1955)** This suit challenged the right of a municipality to maintain segregated golf courses. On 19 July 1951 the manager of a municipally owned golf course in Atlanta, Georgia refused to admit African American citizens. After city officials failed to respond to petitions requesting the desegregation of Atlanta's golf courses, these citizens filed suit in district court. The district court upheld the city's right to maintain segregated golf courses. According to the court, local ordinances requiring segregation in the use of park and recreational facilities were not in conflict with the **Fourteenth Amendment.** Because the city of Atlanta provided no golfing facilities for its African American citizens, the decision allowed time for city officials to provide "separate-but-equal" facilities. The **United States Court of Appeals for the Fifth Judicial Circuit** concurred in this decision. On 7 November 1955 the U.S. Supreme Court reversed the lower courts, ruling that Atlanta could not deny the use of municipally owned golf courses to citizens on the basis of race or color. For the first time the ***Brown v. Board of Education*** decision declaring segregated schools illegal was extended to include other public facilities.

Selected Bibliography *Atlanta Constitution,* 8 November, 24 December 1955; Richard Bardolph, ed., *The Civil Rights Record: Black Americans and the Law, 1849–1970* (1970); Ronald H. Bayor, *Race and the Shaping of Twentieth-Century Atlanta* (1996); David Andrew Harmon, *Beneath the Image of the Civil Rights Movement and Race Relations: Atlanta, Georgia 1946–1981* (1996); *Race Relations Law Reporter,* vol.1 (1957), 14, 146–51.

David A. Harmon

Holmes v. Danner, **191 F. Supp. 394 (M. D. GA., 1961)** This decision represented a victory for opponents of segregated higher education. A U.S. District Court found that the University of Georgia had denied admission to Hamilton Holmes and Charlayne Hunter solely on the basis "of their race and color." Academically qualified applicants, the plaintiffs sued the university in September 1960. In January 1961, they became the institution's first black students under a temporary injunction of the district court. Violent campus demonstrations followed, prompting the university's decision to suspend Holmes and Hunter. The court immediately revoked the suspensions and enjoined state officials from invoking an appropriations statute requiring the cessation of funds to all-white state institutions that admitted blacks. After grudgingly calling for compliance with the federal court orders, Governor Ernest Vandiver convened a special legislative session to amend the appropriations law, which the court had declared unconstitutional. The *Holmes* case was one of the South's numerous battles with the **United States Court of Appeals for the Fifth Judicial Circuit** over the issue of federal interposition in higher education. Unlike some southern states that tried to circumvent court orders by closing schools or by executing new legislation, Georgia resigned itself to desegregation.

Selected Bibliography Numan V. Bartley, *The Rise of Massive Resistance: Race and Politics in the South During the 1950s* (1969); David R. Goldfield, *Black, White, and Southern: Race Relations and Southern Culture, 1940 to the Present* (1990); Frank T. Read and Lucy S. McGough, *Let Them*

Be Judged: The Judicial Integration of the Deep South (1978); "Retreat in Georgia," *Newsweek*, 30 January 1961.

Jack E. Davis

Hooks, Benjamin Lawson (31 January 1925, Memphis, Tenn.–). Executive director of the **NAACP** from 1977–92, Hooks grew up in a relatively elite family of Memphis blacks. He was ordained a Baptist minister but became interested in the law. After military service in World War II, he enrolled in De Paul University, in Chicago, Illinois, where he earned a J.D. degree in 1948. He returned to Memphis to help change the segregated judicial system and became active in the civil rights sit-ins of the 1950s and 1960s. He gained enough support to become assistant public defender of Shelby County in 1961. In 1965 Governor Frank Clement appointed Hooks to fill a vacancy as a Shelby County criminal court judge. The first black in the system, he won election to a full term the following year. He also remained an active minister in the 1950s and 1960s, serving as pastor of the Middle Baptist Church in Memphis and the Greater New Mount Moriah Baptist Church in Detroit, Michigan, where he held bimonthly services. Fulfilling a 1968 campaign pledge, President Richard M. Nixon appointed Hooks to the Federal Communications Commission in 1972, making him the first black to serve on that agency. He received the National Freedom Award in 1998 and in 2003 was serving as distinguished adjunct professor for the Political Science Department of the University of Memphis.

    Selected Bibliography *Current Biography* (1978); "Jimmy's Debt to Blacks—and Others," *Time*, 22 November 1976; "Judge Hook Finally Gets the Job," *Broadcasting*, 17 April 1972; *Who's Who among Black Americans* (1988); http://www.people.memphis.edu.

Thomas D. Cockrell

Hope, John (2 June 1868, Augusta, Ga.–20 February 1936, Atlanta, Ga.). The son of a former slave, Fanny (Mary Francis), and a prosperous Scottish-born businessman, the light skinned John Hope attended Worcester Academy in Massachusetts and Brown University, where he distinguished himself as class orator (1894). As teacher, college president **(Morehouse College, Atlanta University),** and member of numerous committees and commissions, he never wavered from his commitment to racial equality. "If we are not striving for equality," he said in 1896 following **Booker T. Washington's Atlanta Exposition speech,** "in heaven's name for what are we living?" Hope served on the advisory board of the **NAACP,** the executive committee of the **National Urban League,** and as a YMCA field representative on the treatment of black troops in France (1918–19).

    Selected Bibliography Rayford Logan and Michael Winston, eds., *Dictionary of American Negro Biography* (1982); Ridgely Torrence, *The Story of John Hope* (1948).

Loren Schweninger

***Hopwood v. Texas,* 78 F.3d 932; 116 S. Ct. 2581 (1992)** In 1992, Cheryl Hopwood and three other unsuccessful white applicants to the University of

Texas Law School filed suit in federal district court, alleging that the school's affirmative action admissions system violated the **Fourteenth Amendment** and federal civil rights statutes. At the time, the school considered Texas Index scores, a composite of an applicant's undergraduate grade-point average and score on the Law School Admission Test, to rank applicants, but allowed Mexican Americans and African Americans to be placed in the "presumptive admit" category with lower scores than some white students. The district court ruled that the school had violated the plaintiffs' Fourteenth Amendment rights, in accordance with the U.S. Supreme Court's 1978 *Bakke* decision. However, it refused to preclude the law school from using race in its consideration of future applicants. In 1996, in an apparent challenge to the *Bakke* decision, the **United States Court of Appeals for the Fifth Judicial Circuit** ruled that past discrimination on the part of the school had not caused minority underrepresentation at the law school, and thus the race-based admissions process did not serve a narrow remedial purpose. The court prohibited the school from using race for the purpose of obtaining a diverse student body. Immediately after the decision, minority enrollment at the University of Texas Law School dropped precipitously. After the Supreme Court refused to hear the *Hopwood* case the university abandoned further litigation in November 2001 and agreed to pay court costs and the plaintiffs' attorney fees. In effect, the admissions procedures for higher education in the area served by the Fifth Circuit Court (Texas, Mississippi, and Louisiana) became subject to law that did not exist elsewhere in the United States. The Supreme Court's 2003 decisions in *Gratz v. Bollinger* and *Grutter v. Bollinger* changed the situation.

Selected Bibliography Philip T. K. Daniel and Kyle Edward Timken, "The Rumors of My Death Have Been Exaggerated: *Hopwood's* Error in 'Discarding' *Bakke*," *Journal of Law and Education* 28 (July 1999) 391–418; "Constitutional Law–Equal Protection–Affirmative Action–Fifth Circuit Holds that Educational Diversity in No Longer a Compelling State Interest–*Hopwood v. Texas*, 78 F.3d 932 (5th Cir. 1996)," *Harvard Law Review* 110 (January 1997), 775–80; Susan Richardson, "Hopwood Becoming a Matter of Opinion," *Black Issues in Higher Education* 16 (September 2000), 12–13; University of Texas Law School, "*Hopwood v. Texas*," Web site: www.law.utexas.edu/hopwood.

Richard V. Damms

Horizon: A Journal of the Color Line Published in Washington, D.C., between 1907 and 1910, *Horizon* was edited and owned by **W.E.B. Du Bois,** Freeman Murray, and Lafayette M. Henshaw. The unofficial organ of the **Niagara Movement,** it advocated voting rights for blacks and females and the redistribution of wealth. The editorials challenged **Booker T. Washington, Jim Crow** laws, white immigration, and representative government in the South. *Horizon* failed to attract blacks to the Niagara Movement and, after becoming a bimonthly in 1909, it ceased publication.

Selected Bibliography David Levering Lewis, *W.E.B. Du Bois: Biography of a Race, 1868–1919* (1993); August Meier, *Negro Thought in America 1880–1915:Racial Ideologies in the Age of Booker T. Washington* (1973); Elliot Rudwick, *W.E.B. Du Bois: Propagandist of the Negro Protest* (1969).

Jessie M. Carter

Hose, Sam (d. April 1899, Palmetto, Ga.). An African American agricultural worker employed by plantation owner Alfred Cranford near Palmetto, Georgia, Sam Hose was burned at the stake by white Georgians for his self-defense killing of Cranford in April 1899. This lynching was the capstone of a series of racial incidents in Georgia during 1898–99. African American soldiers mobilized for participation in the Spanish-American War were encamped in Georgia and Florida. The resulting racial friction spilled over into Georgia's communities after the troops departed. In Palmetto in March 1899, several local African Americans were lynched as supposed arsonists/ assassins. Sam Hose and Lige Strickland, an African American minister, were similarly accused. Hose was burned and dismembered. Strickland was tortured in the hopes of eliciting a confession that he had directed Hose to kill Cranford. The brutality of these two lynchings drew protests from African Americans and some Northern whites such as Julia Ward Howe. Former Georgia Governor William J. Northern defended the South and justified its use of violence. President William McKinley contended, as other presidents would after him, that lynching was a local matter outside federal jurisdiction. This lynching also took on international dimensions because of the United States' imperial venture in the Philippines following the Spanish-American War. Emilio Aguinaldo, nationalist leader of the Philippine resistance, noted how democracy was restricted to "whites only" whether it involved due process in the United States or building a nation-state for newly liberated peoples of color across the Pacific.

Selected Bibliography *Atlanta Journal* (1898–99); *Boston Evening Transcript* (March–May, 1899); Benjamin Brawley, *A Social History of the American Negro* (1921); W.E.B. Du Bois, *Dusk of Dawn* (1968); Mary Louise Ellis, "'Rain Down Fire': The Lynching of Sam Hose" (Ph.D. diss., Florida State University, 1992); Herbert Shapiro, *White Violence and Black Response from Reconstruction to Montgomery* (1988).

Gregory Mixon

Houston, Charles H. (3 September 1895, Washington, D.C.–20 April 1950, Washington, D.C.). Known as "The First Mr. Civil Rights," Houston graduated from Dunbar High School in Washington, D.C., earned a Phi Beta Kappa key from Amherst College, and received the L.L.B. and J.D. degrees from Harvard University Law School. As professor of law and later dean of **Howard University** Law School, and as chief counsel for the NAACP **Legal Defense and Educational Fund,** Houston was in the vanguard of African American lawyers, including U.S. Supreme Court Associate Justice **Thurgood Marshall,** who developed and utilized legal techniques that eventually led to the 1954 overthrow of the 1896 **separate-but-equal** doctrine.

Selected Bibliography Richard Kluger, *Simple Justice: The History of Brown v. Board of Education and Black America's Struggle for Equality* (1976); Genna Rae McNeil, *Groundwork: Charles Hamilton Houston and the Struggle for Civil Rights* (1983); Loren Miller, *The Petitioners. The Story of the United States Supreme Court and the Negro* (1966); Geraldine R. Segal, *In Any Fight Some Fall* (1975).

Phillip McGuire

Houston Informer   Founded by Houston businessmen Clifton F. Richardson in 1919, the *Informer* was purchased in 1930 by Carter W. Wesley. This prominent attorney combined it with several other newspapers and developed it into one of the largest African American newspaper chains in the United States with papers in Texas, Louisiana, and Alabama. Wesley managed the *Informer* chain until his death in 1969. Under his leadership the *Informer* supported such landmark civil rights cases as **Smith v. Allwright** (1944) and **Sweatt v. Painter** (1950) by providing extensive publicity in the African American community and by soliciting funds to support the cases. Wesley was also personally involved in both cases, providing legal opinions and donating money to pursue them.

Selected Bibliography Nancy Ruth Bessent, "The Publisher: A Biography of Carter W. Wesley" (Ph.D. diss., University of Texas, 1981); Steven F. Lawson, *Black Ballots: Voting Rights in the South, 1944–1969* (1976); Merline Petre, "Black Houstonians and the Separate but Equal Doctrine: Carter W. Wesley versus Lula B. White," *Houston Review* 12 (1990), 23–36; J. William Snorgrass, "America's Ten Oldest Black Newspapers," *Negro History Bulletin* 36 (January–March, 1983), 11–14; Roland E. Wolseley, *The Black Press, U.S.A.* (1990).

W. Marvin Dulaney

Houston Race Riot (1917)   Bitterness among black soldiers returning from Europe after World War I, systematic abridgement of black voting rights in Texas, oppressive conditions, resentment, frustration and anger at assaults upon black soldiers, and the arrest of a black woman caused men of the Third Battalion, Twenty-fourth Infantry, U.S. Army, stationed in Houston, Texas, to mutiny against their white officers, secure arms and munitions, march upon and riot in the city for three hours on 23 August 1917, and leave 15 whites and 4 black soldiers dead and many seriously wounded. In one of the longest courts-martial in military history, 118 men were charged with either disobedience to orders, aggravated assault, mutiny, or murder. One hundred ten men were found guilty of at least one charge and only 7 were acquitted. Eighty-two men were found guilty of all charges and 29 were given death sentences, although only 13 were secretly hanged in April of 1918. Fifty-three were sentenced to prison for life and 28 received prison terms of 2 to 15 years. One man was judged incompetent to stand trial and had all charges dropped. The Houston riot stimulated the establishment of a **NAACP** branch in Houston and prodded the national headquarters to undertake an extensive educational campaign and to seek to secure pardons for the condemned men. Most were paroled by the early 1930s.

Selected Bibliography Robert H. Brisbane, *The Black Vanguard: Origins of the Negro Social Revolution, 1900–1960* (1970); Chandler Davidson, *Biracial Politics: Conflict and Coalition in the Metropolitan South* (1972); Robert V. Haynes, *A Night of Violence: The Houston Riot of 1917* (1976).

Lee E. Williams, II

Howard, Oliver Otis   (8 November 1830, Leeds, Maine–26 October 1909, Burlington, Vt.). A graduate of Bowdoin College, in 1850 and the U.S. Military Academy in 1854, Howard lost an arm and was awarded a Medal of Honor for his service during the Civil War. He fought in most of the major battles in Virginia and participated in General William T. Sherman's famous marches through Georgia and the Carolinas. In the 1870s and 1880s, he campaigned against Apache and Nez Perce Indians. He also served briefly as superintendent of West Point as a result of the problems caused by the presence of black cadet **Johnson C. Whittaker.** Howard retired from the army in 1894, and devoted the remainder of his life to promoting higher education (he helped found Lincoln Memorial University in Harrogate, Tennessee) and campaigning for Republican party candidates. Although he had not been an ardent prewar abolitionist, Howard's opposition to slavery and his deeply held Christian faith earned him the post of commissioner of the Bureau of Refugees, Freedmen, and Abandoned Lands (see **Freedmen's Bureau**). He personally believed that former slaves deserved land, education, and the franchise, but his own political naivete, along with the entrenched opposition of President Andrew Johnson and many Freedmen's Bureau officials, limited his effectiveness. He did succeed in promoting the elementary and secondary education of southern blacks through the Bureau, however, and he was the principal founder of **Howard University** in 1867, which he served as president from 1868 to 1873 and as trustee until three years before his death.

Selected Bibliography John A. Carpenter, *Sword and Olive Branch: Oliver Otis Howard* (1964); Oliver Otis Howard, *Autobiography of Oliver Otis Howard,* 2 vols. (1908); William S. McFeely, *Yankee Stepfather: General O. O. Howard and the Freedmen* (1968).

James Marten

Howard University Established by a charter of the U.S. Congress on 2 March 1867, the main purpose of Howard University was to create "a college for the instruction of youth in the liberal arts and sciences." Its founders were a zealous group of "Radical Republicans," Congregationalists, and former Civil War army officers of whom the most prominent was General **Oliver Otis Howard,** for whom the institution was named. Howard, a Civil War hero and devout Christian, was Commissioner of the Bureau of Refugees, Freedmen, and Abandoned Lands (see **Freedmen's Bureau**). He became the institution's third president from 1869–74 and then served on its board of trustees. During the early years the coeducational institution consisted of normal, preparatory, collegiate, theological, medical, and law departments. More than half of the student population was black. Between 1874 and 1889, Howard University experienced significant academic and student body expansion, creating departments of dentistry and pharmacology. During **Mordecai W. Johnson's** (1926–60) tenure, Howard grew into an outstanding university matriculating many of the nation's outstanding African Americans. Between 1960 and 1967, James M. Nabrit, a leading civil rights lawyer, was president. The faculty and student body played pivotal roles in the civil rights movement. From 1960–89, James E. Cheek presided over the institution's further modernization and expansion, moulding it into one of national stature with over two hundred degree programs on four campuses. In 1990, Franklyn G. Jenifer, became the first alumnus president. In August of 1995, H. Patrick Swygert became the uni-

Graduating law class at Howard University, c. 1900. © Library of Congress.

versity's fifteenth president and Howard continues to grow on its five campuses in the Washington metropolitan area. It consists of 18 schools and colleges, including the Colleges of Dentistry, Medicine and Pharmacal Sciences, School of Architecture, Business Communications, Divinity, Law, and Social Work, and operates a university press, 500-bed teaching hospital, and a radio station (WHUR-FM) and television station (WHMM-TV). It also has one of the world's most comprehensive collections of African and African diaspora, mainly in the Moorland-Spingarn Research Center.

Selected Bibliography Walter Dyson, *Howard University, The Capstone of Negro Education, A History: 1867–1940* (1941); David S. Lamb, ed., *Howard University Medical Department, Washington, D.C.: A Historical Biographical and Statistical Souvenir* (1900); Rayford W. Logan, *Howard University: The First Hundred Years, 1867–1967* (1969); Frederick D. Wilkinson, ed., *Directory of Graduates, Howard University, 1870–1963* (1965). Web site: www.howard.edu.

Glenn O. Phillips

Hughes, Langston (1 February 1902, Joplin, Mo.–22 May 1967, New York, N.Y.). As a columnist, anthologist, translator, playwright, novelist, and poet, Langston Hughes was widely acclaimed among black Americans for his inimitable renderings of black life and racial problems with devastating humor. Throughout his long career, Hughes believed that literature should be used as a weapon to attack social injustice, as is illustrated in his prodi-

Portrait of Langston Hughes by Carl van Vechten, 1936. © Library of Congress.

gious body of poetry from *The Weary Blues* (1926) to *The Panther and the Lash* (1967). Well-known as a poet before he graduated from Lincoln University (Pennsylvania) in 1928, Hughes devoted much of his writing during the 1930s to civil rights and other political issues. He was particularly interested in the infamous **Scottsboro Trials** as an example of class struggle and racial oppression and wrote a proletarian play *Scottsboro Limited* (1931) to draw attention to the "legal lynching." In the 1940s, Hughes's "Simple" stories began appearing as a weekly column in the **Chicago Defender.** Simple, in the words of Arthur P. Davis, grew into "a nationally recognized character and symbol" of the wisdom, humor, and race consciousness of working-class blacks. Until his death, Hughes was one of America's most eloquent spokesmen for racial understanding and human rights.

Selected Bibliography Juda Bennett, "Multiple Passing and the Double Death of Langston Hughes," *Biography* 23 (No. 4, 2000), 670–93; Emily Bernard, ed., *Remember Me to Harlem: The Letters of Langston Hughes and Carl Van Vechten 1925–1964* (2001); Faith Berry, *Langston Hughes: Before and beyond Harlem* (1983); Christopher C. De Santis, ed., *Langston Hughes and the Chicago Defender: Essays on Race, Politics, and Culture, 1942–62* (1995); Donald C. Dickinson, *A Bio-bibliography of Langston Hughes, 1902–1967* (1967); James A. Emanuel, *Langston Hughes* (1967); Donna Akiba Sullivan Harper, *Not So Simple: The "Simple" Stories by Langston Hughes* (1995); Jemi Onwuchekwa, *Langston Hughes: An Introduction to the Poetry* (1985); Arnold Rampersad, *The Life of Langston Hughes* (1986).

Jerry Ward

Humphrey, Hubert Horatio, Jr. (27 May 1911, Wallace, S. Dak.–13 January 1978, Waverly, Minn.). An extraordinary populist orator, Humphrey was the most effective progressive congressman in American history. Believing in government's capacity to do good, he midwifed a host of social democratic programs that gestated a long time before delivery, including federal aid to education, health insurance, vocational training, food stamps, the Peace Corps, the Job Corps, and welfare. Like his idol Franklin D. Roosevelt, he transformed the political landscape permanently, but unlike him was frustrated four times in seeking the presidency.

Among this welter of causes, the empathetic Humphrey chose civil rights as his defining issue. As mayor of Minneapolis, which had only a 1.6 percent black population in the late 1940s, he instituted the Mayor's Council on Human Relations and the nation's first municipal **Fair Employment Practices Committee.** In 1948 at the Democratic party's national convention in Philadelphia, Humphrey delivered a barnburning speech calling for Harry S Truman's undiluted civil rights agenda. That speech made him a national figure and won him a U.S. Senate seat in Republican Minnesota. In the Senate, Humphrey became best known as the most vocal civil rights advocate since Reconstruction. He advocated an antilynching bill, the use of a majority vote to cut off paralyzing filibusters, the removal of all voting impediments, and a civil rights commission to enforce state and federal laws, a proposal that bore fruit in the **Civil Rights Act of 1957.** He also pressed his cause outside the Senate with the National Citizens' Council on Civil Rights and the fledgling Americans for Democratic Action, of which he was chosen permanent chairman.

By the mid-1950s, Humphrey was accepted into the political establishment as he learned to control his abrasive tongue and became friendly with Senate majority leader Lyndon B. Johnson. He became genuinely admired for his ebullient personality, deep knowledge on most complicated government subjects, and tact. In 1961, he was chosen as Senate majority whip, where one of his greatest triumphs was the passage of the **Civil Rights Act of 1964.**

In 1964, Humphrey finally reached national office as Johnson's running mate. He coordinated civil rights activities within the federal government and pushed for the **Voting Rights Act of 1965.** But Johnson ordered his dissenting vice president to toe the line on the growing Vietnam War, a move that destroyed Humphrey's presidential hopes, fractured the Democratic party, and sacrificed Johnson's Great Society programs for the dispossessed of all races.

Selected Bibliography Hubert H. Humphrey, *Moral Crisis: The Case for Civil Rights* (1964); Hubert H. Humphrey, *Beyond Civil Rights* (1964); Hubert H. Humphrey, *The Education of a Public Man: My Life and Politics* (1976); Paula Wilson, *The Civil Rights Rhetoric of Hubert H. Humphrey, 1948–1964* (1996); Carl Solberg, *Hubert Humphrey: A Biography* (1984); Robert Mann, *The Walls of Jericho: Lyndon Johnson, Hubert Humphrey, Richard Russell, and the Struggle for Civil Rights* (1997); Timothy Thurber, *The Politics of Equality: Hubert H. Humphrey and the African Amerian Freedom Struggle* (1999).

Bruce J. Dierenfield

Hurd v. Hodge,* 334 U.S. 24 (1948)** This was a companion case to ***Shelley v. Kraemer (1948), which involved the constitutionality of racially restrictive covenants. Such covenants were widely used to segregate neighborhoods, not just in the South but in other sections of the United States as well. In *Hurd* the Supreme Court reversed enforcement of a racially restrictive neighborhood covenant in the District of Columbia. In *Shelley* the court ruled that judicial enforcement of such covenants was state action and thus forbidden under the **Fourteenth Amendment;** in *Hurd* the court did not address the due process question but instead cited the **Civil Rights Act of 1866,** which guaranteed the right of all citizens equally "to inherit, purchase, sell, hold and convey" real property. If *Hurd* and *Shelley* did not eradicate restrictive covenants, they did make important inroads on discriminatory housing practices.

Selected Bibliography Albert A Dorskinde, "Notes and Comments," *Cornell Law Quarterly* 33 (1947), 293–300; Jack Greenberg, *Race Relations and American Law* (1959); Donald G. Nieman, *Promises to Keep: African-Americans and the Constitutional Order, 1776 to the Present* (1991); Clement E. Vose, *Caucasians Only: The Supreme Court, the NAACP, and the Restrictive Covenant Cases* (1959).

Charles D. Lowery

Hurston, Zora Neale   (7 January 1906, Eatonville, Fla.–28 January 1960, Fort Pierce, Fla.). Probably the most famous female African American writer of the **Harlem Renaissance,** Hurston was a renowned anthropologist, folklorist, and novelist. Her time at **Howard University** (1919–24) enhanced her interest in African American folklore and saw the publication of her first short story. At Barnard (B.A. 1928), Hurston pioneered in the collection and collation of southern African American folktales. Her work includes four published novels; many short stories and nonfiction articles; and editorial board service on the first issue of *Fire!*, an ill-fated magazine jointly organized by some younger members of the Harlem Renaissance. Boldly proclaiming her blackness, Hurston brought ordinary African Americans alive in her folklore and novels.

Selected Bibliography Rose P. Davis, *Zora Neale Hurston: An Annotated Bibliography and Reference Guide* (1997); Robert E. Hemenway, *Zora Neale Hurston: A Literary Biography* (1977); Lillie P. Howard, "Zora Neale Hurston," *Dictionary of Literary Biography* 51 (1987); Lillie P. Howard, *Zora Neale Hurston* (1980); Alice Walker, "Looking for Zora," in Carol Ascher, Louise DeSalvo, and Sara Riddick, eds., *Between Women: Biographers, Novelists, Critics, Teachers, and Artists Write about Their Work on Women* (1984).

Brenda M. Brock

Zora Neale Hurston at the *New York Times* Book Fair, 1937. © Library of Congress.

I

"**I Have a Dream**" The most famous speech of Dr. **Martin Luther King, Jr.**'s, civil rights career was delivered from the steps of the Lincoln Memorial before an integrated mass rally—the **March on Washington** for Jobs and Freedom on 28 August 1963. Climaxing the wave of **nonviolent resistance** protests throughout the summer of 1963, this speech was an act of creative lobbying designed to "inaugurate an era of racial integration and social justice on a national scale." Powerful, elegant, and symbolically significant, "**I Have A Dream**" ranks with King's "**Letter from Birmingham Jail**" as the quintessential statement of the nonviolent protest philosophy. Scholars consider it to be one of the great American speeches of the twentieth century, a peroration worthy of such earlier notable American orators as Patrick Henry, Daniel Webster, and Abraham Lincoln. Echoes of Lincoln's Gettysburg Address resonate throughout the speech. King used emotionally charged language, vivid metaphors, and repetition of phrases to create a powerful cadence and rhythm that elicited a strong response from his audience. His audience was not just the 200,000 people assembled at the Lincoln Memorial. It included an entire nation, many of whose citizens were watching on television, that needed to be awakened to the conditions of racial injustice in America. King moved his followers to continue to work for civil rights and the to pursue the American Dream; he also reminded the nation of its default: black people were yet to receive freedom and equality. As a result of this speech, King emerged as the major spokesman for the civil rights movement and the voice of the nation's moral conscience.

Selected Bibliography Karl W. Anatol and John R. Bittner, "Kennedy on King: the Rhetoric of Control," *Communication Quarterly* 16 (April 1968), 31–34; John Graham, ed., *Great*

Martin Luther King, Jr., speaking at the Lincoln Memorial, 28 August 1963. © National Archives.

American Speeches, 1898–1963, Texts and Studies (1970); David L. Lewis, *King: A Biography* (1970); Philip C. Wander, "The John Birch and Martin Luther King Symbols in the Radical Right," *Western Journal of Speech Communication* 35 (Winter 1971), 4–14; Harris Wofford, *Of Kennedys and Kings* (1980).

Jacquelyn Jackson

Ickes, Harold L. (15 March 1874, Blair County, Pa.–3 February 1952, Washington, D.C.). A former Bull Moose Progressive and civil liberties lawyer, Ickes was a powerful advocate of black equality during Franklin D. Roosevelt's New Deal. Chosen by Roosevelt to be Secretary of Interior in 1933, a post he held until 1946, Ickes also headed the Public Works Administration (PWA). A former president of the Chicago branch of the **NAACP,** Ickes assumed personal responsibility during the early 1930s as "watchdog" for black rights and black people's inclusion within the social and economic programs of the New Deal. Working closely with such black leaders as the NAACP's **Walter Francis White** and economist **Robert C. Weaver,** his chief race relations adviser after 1935, Ickes saw that blacks were appointed to Interior and PWA staff positions, established quotas for black workers on PWA projects, and assured black involvement in low-income housing. He lobbied also for **William Henry Hastie**'s appointment as federal judge to the Virgin

Islands, addressed conventions of the NAACP and **National Urban League,** and ordered eating facilities in the Interior Department integrated. His most public affirmation of civil rights involved securing the Lincoln Memorial for **Marian Anderson**'s celebrated concert following the refusal of the Daughters of the American Revolution to allow her to perform in their convention hall. His introduction of Anderson to a crowd of some seventy-five thousand in 1939 was characterized by the *Journal of Negro Education* as a worthy "rival" to "Lincoln's Gettysburg Address." A committed proponent of New Deal reforms and their importance to black people, Ickes was one of the twentieth century's foremost white racial liberals whose ideas influenced younger liberals of the 1950s and 1960s.

Selected Bibliography John B. Kirby, *Black Americans in the Roosevelt Era* (1980); T. H. Watkins, *Righteous Pilgrim: The Life and Times of Harold L. Ickes, 1874–1952* (1990); Nancy J. Weiss, *Farewell to the Party of Lincoln* (1983); Graham White and John Maze, *Harold Ickes of the New Deal* (1985); Raymond Wolters, *Negroes and the Great Depression* (1970).

John B. Kirby

"If We Must Die" A poem in sonnet form by the Jamaican exponent of negritude, **Claude McKay,** it was first published in the July 1919 issue of the *Liberator*, a New York–based journal edited by Max Eastman. McKay composed the poem in response to the **Red Summer** of 1919, a time when the nation violently attempted to reassert the pre–World War I political and social status quo of unquestioning patriotism and second-class African American citizenship. "If We Must Die" calls for race solidarity and exhorts African Americans to armed self-defense. McKay initially shared the sonnet with fellow black railway porters; even the most jaded were profoundly moved. "If We Must Die" was reprinted in newspapers, recited in churches and became a rallying cry for positive self-consciousness. It is a classic example of the **New Negro movement.**

Selected Bibliography Wayne F. Cooper, *Claude McKay: Rebel Sojourner in Harlem Renaissance* (1987); Wayne F. Cooper, *The Passion of Claude McKay: Selected Poetry and Prose, 1912–1948* (1973); James Richard Giles, *Claude McKay* (1976); James R. Keller, "'A Chafing Savage, Down the Decent Street': The Politics of Compromise in Claude McKay's Protest Sonnets," *African American Review* 28 (1994), 447–56; Claude McKay, *A Long Way From Home* (1937); Tyrone Tillery, *Claude McKay: A Black Poet's Struggle for Identity* (1992).

Bernice F. Guillaume

Indianapolis Freeman The *Indianapolis Freeman*, founded by Edward Elder Cooper, began publication in Indianapolis, Indiana on 14 July 1888. The first black illustrated newspaper in the United States, it provided realistic portrayals of black people. It regularly featured the cartoons of Henry J. Lewis, who was probably the first black political cartoonist in the United States. The paper was also unique in that it did not use a boilerplate, but provided original writing, by black authors. In addition to the news, the paper provided nonpartisan political coverage, articles on the history and literature of African Americans, and coverage of the educational progress of the race. It was considered one of the leading newspapers in the country at the turn of the century. It was published until 1927.

Selected Bibliography Georgetta Merritt Campbell, *Extant Collections of Early Black Newspapers* (1981); Martin E. Dann, *The Black Press, 1827–1890* (1971); George W. Gore, *Negro Journalism* (1922); John F. Marszalek and C. James Haug, "The *Freeman* and Its Ten Greatest Blacks Contest: A People's Poll," *Mid-America* 67 (April–July 1985), 55–68; I. G. Penn, *The Afro-American Press and Its Editors* (1891); Armstead S. Pride and Clint C. Wilson II, *A History of the Black Press* (1997).

Robert A. Bellinger

Interracial Review   Published from 1928 to 1971, the *Interracial Review* was an outgrowth of the work of the Jesuit priest, John LaFarge (1880–1963), who urged the Catholic Church to see the African American "not as a pitiful object of charity . . . but as a mighty factor for national progress and . . . a unique contributor to the fullness of our religious life." The biracial Layman's Union that LaFarge organized was the forerunner of the **Catholic Interracial Council,** founded in New York City in 1936. By 1959, 35 such councils functioned in the United States. The *Review*, which appeared sporadically before the founding of the councils, served as their "clearinghouse for information" and as a forum for continuing advocacy of racial justice and mutual respect.

Selected Bibliography Jay P. Dolan, *The American Catholic Experience* (1985); *The Interracial Review*, 1–40 (1928–71); John LaFarge, *Interracial Justice* (1937; reprint, 1978).

Jo Ann O. Robinson

J

Jackson Advocate   **Percy Greene,** the founder of the *Jackson Advocate*, published this weekly, the oldest black-owned newspaper in Mississippi, from 1938 until 1977. Greene was a long-standing proponent of black voting rights, but his conservatism provoked frequent black protests in the 1960s. He criticized **Martin Luther King, Jr.,** black-instigated violence, public demonstrations, modern-day "carpetbaggers" leading Mississippi voter registration drives, and federally forced integration, while continually expressing fear of a white backlash. Greene urged "responsible" black leaders to work with like-minded whites for gradual black progress. In later years, black leaders accused him of having been paid by the Sovereignty Commission, the state's segregationist agency. Charles Tisdale bought and published the *Advocate* after Greene's death, making it aggressive and at times strident in promoting black interests.

Selected Bibliography *Jackson Advocate*, 29 September 1962, 13 June, 4 July 1964, 14 August 1965; *Jackson Daily News*, 1 June 1982; Julius E. Thompson, *The Black Press in Mississippi, 1865–1986: A Directory* (1988). Web site: www.jacksonadvocate.com.

Eric C. Clark

Jackson, Jesse L.   (8 October 1941, Greenville, S.C.–). A candidate for the Democratic party nomination for president in 1984 and 1988, Jackson is a product of the 1960s civil rights movement. Following his student years at North Carolina Agricultural and Technical University, in Greensboro, North Carolina, and his ordination as a Baptist minister, Jackson joined the **Southern Christian Leadership Conference** (SCLC) during the Selma voting rights campaign. A year later he assisted Dr. **Martin Luther King, Jr.,** in SCLC's Chicago open housing campaign. Although the Chicago campaign was generally regarded as a failure, Jackson was given responsibility for SCLC's "Operation Breadbasket," which utilized economic boycotts to promote the hiring of African Americans and to generate "fair share" contracts for black businesses. In 1970 Jackson broke with SCLC and formed **People United to Save Humanity (Operation PUSH),** a "rainbow coalition" of blacks and whites dedicated to greater economic and political power for the impoverished. PUSH continued to target racially discriminatory corporations through economic boycotts, but Jackson in the mid-1970s expanded its role and his national visibility by speaking against teen violence, drug abuse, and pregnancy. Always eager to challenge local and national politicians unresponsive to black concerns, in 1971 he unsuccessfully ran against Richard Daley for mayor of Chicago. One year later at the Democratic national convention, Jackson and his supporters unseated the Daley-led Illinois delegation. Jackson now regularly promoted Democratic party reform and urged hundreds of blacks to run for state and local office and thousands of African Americans to register to vote. In 1983 Jackson helped elect Harold Washington the first black mayor of Chicago. The successful Chicago campaign and the growing sophistication of black voters prompted Jackson to enter the campaign for the Democratic nomination for president. His "rainbow coalition" campaign of political empowerment of poor people, a concept he first advanced in 1970, allowed him to garner the third highest number of party delegates at the national convention and gave him considerable influence on the party platform. Jackson ran again in 1988, winning nine state primaries. His calls for a Palestinian homeland and his campaign against South African apartheid increased his international stature. The techniques he had developed over two decades as a negotiator also served him well when he arranged the release of an American airman shot down over Syria in 1983 and of 48 prisoners, including 22 Americans from Cuban jails, in 1984. In 1990 during the Persian Gulf Crisis, Jackson also arranged the release of 47 American hostages from Iraq. In the 1990s he held one of the two so-called statehood seats created by the District of Columbia to pressure Congress for statehood. He was always visible on television particularly as a talk show host on CNN. He remained active in the Rainbow Coalition/PUSH. In 1999 he negotiated the release of three captured American soldiers in war-torn Yugoslavia. He received the Presidential Medal of Freedom in 2000, but in 2001 his active role in national and international issues was curtailed when news of his fathering of an illegitimate child surfaced.

Selected Bibliography Elizabeth Drew, *Election Journal: Political Events of 1987–1988* (1989); Jesse Jackson, *Legal Lynching: Racism, Injustice, and the Death Penalty* (1996); *Los Angeles Times,* 3 September 1990; Barbara Reynolds, *Jesse Jackson: America's David* (1985); Karen L. Stanford, "Citizen Diplomacy and Jesse Jackson: A Case Study for Influencing U.S. Foreign Policy toward Southern Africa," *Western Journal of Black Studies* 19 (No. 1, 1995), 19–29.

Quintard Taylor

Jackson, Jimmie Lee   (December 1938, Marion, Ala.–26 February 1965, Selma, Ala.). The shooting and subsequent death of 26-year-old Jimmie Lee

Jackson made him a martyr of the civil rights movement and provoked the **Selma to Montgomery March** of 1965. Alabama State Troopers under the direction of Colonel Al Lingo routed an 18 February 1965 nighttime protest march for voter registration in Marion, Alabama, headed by the Reverend C. T. Vivian. After shutting off the streetlights, the troopers began beating the demonstrators and chasing them into nearby buildings. Several followed Jackson, his mother Viola Jackson, and his 82-year-old grandfather, Cager Lee Jackson, into Mack's Cafe located near the movement headquarters in Zion's Chapel Methodist Church. When troopers hit his mother and grandfather, Jackson charged them, receiving several blows with billy clubs before being shot in the stomach by a trooper identified only as Fowler. Transferred from Perry County Hospital to Good Samaritan in Selma, Jackson languished for eight days during which time Lingo arrested him for assault and battery with intent to kill. No charges were filed against the trooper. The quiet, young church deacon died 26 February 1965. A laborer who cut pulpwood and farmed, Jackson had tried unsuccessfully many times to register to vote. It was during his funeral eulogy for Jackson, that the Reverend **James Bevel** of the **Southern Christian Leadership Conference** suggested a protest march from Marion to Montgomery. The SCLC moved the starting point to Selma where Bloody Sunday had occurred on 7 March 1965.

    Selected Bibliography *Birmingham News*, 19, 27 February 1965; John Dittmer, *Local People: The Struggle for Civil Rights in Mississippi* (1994); Charles E. Fager, *Selma, 1965: The March That Changed the South* (1974); David J. Garrow, *Protest at Selma: Martin Luther King, Jr., and the Voting Rights Act of 1965* (1978); Jack Mendelsohn, *The Martyrs: The Sixteen Who Gave Their Lives for Race Justice* (1966).

Glenn T. Eskew

Jackson, Maynard Holbrook, Jr. (23 March 1938, Dallas, Tex.–24 June 2003, Washington, D.C.). A graduate of **Morehouse College** and of North Carolina Central University Law School, Jackson had no prior political experience when he ran for the U.S. Senate against Herman Talmadge in 1968. He lost the election but the next year won the office of vice-mayor against a white candidate, winning 60 percent of the white vote. In a heated election in 1973 with strong racial overtones, he became the city's first black mayor in a run-off with the incumbent Sam Massell, the city's first Jewish mayor. Jackson was reelected in 1977 and in 1989. As mayor, he helped to ensure to blacks and women economic and political opportunities that had long been denied them by a white business-political elite. He secured for blacks a designated percentage of the construction contracts for the building of the new Atlanta airport and was instrumental in his city's gaining the 1996 Olympics. In 1991 and 1993 *Fortune* magazine named Atlanta as the best U.S. city for business. He was a major figure in the Democratic National Committee and headed Jackson Security Inc., an Atlanta-based investment bank. As a major national speaker, he told black audiences that the key to African American success was "ballot, buck, and book."

Selected Bibliography *(Detroit) Michigan Chronicle,* 24 April 2001, A4; *Atlanta Constitution,* 4, 17, 1973; Henry Hampton and Steve Foyer, *Voices of Freedom: An Oral History of the Civil Rights Movement from the 1950's through the 1980's* (1990); Joint Committee for Political Studies and Johnson Publishing Co., Inc., *Black Profiles of Black Mayors in America* (1977); *New York Times,* 17, 18, 21 October 1973; Carol A. Pierannunzi and John D. Hutcheson, Jr., "Deracialization in the Deep South: Mayoral Politics in Atlanta," *Urban Affairs Quarterly* 27 (1991), 192–201; *Washington Post,* 8 January 1974.

Dorothy A. Autrey

Jeanes (Anna T.) Fund Named for a Philadelphia Quaker, this fund was established in 1905 when Jeanes donated $200,000 for the benefit of African American education in the South. In 1907 she set aside the bulk of her estate to improve African American public schools through sponsorship of the "Jeanes Supervisors," industrial teachers who traveled among African American schools to improve the teaching methods of local untrained teachers. Until 1937 when the Jeanes Fund joined with other philanthropic endeavors to form the Southern Education Foundation, its focus remained the improvement of industrial education for African American rural schools, the training of teachers for extension work, and the support of county agents for the improvement of rural homes and schools.

Selected Bibliography Benjamin Brawley, *Dr. Dillard of the Jeanes Fund* (1971); Raymond B. Fosdick, *Adventure in Giving* (1962); Mabel M. Smythe, ed., *The Black American Reference Book* (1976); Warren Weaver, *United States Philanthropic Foundations* (1967).

Janice M. Leone

Jet Modeled after the small news magazines that proliferated after World War II, *Jet* was the brainchild of ***Ebony*** publisher, John H. Johnson. In 1955 the magazine stunned the black world with a picture that showed the mutilated body of **Emmet Louis Till** at his funeral. *Jet* widely covered the civil rights movement, chronicling the various incidents involving civil rights workers. It followed closely the growing stature of **Martin Luther King, Jr.,** helping to familiarize the black community with his and other civil rights leaders' activities. Its breezy style and wide use of photographs to cover black activities and accomplishments in entertainment, business, sports, and politics made it an appealing magazine. To many black Americans it was and remains their window to the world.

Selected Bibliography Taylor Branch, *Parting the Waters: America during the King Years, 1954–63* (1989); John H. Johnson, *Succeeding against All Odds* (1989); Juan Williams, *Eyes on the Prize,* Episode 1 (1987). Web site: www.jetmag.com.

Charles T. Pete Banner-Haley

Jim Crow The term "Jim Crow" originated with the character in a popular minstrel show of the 1830s who did a song and dance routine to a song called "Jump, Jim Crow." As an historical term, it defines the practice of legal and extralegal racial discrimination against African Americans. When the **Thirteenth Amendment** ended slavery at the close of the Civil War in 1865,

Jim Crow laws and customs became a new means of assuring white supremacy. Beginning in the 1870s, the nation's courts overturned the civil rights legislation of Reconstruction and, in 1896, replaced it with the legal doctrine of **separate-but-equal**. Although local Jim Crow laws and customs varied, they all consistently promoted the systematic segregation, subordination, and dehumanization of African Americans.

Selected Bibliography Catherine A. Barnes, *Journey from Jim Crow: The Desegregation of Southern Transit* (1983); Thomas Borstelmann, "Jim Crow's Coming Out: Race Relations and American Foreign Policy in the Truman Years," *Presidential Studies Quarterly* 29 (No. 3, 1999), 549–69; Glenda Elizabeth Gilmore, "Dating Jim Crow: Chronology as a Tool of Analysis," *Georgia Historical Quarterly* 83 (1999), 58–72; Leonard Williams Levy, *Jim Crow in Boston: The Origin of the Separate but Equal Doctrine* (1974); Neil R. McMillen, *Dark Journey: Black Mississippians in the Age of Jim Crow* (1989); John H. Stanfield, *Philanthropy and Jim Crow in American Social Science* (1985); C. Vann Woodward, *The Strange Career of Jim Crow*, 2nd ed. (1974).

Lillie Johnson Edwards

Jobs for Negroes Movement   The Jobs for Negroes Movement (1929–41), known also as the **"Don't Buy Where You Can't Work" movement,** constituted a wave of picket and boycott movements directed at businesses that excluded African Americans from equitable employment. The movement originated in Chicago in 1929 when an ex–prize fighter Big Bill Tate and A. C. O'Neal, editor of a local paper called the *Whip*, organized a boycott of white merchants who employed no blacks. The Jobs for Negroes Campaigns spread across the country as a major form of African American activism during the 1930s depression. Some of the well known movements were the Future Outlook League in Cleveland, Ohio, the New Negro Alliance in Washington D.C., the Colored Clerks Circle in St. Louis, Missouri, the Prophet Costonie in Baltimore, Maryland, and the *Sentinel* movement in Los Angeles, California. The most turbulent campaigns emerged in Harlem where a mystic named Sufi Abdul Hamid, Episcopalian minister John Johanson (the **Citizens' League for Fair Play**), and the Harlem Labor Union competed in a cauldron of "Action Boycotts" that helped ignite the **Harlem race riot of 1935.** It was the young minister of Abyssinian Baptist Church, **Adam Clayton Powell, Jr.,** who caught the public's attention as his Citywide Coordinating Committee won "jobs for Negroes" in New York Edison Bell Telephone, the New York Bus Company, and the World Fair. Powell forged this movement into a political organization that catapulted him into a seat on the City Council and in 1944 to a long congressional career. The most famous such movement during World War II was **A. Philip Randolph**'s threatened march on Washington that resulted in Franklin Roosevelt's **Executive Order 8802,** which produced the **Fair Employment Practice Committee.** The activism of the boycott movements ended with full employment during World War II and did not appear again until 1955 with Martin Luther King, Jr.'s **Montgomery bus boycott.**

Selected Bibliography Ralph L. Crowder, " Don't Buy Where You Can't Work: An Investigation of the Political Forces and Social Conflict Within the Harlem Boycott of 1935,"

Afro-American in New York Life and History 15 (1991), 7–44; Gary Hunter, "'Don't Buy Where You Can't Work': Black Activism during the Depression Years" (Ph.D. diss., University of Michigan, 1977); Henry McGuinn, "The Courts and the Occupational Status of Negroes in Maryland," *Social Forces* 18 (1939), 256–68.

Gary J. Hunter

Johnson, Charles S. (24 July 1893, Bristol, Va.–27 October, 1956, Louisville, Ky.). One of twentieth-century America's most respected black educators, a sociologist by training, Johnson spent nearly a lifetime studying and interpreting the nation's patterns of race relations. Even before his graduation from the University of Chicago in 1917, his penetrating analysis of America's changing black population trends established him as a leading social scientist. An eyewitness to several race riots during the tumultuous **Red Summer** of 1919, he investigated the causes of Chicago's unrest for an official commission and for the Chicago branch of the **National Urban League.** His coauthorship of the league's report, *The Negro in Chicago*, remains a landmark in social science research. In 1921 Johnson became National Urban League's director of research and investigations and continued his work on race relations. His research, frequently published in the League's official magazine, **Opportunity,** which he founded and edited, clearly revealed that blacks were being systematically excluded from sharing in the American dream. In 1928 he became chairman of **Fisk University**'s Social Sciences Department, shaping its specialty in the field of race relations into one of the nation's most respected. In 1947 he was selected as Fisk's first black president. Enormous administrative responsibilities followed his elevation, but he maintained a busy and prolific research and writing pace. Until his death, he remained a dedicated scholar committed to effecting better understanding between the races.

Selected Bibliography Ernest W. Burgess, Elmer A. Carter, and Clarence Faust, "Charles S. Johnson: Social Scientist, Editor, and Educational Statesman," *Phylon* 17 (Winter 1956), 317–25; Edwin R. Embree, *13 Against the Odds* (1944); Patrick J. Gilpin, "Charles S. Johnson: An Intellectual Biography" (Ph.D. diss., Vanderbilt University, 1973); Todd Lee, "Charles S. Johnson and the Sociology of Race Relations," *Southern Historian* 21 (2000), 56–65; Obituary, *New York Times*, 28 October 1956; Joe M. Richardson, *A History of Fisk University, 1865–1946* (1980); Richard Robbins, *Sidelines Activist, Charles S. Johnson and the Struggle for Civil Rights* (1996).

Robert L. Jenkins

Johnson, Frank M., Jr. (30 October 1918, Delmar, Ala.–23 July 1999, Montgomery, Ala.). President Dwight D. Eisenhower appointed this native Alabamian to the U.S. Federal District Court for Alabama's 23 southeastern counties on 22 October 1955. In 1979 President Jimmy Carter appointed him to the **United States Court of Appeals for the Fifth Judicial Circuit.** During his long tenure on the federal bench, Johnson handed down a series of decisions that brought about political and social changes that impacted not only on Alabama but also on the South and on the nation. He applied the 1954

U.S. Supreme Court *Brown v. Board of Education* desegregation decision to the **Montgomery bus boycott** case, thus incidentally helping to launch the civil rights career of **Martin Luther King, Jr.** He was part of the court that abolished the Alabama poll tax; he ordered Alabama to reapportion its election districts; and he presided over the trial that convicted the murderers of **Viola Fauver Gregg Liuzzo.** He ordered Alabama to integrate all of its school districts, the first statewide desegregation ruling. Throughout these years, his University of Alabama Law School classmate, Governor George C. Wallace, was a constant protagonist, but Johnson's decisions were so significant that many people came to call him the real governor of Alabama. Johnson refused all labels, insisting that his reverence for the law was his only guiding philosophy. In 1992, he assumed senior status and in 1993, he received the American Bar Association's Thurgood Marshall Award. The federal courthouse in Montgomery is named after him. According to a statement about Johnson attributed to Martin Luther King: "That is the man that I know in the United States who gives the meaning to the word justice."

Selected Bibliography Jack Bass, *Taming the Storm: The Life and Times of Judge Frank M. Johnson, Jr., and the South's Fight Over Civil Rights* (1993); "Frank Minis Johnson, Jr., 1918–1999," *Journal of Blacks in Higher Education* 24 (31 July 1999), 128; "Interpreter in the Front Line," *Time* (12 May 1967), 72–78; Robert F. Kennedy, Jr., *Judge Frank M. Johnson, Jr.* (1978); Frank Sikora *The Judge: The Life and Opinion of Alabama's Frank M. Johnson, Jr.* (1992); Tinsley E. Yarbrough, *Judge Frank Johnson and Human Rights in Alabama* (1981).

John F. Marszalek

Johnson, Georgia Douglas (10 September 1877, Atlanta, Ga.–May 1966, Washington, D.C.). An African American poet, playwright, biographer, educator, composer and political appointee, Georgia Johnson graduated from **Atlanta University**'s Normal School in 1893, taught music in Marietta, Georgia, and attended the Oberlin Conservatory of Music in Oberlin, Ohio, from 1902 to 1903. After her 1903 marriage to Henry Lincoln Johnson, creative writing became her metier. Renowned for her lyrical, frank, feminine tone and her use of the "mixed-blood" theme, Johnson was one of the first critically acclaimed female poets of color in the early twentieth century. Her works include *The Heart of a Woman and Other Poems*, 1918; *Bronze: A Book of Verse*, 1922; *An Autumn Love Cycle*, 1928; and *Share My World: A Book of Poems*, 1962. Johnson's plays, *Blue Blood*, 1926, and *Plumes*, 1927, won second and first prizes in **Opportunity** for their respective years. Other plays were published posthumously. She also wrote in collaboration with Gypsy Drago. Additional unpublished works include eighty poems with songs and music titled, *Bridge to Brotherhood*. Johnson produced numerous unpublished short stories, some written under the pseudonym of Paul Tremain. Additional unpublished works include *The Black Cabinet, Being The Life of Henry Lincoln Johnson*, and *White Men's Children*. Johnson was appointed commissioner of conciliation in the Department of Labor by President Calvin Coolidge. **Atlanta University** bestowed a doctor of literature degree on Johnson in 1965.

Selected Bibliography Dorothy F. Henderson, "Georgia Douglas Johnson: A Study of Her Life and Literature" (Ph.D. diss., Florida State University, 1995); Gloria T. Hull, *Color, Sex, and Poetry* (1987); Ann Allen Shockley, *Afro-American Women Writers 1746–1933* (1988); Judith Stephens, "'And Yet They Paused' and 'A Bill to be Passed': Newly Discovered Lynching Dramas by Georgia Douglas Johnson," *African American Review* 33 (1999), 519–22.

Bernice F. Guillaume

Johnson, James Weldon   (17 June 1871, Jacksonville, Fla.—26 June 1938, Wiscasset, Maine). As a poet, critic, anthologist, and novelist, he contributed significantly to the development of twentieth-century African American literature. As a diplomat, lawyer, and executive secretary of the **NAACP,** Johnson left an indelible mark on sociopolitical history. Educated at **Atlanta University** (A.B., 1894; A.M., 1904), he was admitted to the Florida bar in 1898. In 1900 he wrote "Lift Every Voice and Sing," which his brother John Rosamond set to music; the poem has a unique place in black life, having been adopted as "The Negro National Anthem" in the 1930s. Johnson and his brother migrated to New York in 1902, working as a songwriting team until Johnson was appointed United States counsel to Venezuela in 1906 upon the recommendation of **Booker T. Washington.** While in the diplomatic corps (1909–12), Johnson published his only novel *The Autobiography of an Ex-Colored Man* (1912) anonymously. The book did not become popular until it was reissued in 1927. In 1914 Johnson became an editor of *New York Age,* and two years later Joel Spingarn offered him the position of field secretary for the NAACP. Johnson worked diligently in the South to increase the number of NAACP branches and members. In 1917 he organized a silent protest march in New York against lynching and racial oppression and in 1919 made investigations of the race riots that occurred during the **Red Summer.** Serving as NAACP Executive Secretary from 1920 to 1936, Johnson maintained a fairly conservative posture as a key policy maker. He was quite visible, however, in his support of the **Dyer Antilynching Bill** (1921), of **A. Philip Randolph**'s labor organizing efforts, and of efforts to improve living and working conditions for blacks. Johnson resigned from the NAACP in 1930 to accept a chair in creative literature and writing at **Fisk University.** This position gave him time for writing, teaching, and lecturing and relief from the pressures that aggravated his poor health. He remained at Fisk until his death. Johnson's literary activity during his NAACP years was substantial, and he was awarded the **Spingarn Medal** in 1925 for distinguished achievement in writing, diplomacy, and public service. He published *Fifty Years and Other Poems* in 1917 and edited three books in quick succession: *The Book of American Negro Poetry* (1922), *The Book of American Negro Spirituals* (1925), and *The Second Book of Negro Spirituals* (1926). His second and third volumes of poetry were *God's Trombones: Seven Negro Sermons in Verse* (1927) and *Saint Peter Relates an Incident of the Resurrection Day* (1935). Johnson also wrote *Black Manhattan* (1930), an informal history of blacks in New York, *Along This Way* (1933), an urbane autobiography, and *Negro Americans: What Now?*, a thoughtful assess-

Portrait of James Weldon Johnson seated at his desk, 1900–20. © Library of Congress.

ment of race relations. In 1990, the James Weldon Johnson Poetry and Dramatic Arts Competition began, and in 2000 the James Weldon Johnson National Arts Institute was organized. That same year, Johnson was inducted into the Florida Artists Hall of Fame.

Selected Bibliography Herbert Aptheker, "Du Bois on James Weldon Johnson," *Journal of Negro History* 52 (July 1967), 224–27; Hugh Gloster, *Negro Voices in American Fiction* (1948); Judith Erlene Brown Harmon, "James Weldon Johnson, a New Negro: A Study of His Early Life and Literary Career, 1871–1916" (Ph.D. diss., Emory University, 1988); Jacksonville (Florida) *Free Press*, 28 February 2001; "James Weldon Johnson: A Chronology," Oakland *Post*, 17 February 1999; Eugene Levy, *James Weldon Johnson: Black Leader, Black Voice* (1973); Cristina L. Ruotolo, "James Weldon Johnson and the Autobiography of an Ex-Colored Musician," *American Literature* 72 (No. 2, 2000), 259–74; Jean Wagner, *Black Poets of the United States* (1973).

Jerry Ward

Johnson, Mordecai Wyatt (12 January 1890, Paris, Tenn.–11 September 1976, Washington, D.C.). A leading educator, administrator, and champion of educational opportunities, Johnson was the first African American president of **Howard University.** His parents were the Reverend Wyatt and Carolyn Freeman Johnson. He received his earliest education at the Academy of Roger Williams University in Nashville and at Howe Institute in Memphis,

Tennessee. He graduated from Atlanta Baptist College (now **Morehouse College**) in 1911 and then taught English, history and economics there. He continued his studies at the University of Chicago, where he received his bachelor's degree in 1913. He assumed the pastorate of the First Baptist Church of Charleston, West Virginia, in 1916 and received a Master's in Theology degree from Harvard University's School of Divinity in 1922. Johnson was appointed president of Howard University in 1926, became a superb administrator and "one of the great platform orators of his day." One of his talents was the ability to convince southern U.S. congressmen to increase and steadily expand the authorized annual federal appropriations to the University's capital expenditures. Between 1946 and 1960, Howard University received an average of over $1 million annually, in large measure the result of his persistent and skillful efforts.

Selected Bibliography Rayford W. Logan, *Howard University: The First Hundred Years, 1867–1967* (1969).

Glenn O. Phillips

***Johnson v. Virginia*, 373 U.S. 61 (1963)**   It was 27 April 1962, and Ford T. Johnson, Jr., was in traffic court in Richmond, Virginia, for driving with an expired tag. Regulations required that Johnson sit in the section set aside for blacks, but he sat in the white section. When he quietly refused to comply with an order to move to the black section, Johnson, a student at nearby Virginia Union University, was cited for contempt of court. Now he, and the **NAACP,** were in a position directly to challenge the constitutionality of segregated courtrooms. On appeal, the Virginia Supreme Court of Appeals ruled the conviction "plainly right." He took his case to the U.S. Supreme Court, which in April 1963 reversed the Virginia courts on **Fourteenth Amendment** grounds. In a short, unsigned opinion, the nation's high court asserted that "State-compelled segregation in a court of justice is a manifest violation" of "equal protection." By that time, Johnson was a Peace Corp worker in Ghana. He had secured a decision that desegregated southern courtrooms.

Selected Bibliography Loren Miller, *The Petitioners: The History of the Supreme Court of the United States and the Negro* (1966); Peter Wallenstein, *These New and Strange Beings: Conflict, Law, and Change in Twentieth-Century Virginia* (2003).

Peter Wallenstein

Joint Committee on National Recovery   It became critical during the first Hundred Days of the New Deal that someone champion the economic interests of blacks and press for their special needs. One attempt to do so was the establishment of the Joint Committee on National Recovery, formed during the summer of 1933 and initially supported by some twenty groups, the most important of which were the **NAACP** and the **Rosenwald Fund.** Attorney **John P. Davis** and economist **Robert C. Weaver** represented the committee before congressional hearings involved with proposed New Deal legislation. Davis hoped that the committee would combine efforts of existing black and civil rights organizations in representing to the administration the concerns of black Americans and, at the same time, educating black communities to the importance of new federal programs. Unable to obtain support from either the **NAACP** or the Rosenwald Fund, the committee essentially represented the singular efforts of Davis. It had disappeared by 1935. As a result of his experience with the committee, Davis joined **Ralph Johnson Bunche** and labor leader **A. Philip Randolph** to create in 1935 the **National Negro Congress.** The Joint Committee on National Recovery reflected the enormous significance of the changed relationship of the federal government to black people.

Selected Bibliography John B. Kirby, *Black Americans in the Roosevelt Era* (1980); Harvard Sitkoff, *A New Deal for Blacks* (1978); Raymond Wolters, *Negroes and the Great Depression* (1970).

John B. Kirby

Jones, Eugene Kinckle (30 July 1885, Richmond, Va.–11 January 1954, New York, N.Y.). Much of the professional and personal career of Eugene K. Jones was reflected in the organizational history of the early **National Urban League** (NUL). The son of a former slave and free black mother, Jones received a B.A. degree from Virginia Union University and a M.A. from Cornell. Shortly thereafter he became the first field secretary of the National Urban League, which was organized in 1911. In 1917, he succeeded **George Edmund Haynes** as executive secretary of the NUL, a post he held until 1941. During the 1920s the NUL began publishing **Opportunity:** *Journal of Negro Life*, which featured such talented black writers as **Langston Hughes, Countee Cullen,** and **Claude McKay.** Under Jones's direction, the League assumed national prominence. Working with private foundations, corporate institutions, and governmental officials, Jones emphasized securing jobs for blacks within both the private and public sectors. During the New Deal era, he served as a race relations adviser to the Department of Commerce, working closely with black and white administration officials to assure black participation in New Deal programs. Through the efforts of **Lester B. Granger,** whom Jones recruited, the NUL developed closer ties to organized labor. Although less vocal publicly than others in his affirmation of civil rights, Jones was a committed foe of race discrimination and segregation, and he made the NUL a strong organization supporting racial and economic justice.

Selected Bibliography Ralph J. Bunche, "Programs, Ideologies, Tactics, and Achievements of Negro Betterment and Interracial Organizations," (unpublished ms., Carnegie Study, 1940); Guichard Parris and Lester Brooks, *Blacks in the City: A History of the National Urban League* (1971); Nancy J. Weiss, *The National Urban League, 1910–1940* (1974).

John B. Kirby

Jones, LeRoi (Amiri Baraka) (7 October 1934, Newark, N.J.–). Since the 1960s, LeRoi Jones had been a bellwether of changes in black political and artistic thought in the United States. After earning a B.A. (1954) at **Howard University,** Jones established a brilliant career as poet, essayist, and playwright. From the late 1950s to the early 1960s, his Bohemian writings were consistent with the integrationist thrust of the civil rights movement. The production of *Dutchman* (1964), a shockingly honest treatment of racial conflicts, and the publication of *Home* (1966), a collection of social essays, signaled Jones's shift to a nationalist stance. In the year the outcry for **Black Power** created rifts among civil rights workers, Jones changed his name to Amiri Baraka. The anthology he coedited in 1968, *Black Fire,* was a telling record of how many young black writers and thinkers rejected the premises of integration in favor of black nationalist political development. In the 1970s Jones was a political activist in his hometown and on the national scene. As chairman of the Committee for a Unified Newark (1968–75), Jones was instrumental in the election of Kenneth Gibson as the city's first black mayor. He was chairman of the National Black Political Convention (1972), a meeting in which those who wanted to work within traditional political systems could reach no agreement with the black separatists. Although Jones/Baraka has not identified himself with a single political group, his work reflects an intense Marxist critique of politics in a capitalist system. In 2001, he was retired from the State University of New York at Stony Brook and exhibited a collection of his drawings in Santa Monica California. In 2003, the New Jersey General Assembly voted to eliminate the post of state poet he held because of controversy over a poem regarding the 11 September 2001, terrorist attacks.

Selected Bibliography Amiri Baraka, *The Autobiography of LeRoi Jones/Amiri Baraka* (1984); Kimberly W. Benston, *Baraka: The Renegade and the Mask* (1976); Harry J. Elam, Jr., *Taking It to the Streets: The Social Protest Theater of Luis Valdez and Amiri Baraka* (1997); William J. Harris, *The Poetry and Poetics of Amiri Baraka* (1985); Theodore R. Hudson, *From LeRoi Jones to Amiri Baraka* (1973); Henry C. Lacey, *To Raise, Destroy, and Create: The Poetry, Drama, and Fiction of Imamu Amiri Baraka* (1981); *Los Angeles Sentinel,* 7 March 2001; *New York Times,* 2 July 2003; Werner Sollors, *Amiri Baraka/LeRoi Jones: The Quest for a "Populist Modernism"* (1978); Komozi Woodard, *A Nation within a Nation: Amiri Baraka and Black Power Politics* (1999).

Jerry Ward

Jones v. Alfred H. Mayer Co.*, 392 U.S. 409 (1968)**   Previous U.S. Supreme Court cases outlawed segregation ordinances (Buchanan v. Warley,*** 1917) and racially restrictive covenants (***Shelley v. Kraemer,*** 1948; ***Barrows v. Jackson,*** 1953), but they had limited impact on residential segregation practiced by individuals. Decided after passage of the **Civil Rights Act of 1968,** *Jones* immediately outlawed racial discrimination in housing sales and rentals. *Jones* originated in St. Louis County, Missouri when the Alfred H. Mayer Company refused to sell a home to African American Joseph Lee Jones. District and circuit courts rejected Jones's request for an injunction. His U.S. Supreme Court appeal gained support from the **NAACP,** the National Committee against Discrimination in Housing, and the Justice Department. Justice Potter Stewart's controversial (7–2) majority opinion found that the **Civil Rights Act of 1866** "bars all racial discrimination, private as well as public, in the sale or rental of property, and that the statute thus construed, is a valid exercise of the power of Congress to enforce the **Thirteenth Amendment**." Unlike earlier cases, the *Jones* decision attacked housing discrimination directly.

Selected Bibliography Lucius J. Barker and Twiley W. Barker, Jr., *Civil Liberties and the Constitution* (1986); Brian J. L. Berry, *The Open Housing Question: Race and Housing in Chicago, 1966–1976* (1979); Gerhard Casper, "Jones v. Mayer: Clio, Bemused and Confused Muse," *Supreme Court Review* (1968), 89–132; Robert F. Cushman with Susan P. Koniak, *Cases in Constitutional Law* (1989); R. F. Johnson, *Residential Segregation: the State and Constitutional Conflict in American Urban Areas* (1984); Del Menge and George Ramey, "Constitutional Law: The End of Private Racial Discrimination in Housing through Revival of the Civil Rights Act of 1866," *Tulsa Law Journal* 6 (1970), 146–63; Stephen Grant Meyer, *As Long As They Don't Move Next Door: Segregation and Racial Conflict in American Neighborhoods* (2000); Sol Rabkin, *A Landmark Decision on Segregation in Housing: Jones v. Mayer* (n.d.).

James Borchert

Jordan, Barbara Charline (1 February 1936, Houston, Tex.–18 January 1996, Austin, Tex.). Jordan transcended an impoverished background in segregated Houston to graduate magna cum laude from Boston University in 1956. Three years later, she earned a law degree from the same school and returned to her hometown to practice law and work as an assistant for a county judge. In 1960 Jordan directed a local voter registration drive for the John F. Kennedy presidential campaign, which heightened her interest in the politi-

Barbara Jordan at the Democratic National Convention, 1976. © Library of Congress.

cal process. After two failed bids for elected positions, Jordan received 80 percent of the vote in 1966 to become the first black person in history to be elected to the Texas State Senate. Three years later she became the body's speaker pro tem. In 1972 she was elected to the U.S. House of Representatives, which made her the first woman and the first black elected to Congress from Texas. Jordan became part of the 17-member Congressional Black Caucus and fought for the extension of civil rights legislation such as the **Voting Rights Act of 1965.** In 1974, Jordan captivated the nation with her oratorical and analytical skills in a televised speech that eloquently and passionately argued for Richard Nixon's impeachment because of the constitutional abuses he committed during the Watergate episode. Two years later she became the first black woman to deliver the keynote address at the Democratic National Convention, an honor she repeated in 1992. After three terms in the House, Jordan retired in 1979 because of health problems. Despite her battle with multiple sclerosis, Jordan remained active in the struggle for racial equality. She served the Carter and Clinton administrations in advisory capacities, earned numerous doctorates and accolades for her political activism, won the **NAACP's** coveted **Spingarn Medal** in 1992, and taught at the University of Texas until her death in 1996. Jordan's role as a civil rights pioneer continued posthumously, as she became the first black person buried at the Texas State Cemetery in Austin.

Selected Bibliography Barbara Ann Holmes, *A Private Woman in Public Spaces: Barbara Jordan's Speeches on Ethics, Public Religion, and Law* (2000); Barbara Jordan and Shelby Hearon, *Barbara Jordan: A Self-Portrait* (1979); Mary Beth Rogers, *Barbara Jordan: American Hero* (2000).

Michael Butler

Jordan, Michael Jeffery (17 February 1963, Brooklyn, N.Y.–). Michael Jordan was born in Brooklyn, New York, but his family soon moved to Wilmington, North Carolina. He attended the University of North Carolina where legendary coach Dean Smith tutored him. In 1984 the Chicago Bulls drafted Jordan, which team he joined after winning an Olympic gold medal. He signed a huge contract with Nike to market athletic shoes called Air Jordan, which he and Spike Lee successfully marketed. In 1996 Jordan starred in *Space Jam*, which catapulted him into international icon status. Between 1991 and 1993 Jordan led the Bulls to three consecutive NBA championships and also won a second Olympic gold medal. In 1993 Jordan's father was murdered prompting his retirement from basketball and one season of professional baseball. Jordan then returned to basketball where he led the Bulls to three more championships between 1995 and 1999. In 1999 he again retired and became part owner of the Washington Wizards. In 2001 Jordan returned to basketball with the Wizards. He was one of the rare African American athletes who transcended race, one of the most popular figures in the world, building a huge economic empire on shoes, underwear, sports drinks, and other ventures.

Selected Bibliography Charles Barkley, *The Definitive Word on Michael Jordan as Told by His Friends and Foes* (1998); Bob Green, *Hang Time: Days and Dreams with Michael Jordan* (1992);

David Halberstam, *Playing for Keeps: Michael Jordan and the World He Made* (1999); Walter LaFeber, *Michael Jordan and the New Global Capitalism* (1999); Sam Smith, *Jordan Rules* (1992).

Able A. Bartley

Jordan, Vernon Eulion, Jr. (15 August 1935, Atlanta, Ga.–). He received a B.A. degree in political science from De Pauw University in 1957 and a J.D. degree from **Howard University** in 1960. In 1961 he began a civil rights and public service career that spanned two decades. From 1961 to 1963 Jordan served as the field director for the Georgia branch of the **NAACP.** Between 1964 and 1968 he directed the **Voter Education Project** of the **Southern Regional Council.** Jordan then worked for the Office of Economic Opportunity for two years before becoming the executive director of the **United Negro College Fund** in 1970. In 1972 he succeeded the late **Whitney Moore Young, Jr.,** as executive director of the **National Urban League,** which under his leadership increased its affiliates from 99 to 118, its budget from $40 million to $150 million, and its number of employees from 2,100 to 4,200. Jordan also launched a national voter registration drive and campaigns for a national full employment policy and a consumer-oriented national health system. On 29 May 1980, following an address to the Fort Wayne Urban League, Jordan was ambushed and shot. He recovered from his potentially fatal wound and resumed his post as head of the League until 31 December 1981. In 2003 he was in private law practice and partnership with the firm of Akin, Gump, Strauss, Hauer, and Feld in Washington, D.C. During the 1990s, he received national attention because of his friendship for and advice to President Bill Clinton.

Selected Bibliography Les Payne, "Vernon E. Jordan: In the Footsteps of Whitney Young," *Ebony* 27 (July 1972), 98; Harry Ploski and James Williams, eds., *The Negro Almanac: A Reference Work on the African American* (1989); Eleanora W. Schoenebaum, ed., *Political Profiles*, vol. 5 (1979).

Barbara L. Green

Journal of Negro Education Created in 1932 at **Howard University,** this journal reflected in part the growing number of African American scholars in various disciplines during the early decades of the twentieth century. According to its first editor, Charles H. Thompson, Howard University professor of education, the journal was designed to stimulate the collection and dissemination of facts, to critique practices, and to investigate problems surrounding African American education. It remained a major publication in 2003.

Selected Bibliography August Meier and Elliott Rudwick, eds., *Black History and the Historical Profession, 1915–1980* (1986); Mabel Smythe, ed., *The Black American Reference Book* (1976); Charles Thompson, "Why a Journal of Negro Education?" *Journal of Negro Education* 1 (April 1932), 1–4.

Janice M. Leone

The Journal of Negro History In order to seek and publish the records of black Americans, **Carter Goodwin Woodson** founded *The Journal of Negro*

History in Washington, D.C., in 1916 and served as its editor until 1950. The *Journal* was published by the **Association for the Study of Afro-American Life and History.** Under Woodson's guidance, many black scholars were able to publish their work when the major historical journals discriminated against them. The *Journal* also represented an outlet for liberal white scholars whose ideas were rejected by the white historical establishment prior to 1950. Woodson used the *Journal* to advance a positive image of blacks and to challenge a widely held view of racial inferiority. Articles published by Woodson and other scholars, for example, challenged the racist writings of U. B. Phillips and his followers and caused a historiographical shift from emphasis on the master's perspective to that of the slave. In the 1950s and 1960s, many articles on women's history and women authors themselves appeared in the *Journal*, something not regularly occurring in other historical publications. On the *Journal*'s fiftieth anniversary in 1966, **Benjamin Quarles** wrote: "It is pluralistic, it is revolutionary, and it is purposeful." Arthur M. Schlesinger, Sr., hailed it as "an equal member of the family of American historical periodicals." Circulation reached two thousand that year. Due to the preservation of records by the *Journal* and Woodson's efforts to collect primary source material, contemporary scholars have invaluable material on which to draw for their studies. Since 1987, the *Journal* has experienced financial and staff difficulties but it has continued to provide significant scholarly contributions to the study of black life in America despite its erratic publication schedule.

Selected Bibliography Editorial, *Journal of Negro History* 51 (April 1966), 75–97; Jacqueline Goggin, "Countering White Racist Scholarship: Carter G. Woodson and the *Journal of Negro History*," *Journal of Negro History* 68 (Fall 1983), 355–75; Rayford W. Logan and Michael R. Winston, eds., *Dictionary of American Negro Biography* (1982).

Thomas D. Cockrell

Journey of Reconciliation (1947)   In one of the earliest nonviolent **direct action** campaigns of the **Congress of Racial Equality** (CORE), 16 black and white men traveled by bus through the upper South in 1947 to test new federal laws prohibiting segregated services in interstate transportation. Arrests stemming from an incident outside Chapel Hill, North Carolina, resulted in the trial and conviction of four of these riders—**Bayard Rustin** of the **Fellowship of Reconciliation;** law student Andrew Johnson; Worker's Defense League representative Joe Felmet; and New York printer, Igal Rodenko. They were sentenced to 30 days on a road gang, and all but Johnson served 22 days. This journey was a prototype for the more famous journeys of the CORE **Freedom Riders** of 1961.

Selected Bibliography George Houser and Bayard Rustin, *We Challenged Jim Crow* (1947); August Meier and Elliot Rudwick, *CORE: A Study in the Civil Rights Movement, 1942–1968* (1973); James Peck, *Freedom Ride* (1962); Robin Washington, producer, *You Don't Have to Ride Jim Crow* (video documentary, New Hampshire Public Television, 1996).

Jo Ann O. Robinson

Jubilee Singers   The Fisk Jubilee Singers, led by George L. White, began a tour in October 1871 to raise "badly needed money" for financially strapped **Fisk University.** Their initially mixed reception turned into an enthusiastic one after they abandoned the "white man's music" and replaced it with "slave songs." When the tour ended in May 1872, they had performed at the White House and raised $20,000. A European tour, 1873–74, netted nearly $50,000. During their campaigns the black singers were often subjected to indignities, but they continued to travel and popularize the spirituals. Within seven years, the Jubilee Singers collected $150,000 and saved Fisk from financial collapse.

Selected Bibliography J. B. T. Marsh, *The Story of the Jubilee Singers with Their Songs* (1876); Gustavus D. Pike, *The Jubilee Singers, and their Campaign for Twenty Thousand Dollars* (1873); Joe M. Richardson, *A History of Fisk University, 1865–1946* (1980); Andrew Ward, *Dark Midnight When I Rise: The Glory of the Fisk Jubilee Singers* (2001). Web site: www.fisk.edu.

Maxine D. Jones

K

Katzenbach v. McClung, 379 U.S. 294 (1964)   Title II of the **Civil Rights Act of 1964** requires that patrons in places of public accommodation be afforded full and equal service without discrimination. Congress relied heavily on its power to regulate interstate commerce, both because of extensive testimony regarding the effects of segregation on business and commerce, and because of lingering doubts about its ability to regulate private actions. Ollie's Barbecue in Birmingham, Alabama, owned by the McClung family for nearly thirty years, had a takeout service for blacks but would not seat them in the dining room. Because it was located some distance from interstate highways, its clientele was made up largely of local families and workers. Its only possible connection with interstate commerce was the rather tenuous one of having bought and served meat procured from a distributor who obtained it from out-of-state sources. However, the law established that circumstance as sufficient for jurisdiction, and the Court, speaking through Justice Tom C. Clark, upheld the statute. He noted that the commerce power was broad and sweeping, and that in light of the testimony before Congress, legislative discretion in the choice of remedy should be honored. This case may represent an extreme departure from the principle of deciding constitutional issues narrowly in light of the facts of the case.

Selected Bibliography Robert F. Cushman, *Leading Constitutional Decisions* (1992); Harry T. Quick, "Public Accommodations: A Justification of Title II of the Civil Rights Act of 1964," *Western Reserve Law Review* 16 (May 1965), 660–88; George Rossman, ed., "Review of Recent Supreme Court Decisions," *American Bar Association Journal* 51 (1965), 268–69.

James E. Sefton

Katzenbach v. Morgan, **384 U.S. 641 (1966)**   The **Voting Rights Act of 1965** provided for the suspension of literacy tests and other tests and devices in areas where there was reason to believe that such tests and devices discriminated against voters on account of race or color. Section 4(e) protected the right to vote of numerous New York City residents from Puerto Rico. This section "provides that no person who has completed the sixth grade in a public school, or an accredited private school, in Puerto Rico in which the language of instruction was other than English shall be disfranchised for inability to read or write English." The U.S. Supreme Court reversed a lower court ruling that challenged Congress's authority to negate New York English language literacy requirement for voting. It thus affirmed the constitutional authority of Congress to enact "appropriate legislation" to enforce the equal protection clause of the **Fourteenth Amendment.**

Selected Bibliography Thomas I. Emmerson, David Haber, and Norman Dorsen, *Political and Civil Rights in the United States*, vol. 2 (1967); William B. Lockhart, Yale Kamisar, and Jesse H. Choper, eds., *Cases and Materials on Constitutional Rights and Liberties*, 3rd ed. (1970); Bernard Schwartz, ed., *Statutory History of United States Civil Rights*, vol. 11 (1970).

Alfred Young

Kennedy v. Bruce, **298 F. 2d 860 (5th Cir., 1962)**   Attorney General Robert Kennedy, determined to employ the full judicial power of the federal government in order to ensure African Americans of the right to vote, brought action against the registrar of voters in Wilcox County, Alabama. In that impoverished rural county, where blacks outnumbered whites by more than two to one, not a single one of the 6,085 black citizens of voting age was registered. By comparison, 112 percent of eligible whites were registered to vote. The registrar testified in district court that no blacks had been denied a request to register and vote. On appeal, the **United States Court of Appeals for the Fifth Judicial Circuit** reversed the district court, saying that the disparity between the number of white and black voters was too great to accept the defendant's argument that no blacks had been refused the right to register. This case, together with the *United States v. Lynd* case a few months later involving a Mississippi county, gave federal officials the right to examine local voting and registration lists when there were reasonable grounds for assuming that certain voters were being discriminatorily denied their voting rights.

Selected Bibliography Jack Bass, *Unlikely Heroes* (1981); Harvey C. Couch, *A History of the Fifth Circuit Court, 1891–1981* (1984); Frank T. Read and Lucy S. McGough, *Let Them Be Judged: The Judicial Integration of the Deep South* (1978).

Charles D. Lowery

Kerner Commission (National Advisory Commission on Civil Disorders)   At the height of the civil rights movement in 1964 and 1965, race riots erupted in urban ghettoes primarily outside the South. These uprisings demonstrated that civil rights laws alone would not achieve racial equality. Although black northerners generally did not encounter official segregation and disfranchisement, they lacked real economic and political power. Crowded into slums, unable to find adequate jobs, treated harshly by the police, and lacking effective political representation, ghetto dwellers expressed their rage against white exploitation. From 1965–68, approximately half a million blacks in three hundred cities participated in these rebellions, leaving fifty thousand arrested, eight thousand injured, and more than $100 million in damaged property. On 27 July 1967, during another wave of summer violence, highlighted in Newark and Detroit (see **Newark, New Jersey, race riot** and **Detroit race riot**), President Lyndon B. Johnson created the **National Advisory Commission on Civil Disorders,** chaired by Governor Otto Kerner of Illinois. On 1 March 1968, the 11-member, bipartisan panel reported that the United States was "moving toward two societies, one black, one white— separate and unequal;" attributed the underlying causes of the riots to white racism; viewed the black uprisings as a form of political protest; and recommended a massive and costly governmental assault on unemployment, poor housing, and poverty. These suggestions largely went unheeded by the president, who was preoccupied by the Vietnam War, and by white officials angered by violence and weary of expensive social welfare programs.

Selected Bibliography James Button, *Black Violence: Political Impact of the 1960s Riots* (1978); Joe R. Feagin and Harlan Hahn, *Ghetto Revolts* (1973); Michael Lipsky and David J. Olson, *Commission Politics: The Processing of Racial Crisis in America* (1977); National Advisory Commission on Civil Disorders, *Report* (1968); Anthony Platt, ed., *The Politics of Riot Commissions, 1917–1970* (1971).

Steven F. Lawson

Kester, Howard Anderson   (21 July 1904, Martinsville, Va.–12 July 1977, Asheville, N.C.). While attending Lynchburg College, Princeton Theological Seminary, and Vanderbilt University, he became a leader in the fledgling interracial activities of the Intercollegiate Young Men's Christian Association (YMCA), the Student Volunteer Movement, and the **Fellowship of Reconciliation.** In the 1920s he organized an interracial forum among college and seminary students in the Lynchburg, Virginia, area, agitated for the integration of the white YMCA conference center in western North Carolina, and was one of the first white students to attend Negro intercollegiate YMCA conferences in the South. From the late 1920s to the late 1930s, as a freelance activist employed by the Fellowship of Reconciliation and Committee on Economic and Racial Justice, Kester promoted student interracialism, worked for the **Southern Tenant Farmer's Union,** and investigated lynchings, riots, and alleged instances of **black peonage** for the **NAACP** and other groups. From the late 1930s to the mid-1950s, as secretary of the interracial, interdenominational **Fellowship of Southern Churchmen** and as principal of Penn Normal Agricultural and Industrial School, a black institution in South Carolina, Kester labored to build a spirit of Christian fraternity that transcended racial or class distinctions.

Selected Bibliography John S. Bellamy, "If Christ Came to Dixie: The Southern Prophetic Vision of Howard Anderson Kester, 1904–1941" (M.A. thesis, University of Virginia, 1977); Anthony Dunbar, *Against the Grain: Southern Radicals and Prophets, 1929–1959* (1981); John Egerton, *A Mind to Stay Here: Profiles from the South* (1970); Howard Anderson Kester Papers, Southern Historical Collection, The University of North Carolina at Chapel Hill; Howard A. Kester, *Revolt among the Sharecroppers* (1936); Robert F. Martin, "A Prophet's Pilgrimage: The Religious Radicalism of Howard Anderson Kester, 1921–1941," *The Journal of Southern History* 48 (November 1982), 511–30; Robert F. Martin, *Howard Kester and the Struggle of Social Justice in the South, 1904–1977* (1991).

Robert F. Martin

Keyes v. School District No. 1, Denver, Colo., **413 U.S. 189 (1973)** The Supreme Court in June 1973 decided its first case dealing with public school segregation outside of the South, and it held that discriminatory actions of school boards could lead to **de jure segregation,** even in states lacking a statutory or constitutional mandate for dual schooling. Sponsoring the suit filed by local blacks, the **Legal Defense and Educational Fund** of the **NAACP** charged the Denver school board with the deliberate intent to segregate its schools. School officials countered by arguing that social forces, not law, had created the school system's racial imbalance. In a landmark decision, a seven-to-one Supreme Court held that the school board had instituted segregation through "racially inspired" policies, including assigning minority faculty and staff to minority schools, utilizing mobile classrooms at overcrowded black schools, and gerrymandering student-attendance zones and school-site selections. Although the suit uncovered intentional segregation in only one part of the city, the court placed the burden on school authorities to prove that "segregative intent" had not influenced policy throughout the system. The *Keyes* decision facilitated victories against school segregation in other cities outside the South. But these victories, as in Denver, often led to forced busing, a remedy that proved to be controversial.

Selected Bibliography Paul R. Diamond, *Beyond Busing: Inside the Challenge to Urban Segregation* (1985); Jack Goodman, "Constitutional Law-School Desegregation: De Facto Hangs On," *North Carolina Law Review* 52 (1973), 431–32; Laurence R. Marcus and Benjamin D. Stickney, *Race and Education: The Unending Controversy* (1981); William D. Valente, *Law in the Schools* (1980); J. Harvie Wilkinson III, *From Brown to Bakke: The Supreme Court and School Integration, 1954–1978* (1979).

Jack E. Davis

Keys v. Carolina Coach Company, **64 M.C.C. 769 (1955)** This case was decided by the Interstate Commerce Commission (ICC) on 7 November 1955. On 1 September 1953, Sarah Keys, an African American from New York City and a member of the Women's Army Corps stationed at Fort Dix, New Jersey, sued the Carolina Coach Company of Raleigh, North Carolina, which was a member of the National Trailways Bus System. Keys claimed that on 1 August 1952 she had purchased a joint-line ticket for transportation from Trenton, New Jersey to Washington, North Carolina, but that upon arriving at Roanoke

Rapids, North Carolina, she was refused further passage and was subjected by Carolina Coach employees to "false arrest and imprisonment solely because of her race and color." Keys had been sitting in the front half of the bus. Carolina Coach claimed that only white passengers could occupy front seats of the bus, and that its company rules provided the company "full control and discretion as to the seating of passengers." The company's defense was based on the **separate-but-equal** doctrine of the 1896 *Plessy v. Ferguson* decision. At question was section 216 of the Interstate Commerce Act, which made it unlawful for any common carrier by motor vehicle "to subject any particular person . . . to any unjust discrimination or any undue or unreasonable prejudice or disadvantage in any respect whatsoever." Citing a precedent decision in a concurrent railroad case, the ICC declared separate-but-equal as no longer acceptable. Thus the ICC for the first time in its history rejected the separate-but-equal doctrine. Although the *Keys* ruling applied explicitly to seating on buses, implicitly it outlawed segregation in bus company terminals too.

Selected Bibliography Catherine A. Barnes, *Journey from Jim Crow: The Desegregation of Southern Transit* (1983); *Columbia (South Carolina) State* newspaper, 16 July 1955; *New York Times*, 26 November 1955; *Pittsburgh Courier*, 3 December 1955.

Charles A. Risher

Killens, John Oliver (4 January 1916, Macon, Ga.–27 October 1987, Brooklyn, N.Y.). A founder of the Harlem Writers Guild (1952) and tutor to important African American writers, John Oliver Killens was a commanding black voice in the literature of civil rights. He wrote and taught others to write in what he called "a crusade to decolonize the minds of black people." His first novel, *Youngblood* (1954), depicted blacks ready to fight and die for their rights in a small town in Georgia, a place not unlike his native Macon. His second novel, *And Then We Heard the Thunder* (1963), discussed racism in the American military. The protagonist, like Killens, was a law school dropout who served as a commissioned officer in an all black regiment during World War II. His later writing grew much more militant.

Selected Bibliography John Oliver Killens, *Black Man's Burden* (1965); John Oliver Killens, *'Sippi* (1967); John Oliver Killens, *The Cotillion; Or, One Good Bull Is Half the Herd* (1971); Obituary, *New York Times*, 29 October 1987; William H. Wiggins, Jr., "John Oliver Killens," in Thaddius M. Davis and Trudier Harris, eds., *Afro-American Fiction Writers after 1955* (1984).

Thomas J. Davis

King, Alfred Daniel Williams (30 July 1930, Atlanta, Ga.–21 July 1969, Atlanta, Ga.). The younger brother of **Martin Luther King, Jr.,** A. D. assumed a support role in the civil rights movement. He graduated from Palmer Institute in Fedalia, North Carolina, earned a bachelor's degree from **Morehouse College** in Atlanta, Georgia, and attended seminary at the Interdenominational Theological Center at **Atlanta University.** After his home was bombed in Birmingham, Alabama, in May 1963, King led demonstrations calling the city "Bombingham." Moving to Louisville, Kentucky, in

1965, King became pastor at Zion Baptist Church and led a movement for an open housing ordinance there in 1967. After his brother's assassination, he returned to Atlanta to assume the copastorate of Ebenezer Baptist Church. Although he was very active in the **Southern Christian Leadership Conference,** he chose not to seek top administrative positions in the organization. He died in a swimming pool accident at his Atlanta home.

Selected Bibliography Obituary, *Newsweek,* 4 August 1969; Obituary, *New York Times,* 22, 25 July, 1969; Obituary, *Time,* 1 August 1969.

Thomas D. Cockrell

King, Clennon (1921, birthplace unknown–). Teacher, minister and civil rights activist, King first burst into public notoriety in 1957 when students at Alcorn Agricultural and Mining College (now Alcorn State University), in Lorman, Mississippi, where King briefly taught history, protested a series of prosegregation newspaper articles he had written. In June 1958 he attempted to integrate the University of Mississippi summer session to begin work on a doctorate. State police arrested him, and a local judge briefly committed him to the state mental hospital. In 1960 he ran for the U.S. presidency on the Afro-American ticket, and in 1962 he unsuccessfully sought political asylum in Jamaica. While living in California, he was jailed for failing to support his family, but the state supreme court overturned the conviction. He is probably most famous for attempting to integrate President Jimmy Carter's home Baptist church in Plains, Georgia in the last days of the 1976 presidential campaign. His activity caused the church to drop its ban on black members, but eventually the congregation split and King never actually belonged anyway. He was found guilty of election violations when he ran for office in Georgia in the late 1970s and moved to Miami where in the 1980s he founded The Holy King's Divine Mission to take in and feed the homeless. In 1982 he insisted that "America made an error in projecting **Martin Luther King, Jr.,** as some kind of super man and Clennon King as some kind of super kook." During the 1990s he served as pastor of Miami's All Faiths Church of Divine Missions in Overtown in Miami. He frequently ran for public office and had repeated run-ins with black police and public officials including accusations of disorderly conduct and violently resisting arrest. When an opponent was barred from Miami's 1997 mayoral race because of criminal charges and King was allowed to remain in a district municipal election, he was incredulous. He pointed out to a reporter that he too has such a record: "After my 40th jailing, I stopped counting them."

Selected Bibliography "A Feisty Preacher Finds a New Mission," *Newsweek,* 8 February 1982; "I Speak as a Southern Negro," *American Mercury* 6 (January 1958), 23–33; Clennon King entry on electronic data base "Ethnic News Watch"; *Miami Times,* 25 February 1993, 16 October 1997; *New York Times,* 1 November, 1 December, 1976; "One Way to Kill a College," *Time* (18 March 1957); "The Plains Baptists," *Time* (17 October 1977); "Showdown in Plains," *Newsweek,* 2 November 1976; "A Win for Carter in His Backyard," *Time* (22 November 1976).

John F. Marszalek

Coretta Scott King and her husband, Martin Luther King, Jr., 1964. © Library of Congress.

King, Coretta Scott   (27 April 1929, Marion, Ala.–). Her mother, the former Bernice McMurray, and her father, Obadiah Scott, were hardy people who grew up in a world of harsh segregation, racial violence, and hard times but not in a climate of lost black pride and low self-esteem. According to Coretta, she often wondered just how far her father might have gone had he had the chance to receive a high school education. In a family of five, Coretta was described as determined, even aggressive, and "highly intelligent." She attended Lincoln High in Marion and then moved north to Antioch College in Yellow Springs, Ohio. Here, she excelled in music and received a scholarship to Boston's New England Conservatory of Music, where she met the Reverend **Martin Luther King, Jr.** Coretta would later recall their first encounter and remark that Martin was "unlike any other" she had met and that as he was "being prepared" for his journey, she was "being prepared to be his helpmate." They were married in June 1953. In the years that followed, four children were born. An extraordinary person in her own right and as the wife of one of America's great leaders, Coretta's life from 1953 to 1968 was remarkable. She marched hand-in-hand with her husband and nurtured his faith in the dark days of anti–civil rights violence. In 2003 she, along with her family, remained a major force behind the Martin Luther King, Jr. Center for Nonviolent Social Change in Atlanta, Georgia.

Selected Bibliography Coretta Scott King, *My Life with Martin Luther King, Jr.* (1969); Lynn Norment, "The King Family: Keepers of the Dream," *Ebony* (January 1987); Octavia Vivian, *Coretta: The Story of Mrs. Martin Luther King, Jr.* (1970).

LeRoy T. Williams

King, Martin Luther, Jr. (15 January 1929, Atlanta, Ga.–4 April 1968, Memphis, Tenn.). In December 1955 the 26-year-old Martin Luther King, Jr., in his second year as pastor of the Dexter Avenue Baptist Church in Montgomery, Alabama, leapt from the relative obscurity of the southern black clergy into a meteoric career as the nation's preeminent civil rights leader. His achievements, which won for him the Nobel Peace Prize in 1964, ended when he was assassinated by a white sniper in Memphis, Tennessee, in 1968.

Son of the pastor of the prestigious Ebenezer Baptist Church in Atlanta, Georgia, young "M. L." attended segregated Booker T. Washington High School and skipped the ninth and twelfth grades to enter **Morehouse College** in 1944 at the age of 15. In 1947 he was ordained at his father's church, and he received his bachelor's degree from Morehouse the following year. From 1948 to 1951 he attended Crozer Theological Seminary in Pennsylvania, where he was valedictorian and president of the student body. In 1951 he began doctoral study in theology at Boston University (Ph.D., 1955). In Boston he met Coretta Scott, who had left rural Alabama to study voice at the New England Conservatory of Music.

In 1953 Martin and Coretta were married and in 1954, the year of the Supreme Court's school desegregation decision, the couple moved to Montgomery, where King's predecessor at the Dexter church, the Rev. Vernon Johns, was a leader in the city's mobilizing community of civil rights activists. When seamstress **Rosa Parks** sparked the **Montgomery bus boycott** by refusing to give up her seat to a white passenger on 1 December 1955, King was drafted by the veteran leadership to lead the new **Montgomery Improvement Association.** The drama of the boycott and King's eloquence drew national television coverage, and in 1956 a federal court ordered the buses desegregated. In 1958 King published *Stride toward Freedom,* a story of the Montgomery boycott that explained his philosophy of **nonviolent resistance** based on Christian brotherhood and love. In 1959 King moved to Atlanta to head the new **Southern Christian Leadership Conference** and become copastor with his father at Ebenezer.

The sit-in movement of 1960 led to the formation with King's encouragement of the **Student Nonviolent Coordinating Committee,** also headquartered in Atlanta, and also to King's first arrest and jailing (which resulted in the now-famous phone call from Senator John F. Kennedy to Coretta King). The failure of King's **Albany, Georgia, sit-in,** during 1961–62 led to revised nonviolent tactics that in 1963 challenged segregation in Birmingham, Alabama. National revulsion at the televised brutality, led in the spring of 1963 by police chief Eugene "Bull" Connor, was reinforced in August 1963 by King's moving **"I Have a Dream"** address before the Lincoln Memorial in Washington. This momentum, strengthened by President Kennedy's martyrdom in November and by President Lyndon Johnson's commitment, led to the **Civil Rights Act of 1964.** A similar King-led protest against voting discrimination in Selma, Alabama, produced televised police violence and led to the **Voting Rights Act of 1965.**

Fred Shuttlesworth, Ralph Abernathy, and Martin Luther King, Jr., during the Birmingham Confrontation, 1963. © Archives Collections, Birmingham Public Library, Birmingham, Alabama.

When the **Watts race riot** of August 1965 was followed in 1966 by **Stokeley Carmichael**'s **Black Power** challenge to King's nonviolent leadership and then by the massive **Detroit race riot (1967),** King shifted his operations increasingly to the North. His campaign in Chicago in 1966 against job discrimination, poor schools, and slum housing was opposed by Mayor Richard Daley's powerful city machine and was torn by violence from both white ethnic communities and black youth gangs. In 1967 King denounced the Vietnam War, and the FBI intensified its bizarre, secret program to destroy King by bugging his hotel rooms, leaking reports of his Communist associates and his philandering, and attempting through threats to break up his marriage and even to turn his morbid streak toward suicide. In 1968 King called for a **Poor People's March on Washington** to demand withdrawal from Vietnam. But before this march could occur, King was murdered on 4 April 1968, at a motel in Memphis, Tennessee, where he was supporting a strike by black sanitation workers.

The key to King's early leadership was his ability to mobilize a disciplined black peasantry in the South by appealing to their roots in the African American church, while offering brotherhood rather than retribution to the white majority. By drawing televised attacks against nonviolent Negro protesters, King and his allies generated demands by nonsouthern whites that Congress reform the racist South. When King moved northward after 1965, the positive-sum goals of opening southern schools, restaurants, and ballot boxes were replaced by more difficult, zero-sum contests over jobs, promotions, and appointments. King's local victories in the North were few, but the legislative legacy of the congressional reforms of 1964–65 has brought far-reaching change for minorities and women in educational and employment opportunity and electoral districting. Increasingly after 1965, the black social movement split, and King's original protest movement was deeply southern. His leadership radically altered the future for southern blacks, but King also profoundly changed the lives of southern whites, against their fierce resistance.

As King's vision and social agenda, after 1965, expanded beyond black rights toward economic justice, international peace, and human rights, his constituency broadened on the left, but resentment intensified on the right. Like Abraham Lincoln, King was assassinated and martyred in a turbulent and polarized republic. The collective memory of his cause and his courage has eased the pain that divided the nation during his life.

Selected Bibliography Taylor Branch, *Parting the Waters: America in the King Years, 1954–63* (1988); Taylor Branch, *Pillar of Fire: America in the King Years, 1963–1965* (1998); Adam Fairclough, *To Redeem the Soul of America: The Southern Christian Leadership Conference and Martin Luther King, Jr.* (1987); David J. Garrow, *Bearing the Cross: Martin Luther King and the Southern Christian Leadership Conference* (1986); David Levering Lewis, *King: A Critical Biography* (1970).

Hugh Davis Graham

King, R. Edwin, Jr.   (20 September 1936, Vicksburg, Miss.–). A sociologist at the University of Mississippi Medical Center in Jackson, King received a B.A. in sociology at Millsaps College in 1958, and a B.D. from Boston University School of Theology in 1961 followed by a Master's degree in Social Theology in 1963. Active in the civil rights movement, he was arrested in Montgomery, Alabama, in 1960 and in Jackson, Mississippi, in 1963. King and his wife Jeanette worked closely with John R. Salter and **Medgar W. Evers** in the Jackson Movement campaign of 1962 and 1963, and King helped establish the Mississippi Civil Liberties Union. While serving as chaplain at primarily black **Tougaloo College** in Jackson in the 1960s, he initiated attempts by students to attend white churches and led efforts to integrate Jackson's cultural events. King, a native white Mississippian, served as chairperson of the delegation of the **Mississippi Freedom Democratic Party** to the Democratic national convention in 1964. The collapse of his marriage and a divorce in 1983 was the subject of Rosellen Brown's novel *Civil Wars*. In 1994, King denounced the murder trial of Byron de la Beckwith because he thought political pressures predetermined the conviction. He also opposed the opening of the **State Sovereignty Commission** files in Mississippi because he felt it was unfair to those mentioned within. In 2003 King was actively involved in the pro-life movement.

Selected Bibliography Clarice T. Campbell and Oscar Allan Rogers, Jr., *Mississippi: The View from Tougaloo* (1979); Charles Marsh, *God's Long Summer: Stories of Faith and Civil Rights* (1997); John R. Salter, Jr., *Jackson, Mississippi: An American Chronicle of Struggle and Schism* (1978).

Thomas D. Cockrell

Knights of Peter Claver   This Roman Catholic, African American fraternal and mutual aid order, is one of the most visible aspects of Roman Catholicism's black laity. Named after St. Peter Claver (1581–1654), a Jesuit missionary who dedicated himself to the slaves of Carthagena, West Indies, it was founded 7 November 1909 in Mobile, Alabama, by four priests of St. Joseph's Society of the Sacred Heart and three laymen. Five divisions involving male members, as well as female and minor auxiliaries, total 100,000 persons in more than 25 states. The Knights support parish and community activities, youth development, civic improvement, and scholarships for college-bound youths. These are achieved through recreational, insurance, and internal scholarship programs. An important link between the Knights and the larger African American community is found in the Knights' scholarship program at Xavier University of Louisiana, the only historically black, Catholic institution of higher education in the United States. Additionally, the Knights contribute to the **National Urban League,** the **NAACP,** and the **Southern Christian Leadership Council.** Religious activities include collaborative presence at masses and participation in regalia at religious ceremonies.

Selected Bibliography Emanuel J. Abstin, " Catholicism and African-Americans: A Study of Claverism, 1909–1959" (Ph.D. diss., Florida State University, 1998); *Claverite* 70 (June 1989), passim; Cyprian Davis, *The History of Black Catholics in the United States* (1995); John W. Donohue, "Of Many Things," *America* 158 (February 1988), 1; Robert R. MacDonald, John R. Kemp, and Edward F. Haas, eds., *Louisiana's Black Heritage* (1979); Stephen J. Ochs, *Desegregating the Altar: The Josephites and the Struggle for Black Priests, 1871–1960* (1990); Charles B. Rousseve, *The Negro in Louisiana* (1937). Web site: *www.knightsofpeterclaver.com*.

Bernice F. Guillaume

Knights of Pythias   Founded as a fraternal organization by Justice H. Rathbone, a civil service employee, in Washington, D.C., in 1864 in an effort to heal the racial hatreds of the Civil War era, the Pythians rejected a charter application from Philadelphia blacks in 1869. Some black men were still initiated into the mysteries of the order, allegedly because they infiltrated lodges by "passing as whites." By 1880 blacks organized themselves into the Supreme Council of the Knights of Pythias. Attempts to prevent their use of the insignia and the name of the order continued, however, resulting in at least one court case, that in Tennessee in 1911. By the 1930s, black Pythian lodges were found throughout America. In 2003 the organization had over forty thousand members in the United States and Canada.

Selected Bibliography James R. Carnahan, *Pythian Knighthood: Its History and Literature* (1889); W.E.B. Du Bois, ed., *Economic Cooperation among Negro Americans* (1907); E. Franklin Frazier, *The Black Bourgeoisie* (1957); E. A. Williams, *History and Manual of the Colored Knights of Pythias* (1917). Web site: www.pythias.com.

Betty L. Plummer, revised by Marvin Thomas

Knoxville Riot (1968)   The urban riots of the mid-1960s, in particular the **Detroit race riot (1967),** heightened tensions between the African American and white communities. Tennessee was one of the states that instituted riot training for National Guard units. Black leaders in that state charged that "Task Force Bravo," a training exercise to test the mobility of the guard in riot or other emergency situations in the four largest cities of Tennessee, further exacerbated race relations. State officials denied such accusations, and on March 8 troops began the training exercise in the four cities. In an unrelated incident but in this highly emotionally charged setting, a security officer at Knoxville College on March 10, 1968, stopped a car with out-of-state license plates at 2 A.M. on the campus of this predominantly black college. A Knoxville student was arrested and charged with public intoxication, along with a Chicago man, who was booked for criminal trespass. Some 50 to 75 students rioted in protest over the arrest of the two men. A white taxicab driver responded to a call on the campus that morning and later radioed the police for aid. He died as a result of gunshot wounds, and his body and his destroyed vehicle were reported on 11 March 1968. The riot subsided soon thereafter.

Selected Bibliography Lester C. Lamon, *Blacks in Tennessee, 1791–1970* (1981); *New York Times,* 1, 3, 8, 10, 11 March 1968.

Robert A. Calvert

Kowaliga Industrial Community   The Kowaliga Industrial Community was founded in 1896 by **William E. Benson** to arrest black migration to the North by creating a self-sufficient black community in Alabama that combined farming with year-round industrial employment. He bought tracts of land, subdivided some of it into small farms with affordable housing, and established a saw mill, shingle mill, turpentine plant, and plantation store. Education at the Kowaliga School followed the principles espoused by **Booker T. Washington.** Incorporated as the Dixie Industrial Company in 1900 and dependent on the generosity of white northern philanthropists and shareholders, the community was in financial difficulties by the time of Benson's death in 1915 and lost viability not long afterwards.

Selected Bibliography William Benson, "Kowaliga: A Community with a Purpose," *Charities* 15 (7 October 1905), 22–24; W.E.B. Du Bois, ed., *Economic Cooperation among Negro Americans* (1907); Louis R. Harlan, ed., *The Booker T. Washington Papers* (1972–81); Elliott Rudwick, *W.E.B. Du Bois: Voice of the Black Protest Movement* (1982).

Carole Shelton

L

Lake Mohonk Conference   In the spring of 1890 and 1891 the first and second Mohonk conferences were held at Lake Mohonk, New York. They were organized by the Quaker philanthropist Albert K. Smiley at the suggestion of former President Rutherford B. Hayes to discuss the "negro question." Invitations were sent to several hundred representative men and women throughout the country. To ensure the attendance of southern whites, "Smiley decided not to invite any colored people." More than one hundred whites attended. Topics discussed at these conferences included industrial education, the Negro ministry, the Negro family, and public education for the Negro. This was one of the many attempts made during these years to deal with the period's racial situation.

Selected Bibliography James D. Anderson, *The Education of Blacks in the South 1860–1935* (1988); Isabel C. Barrows, ed., *First Mohonk Conference on the Negro Question,* and *Second Mohonk Conference on the Negro Question* (1891, reprint, 1969); *New York Times,* 2, 3, 6 June 1891.

Robert A. Bellinger

Lane v. Wilson, **307 U.S. 266 (1939)**   Following the U.S. Supreme Court's invalidation of Oklahoma's **grandfather clause (*Guinn v. United States,*** 1915), the Oklahoma legislature enacted a law in 1916 providing that all citizens qualified to vote in 1916 who failed to register between 30 April and 11 May 1916, would remain forever disfranchised, except eligible voters in 1914. The effect was that white citizens who were on the voting list in 1914 by virtue of the state's grandfather clause were entitled to vote, whereas African Americans, who had been kept from voting by the clause, would remain disfranchised unless they registered during a limited 12-day period. Robert Lane, an African American, was qualified to vote in 1916 but failed to register during the required time. Denied the right to register in October 1934, he sued, claiming discriminatory treatment resulting from the 1916 statute. The Supreme Court found the procedural requirements for voting discriminatory and invalidated the 1916 legislation. The case's significance lay in the sharp comments of Justice Felix Frankfurter who, in delivering the majority opinion, wrote that the "[**Fifteenth**] **Amendment** nullifies sophisticated as well as simple-minded modes of discrimination. It hits onerous procedural requirements which effectively handicap exercise of the franchise by the colored race although the abstract right to vote may remain unrestricted by race."

Selected Bibliography Loren Miller, *The Petitioners: The Story of the Supreme Court of the United States and the Negro* (1966); "Recent Cases," *University of Chicago Law Review* 6 (1939), 296–301; "Recent Cases," *University of Pennsylvania Law Review* 87 (1939), 348–49.

Alfred Young

Langston, John Mercer (14 December 1829, Louisa Court House, Va.–15 November 1897, Washington, D.C.). A representative figure in the nine-

John Mercer Langston, Minister to Haiti. Photograph by Matthew Brady. © Library of Congress.

teenth-century phase of the civil rights struggle, Langston received his B.A. (1849) and M.A. (1852) from Oberlin College. Admitted to the Ohio bar in 1854, he was an active abolitionist. In 1864 he became president of the National Equal Rights League, a forerunner of the **Niagara Movement** and the **NAACP.** He served as an inspector-general in the **Freedmen's Bureau** (1868–69), where he championed educational and employment rights for newly freed slaves. During the remainder of his life, Langston played significant roles as an educator, diplomat, and politician. He served as dean of the law school (1870–73) and as vice president and acting president of **Howard University** (1873–75). From 1877 to 1885, he was minister resident to Haiti and charge d'affaires to the Dominican Republic. For two years (1885–87), he was president of Virginia Normal and Collegiate Institute. Elected to the House of Representatives from Virginia in 1888, he was much concerned with the harassment of black voters in the South and as a congressman called for vigorous enforcement of the **Fourteenth Amendment.**

Selected Bibliography William F. Cheek and Aimee L. Cheek, *John Mercer Langston and the Fight for Black Freedom, 1829–65* (1989); John Mercer Langston, *From the Virginia Plantation to the Nation's Capitol* (1894, reprint, 1969); Rayford Logan, *Howard University: The First One Hundred Years, 1867–1967* (1969).

Jerry Ward

Larsen, Nella (13 April 1891, Chicago, Ill.–30 March 1964, New York, N.Y.). Best known for her two novels *Quicksand* (1928) and *Passing* (1930), Larsen poignantly portrayed the marginal existence of African American women in American culture. The product of an interracial background, Larsen's books reflected her own experiences. After spending one year at the high school affiliated with **Fisk University** in Nashville, Larsen spent several years at the University of Copenhagen, and subsequently received a degree from New York's Lincoln Training School for Nurses in 1915. Prior to undertaking writing, Larsen pursued careers in nursing and library science. In 1928 the **Harmon Foundation** recognized her work with a bronze medal. In 1930 she received a Guggenheim Fellowship for Creative Writing, the first African American woman to be so honored.

Selected Bibliography Thaddeus M. Davis, "Nella Larsen's Harlem Aesthetic," in Amritjit Singh, William S. Shiver and Stanley Brodwin, eds., *Harlem Renaissance: Revaluations* (1989); Thaddeus M. Davis, *Nella Larson, Novelist of the Harlem Renaissance: A Woman's Life Unveiled* (1994); Charles R. Larson, *Invisible Darkness: Jean Toomer and Nella Larson* (1993); Mary Helen Washington, "Nella Larsen: Mystery Woman of the Harlem Renaissance," *Ms.* 9 (December 1980), 44–50.

Brenda M. Brock

***Lassiter v. Northampton Election Board,* 360 U.S. 45 (1959)** Until Congress barred literacy tests as a qualification for voting in the **Voting Rights Act of 1965** and its subsequent extensions, they were common. In some states the tests disenfranchised blacks only when coupled with such devices as a **grandfather clause,** which typically exempted those individuals eligible to vote on 1 January 1867 and their descendants. The Court invalidated the grandfather clause in 1915 in *Guinn v. United States,* but approved nondiscriminatory literacy tests. When Louise Lassiter attempted to register to vote but was rejected because she refused to take a literacy test, she challenged the requirement on **Fourteenth** and Seventeenth **Amendment** grounds. Although North Carolina's constitution contained a grandfather clause, its applicable 1957 statute did not. The Court, therefore, simply asked whether a literacy test equally applicable to all violated the Constitution. A unanimous Court, referring to *Guinn,* upheld the test. Noting the power conferred upon states in Article I, Section 2, and in the Seventeenth Amendment, which provided that "the Electors in each State shall have the Qualifications requisite for Electors of the most numerous Branch of the State Legislature," the Court concluded that a nondiscriminatory literacy test was a reasonable means of promoting intelligent use of the ballot.

Selected Bibliography Richard Claude, *The Supreme Court and the Electoral Process* (1970); Jack Greenberg, *Race Relations and American Law* (1959); George Rossman, ed., "Review of Recent Supreme Court Decisions," *American Bar Association Journal* 45 (1959), 964.

Earlean M. McCarrick

Lawson, James M., Jr. (22 September 1928, Uniontown, Pa.–). A clergyman, pacifist, and leader of **nonviolent resistance** movements, Lawson gained prominence in the 1960s. Educated at Baldwin-Wallace College, in Berea, Ohio, and Boston University, Lawson helped organize the earliest sit-in demonstrations (November 1959) while he was a divinity student at Vanderbilt University in Nashville, Tennessee. His resultant dismissal in 1960 caused a much-publicized crisis of conscience among the faculty of the Divinity School. Lawson worked actively for the **Student Nonviolent Coordinating Committee** before he accepted a pastorate in Memphis, Tennessee. In 1968 he turned the Memphis garbage collectors' strike into an occasion for focusing national attention on glaring instances of social injustice. Despite **Martin Luther King, Jr.'**s tragic death in this effort, these Lawson-inspired confrontations gained civil rights and economic opportunities for African Americans. As a retired pastor of Holman Methodist Church of Los Angeles, Lawson entered the twenty-first century still working actively for nonviolent solutions to a wide range of social problems.

Selected Bibliography "A Force More Powerful: Nashville 1960; Interview: Rev. James Lawson," in York Zimmerman Inc. and WETA (Copyright 2000), http://www.pbs.org/WETA/forcemorepowerful/Nashville/interview.html; Paul K. Conkin, *Gone with the Ivy: A Biography of Vanderbilt University* (1985); *New York Times,* 8 April 1968; "The Reverend James Lawson: Biographical Sketch," American Friends Service Committee, http://www.afsc.org/lawson.htm; David M. Tucker, *Black Pastors and Leaders: Memphis, 1819–1972* (1975); *Who's Who among Black Americans,* 2nd ed., 1977–1978, vol. 1 (1978).

James R. Chumney

League of Revolutionary Black Workers Inspired by radical elements in the civil rights movement, some African American members of the United

Auto Workers (UAW) in Detroit, Michigan, formed DRUM, FRUM, and ELRUM (i.e., the Dodge, Ford and Eldon Avenue Revolutionary Movements, respectively) in the late 1960s. The League was created to coordinate the efforts of DRUM, FRUM, and ELRUM and to unite "the people" in their revolutionary struggle. Although the league remained in the UAW, the official viewpoint was that "the labor movement as represented by United Mine Workers, Steel Workers, UAW, AFL-CIO, etc. are all the antithesis of the freedom of black people, in particular, and the world in general."

Selected Bibliography James A. Geshwender, *Class, Race, and Worker Insurgency: The League of Revolutionary Black Workers* (1977); "League of Revolutionary Black Workers General Policy Statement, Labor History and League's Labor Program," *Inner City Voice*, 3 February 1971.

Clarence Hooker

Lee, Herbert (1 January 1912, Amite County, Miss.–25 September, 1961, Liberty, Miss.). An Amite County, Mississippi farmer, Lee was one of the first blacks who attempted to register to vote as part of the **Student Nonviolent Coordinating Committee**'s first voter registration effort in Mississippi. He was also active in the local chapter of the **NAACP.** He was shot and killed on 25 September 1961, by State Representative E. H. Hurst in Liberty, Mississippi. Hurst, who claimed he shot Lee in self defense, was acquitted of the crime by a local jury. A witness to the murder, Lewis Allen, later testified to a Justice Department official that Lee had not assaulted Hurst. Allen was killed three years later, allegedly as a result of his testimony.

Selected Bibliography Seth Cagin and Philip Dray, *We Are Not Afraid: The Story of Goodman, Schwerner, and Chaney and the Civil Rights Campaign for Mississippi* (1988); Henry Hampton and Steve Fayer, *Voices of Freedom: An Oral History of the Civil Rights Movement from the 1950s through the 1980s* (1990); Doug McAdam, *Freedom Summer* (1988); Bob Moses, "Mississippi: 1961–1962," *Liberation* (January 1970); Howard Zinn, *SNCC: The New Abolitionists* (1964).

Betsy Sakariassen Nash

Lee v. Macon County Board of Education, **267 F. Supp. 458 (M.D. Ala., 1967)** This case brought about the desegregation of Alabama public schools, which nine years after ***Brown v. Board of Education*** were nearly all still segregated. In January 1963, Detroit Lee and other black parents in Tuskegee, Alabama, county seat of Macon County, sued the County Board of Education seeking an end to biracial schools. A federal district court in Alabama directed the board to admit 13 blacks to the all-white Tuskegee High School in September 1963. The county board attempted to comply but Governor George C. Wallace and the State Board of Education overruled its actions, first postponing the school's opening and then allowing the school to open only when forced to do so by federal court injunction. In January 1964, Wallace and the Board closed Tuskegee High, returned the blacks to the all-black high school in the town, and permitted whites to transfer to segregated white schools in the county. The plaintiffs in the case then sought an injunction to compel the Governor and the Board to end segregation in all Alabama public schools, maintaining that they, not the local boards, were responsible for operating the schools in the state. The federal district court declined the request and only ordered the desegregation of the schools of Macon County. But in 1967, after Wallace and the Board intervened with court-ordered desegregation in the other counties, it ordered Alabama to end its dual system of education. It also forbade state funding for private segregated institutions. The Supreme Court upheld the lower court ruling in 1970.

Selected Bibliography Robert F. Kennedy, Jr., *Judge Frank M. Johnson: A Biography* (1978); Tinsley E. Yarbrough, *Judge Frank Johnson and Human Rights in Alabama* (1981).

Dorothy A. Autrey

Lee v. Mississippi, **332 U.S. 742 (1948)** On 19 January 1948, the U.S. Supreme Court reversed the conviction of Albert Lee, a 17-year-old black Mississippian, on a charge of assault with intent to ravish. Lee had earlier been convicted by the Hinds County Circuit Court, and his conviction had been upheld by the Mississippi Supreme Court.

In his appeals to both the Mississippi Supreme Court and the U.S. Supreme Court, Lee argued that the only basis for his conviction was his confession, which he claimed had been "extorted . . . by threats, force, duress, fear and physical violence." Vague eyewitness testimony, maintained Lee, was the only other evidence against him.

Complicating the case was the fact that Lee also said he had not confessed at all. The Mississippi Supreme Court ruled that Lee could not say that his confession had been coerced and then claim not to have confessed. But the U.S. Supreme Court, in an opinion written by Justice Frank Murphy, ruled that a confession had been made and that the confession was extorted. The case is a significant one in the body of judicial precedents dealing with confessions.

Selected Bibliography *Cases Argued and Decided in the Supreme Court of Mississippi*, vol. 201; *Jackson Clarion-Ledger*,14 April 1947; Harry A. Ploski and James Williams, eds., *The Negro Almanac: A Reference Book on the African American* (1989); Otis H. Stephens, *The Supreme Court and Confessions of Guilt* (1973).

Allen Dennis

Legal Defense and Educational Fund The NAACP Legal Defense and Educational Fund, Inc. was created in 1939 as a tax-exempt corporation to direct the **NAACP**'s civil rights litigation and education programs. Operating independently of the founding organization with an initial staff of two, the fund had grown by the early 1970s to employ some four hundred cooperating attorneys—black and white—on more than six hundred cases annually. Since its inception, the fund has fought for social justice for blacks in the areas of education, employment, administration of justice, voting rights, and housing. Its accomplishments include victories in such landmark civil rights cases as *Sweatt v. Painter* (1950) and *Brown v. Board of Education* (1954). In 2003 it continued its civil rights litigation efforts in court's throughout the nation.

Selected Bibliography Jacqueline L .Harris, *History and Achievement of the NAACP* (1992); NAACP Legal Defense and Educational Fund, *30 Years of Building American Justice* (1970); Warren D. St. James, *Triumphs of a Pressure Group, 1909–1980* (1980); Steven C. Tauber, "The NAACP Legal Defense Fund and the U.S. Supreme Court's Racial Discrimination Decision-Making," *Social Science Quarterly* 80 (1999), 325–40; Mark V. Tushnet, *The NAACP's Legal Strategy against Segregated Education, 1925–1950* (1987). Web site: *www.ldfla.org*.

Robert A. Calvert

Lester, Julius Bernard (27 January 1939, St. Louis, Mo.–). A Jewish African American writer, educator, and folk singer, Lester has been both eloquent supporter and astute critic of **Black Power** politics. He received a B.A. from **Fisk University** in 1960. He was a volunteer for the **Student Nonviolent Coordinating Committee's** (SNCC) **Freedom Summer of 1964** in Mississippi, where he sang at freedom rallies and organized music workshops. He has visited Sweden, Cuba, and Hanoi for SNCC. His late 1960s weekly radio show on WBAI in New York provided a platform for black political views. In 1983 Lester became a Jew. In 2003 he continued as a professor of Judaic/Near Eastern Studies at the University of Massachusetts, Amherst. He has written extensively on Uncle Remus folktales.

Selected Bibliography Julius Lester, *Look Out Whitey, Black Power's Gon' Get Your Mama* (1968); Julius Lester, *Lovesong: Becoming a Jew* (1988); Julius Lester, *To Be a Slave* (1968); Julius Lester, *Uncle Remus: The Complete Tales* (1999).

Linda Ford and Ira Glunts

"Letter from Birmingham Jail" During the violent, tension-filled days of the civil rights movement of the 1960s, the Reverend **Martin Luther King, Jr.,** was often called an outside agitator as he carried the campaign for equality across the American South. After his arrest for leading a protest march in Birmingham, Alabama, King responded on 16 April 1963 from his jail cell to a letter from eight local Christian and Jewish clergymen chiding blacks for "unwise and untimely" activities. These ministers told King to "wait" patiently for justice and equality to come to Birmingham. Writing with a smuggled pen on a variety of surfaces including toilet paper and the margins of the *Birmingham News*, he told his critics why he was in Birmingham, outlined the existing injustices, and explained the tenets of nonviolent protest for social change. To the request for patience, King told of the agony of explaining to young black children why they were denied access to the city's amusement parks and how adult black men were saddled with the commonly used names of "nigger," "boy" and "John." If they understood what it meant to live at a "tiptoe stance" in a racist society and the overwhelming feeling of "nobodiness" experienced by most blacks, King challenged the ministers, they would not ask him to wait. King's lawyers smuggled the long letter out of the jail and the American Friends Service Committee published it, after which it appeared in magazines and newspapers all over the nation. Along with the **"I Have a Dream"** speech, it stands as the most significant statement of the modern nonviolent civil rights movement.

Martin Luther King, Jr., in jail, Birmingham, Alabama. ©
Bettmann/CORBIS.

Selected Bibliography James A. Colaiaco, "The American Dream Unfulfilled, Martin Luther King, Jr. and the 'Letter from Birmingham Jail,'" *Phylon* 45 (March 1984), 1–18; Richard P. Fulkerson, "The Public Letter as a Rhetorical Form: Structure, Logic, and Style in King's 'Letter from Birmingham Jail,'" *Quarterly Journal of Speech* 65 (April 1979), 121–36; C. Eric Lincoln, ed., *Martin Luther King, Jr.* (1970); Wesley T. Mott, "The Rhetoric of Martin Luther King, Jr: Letter from Birmingham Jail," *Phylon* 36 (December 1975), 411–21; Stephen B. Oates, *Let the Trumpet Sound: The Life of Martin Luther King* (1982); Melinda Snow, "Martin Luther King's 'Letter from Birmingham Jail' as Pauline Epistle," *Quarterly Journal of Speech* 71 (August 1985), 318–34.

LeRoy T. Williams

Levitt and Sons Incorporated v. Division Against Discrimination, State of New Jersey, Willie James and Franklin Todd,* 363 U.S. 418 (1959)** In May 1954, during the same month the U.S. Supreme Court handed down its ***Brown v. Board of Education decision, Abraham Levitt and Sons, Inc. began to purchase farmland in Willingboro Township, New Jersey. Already a nationally known pioneer of suburban housing developments (Levittown, New York,

12,000 houses; and Levittown, Pennsylvania, 17,300 houses), Levitt maintained a policy of not selling to Americans of African descent. The New Jersey Conference of **NAACP** branches immediately lobbied the state legislature to expand a state law that already prohibited discrimination in employment, public accommodations, and local schools, to include publicly assisted housing. The amended statute was enacted in 1957. In June of 1958 Levitt announced that his project would be an all-white community and thereafter denied sale to two black men, Willie James, an officer from nearby Fort Dix, and Franklin Todd, an engineer at RCA. James and Todd filed a complaint with the state Division Against Discrimination. While the Division was investigating these complaints, Levitt initiated a suit to stop the terms of the new state law, arguing that the law contained no effective enforcement provisions, and that, if the law was applicable to him, it was an "unconstitutional" restriction of a federal program (FHA Mortgage Insurance) by a state law. These claims were rejected by the appellate and supreme courts of New Jersey and in 1959 by the U.S. Supreme Court, thus ending the use of FHA mortgage insurance to perpetuate residential segregation.

Selected Bibliography Gary Hunter, *Up South: The Civil Rights Movement in Southern New Jersey 1940–1973* (1990).

Gary J. Hunter

Lewis, John (21 February 1940, Pike County, Ala.–). While attending the American Baptist Theological Seminary, Lewis became an early protest leader in the **Nashville Student Movement.** He remained throughout his civil rights career an ardent supporter of **Martin Luther King, Jr.**'s leadership and philosophy of nonviolent **direct action** and went on to play a vital role in the establishment of the **Student Nonviolent Coordinating Committee** (SNCC) He participated in 1961 with the **Freedom Riders** and during the 1963 **March on Washington,** as chairperson of SNCC (1963–66), Lewis delivered that organization's condemnation of American racism and segregation. He demonstrated with King in the civil rights protest at Selma, Alabama. In 1986 Lewis was elected from Georgia to the U.S. House of Representatives and continued serving in that position through 2003.

Selected Bibliography Clayborne Carson, *In Struggle: SNCC and the Black Awakening in the 1960s* (1981); David J. Garrow, *Bearing the Cross: Martin Luther King, Jr., and the Southern Christian Leadership Conference* (1986); Paul Good, "Odyssey of a Man—And a Movement," *New York Times Magazine* (25 June 1967); John Lewis with Michael D'Orso, *Walking with the Wind: A Memoir of the Movement* (1998); Allen Matusow, "From Civil Rights to Black Power: The Case of SNCC, 1960–1966," in Barton J. Bernstein and Allen Matusow, eds. *Twentieth-Century America: Recent Interpretations* (1969); Howard Zinn, *SNCC: The New Abolitionists* (1964).

Marshall Hyatt

Lewis, William Henry (1868, Berkeley, Va.–January 1949, Boston, Mass.). Born the son of former slaves, William Henry Lewis attended Virginia Normal and Industrial Institute before he attended Amherst College, in Amherst,

Massachusetts, where he played on the football team and became the first black man to be named All-American. In 1892 he received his B.A. from Amherst College and was elected class orator. He went on to Harvard Law School, where he was the first black person to play on the Harvard football team. In 1899 he was elected to the Cambridge City Council and in 1902 to the Massachusetts legislature. From 1903 to 1906 he was assistant U.S. attorney general for the Boston area. He was also the head of the Naturalization Bureau for New England (1907), assistant U.S. attorney for New England (1907–11), and assistant U.S. attorney general of the United States (1911–13), the highest appointed black official to that time. He was one of the first blacks admitted to membership in the American Bar Association. From 1913 to 1949 Lewis had a private practice and earned a reputation as "one of Boston's leading criminal lawyers."

Selected Bibliography Walter Christmas, ed., *Negroes in Public Affairs and Government*, vol. 1 (1966); Louis R. Harlan, *Booker T. Washington: The Wizard of Tuskegee, 1901–1915* (1983); Harold Wade, Jr., *Black Men of Amherst* (1976).

Robert A. Bellinger

Little Rock Desegregation Crisis In September 1957, Orval Faubus of Arkansas became the first southern governor to attract worldwide attention by resisting court-ordered school desegregation. Faubus, an Ozark populist reformer who had appointed blacks to party office and who had presided over the quiet integration of state colleges in the state, turned against desegregation to ward off attacks from segregationist opponents as he sought reelection to an unprecedented third term. Expressing fear of mob violence, Faubus joined forces with a group of Little Rock citizens to obtain a state court injunction to prevent integration of Central High School under a plan worked out between the federal court and the local school board. When the injunction was set aside by a federal court order, Faubus called out the National Guard to prevent nine black students from entering the school. Despite President Dwight D. Eisenhower's direct attempts to persuade Faubus to desist, the governor continued his defiance, keeping the troops in place and refusing to recognize the jurisdiction of a federal court over a state governor. In response to a renewed order from the federal court, a mob formed outside the school, attacked black reporters on the scene, and threatened the nine students. As the crowd grew— there were soon thousands of angry protesters in the streets of Little Rock— over the next days, Mayor Woodrow Mann sought Eisenhower's intervention. Although far from enthusiastic about court-ordered school desegregation and no advocate of federal supremacy, Eisenhower was angered by what he saw as Faubus's irresponsible behavior and reluctantly concluded that his administration would have to take action. Federal marshals, who would be used by subsequent administrations to enforce desegregation orders, had not yet been trained for such a task, and Eisenhower was uneasy about using the Arkansas Guard. The President ordered General Maxwell Taylor to send in a thousand highly disciplined troops of the 101st Airborne, and simultaneously national-

Defiant white students at Arkansas's North Little Rock High School block the doors of the school, denying access to six black students enrolled in the school, 9 September 1957. © AP/Wide World Photos.

ized the Arkansas Guard to remove them from the governor's control. As soon as order had been established and the federal court directive carried out, Eisenhower replaced the Airborne troops with units from the Arkansas National Guard, who remained on duty in Little Rock until the end of that school year.

Selected Bibliography Stephen E. Ambrose, *Eisenhower: The President* (1984); Jack Bass and Walter DeVries, *The Transformation of Southern Politics: Social Change and Political Consequence since 1945* (1976); Daisy Bates, *The Long Shadow at Little Rock: A Memoir* (1962); Will Counts, *A Life Is More Than a Moment: The Desegregation of Little Rock's Central High* (1999); Cory Fraser, "Crossing the Color Line in Little Rock: The Eisenhower Administration and the Dilemma of Race for U.S. Foreign Policy," *Diplomatic History* 24 (No. 2, 2000), 233–64; Tony A. Freyer, *The Little Rock Crisis: A Constitutional Interpretation* (1984); Tony A. Freyer, "The Little Rock Crisis Reconsidered," *Arkansas Historical Quarterly* 56 (No. 3, 1997), 361–70; Elizabeth Jacoway and Fred C. Williams, eds., *Understanding the Little Rock Crisis: An Exercise in Remembrance and Reconciliation* (1999).

Allen Kifer

Liuzzo, Viola Fauver Gregg (11 April 1925, California, Pa.–25 March 1965, Lowndes County, Ala.). Viola Liuzzo grew up in Tennessee and Georgia, married Anthony J. Liuzzo, an official with a Teamsters union local, and worked as a medical laboratory assistant in Detroit, Michigan, hospitals. After watching on television the "bloody Sunday" clash in Selma, Alabama, she drove alone to Selma. A week later she drove to Montgomery for the last leg of the march. After the march she and LeRoy Moton, a young black man, ferried marchers back to Selma. On a return trip to Montgomery, four Ku Klux Klansmen pulled beside Liuzzo's car on highway 80 and fatally shot her in the head; Moton escaped uninjured.

The Klansmen were acquitted in her death in state court in 1965. The testimony of Gary Thomas Rowe, Jr., an FBI informant, helped convict William Orville Eaton, Eugene Thomas, and Collie LeRoy Wilkins, Jr., in 1966 of violating Liuzzo's civil rights. In 1978 the three charged that Rowe had fired the fatal shot, and he was indicted for murder. Federal courts ruled that he could not be tried, and a Justice Department inquiry found "no credible evidence" that Rowe had fired the shot. In 1983 a federal court rejected the Liuzzo family's two million dollar negligence suit against the FBI in Liuzzo's death.

Selected Bibliography Charles E. Fager, *Selma, 1965: The March That Changed the South* (1974); Jack Mendelson, *The Martyrs: Sixteen Who Gave Their Lives for Racial Justice* (1966); Southern Poverty Law Center, *Free at Last* (1989); Mary Stanton, *From Selma to Sorrow: The Life and Death of Viola Liuzzo* (1998).

Charles W. Eagles

Locke, Alain Leroy (13 September 1885, Philadelphia, Pa.–9 June 1954, New York, N.Y.). Locke, graduated magna cum laude from Harvard in 1907, was the first black man to be selected a Rhodes Scholar. His triumph was tarnished when he was denied admission to five Oxford colleges before Hertford College accepted him. Three years at Hertford were followed by another year at the University of Berlin. He took a teaching position at **Howard University** in 1912, and, at the same time, continued his studies; in 1924 he received a Ph.D. from Harvard. Locke became a popular and outstanding teacher at Howard, but he was fired in 1925 in the midst of student and faculty unrest. When students, alumni, and the public protested his dismissal, he was not only reappointed to the faculty but he also became a personal advisor to **Mordecai Wyatt Johnson,** the school's first black president. The new administration placed greater emphasis on black life and problems and helped make the school the major African American educational institution and a leader in the civil rights struggle. This change was a reflection of what Locke called "the **New Negro Movement**"—a development of black pride as a necessary prerequisite to the civil rights movement. His work in adult education led him to be elected president of the American Association for Adult Education in 1945, making him the first black national-level president of a predominantly white educational association. An immensely productive scholar, Alain Locke well represents the **Harlem Renaissance** that he personally described as "an artistic awakening of racial self-consciousness and a collective self-renewal for black people." Not only was he its chief philosopher and art critic, but he also played a significant part in helping others advance in their own careers. Among his most important works are *The New Negro* (1925), *The Negro in America* (1933); *The Negro in Art: A Pictorial Record of the Negro Artist and the Negro Theme in Art* (1940), and numerous other books and articles. At his death, he was working on *The Negro in American Culture* (completed by Margaret Just Butcher and published in 1956).

Selected Bibliography Rudolph A. Cain, "Alain Leroy Locke: Crusader and Advocate for the Education of African American Adults," *Journal of Negro Education* 64 (No. 1, 1995), 87–99; Laverne Gyant, "Contributors to Adult Education: Booker T. Washington, George Washington Carver, Alain L. Locke, and Ambrose Caliver," *Journal of Black Studies* 19 (September 1988), 97–110; Alain LeRoy Locke, *Race Contacts and Interracial Relations* (1992); Rayford W. Logan and Michael R. Winston, eds., *Dictionary of American Negro Biography* (1982); Winston Napier, "Affirming Critical Conceptualism: Harlem Renaissance Aesthetics and the Formation of Alain Locke's Social Philosophy," *Massachusetts Review* 39 (No. 1, 1998), 93–112; Wilhelmena S. Robinson, *Historical Negro Biographies* (1969); Jeffrey C. Stewart, *The Critical Temper of Alain Locke: A Selection of His Essays on Art and Culture* (1983); Johnny Washington, *A Journey into the Philosophy of Alain Locke* (1994).

Gary B. Mills

Lockwood, Lewis C. (birth and death information unknown). Soon after the start of the Civil War, the **American Missionary Association** (AMA), a nonsectarian organization founded in 1846 and dominated by white abolitionists, contacted General **Benjamin Franklin Butler** at Fortress Monroe, Virginia about the status of the "contrabands." Butler said he intended to let the former slaves live in freedom. Consequently, the AMA sent the Reverend Lewis C. Lockwood as the first missionary to freed people. He conferred with the freedmen at Fortress Monroe, establishing schools and organizing church meetings. He also wrote back to the AMA for clothing, supplies, and additional missionaries. All this activity took place near the site where the first blacks had arrived in British America in 1619. The one room school, under the direction of Mary S. Peake, a local black woman, was at first conducted in the former home of ex-president John Tyler. It is usually considered the cradle of the later famous **Hampton Institute.** Lockwood remained in the area for 13 months and enrolled seven thousand students in the day and night schools and five thousand students in the Sunday Bible study. "This is not a day of small things," he surmised, "but already a day of great things."

Selected Bibliography Lewis C. Lockwood, *Mary S. Peake, The Colored Teacher at Fortress Monroe* (1864; reprint, 1969); Benjamin Quarles, *The Negro in the Civil War* (1953); James M. McPherson, *The Struggle for Equality: Abolitionists and the Negro in the Civil War and Reconstruction* (1964); Benjamin Quarles, *The Negro in the Civil War* (1953).

John F. Marszalek

Logan, Rayford Whittingham (7 January 1897, Washington, D.C.–4 November 1982, Washington, D.C.). A scholar and public servant who focused on racial injustice at home and abroad, particularly in the Caribbean basin and Africa, Rayford W. Logan was a Phi Beta Kappa graduate of Williams College (B.A., 1917; M.A., 1929) and Harvard University (M.A., 1932; Ph.D., 1936). He worked with **W.E.B. Du Bois** and served during the 1920s as secretary of Pan-African congresses in Paris, London, Lisbon, and New York. He served in the U.S. State Department's inter-American Affairs

Bureau and chaired the federal committee on participation of blacks in national defense from 1940 to 1945. A pioneer in what he always preferred to call "Negro History," Logan taught history at Virginia Union University (1925–30), **Atlanta University** (1933–38), and **Howard University** (1938–65; emeritus, 1965–82). He authored numerous books and scholarly articles. The **NAACP** awarded Logan its **Spingarn Medal** in 1980.

Selected Bibliography Obituary, *Washington Post,* 7 November 1982; Obituary, *New York Times,* 6 November 1982; James A. Page and Jae Min Roh, comps., *Selected Black American, African, and Caribbean Authors: A Bio-Bibliography* (1985).

Thomas J. Davis

Lomax, Louis E. (16 August 1922, Valdosta, Ga.–31 July 1970, Santa Rosa, N.M.). A prolific black writer, Lomax was a contemporary interpreter of the civil rights movement. A 1942 graduate of Paine College in Augusta, Georgia, and the recipient of master's degrees from American University (1944), and Yale University (1947), Lomax worked as a newspaperman from 1941–58. He became a freelance writer and briefly (1964 to 1968) worked as a broadcast news commentator. In the fall of 1969, he joined the faculty of Hofstra University, in Hempstead, New York. Lomax's first major book *The Reluctant African,* won the Annisfied-Wolf Award in 1960, but he is probably best known for his *The Negro Revolt* (1962), an early analysis of the civil rights movement. He was a strong believer in equal rights but told college administrators that they should not give in to unreasonable black student demands or treat blacks preferentially. At the same time, he defended rebellious young people as being correct about society's deficiencies. He also denounced moderation as being irrelevant in the face of the long travails of the black masses. At the time of his death, Lomax was working on a three-volume history of black Americans. In addition to the books listed above, Lomax wrote: *When the Word is Given; A Report on Elijah Muhammad, Malcolm X, and the Black Muslim World* (1963); *Mississippi Eyewitness: The Three Civil Rights Workers, How They Were Murdered* (1964); *Thailand, The War That Is, The War That Will Be* (1967); *To Kill a Blackman* (1969).

Selected Bibliography Eric Foner, ed., *America's Black Past: A Reader in Afro-American History* (1970); *New York Times,* 1 August 1970.

John F. Marszalek

Lombard v. Louisiana,* 373 U.S. 267 (1963)** Only public education was directly affected by ***Brown v. Board of Education. Numerous state and local segregation laws governing aspects of public accommodations were left intact. Civil rights activists, believing such laws were immoral and unconstitutional, practiced civil disobedience and peacefully violated them, thus subjecting themselves to criminal prosecution for trespass, disorderly conduct, or criminal mischief. The situation that gave rise to *Lombard v. Louisiana* was slightly different from other sit-in cases in that no state law or local ordinance required the management of McCrory Five and Ten Cent Store to deny service at its lunch counter to blacks. Both the mayor and the superintendent of police, however, had made recent public statements condemning sit-ins and stating that they would not be tolerated. The Supreme Court reversed the convictions that had been obtained under Louisiana's criminal mischief statute. Writing for the majority, Chief Justice Earl Warren denied that there had been merely private discrimination. Although no law required management to deny integrated service, the state could "achieve the same result by an official command which has at least as much coercive effect as an ordinance." There had been "state action" prohibited by the equal protection clause of the **Fourteenth Amendment.**

Selected Bibliography Abe Fortas, *Concerning Dissent and Civil Disobedience* (1968); Note, "State Action—Sit-Ins—Municipal Ordinances and Statements by Municipal Officials," *Arkansas Law Review* 18 (Spring 1964), 118–20; Louis H. Pollak, "The Supreme Court: 1962 Term," *Harvard Law Review* 77 (November 1963), 127–31.

Patricia A. Behlar

Long Hot Summer (1966) In 1966 the cry of "Burn, Baby, Burn" and the violent destruction of white business property in the ghettos reflected an outburst of suppressed black anger and pride. In March a recurrence of violence in the **Watts race riot** in the Los Angeles area left two dead and caused further property damage. In Chicago, Illinois, three nights of rioting, 12–15 July left two dead and over four hundred people arrested. Violence continued when marchers for desegregation, led by **Martin Luther King, Jr.,** in the Chicago suburb of Cicero, were stoned by a white mob of nearly four thousand. As black rage spread to Dayton, Ohio; Milwaukee, Wisconsin; Detroit, Michigan; San Francisco, California; and Cleveland, Ohio; President Lyndon B. Johnson called out the National Guard. On July 18 the black area of Hough in Cleveland exploded. Six days of rioting left 4 dead, 50 injured, 164 persons arrested, and widespread property damage. On 9 August Detroit's Kercheval area continued this pattern with three days of rioting. The long hot summer of 1966 reflected a paradoxical change in the pursuit of social change in America, from a **nonviolent** multiracial civil rights movement to one of **Black Power.**

Selected Bibliography Issac Balbus, *The Dialectics of Legal Repression* (1982); *Kerner Commission Report of the National Advisory Commission on Civil Disorders* (1968); J. Paul Mitchell, ed., *Race Riots in Black and White* (1970); Bayard Rustin, "The Lessons of the Long Hot Summer," *Commentary* 44 (1967), 39–45; Harvard Sitkoff, *The Struggle for Black Equality, 1954–1980* (1981).

Malik Simba

Longview Race Riot (1919) This riot in a small northeast Texas town sprang from the lynching of a black man in June, 1919 for the alleged rape of a white woman. A local black school teacher, Samuel L. Jones, reported in the *Chicago Defender* that the white woman despaired the loss of her black lover. Whites also became annoyed at Dr. C. P. Davis, who formed the Negro Business Men's League to prevent the exploitation of black cotton farmers in the area. Such black unity alarmed whites who decided to teach blacks a lesson by attacking the author of the *Defender* story. A white mob came to get Jones who sought refuge in Davis's home where the physician and members of the Negro Business Men's League used their weapons to protect him. In the gun battle, several whites were wounded. The retreating whites then set fire to black homes and businesses, including Dr. Davis's office. During the melee, a black school principal was flogged and several prominent blacks were run out of town. Texas Rangers arrived on 12 July 1919 to restore order.

Selected Bibliography Robert H. Brisbane, *The Black Vanguard* (1970); John Hope Franklin and Alfred A. Moss, Jr., *From Slavery to Freedom*, 8th ed. (2000); William M. Tuttle, Jr., "Violence in a 'Heathen' Land: The Longview Race Riot of 1919," *Phylon* 33 (1972), 324–33; Arthur I. Waskow, *From Race Riot to Sit-in: 1919 and the 1960s: A Study in the Connections between Conflict and Violence* (1966).

Lee E. Williams, II

Louis, Joe (13 May 1914, Chambers County, Ala.–12 April 1981, Las Vegas, Nev.). Born Joe Louis Barrow in a sharecropper's cabin in rural Alabama, Louis lost his father to a mental breakdown when he was two years old. In 1916 his mother married Pat Brooks who in 1926 moved the family to Detroit, Michigan, for economic betterment. Young Joe, a quiet child with a speech impediment, learned how to box for self-protection in his tough neighborhood. His first amateur fight saw him knocked down several times, but the

Joe Louis, 1941. © Library of Congress.

next time he climbed into the ring he won the 1933 Detroit Golden Gloves Light Heavyweight Championship. He turned professional under black managers and quickly rose to the top of the heavyweight class. In 1935 he defeated Primo Carnera and Max Baer, but in 1936 the German champion, Max Schmeling, knocked him out. In 1936 he defeated James J. Braddock for the world heavyweight championship, and in one of the most famous battles in ring history he demolished Schmeling in the first round of their 1938 rematch. He took on all comers, spent World War II in the U.S. Army Special Services, and retired in 1949 having defended his title 25 times and holding the championship a record number of years. His later comeback attempt was a failure.

Joe Louis was the first universally admired black athlete. To African Americans, he represented black success in the white world; to whites, he was the nonthreatening symbol of American patriotism. When he defeated Schmeling, the American public saw it as a victory of American democracy over German Nazism. His World War II activities further buttressed his patriotic reputation. Although he was hardly the paragon of virtue he was made out to be and although he always remained silent on race relations, Joe Louis is a major figure in the civil rights movement. He opened doors for later black athletes and helped make possible black successes in American society as a whole. Sports writer Jimmy Cannon's famous line perhaps summarized Joe Louis's image in the American mind most succinctly: "He is a credit to his race—the human race."

Selected Bibliography John U. Bacon, "He Ain't Gentle, But He's a Real Gentlemen," *Michigan History* 81 (No. 5, 1997), 10–15; Lenwood G. Davis, *Joe Louis: A Bibliography of Articles, Books* . . . (1983); Art Evans, "Joe Louis as a Key Functionary: White Reactions toward a Black Champion," *Journal of Black Studies* 16 (No. 1, 1985), 95–111; Chris Mead, *Champion-Joe Louis: Black Hero in White America* (1985), condensed in *Sports Illustrated*, 16, 23 September 1985; Barney Nagler, *Brown Bomber* (1972).

John F. Marszalek

Louisville, New Orleans, and Texas Railway Company v. Mississippi, 133 U.S. 587 (1890)

In March 1888 Mississippi became the second southern state to enact legislation requiring all railroads doing business in the state, except for street railways, to segregate passengers by race. The law mandated that carriers had to provide separate passenger cars for each race, or to provide separate facilities in each car. The Louisville, New Orleans, and Texas Railroad challenged the law in the state's courts, claiming that the new law was burdensome to railroads and that it interfered with interstate commerce. The state supreme court upheld the law in 1889, and the case was appealed directly to the U.S. Supreme Court. On 3 March 1890 the highest court rendered its decision in favor of the state of Mississippi. The majority opinion written by Justice David Brewer declared that the state may compel a railway "to provide separate cars or compartments . . . equal in accommodations . . . to be used separately by individuals of both races," but it reserved judgment as to whether the state could require individuals to use separate facilities. The court would render that judgement six years later in the **Plessy v. Ferguson** case. This 1890 case, however, did send a legal signal to the southern states. By 1891 six other states had also enacted separate coach laws.

Selected Bibliography Charles A. Lofgren, *The Plessy Case: A Legal-Historical Interpretation* (1987); Catherine A. Barnes, *Journey from Jim Crow: The Desegregation of Southern Transit* (1983).

Larry T. Balsamo

Loving v. Virginia, **388 U.S. 1 (1967)** Richard Perry Loving was white; Mildred Delores Jeter was not; therefore, Virginia law prohibited their marriage. They went to Washington, D.C., in June 1958 to be married, and then they lived together in Caroline County, Virginia. Convicted in January 1959 of violating the state's antimiscegenation law, they were given the minimum sentence the law permitted, one year each in jail (although the law required the penitentiary), such sentence to be suspended if they left the state for 25 years. They moved to Washington, D.C., but in 1963 they initiated a challenge to the constitutionality of the law that had led to their banishment. In March 1966, the Virginia Supreme Court of Appeals upheld the statute and the conviction (206 Va. 924), but, in June 1967, the U.S. Supreme Court unanimously ruled that the **Fourteenth Amendment**'s "equal protection" and "due process" provisions denied any state the authority to use racial classifiers to determine which citizens could intermarry. Such statutes fell in the 16 states where they were still on the books.

Selected Bibliography ACLU Papers, Princeton University; Peter Wallenstein, *Tell the Court I Love My Wife: Race, Marriage, and the Law—An American History* (2002).

Peter Wallenstein

Lowery, Joseph E. (6 October 1921, Huntsville, Ala.–). This United Methodist minister was a pioneer of the modern civil rights movement, perhaps most significantly in his role as one of the several cofounders along with **Martin Luther King, Jr.,** of the **Southern Christian Leadership Conference** (SCLC). He served as a vice president of the SCLC in its earliest years, was chairman of the board from 1967–77, and then long served as president. Lowery began his ministerial career in 1952 at Mobile, Alabama's, Warren Street United Methodist Church. From 1964–68 he pastored St. Paul United Methodist Church in Birmingham, Alabama, and in 1968 he began his longest assignment when he became pastor at the Central United Methodist Church in Atlanta, Georgia. He led civil rights activities in Mobile, in Nashville, Tennessee, and Birmingham, and he was part of the historic *Sullivan v. New York Times* libel decision. He has also led antiapartheid efforts against South Africa. Despite these significant activities, Lowery has been overshadowed by more famous civil rights advocates. Even after King's death and **Ralph David Abernathy**'s retirement, Lowery's ascension to head the SCLC did not make his name a household word. Even the most thorough account of the SCLC during the days of Martin Luther King mentions him only in passing. In 1998 he retired from his 20-year term as president of the SCLC and the pastorship of Central United Methodist Church. In 2000 he was the first recipient of the Walter P. Reuthers Humanitarian Award. In 2003, he continued his public involvement, serving as chairman of the Black Leadership Forum, which he had helped co-found in the late 1970s.

Selected Bibliography Adam Fairclough, *To Redeem the Soul of America, The Southern Christian Leadership Conference and Martin Luther King, Jr.* (1987); Ron Harris, "Dr. Joseph Lowery, The Man Who's Reviving SCLC," *Ebony* 35 (November 1979), 53–56; Philadelphia *Tribune* 12 January 2001; *Who's Who in America*, 44th ed. (1986–87).

John F. Marszalek

Lowndes County Freedom Organization   The Lowndes County Freedom Organization (LCFO) was created during the early spring of 1965 in Lowndes County, Alabama, by members of the **Student Nonviolent Coordinating Committee** (SNCC) in an effort to counteract the political domination of the white supremacist state Democratic party. Pointing to the 1964 failure of the **Mississippi Freedom Democratic Party,** SNCC activist **Stokely Carmichael** argued that the time had come for an independent black political party. Lowndes County, whose population of fifteen thousand included twelve thousand blacks, none of whom were registered to vote at the beginning of 1965, was a promising starting point for such an independent movement. The LCFO

Blacks waiting to vote in Lowndesboro precinct, Alabama, November 1966. © Carl and Ann Braden Collection, Wisconsin Historical Society.

became the first political organization in the civil rights movement to be identified with the symbol of the black panther. Chosen as a contrast to the Democratic party's symbol, the white rooster, the panther was viewed by LCFO members as a representation of the power and determination of its organization and would later be adopted as the symbol of the **Black Panther** movement in Oakland, California. The LCFO proved its strength in a 8 May 1965 local election when nine hundred of two thousand registered blacks in Lowndes County risked their personal safety and followed LCFO instructions to "Vote the panther, then go home." The LCFO proved significant to the civil rights movement by defining the growing differences between SNCC and the **Southern Christian Leadership Conference.** The latter had urged Lowndes County blacks to remain in the Democratic party. LCFO also furthered the development of independent black political activity.

Selected Bibliography Bettye Collier-Thomas and V. P. Franklin, eds., *Sisters in the Struggle: African American Women in the Civil Rights–Black Power Movement* (2001); Townsend Davis, *Weary Feet, Rested Souls: A Guided History of the Civil Rights Movement* (1998); Adam Fairclough, *To Redeem the Soul of America: The Southern Christian Leadership Conference and Martin Luther King, Jr.* (1987); Raymond L. Hall, *Black Separatism in the United States* (1978); Henry Hampton and Steve Fayer, *Voices of Freedom: An Oral History of the Civil Rights Movement from the 1950s through the 1980s* (1990); Edward Peeks, *The Long Struggle for Black Power* (1971); Emily Stoper, *The Student Non-Violent Coordinating Committee: The Growth of Radicalism in a Civil Rights Organization* (1989).

JoAnn D. Carpenter

Lucy, Autherine Juanita (5 October 1929, Marengo County, Ala.–). A tenant farmer's daughter and the youngest of 10 children, Lucy had earned an undergraduate degree from Miles College, a black Methodist institution in Birmingham in 1952. For the next four years she taught high school English and Sunday school in Birmingham. In March, April, and September 1956 national attention centered on her when the University of Alabama at Tuscaloosa, after a three-year court fight, admitted her as its first black student. Twenty-six-year-old Lucy sought a graduate degree in library science. The disruption at the school caused by mob violence of white segregationists, some from outside the Tuscaloosa area, compelled the university's board of trustees to expel Lucy for her own safety and because she accused the university of conspiring with the white mob against her. Lucy's bravery and courage came at a time when blacks, as exemplified in the two-month-old **Montgomery bus boycott,** had come to understand that they could meet the challenge of segregationists. In 1992, Lucy received a master's degree in elementary education from the university that had expelled her 36 years earlier.

Selected Bibliography John Hope Franklin and Alfred A. Moss, Jr., *From Slavery to Freedom: A History of Negro Americans*, 8th ed. (2000); Gilbert Osofsky, *The Burden of Race: A Documentary History of Negro-White Relations in America* (1967); Harry A. Ploski and James Williams, eds., *The Negro Almanac: A Reference Work on the Afro-American* (1983); *Progressive* 48 (July 1984), 15–19.

Linda Reed

Lucy v. Adams, **134 F. Supp. 235 (W.D. Ala., 1955)**   Autherine Lucy and Polly Myers applied for admission to the University of Alabama in 1950. They were eminently qualified, both having performed well at a segregated college. They completed their registration by mail and enrolled for the fall term. They had arranged for classes and received dormitory assignments in advance. School officials turned them away when they arrived on campus. After dealing with the school for more than a year, the women sued. A federal judge ruled in their favor. The university could not deny them admission because of their race. The university successfully appealed this decision. Attorneys for Lucy then carried the case to the U.S. Supreme Court. That winter, the university reluctantly admitted Autherine Lucy. It denied enrollment to Myers, however, because of her marital status and alleged misconduct. Violence followed. Throngs of students and townspeople staged riots by burning crosses to protest the admission of a "Negro." University officials dismissed Lucy temporarily, supposedly for her own safety. The board of trustees later expelled her for allegedly making accusations about the university's racial policy. The state legislature supported this action and threatened to stop appropriations to "Negro" colleges and to discontinue its out-of-state tuition program for minority students.

Selected Bibliography Thomas I. Emerson, David Haber, and Norman Dorsen, *Political and Civil Rights in the United States* (1967); "Free Choice Plan Is Likely to Come before Alabama Legislature in May," *Southern School News* (April 1957); Raymond Wolters, *The Burden of Brown: Thirty Years of School Desegregation* (1984).

Stephen Middleton

Lynch, John Roy   (10 September 1847, Vidalia, La.–2 November 1939, Chicago, Ill.). Mississippi Reconstruction black politician, Republican party leader, businessman, army officer, and lawyer, Lynch was a leading figure in black America during the late nineteenth and early twentieth centuries. Born to an Irish immigrant and his slave wife, he lived in slavery until 1863. Appointed a justice of the peace in 1869, he was also almost immediately elected to the Mississippi House of Representatives and in 1872 became its speaker. That same year he was elected for the first of his three terms to the U.S. House of Representatives. His staunch support for the **Civil Rights Act of 1875** was his major accomplishment. He was also the first black man to be a keynote speaker at a national political convention (1884). He held several governmental and army posts in Republican administrations, was active in real estate and law in Mississippi, Washington, and Chicago, and published a revisionist book and two articles on Reconstruction in **The Journal of Negro History.** Upon his death he was buried at the Arlington National Cemetery with full military honors.

Selected Bibliography Rayford W. Logan and Michael R. Winston, eds., *Dictionary of American Negro Biography* (1982); John R. Lynch, *The Facts of Reconstruction* (1918); John R. Lynch, "Some Historical Errors of James Ford Rhodes," *Journal of Negro History* 2 (October 1917), 345–68; John R. Lynch, "More about the Historical Errors of James Ford Rhodes," *Journal* *of Negro History* 3 (April 1918), 139–57; John R. Lynch, *Reminiscences of an Active Life* (1970); James A. McLaughlin, "John R. Lynch" (Ph.D. diss., Ball State University, 1981); George A. Sewall, *Mississippi Black History Makers* (1977).

John F. Marszalek

Lynching   In this extralegal practice members of a mob, using some form of injury or execution, punish an individual for allegedly breaking some law or local custom. The origin of the term can be traced to Revolutionary Virginia where an American colonel, Charles Lynch, established an extralegal court, punishing suspected criminals and Tories. In time, "lynching" became a popular means for social control on the southern and western frontiers.

Throughout the history of lynching, a variety of methods were employed: floggings, brandings with acid, tarring and feathering, hangings, burnings, and dragging behind automobiles. From Reconstruction to the middle of the twentieth century, lynching was primarily used to intimidate, degrade, and control black people in the southern and border states. Increasingly during this period the use of the term *lynching* became associated with mob action resulting in death. The most reliable statistics, gathered by the **Tuskegee Institute,** show that from 1882 to 1968 at least 4,743 deaths by lynching occurred (nearly

Two African American men, lynched, Marion, Indiana, 1930. © Library of Congress.

three-fourths were black), mostly in the South. In the 10 years from 1 January 1918 through 1927, at least 39 blacks were burned alive. White Southerners perpetuated the myth that lynching was necessary to protect white women from assaults by black men. In fact, less than 30 percent of the recorded lynchings of blacks related to this particular crime. Organizations such as the **Association of Southern Women to Prevent Lynching** (ASWPL), founded in 1930, fought lynching at the local level. The **NAACP** lobbied unsuccessfully to obtain a federal antilynching bill. After 1921 the number of reported lynchings declined, possibly as a result of the attention focused on the practice. Finally, the **Civil Rights Act of 1968** authorized the federal government to intervene if citizens were being deprived of their constitutional rights, whether or not death resulted.

Selected Bibliography James Elbert Cutler, *Lynch-Law: An Investigation into the History of Lynching in the United States* (1905); Neil R. McMillen, *Dark Journey: Black Mississippians in the Age of Jim Crow* (1989); Walter White, *Rope and Faggot: A Biography of Judge Lynch* (1929); Robert L. Zangrando, *The NAACP Crusade against Lynching, 1909 to 1950* (1980).

Horace D. Nash

***Lyons v. Oklahoma*, 332 U.S. 596 (1944)** This case originated in Oklahoma in 1939 when the police arrested W. D. Lyons, a black man, for allegedly murdering Elmer Rogers, a white man, and his family. Lyons was an unsettled 22-year-old whom the police regularly suspected for most area crimes. After a 10-hour interrogation, which included a beating, Lyons confessed. After he was convicted and sent to prison, he admitted having committed the crime on two separate occasions. His attorneys appealed his conviction, and the Supreme Court ruled that the police had coerced Lyons's confession. Because he had confessed voluntarily on two successive occasions, however, the Court approved those confessions, holding that the first confession did not control the later ones. Satisfied that it had protected Lyons's civil rights, the Court upheld his conviction.

Selected Bibliography "Recent Cases," *George Washington Law Review* 13 (1944), 109–11; Paul G. Kauper, *Constitutional Law* (1966); Otis H. Stephens, *The Supreme Court and Confessions of Guilt* (1973); Mark V. Tushnet, *Making Civil Rights Law: Thurgood Marshall and the Supreme Court, 1936–1961* (1994).

Stephen Middleton

M

McDew, Charles   (23 June 1938, Massillon, Ohio–). As a student at South Carolina State College, McDew organized some four hundred students in lunch counter demonstrations in Orangeburg, South Carolina. He was active on the Freedom Ride Coordinating Committee and served as **Student Nonviolent Coordinating Committee** (SNCC) chairman. He participated in the 1961 protests in McComb, Mississippi, over the murder of **Herbert Lee** and the arrest of Brenda Travis. In 1962 he was arrested along with Bob Zellner in Baton Rouge, Louisiana, on criminal anarchy charges. Subsequently, the charges were dropped. Much of McDew's expertise was used by SNCC to raise funds in the northern states. In June 1963 he was replaced as SNCC chairman by **John Lewis.** In 1988 he attended a SNCC reunion at Shaw University in Raleigh North Carolina.

Selected Bibliography Clayborne Carson, *In Struggle: SNCC and the Black Awakening of the 1960s* (1981); James Forman, *The Making of Black Revolutionaries* (1985); Casey Hayden, Howard Zinn, Charles McDew, and Bob Mantis, "Old Hands, Young Blood: Student Activist of the 60s Meet Campus Organizers of the 80s," *Southern Exposure* 16 (No. 2, 1988), 46–53; Howard Zinn, *SNCC: The New Abolitionists* (1964).

Ray Branch

McDonald v. Key, **224 F.2d 608 (1955)**   One technique used by some southern states to discourage, harass, and defeat black candidates for public office was the racial identification requirement; it was particularly popular in the "massive resistance" period following the Supreme Court's 1954 invalidation of racial segregation in public education. Oklahoma had such a requirement; its constitution defined "Negro" as a person of African descent; all others were considered "white." Statutory law required blacks to be racially identified on ballots; all others were presumed white and were racially unidentified. A. B. McDonald, a black aspirant for U.S. senator, sued members of the state election board for placing "Negro" after his name on the ballot, alleging that the statutory requirement violated the equal protection clause of the **Fourteenth Amendment.** The federal district court dismissed his complaint, holding that the designation of race was descriptive, not discriminatory. The Court of Appeals for the Tenth Circuit reversed this decision. The appellate court held that the requirement that candidates of only one race be identified while candidates of other races were racially unidentified discriminated against blacks and therefore violated the equal protection clause. The board members appealed to the Supreme Court, which refused to hear the case.

Selected Bibliography Richard Claude, *The Supreme Court and the Electoral Process* (1970); Jack Greenberg, *Race Relations and American Law* (1959).

Earlean M. McCarrick

McGill, Ralph (5 February 1898, Soddy, Tenn.–3 February 1969, Atlanta, Ga.). A "Southern Liberal," this editor and publisher of the *Atlanta Constitution* was a loyal critic of the South, especially its racial mores. He entered Vanderbilt University, in Nashville, Tennessee, in 1917 for a year, left for a brief stint in the U.S. Marine Corps, and returned to the university in 1919. He promised to be a typical student—an athlete, fraternity member, and newspaper staffer—but his activism, outspokenness, and love of practical jokes resulted in his expulsion in April 1921. He then began his journalistic career with the *Nashville Banner*. In 1929 he left the *Banner* to become assistant sports editor of the *Atlanta Constitution*, then its associate editor in 1938, editor in 1942, and publisher in 1960. Paralleling his career was an impressive record of community service including numerous volunteer positions in support of education, Brotherhood Week, and other social causes. Although best known for his support of civil rights in the sixties, McGill actually advocated minority rights in the thirties, forties, and fifties, before it was fashionable to do so. His early views were more liberal than those of most people, but he did accept the doctrine of **separate but equal.** Although most white southerners considered him a "flaming liberal," by his own admission McGill could never be a crusader—because he could always see both sides of the issue even while criticizing one or the other. The best phrase to describe him would be the one others have applied to him; "the conscience of the South." Ralph McGill received numerous honors for his achievements, including a Pulitzer Prize for editorial writing (1958); the Medal of Freedom (1964); and at least nineteen honorary degrees. In addition to his other types of writing, he authored *The South and the Southerner.*

Selected Bibliography Barbara Barksdale Clowse, *Ralph McGill: A Biography* (1998); Cal M. Logue, *Ralph McGill: Editor and Publisher* (1969); Ralph McGill, *No Place to Hide: The South and Human Rights,* 2vols. (1984); Ralph McGill, *The South and the Southerner* (1959, 1963); Harold Martin, *Ralph McGill, Reporter* (1973).

Gary B. Mills

McKay, Claude (15 September 1889, Sunny Ville, Jamaica–22 May 1948, Chicago, Ill.). One of the best-known writers of the **Harlem Renaissance,** McKay migrated from Jamaica to the United States in 1912, and studied agriculture at **Tuskegee Institute** for several months and at Kansas State College for two years (1912–14). Abandoning his studies for a writing career in New York, McKay published his first volume of American poetry, *Harlem Shadows*, in 1922. This acclaimed book was followed by the novels *Home to Harlem* (1928), *Banjo* (1929), and *Banana Bottom* (1933), a collection of short stories *Gingertown* (1932), his autobiography *A Long Way from Home* (1937), a study of black urban culture *Harlem: Negro Metropolis* (1940), and the posthumous collection *The Selected Poems of Claude McKay* (1953). McKay did not become an American citizen until 1940. Viewing American racial problems from a West Indian perspective, McKay wrote poems reflecting nostalgia for his homeland, interest in the African continent and in the phenomenon of the city, and ambivalence about race in the United States. His main contributions to discourse about civil rights is to be located in such poems as **"If We Must Die,"** "America," "White House," "Baptism," and "The Lynching," models of the militant statement, and in his poems, essays, and reviews for Max Eastman's leftist magazine *The Liberator*.

Selected Bibliography Stephen H. Bronz, *Roots of Negro Racial Consciousness* (1964); Wayne F. Cooper, *Claude McKay: Rebel Sojourner in the Harlem Renaissance : A Biography* (1987); Arthur P. Davis, *From the Dark Tower: Afro-American Writers, 1900 to 1960* (1974); James R. Giles, *Claude McKay* (1976); James R. Keller, "'A Chafing Savage, Down the Decent Street': The Politics of Compromise in Clause McKay's Protest Sonnets," *African American Review* 28 (No. 3, 1994), 447–56; Tyrone Tillery, *Claude McKay: A Black Poet's Struggle for Identity* (1992).

Jerry Ward

McKissick, Floyd B. (9 March 1922, Asheville, N.C.–28 April 1991, Durham, N.C.). A black lawyer, judge, civil rights activist, businessman, and minister, McKissick's leadership role in the 1960s national civil rights movement capstoned nearly a lifetime of opposition to racial barriers. Educated at Atlanta's **Morehouse College** and North Carolina College, he desegregated the University of North Carolina Law School in 1951 and became its first black graduate. Establishing a law practice in Durham, he joined with black college students in 1960 when they launched the sit-in movement to protest segregated eating facilities. Their demonstrations dramatically escalated civil rights activities in North Carolina, and McKissick played an integral role in the effort. A longtime advisor to state **NAACP** youth groups, he concentrated much of his civil rights and legal activities on their behalf. Especially notable was his work in organizing and defending student demonstrators seeking to desegregate Durham's public accommodations.

McKissick gained national prominence as a civil rights activist through his association with the **Congress of Racial Equality** (CORE). In 1947, as a young army veteran, he had participated in CORE's earliest freedom rides, and when CORE established a Durham chapter in 1962, McKissick was named director. Under his leadership, Durham's branch flourished. His role in planning and organizing the massive demonstrations and negotiations of North Carolina's "Freedom Highways" campaign helped desegregate a major motel chain and gave him considerable influence in the national organization as well. In 1963, CORE named him National Chairman, a titular leadership post that came in response to the demands of more militant elements for a shift in emphasis in the civil rights program, and a larger black-led role in the group's governing structure. Afterward, McKissick moved closer to the increasingly influential militant camp, which proved advantageous to his aspirations. In 1966, he replaced **James Farmer** as national director.

By then, much of his race relations and civil rights philosophy had changed perceptibly. Disillusioned over a lack of substantive change in America's racial order, he became an exponent of **Black Power.** Although its meaning was unclear, the slogan frightened concerned moderate black leaders and conservative whites, many of whom abandoned the organization. McKissick and CORE embraced it and were branded as militants. Thereafter, McKissick increasingly directed CORE's attention to persistent black ghetto problems, but little of consequence was achieved. Nevertheless, he helped focus national concern on an area heretofore neglected in the general thrust of civil rights activism. In 1968, McKissick left CORE to launch his ambitious, but unsuccessful, "Soul City" model town and industrial project in rural North Carolina. At his death in April of 1991 he was serving as pastor of Soul City's First Baptist Church and capping a long legal career as a recent appointee to a North Carolina judgeship.

Selected Bibliography James Farmer, *Lay Bare the Heart: An Autobiography of the Civil Rights Movement* (1985); Floyd B. McKissick, *Three-Fifths of a Man* (1969); Floyd B. McKissick, "The Way to a Black Ideology," *Black Scholar* 1 (1969), 14–17; August Meier and Elliott Rudwick, *CORE: A Study in the Civil Rights Movement, 1942–1968* (1973); Charles Moritz, ed., *Current Biography Yearbook* (1968); Obituary, *New York Times*, 30 April 1991; Fred C. Shapiro, "The Successor to Floyd McKissick May Not Be So Reasonable," *The New York Times Magazine* (1 October 1967); "Soul City," *Newsweek* (14 August 1972).

Robert L. Jenkins

McLaughlin v. State of Florida, **379 U.S. 184 (1964)** This U.S. Supreme Court case involved the reversal of a lower court conviction of an unmarried interracial couple, Dewey McLaughlin and Connie Hoffman, also known as Connie Gonzalez. Florida law subjected unmarried interracial couples to a different standard of punishment than unmarried same-race couples. The conviction was reversed on 11 points of constitutional law. Five points were of primary significance to civil rights: (1) the defendants were convicted unfairly by a Florida statute that denied equal protection under the law to unmarried interracial couples; (2) the Florida statute did not adhere to the central purpose of the equal protection clause, which was to eliminate discrimination emanating from state official sources; (3) the Florida statute had racial classifications that were not relevant to any constitutionally acceptable legislative purpose; (4) the Florida court was not sensitive to policies of equal protection where state power used racial classifications in criminal statutes; and (5) an invidious form of discrimination was maintained through Florida's legal treatment of the same quality offense by different people in a different manner.

Selected Bibliography Derrick A. Bell, Jr., *Race, Racism, and American Law* (1980); Thomas I. Emerson, David Haber, and Norman Dorsen, *Political and Civil Rights in the United States* (1967); Loren Miller, *The Petitioners: The Story of the Supreme Court of the United State and the Negro* (1966); *New York Times*, 28 April, 8 December 1964; George Rossman, ed., "Review of Recent Supreme Court Decisions," *American Bar Association Journal* 51 (1965), 270.

Donald Cunnigen

McLaurin v. Oklahoma State Regents, **339 U.S. 637 (1950)** When he was almost seventy years old, George McLaurin decided he wanted to earn a doctorate in education. The University of Oklahoma admitted him but made him sit in the hallway at the classroom door, study inconspicuously on the library balcony, and eat in sequestration. He finally gained a classroom seat, but it was set apart and marked "reserved for colored." A unanimous Supreme Court, in an opinion by Chief Justice Fred Vinson, had little difficulty in finding that this treatment constituted a denial of equal protection under the **Fourteenth Amendment.** Once admitted, students may not be treated differently based on race. Like all cases of this type, the basic issue was the extent to which race may be used as an acceptable classification of persons for legal purposes. In a companion case, Vinson made it clear that the Court would maintain its tradition of deciding constitutional issues as narrowly as possible and only in the context of the specific facts presented by the case at hand. For that reason, the *McLaurin* case did not occasion a full scale review of the **separate-but-equal** doctrine, although it did serve as an obvious stepping stone to the 1954 decision that outlawed segregation (see *Brown v. Board of Education*).

Selected Bibliography Richard Kluger, *Simple Justice: The History of Brown v. Board of Education and Black America's Struggle of Equality* (1975); Irving Lefberg, "Chief Justice Vinson and the Politics of Desegregation," *Emory Law Journal* 24 (1975), 243–312; Mark V. Tushnet, *The NAACP's Legal Strategy against Segregated Education, 1925–1950* (1987); Melvin I. Urofsky, *A March of Liberty* (1988).

James E. Sefton

McQueen, Thelma "Butterfly" (8 January 1911, Tampa, Fla.–22 December 1995, Augusta, Ga.). Pioneering African American dancer, performer, and movie actress, McQueen first lived in Tampa and Augusta, before moving to Long Island, New York, where her mother worked as a maid. She graduated from the Babylon High School on Long Island, New York. Her mind set on becoming a performer, McQueen studied ballet and modern dance in New York City at Venezuela Jones's Negro Youth Project in the mid 1930s. Her spectacular off-Broadway performance on the Butterfly Ballet in *A Midsummer Night's Dream* earned her acclaim and a new name. She won leading roles in *Brown Sugar* (1936), *Brother Rat* (1937), and *What a Life* (1938). While per-

321

forming in the Benny Goodman–Louis Armstrong musical *Swingin' the Dream*, she caught the eye of David Selznick and was offered the role of Prissy, the maid, in the important epic film *Gone with the Wind* (1939). McQueen became the most famous African American actress of the early forties for her line "Lawdy, Miz Scarlett, I don't know nuthin 'bout birthin.'" She then starred in *Affectionately Yours* (1941), *Mildred Pierce* (1945), and *Duel in the Sun* (1947). However, McQueen's resolute refusal to continue to play "handkerchief head parts" almost ended her acting career, because little else was then available for dark-skinned African American actresses. Only in the late 1960s did she reappear in two off-Broadway musicals. She also appeared as Oriole in the television series *Beulah* before moving to other interests. She returned to Georgia and became involved in nursing and child welfare issues and services. By the early 1970s, she returned to New York City, enrolled in college and in 1975, at the age of 64, graduated with a bachelor's degree from the City College of New York. She produced and starred in bilingual plays especially at Harlem Public School Number 153. She also received minor acting roles in *Amazing Grace* (1974) and *The Mosquito Coast* (1986). In 1979, she won an Emmy Award for her role in a children's TV special. But in these years she spent most of her time in community work. In 1989, she appeared in the fiftith-anniversary celebration of *Gone with the Wind* and received wide recognition from a new generation for her work and her earlier stance against racism in America's performing arts industry. At the age of 84, McQueen died from burns received in a fire at her home in Augusta, Georgia.

Selected Bibliography Donald Bogle, *Blacks in American Film and Television* (1988); Thomas Cripps, *Slow Fade to Black: The Negro in American Film, 1900–1946* (1977); Eileen Landay, *Black Film Stars* (1973); Gary Null, *Black Hollywood: The Negro in Motion Pictures* (1975).

Glenn O. Phillips

Malcolm X (Malcolm Little; also used adopted religious name, El-Hajj Malik El-Shabazz) (19 May 1925, Omaha, Nebr.–21 February 1965, New York, N.Y.). One of the so-called black militants of the civil rights movement, he was the voice of the northern big city ghettoes. While blacks fought segregation in the South, he kept the frustration of their northern brethren in view.

Born the son of a Baptist preacher and **Marcus Mosiah Garvey** organizer, Malcolm Little experienced firsthand the brutality of American racism. Antiblack hate groups burned his house in Lansing, Michigan, and murdered his father. Welfare agencies broke up his family; his mother was committed to a mental institution, and he found himself in a detention home run by a paternalistic but racist white couple. He quit school after the eighth grade and drifted to Boston and eventually to Harlem, where he became involved in drugs, gambling, and prostitution. Returning to Boston, he was arrested for burglary and was sentenced to ten years in prison.

During the six and a half years he spent in prison, he used his time to discover the Lost-Found Nation of Islam **(Black Muslims).** When he left prison in 1952 he replaced his "slave name" of Little with an X, and he became actively involved as a Muslim recruiter. In 1954 he became minister of Harlem's Temple Number 7. He became famous quickly, rivaling Muslim leader, Elijah Muhammad (see **Elijah Poole**) in public notoriety. He organized mosques all over the country and in 1961 began *Muhammad Speaks,* the order's official newspaper. In 1958 he married Betty X Shabazz, with whom he had six children.

A major crisis came in 1963 when Malcolm X, already a symbol of unyielding black hatred for whites, said that President John F. Kennedy's assassination was a matter of "the chickens coming home to roost." (White society hatred, developed to suppress blacks, had reached out to cut down the president.) Elijah Muhammad, who for several years had begun to suspect his ever more successful lieutenant, suspended Malcolm for his remark. Malcolm resigned from the Black Muslims on 12 March 1964.

This split, like his years in prison, he used to further his education. He left for Mecca in April 1964 and toured the Middle East, where he met nonblacks who were not racists. As a result, he tempered his antiwhite rhetoric. He now blamed racism on western culture and founded the **Organization of Afro-American Unity** to unify blacks and to cooperate with sympathetic whites to arrest its scourge. He made another trip to Africa, but he remained too controversial to gain a broad following either among blacks or whites.

Malcolm X giving a speech. © Library of Congress.

On 14 February 1965 unknown assailants firebombed his house, and on 21 February 1965 he was gunned down during a New York speech. Three Black Muslims were found guilty of the crime, but scholars dispute the validity of their convictions.

Malcolm X had few concrete accomplishments, but his legacy is important, nonetheless. To white America, he was a teacher of hate, the symbol of "black pride": the refusal to apologize for one's blackness or to beg for what was inherently due any human being. He helped push a civil rights movement he did not support to take a more radical stance.

Selected Bibliography George Breitman, ed., *Malcolm X Speaks* (1965); Perry Bruce, *Malcolm: The Life of a Man Who Changed Black America* (1991); Louis A. De Caro, Jr., *Malcolm and the Cross: The Nation of Islam, Malcolm X, and Christianity* (1998); Louis A. De Caro, Jr., *In the Side of My People: A Religious Life of Malcolm X* (1995); Michael Eric Dyson, *Making Malcolm X: The Myth and Meaning of Malcolm X* (1995); David Gallen, *Malcolm X: As They Knew Him* (1992); Peter Goldman, *The Death and Life of Malcolm X* (1979); Malcolm X, *The Autobiography of Malcolm X* (1965); Robert L. Jenkins and Mfanya D. Tryman, *Malcolm X Encyclopedia* (2002); William W. Saler, Jr., *From Civil Rights to Black Literature: Malcolm X and the Organization of Afro-American Unity* (1994).

John F. Marszalek

Mansfield, Texas, School Integration Crisis (1956) Mansfield, 17 miles southeast of Fort Worth, compelled its 58 black students in 1956 either to attend a segregated elementary school, which had no indoor toilets, or to ride public buses to Fort Worth in order to attend high school. A federal court ordered it to allow blacks to attend its neighborhood public school, the first school district in Texas to be so ordered. Hundreds of angry parents daily ringed the white school, preventing black enrollment. The mob took over the town, as the mayor and others left the community. Governor Allan Shivers dispatched Texas Rangers to uphold segregation, and President Dwight Eisenhower did not interfere in the election year. In this and many other communities throughout the South and Southwest, the implementation of the 1954 *Brown v. Board of Education* decision was postponed for years.

Selected Bibliography Robert Burk, *The Eisenhower Administration and the Civil Rights Movement* (1984); George N. Green, *The Establishment in Texas Politics: The Primitive Years, 1938–1957* (1979); John Howard Griffin and Theodore Freedman, "Mansfield, Texas: A Report of the Crisis Situation Resulting from Efforts to Desegregate the School System," Anti-Defamation League; *Texas Observer*, 5, 12 September 1956; Robyn Ladino, *Desegregating Texas Schools: Eisenhower, Shivers, and the Crisis at Mansfield High* (1996).

George N. Green

March against Fear.   See Meredith March.

March on Washington   In 1963 **A. Philip Randolph,** who headed the **March on Washington Movement** in 1941, began to plan a second march. He involved **Martin Luther King, Jr., Roy Wilkins** of the **NAACP, James Farmer** of the **Congress of Racial Equality, Whitney M. Young, Jr.,** of the

National Urban League, and John Lewis of the Student Nonviolent Coordinating Committee, together with four whites—Mathew Ahmann, Dr. Eugene Carson Blake, Rabbi Joachim Prinz, and Walter P. Reuther for the organizing committee. Bayard Rustin was the person most responsible for the planning and efficient organizing of the demonstration. On 28 August 1963, over two hundred thousand people took part in the March on Washington, a peaceful demonstration of one hundred seventy thousand black Americans and thirty thousand white Americans. While they marched they sang the anthem of the civil rights movement, "We Shall Overcome," and carried banners and placards that called for decent housing and "Jobs and Freedom." The marchers assembled first on the grounds of the Washington Monument, where a distinguished group of white and black stars entertained them. Joan Baez sang the anthem of the movement, and Mahalia Jackson stirred the crowd with her powerful rendition of Negro spirituals. President John F. Kennedy endorsed the march, although he feared that violence might erupt and embarrass his administration. The march was also endorsed by several leading members of the Senate, including Hubert H. Humphrey, Jr., Jacob Javits, and George Aiken. The one great blow to the organizers was the failure of the executive council of the AFL-CIO to join. The program consisted mainly of speeches, and the list of speakers was long. After nine distinguished speakers

The March on Washington, August 28, 1963. © National Archives.

had raised their voices against injustice, King rose to the strains of the "Battle Hymn of the Republic." The crowd and the millions watching on television at home listened with a new expectancy. "I have a dream," he said, "that one day this nation will rise up and live out the true meaning of its creed: 'We hold these truths to be self-evident, that all men are created equal. . . .'" He dreamed of his brotherhood in Georgia and an end to oppression in Mississippi (see **"I Have a Dream"**). The press proclaimed the march a success. President Kennedy was pleased that the predicted violence and vandalism did not occur. The civil rights leaders were satisfied with their efforts and knew that 28 August 1963, had been a day never to be forgotten.

Selected Bibliography Taylor Branch, *Parting the Waters: America in the King Years 1954–1963* (1988); Clayborne Carson, *In Struggle: SNCC and the Black Awakening of the 1960s* (1981); David J. Garrow, *Bearing the Cross: Martin Luther King, Jr., and the Southern Christian Leadership Conference* (1986); Thomas Gentile, *March on Washington: August 28, 1963* (1983); David Levering Lewis, *King: A Critical Biography* (1970); Benjamin Muse, *The American Negro Revolution: From Nonviolence to Black Power, 1963–1967* (1968); Stephen B. Oates, *Let the Trumpet Sound: The Life of Martin Luther King, Jr.* (1982).

Arvarh E. Strickland

March on Washington Movement This movement came as a response to employment discrimination at the beginning of World War II. The idea for a march came in 1941 during a meeting of civil rights groups in Chicago. **A. Philip Randolph** liked the idea, and two weeks later, he began planning for a nationwide mass demonstration to protest against discrimination in defense industries. In May 1941, Randolph issued a "Call to Negro America to March on Washington for Jobs and Equal Participation in National Defense on July 1, 1941." Black organizations and the black press rallied to the cause. Local groups formed branches of the March on Washington Movement throughout the country. By June, estimates of the number expected to participate were as high as 100,000. At this point, the Roosevelt administration could no longer ignore the movement. When other efforts to have Randolph and the other leaders call off the march failed, President Franklin D. Roosevelt agreed to issue **Executive Order 8802,** which declared it national policy "to encourage full participation in the national defense program by all citizens of the United States, regardless of race, creed, color of national origin." The president also established the **Committee on Fair Employment Practices** to oversee the policy.

Selected Bibliography Herbert Garfinkel, *When Negroes March: The March on Washington Movement in the Organizational Politics for FEPC* (1959); Louis Ruchames, *Race, Jobs, and Politics: The Story of the F.E.P.C.* (1953); Harvard Sitkoff, *A New Deal for Blacks: The Emergence of Civil Rights as a National Issue* (1978).

Arvarh E. Strickland

Margold, Nathan Ross (21 July 1899, Jassy, Rumania–16 December 1947, Washington, D.C.). Born the son of migrants to the United States, in 1919 Margold earned an associate degree from the College of New York, and in

1923 an LL.B. cum laude from Harvard University Law School. In 1924 he was admitted into the New York Bar Association and went on to practice successfully as a private attorney. He was also a law professor at Harvard, the legal adviser for Indian Affairs at the Brookings Institute, and a special assistant to the U.S. attorney general. The most distinguished part of his career, however, related to his service from 1930 to 1933 as special counsel to the **NAACP.** After the stock market crash in 1929, the NAACP hired Margold to develop an agenda for improving African American rights. He prepared a detailed book-length study that called for an attack on school segregation and the **separate-but-equal** clause created by the U.S. Supreme Court in its 1896 *Plessy v. Ferguson* decision. That doctrine was the legal foundation of segregation in the United States. The Margold Report argued for an attack on segregation based on the fact that underfunded black southern schools were not equal. The Margold Report became the bible of the NAACP's legal campaign as well as the premier document of its **Legal Defense and Educational Fund** organization.

Selected Bibliography Jonathan Kaufman, *Broken Alliance* (1988); Genna Rae McNeil, *Groundwork* (1983); Mark V. Tushnet, *The NAACP's Legal Strategy against Segregated Education, 1925–1950* (1987); Vibert L. White, "Developing the 'School' of Civil Rights Lawyers: From the New Deal to the New Frontier" (Ph.D. diss., The Ohio State University, 1988).

Vibert L. White

Marshall, Burke (1 October 1922, Plainfield, N.J.–2 June 2003, Newtown, CT). A veteran of World War II, he was a practicing attorney in Washington, D.C., until he became assistant attorney general of the United States in charge of the Civil Rights Division, 1961–65. While serving in this post during the Kennedy and Johnson administrations, he directed the federal government's efforts to integrate the University of Mississippi in 1962 and served as a negotiator between Birmingham, Alabama, city officials and civil rights leaders during the 1963 desegregation campaign. Marshall also assisted in drafting the **Civil Rights Act of 1964.** He became a familiar figure because of television's coverage of his front line integration activities. In 1976 he was named chairman of the National Advisory Commission on Selective Service. He later served as Nicholas Katzenbach Professor of Law at Yale University.

Selected Bibliography Taylor Branch, *Parting the Waters: America in the King Years, 1954–1963* (1988); Carl M. Brauer, *John F. Kennedy and the Second Reconstruction* (1977); Joseph Goldstein, Burke Marshall and Jack Schwartz, eds., *The My Lai Massacre and Its Cover-Up: Beyond the Reach of Law* (1976); Burke Marshall, *Federalism and Civil Rights* (1964); New York Times, June 3, 2003.

Quintard Taylor

Marshall, Thurgood (2 July 1908, Baltimore, Md.–24 January 1993, Washington, D.C.). Lawyer, federal judge, Solicitor General, and U.S. Supreme Court justice, Marshall played a major role in the civil rights movement of the twentieth century. It is no exaggeration to title him "the lawyer of civil rights." Marshall was born in the year that the Springfield, Illinois, race

Thurgood Marshall (right) standing with Roy Wilkins and Walter White. © Library of Congress.

riot caused the birth of the **NAACP.** His father was chief steward for a number of important white social clubs, and his mother taught in a segregated black elementary school in Baltimore. His parents' example of racial pride, dignity, and learning helped mold his personality. In 1926 he began college studies at the all-black Lincoln University, holding odd jobs to defray expenses. He graduated in 1930 cum laude and entered **Howard University** Law School. At Howard he met **Charles H. Houston,** his later mentor, the school's assistant dean and later NAACP's legal counsel. Marshall graduated in 1933 at the head of his class and for the next five years practiced law in Baltimore and served as that city's NAACP chief counsel. In 1938, after two years of service as Houston's assistant at the NAACP legal office, Marshall became chief counsel himself. In 1939, the NAACP formed the **Legal Defense and Educational Fund** as a separate entity, and Marshall was its first director. It was in this capacity for the next 22 years that Marshall made his most profound impact on civil rights. He traveled all over the South and also argued before the Supreme Court in a variety of civil rights cases. Seldom combative, he usually stated his carefully prepared arguments in a calm, temperate voice. Without doubt, his most famous case was *Brown v. Board of Education* (1954), which resulted in the overthrow of the nineteenth-century *Plessy v. Ferguson* (1896), the constitutional underpinning for segregation.

Marshall continued his civil rights litigation until President John F. Kennedy nominated him to the Second Circuit Court of Appeals on 23 September 1961. Despite determined southern opposition, the Senate finally confirmed him on 11 September 1962. For the next four years, Marshall wrote over 100 opinions on a variety of subjects, but his civil rights and criminal law opinions stand out. On 13 July 1965 President Lyndon Johnson nominated him to be Solicitor General, and this time Johnson's political acumen prevented a repetition of the earlier opposition. As the nation's first black solicitor general, Marshall argued a wide variety of legal issues and gained experience and more respect. On 13 June 1967, President Johnson nominated Marshall to the Supreme Court. Once again southern senators unsuccessfully fought his nomination. On 1 September 1967 he took his seat as the nation's first and only black Supreme Court justice. Marshall was a consistent member of the court's so-called liberal wing, continuing his lifetime support of individual rights. The presidency of Ronald Reagan proved to be a particularly difficult time for him, and in 1987 he told a television interviewer that Reagan had the worst presidential record on civil rights since Woodrow Wilson. Because of age and health considerations, and because he felt increasingly isolated on a conservative court, he resigned on 27 June 1991 after writing a strong dissent against a conservative majority decision in *Payne v. Tennessee*. During the few years before he died, ill health limited his activities, but he continued to speak out forthrightly on contemporary issues.

Selected Bibliography Howard Ball, A *Defiant Life : Thurgood Marshall and the Persistence of Racism in America* (1998); Roger Goldman, *Thurgood Marshall Justice for All* (1992); John P. MacKenzie, "Thurgood Marshall," in Leon Friedman and Fred L. Israel, eds., *The Justices of the United States Supreme Court 1789–1969* (1969); Thurgood Marshall, "Race and the Constitution," *Social Policy* 18 (No. 1, 1987) 129–30; Mark V. Tushnet, *Making Constitutional Law: Thurgood Marshall and the Supreme Court, 1961–1991* (1997); Juan Williams, *Thurgood Marshall, American Revolutionary* (1998).

John F. Marszalek

Mason, Lucy Randolph   (26 July 1882, Clarens, Va.–6 May 1959, Atlanta, Ga.). "Miss Lucy," as she came to be known, was a social worker and union organizer for the Congress of Industrial Organizations (CIO). She was born the daughter of an Episcopalian priest and the heir of numerous American founding fathers. She began her career in 1914 as Industrial Secretary of the Richmond Young Women's Christian Association, eventually becoming its General Secretary. In 1931 she toured the South on behalf of women and child labor reform and wrote a pamphlet entitled *Standards for Workers in Southern Industry*. From 1931 to 1937 she was general secretary of the National Consumers League. From 1937 to 1941 she was at the height of her influence as southeastern public relations officer for the CIO. In this position, she utilized her southern roots and, less so, the threat of legal action or the intervention of her friend **Eleanor Roosevelt,** to help bring unions and labor reform to all parts of the South. Overcoming her own racial views, she matter-of-factly tried to organize both blacks and whites into single unions, thus causing at least a small chink in the wall of segregation.

Selected Bibliography *Atlanta Constitution*, 7, 9 May 1959; L. Lader, "Lady and the Sheriff," *New Republic* 118 (5 January 1948), 17–19; Lucy Randolph Mason, *To Win These Rights: A Personal Story of the CIO in the South* (1952); *New York Times*, 8 May 1959; *Dictionary of American Biography*, Supplement 6 (1980); John A. Salmond, *Miss Lucy of the CIO: The Life and Times of Lucy Randolph Mason, 1882–1959* (1988).

John F. Marszalek

Maverick, Maury (23 October 1895, San Antonio, Tex.–7 June 1954, San Antonio, Tex.). As a member of the U.S. House of Representatives from 1935 to 1939, Maverick gained a national reputation for his uncompromising defense of civil liberties and civil rights. He battled to prevent passage of bills abridging freedom of speech, and he was the only southerner to support the Gavigan antilynching bill. Maverick was defeated for reelection in 1938 and was then elected mayor of San Antonio. His popularity was eroded by his insistence on allowing the **Communist Party** to meet in the city auditorium and attempting to protect the Communists from rioters.

Selected Bibliography Richard B. Henderson, *Maury Maverick: A Political Biography* (1970); Maury Maverick Papers, University of Texas, Austin.

Bernard Donahoe

Mayor and City Council of Baltimore City v. Dawson*, 350 U.S. 877 (1955)** Robert M. Dawson filed suit in federal district court challenging racially segregated public beaches, arguing that compulsory segregation violated the equal protection clause of the **Fourteenth Amendment.** The district judge dismissed the suit. Although the Supreme Court's 1954 ***Brown v. Board of Education opinion specifically invalidated segregation only in education, it clearly called into question the constitutionality of compulsory segregation in any area. The district judge in *Dawson*, however, relied on pre-*Brown* Supreme Court and lower court decisions upholding segregation. The Court of Appeals for the Fourth Circuit reversed the district court, relying not only on *Brown* and its companion case of ***Bolling v. Sharpe*** outlawing educational segregation in Washington, D.C., but also on earlier Supreme Court opinions prohibiting racial discrimination in interstate commerce, within schools, and in the sale of property. The U.S. Supreme Court's opinion in its entirety was: "The motion to affirm is granted and the judgment is affirmed." That is, it simply upheld the court of appeals without comment. By 1955, the Supreme Court found it unnecessary to explain any further than it had done in *Brown* why states could not require segregation; in subsequent cases, it similarly invalidated state-required segregation in other public facilities with little or no discussion.

Selected Bibliography Albert P. Blaustein and Clarence Clyde Ferguson, Jr., *Desegregation and the Law: The Meaning and Effect of the School Segregation Cases* (1962); Albert P. Blaustein and Robert L. Zangrando, *Civil Rights and the American Negro: A Documentary History* (1968); Jack Greenberg, *Race Relations and American Law* (1959); C. Herman Pritchett, *Constitutional Civil Liberties* (1984).

Earlean M. McCarrick

Mays, Benjamin Elijah (1 August 1894, Epworth, S.C.–28 March 1984, Atlanta, Ga.). As a minister-educator and sixth president (1940–67) of Atlanta's **Morehouse College,** Mays's life developed naturally from three important experiences in his early life. Witnessing a lynch party intimidate his father made him a lifelong and eloquent foe of American racism. His early thirst for education and sense of calling to the Baptist ministry (ordained, 1921) further shaped his professional career. Interspersed with his graduations from Bates College (B.A., 1920) and the University of Chicago Divinity School (M.A., 1925; Ph.D., 1935), he and Joseph W. Nicholson published *The Negro's Church* (1933), the first sociological study of African American religion. From the deanship (1934–40) of **Howard University**'s School of Religion through his administration of Morehouse, Mays rose to become one of the most respected prophetic voices against segregation in the American black community, his articles and speeches often receiving nationwide black press coverage. He gave major addresses at over 250 colleges and received 28 honorary doctorates. He became a ministerial model for a young **Martin Luther King, Jr.,** who, by Mays's example, became convinced that one could combine a keen intellect with religious fervor and a prophetic consciousness. After King rose to leadership in the civil rights movement, Mays remained an unofficial senior advisor and delivered the eulogy at King's funeral. In 1970 he was elected the first African American president of the Atlanta School Board.

Selected Bibliography Lawrence Edwards, ed., *Walking Integrity: Benjamin Mays, Mentor to Martin Luther King, Jr.* (1998); Benjamin E. Mays, *Born to Rebel: An Autobiography* (1971); Benjamin E. Mays, *Disturbed About Man* (1969); Benjamin E. Mays, *The Negro's God* (1938); Obituary, *Time*, 9 April 1984; Henry J. Young, *Major Black Religious Leaders since 1940* (1979).

Andrew M. Manis

Memphis Race Riot (1866) Immediately after the Civil War, there was continual friction between the city's predominantly Irish police force and the black Union soldiers stationed there who were waiting to be mustered out of federal service. The police force was well armed but poorly disciplined, and the city's government was both corrupt and inefficient. The local press and the white populace were hostile to and uneasy with the presence of large numbers of armed and indifferently disciplined black troops in the community. Restless black soldiers were widely accused of committing acts of violence and theft. The riot began on 1 May 1866 when police attempted to arrest a black driver involved in a traffic accident with a white teamster. A group of black soldiers intervened. Gunfire swept the streets of Memphis. White civilians from the surrounding area soon joined with the police in attacking black neighborhoods in the southern part of the city. Fighting came to an end on 4 May 1866 after the intervention of regular U.S. troops. A congressional committee blamed the riot on the city's poor government and the police. Forty-eight people died, two of them white. Dozens were injured. Four black churches, 12 black schools, and 91 black dwellings were destroyed.

Selected Bibliography Eric Foner, *Reconstruction; America's Unfinished Revolution, 1863–1877* (1988); Jack D. L. Holmes, "The Underlying Causes of the Memphis Race Riot of 1866,"

Tennessee Historical Quarterly 17 (September 1958), 195–223; Bobby L. Lovett, "Memphis Riots: White Reaction to Blacks in Memphis, May 1865–July 1866," *Tennessee Historical Quarterly* 38 (Spring 1979), 9–33; George C. Rable, *But There Was No Peace: The Role of Violence in the Politics of Reconstruction* (1984); James Gilbert Ryan, "The Memphis Riots of 1866: Terror in a Black Community During Reconstruction," *Journal of Negro History* 62 (July 1977), 243–58.

Larry T. Balsamo

Menard, John Willis (3 April 1838, Kaskaskia, Ill.–8 October 1893, Washington, D.C.). Educated in Sparta, Illinois, and at Iberia College in Ohio, he became the first African American to be elected to Congress. During the Civil War, he was a clerk in the Department of the Interior. Following the war, Menard moved to New Orleans, Louisiana, and became active in Republican party politics, winning the party's nomination in 1868 to fill the unexpired term of one James Mann who died in August of that year. A bizarre three-way contest for the seat developed when Caleb S. Hunt challenged Menard's election and Simon Jones, a Republican, contested the right of the deceased James Mann to have held the seat. The case was referred to the committee on elections where it was decided it was "too early" to admit an African American to the United States Congress. Hence, Menard may be credited as the first African American *elected* but not the first to "serve" in the House of Representatives. In 1869, after the Fortieth Congress refused to seat Menard, he was appointed inspector of customs of New Orleans and, later, commissioner of streets. In addition to his political activities, Menard was editor of a newspaper, *The Free South*, which was later renamed *The Radical Standard*. Both these papers carried on an unceasing campaign for black civil rights.

Selected Bibliography Philip S. Foner, ed., *The Voice of Black America: Major Speeches by Negroes in the United States, 1797–1971* (1972); Philip S. Foner and George E. Walker, eds., *Proceedings of the Black National and State Conventions, 1865–1900*, vol. 1 (1986).

George E. Walker

Meredith, James Howard (25 June, 1933, Kosciusko, Miss.–). An African American civil rights activist in the 1960s and currently a conservative Republican, James Meredith received his early education in Mississippi and Jacksonville, Florida. He attended Jackson State College from 1960 to 1962. He won a major civil rights victory when he became the first black to gain admission to the University of Mississippi. Although federal troops were sent to protect his right to attend the university, Meredith's presence was continuously opposed by students and state officials. Despite such opposition, Meredith succeeded in earning his B.A. He continued his education at the University of Ibadan in Nigeria, West Africa, from 1964 to 1965 and at Columbia University where he earned his J.D. in 1968. Following publication in 1966 of his autobiography entitled *Three Years in Mississippi*, Meredith was shot and wounded as he and others carried out a civil rights march there (see **Meredith March**). Before he was shot, Meredith had told an interviewer that blacks would not achieve their civil rights objectives through nonviolent means. If blacks wanted their rightful place in America, he later insisted, they

James Meredith, about the time of his 1966 "March against Fear." © Library of Congress.

would have to struggle aggressively for it. Meredith, however, began to change from being a militant civil rights activist to a moderate one in the late 1960s. He became, for example, a stockbroker and then an investor. Meredith's new entrepreneurship was viewed by some as an attempt on his part to establish a model for black entrepreneurs. Others, however, viewed it as an abandonment of the civil rights movement. Despite these views, Meredith's positions on civil rights continued to be moderate ones until the 1980s. He became a Republican candidate for the U.S. Congress in 1972, but he did not abandon his attack on racial injustices. By the 1980s, however, Meredith had become a bona fide conservative Republican. During the 1988 presidential election he called on blacks to support the Republican party, asserting that only through that party would blacks be treated as full citizens. He declared in 1988 that "the greatest enemy" of African Americans were the liberal whites and their black counterparts. He also strongly opposed divestment in South Africa. In 1989, Meredith became the first professional black to serve on the staff of North Carolina Senator Jesse Helms, an extreme conservative who opposed making the birthday of **Martin Luther King, Jr.,** a national holiday and voted against civil rights bills. In 1997, Meredith published *Mississippi: A Volume of Eleven Books*. In 2003 he continued lecturing on conservative topics.

Selected Bibliography *Contemporary Authors* (1979); James H. Meredith Papers, University of Mississippi, Oxford, Mississippi; James H. Meredith, *Three Years in Mississippi* (1966); *Washington Times*, 7 September 1988; "White House Camp-In," *Newsweek*, 18 April 1966.

Amos J. Beyan

Meredith March   In the early afternoon of 5 June 1966, **James Howard Meredith** began a solitary inspirational "March against Fear." When he was wounded by a sniper's bullet one day after beginning his trek from Memphis, Tennessee, to Jackson, Mississippi, civil rights leaders rallied to his cause. After much haggling and mutual suspicion among the members of the leadership corps and after Meredith permitted them to continue in his name, the march resumed, led by **Martin Luther King, Jr., Stokely Carmichael,** and **Floyd McKissick.** What had begun as one man's protest against racism became a major media event, highlighted by arrests, by public displays of white prejudice, and by the charisma of King. Aware of King's mass appeal, Carmichael took advantage of his presence to popularize his new slogan, **"Black Power."** On 25 June, Meredith rejoined the march, which arrived in Jackson the following day. The march itself accomplished little in terms of concrete legislation. As the first major demonstration to occur after passage of the **Voting Rights Act of 1965,** it signaled the onset of a new, more militant phase of the movement, which would find success elusive in the waning years of civil rights activism.

Selected Bibliography Paul Good, "The Meredith March," *New South* (Summer 1966), 216; Joyce Ladner, "What Black Power Means to Negroes in Mississippi," in August Meier, ed., *The Transformation of Activism* (1970); Neil R. McMillen, "Black Enfranchisement in Mississippi: Federal Enforcement and Black Protest in the 1960s," *Journal of Southern History* (August 1977), 351–72; Harvard Sitkoff, *The Struggle for Black Equality, 1954–1980* (1981); Thomas A. Upchurch, "James Meredith," in Waldo E. Martin and Patricia Sullivan, eds., *Civil Rights in the United States* (1999); Milton Viorst, *Fire in the Streets: America in the 1960s* (1979); Nancy J. Weiss, "Creative Tensions in the Leadership of the Civil Rights Movement," in Charles W. Eagles, ed., *The Civil Rights Movement in America* (1986).

Marshall Hyatt

***Meredith v. Fair,* 305 F.2d 343 (5th Cir., 1962)**   The decision of the **United States Court of Appeals for the Fifth Circuit** in New Orleans, Louisiana, on 25 June 1962 to force the admission of **James H. Meredith,** a black Mississippian, to the University of Mississippi marked the first desegregation of a public school in the state. Twice rejected in 1961 by university authorities, Meredith had filed a complaint with the district court on 31 May 1961 charging racial bias. Rejecting the charge, the court ruled that Meredith was denied admission not because of his race but because he had failed to fulfill admission requirements. On appeal from Meredith, the Fifth Judicial Circuit Court reversed the district court's ruling. By a two-to-one decision, the circuit court's three-judge panel held that Meredith had indeed been denied admission solely because of his race and that Mississippi was maintaining a policy of segregating state schools. The circuit court instructed the district court to issue an injunction commanding the university officials to refrain from activities barring Meredith's admission to the school. The decision initiated a bitter struggle between the federal government and Mississippi authorities over Meredith's admission to the University of Mississippi.

Selected Bibliography Russell H. Barrett, *Integration at Ole Miss* (1965); Walter Lord, *Mississippi: The Past That Would Not Die* (1965); William J. Kupense, Jr., "Note," *Cornell Law Quarterly* 48 (1963), 743–53; James H. Meredith, *Three Years in Mississippi* (1966); Lester A. Sobel, ed., *Civil Rights, 1960–1966* (1967).

Amm Saifuddin Khaled

Merrick, John   (1859, Clinton, N.C.–6 August 1919, Durham, N.C.). Born a slave, Merrick worked at menial jobs in his youth, but by 1881 he had begun to display his natural talent for business. He joined a barber, John Wright, in a partnership; by 1896, he owned five barbershops, two for blacks and three for whites in Durham, North Carolina. Some of his customers included James B. Duke and William Jennings Bryan. He persuaded the Duke family to fund Lincoln Hospital in 1901, which became one of the leading black hospitals in the South. One of his greatest accomplishments was the founding of the **North Carolina Mutual Life Insurance Company** in 1898 with over $16 million of insurance in force by 1919.

He accompanied **Booker T. Washington** on his South Carolina tour in 1910, and he shared the black spokesman's economic ideology. Among Merrick's other contributions to the business community were banks, real estate, and drug stores.

Selected Bibliography Russell J. Adams, *Great Negroes: Past and Present* (1969); William J. Kennedy, *The North Carolina Mutual Story* (1970); Alain Locke, ed., *The New Negro: An Interpretation* (1925); Rayford W. Logan and Michael R. Winston, eds., *Dictionary of American Negro Biography* (1982).

Thomas D. Cockrell

The Messenger   Edited in New York by **A. Philip Randolph** and Chandler Owen, and billing itself as the "Only Radical Newspaper in America," *The Messenger* first appeared in November 1917. It endorsed black labor unions, women's suffrage, the Russian Revolution, and socialism. It attacked World War I, capitalism, Garveyism, and on occasion, the **NAACP.** The Old Negro, the editors charged, as represented by **W.E.B. Du Bois, Kelly Miller,** and **James Weldon Johnson,** were stooges of the white establishment. The magazine's black contributors included **Eugene K. Jones, George S. Schuyler,** and **T. Thomas Fortune.** By the 1920s *The Messenger* opposed the brutality of Bolshevism and included columns on music, theater, sports, and college life. The newspaper was a victim of financial reverses; the last issue appeared in 1928 endorsing Alfred E. Smith for president, proclaiming: "A Catholic President and a mixed cabinet of Jews, theists, Negroes and Indians would be an excellent thing for the soul of America." *The Messenger* remains an indispensable source for the study of the **Harlem Renaissance**'s compelling vitality.

Selected Bibliography Jervis Anderson, *A. Philip Randolph: A Biographical Portrait* (1973); William H. Harris, *Keeping the Faith: A. Philip Randolph, Milton P. Webster, and the Brotherhood of Sleeping Car Porters, 1925–1937* (1977); Theodore Kornweibel, *No Crystal Star: Black Life and the Messenger, 1917–1928* (1975).

Richard W. Resh

Mfume, Kweisi (24 October 1948, Baltimore, Md.–). Born Frizell Gray, he graduated from Morgan State University in 1976, and earned a Master's degree from the Johns Hopkins University in 1989. He was first elected to Congress in 1987 and continued holding his seat in the House of Representatives until 1996, when he resigned to become president of the **NAACP.** In that capacity, Mfume has helped reinvigorate the declining organization, clearing its debt and increasing its membership. In 2003 he remains one of the most visible and influential spokesmen for African Americans.

Selected Bibliography Mfume Kweisi and Ron Stadgill II, *No Free Ride: From the Mean Streets to the Mainstream* (1996); Jessie Carney Smith, ed., *Notable Black American Men* (1999).

Thomas Adams Upchurch

Michaux, Solomon Lightfoot (7 November 1884, Buckroe, Va.–29 October 1968, Washington, D.C.). It was Michaux's natural talents, fervor, and kindness, rather than education, that led him to reach the pinnacle of his ministry. He had a true gift for attracting and holding audiences. In the words of **Edward Franklin Frazier,** the sermons of this "Happy Am I Prophet" consisted "chiefly of tirades against sin, rowdy women, slot machines, whiskey, beer, and gamblers." His early career was undistinguished until he established the Church of God Movement in Newport News, Virginia, complete with local radio broadcasts. In 1928 he built a Church of God in the nation's capital where his radio—and later television—broadcasts went national. By 1934 his broadcasts were carried by more than 50 radio stations, allowing him to reach an estimated audience of twenty-five million. He also published a popular monthly paper called *Happy News,* issued a songbook *(Spiritual Happiness-Making Songs)*, and organized a group of religious singers for public appearances. His Happy News Café fed thousands at a penny a meal, and his Mayfair Mansion was one of the largest black housing developments in the country. His popularity peaked in the mid-1930s and began a slow decline into the early 1940s. By mid-decade he had faded away to mere local popularity. While some black leaders criticized his style and methods, Michaux helped to call the attention of whites to black problems, especially because of his close contacts with high government officials who considered him to be a spokesman for black religious groups.

Selected Bibliography E. Franklin Frazier, *The Negro Church in America* (1964); Constance McLaughlin Green, *The Secret City: A History of Race Relations in the Nation's Capital* (1967); Rayford W. Logan and Michael R. Winston, eds., *Dictionary of American Negro Biography* (1982); J. Gordon Melton, *Biographical Dictionary of American Cult and Sect Leaders* (1986); Lillian Ashcraft Webb, *About My Father's Business: The Life of Elder Michaux* (1981).

Gary B. Mills

Milholland, John E. (20 May 1860, Lewis, N.Y.–29 June 1925, New York, N.Y.). A wealthy, white, New York businessman who became an advocate of anti-imperialist and racial causes, Milholland began his career as a newspaperman and later became a manufacturer of pneumatic tube equipment. In 1903 he formed the interracial Constitution League for the purposes of establishing the rights of blacks through legal test cases. Founder of the New York Republican State Club, he was one of the leading critics of the government's handling of the 1906 **Brownsville, Texas, affray.** An early supporter of the philosophical underpinnings of **Tuskegee Institute,** he broke with **Booker T. Washington** over Washington's accommodationist views. In 1909 he was active in the founding of the **NAACP.**

Selected Bibliography Charles Flint Kellogg, *NAACP: A History of the National Association for the Advancement of Colored People* (1967); David Levering Lewis, *W.E.B. Du Bois: Biography of a Race, 1868–1919* (1993); August Meier, *Negro Thought in America, 1880–1915* (1963); Obituary, *New York Times,* 1 July 1925.

Ray Branch

Miller, Kelly   (18 July 1863, Winnsboro, S.C.–29 December 1939, Washington, D.C.). An African American education administrator and scholar, Miller received his early education at Fairfield Institute in Winnsboro. Following his studies there, he enrolled at **Howard University** where he earned his undergraduate degree in 1886. Miller did advanced studies at Johns Hopkins University, but financial reasons prevented him from graduating. After leaving Johns Hopkins, Miller taught at a high school in Washington, D.C. until he was offered teaching and administrative positions at Howard University in 1890. As a Dean of the College of Arts and Sciences at Howard, he redesigned the curriculum to address the problems faced by blacks. During his deanship, student enrollment increased. Although he was an integrationist, Miller was also an admirer of such radical black nationalists as Nat Turner, David Walker, Denmark Vesey, and Toussaint L'Ouverture.

Selected Bibliography Horace M. Bond, *Black American Scholars: A Study of Their Beginnings* (1972); Kelly Miller, *An Appeal to Conscience: America's Code of a Caste, A Disgrace to Democracy* (1918); Kelly Miller, *Out of the House of Bondage* (1914); Wilson M. Moses, *The Golden Age of Black Nationalism, 1850–1925* (1978); Earl E. Thorpe, *The Mind of the Negro: An Intellectual History of Afro-Americans* (1970).

Amos J. Beyan

Miller v. Johnson, 515 U.S. 900 (1995)   In this five-to-four ruling on a Georgia redistricting plan, the U.S. Supreme Court further tightened the limits that it had put on creating majority-black congressional districts in *Shaw v. Reno.* A district did not have to look bizarre on its face to violate the equal protection clause of the **Fourteenth Amendment,** the court held. It was enough to show that "race was the predominant factor motivating the legislature's decision to place a significant number of voters within or without a particular district." The decision has been sharply criticized for ignoring a political community of interest among blacks and for tacitly invalidating key provisions of the **Voting Rights Act.**

Selected Bibliography J. Morgan Kousser, *Colorblind Injustice, Minority Voting Rights and the Undoing of the Second Reconstruction* (1999); Stephan Thernstrom and Abigail Thernstrom, *America in Black and White: One Nation Indivisible* (1997); Carol M. Swain, "The Future of Black

Representation," in Stephen Steinberg, ed., *Race and Ethnicity in the United States, Issues and Debates* (2000), 172–78.

Manfred Berg

Milliken v. Bradley, **418 U.S. 717 (1974)**   In most northern cities, statutory school segregation had never existed or it had long since been done away with by the 1970s. Yet despite the absence of forced segregation, the school systems in metropolitan cities remained divided along racial lines. The inner cities, for the most part, were predominantly black, while the suburbs were almost entirely white. Black organizations like the **NAACP** found this situation intolerable. As long as racial imbalance continued in urban schools, they argued, blacks would receive an inferior education. In ***Swann v. Charlotte-Mecklenburg Board of Education*** (1971), the Supreme Court seemed to agree, maintaining that cities must bus students out of their neighborhoods if this was necessary to achieve integration. In *Milliken*, however, the Court rejected five to four a plan to integrate Detroit's schools with those of the outlying suburban areas. Writing for the majority, Chief Justice Warren Burger stated that there was no evidence that the suburban districts had operated segregated schools. The Court, he concluded, could not impose a busing plan on all school districts in order to remedy segregation in one district. The Court's ruling came in the wake of angry protests in Boston, Denver, and Pontiac, Michigan. Many white parents denounced what they saw as the destruction of the neighborhood school. This public opposition, together with the Court's moderate stance, slowed the process of metropolitan integration.

Selected Bibliography Derrick A. Bell, Jr., *Race, Racism, and the Law*, 2nd ed. (1980); Vincent Blasi, ed., *The Burger Court: The Counter-Revolution That Wasn't* (1983); Paul R. Diamond, *Beyond Busing: Inside the Challenge to Urban Segregation* (1985); J. Harvey Wilkinson, *From Brown to Bakke: The Supreme Court and School Integration, 1954–1978* (1979); Rowland L. Young, "Supreme Court Report," *American Bar Association Journal* 60 (1974), 1261–62.

Phillip A. Gibbs

Million Man March   The crowning achievement of **Louis Farrakhan** as the leader of the Nation of Islam was the Million Man March, the largest gathering of African Americans in the history of the United States. This historic event occurred on 16 October 1995, in Washington, D.C. The purpose of the Million Man March was to inspire black men to become more vocal advocates of racial, economic, and social justice in their communities. Reminiscent of the demonstrations of the Civil Rights era, the Million Man March was one of the most memorable civil rights events of the last decade of the twentieth century. It had its critics, but the day of atonement and black male solidarity was a stunning success.

Selected Bibliography Michael H. Cottman, *Million Man March* (1995); Florence Hamlish Levinsohn, *Looking for Farrakhan* (1997); Manning Marble, *Speaking Truth to Power* (1996); Kim Martin Sadler, ed., *Atonement: The Million Man March* (1996).

Leonne M. Hudson

The Million Man March takes place on the Mall in Washington, D.C., 16 October 1995, with the Capitol in the background, and a jumbo video screen featuring Nation of Islam leader Louis Farrakhan speaking to the right. © AP/Wide World Photos.

Mills v. Board of Education of Anne Arundel County, **30 F. Supp. 245 (D.Md., 1939)** Walter Mills, principal of a black school, challenged the constitutionality of a Maryland statute prescribing differing minimum salaries for white and black teachers in the state's segregated schools. He argued that the statute, on its face and in its application, violated the equal protection clause of the **Fourteenth Amendment.** The statutory minimum annual salary was $1,250 for white teachers and $765 for black teachers. Mills's initial suit against the state board of education was dismissed because, among other reasons, he had failed to include the county board as a defendant. He then instituted this suit against the county board. The federal district court found it unnecessary to determine whether the statute was unconstitutional on its face, noting that the statute did not necessarily require lower salaries for blacks. The court, however, held that its application was discriminatory and therefore unconstitutional—*no* black teacher in Anne Arundel county received as high a salary as *any* white teacher and the actual salaries of white teachers were twice as high as that of black teachers; it ordered a cessation of salary discrimination based on race. The court, however, refused Mills's request to order the board not to pay black teachers less than white teachers.

Selected Bibliography Jack Greenberg, *Race Relations and American Law* (1959); Richard Kluger, *Simple Justice: The History of Brown v. Board of Education and Black America's Struggle for Equality* (1976); "Recent Cases," *Harvard Law Review* 53 (1940), 669–71.

Earlean M. McCarrick

Miscegenation (Interracial Marriage)   Miscegenation, a term that originated during the Civil War, refers to interracial sex, interracial marriage, and laws banning either. Most American colonies and states enacted laws against marriages between Caucasians and African Americans. Maryland passed the first such law in 1664, when it declared that any white woman who married a slave would become a servant for as long as her husband lived, and her children would be born into slavery. In 1866, every southern state had such a law, and many northern and western states did too. Congressional Reconstruction brought an end to such legislation in seven southern states—every state of the former Confederacy except Virginia, Tennessee, North Carolina, and Georgia—but these states all restored their laws by the 1890s. Meanwhile, the U.S. Supreme Court upheld a related law in *Pace v. Alabama* (1883). Some twentieth-century laws (for example, in California and Mississippi) banned Caucasians from marrying either Asian Americans or African Americans. At the end of World War II, 30 states still had laws against interracial marriage, but the California Supreme Court overturned that state's law in 1948, and by 1965 only the 17 southern states retained such laws. The U.S. Supreme Court's 1964 decision in **McLaughlin v. Florida** overturned *Pace v. Alabama*, and its 1967 decision in **Loving v. Virginia** threw out the laws against interracial marriage everywhere—the last **Jim Crow** laws to fall.

Selected Bibliography Peter Wallenstein, *Tell the Court I Love My Wife: Race, Marriage, and the Law—An American History* (2002).

Peter Wallenstein

Mississippi Freedom Democratic Party   The Mississippi Freedom Democratic Party (MFDP) was organized during the summer of 1964 by members of the **Student Nonviolent Coordinating Committee** and other participants of the **Freedom Summer of 1964** project. The party was designed to challenge the power of the state Democratic party, which in June had included in its platform a clause rejecting civil rights and opposing the national party's commitment to that cause. Charging that the state regulars were disloyal to the national party, the MFDP attempted in August 1964 to secure delegate representation at the national Democratic convention being held in Atlantic City, New Jersey. **Hubert Humphrey** and Walter Mondale, working to preserve what was supposed to be an effortless renomination for Lyndon Johnson at the convention, proposed a compromise calling for Mississippi regulars to be seated if they swore loyalty to the national party and providing for the creation of two "at large" seats to be filled by members of the MFDP. The compromise failed when all but three of the party regulars walked out of the convention while the entire MFDP delegation, led by grass roots activist, **Fannie Lou Hamer,** was removed from the convention floor when they attempted to take the seats of the party regulars. The struggle of the MFDP promoted greater interest among many civil rights activists for the creation of a stronger independent black organization within the movement.

Selected Bibliography James C. Cobb, *The Most Southern Place on Earth: The Mississippi Delta and the Roots of Southern Regional Identity* (1992); Bettye Collier-Thomas and V. P. Franklin, eds., *Sisters in the Struggle: African American Women in the Civil Rights–Black Power Movements* (2001); Henry Hampton and Steve Fayer, *Voices of Freedom: An Oral History of the Civil Rights Movement from the 1950s through the 1980s* (1990); Chana Kai Lee, *For Freedom's Sake: The Life of Fannie Lou Hamer* (2000); Kay Mills, *This Little Light of Mine: The Life of Fannie Lou Hamer* (1994); Lynne Olson, *Freedom's Daughters: The Unsung Heroines of the Civil Rights Movement from 1830–1970* (2001); Kenneth O'Reilly, *Racial Matters: The FBI's Secret File on Black America, 1960–1972* (1989); Juan Williams, *Eyes on the Prize: America's Civil Rights Years, 1954–1965* (1987).

JoAnn D. Carpenter

Missouri ex rel. Gaines v. Canada, 305 U.S. 337 (1938)   Missouri denied Lloyd Gaines, a graduate of Lincoln University, in Jefferson City, Missouri, admission to the University of Missouri law school solely because of his race. Since Missouri had no law school for blacks, based allegedly on a lack of demand, the state paid tuition at law schools in Kansas, Nebraska, Iowa, or Illinois that would accept nonresident blacks. Chief Justice Charles Evans Hughes found this practice to be a denial of equal protection of the laws. He noted that Gaines had a right to admission to the university in the absence of "other and proper provision for his legal training within the state." Demand was a legitimate basis for state policy, but where a service was in fact provided, substantial equality of treatment was mandatory. The case is less a desegregation case than it is a further interpretation of the **separate-but-equal** rule in specific circumstances. However, it also marks the first of a 15-year series of cases that would conclude with **Brown v. Board of Education** in 1954.

Selected Bibliography Daniel T. Kelleher, "The Case of Lloyd Lionel Gaines: The Demise of the 'Separate-but-Equal' Doctrine," *Journal of Negro History* 56 (October 1971), 262–71; Richard Kluger, *Simple Justice: The History of Brown v. Board of Education and Black America's Struggle for Equality* (1976); Donald G. Neiman, *Promises to Keep: African-Americans and the Constitutional Order, 1779 to Present* (1991); Bernard H. Nelson, *The Fourteenth Amendment and the Negro since 1920* (1967); Mark V. Tushnet, *The NAACP's Legal Strategy against Segregated Education, 1925–1950* (1987).

James E. Sefton

Mitchell, Arthur W.   (22 December 1883, Chambers County, Ala.–May 1968, Petersburg, Va.). His election to the U.S. House of Representatives in 1934 marked a significant turning point in twentieth-century black politics. Running as a New Deal Democrat, Mitchell defeated black Republican **Oscar Stanton De Priest** (elected in 1928), which symbolized the enormous importance of Franklin D. Roosevelt's New Deal on black political life. The son of ex-slaves and raised in rural Alabama, Mitchell worked as office boy for **Booker T. Washington.** Imbued with Washington's philosophy, he studied at Talledega College and Snow Hill Normal and Industrial Institute and, in 1908, he founded his own school, Armstrong Agricultural College. Following service in World War I, he migrated to Chicago, where he became involved in real estate and law, joined the Republican party, and in 1928 served on the staff of Herbert Hoover's presidential campaign. Unable to break into De Priest's Republican organization, disillusioned with Hoover's depression policies, and inspired by the New Deal, Mitchell became a Democrat in 1934. Backed by local Democrats, he narrowly defeated De Priest and, during his eight years in Congress, distinguished himself primarily as a loyal Roosevelt supporter. His most celebrated civil rights effort came with his law suit against the Pullman Company for refusing him accommodations in the white section of the railway car. As a result of his legal action, the U.S. Supreme Court overturned the segregation policies of the Interstate Commerce Commission (see *Mitchell v. United States*). Mitchell's support of other civil rights issues, such as antilynching legislation, was less forceful and during the thirties he was often criticized by such black leaders as **Walter White** of the **NAACP.** He retired from Congress in 1942.

Selected Bibliography Dennis S. Nordin, *The New Deal's Black Congressmen: A Life of Arthur Wergs Mitchell* (1997); Christopher Robert Reed, "A Study of Black Politics and Protest in Depression-Decade Chicago: 1930–1939" (Ph.D. diss., Kent State University, 1982); Nancy J. Weiss, *Farewell to the Party of Lincoln* (1983); Robert L. Zangrando, *The NAACP Crusade Against Lynching, 1909–1950* (1980).

John B. Kirby

Mitchell, Clarence Maurice, Jr. (8 March 1911, Baltimore, Md.–18 March 1984, Washington, D.C.). For about 30 years, Clarence M. Mitchell, Jr., was the most conspicuous civil rights lobbyist in the halls of Congress, whose admirers called him "the 101st Senator." Born and raised in Baltimore, he received an A.B. degree from Lincoln University in Pennsylvania in 1932 and began working as a journalist for the *Baltimore Afro-American*. After stints with the Negro Youth Administration and the **National Urban League,** Mitchell joined the **Fair Employment Practices Committee** (FEPC) in 1942. With the FEPC expiring in 1946, he moved on to the **NAACP's** Washington Bureau, at first as its labor secretary and then as the head of the bureau. He also became the chairman of the **Leadership Conference on Civil Rights,** a coordinating committee of more than sixty organizations interested in promoting civil rights. During the momentous congressional battle for the civil rights legislation of the 1950s and 1960s, Mitchell was a highly visible and effective lobbyist who viewed bipartisanship as a key to success. Despite his enormous workload, he earned a law degree from the University of Maryland in 1962. For his untiring labor in the cause of civil rights, Mitchell received many honors, including a nomination to the U.S. delegation at the United Nations, the NAACP's **Spingarn Medal,** and the Presidential Medal of Freedom.

Selected Bibliography Hugh Davis Graham, *The Civil Rights Era: Origins and Development of National Policy* (1990); Denton L. Watson, *Lion in the Lobby: Clarence Mitchell, Jr's Struggle for the Passage of Civil Rights Laws* (1990).

Manfred Berg

Mitchell, Harry Leland (H. L.) (14 June 1906, near Halls, Tenn.–2 August 1989, Montgomery, Ala.). An agricultural day laborer as a boy and a sharecropper in his early teens, Mitchell understood well the problems of the rural poor. By the time he had graduated from high school he had become an atheist, evolutionist, and Socialist. In 1932, after hearing a speech by Norman Thomas, he joined the Socialist party and organized a local in Tyronza, Arkansas. Two years later, with Thomas's encouragement, he and Henry Clay East helped a small interracial band of sharecroppers around Tyronza to organize the **Southern Tenant Farmers' Union** (STFU). Throughout the remainder of the decade, the STFU, with Mitchell as secretary, attracted national attention to the plight of the South's croppers and tenants.

In the mid-1940s a remnant of the faction-ridden STFU became the National Farm Labor Union, later the National Agricultural Workers Union, with Mitchell as president. From 1948 to 1960 Mitchell directed the union's activities and lobbied in Washington on behalf of black, Hispanic, and white farmers and farm laborers in the South and West. In 1960, after the union was absorbed by the Amalgamated Meat Cutters and Butcher Workmen of North America, he became an organizer for an affiliate of the Amalgamated Meat Cutters and worked among food and agricultural laborers in the South. Mitchell was sometimes frustrated by what he considered the conservatism, bigotry, and narrowly economic aims of the labor establishment. Consequently, in 1969 he helped organize the Southern Mutual Help Association, which undertook educational, health, and housing projects among the black and white rural poor of Louisiana. Following his retirement in 1973, Mitchell devoted his remaining years to perpetuating the memory of the pioneering interracial work of the Southern Tenant Farmers' Union.

Selected Bibliography Donald H. Grubbs, *Cry from the Cotton: The Southern Tenant Farmers' Union and the New Deal* (1971); H. L. Mitchell, *Mean Things Happening in This Land: The Life and Times of H. L. Mitchell, Co-Founder of the Southern Tenant Farmers' Union* (1979); H. L. Mitchell, *Roll the Union On: A Pictorial History of the Southern Tenant Farmers' Union, as Told by Its Co-Founder, H. L. Mitchell* (1987).

Robert F. Martin

Mitchell, John R., Jr. (11 July 1863, Richmond, Va.–3 December 1929, Richmond, Va.). Mitchell took over management of the struggling *Richmond Planet* in 1884 and made it into a major black newspaper. The *Planet* forthrightly battled the rising tide of late nineteenth-century segregation, discrimination, and lynching, taking a more militant position than most black newspapers. When Richmond's street cars were segregated in 1904, Mitchell led the boycott that bankrupted the transportation company. His life was frequently threatened because of his paper's strong stands, but he fearlessly stood up to the threats. His close connections with the Republican party did not prevent his newspaper from criticizing the GOP when he thought it appropriate, for example, over the issue of American imperialism. But he remained in the party all his life. He served on the Richmond City Council from 1888–96, attended several national Republican conventions, and in 1921 unsuccessfully ran for governor on an all-black ticket. He founded the Mechanics Savings

Bank in 1902 and later became the first black member of the American Bankers' Association. When he died in 1929, his son Roscoe briefly succeeded him at the *Planet*, but the paper was sold in 1938.

Selected Bibliography Ann F. Alexander, "Black Protest in the New South: John Mitchell, Jr., and the Richmond Planet" (Ph.D. diss., Duke University, 1973); Willard B. Gatewood, Jr., "A Negro Editor on Imperialism: John Mitchell, 1898–1901," *Journalism Quarterly* 49 (1972), 43–50, 60; Rayford W. Logan and Michael R. Winston, eds., *Dictionary of American Negro Biography* (1982); Henry Lewis Suggs, ed., *The Black Press in the South, 1865–1979* (1983).

John F. Marszalek

Mitchell v. United States, **313 U.S. 80 (1941)**   Early challenges to segregation in interstate travel failed, but civil rights lawyers began to achieve some success on the eve of World War II. In 1937 U.S. Representative Arthur W. Mitchell boarded a train in Chicago en route to Hot Springs, Arkansas. He obtained first-class accommodations on a nonsegregated basis. When he reached Arkansas, the conductor ordered him to move to a segregated car so that the company could comply with a local segregation law. Mitchell objected but ultimately complied to avoid arrest. He filed charges against the railroad company before the Interstate Commerce Commission (ICC). When the ICC dismissed the complaint on grounds that there was insufficient "colored traffic on the lines" to justify a first coach for blacks, Mitchell appealed to the Supreme Court after a district court ruled for the ICC. The Court ruled in his favor, holding "that separate coach laws of the several states do not apply to interstate commerce." Most southern states ignored the ruling, however, and segregation prevailed in interstate travel into the 1960s.

Selected Bibliography Richard Bardolph, ed., *The Civil Rights Record: Black Americans and the Law, 1849–1970* (1970); Catherine A. Barnes, *Journey from Jim Crow: The Desegregation of Southern Transit* (1983); Derrick A. Bell, Jr., *Race, Racism, and American Law* (1980); Scott D. Breckinridge, Jr., "Effect of *Mitchell v. United States* on the Duty of the Common Carrier in Kentucky toward the Negro Passenger," *Kentucky Law Journal* 30 (1942), 247–50; "Recent Cases," *George Washington Law Review* 10 (1941), 229–31; "Recent Decisions," *Michigan Law Review* 39 (1941), 1414–17.

Stephen Middleton

Montgomery Bus Boycott   Sparked by the arrest of **Rosa Parks** for refusing to relinquish her seat to a white man and move to the back of a Montgomery, Alabama, City Lines bus, as was mandated by that city's segregation ordinance, the 381-day bus boycott began in December 1955 and continued without interruption until 21 December 1956. At that time the U.S. Supreme Court upheld an earlier three-judge federal court decision maintaining that segregation on a common carrier violated the due process and equal protection of the law clauses of the **Fourteenth Amendment** (see *Browder v. Gayle*). Beyond integrating the Montgomery buses, this precedent-setting decision allowed the nascent civil rights movement to adopt the Fourteenth Amendment as a formidable weapon against all forms of **de jure segregation.** The boycott itself also gave **Martin Luther King, Jr.,** national visibility as a

Rosa Parks arrives at circuit court on 24 February 1956 to be arraigned in the Montgomery bus boycott. © AP/Wide World Photos.

civil rights spokesperson. His leadership of the boycott began when he was elected president of the newly established **Montgomery Improvement Association,** which organized and coordinated the protest. This visibility gave King a platform from which he could articulate his philosophy of nonviolent **direct action** and keep it in the forefront of civil rights tactics and ideology. The boycott's success motivated many similarly fashioned protests throughout the South. Victory in Montgomery was achieved because of the strong grass-roots organizing efforts of individuals such as **E. D. Nixon, Ralph Abernathy,** and **Fred L. Shuttlesworth,** and the support of such advisors as **Bayard Rustin** and Stanley Levison. Additionally, the **NAACP** provided valuable legal support and handled the case as it went through the judicial process. As a direct and enduring legacy of the boycott, King in 1957 established the **Southern Christian Leadership Conference,** intended to organize black clergymen "to assert their human dignity through nonviolent protest against segregation."

Selected Bibliography Taylor Branch, *Parting the Waters: America in the King Years 1954–1963* (1988); Adam Fairclough, *To Redeem the Soul of America: The Southern Christian Leadership Conference and Martin Luther King, Jr.* (1987); David J. Garrow, *Bearing the Cross: Martin Luther King, Jr., and the Southern Christian Leadership Conference* (1986); Martin Luther King, Jr., *Stride toward Freedom: The Montgomery Story* (1958); Aldon D. Morris, *The Origins of the Civil Rights Movement: Black Communities Organizing for Change* (1984); Jo Ann Gibson Robinson, *The Montgomery Bus Boycott and the Women Who Started It: The Memoir of Jo Ann Gibon Robinson* (1987); Norman W. Walton, "The Walking City: A History of the Montgomery

Boycott—Part I," *Negro History Bulletin* 20 (October 1956), 17–21; Norman W. Walton, "The Walking City: A History of the Montgomery Boycott—Part II," *Negro History Bulletin* 20 (November 1956), 27–33; Norman W. Walton, "The Walking City: A History of the Montgomery Boycott—Part III," *Negro History Bulletin* 20 (February 1957), 102–4; Norman W. Walton, "The Walking City: A History of the Montgomery Boycott—Part IV," *Negro History Bulletin* 20 (April 1957), 147–52, 166.

Marshall Hyatt

Montgomery Improvement Association When African Americans in Alabama's capital decided, at a mass meeting on the evening of 5 December 1955, to continue the one-day-old **Montgomery bus boycott** of the city's seg-regated buses, they formed this organization to lead and coordinate the boy-cott. **Martin Luther King, Jr.,** was elected president, and leaders of the black churches and civic organizations in the city made up its 35-member executive board. Its finance and transportation committees created a free transportation system for the tens of thousands of black people in Montgomery who were affected by the boycott. The Montgomery Improvement Association (MIA) provided this service without interruption for the duration of the 11-month boycott, despite acts of intimidation and attempts by the city and state to close down the operation. It held weekly meetings and published *The MIA Newsletter* to keep people informed of developments. After failing to get the city to agree to limited desegregation of the buses, the MIA filed suit in fed-eral court on 1 February 1956, challenging the constitutionality of the bus seg-regation ordinances. On 16 November 1956, the U.S. Supreme Court upheld the lower court's ruling that the segregation of Montgomery's buses was uncon-stitutional (see *Browder v. Gayle*). After the boycott, the MIA continued to serve the black people of Montgomery in the civil rights movement it had helped initiate, and it became an affiliated member of the **Southern Christian Leadership Conference.**

Selected Bibliography Taylor Branch, *Parting the Waters: America in the King Years, 1954–1963* (1988); David J. Garrow, *Bearing the Cross: Martin Luther King, Jr., and the Southern Christian Leadership Conference* (1986); Aldon D. Morris, *The Origins of the Civil Rights Movement: Black Communities Organizing for Change* (1984); Martin Luther King, Jr., *Stride toward Freedom: The Montgomery Story* (1958); Jo Ann Gibson Robinson, *The Montgomery Bus Boycott and the Women Who Started It* (1987); Lamont H. Yeakey, "The Montgomery, Alabama, Bus Boycott, 1955–56" (Ph.D. diss., Columbia University, 1979).

Gloria Waite

Moody, Anne (15 September 1940, Centreville, Miss.–). Civil rights activist, writer, and lecturer, Anne Moody attended Natchez Junior College and received a bachelor's degree from **Tougaloo College.** While a student, she and two other young blacks were among the first sit-in demonstrators at a Jackson, Mississippi, Woolworth's lunch counter. Later she was jailed on sev-eral occasions for her participation in marches and demonstrations. She con-tinued to recruit high school and college students and she conducted workshops on self-protection tactics. In 1963 Moody expanded her activities by going to work for the **Congress of Racial Equality** in Canton, Mississippi. Having earned a national reputation, Moody became a Civil Rights Coordinator at Cornell University (1964–65). She has described her involvement in the civil rights movement in her *Coming of Age in Mississippi* (1968), which received several awards, including the American Library Association's "Best Book of the Year Award." In 1975, she published *Mr. Death: Four Stories*. In 2003 Moody resided in New York City, living a nonpublic life.

Selected Bibliography Marianna W. Davis, ed., *Contributions of Black Women to America*, vol. 2 (1982); Gerda Lerner, ed., *Black Women in White America: A Documentary History* (1972); Anne Moody, *Coming of Age in Mississippi* (1968); Anne Moody, *Mr. Death: Four Stories* (1975); George A. Sewell, *Mississippi Black History Makers* (1977); "Voices from the Gaps: Women Writers of Color: Anne Moody," http://voices.cla.umn.edu/authors/annemoody.html.

Betty L. Plummer

Moore, Amzie (23 September 1911, border of Carroll and Grenada Counties, Miss.–1 February 1982, Mound Bayou, Miss.). An African American businessman and civil rights activist in the 1950–60 decade of mass protestations, Moore was more interested in overthrowing segregationist regimes in Mississippi than in desegregation. He concentrated on voter registration and is credited with helping move Bolivar County, Mississippi, into the civil rights era. Elected president of the Cleveland, Mississippi, **NAACP** in 1955 and a founder of the Delta's Regional Council of Negro Leadership, Moore persuaded **Robert Moses,** working for the **Student Nonviolent Coordinating Committee** (SNCC), that voter registration should be its focus for Mississippi and that local youth along with SNCC volunteers should be used in the effort.

Selected Bibliography Taylor Branch, *Parting the Waters: America in the King Years of Mass Demonstrations, 1954–1963* (1988); Clayborne Carson, *In Struggle. SNCC and the Black Awakening of the 1960s* (1982); John Dittmer, *Local People: The Struggle of Civil Rights in Mississippi* (1994); Charles W. Eagles, ed., *The Civil Rights Movement in America* (1986); *New York Times*, 7 February 1982.

Nancy E. Fitch

Moore, Harry T. (18 November 1905, Mims, Fla.–25 December 1951, Mims, Fla.). Florida Coordinator of the **NAACP,** he attacked racism along a variety of fronts. A former school teacher, he led the challenge against unequal salaries for black educators. Following the outlawing of the **white primary** by the U.S. Supreme Court in 1944, he formed the Florida Progressive Voters League, which succeeded in tripling the enrollment of registered black voters. Moore was also involved in protesting the convictions of three black men for the rape of a white woman in Groveland, Florida in July 1949. Two years later after the U.S. Supreme Court ordered a new trial, Sheriff Willis McCall of Lake County shot and killed one unarmed prisoner and wounded another in his custody. Moore called for the sheriff's suspension. A month after the shooting on Christmas Day 1951, a bomb shattered Moore's house, killing the NAACP leader and his wife. Although members of the Ku Klux Klan were

Harry T. Moore. © Library of Congress.

suspected of the crime, the assailants were never brought to trial. In 1955 Governor LeRoy Collins reopened the case and commuted the death sentence of the surviving prisoner.

Selected Bibliography Gloster Current, "Martyr for a Cause," *Crisis* 59 (February 1952), 72–81, 133–34; Ben Green, *Before His Time: The Untold Story of Harry T. Moore* (1999); Steven F. Lawson, *Black Ballots: Voting Rights in the South, 1944–1969* (1976); Steven F. Lawson, David R. Colburn, and Darryl Paulson, "Groveland: Florida's Little Scottsboro," *Florida Historical Quarterly* 65 (July 1986), 1–26.

Steven L. Lawson

Moore v. Dempsey, 261 U.S. 86 (1923) This 1923 U.S. Supreme Court decision upheld the constitutional right of fair trial and due process of law. In 1919, responding to the exploitation of black sharecroppers and tenant farmers by white merchant/planters, Robert L. Hill, a black veteran of World War I, organized in Arkansas the self-help Farmers Progressive Household Union of America. Its aim was to "advance the interests of the Negro." Fearing the worst, a white deputy and assistant approached a mass church meeting of the Union; gunfire erupted, which left both the deputy and his assistant wounded. A subsequent race riot unofficially left nearly 200 blacks dead. The surviving members of the union were rounded up and tried for murder. Upon a howling mob's insistence, the jury quickly sentenced 12 to death and 67 to lengthy prison sentences. Attorneys for the **NAACP** won appeals for the convicted on the grounds that the racist hysteria of the moment led to a trial in name only. The Supreme Court agreed with this assessment and overturned the convictions.

Selected Bibliography Richard Kluger, *Simple Justice: The History of Brown v. Board of Education and Black America's Struggle for Equality* (1976); Loren Miller, *The Petitioners: The Story of the Supreme Court of the United States and the Negro* (1966).

Malik Simba

Moore, William L. (28 April 1927, Binghamton, N.Y.–23 April 1963, Etowah County, Ala.). William Moore planned in 1963 to walk from Chattanooga, Tennessee, to Jackson, Mississippi, and deliver a letter protesting the state of race relations to Governor Ross Barnett. The Baltimore postmaster had been raised in Mississippi but deplored in his communication to Barnett the state's reputation as "the most backward and most bigoted in the land." Moore specifically objected to segregated public accommodations in the South. The 35-year-old white man, pushing a cart with his possessions before him, began the solitary journey on 21 April. Heading south, with signs reading "Eat at Joe's—Both Black and White" and "Equal Rights For All" attached to him, Moore crossed into Alabama. He recorded in his diary a white woman's encouragement and the "nigger lover" taunts of others. Moore pushed on, sleeping one night in a school bus. In Etowah County, as he walked along a remote stretch of U.S. Highway 11, he was shot and killed on the evening of 23 September. Both President John Kennedy and Governor George Wallace, unusual allies, condemned the crime. Two individuals were questioned but the murderer went unpunished. Moore's undelivered letter to Governor Barnett was opened and read. It said that "the white man cannot be truly free himself until all men have their rights."

Selected Bibliography Taylor Branch, *Parting the Waters: America in the King Years 1954–1963* (1988); *Gadsden (Alabama) Times*, 24 April 1973; *Montgomery Advertiser*, 24–26 April 1963.

William Warren Rogers, Jr.

Morehouse College Established in 1867 as Augusta Institute, Morehouse College moved to Atlanta, Georgia, in 1879 where it became known as the Atlanta Baptist Seminary. In 1897 the name was changed to the Atlanta Baptist College. Throughout these years there was repeated debate over the issue of white versus black control of the institution, but it was not until **John Hope** became president in 1906 that a black man first held that post. Through the influence of **Booker T. Washington,** Hope was able to raise badly needed funds for the school, but his action temporarily alienated **W.E.B. Du Bois.** In 1913 the school's name was changed to Morehouse College in honor of the Secretary of the American Baptist Home Mission Society. The college grew and in 1929 joined with Spelman College and **Atlanta University** in a successful cooperative venture that continues to the present day. In 1935 **Benjamin E. Mays** ascended to the presidency and, like John Hope, put his mark on the school. Mays was also a major national black figure. Morehouse is perhaps most often remembered as the alma mater of **Martin Luther King, Jr.,** but it also produced many black professionals, businessmen, and other important civil rights leaders. Morehouse students also played an active role in the 1960s desegregation struggles in Atlanta.

Selected Bibliography Benjamin Brawley, *History of Morehouse College* (1917); Addie Louis Joyner Butler, *The Distinctive Black College: Talladega, Tuskegee, and Morehouse* (1977); Leroy Davis, *A Clashing of the Soul: John Hope and the Dilemma of African American Leadership and Black Higher Education in the Early Twentieth Century* (1998); Benjamin E. Mays, *Born to Rebel: An Autobiography* (1971); Dereck Joseph Rovaris, " Developer of an Institution, Dr. Benjamin E. Mays, Morehouse College President, 1940–1957" (Ph.D. diss., University of Illinois, Urbana-Champagne, 1990); Web site: www.morehouse.edu.

John F. Marszalek

Morgan, Charles, Jr. (11 March 1930, Cincinnati, Ohio–). A native of Kentucky, Morgan was educated at the University of Alabama and practiced law in Birmingham from 1955 to 1963. On 16 September 1963, the day after a bomb killed four black girls in the Sixteenth Street Baptist Church, Morgan told the Young Men's Business Club, "We all did it. Every last one of us is condemned for that crime. . . . Birmingham is not a dying city. It is dead." Within weeks he left Birmingham. From 1964 to 1972 Morgan directed the southern regional office of the **American Civil Liberties Union** (ACLU) and later (1972–76) headed the ACLU's Washington, D.C., office. Having established the one man–one vote doctrine in *Reynolds v. Sims,* Morgan attacked institutional racism. He defeated racial discrimination on juries (*White v. Crook, Bailey v. Wharton,* and **Whitus v. Georgia**) and segregation in Alabama prisons (*Lee v. Washington*). In 1966 he represented **Julian Bond,** who had been denied a seat in the Georgia legislature after speaking against the war in Vietnam. A historian of the ACLU has called Morgan "the only other charismatic figure in ACLU history besides Roger Baldwin." In 1987, Morgan was the attorney in Sears's successful court victory over the EEOC in a sex discrimination case.

Selected Bibliography *EEOC v. Sears* .839 F.2d 302; Charles Morgan, Jr., *One Man, One Voice* (1979); Charles Morgan, Jr., *A Time to Speak* (1964); Fred Powledge, "Profiles (Charles Morgan, Jr.)," *New Yorker,* 25 October 1969; Samuel Walker, *In Defense of American Liberties: A History of the ACLU* (1990).

Charles W. Eagles

Morgan v. Virginia, 328 U.S. 373 (1946) Irene Morgan climbed aboard a Richmond, Virginia, Greyhound bus on 14 July 1944 in Gloucester County, Virginia. She had a ticket to Baltimore, Maryland, the destination of the bus. A short while later, the bus driver ordered her and another African American woman to move two rows back to the last row so that four of six white passengers who were standing could be seated. A Virginia state law dating from 1930 required seating segregation by rows, and it required the bus driver to take the action he did. When Morgan chose to remain in her seat, she was forcibly removed and subsequently convicted of violating the law and resisting arrest. On appeal, the Virginia Supreme Court of Appeals unanimously sustained the segregation statute and its application to her (184 Va. 24). By a seven-to-one margin, however, the U.S. Supreme Court invalidated the law as it applied to interstate passengers. The state's police power under the Tenth Amendment might require segregation among intrastate passengers, but, according to the new interpretation of the Interstate Commerce Clause, it could not also reach interstate passengers. The court had issued its ruling, but only after two more decades would such segregation requirements—in intrastate and interstate travel alike—finally fall, particularly in the Deep South.

Selected Bibliography Catherine A. Barnes, *Journey from Jim Crow: The Desegregation of Southern Transit* (1983); Gilbert Ware, *William Hastie: Grace under Pressure* (1984).

Peter Wallenstein

Morial, Ernest N. "Dutch" (9 October 1929, New Orleans, La.–23 December 1989, New Orleans, La.). Upon receiving his undergraduate education from Xavier University of New Orleans in 1951, Morial was among the first black students to enroll in law school at Louisiana State University (LSU). Accelerating his studies, he became the LSU law school's first black graduate in 1954. Together with his law partner **A. P. Tureaud,** he hammered away at the walls of segregation and discrimination that made New Orleans a divided city. As attorneys for the **Legal Defense and Educational Fund** of the **NAACP,** they filed suits that brought an end to segregation in New Orleans schools, places of public entertainment, municipal facilities, buses, and taxicabs. Morial was president of the New Orleans Branch of the **NAACP** from 1963 to 1965. He became the first black to serve as assistant U.S. attorney in the state of Louisiana (1965 to 1967). In 1967 he won a seat in the Louisiana House of Representatives, becoming the first black to sit in the legislature since the end of the nineteenth century. He held the seat from 1968 to 1970, when Governor John McKeithen appointed him to fill an unexpired term on the Orleans Parish Juvenile Court in 1970. The first black to sit on that bench, he was also the first of his race to win election to the state's Fourth Circuit Court of Appeals, where he served from 1973 to 1977. In 1977 he emerged victorious from a hotly contested mayoral race to become the first black mayor of New Orleans. Morial's assertiveness endeared him to thousands of ordinary black people throughout Louisiana, who took vicarious pleasure in witnessing him "stand up" to white symbols of power. As a champion of the poor and dispossessed of all races, he used his intellect, courage, and skills as an attorney to broaden the boundaries of freedom for all people. When his election as mayor catapulted him into greater national prominence and the presidency of the U.S. Conference of Mayors, he used that office to marshal support for the continuation of General Revenue Sharing programs, Community Services Block Grants, and other federal programs designed to enable financially strapped cities to provide services for the poor.

Selected Bibliography Arnold R. Hirsch, *Dutch Morial: Old Creole in the New South,* Working Paper No. 4, College of Urban & Public Affairs, University of New Orleans (1990); Arnold R. Hirsch, "Simply a Matter of Black and White: The Transformation of Racial Politics in Twentieth Century New Orleans" (unpublished manuscript, 1989); Ernest N. Morial, Mayor, City of New Orleans (short political biography in author's possession; no date); Ernest Nathan Morial Papers, Amistad Research Center, Tulane University; *The New Orleans Times-Picayune,* 25 December 1989; Ernest N. Morial and Marion Barry, Jr., *Rebuilding America's Cities: A Policy Analysis of the U.S. Conference of Mayors* (1986).

Joe Louis Caldwell

Morrill Act (1890) The first Morrill Act (the Morrill-Wade Land-Grant College Act of 1862) inaugurated substantial federal support for higher education—emphasizing agriculture and engineering—in every state, and the second Morrill Act (the 1890 Morrill-McComas Act) increased the amount of funding. Across the South, however, black students were excluded from the "colleges of 1862," although Virginia and Mississippi each apportioned some of the 1862 money to a black school. The 1890 act made funding conditional on black access, but segregation was acceptable if a state made an "equitable division" of its funds between a "college for white students" and an "institution for colored students," so all 17 southern states divided the money between schools for each race. Although dependent on the Morrill Act money, with most state money going to white schools, the "colleges of 1890" provided employment and education for many black southerners. In the early years, few black land-grant schools offered baccalaureate degrees, and none had graduate programs. By World War II, states recognized that they had to upgrade the black schools to forestall desegregation. In the early 1960s, those schools were centers of civil rights activity, as when four students at North Carolina Agricultural and Technical College began the **Greensboro sit-in.** Desegregation at all of the South's "colleges of 1862" began by 1965, but, at the beginning of the twenty-first century, African American enrollment remained higher at many of the "colleges of 1890."

Selected Bibliography Jean L. Preer, *Lawyers v. Educators: Black Colleges and Desegregation in Public Higher Education* (1982); Peter Wallenstein, *Virginia Tech, Land-Grant University, 1872–1997: History of a School, a State, a Nation* (1997).

Peter Wallenstein

Morrison, Toni (18 February 1931, Lorain, Ohio–). Toni Morrison, born Chloe Anthony Wofford, earned a Bachelor of Arts degree at Howard University and a Master of Arts from Cornell University. She also received honorary degrees from Oberlin College, Dartmouth College, Bryn Mawr College, and Yale University. Morrison has been the Robert F. Goheen Professor of the Humanities at Princeton University since 1989. The author of seven novels and a host of other works, her skillful use of language has illuminated the lives and struggles of African American women and legitimized the slave experience. Her works demonstrate the extent to which sexist actions have oppressed African American women. After black writers published a controversial letter in the *New York Times Book Review* accusing the Nobel Prize Committee of prejudicial treatment of Morrison, in what many considered was actually pressure on the Pulitzer Prize Committee, her novel, *Beloved,* won the 1988 Pulitzer Prize for fiction and the Robert F. Kennedy award. Toni Morrison later became the first African American writer to win a Nobel Prize for literature. She ranks among the great writers of the twentieth century.

Selected Bibliography Eberhard Alsen, "Toni Morrison," in Emmanuel S. Nelson, ed., *Contemporary African American Novelists: A Bio-Bibliographical Critical Sourcebook* (1999); Patrick Bryce Bjork, *The Novels of Toni Morrison: The Search for Self and Place within the Community* (1992); Karen Carman, *Toni Morrison's World of Fiction* (1993); Douglas Century, *Toni Morrison* (1994); Jan Furman, *Toni Morrison's Fiction* (1996).

Cassandra August

Morrow, Everette Frederic (20 April 1909, Hackensack, N.J.–19 July 1994, New York, N.Y.). From 1955 to 1961 Morrow served as administrative officer for special projects for President Dwight D. Eisenhower, the first black appointed to a president's executive staff. This was one of several important positions he held in his career as public servant, businessman, and civil rights activist. Morrow graduated from Bowdoin College, in Brunswick, Maine, in 1930 and later from Rutgers University Law School. After college he worked for the **National Urban League** and subsequently for the **NAACP.** A major in the U.S. Army during World War II, he agitated for the rights of blacks in a segregated and discriminatory armed forces. In 1949 he was the first black writer hired by CBS in its Public Affairs Department, and he left that position in 1952 to serve on President Eisenhower's election campaign staff. As White House aide in the Eisenhower White House, he was not always successful in influencing administration racial policies; yet his voice was one of reason in the tension-filled days of the early civil rights movement. Morrow held a number of subsequent jobs, the most important of which was vice president for the Bank of America. He retired in 1975, but became an executive associate at the Educational Testing Service of Princeton, New Jersey.

Selected Bibliography Robert Frederick Burk, *The Eisenhower Administration and Black Civil Rights* (1981); "E. Frederic Morrow—Whatever Happened To," *Ebony* 38 (December 1982), 120; E. Frederic Morrow, *Black Man in the White House: A Diary of the Eisenhower Years* (1963); E. Frederic Morrow, *Forty Years a Guinea Pig* (1980); Obituary, *New York Times*, 21 July 1994.

Dorothy A. Autrey

Moses, Robert (23 January 1935, Harlem, N.Y.–). A shy, soft-spoken individual, Robert Moses was the driving force behind the **Student Nonviolent Coordinating Committee** (SNCC). Born and raised in Harlem, Moses was quickly recognized as a gifted youth and he distinguished himself by mastering the Chinese philosophy of Laotze. While he was a Harvard graduate student, majoring in philosophy and teaching grade school, he heard of the civil rights movement in the South. Armed with a knowledge of French existentialist Albert Camus, a renewed interest in Eastern religions, and an interest in pacifist thought, Moses left his studies and immersed himself in the movement. The newly formed SNCC found in Moses a leader of rare courage and strong principles. In many respects, Robert Moses was the embodiment of the early SNCC belief in a "Beloved Community." He endured numerous beatings and jailings. He was also a masterful strategist who backed the move to involve white students in the Voter Registration Drive of 1964 (see **Freedom Summer of 1964**). Moses gave SNCC a vision and methods of operation, especially the idea of participatory democracy. Frustrated and saddened over the organization's later shift to **Black Power,** Moses left it. He traveled to Africa and then returned to Harvard to pursue his doctorate in philosophy.

Selected Bibliography Taylor Branch, *Parting the Waters: America during the King Years, 1954–1963* (1988); Eric R. Burner, *And Gently He Shall Lead Them: Robert Parris Moses and Civil Rights in Mississippi* (1994); Clayborne Carson, *In Struggle: SNCC and the Black Awakening of the*

1960s (1981); James Forman, *The Making of Black Revolutionaries* (1985); Robert Weisbrot, *Freedom Bound: A History of America's Civil Rights Movement* (1990); Howard Zinn, *SNCC: The New Abolitionists* (1964).

Charles T. Pete Banner-Haley

Motley, Constance Baker (14 September 1921, New Haven, Conn.–) Born in Connecticut of recently emigrated West Indian parents, she studied law at Columbia University. While still a law student, she began to work for the **Legal Defense and Educational Fund** of the **NAACP.** Upon graduating, she went to work full-time for the fund, which at that time was fully engaged in an assault on the dual school system. As a black female lawyer, she faced many professional obstacles, but she was undeterred by the challenge. She gained widespread recognition for her defense of civil rights. In 1948, soon after finishing law school, she made her first trip to Mississippi, where she argued a wage equalization case for black teachers. Before she left the organization in 1964, Motley successfully argued nine NAACP cases before the Supreme Court, including **Autherine Lucy**'s suit for admission at the University of Alabama and **James Meredith**'s case for admission to the University of Mississippi. In 1964 she entered politics and won a seat in the New York Senate, thereby becoming the first African American female ever to sit in that state's upper chamber. The following year she won election to the position of Manhattan Borough President. In 1966 President Lyndon B. Johnson

Constance Baker Motley, about the time President Lyndon Johnson made her the first black woman federal judge. © Library of Congress.

appointed her to the U.S. District Court for Southern New York, making her the nation's first black woman federal judge. In 1982 she became chief judge and served in that capacity until 1986 when she assumed the status of senior judge. Since her retirement Judge Motley has remained active in civil and professional areas and has published extensively in legal and professional journals. She has received many honorary degrees, including the LL.D from **Howard,** Brown, Princeton, and Tulane as well as other prestigious universities. In 2003, she received the NAACP **Spingarn Medal.**

Selected Bibliography Jack Bass, *Unlikely Heroes* (1981); Floris Barnett Cash, "Constance Baker Motley," *Notable Black American Women,* vol. 1 (1992), 779–82; Constance Baker Motley, *Equal Justice under the Law: An Autobiography* (1998); *The Negro Almanac* (1971); *New York Times,* 11 September 1963; *Who's Who in Colored America,* 7th ed. (1950).

Charles D. Lowery

Moton, Robert Russa (26 August 1867, Rice, Va.–31 May 1940, Capahoosie, Va.). An African American intellectual and college administrator, Moton studied at **Hampton Institute** and earned his M.A. degree at Harvard University. He also studied at Wilberforce University, Oberlin College, William and Mary College, and **Howard University** and received an Litt.D. from Lincoln University in Pennsylvania. Moton was associated with Hampton Institute until he was appointed to replace **Booker T. Washington** as the chief administrator of **Tuskegee Institute** in 1915. He played a significant role in forming the National Negro Finance Corporation, and in the early 1920s he was among the sponsors of the **National Urban League,** an organization founded in 1911 to address problems of urban black dwellers. He also served on a committee established by the federal government to deal with discrimination against black troops during the First World War. Moton was instrumental in the appointment of **Emmett J. Scott,** a former Booker T. Washington aide, as a special assistant to the Secretary of War during the First World War. Moton was sent to France by President Woodrow Wilson to investigate the grievances and allegations brought against the African American troops by their white officers. Although the main objective of his mission was to appease the black troops in France, Moton was able to bring black grievances to the attention of President Wilson.

Selected Bibliography Wilson J. Moses, *The Golden Age of Black Nationalism, 1850–1925* (1978); Robert R. Moton, *Finding a Way Out: An Autobiography* (1921); Robert R. Moton, *What the Negro Thinks* (1929).

Amos J. Beyan

Mound Bayou Founded in the Mississippi Delta (Bolivar County) in 1887 by the freedmen Isaiah T. Montgomery and Benjamin T. Green, this town was conceived as a refuge from white supremacy, a nationalist utopia built, governed, and occupied exclusively by blacks. A cotton center sustained and surrounded by a larger black agricultural colony of small black landowners and sharecroppers, it was the most celebrated of the several all-black towns formed in the United States during a period of mounting white racism and reactive black separatism. The community briefly flourished through the entrepreneurial skills and energy of its first citizens (Montgomery and Charles Banks), the endorsement of **Booker T. Washington,** and the patronage of such northern philanthropists as Andrew Carnegie. In its heyday, on the eve of World War I, this town of eight hundred inhabitants boasted a bank, a cotton seed oil mill, public and parochial schools, a newspaper, a railroad depot, a telephone exchange and utilities company, and numerous businesses offering "nearly every necessity of the retail and supply trade." Although town leaders valiantly struggled to make it a model of black capitalism, self-help, and group consciousness, it declined rapidly after World War I. Victimized by a modernizing economy, heavy rural-to-urban migration, increased consumer mobility, and a racial system designed to keep African Americans economically dependent on whites, Mound Bayou was described in 1940 by a sympathetic traveler as "more dead than alive." And so it remains in the early twenty-first century.

Selected Bibliography Norman Crockett, *The Black Towns* (1979); Janet Sharp Hermann, *Pursuit of a Dream* (1981); Neil R. McMillen, *Dark Journey: Black Mississippians in the Age of Jim Crow* (1989); Mary Woodson, *Police Brutality in Mound Bayou, Mississippi in 1965* (1996).

Neil R. McMillen

Moynihan Report (1965) Assistant Secretary of Labor and Director of the Office of Policy Planning and Research in 1963, later New York (D) senator, Daniel Patrick Moynihan authored *The Negro Family: The Case For National Action,* popularly known as the "Moynihan Report." The report had been classified "For Official Use Only" until it became the basis for President Lyndon B. Johnson's address at **Howard University**'s commencement 4 June 1965. The report argued that the deterioration of the black family was rooted in slavery and Reconstruction, which had forced black society into a matriarchal structure with "often reversed roles of husband and wife." The deteriorated state of the African American family was viewed as the fundamental source of weakness of the black community, resulting in a cycle of (1) matriarchy, (2) poor school achievement, (3) higher rates of delinquency, (4) alienation of men, (5) higher drug addiction, (6) and welfare dependency and poverty. The report ended by stating, "The policy of the U.S. is to bring Negro Americans to full and equal sharing in responsibilities and rewards of citizenship. To this end, the programs of the federal government bearing on this objective shall be designed to have the effect, directly or indirectly, of enhancing the stability and resources of the Negro family." Widely discussed in the media, the controversial report was viewed by many as an attack on the black family, as a threat to the integrity of the social sciences, and to the autonomy of social agencies.

Selected Bibliography Herbert G. Gutman, *The Black Family in Slavery and Freedom, 1750–1925* (1976); Godfrey Hodgson, *The Gentlemen from New York: Daniel Patrick Moynihan—A Biography* (2001); Daniel Patrick Moynihan, *The Negro Family: The Case for National Action* (1965); Jeffrey O'Connell and Richard F. Bland, "Moynihan's Legacy," *Public Interest* 142 (2001), 95–106; Lee Rainwater and William L. Yancey, *The Moynihan Report and the Politics of Controversy* (1967).

Clarence Hooker

Muhammad, Elijah.   See Poole, Elijah.

Muhammad Speaks   This newspaper was the national organ of the **Nation of Islam** from 1960 to 1975. Created by Elijah Muhammad (see **Elijah Poole**), the paper served as the chief propaganda voice of the movement. It was initially headed by **Malcolm X** of Muhammad's New York Temple. Under his direction *Muhammad Speaks* evolved from a monthly to a weekly paper. During the 1970s the Nation of Islam claimed that the organ had the largest circulation of any black newspaper in the United States. In fact, in 1975 it had 500,000 readers located not only in the United States but also in the West Indies, Central and South America, and Europe. *Muhammad Speaks* reported on social, religious, and political issues that affected black people throughout the world. But foremost, it was the Nation of Islam's voice to the world representing the philosophies of Elijah Muhammad.

Selected Bibliography Peter Goldman, *The Death and Life of Malcolm X* (1979); Robert L. Jenkins and Mfanya D. Tryman, *The Malcolm X Encyclopedia* (2002); C. Eric Lincoln, *The Black Muslim in America* (1963); Malcolm X, *The Autobiography of Malcolm X* (1965); Web site: www.muhammadspeaks.com.

Vibert L. White

Muhammad, Wallace D. (Imam Warith Deen Mohammed)   (30 October 1933, Chicago, Ill.–   ). Son of Elijah Muhammad (see **Elijah Poole**) and Clara Muhammad, Wallace Muhammad became the spiritual leader of the **Black Muslims** on the death of his father in 1975. An orthodox Muslim, he stood as leader against various separatist splinter movements and brought the **Nation of Islam** into conformity with world Islam, beginning the "decultification" of the sect by lifting the ban on white membership, making certain internal reforms, releasing financial information about the Nation, and even changing its name to the American Muslim Mission. This trend was traceable as far back as 1960 when, as minister of the Philadelphia temple, Muhammad helped to launch a fund drive for a **NAACP** regional executive, a clear reversal of previous Black Muslim practices. In 1961, he was imprisoned for refusing to accept government service in place of draft-imposed military service. When his father died in 1975, Muhammad took the name W. Deen Mohammed and became the Nation of Islam's new leader. He later broke with the Nation of Islam and in 2003 headed the Muslim American Society with membership open to all races.

Selected Bibliography Zafar Ishaq Ansari, "W. D. Muhammad: The Making of a 'Black Muslim' Leader (1933–1961)," *American Journal of Islamic Studies* 2 (No. 2, 1985), 245–62; C. Eric Lincoln, *The Black Muslims in America* (1961); C. Eric Lincoln, *Race, Religion, and the Continuing American Dilemma* (1984); *New York Times,* 17 June 1975; Web site: http://www.wdmonline.com.

Ray Branch

Muir v. Louisville Park Theatrical Association, **347 U.S. 971 (1954)**   This case extended the principle of the unconstitutionality of racial segregation to public facilities that are leased to nonpublic entities. James W. Muir, a black resident of Louisville, Kentucky, was refused the purchase of a ticket to a production in a city owned amphitheater that had been leased to a nonprofit theatrical association. Muir brought suit claiming that the equal protection clause of the **Fourteenth Amendment** prohibits racial segregation in publicly owned facilities. The lower courts rejected the claim on the grounds that, although the city owned the facility, it was leased to a nonpublic entity to which the Fourteenth Amendment did not apply. In the landmark *Brown v. Board of Education* school desegregation case of 1954, the Supreme Court ruled that racial segregation in public education violates the equal protection clause of the Fourteenth Amendment. Through a series of unanimous opinions, the court summarily extended this principle to all public facilities. In *Muir*, the Supreme Court vacated the lower court decision and in a terse unanimous opinion ordered that its ruling in *Brown* be applied to publicly owned facilities whether operated by a public body or leased to a nonpublic entity.

Selected Bibliography Henry J. Abraham, *Freedom and the Court: Civil Rights and Liberties in the United States* (1988); Derrick A. Bell, Jr., *Race, Racism, and American Law* (1980).

Frederick G. Slabach

Murray, Anna Pauline "Pauli"   (20 November 1910, Baltimore, Md.–1 July 1985, Pittsburgh, Pa.). The daughter of William Henry and Agnes Georgianna Fitzgerald Murray, she was orphaned at an early age and reared by her grandmother and aunts in Durham, North Carolina. She is remembered principally as the first black woman Episcopal priest (ordained in 1977) and as a cofounder of the National Organization for Women (NOW), but her remarkably varied career included the law, academics, and creative writing as well. After graduating from Hunter College, in New York, she unsuccessfully attempted to desegregate the University of North Carolina School of Law in 1938. During several years of civil rights activism, she was arrested for refusing to sit at the back of a bus in Virginia in 1940 and for organizing sit-ins in Washington, D.C. Law degrees subsequently earned at **Howard University** and the University of California, Berkeley, prepared her for stints as deputy attorney general of California in 1946, attorney for the American Jewish Congress, 1946–47, and a private law practice in New York City, 1956–60. She later taught at the University of Ghana, Benedict College, Brandeis University, and Boston University. Her writings include a volume of poetry, *Dark Testament, and Other Poems* (1970) and two autobiographical books, *Proud Shoes: The Story of an American Family* (1956) and *Song in a Weary Throat: An American Pilgrimage* (1987), which document her unusual life and family background.

Selected Bibliography Pauli Murray, *Song in a Weary Throat: An American Pilgrimage* (1987); Obituary, *New York Times*, 4 July 1985.

Brenda M. Eagles

Muste, Abraham John   (8 January 1885, Zierkzee, the Netherlands–11 February 1967, New York, N.Y.). Clergyman, labor organizer, civil liberties advocate, and preeminent leader of the American peace movement, he championed racial justice. In the 1930s he fought union racism. During World War II he encouraged conscientious objectors' struggles against segregation in federal prisons and civilian public service camps. As executive secretary of the **Fellowship of Reconciliation** (FOR), he authorized the founding of the **Congress of Racial Equality** (CORE) and allocated staff and money for its early projects. An essay he wrote in 1943, "What the Bible Teaches about Freedom," was distributed widely in African American churches and organizations.

Through FOR and, after 1953, the War Resisters League, Muste mentored numerous civil rights activists, including **Bayard Rustin** and **James Lawson.** He prodded **Martin Luther King, Jr.,** to take a bolder stand against war. Conversely, he urged peace advocates to attack racism. He was a key advisor in the **Albany, Georgia, sit-in,** sparked when an interracial "Quebec to Guantanamo" peace team was arrested in 1963. Muste worked fervently to unite the peace and civil rights movements against the war in Vietnam. He died in February 1967 but would have been gratified that half a million antiwar demonstrators attended the April 15 rally that he had helped plan and that featured as principal speaker Martin Luther King, Jr.

Selected Bibliography Barbara Deming, *Prison Notes* (1966); Nat Hentoff, *Peace Agitator: The Story of A. J. Muste* (1982); Nat Hentoff, ed., *The Essays of A. J. Muste* (2001); Jo Ann O. Robinson, *Abraham Went Out: A Biography of A. J. Muste* (1981).

Jo Ann O. Robinson

The Myth of the Negro Past   This ground-breaking 1941 monograph written by anthropologist **Melville J. Herskovits** (1895–1963), was aimed at disproving the myth that people of African descent had no past. Sophisticated institutions had existed in Africa and blacks in the Americas evolved distinct cultures. Herskovits charted Africanisms within African American communities, and by so doing, stimulated heated debates concerning cultural primacy in African American life. This book, connected with African independence and civil rights movements, challenged the supremacist notion that European culture singularly triumphs when in contact with non-Western societies. It served as one engine to African American and African Diaspora Studies.

Selected Bibliography Robert Baron, "Africa in the Americas: Melville J. Herskovits, Folkloristic and Anthropologist Scholarship, 1923–1941" (Ph.D. diss., University of Pennsylvania, 1994); W.E.B. Du Bois, "Review of *The Myth of the Negro Past* by Melville J. Herskovits," *The Annals of the American Academy* 222 (1942), 226–27; Jerry B. Gershenhorn, "Melville J. Herskovits and the Racial Politics of Knowledge" (Ph.D. diss., University of North Carolina, 2000); Melville J. Herskovits, *The Myth of the Negro Past,* with new introduction by Sidney Mintz (1990); W. Jackson, "Melville J. Herskovits and the Search for Afro-American Culture," in G. W. Stocking, Jr., ed., *Malinowski, Rivers, Benedict, and Others* (1986); George E. Simpson, *Melville J. Herskovits* (1973).

Lisa Brock

N

NAACP.   See National Association for the Advancement of Colored People.

NAACP v. Alabama, 377 U.S. 288 (1964)   The last of four cases brought by the Alabama branch of the **NAACP** before the U.S. Supreme Court (1958–64), this case was an attempt to prevent Alabama from ousting the organization from the state. In June 1956, Alabama's attorney general sued the NAACP to bar it from the state, charging that it had not registered as an out-of-state corporation. Meanwhile, the Alabama circuit court ordered the group to submit its membership lists and numerous other records or incur a $100,000 fine. In *NAACP v. Alabama* (1958) a unanimous Supreme Court ruled that this Alabama requirement violated NAACP members' rights to freedom of association. It vacated the fine and ordered the Alabama court to try the case on its merits. The court refused to do so, forcing the NAACP to return to the Supreme Court two additional times (1959, 1961) before the Alabama court ruled on the original charges. In 1962, it permanently banned the NAACP from doing business in the state. A unanimous Supreme Court in 1964 overturned this decision, ruling that the "freedom of individuals to associate for the collective advocacy of ideas" was a fundamental constitutional right. The Court ordered Alabama to qualify the NAACP as a legal organization.

Selected Bibliography Richard Bardolph, ed., *The Civil Rights Record: Black Americans and the Law, 1849–1970* (1970); Taylor Branch, *Parting the Waters: America in the King Years, 1954–1963* (1988); "Case Comments," *University of Pennsylvania Law Review* 112 (1963), 148; Ann Fagan Ginger, *The Law, the Supreme Court, and the People's Right* (1974); Loren Miller, *The Petitioners: The Story of the Supreme Court of the United States and the Negro* (1966).

Dorothy A. Autrey

NAACP v. St. Louis–San Francisco Railroad, 297 I.C.C. 335 (1955)   Jim Crow practices in interstate public transportation suffered a major defeat with this decision. For the first time, the Interstate Commerce Commission (ICC) rejected the separate but equal doctrine of **Plessy v. Ferguson,** and banned racial segregation on trains and in waiting rooms serving interstate travelers. The **NAACP** argued its case against 15 southern railway companies before a hearing of the ICC in July 1954. With evidence compiled over a three-year period and assistance from the Justice Department as amicus curiae, the NAACP demonstrated the existence of Jim Crow policies on all but one of the defendant railways. Building on the recent decision in **Brown v. Board of Education,** the ICC determined that segregated facilities subjected "Negro passengers to undue and unreasonable disadvantages" in violation of the Interstate Commerce Act. It then ordered that discriminatory policies be "removed" by 10 January 1956. In the companion case of **Key v. Carolina Coach Company,** the ICC extended its order to buses and terminals; however, the decisions did not cover railway station restaurants or intrastate travel. As a result, many southern states managed to circumvent the rulings until the ICC issued a new decree in 1961 that abolished segregation in any facility that jointly served interstate and intrastate passengers.

Selected Bibliography Catherine A. Barnes, *Journey from Jim Crow: The Desegregation of Southern Transit* (1983); Minnie Finch, *The NAACP: Its Fight for Justice* (1981); *New York Times*, 26, 27 November 1955; Robert W. Steele, "Recent Decision," *Michigan Law Review* 54 (1956), 1175–77.

Jack E. Davis

Nashville Sit-Ins   On 12 February 1960, about forty college students, primarily from **Fisk University** and the American Baptist Theological Seminary, staged a sit-in at Woolworth's lunch counter with the intention of integrating eating establishments in Nashville, Tennessee. Well-organized and counseled by Vanderbilt University theology student, **James Lawson,** to use passive resistance or the Gandhi method, they sat quietly at the counter. Their numbers increased daily; white hecklers harassed them and hundreds of protesters were arrested. A city biracial committee was formed, and by May the downtown lunch counters began integrating. These sit-ins and others contributed to the formation of the **Student Nonviolent Coordinating Committee** and eventually to the **Civil Rights Act of 1964.**

Selected Bibliography Kenneth B. Clark, "The Civil Rights Movement: Momentum and Organization," *Daedalus* 95 (Winter 1966), 239–67; David Halberstam, *Children* (1999); *Knoxville News Sentinel*, 15 March 1960; John Lewis and Michael D'orso, *Walking with the Wind: A Memoir of the Movement* (1998); Ruth Searles and J. Allen Williams, Jr., "Negro College Students' Participation in Sit-Ins," *Social Forces* 40 (March 1962), 215–20. Harvard Sitkoff, *The Struggle for Black Equality, 1954–1980* (1981).

Jane F. Lancaster

Nashville Student Movement   Under the leadership of **James Lawson,** Diane Nash, and **John Lewis,** the Nashville Student Movement, in Nashville,

Tennessee, was one of the largest and best-organized student groups to conduct nonviolent sit-ins during the early 1960s. Noted for its careful, disciplined protests, preceded by workshops on nonviolent philosophy and tactics and tests of prospective targets, the group met with a fair degree of success in desegregating some Nashville public accommodations and calling attention to instances of discrimination throughout the city. As an organization, it played a pivotal role in the Shaw University retreat out of which the **Student Nonviolent Coordinating Committee** emerged in 1960.

Selected Bibliography Taylor Branch, *Parting the Waters: America in the King Years 1954–1963* (1988); Clayborne Carson, *In Struggle: SNCC and the Black Awakening in the 1960s* (1981); Harvard Sitkoff, *The Struggle for Black Equality, 1954–1980* (1981); Charles U. Smith, "The Sit-Ins and the New Negro Student," *Journal of Intergroup Relations* 2 (Summer 1961), 223–29; David E. Sumner, "The Nashville Student Movement, *American History Illustrated* 23 (1988), 28–31; Milton Viorst, *Fire in the Streets: America in the 1960s* (1979).

Marshall Hyatt

Nation of Islam.   See Black Muslims.

National Advisory Commission on Civil Disorders.   See Kerner Commissioner.

National Association for the Advancement of Colored People   Shocked by the violence directed against black people in the **Springfield, Illinois, race riots of 1908,** William English Walling, a reporter who had covered the riots, **Mary White Ovington,** New York social worker and third generation abolitionist, and Henry Moskowitz, another social worker, called for a conference on the so-called Negro problem to be held on Abraham Lincoln's birthday in 1909. Quick to join this group were other "neo-abolitionists" such as **Oswald Garrison Villard,** the grandson of William Lloyd Garrison, members of the **Niagara Movement** including **W.E.B. Du Bois,** and a prominent group of progressives including Jane Addams, John Dewey, **Ida Wells Barnett,** and William Dean Howells. In 1910 the National Association for the Advancement of Colored People (NAACP) was formally founded with **Moorfield Storey,** a distinguished Boston attorney, as the first president.

The founding of the NAACP was a clear rejection by northern white and black progressives of **Booker T. Washington**'s accommodationist approach. Instead of accommodation, the NAACP strategy was to use publicity, protest, and legal redress to fight for equality and justice for African Americans. The first national publicity campaign was directed against **lynching.** Indeed, when the NAACP was founded, lynchings were still averaging about 70 a year. By 1940 the number had dropped to four a year. In large part the reduction was due to the creation of public awareness through the publication of *Thirty Years of Lynching in the United States, 1889–1918* as well as pamphlets and speakers on the subject. Although their efforts were directed toward reducing

The NAACP big four confer on a policy problem. Seated, left to right, Roy Wilkins, Walter White, and Thurgood Marshall, standing is Henry Lee Moon. © Library of Congress.

the number of lynchings, the NAACP was never able to secure a federal anti-lynching bill.

The most important work of the Association has been its legal approach to the redress of racial grievances. The NAACP, first through organizationally retained lawyers, then through its legal bureau and now finally through the NAACP **Legal Defense and Educational Fund,** is partially or wholly responsible for striking down the **grandfather clause,** restrictive covenants by city ordinance, **white primaries,** all-white juries, and public facility segregation (most notably school segregation).

Because of its legal approach to the redress of racial grievances, the NAACP has always been acutely sensitive to and aware of nominations to the Supreme Court. The NAACP's first successful national campaign was a lobbying/publicity campaign directed against the Supreme Court nomination of John J. Parker in 1930. The NAACP, along with the American Federation of Labor and later Senate Democrats and progressive Senate Republicans, was able to defeat this nomination. The NAACP has also been successful in helping to defeat the Supreme Court nominations of Judge Clement F.

Haynesworth (1969), Judge G. Harold Carswell (1970), and Judge Robert H. Bork (1986).

Other successful publicity campaigns were the **"Don't Buy Where You Can't Work" movement** in the 1940s, and perhaps most importantly the 1963 **March on Washington** to help gain passage of what became the **Civil Rights Act of 1964.** The desegregation of the United States is in a large measure due to the efforts of the NAACP and surely will be one of its most enduring legacies.

Selected Bibliography Kenneth W. Goings, *The NAACP Comes of Age: The Defeat of Judge John J. Parker* (1990); Charles F. Kellogg, *NAACP: A History of the National Association for the Advancement of Colored People* (1967); James McPherson, *The Abolitionist Legacy: From Reconstruction to the NAACP* (1975); Web site: www.naacp.org.

Kenneth W. Goings

National Association for the Promotion of Labor Unionism among Negroes Founded in 1919 by **A. Philip Randolph** and Chandler Owen, socialist editors of the *Messenger,* this group encouraged blacks to join with whites in a united, interracial, class-based labor movement. Located in New York, its advisory board members included such prominent white socialists as Morris Hilquit and Rose Schneiderman. Short-lived, the association disbanded in the early 1920s. Still, it remains one of the earliest and most significant interracial attempts to combine all workers into the organized labor movement and thus improve the general condition of the entire working class.

Selected Bibliography Philip S. Foner and Ronald L. Lewis, eds., *The Black Worker: A Documentary History from Colonial Times to the Present,* vol. 5: *The Black Worker from 1900 to 1919* (1980); Charles L. Franklin, *The Negro Labor Unionist of New York* (1936); "The Negro and the American Federation of Labor" and "Our Reason for Being," *Messenger* 8 (August 1919), 10–12; Paula Pfeffer, *A. Philip Randolph: Pioneer of the Civil Rights Movement* (1990); Sterling D. Spero and Abraham L. Harris, *The Black Worker: The Negro and the Labor Movement* (1974).

Robert Cvornyek

National Association of Colored Women Founded in 1896 in Washington, D.C., the National Association of Colored Women (NACW) united the National League of Colored Women, the National Federation of Afro-American Women, and over 100 other clubs. In the preamble to its constitution, the organizers stated their intention "to furnish evidence of the moral, mental and material progress made by people of color through the efforts of our women. . . ." Ten years after its founding, the association had grown considerably and was addressing issues crucial to the progress of the race, such as **lynching,** the convict lease system, and education. During World War I, the association boasted a membership of 300,000, with departments concentrating on suffrage, education, rural life conditions, motherhood, health conditions, and lynching. Among the special projects undertaken by the NACW was an agreement to assist the Frederick Douglass Memorial and Historical Association in restoring Douglass's home in Anacostia, in Washington, D.C.

In 1916 the women pledged to clear the home of all indebtedness and to restore it to its former beauty in order that black youth might visit an historical site associated with a great black leader. Apparently it ceased existence around 1920.

Selected Bibliography Elizabeth L. Davis, *Lifting as They Climb: The National Association of Colored Women* (1933); Gerda A. Lerner, ed., *Black Women in White America: A Documentary History* (1972); Stephanie J. Shaw, "Black Club Women and the Creation of the National Association of Colored Women," *Journal of Women's History* 3 (No. 2, 1991), 10–25; Mary Church Terrell, *A Colored Woman in a White World* (1940).

Betty L. Plummer

National Baptist Convention, USA Founded in 1895 with headquarters in Nashville, Tennessee, in response to inferior racial treatment received by African American Baptists working within and for the white Southern and Northern Baptist Conventions, the new all-black convention sent missionaries to West Africa, established five independent black Baptist colleges, and a publishing board. Since 1924 the National Baptists and the Southern Baptists have operated jointly American Baptist Seminary [now College] in Nashville. And in the 1960s, a number of its students, including **John Lewis,** were leaders in the civil rights movement. The National Baptist Convention has become the largest African American denomination in the world, with eight million members in 1984. But in 1915, there was a split and the National Baptist Convention of America was organized. In 1961, another split (in part related to civil rights issues) established the Progressive National Baptist Convention. This second split resulted from the opposition of National Baptist Convention President Joseph H. Jackson's to **Martin Luther King, Jr.'s** social activism. In 1982, Theodore J. Jemison, a former civil rights leader, became Convention president. In 1989, the Convention's new headquarters in Nashville were dedicated. In 1994 Henry Lyons became president, but was convicted of grand theft and racketeering in 1999 and sentenced to five and a half years in prison. He was found guilty of taking $5 million in convention funds. William J. Shaw of Philadelphia became the new president.

Selected Bibliography Adam Fairclough, *To Redeem the Soul of America: The Southern Christian Leadership Conference and Martin Luther King, Jr.* (1987); Miles M. Fisher, *Short History of the Baptist Denomination* (1933); Joseph H. Jackson, "National Baptist Philosophy of Civil Rights," in Milton C. Sernett, ed., *Afro-American Religious History: A Documentary Witness* (1985); Emmanuel L. McCall, *Black Church Life-Styles* (1986); James M. McPherson, *The Abolitionist Legacy: From Reconstruction to the NAACP* (1975); Charles L. Sanders, "$10 Million Headquarters Signals New Course For National Baptist Convention, U.S.A., Inc.," *Ebony* (October 1989); Charles Whitaker, "Introducing Dr. William J. Shaw," *Ebony* (February 2000); Web site: www.nationalbaptist.com.

Lawrence H. Williams

National Brotherhood Workers of America Established in 1919, the National Brotherhood Workers of America (NBWA) reflected the move toward independent black unions following World War I. Under the leadership of T. J. Pree and R. T. Simms, the NBWA planned to organize and federate all African American workers and thus counteract the discriminatory policies of unions affiliated with the American Federation of Labor. Membership remained concentrated in Virginia's Tidewater area, but, at its peak, the Brotherhood attracted thousands of workers in 12 states and the District of Columbia. The short-lived NBWA collapsed in 1921, but not before it addressed squarely the issue of racial discrimination in the organized labor movement and offered black workers an alternative means of fighting employers and challenging white-controlled unions for economic justice.

Selected Bibliography Philip S. Foner, *Organized Labor and the Black Worker, 1619–1981* (1982); Philip S. Foner and Ronald L. Lewis, eds., *The Black Worker: A Documentary History from Colonial Times to the Present, vol. 5: The Black Worker from 1900 to 1919* (1980); "The National Brotherhood Association," *Messenger* 8 (August 1919), 7; "Report of Resolutions Committee of the National Brotherhood Workers of America," *Messenger* 11 (December 1919), 16–19; Sterling D. Spero and Abraham L. Harris, *The Black Worker: The Negro and the Labor Movement* (1974).

Robert Cvornyek

National Catholic Conference for Interracial Justice Founded in 1960, in Washington, D.C., as the successor to the **Catholic Interracial Council,** the National Catholic Conference for Interracial Justice (NCCIJ) is a nonprofit organization historically focused on generating concern for interracial justice in the white community and fostering black-white dialogue and common action. Early accomplishments included cochairing the 1963 **March on Washington,** mobilizing Catholics to join the 1965 **Selma to Montgomery March,** and calling for federal legislation against civil rights violence in the South. It has also promoted integrated Catholic education and greater sensitivity to minority concerns within inner-city Catholic schools. With the growing numbers of Hispanic, Asian American, and Native American Catholics, the NCCIJ has broadened its agenda to include the creation of a multiracially and multiculturally inclusive Catholic church in the United States.

Selected Bibliography John Hope Franklin and Alfred A. Moses, *From Slavery to Freedom: A History of African Americans,* 8th ed. (2000); National Catholic Conference for Interracial Justice, "A Future without Racism" and "Still Building Bridges between Races and Cultures," *Commitment* (pamphlets published by NCCIJ, 3033 Fourth Street, N. E., Washington, D.C.); Web site: www.nccij.org.

Andrew M. Manis

National Committee to Abolish the Poll Tax In 1938, encouraged by President Franklin D. Roosevelt, progressive southerners formed the **Southern Conference for Human Welfare** to seek ways of extending economic and political democracy to their region. Two of its members, Joseph Gelders and **Virginia Foster Durr** of Alabama, headed a Civil Rights Committee to persuade Congress to repeal the **poll tax** in the eight southern states that had imposed it. In 1941, they chartered a separate **National Committee to Abolish**

the Poll Tax, consisting of labor, liberal, and civil rights groups. Actively cooperating with the NAACP, the anti–poll tax federation nevertheless stressed that impoverished southern whites would benefit more than disfranchised blacks from abolition of the suffrage burden. Headquartered in Washington, D.C., the committee lobbied for several bills that won House approval but failed in the Senate. Although the organization collapsed in 1948, it succeeded in turning public opinion in the South against the poll tax. By the mid-1950s Georgia, South Carolina, and Tennessee had abolished their restrictions, while Alabama had reduced its required payment. In 1964, the ratification of the Twenty-fourth Amendment removed the poll tax requirement in national elections, and two years later in *Harper v. Virginia State Board of Elections* the U.S. Supreme Court eliminated it in state and local elections.

Selected Bibliography Virginia Durr, *Outside the Magic Circle* (1985); Thomas A. Krueger, *And Promises to Keep: The Southern Conference for Human Welfare, 1938–1948* (1967); Steven F. Lawson, *Black Ballots: Voting Rights in the South, 1944–1969* (1976); Frederic D. Ogden, *The Poll Tax in the South* (1958); Patricia Sullivan, *Days of Hope: Race and Democracy in the New Deal Era* (1996).

Steven F. Lawson

National Conference of Negro Youth   The National Conference of Negro Youth grew out of its New Deal umbrella organization, the National Youth Administration, a Works Progress Administration subsidiary. Mary McLeod Bethune was the moving spirit behind the conference. As the unofficial head of President Franklin D. Roosevelt's Black Cabinet, she utilized government facilities and goodwill to promote a series of conferences focused on the problems of black Americans. One of the most notable of these conferences was a three-day affair held in Washington, D.C., in 1937. An important aim was the enhancement of federal programs for black Americans. Other concerns were increased economic opportunities for blacks, an upgrading of educational and recreational facilities for black youth, better housing and health care, and equal protection under the law. Eleanor Roosevelt addressed the conference, along with several members of her husband's cabinet. The National Conference of Negro Youth, and the other Washington conferences, garnered unprecedented national publicity for the plight of black Americans. By reiterating the litany of demands articulated by the NAACP, the National Urban League, and the National Negro Congress, this effort gave impetus to the civil rights movement.

Selected Bibliography Ralph J. Bunche, *The Political Status of the Negro in the Age of FDR*, edited with an introduction by Dewey W. Grantham (1973); Harvard Sitkoff, *A New Deal For Blacks: The Emergence of Civil Rights as a National Issue: The Depression Decade* (1978); Joyce B. Ross, "Mary McLeod Bethune and the National Youth Administration: A Case Study of Power Relationships in the Black Cabinet of Franklin D. Roosevelt," *Journal of Negro History* 60 (January 1975), 1–29; Charles H. Wesley, *International Library of Afro-American Life and History: The Quest for Equality: From Civil War to Civil Rights* (1976).

Joe Louis Caldwell

National Council of Negro Women Educator **Mary McLeod Bethune** founded the National Council of Negro Women (NCNW) in New York City in December 1935, and served as its president until her retirement in 1949. Bethune united the major national African American women's associations into the NCNW, focusing activities on racial discrimination, the enhancement of better international relationships, and national liberal causes. The NCNW served as a clearinghouse for federal legislation affecting women and children, sponsored an archives, and published the quarterly, *Aframerican Woman's Journal*. As president of the NCNW, Bethune strengthened the organization by establishing chapters in major cities and, with a generous donation from Marshall Field III, was able to purchase a permanent headquarters building in Washington, D.C.

Selected Bibliography Franklin Fosdick, "War among the Women," *Negro Digest* 8 (February 1950), 21–25; Stanley S. Jacobs, "The Story of Mary Bethune," *This Month* (March 1947), 110–13; Edward T. James and Janet Wilson James, eds., *Notable American Women* (1971); Web site: www.ncnw.com.

Janice M. Leone

National Equal Rights League The first National Equal Rights League was founded in 1864 to promote the civil rights of African Americans. **John Mercer Langston** was chosen to be the first president. A second league was started in the early 1900s by **William Monroe Trotter,** a central figure in the **Niagara Movement** from which eventually came the **National Association for the Advancement of Colored People** (NAACP). He was also part of a group **W.E.B. Du Bois** called the "Talented Tenth," which insisted upon equal rights for African Americans. However, Trotter's National Equal Rights League competed with Du Bois and the NAACP for the allegiance of integrationists, black and white. The league was unsuccessful because of Trotter's discordant tactics and the NAACP's more moderate approach. In 1903 Trotter gained national attention in the so-called **Boston Riot** by publicly confronting **Booker T. Washington** in a local church, and in 1908 he opposed William Howard Taft's election to the presidency. He again made headlines by criticizing the racial policies of President Woodrow Wilson and by meeting with presidents Warren G. Harding and Calvin Coolidge to protest racial segregation in the federal government. In the 1920s he tried to connect the league to **Marcus Garvey**'s movement and the **African Blood Brotherhood,** but, instead, the league dissolved.

Selected Bibliography Howard H. Bell, ed., *Minutes of the Proceedings of the National Negro Conventions, 1830–1964* (1969); Robert Brisbane, *The Black Vanguard: Origins of the Negro Social Revolution, 1900–1960* (1970); Stephen Fox, *The Guardian of Boston: William Monroe Trotter* (1970); Charles V. Hamilton, *Du Bois's "Two-ness" and the Dual Agenda* (1993); David Levering Lewis, *W.E.B. Du Bois: Biography of a Race* (1993); Charles V. Willie, Antoine M. Garibaldi, and Wornie L. Reed, eds., *The Education of African Americans* (1991).

Marvin Thomas

National Freedmen's Relief Association Urged on by leaders of the **American Missionary Association,** opponents of slavery in New York City established the National Freedmen's Relief Association on 22 February 1862. The organization sought to aid ex-slaves on the South Carolina sea islands by providing instructors for schools, direction for the cultivation of plantations, and supplies. In 1863 the association joined similar groups to advocate organization of what would become the **Freedmen's Bureau.** The association in 1865 cooperated with other societies to support black schools across the South through the American Freedmen's Aid Commission, which expanded into the American Freedmen's Union Commission from 1866 to 1868.

Selected Bibliography Robert C. Morris, *Reading, 'Riting, and Reconstruction: The Education of Freedmen in the South, 1861–1870* (1981); Willie Lee Rose, *Rehearsal for Reconstruction: The Port Royal Experiment* (1964).

Alwyn Barr

National Medical Association Founded in Atlanta, Georgia, in 1895 by a group of black men attending the Cotton States and International Exposition, the National Medical Association (NMA) was designed as a national organization for black physicians, dentists, and pharmacists. Specifically, its purpose was to unite "men and women of African descent who are legally and honorably engaged in the cognate professions of medicine, surgery, pharmacy and dentistry." Since its inception, members of the NMA have struggled to end any discrimination and segregation directed toward health care professionals and discrimination in health care facilities. During World War II the NMA opposed the construction of segregated Veterans Administration hospitals. In 1945 representatives from the NMA and other black groups met with the Director of the Veterans Administration to discuss policies for the complete integration of the veterans hospital system. At the same time, the NMA opposed federal funding for segregated hospitals for the general population. It was especially critical of the Hill-Burton Hospital Construction Act (1946) with its **separate-but-equal** clause, which allowed for further creation of **Jim Crow** hospitals at government expense. During the civil rights crusade of the 1960s and 1970s the NMA intensified its campaign to end segregation in hospital facilities and demanded that black physicians and surgeons be allowed privileges in all hospitals.

Selected Bibliography Benjamin F. Mays, "The Diamond Jubilee of the National Medical Association," *Journal of the National Medical Association* 62 (November 1970), 408–10; Herbert M. Morais, *The History of the Negro in Medicine* (1967); Charles E. Odegaard, *Minorities in Medicine* (1977); Dietrich C. Reitzes, *Negroes and Medicine* (1958); Web site: www.nmanet.org.

Betty L. Plummer

National Negro Business League The idea for such an organization may have come from **W.E.B. Du Bois,** but **Booker T. Washington** created it in 1900 in Boston. It sought to achieve racial economic independence in an increasingly commercial age. The first annual meeting drew 300 delegates, representing business and the professions. In 1915, 3,000 delegates from 300 chapters attended its convention. Total membership, in 36 states and West Africa, ranged from 5,000 to 40,000. Life memberships at $25 each reached nearly 100 by 1915, and two philanthropists—**Julius Rosenwald** and Andrew Carnegie—contributed generously. Many local chapters existed only on paper, however, while others were torn by internecine personal disputes. Washington resolutely staffed the league with his conservative loyalists. **Lynching,** segregation, and race riots incurred only oblique condemnation. Instead, the league concentrated on self-help, race loyalty, and material success. Offering encouragement and commercial instruction, the league remained, until Washington's death, an integral part of the Tuskegee Machine, a resolute opponent of more radical black organizations. In the 1930s, it emphasized interracial cooperation because black "progress will tend to strengthen the whole structure of American business. . . ." During World War II, the league promoted victory gardens, thrift, and the easing of racial tensions.

Selected Bibliography John H. Burrows, *The Necessity of Myth: A History of the National Negro Business League* (1988); Louis R. Harlan, "Booker T. Washington and the National Negro Business League," in William G. Shade and Roy C. Herrenkohl, eds., *Seven on Black: Reflections on the Negro Experience in America* (1969); August Meier, *Negro Thought in America, 1880—1915* (1963).

Richard W. Resh

National Negro Congress   The National Negro Congress (NNC), although it never established itself as a mass movement, was a notable attempt at racial solidarity. Founded at **Howard University** in 1935, its call to membership was made to all African Americans and their organizations, churches, unions and political groups. The NNC urged unionization of African American women workers, desegregation of public accommodations and schools, and protection of migrant workers. It lobbied for antilynch legislation and against fascism. Its first president, **A. Phillip Randolph,** cautioned the 800 delegates against **Communist Party** infiltration in the first meeting held in Chicago, Illinois, in 1936. By 1940, the NNC was a Communist-controlled group and remained under Federal Bureau of Investigation surveillance until the 1950s.

Selected Bibliography Robert L. Allen, *Reluctant Reformers* (1974); Thomas Fleming, *Reflections on Black History for the Columbus Free Press,* http://www.freepress.org/Backup/Unixbackup/pubhtml/fleming/fleming.html; Scholarly Resources Microfilm, "FBI Files," 1986; Mark I. Solomon, *The Cry Was Unity: Communists and African Americans, 1917–1936* (1998); Monroe Work, ed., *Negro Year Book: 1937–1938* (1937).

Aingred G. Dunston

National Urban League   Officials of this organization consider it the most versatile of the groups founded for the advancement of black Americans. The seventieth-anniversary *Journal,* published in 1980, summed up the role of the league as being "a provider of direct services; a research institution; a laboratory in which human development programs are conceived and implemented; an advocate for civil rights, equity and justice; a catalytic force that unites diverse people in pursuit of unselfish goals; a dreamer and a doer." In October 1911, three organizations that had been formed between 1905 and 1910 to help black migrants adjust to urban life merged to form the National Urban League. At first, the league was primarily a New York organization, but the founders intended that it become a national movement. The first directors, **George E. Haynes** and **Eugene Kinckle Jones,** led in developing programs and structures applicable to cities throughout the country. The mass migration of black workers to northern cities during World War I accelerated the league's growth. Soon, there were branches in most industrial cities. Throughout its history the league has participated in efforts to end discrimination within the ranks of organized labor and in federal programs. **Lester B. Granger,** who became executive director in 1941, worked to foster the integration of the armed forces. From 1923 to 1948, the league published the magazine *Opportunity,* which contained articles on black life and served as a medium of expression for black writers and artists. After **Whitney M. Young, Jr.,** became executive director in 1961, the league became an active participant in the civil rights movement. League branches were established in many southern cities. In 1968, in response to the **Black Power movement** and to the urban violence of the 1960s, the league directed more of its resources to helping the underclass in black communities. Young called these efforts to aid high school dropouts, launch voter registration drives, promote community health, and start neighborhood improvement programs the league's "New Thrust" approach. In 1977, the title of the organization's executive was changed from executive director to president. The league's work in civil rights and in community improvement have continued under Young's successors, **Vernon E. Jordan, Jr.** (1972), John Jacob (1982), and Hugh B. Price (1994). Price has been faced with the challenge of positioning his organization to protect the economic gains made by African Americans since the 1960s in the face of forces seeking to roll back these gains and end affirmative action.

Selected Bibliography Jesse Thomas Moore, Jr., *A Search for Equality: The National Urban League, 1910–1961* (1981); National Urban League, *70th Anniversary* (1980); Guichard Parris and Lester Brooks, *Blacks in the City: A History of the National Urban League* (1971); Arvarh E. Strickland, *History of the Chicago Urban League* (1966 and 2001); Nancy J. Weiss, *The National Urban League, 1910–1940* (1974); Nancy J. Weiss, *Whitney M. Young, Jr., and the Struggle for Civil Rights* (1990); Web site: www.nul.org.

Arvarh E. Strickland

Native Son   Chosen as a Book of the Month Club selection when it was published in 1940, *Native Son* gave American readers "a terrible picture of reality which they could see and feel and yet not destroy." **Richard Wright** created a searing indictment of institutionalized racism in his novel, for he believed society could not continue to ignore the probable results of its having created the conditions for an underclass in its urban ghettoes. The novel challenged and continues to challenge readers regardless of their attitudes about civil rights. It exposes in graphic episodes the deep resentments bred by what **Margaret**

Walker Alexander has aptly termed "the psychic wound of racism." Through his archetypal hero Bigger Thomas, Wright shows how the poverty and ignorance born of rigid segregation and discrimination can erupt in violence. As a fictional treatment of the sociology of racism, *Native Son* remains unsurpassed as a portrayal of what happens in America's inner cities. *Native Son* provided a prophetic vision of the hatreds unleashed in the urban riots of the 1960s.

Selected Bibliography Richard Abcarian, ed., *Richard Wright's Native Son: A Critical Handbook* (1970); Houston A. Baker, Jr., ed., *Twentieth-Century Interpretations of* Native Son (1972); Katherine Fishburn, *Richard Wright's Hero* (1977); Joyce Ann Joyce, *Richard Wright's Art of Tragedy* (1986); Richard Macksey and Frank E. Moorer, eds., *Richard Wright: A Collection of Critical Essays* (1984); James Smethurst, "Invented by Horror: The Gothic and African-American Literary Ideology in *Native Son,*" *African American Review* 35 (No. 1, 2001), 29–40; Margaret Walker, *Richard Wright, Daemonic Genius: A Portrait of the Man, A Critical Look at His Works* (1988).

Jerry Ward

Neal, Claude (date and place of birth unknown–27 October 1934, Greenwood, Fla.). This 23-year-old illiterate black man was lynched in Greenwood, in Jackson County, Florida, on 27 October 1934 for the alleged rape and murder of a young white woman. He was arrested on circumstantial evidence and placed in concealed confinement in Brewton, Alabama. Some men from Jackson County easily abducted Neal and returned him to Florida, where Neal was castrated, forced to eat his penis and testicles, and "horribly mutilated." **Walter Francis White** of the NAACP called Neal's lynching "one of the most bestial crimes ever committed by a mob." Neal's lynching received widespread media and newspaper coverage that White utilized to garner support for a proposed federal antilynching bill.

Selected Bibliography Walter T. Howard, "Vigilante Justice: Extra-Legal Executions in Florida, 1930–1940" (Ph.D. diss., The Florida State University, 1987); Lynching File, Florida State Archives, Tallahassee; James R. McGovern, *Anatomy of a Lynching: The Killing of Claude Neal* (1982); James R. McGovern and Walter T. Howard, "Private Justice and National Concern: The Lynching of Claude Neal," *The Historian* 43 (August 1981), 546–59; National Association for the Advancement of Colored People, *The Lynching of Claude Neal* (1934).

Maxine D. Jones

***Neal v. Delaware,* 103 U.S. 370 (1880)** William Neal was a black man accused of rape. At his trial in a Delaware court, Neal's defense attorney moved to dismiss the all-white jury because blacks were systematically and completely excluded from juries in the state. The trial court refused to consider the motion, and Neal was convicted and sentenced to death. In reviewing the trial court's action, the chief justice of Delaware's highest appeals court admitted that blacks were and had always been excluded from juries but explained the phenomenon with the observation that "the great body of black men residing in this State are utterly unqualified by want of intelligence, experience or moral integrity, to sit on juries." When Neal appealed his conviction to the U.S. Supreme Court, the state attorney general also admitted that the state purposefully excluded blacks from juries.

Justice **John Marshall Harlan,** writing for the majority of the Court, declared that the state's open admission of the exclusion of blacks from juries presented a prima facie case of denial "of that equality of protection which has been secured by the Constitution and laws of the United States." He explained that, while the Court would generally presume that states were acting within the dictates of the **Fourteenth** and **Fifteenth Amendments,** the Delaware chief justice's "violent presumption" that all blacks were "utterly disqualified" for jury service, without further inquiry, denied Neal his constitutional rights. The Supreme Court reversed Neal's conviction and instructed the new trial court to grant him a hearing on his motions challenging the all white jury.

Although the Supreme Court decision guaranteed Neal a hearing, it in no way guaranteed that blacks would serve on future juries. It only prevented states from recognizing the total exclusion of blacks from juries and cavalierly refusing to consider, even cursorily, the possibility of racial discrimination.

Selected Bibliography Charles Fairman, *History of the Supreme Court of the United States, vol. 7: Reconstruction and Reunion 1864–1888 Part II* (1986); Loren Miller, *The Petitioners: The Story of the Supreme Court of the United States and the Negro* (1966); Harvey B. Rubenstein, "The Case of the 'Violent Presumption': Another Delaware Controversy That Shaped the Constitution," *Delaware Lawyer* 6 (1988), 46.

Kenneth DeVille

Nearing, Scott (6 August 1883, Morris Run, Pa.–23 August 1983, Harborside, Vt.). A socialist/pacifist dedicated to civil liberties, Nearing

Scott Nearing, c. 1915. © Library of Congress.

thought society should "provide a good life for all." He attended the University of Pennsylvania (Ph.D. in Economics, 1909), served on child labor committees, and gained notoriety by getting fired from teaching positions at the University of Pennsylvania (1915) and Toledo University (1917) because of his antiwar views. Later, Nearing taught at the Rand School, was a socialist candidate for Congress, and then a farmer. He wrote two books on racism: *Black America* (1924), urging black workers to join whites in a worker's party, and the novel *Free Born* (1932), the violent tale of a black laborer leading a Pennsylvania coal strike.

Selected Bibliography Scott Nearing, *The Making of a Radical: A Political Autobiography* (1972); John A. Saltmarsh, *Scott Nearing: An Intellectual Biography* (1991); Stephen J. Whitfield, *Scott Nearing: Apostle of American Radicalism* (1974).

Linda G. Ford

Negro American Labor Council   Organized in May 1960 as a gathering of black and white trade unionists, the Negro American Labor Council was formed to promote increased black membership in labor unions and black advancement within union administrations. The council's most notable accomplishment was its leadership in organizing the 1963 **March on Washington.** Council President **A. Philip Randolph** was already planning an "Emancipation March to Washington for Jobs," which had aroused little interest. Dr. **Martin Luther King, Jr.,** heard of Randolph's fading proposal and decided to adopt the idea and expand the scope of the march. Forty thousand union members participated under the council's auspices. The Negro American Labor Council was replaced in 1972 by the **Coalition of Black Trade Unionists,** which has continued to seek greater black participation in organized labor.

Selected Bibliography Adam Fairclough, *To Redeem the Soul of a Nation: The Southern Christian Leadership Conference and Martin Luther King, Jr.* (1987); Philip S. Foner and Ronald L. Lewis, eds., *Black Workers: A Documentary History from Colonial Times to the Present* (1989); Paula F. Pfeffer, *A Philip Randolph: Pioneer of the Civil Rights Movement* (1990).

Randall L. Patton

The Negro Artisan   Written and edited by **W.E.B. Du Bois** in 1902, it was the first comprehensive study of black workers. It exhaustively documented the exclusionary practices of labor unions and the growing frustration of black skilled workers. Arguably the best study in the **Atlanta University Conference for the Study of Negro Problems,** *The Negro Artisan* also provided Du Bois with the empirical data that underlined his growing opposition to industrial education. The monograph combined an historical narrative with surveys of artisans, employer attitudes, training schools, and union practices. It established the standard approaches in black labor history for the next 50 years. In 1912 Du Bois investigated black workers again in his 10-year repeating cycle of comprehensive studies.

Selected Bibliography Herbert Apetheker, ed., *The Correspondence of W.E.B. Du Bois,* vol. 1 (1973); W.E.B. Du Bois, ed., *The Negro Artisan* 7 (Atlanta, 1902); W.E.B. Du Bois and Augustus Dill, eds., *The Negro American Artisan* 14 (Atlanta, 1912); Francille Rusan Wilson, *The Segregated Scholars: Black Labor Historians, 1895–1950* (2002); Elliot Rudwick, "W.E.B. Du Bois as a Sociologist," in James Blackwell and Morris Janowitz, eds., *Black Sociologists: Historical and Contemporary Perspectives* (1975).

Francille Rusan Wilson

Negro History Bulletin **Carter G. Woodson** founded this magazine in October 1937 under the auspices of the **Association for the Study of Afro-American Life and History** (ASALH) and served as its managing editor. The initial subscription was one dollar a year and targeted an audience that professional or scholarly publications would not ordinarily reach. Combining scholarly and popular topics, the *Bulletin* early enjoyed a large circulation, which reached 5,000 in 1966 and 7,500 in 1984. The publication provided an invaluable service to black school children by promoting black culture and history and filling gaps in textbooks, which often neglected black contributions to America's past. During the 1980s the *Bulletin* failed to meet scheduled publication dates due to a lack of staffing resulting from financial difficulties experienced by the ASALH. In 2003, the last published issue was volume 64 (2001).

Selected Bibliography Rayford W. Logan and Michael R. Winston, eds., *Dictionary of American Negro Biography* (1982); Publication Information, *Negro History Bulletin* 1 (October 1937), 47 (July–December 1984).

Thomas D. Cockrell

Negro History Week During the second week of February 1926, Negro History Week was first commemorated to highlight the outstanding accomplishments of African Americans, and to call attention to their history. The concept was most vigorously promoted by Dr. **Carter G. Woodson,** the initiator of the observance. This week was selected to coincide with the birth dates of **Frederick Douglass** and Abraham Lincoln. This week-long activity's primary purpose, according to Woodson, was "to stage dramatizations and other exercises in order to demonstrate the role of the Negro in the past and secure for the race the same considerations in the curriculum that we give others." He was ably supported by the active members of the **Association of the Study of Negro Life and History.** During the peak years of the civil rights era and to the mid-1970s an increasing demand was made by a wide cross-section of the African American community to extend the celebration period. This led to expanding the observance to all four weeks of February, which then became Black History Month.

Selected Bibliography Albert N. D. Brooks, "Proud American Day," The Association for the Study of Negro Life and History, Washington, D.C. (1956); Nerissa L. Milton, "Negro History Week, 1958," The Association for the Study of Negro Life and History, Washington, D.C. (1958); Edgar A. Toppin, "Carter Woodson Began Black History Week," *Washington Afro-American,* 8 February 1975.

Glenn O. Phillips

Newsboy in Chicago selling the *Chicago Defender*, a leading black newspaper, 1942. © Library of Congress.

Negro Newspaper Publishers' Association   Established in 1940, the Negro Newspaper Publishers' Association is currently known as the National Newspaper Publishers Association. It met the need of African American publishers to establish a relationship between the black press and black business. It improved its members' advertising capabilities and unified their editorial stance on all African American issues. It was instrumental in breaking the color barrier in the Congressional Press Galleries in 1947, and two of its members broke other social barriers when they traveled with President Harry S Truman in 1948. In 2003, the association remained vibrant, giving annual awards and maintaining a Hall of Fame.

   Selected Bibliography *Encyclopedia of Associations* (1990); Lawrence Hogan, *A Black National News Service: The Associated Negro Press and Claude Barnett, 1919–1945* (1984); Web site: www.nnpa.org.

Jessie M. Carter

Negro People's Theater   This Harlem-based theatrical company was the first of many independent theater groups established in the 1930s. The founders, **Rose McClendon,** Dick Campbell, and Muriel Rahn, sought to create a cultural platform from which real drama about black life, with black actors and actresses devoid of denigrating stereotypes, could be performed. The company presented its version of Clifford Odets's *Waiting for Lefty* in 1935 and in conjunction with the New Theater League, presented Odets's *Remember*, a play about a black family on relief, during the same year. These were the only productions of this theater company.

Selected Bibliography Malcolm Goldstein, *The Political Stage: American Drama and Theater of the Great Depression* (1974); Errol Hill, ed., *The Theater of Black Americans* (1980); Loften Mitchell, *Black Drama: The Story of the American Negro in the Theater* (1967); Jay Plum, "Rose McClendon and the Black Units of the Federal Theater Project: A Lost Contribution," *Theater Survey* 33 (1992), 144–53.

Malik Simba

Negro Spiritual An oral record and classic folk expression of African Americans, the Negro spiritual became a major source of communication for African Americans who refused to reconcile themselves to slavery. The Negro spiritual, first sung on southern plantations, was probably shaped by a mixture of African musical influences, hymns sung in white churches, and music by white composers. It is a vehicle for understanding African American slave experiences, which provided a medium of black communication that mitigated the debilitating effects of slavery. The Negro spiritual also indicated that slavery was not a closed institution; that the process of dehumanization was not complete; that African Americans were able to maintain their essential humanity; and that African Americans were aesthetically and morally equal to whites. Furthermore, the Negro spiritual represented the sorrow, escape, relief, and rebellious nature of the African American. From its beginning in American musical culture, the Negro spiritual has contained some persistent themes that have helped to explain the African American ethos in antebellum as well as in postbellum America. The following are major ideas that permeated these songs: the obtaining of physical freedom in the secular world; death and resurrection in celestial happiness, freedom from white oppression; despair intertwined with confidence and joy; and the notion that African Americans were God's chosen people. Early in its history, the Negro spiritual was denigrated and maligned. As African Americans allegedly had made no worthwhile contributions to shaping American culture, the Negro spirituals were viewed with contempt. It was through the efforts of the famed **Jubilee Singers** of **Fisk University** that the Negro spiritual was rescued from obscurity. This group, organized about 1875, popularized this music and enhanced its acceptance throughout the world.

Selected Bibliography Pamela T. Burns, "The Negro Spiritual: From the Southern Plantations to the Concert Stages of America" (Ph.D. diss., University of Alabama, 1994); James H. Cone, *The Spirituals and the Blues: An Interpretation* (1972); Miles Mark Fisher, *Negro Slave Songs in the United States* (1953); James Weldon Johnson and Rosamund Johnson, *The Book of American Negro Spirituals* (1926); Lawrence W. Levine, *Black Culture and Black Consciousness: Afro-American Folk Thought from Slavery to Freedom* (1977); Alain Locke, "The Negro Spirituals," in Alain Locke, ed., *The New Negro* (1925); J. B. T. Marsh, *The Story of the Jubilee Singers: With Their Songs* (1881).

Phillip McGuire

The Negro Worker This pamphlet, written by **Abram L. Harris** for the National Committee for Labor Action, addressed the problems African Americans were having in the "entire labor movement." Depicting the problem as one of vital concern, the essay provided statistics for the number of African American workers involved in the unions, which amounted to 45,000 in affiliated and 11,000 in independent unions. It listed 26 unions with racial bars, including the names of 11 American Federation of Labor and 13 unaffiliated unions. It further claimed that, in 1930, 9 federated and 10 unaffiliated unions had provisions in their constitutions barring blacks from membership.

Selected Bibliography Abram L. Harris, *The Negro Worker* (1930); Ray Marshall, *The Negro Worker* (1967).

Jessie M. Carter

Negro World Published from 1919 to 1933 by **Marcus Garvey** as the official organ for the **Universal Negro Improvement Association** and editorialized as "a newspaper devoted solely to the interests of the Negro race," the paper repeated Garvey's nationalist aims and reflected his strong personality. His message—that black people are beautiful, are overwhelmed with white oppression, and should rid themselves of self-hatred—was as uncompromisingly adamant as that found in any other major African American newspaper of the period. Along with promoting his shipping line, the editorials criticized men like **W.E.B. Du Bois** for being intellectual pawns of whites.

Selected Bibliography Nathan Irvin Huggins, *Harlem Renaissance* (1979); Amy Jacques-Garvey, *Philosophy and Opinions of Marcus Garvey* (1971).

Jessie M. Carter

New England Freedman's Aid Society An outgrowth of the Boston Educational Commission, this organization begun on 7 February 1862, was the first among many nonsectarian freedman's aid societies. Its goal, according to its secretary J. H. Chapin, was "to pave the way for a good free school system at the South open alike to all races and colors." Consequently, it sent its first group of teachers to Port Royal, South Carolina, in March 1862. In 1865 the society affiliated with the American Freedman's Aid Commission, a coalition of nondenominational societies in the Northeast and Midwest. It was also instrumental in the **Freedmen's Bureau**'s establishment in March 1865. By January 1871, however, its work decreased because of the rise of southern public education and black self-help. It gave up all normal school work in 1874, with the exception of two schools in Virginia and Georgia.

Selected Bibliography Ronald Buchart, *Northern Schools, Southern Blacks and Reconstruction, Freedmen's Education, 1862–1875* (1980); Robert C. Morris, *Reading, 'Riting, and Reconstruction: The Education of Freedmen in the South, 1861–1871* (1981); Julius H. Parmelee, "Freedmen's Aid Societies, 1861–1871," U.S. Department of the Interior, Office of Education, *Bulletin* (No. 38, 1916), 268–300; Willie Lee Rose, *Rehearsal for Reconstruction: The Port Royal Experiment* (1964); Henry Lee Swint, *The Northern Teacher in the South, 1862–1870* (1967).

Judith N. Kerr

New Negro Alliance   The New Negro Alliance began in Washington D.C. during the summer of 1933 as a picketing and boycott movement directed at businesses and chain stores operating in African American neighborhoods without black workers. Organized by Frank Thorne, **William Hastie,** and Beford Lawson, the alliance was one of several dozen **Jobs for Negroes Movement** campaigns launched in black neighborhoods in cities across the nation during the depression of the 1930s. Picketing had to be suspended when the Kauffman Five and Dime and Sanitary Drug Store secured a temporary court injunction contending that the pickets were "unlawful assemblies that restrained trade, endangered lives of pedestrians that could result in violent riots." While William Hastie (later the first African American appointed to the federal bench) appealed the injunction, the alliance organized neighborhoods in support of a civil rights law, set up a community school to train clerks and managers, and established several citywide recreational programs. By 1938 when the U.S. Supreme Court agreed that African Americans did have the right to use pickets to address racial discrimination, the New Negro Alliance had established itself as a vital community institution in Washington, D.C., that would last until the 1950s.

Selected Bibliography *Baltimore Afro-American,* 27 January 1934; Gary Hunter, "'Don't Buy Where You Can't Work': Black Activism During the Depression Years" (Ph.D. diss., University of Michigan, 1977); Michele F. Pacifico, "Don't Buy Where You Can't Work: The New Negro Alliance of Washington," *Washington History* 6 (1994), 66–88.

Gary J. Hunter

New Negro Movement   This post–World War I movement merged two streams of African American consciousness: social and civil equality, and cultural identity. Black intellectuals and artists broke with the nineteenth century's social and intellectual tradition of accommodation and attempted to build a new concept of race and to define a culture rooted in Africa, not Europe. "Militant" African Americans announced that they would use physical action in self-defense to achieve equality, while artists exploited the beauty and richness of blackness. **Alain Locke**'s *The New Negro* (1920) showcased the affirmation of the artistic self-consciousness of the Negro's human and cultural worth, the sense of an urgent need for self-assertion and militancy, and the belief in a culturally enriched past in America and Africa.

Selected Bibliography Nathan Irvin Huggins, *The Harlem Renaissance* (1971); David Levering Lewis, *When Harlem Was in Vogue* (1979); Wilson J. Moses, *The Golden Age of Black Nationalism, 1850–1925* (1978); Gary D. Wintz, *Black Culture and the Harlem Renaissance* (1988).

Thaddeus M. Smith

New Orleans Race Riot (1866)   By the summer of 1866, portents of political conflict in Louisiana were unmistakable. Unionist Governor James Madison Wells was moving closer to the so-called **Radical Republicans** of both races who were centered in New Orleans. Wells had taken the unusual step, with Radical support, of calling the 1864 constitutional convention back in session. The convention was to meet on 30 July 1866 in New Orleans. The convention and its main goal, black suffrage, were both bitterly opposed by the Democrat controlled state legislature, the Democrat mayor of New Orleans who promised to arrest delegates, and the city's Democrat press. Delegates convened about noon on the appointed day. At the same time several hundred blacks marching in support of the convention were set upon by a large crowd of police and white civilians near the convention site. Amidst shooting and wild disorder, the white mob pursued the marchers to the nearby Mechanics' Institute, where they forced entry, and proceeded to beat, stab, and shoot delegates and their supporters. In midafternoon federal troops arrived and brought order. The day of violence was less a riot than a police-led massacre that had distinct political overtones. Of the 36 dead, all but one was a black or white Republican.

Selected Bibliography Joseph G. Dawson, *Army Generals and Reconstruction: Louisiana: 1862–1877* (1982); George C. Rable, *But There Was No Peace: The Role of Violence in the Politics of Reconstruction* (1984); Joe Gray Taylor, *Louisiana Reconstructed, 1863–1877* (1974); Ted Tunnell, *Crucible of Reconstruction: War, Radicalism, and Race in Louisiana, 1862–1877* (1984); Gilles Vandal, *The New Orleans Riot of 1866: Anatomy of a Tragedy* (1983).

Larry T. Balsamo

New Orleans Race Riot (1874). See Battle of September 14th (or Canal Street) 1874.

New Orleans Race Riot (1900) The New Orleans race riot of 1900 started on 23 July and lasted five days. Race relations were especially tense that summer as poor whites were being displaced from their jobs by African American migrants from rural areas, and African Americans were resentful of increasing restrictions as segregation was more strictly enforced. The violence began when Robert Charles, a member of the International Migration Society who had been outraged by the story of the 1899 lynching and mutilation of **Sam Hose** in Georgia, scuffled with a police officer. They exchanged pistol shots, and both were wounded. Charles killed 2 pursuing police officers. Before he died in a hail of bullets on 27 July, he had killed 7 whites, including 3 police officers; wounded 8 whites seriously, including 3 additional police officers; and wounded an additional 12 whites slightly. During this time a white mob that had broken into roving gangs randomly attacked African Americans, killing 8, severely injuring 21, and beating approximately 50 others. The mob also burned the best African American school in Louisiana. Five whites were hospitalized. In all probability only Mayor Paul Capdeville's swift action in deputizing 1,500 special police and deploying state militia troops prevented more extremes in white violence.

Selected Bibliography William Ivy Hair, *Carnival of Fury: Robert Charles and the New Orleans Race Riot of 1900* (1976); Dale A. Somers, "Black and White in New Orleans: A Study in Urban Race Relations, 1865–1900," *The Journal of Southern History* 40 (February 1974), 19–42;

Daphne Spain, "Race Relations and Residential Segregation in New Orleans: Two Centuries of Paradox," *The Annals of the American Academy of Political and Social Science* 441 (January 1979), 82–96.

Lorenzo Crowell

New Orleans Tribune (La Tribune de la Nouvelle-Orleans) The *New Orleans Tribune* was the first African American daily newspaper in the United States. With a bilingual format, the *Tribune* was published from 21 July 1864 to 27 April 1868, with intermittent revivals between 1868 and 1871. It supplanted an earlier Afro-Creole newspaper, *L'Union,* and paralleled the biracial publication, *Louisianan.* The *Tribune*'s founder and publisher was Louis Charles Roudanez, M.D. (1823–90), a Louisiana free Creole. Editors included Paul Trevigne and Jean-Charles Houzeau, the latter a Belgian scientist who actively participated in liberation causes in Europe and the United States. The *Tribune* uncompromisingly supported universal suffrage and counseled against blind loyalty to the Republican party. This position, along with counter-Reconstruction impulses, contributed to factionalism in the African American community and in the newspaper's management. Nonetheless, the *Tribune* served as an important document of African American political consciousness during the immediate postbellum era.

Selected Bibliography John W. Blassingame, *Black New Orleans, 1860–1880* (1973); Rodolphe Lucien Desdunes, *Our People and Our History* (1911; reprint, 1973); Jean-Charles Houzeau, *My Passage at the New Orleans Tribune* (1870; reprint, 1984); Robert R. MacDonald, John R. Kemp, and Edward F. Haas, eds., *Louisiana's Black Heritage* (1979).

Bernice F. Guillaume

New York Age **T. Thomas Fortune** and Jerome B. Peterson founded the *New York Age* in 1886. Fortune used the paper to promote political awareness among black readers, and he urged blacks to place race before party. Under his aggressive leadership, the *New York Age* championed the civil rights of blacks, bemoaned the stereotypical black characters depicted on New York stages, and sounded a clarion call for black southerners to migrate north. During his tenure, Fortune's temperamental nature and his excessive drinking caused inconsistencies in the *New York Age's* editorials. However, his radical posture on the question of race shaped the paper's protest image. Financial ties to **Booker T. Washington** did not prevent Fortune from denouncing President Theodore Roosevelt, Washington's political ally, for his role in the infamous **Brownsville, Texas, affray.** Fortune launched a blistering attack against Roosevelt in the *New York Age*. When Fortune, after suffering a physical and mental breakdown, sold his share of the *New York Age* in 1907, the heyday of its role in the forefront of civil rights protest journalism had passed.

Selected Bibliography John Hope Franklin and Alfred A. Moss, Jr., *From Slavery to Freedom: A History of Negro Americans,* 8th ed. (2000); August Meier, *Negro Thought in America, 1880–1915* (1966); James Dolores Nutter, "Coverage of Marcus Garvey by the New York Age and the New York *Times: A Comparative Historical Analysis*" (Ph.D. diss., Howard University, 1991); Gilbert Osofsky, *Harlem: The Making of a Ghetto Negro New York, 1890–1930* (1963); Emma Lou Thornbrough, "More Light on Booker T. Washington and the New York Age," *Journal of Negro History* 43 (1958), 30–49; Emma Lou Thornbrough, *T. Thomas Fortune: Militant Journalist* (1972).

Joe Louis Caldwell

Newark, New Jersey, Race Riot (1967)   This riot was one of the most destructive of the many "civil disturbances" that swept American cities during the "long, hot summers" of the late 1960s. Newark was a city of over 400,000, the thirtieth-largest metropolitan area in the United States. It had serious social and economic problems. "White flight" during the 1950s and early 1960s had transformed it from a majority white to a majority black city. The city's tax base also shrank as white businesses fled the inner city, and city revenues could not keep pace with increased social needs. Inadequate educational opportunities, combined with racial discrimination, had a ripple effect on the city's economy: by 1967, over 24,000 adult black males were unemployed. The white community, despite its minority status, maintained control over the city's government. Complaints of police brutality escalated but were generally brushed aside. Black anger at this indifference erupted into a riot. It began on 12 July, when police beat a black cab driver after arresting him. Protesters gathered at the police station near the Hayes Homes housing project. A fire-

Firemen spray water on burning buildings during the riot in Newark, New Jersey, 1967. © AP/Wide World Photos.

bomb hit the wall of the station house. Police charged out of the building, clubbing everyone within reach and triggering a four-day riot. Angry protesters looted local businesses. The 1,300-man Newark police force was augmented by 475 state troopers and over 4,000 National Guardsmen. The guardsmen often fired on suspected looters or snipers, killing 21 blacks, most of them bystanders, including 2 children. Two whites, a policeman, and a fireman were killed. The riot caused over 10 million dollars in property damage.

Selected Bibliography Jules Archer, *Riot! A History of Mob Action in the United States* (1974); David M. Gerwin, "The End of Coalitions: The Failure of Community Organizing in Newark in the 1960s" (Ph.D. diss., Columbia University, 1998); Tom Hayden, *Rebellion in Newark* (1976); Andrew Kopkind, "White on Black: The Riot Commission and the Rhetoric of Reform," in Anthony Platt, ed., *The Politics of Riot Commissions, 1917–1970* (1971); *Report of the National Advisory Commission on Civil Disorders* (1968).

Randall L. Patton

Newton, Huey P. (17 February 1942, Monroe, La.–22 August 1989, New Orleans, La.). Capitalizing on the growing militancy in urban black communities, Huey P. Newton, a former college student, cofounded the **Black Panther party** with **Bobby Seale** in October 1966. Newton, Seale, and **Eldridge Cleaver,** whose prison writings titled *Soul on Ice* became a national best seller, embraced Marxist Leninism as they led the paramilitary organization through much of the late 1960s. However, Newton himself emerged as the principal symbol of the party when in October 1967 he was arrested for the murder of an Oakland, California, policeman. His case, becoming a cause celebre among black and leftist groups, prompted a "Free Huey" campaign across the nation. Panther membership in the San Francisco Bay area soared from 60 to several hundred, and new chapters sprang up across the United States. Newton was convicted of voluntary manslaughter in July 1968, but two years later the California Supreme Court overturned the conviction and he was released from prison. Nonetheless the fortunes of the party declined considerably during the years of his imprisonment. In 1970 Eldridge Cleaver led a dissident faction out of the party. The Panthers were also targeted by the Federal Bureau of Investigation, which mounted a national campaign to disrupt their activities. Membership declined from 2,000 in 1968 to fewer than 1,000 before being further reduced by the schism with Eldridge Cleaver. By the early 1970s Newton shifted the party's focus to voter registration campaigns and the establishment of free health clinics. Newton's personal fortunes also declined. In and out of jail on a series of criminal charges, including the murder of a teenage prostitute, he was killed in August 1989 outside an Oakland crack house, allegedly by a drug dealer whom he had robbed.

Selected Bibliography Curtis J. Austin, "The Role of Violence in the Creation, Sustenance, and Destruction of the Black Panther Party" (Ph.D. diss., Mississippi State University, 1998); *Current Biography*, February 1973; Jack Lule, "News Strategies and the Death of Henry Newton," *Journalism Quarterly* 70 (No. 2, 1993), 287–99; Obituary, *New York Times*, 23 August 1989; Bobby Seale, *Seize the Time* (1970).

Quintard Taylor

Niagara Movement   Founded in 1905 on the Canadian side of Niagara Falls and organized under the leadership of **W.E.B. Du Bois,** this short-lived movement was the principal forerunner of the **NAACP.** In its declaration of principles, radical organizers drew up a plan for aggressive action and demanded, among other things, manhood suffrage, equal economic opportunities, equal educational opportunities, a healthier environment, an end to segregation, and full civil rights. At the same time, the organizers acknowledged that African Americans had duties to fulfill—a duty to vote, work, obey the laws, respect the rights of others, be clean and orderly, and respect themselves as well as others.

Selected Bibliography Herbert Aptheker, ed., *A Documentary History of the Negro People in the United States*, vol. 2 (1951); Francis L. Broderick and August Meier, eds., *Negro Protest Thought in the Twentieth Century* (1965); S. P. Fullinwider, *The Mind and Mood of Black America* (1969); Elliott M. Rudwick, "The Niagara Movement," *Journal of Negro History* 42 (1957), 177–200.

Betty L. Plummer

Ninety-ninth Pursuit Squadron   For black Americans during World War II, this unit symbolized both achievement and inequality. Because of black insistence, the War Department in September, 1940, established the Civilian Pilot Training Program at Tuskegee, Alabama (see **Tuskegee Airmen**). The entirely black squadron, organized in October, 1942 and commanded by Col. **Benjamin O. Davis, Jr.,** was sent to the Mediterranean theater in April 1943. The maligned and undermanned unit gained combat experience over Sicily and Italy; at Anzio in January, 1944 it downed 18 enemy planes. This performance earned the squadron two Distinguished Unit Citations and prompted the Air Corps command to employ additional black pilots in combat. The 450 pilots of the all-black 332nd Fighter Group, which included the 99th, ultimately flew thousands of sorties in Europe. In more than 200 missions over Germany in 1945, no allied bomber fell to enemy fighters when escorted by Tuskegee airmen, of whose number 85 won the Distinguished Flying Cross during the war.

Selected Bibliography Charles E. Francis, *The Tuskegee Airmen: The Story of the Negro in the U.S. Air Force* (1955); Bernard C. Nalty, *Strength for the Flight: A History of Black Americans in the Military* (1986); Alan M. Osur, *Blacks in the Army Air Forces During World War II* (1977); Robert A. Rose, *The Lonely Eagles: The Story of America's Black Air Force in World War II* (1946); Lawrence P. Scott and William M. Womack, Sr., *Double V: The Civil Rights Struggle of the Tuskegee Airmen* (1994).

James B. Potts

Nixon, Edgar Daniel   (12 July 1899, Montgomery, Ala.–25 February 1987, Montgomery, Ala). Commonly regarded by Alabamians as the father of the civil rights movement, through five decades E. D. Nixon led the struggle for civil rights in that state. During the 1920s and 1930s he advanced the cause for black justice in the **Brotherhood of Sleeping Car Porters and Maids** as the founder and president of the state's branch of that organization. In 1944 as president of the Voters' League of Montgomery, he led a march to the court house to demand the vote for blacks. During the 1950s he took an active role in desegregating Alabama's public schools. In the 1960s and 1970s he worked for various civil rights acts and **affirmative action** programs. However, it was his participation in the Brotherhood of Sleeping Car Porters Union between 1928 and 1964 and in the **Montgomery Improvement Association** that gave him the nickname "Mr. Civil Rights."

In 1928 E. D. Nixon joined the Brotherhood of Sleeping Car Porters. He soon assumed a leadership role in that organization, and he became the leading advocate in Alabama for black justice and equality. At the same time he became the president of the Alabama **NAACP.** When **Rosa Parks** was arrested in December 1955 for refusing to move to the rear of a Montgomery city bus, Nixon bailed her out of jail and was one of the leading figures in the **Montgomery bus boycott.** He helped to create the Montgomery Improvement Association (MIA), which launched the civil rights career of **Martin Luther King, Jr.** Nixon called the meeting of Montgomery's major black leaders at the Dexter Avenue Baptist Church, where King was minister, to discuss the formation of a civil rights campaign. It was at this meeting that the young King was chosen spokesman of the movement. Unfortunately, after the great victory in the bus campaign, Nixon and King had a major disagreement and parted

E. D. Nixon (left) with Adam Clayton Powell at a New York City political rally. © Library of Congress.

company. After the boycott Nixon continued his advocacy of civil rights throughout the 1960s and 1970s, but he never achieved the national prominence of some other black leaders. In 1975 he was appointed to the U.S. Commission on Civil Rights for the State of Alabama and also to the Montgomery County Board of Pensions and Security. In 1985 he received the NAACP's **Walter White** Award. During his later life, Nixon was criticized by civil rights groups for endorsing George Wallace for governor. His defense was that Wallace had never been a racist; he was, rather, a smart politician.

Selected Bibliography Lewis V. Baldwin and Aprille V. Woodson, *Freedom Is Never Free: A Biographical Portrait of Edgar Daniel Nixon* (1992); Richard Blake Dent, "The Man behind the Movement: E. D. Nixon Remembers," *Tusk*, 4 February 1982; "E. D. Nixon," *Economic Spirit* (July 1979), 4; "A Fierce Black Eye," *Montgomery Advertiser*, 17 November 1981; Rheta Grimsley Johnson, "The End of One Man's Struggle," *The Commercial Appeal*, Viewpoint, 4 March 1987; Lynn Lanier, "E. D. Nixon: Leader of the Times," *(Montgomery) Alabama Journal*, 17 May 1974; "Profile of Dr. E. D. Nixon," *Montgomery-Tuskegee Times*, 23–29 August 1979.

Vibert L. White

Nixon v. Condon, 286 U.S. 73 (1932) Together with **Nixon v. Herndon** (1927), **Grovey v. Townsend** (1935), and **Smith v. Allwright** (1944), this was one of four Supreme Court cases brought by black Texans, supported by the **NAACP,** that overturned Democratic **white primary** laws. In 1923, the Texas legislature provided that "in no event shall a negro be eligible to participate in a Democratic party election." Challenged by Dr. L. A. Nixon, a black El Paso physician, the Court declared the Texas law a "direct infringement of the **Fourteenth Amendment**" in *Nixon v. Herndon*. The Texas legislature's response was to delegate voter qualifications for primary elections to the party's executive committee, which promptly excluded blacks from the Democratic primary.

Urban black Texans immediately challenged the exclusion. The NAACP championed El Paso blacks, and, in *Nixon v. Condon*, the Supreme Court held the Texas law unconstitutional by a slender five to four majority. Relying upon the Fourteenth Amendment, the Court majority decreed that the Executive Committee acted as state agent under the statute and violated black rights by eliminating them from the primary. "A narrow and incomplete victory," the decision left the door open and the state essentially returned to the pre-1923 policy; the Democratic party controlled its membership. In a party convention, white Democrats barred blacks. Not until 1944, after another decade of struggle, was the white primary abolished.

Selected Bibliography J. Alston Atkins, *The Texas Negro and His Political Rights: A History of the Fight of Negroes to Enter the Democratic Primaries of Texas* (1932); Conrey Bryson, *Dr. Lawrence A. Nixon and the White Primary* (1974); Bruce A. Glasrud, "Blacks and Texas Politics during the Twenties," *Red River Valley Historical Review* 7 (Spring 1982), 39–53; Darlene Clark Hine, *Black Victory: The Rise and Fall of the White Primary in Texas* (1979); Walter Lindsey, "Black Houstonians Challenge the White Democratic Primary, 1921–1944" (M.A. thesis, University of Houston, 1969); Samuel Paschal Wilson, "The White Primary Laws in Texas from 1923–1953" (M.A. thesis, Southwest Texas State University, 1971).

Bruce A. Glasrud

Nixon v. Herndon, **273 U.S. 536 (1927)** In 1923 the Texas legislature passed a law barring African Americans from its primary elections. The law stated that "in no event shall a Negro be eligible to participate in a Democratic Party primary election held in the state of Texas." The Democratic party in El Paso enforced this statute in 1924, when it created the **white primary.** Because Texas was a one-party state, whoever won the primary automatically won the election. This practice rendered the regular election moot. Dr. Lawrence A. Nixon brought suit when an El Paso registrar denied him suffrage solely because of his race. His attorneys argued that the **Fifteenth Amendment** provided him immunity from racial discrimination. The Supreme Court agreed and held unconstitutional the Texas white primary law. It ruled that the Fifteenth Amendment protected eligible black citizens from discrimination at the polls. Congress had adopted the amendment, the Court asserted, to "protect the blacks from discrimination against them." Although the *Nixon* case outlawed the white primary, southern states adopted new strategies to disfranchise blacks.

Selected Bibliography Derrick Bell, Jr., *Race, Racism, and American Law* (1980); Conrey Bryson, *Dr. Lawrence A. Nixon and the White Primary* (1974); Darlene Clark Hine, *Black Victory: The Rise and Fall of the White Primary in Texas* (1979); "Notes and Comments," *Marquette Law Review* 11 (1927), 259–60; "Recent Cases," *Nebraska Law Bulletin* 6 (1928), 212–14.

Stephen Middleton

Nonviolent Resistance Nonviolent resistance is a method for effective social change that employs such instruments as strikes, sit-ins, boycotts, fasts, and civil disobedience. The use of these means by religious dissenters, abolitionists, advocates for women's rights, and labor union organizers is a significant theme in U.S. history. *The Essay on Civil Disobedience* by Henry David Thoreau (1849) is a seminal statement of nonviolent resistance theory. Mohandas Gandhi drew on Thoreau in fashioning the movement that forced Great Britain from India in 1947. Civil rights advocates in the United States drew on Gandhi.

"It may be through the Negroes that the unadulterated message of nonviolence will be delivered to the world," Gandhi told Dr. Howard Thurman in 1936. Adaptations of Gandhi's *Satyagraha* ("Soul Force") characterized the **March on Washington Movement** of **A. Philip Randolph** and, until the era of **Black Power,** the methods of the **Congress of Racial Equality** and the **Student Nonviolent Coordinating Committee.**

Faith in nonviolent resistance sustained **Martin Luther King, Jr.,** and remained the hallmark of the **Southern Christian Leadership Conference,** which he founded. "Christ showed us the way," he averred, "and Mahatma Gandhi showed us it would work." He insisted that nonviolent resistance was "the only morally and practically sound method open to oppressed people in their struggle for freedom," and that it was the key to lasting and profound change. Its "transforming power," he declared, "can lift a whole community to new horizons of fair play, goodwill and justice."

Selected Bibliography Peter Ackerman and Jack Duvall, *A Force More Powerful: A Century of Nonviolent Conflict* (2000); Joan V. Bondurant, *Conquest of Violence: The Gandhian Philosophy of Conflict* (1965); Severyn T. Bruyn and Paula M. Rayman, eds., *Nonviolent Action and Social Change* (1979); Robert Cooney and Helen Michalowski, *The Power of the People: Active Non-Violence in the United States* (1977); Sudarshan Kapur, *Raising Up a Prophet: The African American Encounter with Gandhi* (1992); August Meier, Elliott Rudwick, and Francis L. Broderick, eds., *Black Protest Thought in the Twentieth Century* (1980); Roger Powers and William Vogele, eds., *Protest, Power, and Change: An Encyclopedia of Nonviolent Action From ACT-UP to Women's Suffrage* (1997).

Jo Ann O. Robinson

Norfolk Journal and Guide   Originally called the *Gideon Safe Guide*, then the *Lodge Journal and Guide*, this newspaper began in 1900 as the official newspaper of the Supreme Lodge Knights of Gideon. **P. B. Young** purchased it in 1910 and eventually adopted the motto "Build Up, Don't Tear Down" in espousing the accommodationist philosophy of **Booker T. Washington.** Its circulation grew steadily, reaching its peak in the post–World War II years and becoming one of the nation's major black newspapers. It consistently took a conservative position on race relations, reflecting its editor-publisher's viewpoint. It remained cautious during the civil rights years, much to the dismay of more activist African Americans. In 2003 it continued weekly publication under the title the *New Journal and Guide*. The Young family's connection with the paper ended in 1967.

Selected Bibliography *Atlanta Inquirer*, 17 March 2001; Henry Lewis Suggs, *P. B. Young, Newspaperman: Race, Politics, and Journalism in the New South 1910–1962* (1988); Henry Lewis Suggs, ed., *The Black Press in the South, 1865–1979* (1983); Web site: www.njournalg.com.

John F. Marszalek

Norris v. Alabama, 294 U.S. 587 (1935)   In 1932 the Supreme Court reversed the first rape convictions of Clarence Norris and the eight other "Scottsboro Boys" (see **Scottsboro Trials**) due to deprivation of their constitutional right to counsel. The state of Alabama retried the defendants and convicted them again. Norris appealed his second conviction on the ground that blacks had been deliberately excluded from the jury. The Supreme Court agreed. Chief Justice Charles Evans Hughes noted that no blacks had served on juries in the counties in question for many decades, even though qualified blacks were available to serve. State law did not overtly discriminate, but local officials had evolved their own customary ways of excluding blacks. The Court found that the exclusion had been systematic and racially motivated, and it was thus a violation of the equal protection clause of the **Fourteenth Amendment.** The ruling was not surprising, since it had precedents going back even to the 1880s, a period when the Court showed concern for impartial administration of justice, if not for civil rights generally. Following various retrials and appeals, Norris escaped and vanished. He surfaced many years later in Michigan and returned to Alabama upon extradition to receive a ceremonial pardon from Governor George Wallace.

Selected Bibliography J. F. Barbour, Jr., "Note and Comment," *Mississippi Law Journal* 8 (1935), 196–204; Dan T. Carter, *Scottsboro* (1969); Robert F. Cushman, *Cases in Constitutional Law* (1979); James Goodman, *Stories of Scottsboro* (1994); Donald G. Neiman, *Promises to Keep: African-Americans and the Constitutional Order, 1776 to the Present* (1994).

James E. Sefton

The North Carolina Mutual Life Insurance Company   Chartered in 1899, the North Carolina Mutual Life Insurance Company, an industrial insurer with a philanthropic impulse, has played a pivotal role in the economic, political, and social lives of black North Carolinians throughout the twentieth century. The genius behind this pioneering black business was **John Merrick,** an ex-slave who, along with Dr. Aaron McDuffie and a grocer named **Charles Clinton Spaulding,** gave leadership to the company. Expanding rapidly, it was doing business in 12 states and the District of Columbia by 1915. In keeping with the tenor of the times, the leadership of the company touted the principle of black self-help during the first 50 years of its existence. The influence of **Booker T. Washington** was unmistakable. Never aloof from the everyday affairs of the black community, Merrick and his colleagues were involved in the civil rights struggles in North Carolina both publicly and behind the scene. Spaulding lobbied the legislature strenuously for better funding for black colleges in North Carolina. During the thirties he threw the resources of the company, and his personal prestige, behind the fight for equalization of pay for black teachers in the state. At first his support of the **NAACP** was cautious, but in time he became a staunch supporter. Spaulding died in 1952, having husbanded the company through good times and bad. He meshed entrepreneurship with a social philosophy oriented toward race pride. North Carolina Mutual was what he and his colleagues made it, a monument to black enterprise, a landmark of the new South, and a testament to the twin desires of black economic progress and equal rights for all peoples. In 2003 it is the largest black-owned insurance company in America, ranking in the top 10 percent of all American life insurance companies.

Selected Bibliography John Hope Franklin and Alfred A. Moss, Jr., *From Slavery to Freedom: A History of Negro Americans*, 8th ed. (2000); Los Angeles *Sentinal*, 3 March 1999, A9; August Meier, *Negro Thought in America: 1880–1915* (1963); Walter B. Weare, *Black Business in the New South: A Social History of the North Carolina Mutual Life Insurance Company* (1973); Web site: www.ncmutuallife.com.

Joe Louis Caldwell

Northern Student Movement   Founded in New Haven, Connecticut, during the spring of 1961 by Yale University student, Peter Countryman, the Northern Student Movement (NSM) initially consisted of northern, white college students eager to join the burgeoning civil rights movement. These students entered the northern ghettos in 1962 with the simple goal of tutoring disadvantaged inner-city blacks. By 1965, NSM's inner-city experience had resulted in dramatic changes. Led by William Strickland, a black activist who succeeded Countryman as NSM's Executive Director in 1963, NSM evolved into a primarily black organization concerned with mobilizing northern black communities. Its strategy involved using tutorials to gain community trust, recruiting a core of indigenous leaders, and then expanding to work on broader inner-city problems, such as poverty, substandard housing, unemployment, poor education, police brutality, and welfare rights. Ultimately, NSM members hoped to ignite an independent, black political movement capable of empowering inner-city blacks and mounting a direct challenge to existing racist institutions. NSM amassed 65 campus affiliates nationwide and established community action projects in Boston, Chicago, Detroit, Hartford, New York, and Philadelphia. NSM members created a Freedom Library in Philadelphia, waged rent strikes in Harlem, confronted police brutality in Detroit, and helped coordinate public school boycotts in Boston, Chicago, and New York.

Selected Bibliography *Students for a Democratic Society Papers, 1958–1970*, series 2A, National Office (Fall 1962–August 1965), reel 9, "Related Groups no. 113"; *The Northern Student Movement, 1962–1965* (n.d.), Glen Rock, N. J., Microfilming Corporation of America (1977).

Mark E. Medina

Norton, Eleanor Holmes   (13 June 1937, Washington, D.C.–). The eldest of three girls born to working-class parents, Eleanor Holmes Norton was educated in segregated public schools in Washington, D.C., and earned her high school diploma from the District's only college preparatory school for blacks—Dunbar High School. She graduated from Antioch College in 1960 and received her M.A. from Yale Graduate School in 1963 and her LL.B. from Yale Law School in 1964. Her specialty in civil liberties led to an appointment as assistant legal director of the **American Civil Liberties Union,** a post she held from 1965 to 1970. In chairing the New York City Commission on Human Rights (1970–77) and the **Equal Employment Opportunity Commission** (1977–81)—the only woman to chair the latter— she revitalized both agencies. By spearheading its 1978 reorganization, she brought the EEOC into the forefront as the lead agency in the enforcement of equal employment opportunity. Between 1982 and 1990 Norton was a faculty member at the Georgetown University Law Center, when she took a leave of absence to seek political office. Despite a last second discovery that her husband had not filed their local income taxes for seven years, she won the nonvoting delegate seat from the District of Columbia to the U.S. House of Representatives in the 1990 election and won reelection campaigns in each succeeding congressional election through 2002. Described as "One of the Most Powerful Women in Washington" by the *Washingtonian Magazine* in

President Jimmy Carter at the 1977 swearing-in ceremony for (left to right) Patricia Derian, Virginia McCarty, and Eleanor Holmes Norton. © Jimmy Carter Library.

1989, Norton has received honorary doctorates from more than fifty universities. In 2001, she was a leader in the formation of the Commission on Black Men and Boys, funded through the U.S. Department of Labor. In 2003 she also continued as a leading proponent of statehood for the District of Columbia.

Selected Bibliography "America's 100 Most Important Women," *Ladies Home Journal* (November 1988), 47–48, 223; Ed Gordon, "Dialogue with Eleanor Holmes Norton," *Emerge* (August 1990), 11–12; Richette Haywood, "A Black Woman's Place Is in the . . . House of Representatives," Eleanore Holmes Norton Takes D.C. Seat," *Ebony* 46 (January 1991): 104–6; Brian Lanker, *I Dream a World* (1989); Leslie Milk, "100 Most Powerful Women," *Washingtonian Magazine* (September 1989), 132–35; Eleanor Holmes Norton, "Yes, A Denial of Human Rights," *ABA Journal* 79 (August 1993), 46–49.

Jennifer J. Beaumont

Not without Laughter   An incisive and convincing psychological study of interracial, intrafamilial relationships in a racially oppressive small Midwestern town, **Langston Hughes**'s first novel (1930) heralded a new spirit and direction in the canon of black literature—the advent of a racial consciousness committed to the affirmation, spirit, and rich heritage of the folk experience. In this novel, Hughes, an acclaimed innovative stylist, rejected the exoticism of the plantation tradition and the conservatism of his progenitors, and adopted black folk materials and cultural tradition—the **blues,** black idiom, folk laughter—to reveal the complexity of black life. Forging beyond the limitations of romanticism, Langston Hughes pioneered the rise of a realistic Negro literature.

Selected Bibliography James Emanuel, *Langston Hughes* (1967); Edward J. Mullen, ed., *Critical Essays on Langston Hughes* (1989); Thermon B. O'Daniel, ed., *Langston Hughes, Black Genius* (1971); Armstead Rampensad, *The Life of Langston Hughes* (1986); Amritjit Singh, *The Novels of the Harlem Renaissance* (1976).

Jacquelyn Jackson

O

Odum, Howard Washington (24 May 1884, Bethlehem, Ga.–8 November 1954, N.C.). A white southern sociologist dedicated to improving race relations in the region, Odum was chairman of the **Commission on Interracial Cooperation** from 1937–44. He was influential in developing the **Southern Regional Council,** a major white southern liberal civil rights group. He received his undergraduate degree from Emory College and his graduate education from the University of Mississippi, Clark University, and Columbia University. He held positions at the University of Georgia, Emory College, and the University of North Carolina. He founded the *Journal of Social Forces* and the Institute for Research in Social Sciences, which explored civil rights issues.

Selected Bibliography Wayne Douglas Brazil, "Howard W. Odum, The Building Years 1884–1930" (Ph.D. diss., Harvard University, 1975); Howard W. Odum, *An American Epoch* (1930); Howard W. Odum, *Southern Regions of the United States* (1936); Rupert B. Vance and Katherine Jocher, "Howard W. Odum," *Social Forces* 33 (March 1955), 203–17.

Donald Cunnigen

Office of Federal Contract Compliance Programs Created in the fall of 1965 by Labor Secretary W. Willard Wirtz, the Office of Federal Contract Compliance (OFCC) Programs was charged with enforcing nondiscrimination in employment by government contractors and in federally assisted construction programs. This was required by President Lyndon B. Johnson's **Executive Order 11246** of September 1965, which designated the Labor Department as the principal agency for coordinating contract compliance under Title VI of the **Civil Rights Act of 1964.** In early 1966 Wirtz appointed Edward K.

Sylvester to head the OFCC, and under Sylvester the office developed a preaward program that compelled bidders on contracts of $1 million or more to first be reviewed and approved for compliance with the executive order. Following unsuccessful experiments with construction contracts in St. Louis, San Francisco, and Cleveland, the OFCC developed in Philadelphia a formula that required bidders to set numerical goals for minority employees. Builders complained that the minority goals required under Title VI enforcement amounted to racial quotas, which were banned by Title VII, and that the OFCC should place the onus of desegregation at the source of discrimination: the hiring-hall system required by labor union contracts. In November 1968, Comptroller-General Elmer Staats ruled that the **Philadelphia Plan** illegally required contractors to set racial quotas in hiring. The OFCC's affirmative action program was revived in 1969, however, by President Richard M. Nixon's Secretary of Labor, George P. Shultz. Its effect was to split the liberal Democratic coalition between civil rights groups and organized labor. In April 1970, the Third Circuit Court of Appeals upheld the Philadelphia Plan in a suit brought by Pennsylvania contractors. Shortly thereafter the Nixon administration expanded the goals-and-timetables requirements for minorities and women to apply to all federal contractors. These policies were continued under the Ford and Carter administrations. By the time Ronald Reagan became president in 1981, the OFCC program had become sufficiently entrenched that the Labor Department, under Secretary William Brock, was able to defeat conservative attacks on its minority preferences led by Attorney General Edwin Meese. Its thrust since 1992 has been toward enforcing compliance with the American Disability Act (ADA).

Selected Bibliography Nelson A. Bruce and Mary Lou Christie, "Affirmative Action Requirements for the Construction Industry Under Executive Order 11246," in David A. Corpus and Linda Rosenweig, eds., *The OFCC and Federal Contract Compliance* (1981); Hugh Davis Graham, *The Civil Rights Era* (1990); Web site: www.dol.gov/dol/esa/public/ofcp_org.htm.

Daniel Gomes

Office of Minority Business Enterprise On 5 March 1969, President Richard Nixon established, by executive order, the Office of Minority Business Enterprise within the Commerce Department. Attempting to ameliorate some of the causal conditions of racial turbulence, Nixon planned to use this office to spur **Black Capitalism.** The OMBE was charged with coordinating all efforts to expand minority businesses. In October, the OMBE implemented Project Enterprise, which established the Minority Enterprise Small Business Investment Company. This company offered "venture capital and long term credit" to minority businesses but did not provide the "support necessary for the second stage of growth;" therefore, a high failure rate resulted among these businesses. In 1979, the OMBE became the Minority Business Development Agency. It still exists; in 2000 it granted $31 million to minority businesses.

Selected Bibliography Edward W. Brooke, "Black Business: Problems and Prospects," *Black Scholar* 6 (1975), 2–7; Theodore Cross, *The Black Power Imperative* (1984); Roy F. Lee, *The*

Setting for Black Business Development (1972); Maurice H. Stans, "Richard Nixon and His Bridges to Human Dignity," *Presidential Studies Quarterly* 26 (1996), 179–83; Gerald Whittaker, ed., *Minority Business: The Second Stage of Growth* (1977).

Malik Simba

Open (or Fair) Housing Act (1968)   Part of the **Civil Rights Act of 1968** signed by President Lyndon B. Johnson on 11 April, this act was the last major civil rights legislation of the 1960s. The passage of open housing legislation was a surprise, considering the declining enthusiasm for such a bill in Congress. The summers of urban violence after the **Watts race riot** of 1965 had produced white "backlash" against civil rights protests and had reduced the likelihood of new legislation. An open housing bill was originally sent to Congress by President Johnson in 1966. The House of Representatives passed it, but opposition from minority leader Everett Dirksen, a Republican from Illinois, and a filibuster by southern Democrats doomed the measure in the Senate. No action was taken during 1967, but early in 1968 a bill protecting civil rights workers was passed by the House and was amended in the Senate to include the dormant open housing measure. Again a southern-led filibuster occurred, but cloture was voted after Dirksen switched sides and supported the bill. The Open Housing Act prohibited discrimination on the basis of race in 80 percent of all rental and sale housing. In a political compromise the law also expanded federal protection for civil rights workers, and an antiriot provision provided tougher criminal penalties for activities that caused civil disturbances. The Open Housing Act of 1968 had an ambiguous legacy; housing discrimination was made a national crime, but federal enforcement was hampered by small budgets and weak penalties.

Selected Bibliography Hugh Davis Graham, "Race, History, and Policy: African Americans and Civil Rights since 1994," *Journal of Policy History* 6 (1994), 12–39; Hugh Davis Graham, "The Surprising Career of Federal Fair Housing Law," *Journal of Policy History* 12 (2000), 215–32; U.S. Commission on Civil Rights, *The Federal Fair Housing Enforcement Effort* (1979).

William J. Thompson

Opportunity   The official publication of the **National Urban League,** *Opportunity* first appeared in January 1923. **Charles S. Johnson,** its first editor, intended it to be a factual presentation of employment opportunities for black urban residents and future migrants. Research properly conducted, he believed, would blunt prejudice, reduce discrimination, and encourage interracial cooperation. Articles covered a wide range of topics: child placement, health, the labor market, housing, history, and international affairs. The arts were also represented. **Claude McKay, Langston Hughes, Alain Locke,** and **Countee Cullen** make their appearances at a time when few white magazines would publish any African American authors. In 1928, Elmer A. Carter assumed editorship, and *Opportunity* opened its pages to such prominent white writers as H. L. Mencken, Pearl Buck, and Clarence Darrow. During the Great Depression, the journal increasingly dealt with unemployment and supported the New Deal. An increasing financial burden to the Urban League, it ceased publication in 1949. Some 40 percent of its readership was white, and it never equaled the circulation of the **NAACP's *Crisis*.** It has been criticized by some scholars for overemphasizing black success stories and underplaying racial violence; nevertheless, it is an important source for the study of African American life.

Selected Bibliography Jesse T. Moore, *A Search for Equality: The National Urban League, 1910–1961* (1989); Guichard Parris and Lester Brooks, *Blacks in the City: A History of the National Urban League* (1971); Nancy Weiss, *The National Urban League: 1910–1940* (1974); Sondra K. Wilson, ed., *The Opportunity Reader: Selections from the Urban League's Opportunity Magazine* (1999).

Richard W. Resh

Orangeburg, South Carolina, Massacre (1968)   This event was the climax of a struggle between black college students and local segregationists that went back to a failed attempt in 1963 to integrate local lunch counters. In 1967 a student chapter of the **NAACP** was organized at South Carolina State College with John Stroman as its leader. The students tried with no success to get Harry Floyd to integrate his All Star Bowling Lanes, and on the night of 5 February 1968, Stroman led a group to the bowling alley. Some students got in, but the bowling alley was closed. The following night the students returned in larger numbers and **Student Nonviolent Coordinating Committee** organizer Cleveland Sellers was also present. This time law officials were waiting. General disorder erupted, and several students, including coeds, were beaten. On the college campus the next day a student grievance committee made plans for a march on city hall and a boycott of local businesses unless grievance demands were met. No agreements could be reached between students and city officials. The mood grew tense. Governor Robert E. McNair activated additional National Guardsmen to reinforce the highway patrolmen who were already on the scene. By the morning of 8 February an eerie calm had settled over the campus, and acting President M. Maceo Nance instructed the students to stay on campus. That evening a group of students attempted to start a bonfire on the edge of the campus near the command post of the patrolmen. When a fencepost was thrown and struck an officer, the other patrolmen thought that the officer had been shot and they opened fire. In a few seconds 30 students were shot, 3 of whom were killed. The press claimed that shots had been exchanged, but later investigation proved that no student had fired a single shot. Governor McNair declared a state of emergency. Cleveland Sellers was arrested and found guilty of inciting a riot, although his conviction was later overturned. Nine of the patrolmen involved were tried, but all were found "not guilty." Later legal action, however, required Harry Floyd to desegregate his bowling alley.

Selected Bibliography *Charlotte Observer*, 9, 10 February 1968; Jack Nelson and Jack Bass, *The Orangeburg Massacre* (1970); *Orangeburg Times and Democrat*, 7, 8, 9, 10 February 1968.

Charles A. Risher

Organization of Afro-American Unity (OAAU). The Organization of Afro-American Unity was established in 1965 by **Black Muslim** leader **Malcolm X** after his break with Elijah Muhammad (see **Elijah Poole**), the leader of the Nation of Islam. In the name of universal brotherhood of Islam, OAAU sought to make common cause with the Third World nations. In effect, Malcolm X moved from civil rights to human rights. His premature death at the hands of an assassin on 21 February 1965 halted OAAU's activities. Although Malcolm's sister, Ella Mae Collins, assumed leadership of the organization, it soon became inactive.

Selected Bibliography John H. Bracey, *Black Nationalism in America* (1970); Robert C. Twombly, *Blacks in White America since 1865: Issues and Interpretations* (1971); Malcolm X and Alex Haley, *The Autobiography of Malcolm X* (1965); Robert L. Jenkins and Mfanya D. Tryman, *The Malcolm X Encyclopedia* (2002).

Amm Saifuddin Khaled

Ovington, Mary White (11 April 1865, Brooklyn, N.Y.–15 July 1951, Auburndale, Mass.). The granddaughter of an abolitionist and the daughter of a post–Civil War "abolitionist," the wealthy white Ovington attended the 1906 meeting of the **Niagara Movement** as a reporter for the *New York Evening Post*. In 1909 she answered the call that went out for a conference to organize what became the **NAACP** to protest "present evils" affecting blacks and to ask that a new struggle be initiated to obtain civil and political liberty for all. In 1911 she wrote *Half a Man: The Status of the Negro in New York*.

Ovington's stand with the NAACP was all the more significant because the interracial organization had formed when Progressives paid little attention to the needs of blacks and when **lynching** increased each year. Between 1910 and 1941, Ovington held important offices in the NAACP for longer periods than any of the organization's other officials. Having worked persistently for racial equality all of her life, the aging Ovington still understood that much more had to be done. Indeed, she died only three years before the **Brown v. Board of Education** decision of 1954.

Selected Bibliography W.E.B. Du Bois, *The Autobiography of W.E.B. Du Bois: A Soliloquy on Viewing My Life from the Last Decade of Its First Century* (1968); B. Joyce Ross, *J. E. Spingarn and the Rise of the NAACP, 1911–1939* (1972); Carolyn Wedin, *Inheritors of the Spirit: Mary White Ovington and the Founding of the NAACP* (1998).

Linda Reed

Owens, Jesse (12 September 1913, Oakville, Ala.–31 March 1980, Tucson, Ariz.). With four gold medals emblazoned around his neck, three for individual feats, the other as part of a relay team, Jesse Cleveland Owens was catapulted into instant fame during the 1936 Olympic games held in Berlin and attended by Adolf Hitler, Chancellor of Germany. Owens was the tenth and last child of an impoverished southern sharecropper in northern Alabama who with millions of other African Americans migrated to the North for a better life. Cleveland, Ohio became the Owenses' home, the place where Jesse

Jesse Owens (left) with Ralph Metcalfe at the 1936 track and field meet at Randall's Island Stadium in New York. © Library of Congress.

encountered the complexities of northern racism and the institutions that educated and excited him about athletics and success. A white coach, whose background was poor Pennsylvania Irish, nurtured, tutored and honed his talents. He enrolled at Ohio State University but never graduated. Shortly after his Olympic triumph, Jesse turned his energies in pursuit of the American Dream. He plunged into a myriad of investments, worked for public relations firms, lent his name to commercial products, crisscrossed the country delivering inspirational talks, stumped for Republican presidential candidates, attended Olympic games as a goodwill ambassador, managed black basketball and softball teams, worked for the Works Projects Administration, and professionally competed against other runners. His was a middle-class existence that was constantly forced to cope with the realities of racist practices. Toward the end of his life, his conservative approach to racial issues was criticized by **Black Power** advocates, but Owens held steadfast to his ideas of patriotism, opportunity, and nonconfrontation.

Selected Bibliography William J. Baker, *Jesse Owens: An American Life* (1986); Jesse Owens, *Blackthink: My Life as Black Man and White Man* (1970).

Joseph Boskin

Oxley, Lawrence Augustus (17 May 1887, Boston, Mass.–2 July 1973, Washington, D.C.). A veteran social worker, Oxley began his career as a teacher at St. Augustine's College, Raleigh, North Carolina. Subsequently, he developed social surveys of the black communities in Washington, D.C.; Louisville, Kentucky; Cincinnati, Ohio; Chicago, Illinois; North Carolina; and Little Rock, Arkansas. After serving as the director of Negro Work for the North Carolina State Board of Charities and Public Welfare, Oxley became a member of Franklin D. Roosevelt's **Black Cabinet** as special assistant to the secretary of labor. Later, he was the director of special projects, National Council of Senior Citizens.

Selected Bibliography *Jet*, 19 July, 21 September 1973; John Kirby, ed., *New Deal Agencies and Black America in the 1930s* (1984); Obituary, *Washington Post*, 5 July 1973; *Who's Who in Colored America, 1940* (1940).

Ray Branch

P

Pace v. Alabama, 106 U.S. 583 (1882)   This miscegenation case challenged an Alabama law that dictated greater punishment for adultery between an interracial couple than between a same race couple. Tony Pace, a black man, and Mary J. Cox, a white woman, were convicted under the law and received the minimum sentence of two years each at hard labor. An unmarried couple of the same race would have been fined $100, and could have served six months in prison. In a unanimous decision, the Supreme Court upheld the state law, claiming that it was not in violation of the equal protection clause of the **Fourteenth Amendment** of the Constitution or civil rights legislation because it applied the same punishment to both offenders and therefore was not discriminatory. The court said that equal protection guaranteed a person, regardless of race, the same punishment for the same offense. The rationale for the decision was that both blacks and whites who crossed racial barriers to engage in such acts were punished equally. The Alabama law and 15 similar laws in other southern states were overturned in 1967, when the Supreme Court declared antimiscegenation laws invalid under the Fourteenth Amendment in the case *Loving v. Virginia.*

Selected Bibliography Richard Bardolph, ed., *The Civil Rights Record, Black Americans and the Law, 1849–1970* (1970); Derrick A. Bell, Jr., *Race, Racism, and American Law* (1980); Robert F. Cushman, *Cases in Constitutional Law,* 4th ed. (1975); Robert J. Sickels, *Race, Marriage, and the Law* (1972).

Carol Wilson

Pan-African Movement   Begun at the beginning of the twentieth century, this world view especially appealed to black intellectuals. It seeks to unite peoples of African ancestry around the world to help systematically emancipate their race from further socioeconomic and political discrimination and to restore the dignity of the African motherland. Pan-Africanism emerged as a coordinated international movement in the early twentieth century with plans to help liberate the continent of sub-Sahara Africa and Africans living abroad from colonialism and imperialism. The early dialogue was international in scope and included Africans, African Americans, and West Indians. One early organizer, Henry S. Williams, a Trinidadian lawyer, created the first All African Association in London in September, 1897. He spearheaded the first Pan-African conference in London on 23–25 July 1900, which was attended by 33 delegates from Africa, the Caribbean, the United States, and Canada. The first follow-up conference in the United States was sponsored by **Tuskegee Institute** in 1914. **W.E.B. Du Bois** played a key role in "giving reality to the dream before its world-wide acceptance" in the post–World War I years. Seven Pan-African Congresses were held between 1919 and 1963, in Europe, the United States, and Africa. During the civil rights period, a large percentage of African Americans were strong supporters of the Pan-African movement.

Selected Bibliography Stokely Carmichael, *Stokely Speaks: Black Power Back to Pan Africanism* (1971); Imanuel Geiss, *The Pan-African Movement: A History of Pan Africanism in America* (1974); Robert A. Hill, ed., *Pan African Biography* (1987); Tony Martin, *The Pan African Connection: From Slavery, to Garvey and Beyond* (1984); George Padmore, *Pan-Africanism or Communism?* (1956).

Glenn O. Phillips

Parks, Rosa (4 February 1913, Tuskegee, Ala.–). A Negro seamstress educated at Alabama State College in Montgomery, Rosa Parks became during the 1950s a simple but powerful symbol of Negro protest against segregation. Perhaps nowhere in the South was the color line more rigidly enforced than on Montgomery's city buses. On 1 December 1955 Rosa Parks boarded a city bus. Finding no vacancy in the black section, she took a seat toward the front. When she refused to move to the rear, she was arrested and jailed. Montgomery's black leaders rushed to her support. A year earlier they had received promises from the city commission and bus authority that changes would be made in the segregation of the city's buses. Nothing had happened, however, and black leaders decided that direct action was necessary. **Martin Luther King, Jr., E. D. Nixon,** and others rallied the black community and organized the **Montgomery bus boycott.** That boycott and its symbol, Rosa Parks, helped usher in the Negro revolt and catapulted Martin Luther King, Jr., and nonviolent **direct action** into national prominence. To escape economic and social reprisal, Rosa and Raymond Parks fled Montgomery in 1957 and relocated in Detroit, Michigan, where Rosa served on the staff of U.S. Representative John Conyers, Democrat, from 1967 to 1988. After leaving his staff she toured the country speaking about the civil rights struggle and urging young people to continue to fight for justice and equality. In 1979 she won the

Rosa Parks sitting on the bus. © Bettmann/CORBIS.

Spingarn Medal, and two decades later she was awarded the Congressional Medal of Honor. That prestigious award acknowledged her exceptional role in the struggle for racial justice and democracy not just in Alabama but the entire nation. In 2003 a made-for-television motion picture about her life won an **NAACP** Image Award.

Selected Bibliography *Alabama Journal*, 1 December 1973; Taylor Branch, *Parting the Waters: America in the King Years, 1954–1963* (1988); Douglas Brinkley, *Mine Eyes Have Seen the Glory: The Life of Rosa Parks* (2000); Eric Foner, ed., *America's Black Past: A Reader in Afro-American History* (1970); Kai Friese, *Rosa Parks: The Movement Organizes* (1990); George R. Metcalf, *Black Profiles* (1980); *Montgomery Advertiser*, 15 January, 2 December 1980; Rosa Parks, *Quiet Strength: The Faith, the Hope, and the Heart of a Woman Who Changed a Nation* (1994); Rosa Parks with Jim Haskins, *Rosa Parks: My Story* (1992); Jo Ann Gibson Robinson, *The Montgomery Bus Boycott and the Women Who Started It: The Memoir of Jo Ann Gibson Robinson* (1987); J. Mills Thornton III, "Challenge and Response in the Montgomery Bus Boycott of 1955–1956," *The Alabama Review* 33 (July 1980), 163–235; Roberta Hughes Wright, *The Birth of the Montgomery Bus Boycott* (1991).

Charles D. Lowery

***Pasadena Board of Education v. Spangler*, 427 U.S. 424 (1976)** This 1976 U.S. Supreme Court decision concerned resegregation of schools after desegregation. The problem arose in Pasadena, California where segregation was found to be recurring because whites were moving out of the district and minorities, including blacks, were moving in. Busing was blamed for this situation. In 1970, a federal district court had ruled that there could be no school in the Pasadena district with a majority of minority students. The court authorized the school officials to make yearly readjustments in the racial composition of the schools. Reversing this decision in 1976, the Supreme Court ruled by a six-to-two vote that once desegregation was accomplished in the schools, court authority was not required to make annual readjustments. In Pasadena, the court said, the changes in the racial composition of the schools had occurred because of normal human migration and not from any official action. Justices Thurgood Marshall and William Brennan, however, said that Pasadena schools had never been truly desegregated due to the noncooperation of the school authorities. The Pasadena problem of resegregation after desegregation was in fact representative of similar problems in many other districts throughout the nation.

Selected Bibliography Paul R. Dimond, *Beyond Busing: Inside the Challenge to Urban Segregation* (1985); Bruce E. Fein, *Significant Decisions of the Supreme Court, 1975–1976* (1977); "Court Turning against Reverse Discrimination," *U.S. News and World Report* (12 July 1976); J. Harvis Wilkinson III, *From Brown to Bakke: The Supreme Court and School Integration* (1979); Perry A. Zirkel, ed., *A Digest of Supreme Court Decisions Affecting Education* (1978).

Amm Saifuddin Khaled

Patton v. Mississippi, **332 U.S. 463 (1947)** This Supreme Court case involved a black petitioner named Eddie "Buster" Patton who was indicted by an all-white grand jury, and was tried and convicted by an all-white petit jury in Lauderdale County, Mississippi. The **NAACP** defense team, led by **Thurgood Marshall,** argued that Patton had been denied his constitutional rights under the **Fourteenth Amendment** because blacks had been systematically excluded from jury duty for at least the past thirty years. Mississippi, represented by its attorney general, argued that jurors were selected from voting lists and, because there were few or no black voters on the list, the state had not discriminated when it had selected an all-white jury. Justice Hugo Black, in a unanimous decision for the Court, declared that "when a jury selection plan whatever it is, operates in such a way as always to result in the complete and long-continued exclusion of any representative at all from a large group of Negroes, or any other racial group, indictments and verdicts returned against them by juries thus selected cannot stand." Black went on to note that Patton was not necessarily free, but if Mississippi were to indict and try him again, the juries would have to be more representative of the state's population.

Selected Bibliography Robert S. Harris, *The Quest for Equality: The Constitution, Congress and the Supreme Court* (1960); C. Herman Pritchett, *Civil Liberties and the Vinson Court* (1954); "Recent Cases," *George Washington Law Review* 16 (1948), 426–29.

Kenneth W. Goings

Payne, Ethel L. (1912, Chicago, Illinois–28 May 1991, Washington, D.C.). Ethel L. Payne, often called "the first lady of the black press," became the first African American woman to join the White House press corps in 1951. A journalism graduate of Northwestern University, Payne was working in Tokyo in 1949 and keeping a journal about discrimination against American black servicemen when journalists urged her to send her work to the *Chicago Defender.* Her stories impressed **John H. Senstacke,** publisher and editor of the paper, who hired her as the Washington political correspondent. Payne's persistence in raising civil rights–related questions at the White House news conferences of Dwight D. Eisenhower prompted a presidential fit of temper in 1955. When she asked about his position on segregation, Eisenhower angrily retorted: "What makes you think I am going to give special favoritism to special interests? I am the president of all the people." Eisenhower became so irritated with her that he seldom called on her for questions for the remainder of his presidency.

Payne had a special reputation for reporting on international affairs, having interviewed Chinese Premier Chou En-Lai and African dictator Idi Amin. She covered her first international conference in Bandung, Indonesia, in 1956 at a time when black newspapers were not covering international news.

Driven by a "great sense of indignation for people who couldn't defend themselves," and Frederick Douglass's admonition to "agitate, agitate, agitate," Payne was not reserved about pushing civil and human rights issues into print or playing an active role in causes. She wrote about discrimination against African Americans in the armed forces and the federal government. She marched in civil rights demonstrations and campaigned through letters, petitions, and other means to secure the freedom in South Africa of Nelson Mandela.

Selected Bibliography *New York Times,* 29 April 1955; Ethel L. Payne, "Loneliness in the Capitol: The Black National Correspondent," in Henry G. La Brie III, ed., *Perspectives of the Black Press: 1974* (1974); Rodger Streitmatter, "No Taste for Fluff: Ethel L. Payne, African-American Journalist," *Journalism Quarterly* 68 (1991), 528–40; Rodger Streitmatter, "African-American Women Journalists and their Male Editors: A Tradition of Support," *Journalism Quarterly* 70 (1993), 276–86; *Washington Post,* 27 April 1955, 1 June 1991.

Danny Blair Moore

Peabody Education Fund The Peabody Education Fund was established in 1867 by merchant and banker George Peabody (1795–1869), a New Englander who made his fortune in Baltimore and London and was known for his widespread philanthropy in both the United States and Great Britain. Peabody's endowment of the education fund provided for "the promotion and encouragement of intellectual, moral, or industrial education among the young people of the more destitute portions of the Southern and Southwestern states of our Union." The fund supported education for both black and white students, primarily through aid in establishing and maintaining public schools and teachers' training schools. Over the years, the 56 trustees of the Peabody

Fund, who included Presidents Grover Cleveland and Theodore Roosevelt, chose a policy of passive acceptance of racial segregation in education. The fund, the first of many established by northern philanthropists to aid southern and/or Negro education, distributed over $3,500,000 before liquidating in 1914. At that time, $350,000 of the principal was given to the **Slater Fund,** devoted solely to the support of education for African Americans, and the rest was given to the Peabody Normal College, a white teachers' college in Nashville, Tennessee.

Selected Bibliography Henry Allen Bullock, *The History of Negro Education in the South from 1619 to the Present* (1967); George A. Dillingham, *The Foundation of the Peabody Tradition* (1989); "Legacy of George Peabody: Special Bicentenary Issue," *Peabody Journal of Education* 70 (April 1996); Franklin Parker, *George Peabody: A Biography* (1971).

Suzanne Ellery Greene Chapelle

People against Racism An all-white organization that evolved out of the Detroit branch of the **Northern Student Movement** (NSM), People against Racism (PAR) was established in 1965 by white activist Frank Joyce as a response to two beliefs: racism was fundamentally a white problem, and white activists should not be organizing in black communities. PAR's goal was to educate and organize white communities, to confront racist institutions, and to support the black movement, when possible and requested. By combining research, education, organization, and action with an historical analysis of American racism, PAR hoped to create a strong, antiracist faction within the white community. Although PAR disappeared in the early 1970s, its existence was important to both the civil rights movement and American society. By stressing that racism was a white problem, the group made it clear that apathetic white Americans were nearly as much of the problem as outspoken racists. PAR also revealed the high level of commitment and dedication that would be required to produce meaningful change in the white community. PAR's ideas are still considered to be an advanced and sophisticated analysis of American racism.

Selected Bibliography "A Collection of Racist Myths" and "Repression in America: Law, Order, and the White Backlash," Kansas Collection, University of Kansas, Lawrence; Harvard Sitkoff, *The Struggle for Black Equality, 1954–1980* (1981); Students for a Democratic Society Papers, 1958–70, series 3, section VII (1965–69), reel 31, "Related Groups—United States #167," Glen Rock, New Jersey, Microfilming Corporation of America (1977).

Mark E. Medina

People United to Save Humanity (Operation PUSH). This Chicago-based black economic rights organization was founded by **Jesse Jackson** in 1971 after his break with the **Southern Christian Leadership Conference.** Worried that civil rights, unaccompanied by economic advancement, would be meaningless, PUSH leadership worked toward obtaining support from big business. Using massive boycotts of products and services, PUSH forced companies such as Coca-Cola, Seven-Up, Burger King, and Kentucky Fried Chicken to increase black employment as well as to deposit company funds in black banks.

During the early 1980s, PUSH's boycott strategy indeed helped blacks come closer to their dream of equal employment opportunity. In the late 1990s, the Rainbow/PUSH Coalition began, as PUSH founder and leader Jesse Jackson continued to expand his economic activities. The 2001 disclosure of Jackson's fathering of an illegitimate child created controversy for PUSH and all the other organizations Jackson headed.

Selected Bibliography John Martin Burke, *Civil Rights: A Current Guide to the People, Organization, and Events* (1974); Theodore Cross, *The Black Power Imperative: Racial Inequality and the Politics of Nonviolence* (1984); Web site: www.rainbowpush.org.

Amm Saifuddin Khaled

Pepper, Claude Denson   (8 September 1900, Dudleyville, Ala.–30 May 1989, Washington, D.C.). Claude Pepper, the son of poor Alabama cotton farmers and heir to the state's populist tradition, rose to become the South's leading liberal Democratic congressman. Most of his proposals for government help for the powerless became laws decades later. Pepper rose quickly in political life. He earned Phi Beta Kappa honors from the University of Alabama in 1921 and received his law degree from Harvard before moving to Florida to practice law. In 1929, Pepper was elected to the Florida legislature and staked out liberal positions on two controversial issues that marked his entire public life—senior citizen benefits and civil rights for blacks. He pushed through a popular bill exempting persons over 65 years of age from having to obtain a fishing license. But when he refused to censure Eleanor Roosevelt for inviting a black man to a White House tea, his constituents turned him out of office. Pepper reached the U.S. Senate in 1936 after highly publicized service as a state government attorney. He was an unabashed New Deal liberal, even going beyond FDR's proposals to call for national health insurance, **poll tax** repeal, and permanent federal agencies for public works and the arts. After World War II, Pepper's liberal crusade played poorly in Florida. His support for a permanent **Fair Employment Practices Commission,** his filibuster against the Taft-Hartley Bill, and his opposition to the Truman aid package to Greece and Turkey, conveyed to some constituents the impression that Pepper was nothing more than a "Nigger-lover," a "Red Pepper," and a "wily, oily-tongued apologist" for northern union bosses. In 1950 Pepper was bounced from office. After his stunning defeat, Pepper practiced law until he won the new House seat in growing Dade county in 1962. He was one of the few southerners to back John F. Kennedy's New Frontier and Lyndon B. Johnson's Great Society, including the Medicare programs for the elderly of all colors and the epic **Civil Rights Act of 1964** and the **Civil Rights Act of 1965.** Later he gained fame as the chief defender of the elderly, particularly as chairman of the House Select Committee on Aging.

Selected Bibliography Claude Denson Pepper with Hays Gorey, *Pepper: Eyewitness to a Century* (1987); Tracy Danese, *Claude Pepper and Ed Ball: Politics, Purpose, and Power* (2000); John Egerton, "Courtly Champion of America's Elderly," *New York Times Magazine* (29 November 1981), 125–31; Bill Keller, "I, Claude," *New Republic* 188 (7 March 1983), 16–18; Obituary, *New York Times*, 31 May 1989.

Bruce J. Dierenfield

Peterson v. Greenville, 373 U.S. 244 (1963)   Ten African American youth, including James Richard Peterson, entered the S. H. Kress store in Greenville, South Carolina, on 9 August 1960 and seated themselves at the lunch counter. The Greenville police arrested them, and a district court convicted them of trespass. On 21 May 1963 the U.S. Supreme Court threw out the conviction on the ground that the Kress management had excluded the petitioners from the lunch counter solely because of their race. Such private actions abridging individual rights, however, would not have violated the equal protection clause of the **Fourteenth Amendment** had the state not been involved. In this case, Chief Justice Earl Warren said that the city of Greenville, an agency of the state, had an ordinance requiring separation of the races in restaurants. The court ruled that it was unconstitutional for a state or a community to require segregation in a business and that the state could not use the police power to enforce such segregation. The *Peterson* case was typical of a series of Supreme Court decisions outlawing segregation in privately owned businesses.

Selected Bibliography Alexander M. Bickel, "Civil Rights Boil-Up," *New Republic* (8 June 1963), 10–14; James E. Clayton, *The Making of Justice: The Supreme Court in Action* (1964); "In High Court: A Blanket Rule against Segregation?" *U.S. News and World Report* (3 June 1963); Milton R. Konvitz, *Expanding Liberties: Freedom's Gains in Postwar America* (1966); George Rossman, ed., "Review of Recent Supreme Court Decisions," *American Bar Association Journal* 49 (1963), 1012.

Amm Saifuddin Khaled

Phelps-Stokes Fund   The Phelps-Stokes Fund was established with a bequest from white philanthropist Caroline Phelps Stokes in 1911 for "the education of Negroes both in Africa and the United States, North American Indians and needy . . . white students," and for improved housing in New York City. The Fund set up schools in Africa, endowed schools in the United States for black youth (at first supporting **Booker T. Washington**'s industrial training program), and conducted studies of African, African American and Native American education in both the United States and Africa. It established residences for black working women in New York and published works about black Americans and their accomplishments. A Fund president conceived the idea for the **United Negro College Fund.** In the twenty-first century, the Fund provides scholarships, develops educational programs that serve blacks and Native Americans, and examines the treatment of minorities in New York's state courts.

Selected Bibliography Edward Berman, "American Influence on African Education: The Role of the Phelps-Stokes Fund's Education Commission," *Comparative Education Review* 15 (June 1971), 132–45; *Educational Adaptations: Report of Ten Years Work of the Phelps-Stokes Fund, 1910–1920* (1920); Phelps-Stokes Fund Papers, Schomburg Center for Research in Black Culture, New York City; *Twenty Year Report of the Phelps-Stokes Fund 1911–1931* (1932); Anson Phelps Stokes, *Negro Status and Race Relations in the United States, 1911–1946* (1948).

Cheryl Greenberg

407

Philadelphia Plan Following a 1967 investigation of problems of compliance with **Executive Order 11246** in Philadelphia, Pennsylvania, construction trades, the Labor Department, headed in 1969 by Secretary George F. Shultz, developed a plan for extending minority employment in that city. The Philadelphia Plan required that individuals bidding on contracts of $500,000 or more submit an acceptable **affirmative action** program that outlined specific numerical goals for minority group employment. Contractors responded by claiming that such goals amounted to racial quotas, which were banned by Title VII of the **Civil Rights Act of 1964.** In November 1968, Comptroller-General Elmer Staats ruled that the Philadelphia Plan illegally required contractors to set racial quotas, and the Plan was suspended. Following hearings that produced evidence of continuing discrimination by the Philadelphia construction unions, Assistant Secretary of Wage and Labor Standards Arthur Fletcher supervised the design of a revised plan. As a gesture toward the antiquota language of Title VII, the June 1969 plan now suggested a target range expressed as a percentage, rather than a numerical, goal. Under its provisions, prospective bidders were required to commit to a target range of minority (now defined as "Negro, Oriental, American Indian and Spanish Surnamed Americans") manpower utilization and a timetable for its accomplishment. In September Fletcher's implementation memorandum set five-year target ranges. In December 1969, the Nixon administration defeated an attempt by Congress to ban the plan. To revive the plan, Labor Secretary Shultz issued an order in February 1970 that required all bidders, not just construction contractors, to submit an affirmative action plan within 120 days of signing a contract. An acceptable program required an analysis of all major job categories to identify underutilization of minorities. In March 1970 a suit brought against the Philadelphia Plan by Pennsylvania contractors was dismissed in federal district court. The Third Circuit Court of Appeals upheld the Plan in April 1971.

Selected Bibliography Hugh Davis Graham, *The Civil Rights Era* (1990); Dean J. Kotlowski, "Richard Nixon and the Origins of Affirmative Action," *Historian* 60 (1998), 523–41; Nicholas Pedriana and Robin Stryker, "Political Culture Wars 1960s Style: Equal Employment Opportunity–Affirmative Action Law and the Philadelphia Plan," *American Journal of Sociology* 103 (1997), 633–91; U.S. Congress, Senate, Committee on the Judiciary, Subcommittee on the Separation of Powers, *The Philadelphia Plan: Hearing Before the Subcommittee on the Separation of Powers*, 91st Cong., 1st sess., 27–28 October 1969.

Nancy Diamond

Phylon Founded in 1940 by **W.E.B. Du Bois,** *Phylon* emerged, almost immediately, as the preeminent journal of scholarly and intellectual thought in the African American community. The editorial board was a virtual who's who of African American intellectuals of the period. It included Horace Mann Bond, **Rayford Logan,** Mercer Cook, and **William S. Brathwaite.** *Phylon*'s stature was due, predominantly, to the fact that the journal was in many ways a personification of Du Bois's own intellectual rigor and scholarship. *Phylon* closely followed the research staked out in Du Bois's earlier **Atlanta University,** scholarly monographs on black history; yet, *Phylon* appealed to a much wider intellectual public, and that appeal placed it among the "best university journals in the nation" in 1956. It ceased publication in 1989.

Selected Bibliography Herbert Aptheker, ed., *The Correspondence of W.E.B. Du Bois* (1968); Walter C. Daniel, *Black Journals of the United States* (1982); W.E.B. Du Bois, *The Autobiography of W.E.B. Du Bois* (1968); Alexa B. Henderson and Janice Sumler-Edmond, eds., *Freedom's Odyssey: African-American History Essays from Phylon* (1999).

Maghan Keita

Pinchback, Pinckney Benton Stewart (10 May 1837, Macon, Ga.–21 December 1921, Washington, D.C.). The son of Major William Pinchback by the newly manumitted, racially mixed Eliza Stewart, he was said to have been so light in appearance that he was often "mistaken for a white man." His education at Cincinnati came to an abrupt halt in 1849 when his father died without adequately providing for Eliza and her offspring; thus at 12 years of age, Pinckney began to work on riverboats to help support his family. Entering Union service at New Orleans during the Civil War, he was placed in charge of recruiting black troops and was made a captain in the Louisiana Native Guards. He demanded that blacks be given political rights, and he protested

Photograph of Pinckney Pinchback, governor of Louisiana, by Matthew Brady. © Library of Congress.

the treatment of black troops. His outspokenness cost him promotions and compelled him to resign in September 1863. When he subsequently raised a cavalry company of free men of color, the Union army refused to muster it into service. He left Louisiana for Ohio in disappointment. Returning to New Orleans after the war, he became a delegate to the constitutional convention of 1867–68, where his proposals for free public education and civil rights aided his election to the state senate in 1868. He continued to push such measures both in office and in the *New Orleans Louisianian*, which he founded in 1871. After the death of Lieutenant Governor Oscar J. Dunn in November 1871, the senate elected Pinchback to the post. Forty-three days before his term ended, Governor Henry Clay Warmoth was impeached; and from December 9, 1872, until January 13, 1873, Pinchback served as the nation's first black governor. In 1872 he was elected to both the U.S. House of Representatives and the U.S. Senate, but he was not allowed to take either seat when enemies within his own party conspired with Democrats against him. He was appointed to the state board of education in 1877, was elected a state constitutional-convention delegate in 1879, and was appointed surveyor of customs at New Orleans. In 1885 he left Louisiana and eventually settled in Washington, D.C., where he remained active in politics and civil rights well into the twentieth century.

Selected Bibliography James Haskins, *Pinckney Benton Stewart Pinchback* (1973); Joe Gray Taylor, *Louisiana Reconstructed, 1863–1877* (1974); Rayford W. Logan and Michael R. Winston, eds., *Dictionary of American Negro Biography* (1982).

Gary B. Mills

Pittsburgh Courier   Founded in 1910 by Edwin N. Harleston, the *Pittsburgh Courier* quickly came under the editorship of **Robert Vann,** an attorney, who with the help of Ira Lewis, was eventually to make it one of the nation's leading black newspapers. At first, however, it struggled financially and mainly promoted Vann's career. By the 1920s the newspaper had a city and a national edition with circulation of approximately 55,000. It had also built its own printing plant. In the 1930s the paper helped convince blacks to switch from the Republican to the Democratic party. By 1937 it was the nation's leading black newspaper with around 150,000 subscribers all over the nation. Vann died in 1940 but during World War II the newspaper conducted an effective Double V for victory campaign—against the overseas enemy and against discrimination at home. It reached its circulation peak of 357,212 in 1947, but Ira Lewis died in 1948, and during the civil rights struggle white newspapers began to cover black news, so its circulation slid disastrously. The newspaper continued in business in the twenty-first century as the *New Pittsburgh Courier*, remaining one of the major black newspapers in the nation.

Selected Bibliography Andrew Buni, *Robert L. Vann of the Pittsburgh Courier: Politics and Journalism* (1974); Patrick S. Washburn, "The Blood Press: Homefront Clout Hits a Peak in World War II," *American Journalism* 12 (Fall 1995), 359–66; Nancy J. Weiss, *Farewell to the Party of Lincoln* (1983).

John F. Marszalek

Plessy v. Ferguson, 163 U.S. 537 (1896)   The "separate but equal" doctrine upheld by the Supreme Court in the 1896 *Plessy v. Ferguson* decision constituted a major legal barrier to equal rights for Negroes for more than half a century. The decision was one of a long series of Court opinions beginning in the 1870s—the **Slaughter House Cases, United States v. Reese, United States v. Cruikshank,** the **Civil Rights Cases**—that eroded rights and privileges gained by blacks during Reconstruction and guaranteed by the **Fourteenth** and **Fifteenth Amendments.** The *Plessy* principle, by rendering all but meaningless the Fourteenth Amendment's equal protection clause, provided the constitutional basis for a plethora of southern **Jim Crow** laws that accompanied the reestablishment of white supremacy after 1876.

A Louisiana statute of 1890 required all railroad companies operating in the state to provide equal but separate accommodations for black and white passengers. Homer A. Plessy, an African American who often passed as white, was arrested for refusing to vacate a seat in a white compartment of a Louisiana train. He instituted action to restrain enforcement of the 1890 law on grounds that it was unconstitutional. Losing in the state courts, he appealed to the Supreme Court. In the *Civil Rights Cases* of 1883 the Court had said that the federal government could protect blacks from segregation and discrimination arising from state action, but that private "invasion of individual rights" was not prohibited. In the *Plessy* decision state action was at issue, however, and the Court seemingly ignored the distinction between private and state action it had delineated earlier. The Louisiana Jim Crow statute, said the Court, did not deprive African Americans of equal protection of the laws. The Fourteenth Amendment "could not have been intended to abolish distinctions based upon color," and laws permitting or even requiring separation of the races did not necessarily imply the inferiority of either race to the other. Such laws, continued the Court, were clearly authorized by the Constitution under the police power of the states. And although every exercise of the police power must be reasonable, there was nothing unreasonable in the Louisiana statute requiring the separation of the two races in public conveyances.

Registering a vigorous lone dissent, Justice **John Marshall Harlan** insisted, "Our Constitution is color-blind, and neither knows nor tolerates classes among citizens." His prediction that "the judgment this day rendered will, in time, prove to be quite as pernicious as the decision made by this tribunal in the Dred Scott Case" was sound prophecy. With the *Plessy* decision, the separate but equal formula became the new constitutional orthodoxy that prevailed until 1954.

Selected Bibliography Catherine A. Barnes, *Journey from Jim Crow: The Desegregation of Southern Transit* (1983); Thomas Brooks, *Plessy v. Ferguson: A Brief History with Documents* (1997); Charles A. Lofgren, *The Plessy Case: A Legal-Historical Interpretation* (1987); Otto H. Olsen, *The Thin Disguise: Turning Points in Negro History, Plessy v. Ferguson, A Documentary Presentation* (1967); Mark V. Tushnet, *The NAACP's Legal Strategy against Segregated Education, 1925–1950* (1987); C. Vann Woodward, *The Strange Career of Jim Crow*, 2nd ed. (1974).

Charles D. Lowery

Poll Tax   The poll tax, levied per head, had to be paid in order to vote. It was once considered a reform measure because it was less restrictive than property requirements. However, southern states adopted the poll tax after the Civil War to get around the **Fifteenth Amendment,** a constitutional change that guaranteed the vote to freed slaves. In fact, the poll tax kept many poor men, black and white, who were unable to pay the tax, from voting. The Twenty-fourth Amendment (1964) outlawed the poll tax for federal elections, but failure to ban poll taxes in state and local elections made the amendment largely ineffective. Congress in the **Voting Rights Act of 1965** authorized federal intervention to register voters, and the U.S. Supreme Court, considering the Virginia poll tax in *Harper v. Virginia State Board of Elections* (1966), ruled that the **Fourteenth Amendment** made the levying of a poll tax for any election unconstitutional. That year, too, lower courts outlawed the remaining poll tax laws in Alabama, Mississippi, and Texas.

Selected Bibliography J. Morgan Kousser, *The Shaping of Southern Politics: Suffrage Restriction and the Establishment of the One-Party South, 1880–1910* (1974); Paul Lewinson, *Race, Class, and Party: A History of Negro Suffrage and White Politics in the South* (1965); Jack C. Plano and Milton Greenberg, *The American Political Dictionary* (1985); Frank Broyles Williams, *Poll Tax as a Suffrage Requirement in the South, 1870–1901* (1973).

Marvin Thomas

Pollock v. Williams, 322 U.S. 4 (1944)   This case was one of a series of important black peonage cases in which the Supreme Court, between the years 1911 and 1944, helped to sustain the national antipeonage campaign then being waged by African Americans. The circumstances of the case closely parallel those of earlier important peonage cases such as **Bailey v. Alabama** (1911), **United States v. Reynolds** (1914), and **Taylor v. Georgia** (1942). James Pollock was a black resident of Florida who accepted a cash advance from an employer and then failed to provide the promised services. His actions violated a Florida statute typical of laws passed by southern states after Reconstruction permitting the arrest of blacks for vagrancy, breach of labor contracts, and other crimes. The laws were used by southern planters and others to create a pool of cheap black labor and to prevent indebted employees from leaving their service. The Florida trial court held that Pollock's breach of the labor contract into which he had entered was prima facie evidence of intent to defraud his employer. The Supreme Court reversed the lower court and ruled that the Florida statute violated the **Thirteenth Amendment** and federal antipeonage laws. *Pollock* dealt a death blow to southern black peonage. A few prosecutions were filed by the **Civil Rights Section, Justice Department** in the 1950s, but for all practical purposes black peonage disappeared after *Pollock*.

Selected Bibliography Pete Daniel, *The Shadow of Slavery: Peonage in the South, 1909–1969* (1972); Loren Miller, *The Petitioners: The Story of the Supreme Court of the United States and the Negro* (1966); Edgar Bronson Talman, "Review of Recent Supreme Court Decisions," *American Bar Association Journal* 30 (1944), 297–99; Melvin I. Urofsky, *A March of Liberty: A Constitutional History of the United States* (1988).

Charles D. Lowery

Poole, Elijah (Elijah Muhammad) (7 October 1897, Sandersville, Ga.—25 February 1975, Chicago, Ill.). The son of sharecroppers and former slaves, Elijah Poole, who later took the name Elijah Muhammad, rose to prominence as the spiritual leader of the **Nation of Islam,** commonly known as the **Black Muslims.** By the 1960s he had become a powerful symbol of black nationalism, not only to his religious movement but also to the mushrooming secular **Black Power** movement. At the time of his death in 1975, he had become a controversial figure for his militant racial views, such as derogating whites as incorrigible "blue-eyed devils," and his well-publicized feud with his former lieutenant, **Malcolm X,** whose assassination in 1965 has been attributed to three of Poole's zealous followers.

Poole left Georgia for the North in 1923, settling finally in Detroit, Michigan where he met W. D. Fard, who claimed to be "Allah," the self-annointed leader of the "Lost-Found Nation of Islam in the Wilderness of North America." After Fard's unexplained disappearance in 1934, Poole, who came now to be known as Elijah Muhammad the "Apostle" or "Prophet," assumed control of the fledgling Nation of Islam, a position he held until his death. Under Muhammad's leadership, the Nation of Islam grew into a Chicago-based, religious–black nationalist organization whose national membership, located primarily in the urban North, ranged between 50,000 and 250,000. Muhammad preached his doctrines of racial separation, self-help, self-defense, and racial dignity (a direct precursor to Black Power) through his powerful speeches and through such written works as the Black Muslim weekly tabloid, *Muhammad Speaks*, and his *Message to the Black Man* (1965). As the contemporary civil rights movement peaked in the 1960s, Elijah Muhammad remained a controversial figure: suspect in the eyes of moderate integrationists and revered in the minds of militant Black Power advocates.

Selected Bibliography Claude Andrew Clegg, *An Original Man: The Life and Times of Elijah Muhammad* (1997); Karl Evanzz, *The Messenger: The Rise and Fall of Elijah Muhammad* (1999); "Guide to the Microfilm Edition of the FBI File on Elijah Muhammad (1996); Obituary, *New York Times*, 29 February 1975; Joe Wood, ed., *Malcolm X: In Our Image* (1992);

Irvin D. S. Winsboro

Poor People's March on Washington (Poor People's Campaign). The last major demonstration planned by **Martin Luther King, Jr.,** and the **Southern Christian Leadership Conference,** this protest was designed "to force Americans to face the fact that America is a racist country," and that her racism had impoverished thousands. King argued that the right to vote and to eat in any establishment failed to affect living conditions. The poor needed something more. Among the demands of this campaign were full employment, a guaranteed annual income, and construction funds for low cost housing. Because it was essential to make the federal government aware of the plight of the poor, King proposed a mule cart procession, involving thousands, that would begin around April 22, 1968, in Mississippi and terminate in Washington, D.C. There, the participants would construct a shanty town close to the federal buildings. He suggested that demonstrators might bring some shanties from Mississippi on flat bed trucks to further dramatize the poverty in America. His assassination temporarily halted preparations for the campaign, but **Ralph David Abernathy,** King's successor, vowed to lead the demonstrators to Washington as King had planned. Nine caravans (buses and cars) of people converged on Washington where they built a plywood shanty town—**Resurrection City**—within walking distance of the White House. The campaign proved unsuccessful.

Selected Bibliography Robert T. Chase, "Class Resurrection: The Poor People's Campaign of 1968 and Resurrection City" *Essays in History* 40 (1998), www.etext.lib.virginia.edu/journals/eh; Charles E. Fager, *Uncertain Resurrection: The Poor People's Washington Campaign* (1969); Gerold Frank, *An American Death* (1972); David J. Garrow, *Bearing the Cross: Martin Luther King and the Southern Christian Leadership Conference* (1988).

Betty L. Plummer

Portsmouth, Virginia, Sit-Ins (1960)   The sit-in movement in Virginia began in February 1960. These demonstrations were part of a movement that had originated in Greensboro, North Carolina, and had spread quickly first to other North Carolina cities and then to Hampton, Norfolk, and Portsmouth in Virginia. Although students from Virginia State College, **Hampton Institute,** and Norcom High School were among the participants, the movement was primarily an effort organized by the **NAACP.** Students from Hampton Institute staged sit-ins at the Woolworth Store in Hampton and a Hampton drugstore lunch counter. The sit-ins spread to the Norfolk-Portsmouth area when P. L. Artis sought to be served breakfast and later lunch at Bradshaw-Diehl's Department Store. At the same time 18 blacks entered Rose's and took seats at the lunch counter, and 38 blacks asked to be served at Norfolk's Woolworth counter. In each case the sit-ins were orderly and no arrests were made. The following week about 150 black students demonstrated at Rose's in Portsmouth. The situation evolved into fist fights between white and black youths. Later, when a crowd of some 3,000 assembled at the shopping center, 27 persons, white and black, were arrested for various disturbances. As a result of these events, some establishments closed their lunch counters for the next several days. Eventually, court orders and voluntary action by some store owners permanently desegregated the facilities.

Selected Bibliography *Norfolk Ledger Dispatch*, 13, 15, 16 February 1960; *Virginia Pilot*, 17, 18 February 1960.

Charles A. Risher

Poston, Theodore "Ted" Roosevelt Augustus Major   (4 July 1906, Hopkinsville, Ky.–11 January 1974, Brooklyn, N.Y.). Poston began his career with the family newspaper, *The Contender*, in Hopkinsville, Kentucky. In 1929 he went to work for Harlem's **Amsterdam News,** becoming city editor in 1934 and taking an active part in the *News* strike of 1934. During World War II, he served as chief of the Negro News Desk in the Office of War Information.

After the war, he was hired by the *New York Post*, and he became the first black columnist to work full time for a New York daily. Poston's byline ran in the *Post* for 33 years.

Selected Bibliography James Forman, *The Making of Black Revolutionaries* (1985); Kathleen Hauke, *Ted Poston: Pioneer American Journalist* (1998); Obituary, *New York Times,* 12 January 1974; Roi Ottley, *New World A-Coming* (1943); Ted Poston, "My Most Humiliating Jim Crow Experience," *Negro Digest* 2 (April 1944), 55–56; Theressa Rush, Carol Myers, and Esther Arata, *Black American Writers Past and Present: A Biographical and Bibliographical Dictionary* (1975).

Ray Branch

Powell, Adam Clayton, Jr. (29 November 1908, New Haven, Conn.–4 April 1972, Miami, Fla.). Easily the nation's most recognized African American politician from the 1940s to the 1960s, Adam Clayton Powell, Jr., was heir to one of the nation's largest black congregations—Abyssinian Baptist Church in New York City's Harlem. He grew up in the middle of what he would later call **"black power,"** listening to his father and to the black nationalist **Marcus Garvey.** Educated at Colgate University, in Hamilton, New York (A.B., 1930), Columbia University, in New York

Adam Clayton Powell, Jr. © Library of Congress.

(M.A., 1932), and Shaw University, in Raleigh, North Carolina (D.D., 1935), Powell succeeded his father as pastor in 1937 and became a force in city politics as he led demonstrations to force major employers in Harlem to hire blacks. He was elected in 1941 to New York's city council and in 1945 to the U.S. House of Representatives, where he served for 11 successive terms. With characteristic panache, he broke the racial barriers in congressional service facilities, pushed to admit black journalists to the press galleries, and pioneered the use of the power of the federal purse to punish segregation. He sought, for instance, to deny federal funds to any public project that discriminated. As chair of the House Committee on Education and Labor (1960–67) he managed enactment of numerous laws from minimum wage to antipoverty.

Selected Bibliography P. Allan Dionisopoulos, *Rebellion, Racism, and Representation: The Adam Clayton Powell Case and Its Antecedents* (1970); Charles V. Hamilton, *Adam Clayton Powell, Jr.: The Political Biography of an American Dilemma* (1991); Adam Clayton Powell, *Adam by Adam: The Autobiography of Adam Clayton Powell, Jr.* (1971); Wil Haygood, *King of the Cats: The Life and Times of Adam Clayton Powell, Jr.* (1993).

Thomas J. Davis

Powell v. Alabama, **287 U.S. 45 (1932)** In 1931 Ozie Powell and the eight other teenage "Scottsboro Boys" (see **Scottsboro Trial**) stood trial for the alleged rape of two white women, a capital offense. The trial judge somewhat casually appointed all members of the local bar as their counsel and invited anyone willing to help to do so. At trial the same day, all received death sentences, which (except for one juvenile) the state supreme court affirmed. This first of two appeals to the Supreme Court focused on the inadequacy of trial counsel, in violation of the Sixth Amendment and the due process clause of the **Fourteenth Amendment.** Justice George Sutherland, for the seven-to-two majority, reversed the convictions. He combined sociological considerations with a historic review of due process back to the Magna Carta. Counsel was a necessary part of any hearing, and because the defendants were "young, ignorant, illiterate, surrounded by hostile sentiment, hauled back and forth under guard of soldiers," and charged with the community's most atrocious crime, effective counsel was vital. This case marked the first incorporation of any element of criminal due process from the Bill of Rights into the Fourteenth Amendment. Such incorporation seemed to be precluded by *Hurtado v. California* (1884), but "compelling circumstances" supported this exception. The subsequent retrials led to **Norris v. Alabama** (1935), another appeal on a different issue.

Selected Bibliography Dan T. Carter, *Scottsboro* (1969); Robert F. Cushman, *Leading Constitutional Decisions* (1992); James Goodman, *Stories of Scottsboro* (1994); Donald G. Neiman, *Promises to Keep: African-Americans and the Constitutional Order, 1776 to Present* (1991); "Notes," *University of Pennsylvania Law Review* 81 (1933), 337–38; "Recent Decisions," *Columbia University Law Review* 32 (1932), 1430–31.

James E. Sefton

Powers v. Ohio, 499 U.S. 400 (1991)   The Supreme Court held, in a seven to two opinion written by Justice Anthony M. Kennedy, that a criminal defendant can object to race-based exclusions of jurors through peremptory challenges, regardless of whether the defendant and the excluded jurors are the same race. The equal protection clause prohibits a prosecutor from using the state's peremptory challenges to exclude potential jury members solely on the basis of their race. In *Powers,* the defendant was a white man indicted and convicted of murder charges, who objected to the prosecution's peremptory challenges of prospective black jurors. The Supreme Court had previously held in 1986 in *Batson v. Kentucky* that a prosecutor's use of racially discriminatory peremptory challenges violated the **Fourteenth Amendment.** In *Batson,* however, the defendant was black and so were the excluded jurors. Despite the difference in racial identity between the defendant and the excluded jurors, the majority on *Powers* held that a white criminal defendant had standing to raise the third-party equal protection claims of black jurors excluded by the prosecution because of their race. In dissent, Justice Anton Scalia, joined by Chief Justice William Rehnquist, argued that the majority's opinion was a clear departure from prior law in the area of equal protection and standing.

Selected Bibliography Stephen R. DiPrima, "Note: Selecting a Jury on Federal Criminal Trials after *Batson* and *McCollum,*" *Columbia Law Review* 95 (May 1995), 888–928; A. Leon Higginbotham, *Shades of Freedom: Racial Politics and Presumptions of the American Legal Process* (1996); Randall Kennedy, *Race, Crime, and the Law* (1997).

Elizabeth M. Smith

Prayer Pilgrimage to Washington (1957)   The Prayer Pilgrimage was a mass rally held in Washington, D.C., to demonstrate support for the proposed **Civil Rights Act of 1957.** The idea for the Pilgrimage came out of a meeting of the **Southern Christian Leadership Conference** in February 1957. Originally, the concept of the march had been to protest President Dwight D. Eisenhower's earlier failure to meet with a group of black leaders led by **A. Philip Randolph.** Randolph, **Martin Luther King, Jr.,** and **Roy Wilkins** organized the protest. Held on 17 May, the third anniversary of the *Brown v. Board of Education* decision, the Prayer Pilgrimage drew a disappointing crowd of between 15 and 25 thousand; organizers had predicted a turnout of 50 thousand. Randolph presided. The crowd heard Mahalia Jackson sing and listened to speeches by Wilkins, **Adam Clayton Powell, Mordecai Johnson, Fred Shuttlesworth,** and others. Entertainers such as Sammy Davis, Jr., Ruby Dee, Sidney Poitier, and Harry Belafonte made appearances, as did baseball great **Jackie Robinson.** King spoke last, and his speech, in which he repeatedly demanded "give us the ballot," drew the greatest response from the crowd. The event helped establish King's position as a national leader.

Selected Bibliography Taylor Branch, *Parting the Waters: America in the King Years, 1954–1963* (1988); Adam Fairclough, *To Redeem the Soul of America: The Southern Christian Leadership Conference and Martin Luther King, Jr.* (1987); David J. Garrow, *Bearing the Cross:*

Seated on speakers' platform at the May 17, 1957 Prayer Pilgrimage for Freedom in Washington, D.C. are (left to right) Roy Wilkins, A. Philip Randolph, Rev. Thomas Kilgore, Jr., and Dr. Martin Luther King, Jr. © Library of Congress.

Martin Luther King and the Southern Christian Leadership Conference (1986); David Levering Lewis, *King: A Critical Biography* (1970).

Michael S. Mayer

Price, J[oseph] C[harles] (10 February 1854, Elizabeth City, N.C.–25 October 1893, Salisbury, N.C.). One of the most prominent African American educators of his generation, Price's career was established after his graduation from Lincoln University in Pennsylvania in 1881, when the African Methodist Episcopal Zion Church enlisted him to embark on a speaking tour of England on behalf of a struggling denominational school named Zion Wesley Institute. Price raised nearly 10,000 dollars for Zion Wesley and was named president of the institute in 1882. He built the Salisbury, North Carolina school into a four-year liberal arts institution named Livingstone College. Subsequent speaking tours established Price not only as a minister but also as an advocate of education and civil rights in the post-Reconstruction South. In North Carolina, Price fought for a state supported college for his race and pleaded for federal funds for education. Price received national attention in 1890 after he was elected president of the **Afro-American League,** an organization founded by *New York Age* editor **T. Thomas Fortune** for the legal protection of blacks. For the next three years Price continued to address civil rights as a national concern, denouncing separate car laws and defending black suffrage. Price's promise as a national leader ended abruptly when he died of Bright's disease in 1893 at the age of 39.

Selected Bibliography Daniel W. Crofts, "The Blair Bill and the Elections Bill: The Congressional Aftermath to Reconstruction" (Ph.D. diss., Yale University, 1968); Lenwood Davis, "A History of Livingstone College, 1879–1957" (D.A. thesis, Carnegie-Mellon University, 1963); Frenise A. Logan, *The Negro in North Carolina 1876–1894* (1964); August Meier, *Negro Thought in America: 1880–1915: Racial Ideologies in the Age of Booker T. Washington* (1966); William J. Walls, *Joseph Charles Price, Educator and Race Leader* (1943); Thomas A. Upchurch, "The Billion Dollar Congress and Black America: Debating the Race Problem on the Eve of Jim Crow, 1889–1991" (Ph.D. diss., Mississippi State University, 2001); Paul Yandle, "Joseph Charles Price and the Southern Problem" (M.A. thesis, Wake Forest University, 1990).

Paul Yandle

Price, Leontyne (10 February 1927, Laurel, Miss.–). "The prima donna absoluta," she earned a B.A. from Central State University in 1948 and pursued additional voice training at the Julliard School in New York and with Florence Page Kimball in New York. Despite the reluctance of the American opera world to permit blacks to sing major roles at the leading opera houses, she dreamed of singing at the Metropolitan Opera. In 1959 she was offered that opportunity, but she refused the part of Aida, choosing to wait and make her debut in a role where race was insignificant. In 1961 when she sang the role of Leonora in *Il Trovatore* she became the first black woman to sing a major role on opening

Portrait of Leontyne Price, 1951. © Library of Congress.

night at the Met. In 2003, she remained a major voice in America music. She is the recipient of a variety of awards and recognitions, including 19 Grammys and the Presidential Medal of Freedom. In late 2002, a rediscovered recording of her famous 1965 Carnegie Hall debut recital was issued.

Selected Bibliography John P. Davis, ed., *The American Negro Reference Book* (1966); Marianna W. Davis, ed., *Contributions of Black Women to America*, vol. 1: *The Arts, Media, Business, Law, Sports* (1982); Hugh Lee Lyon, *Leontyne Price: Highlights of a Prima Donna* (1973); William C. Matney, ed., *Who's Who among Black Americans* (1988); George A. Sewell, *Mississippi Black History Makers* (1977).

Betty L. Plummer

Project C See Birmingham Confrontation.

Public School Busing Court-ordered busing to achieve racial desegregation of the public schools in areas where dual systems once existed resulted from the 1971 *Swann v. Charlotte-Mecklenburg Board of Education* decision, the national test case for busing. Busing, the Supreme Court said in its unanimous but controversial ruling, was a legal remedial tool to fulfill the intent of the 1954 *Brown v. Board of Education* decision. Transporting students to ameliorate school board-imposed segregation violated no one's constitutional rights, said the Court. "Every available technique," including massive crosstown busing and the redrawing of school districts, should be employed to correct persistent racial imbalances in the public schools. President Richard M. Nixon, who praised the ideal of the neighborhood school and predictably denounced busing because it challenged his administration's legal position on school desegregation issues, tried unsuccessfully to get Congress to pass legislation limiting busing. Such legislation was passed during the presidency of Gerald Ford.

In 1973–74, busing became a politically volatile topic outside the South when northern cities came under judicial scrutiny. In 1974 Boston became the center for northern urban opposition to the use of the school bus to integrate the city school system. The federal courts stood firm, however, and proponents of integration beat back a serious attempt to pass a constitutional amendment against court-ordered busing. As the Supreme Court became more conservative, however, it issued a series of decisions in the late 1970s and 1980s that rejected busing as a means of integration. Many blacks were not entirely unhappy at this turn of events because it was their children, not those of white parents, that were usually bused. By the beginning of the twenty-first century the school bus was no longer an important civil rights vehicle; busing is widely viewed by both black leaders and white liberals as a failure, and urban schools remain de facto segregated.

Selected Bibliography Judith Bentley, *Busing the Continuous Controversy* (1982); Bernard R. Boxill, *Blacks and Social Justice* (1984); Paul R. Dimond, *Beyond Busing* (1985); Frye Gaillard, *The Dream Long Deferred* (1988); Edward Keynes, *The Courts vs. Congress* (1989); Bernard Schwartz, *Swann's War* (1986).

Jessie M. Carter

Q

Quarles, Benjamin (23 January 1904, Boston, Mass.–16 March 1996, Mitchellville, Md.). A renowned African American historian, Quarles earned his B.A. at Shaw University, in Raleigh, North Carolina, and his M.A. and Ph.D. at the University of Wisconsin. He lectured at Shaw and Dillard Universities before moving to Morgan State University, a predominantly black institution in Maryland. There, Quarles taught history and became the chairperson of the History Department. He became well known for his many outstanding publications including: *Frederick Douglass* (1948); *Allies for Freedom: Blacks and John Brown* (1974); *The Negro in the Civil War* (1953); *The Negro in the American Revolutionary War* (1960); *The Negro in the Making of America* (1964); and *Black Abolitionists* (1969). Quarles provided concrete evidence in these works to support his main argument that blacks have always played a significant role in the development of America.

   Selected Bibliography *Directory of American Scholars*, 8th ed. (1982); *Afro-American Encyclopedia* (1974); *Quarles: Memorial Convocation Celebrating the Life and Legacy of Dr. Benjamin A. Quarles* (1997).

Amos J. Beyan

R

Race Relations Law Reporter This journal was started by the Vanderbilt University School of Law in Nashville, Tennessee, in February 1956 with funding provided by the Fund for the Republic, Inc. In 1959 the **Southern Education Reporting Service** took over management functions for the *Reporter,* but the law school continued to edit it. Originally a bimonthly, the journal became a quarterly in the spring of 1959. Over the years most of its support came from the Ford Foundation. The *Reporter* aimed to "report the materials in all fields where the issue of race and color is presented as having legal consequence" by systematically compiling the primary documents in the field. It included the texts of decisions by the U.S. Supreme Court, lower federal courts, and state courts; federal and state legislation; administrative rules, regulations, and orders; opinions of state attorneys general; and a sampling of local ordinances. Editors provided case summaries and occasionally abridged and summarized documents. Lacking financial support the *Reporter* ended publication in the winter of 1967 and was succeeded from May 1969 to March 1972 by the Vanderbilt Law School's briefer *Race Relations Law Survey.*

Selected Bibliography *Race Relations Law Reporter; Southern School News.*

Charles W. Eagles

Racial Profiling Racial profiling consists of using race, ethnicity, or national origin as a determining factor in action taken. It ranges from employers requiring applicants to list race or ethnicity on forms, to law enforcement officials using statistical profiles to decide who to stop and search in airports, malls, and other places. Because of increasing drug trafficking in the last decades of the twentieth century, racial profiling was especially associated with law enforcement officials who were accused of stopping and searching a high number of African American male motorists in the hopes of seizing contraband. An expanded form of profiling, the CARD system, which included class, age, race, and dress, was also used. Racial profiling has resulted in numerous court cases, congressional hearings, and much legislation. Past studies have proved its ineffectiveness, and several national organizations and police departments are working to eradicate it. Both President Bill Clinton and George W. Bush have called for it to end. Whether targeted at African Americans, Native Americans, Japanese Americans, Muslim Americans, or others, total elimination of racial profiling may prove futile because it is often predicated on world events.

Selected Bibliography Gene Callahan and William Anderson, "The Roots of Racial Profiling: Why Are Police Targeting Minorities for Traffic Stops?" *Reason* 33 (August–September 2001), 32–40; Angie Cannon, "DWB: Driving While Black," *U.S. News and World Report*, 15 March 1999; Robert M. Entman and Andrew Rojecki, *The Black Image in the White Mind: Media and Race in America* (2001); David A. Harris, *Profiles in Injustice: Why Police Profiling Cannot Work* (2002); Kenneth Meeks, *Driving While Black: Highways, Shopping, Malls, Taxicabs, Sidewalks: How to Fight Back if You Are a Victim of Racial Profiling* (2000).

Jane F. Lancaster

Radical Reconstruction   This term, also called Military Reconstruction and Congressional Reconstruction, refers to the period from 1867 to 1876, when Congress asserted control over readmission of former Confederate states into the Union. Radical Reconstruction was initiated in 1867 with the passage of a series of Reconstruction Acts. The first act, passed on 2 March 1867, divided the conquered South into five military districts, each under the control of a general appointed by the president. States were directed to convene constitutional conventions in which former slaves could participate, and to frame new state constitutions providing for black citizenship and suffrage. Supplemental acts insured implementation by instructing federal commanders to expedite elections, register voters, and convene constitutional conventions. Some historians argue that Radical Reconstruction is a misnomer. After all, former slaves were not distributed real property or other compensations that would have radically altered the distribution of wealth and influence in the South. Another group contends, however, that granting blacks suffrage (considering that in 1867 18 of 25 northern states refused blacks the vote) made Reconstruction radical. During the period, blacks became politically active in the South and gained valuable experience.

Selected Bibliography Robert Cruden, *The Negro in Reconstruction* (1969); W.E.B. Du Bois, *Black Reconstruction in America* (1935); Eric Foner, *Reconstruction, 1863–1977* (1988); John Hope Franklin, *Reconstruction: After the Civil War* (1961); Rembert W. Patrick, *The Reconstruction of the Nation* (1967); Kenneth Stampp, *Reconstruction: An Anthology of Revisionist Writings* (1969); Hans L. Trefousse, *The Radical Republicans: Lincoln's Vanguard for Racial Justice* (1969); Allen W. Trelease, *Reconstruction: The Great Experiment* (1971).

Wali Rashash Kharif

Radical Republicans   The most advanced group of Republicans, they advocated resistance to the slaveholders before the Civil War, emancipation during the conflict, and civil rights for the freedmen afterward. Never an organized faction, they differed among themselves on issues other than slavery and race. The radicals took an active part in the founding of the Republican party, its early struggles in Congress, and in opposing compromise during the secession crisis. Their relations with Abraham Lincoln were controversial; his end aims were similar to theirs, but he had a better sense of timing and angered them by moving too slowly against slavery. Yet he was able to make use of their pressure to move forward in spite of conservative opposition, so that emancipation became a fact before the war was over. At first the radicals greeted the accession of Andrew Johnson with pleasure. But when the new president unfolded his conservative program of Reconstruction, they became his most determined opponents. Because they were a minority, they were never able to frame Reconstruction measures exactly to their liking; nevertheless, their relentless pressure induced the majority of Congress to override his veto of the **Civil Rights Act,** pass the **Fourteenth Amendment** and, with the Reconstruction Acts, inaugurate Congressional Reconstruction. And while they were unable to convict Johnson in the impeachment trial, they did succeed in passing the **Fifteenth Amendment,** which enfranchised the blacks. During the 1870s their influence began to wane. Advancing age and death removed the most active; lessening interest in Reconstruction made it difficult to sustain the Republican governments in the South, and the disputed election of 1876 led to the compromise of the following year involving the inauguration of Rutherford B. Hayes in return, in part, for the removal of federal troops from the statehouses in the South, so that Reconstruction ended.

Selected Bibliography Michael Les Benedict, *A Compromise of Principle* (1974); Allan G. Bogue, *The Earnest Man* (1981); Hans L. Trefousse, *The Radical Republicans: Lincoln's Vanguard for Racial Justice* (1968); T. Harry Williams, *Lincoln and the Radicals* (1941).

Hans L. Trefousse

Rainey, Homer P.   (19 January 1896, Clarksville, Tex.–19 December 1985, Boulder, Colo.). Rainey, who held degrees from Austin College and the University of Chicago, had a distinguished career in education when he was hired as president of the University of Texas in 1939. He soon alienated the ultraconservative board of regents, who complained that Rainey wanted to improve educational opportunities for blacks in Texas and that he favored equal rights in general. The regents fired him in 1944, largely because of his defense of academic freedom. African Americans, voting in Democratic primaries for the first time in 1946, overwhelmingly supported Rainey for governor, but he lost the runoff and left the state.

Selected Bibliography Alice Cox, "The Rainey Affair: A History of the Academic Freedom Controversy at the University of Texas, 1938–1946" (Ph.D. diss., University of Denver, 1970); George N. Green, *The Establishment in Texas Politics: The Primitive Years, 1938–1957* (1979); "Rainey, Homer P.," *Current Biography* (1946); Homer Rainey Biographical File, Barker Texas

History Center, University of Texas at Austin; Homer Rainey Papers, University of Missouri Library, Columbia.

George N. Green

Rainey, Julian D.   (1889–30 March 1961, Boston, Mass.). A graduate of the City College of New York and the Suffolk Law School, in Boston, Massachusetts, Rainey was the first black to serve as corporation counsel for the city of Boston. He held this position from 1929 to 1932, when he left to become special assistant to the U.S. attorney general, a position he held until 1944. Assistant to the Democratic national chairman, Rainey also functioned as a counsel for the **NAACP.**

Selected Bibliography Obituary, *New York Times*, 1 April 1961; John C. Smith, *Emancipation: The Making of the Black Lawyer, 1844–1944* (1993).

Ray Branch

Randolph, A. Philip   (15 April 1889, Crescent City, Fla.–16 May 1979, New York, N.Y.). A leading African American labor unionist and civil rights activist, Randolph received his high school education in Jacksonville, Florida, and his postsecondary education at City College of New York. While in New York, Randolph served as an elevator operator, a porter, and a waiter. In 1917

A. Philip Randolph before the Lincoln Memorial during the 1963 March on Washington. © National Archives.

he and Chandler Owen launched a radical magazine, *The Messenger,* to address the social injustices blacks experienced. Randolph was arrested in Cleveland, Ohio, by federal marshals, because he opposed black support for World War I. Randolph's short term imprisonment did not deter him from his militant civil rights and union activities. He organized black porters into a union, founding the **Brotherhood of Sleeping Car Porters and Maids** in 1925. Despite opposition to the newly founded union from other unions and the Pullman company, its membership and bargaining power continued to increase. In 1941 Randolph warned the administration of President Franklin D. Roosevelt that, if the discriminatory hiring practices of companies that received federal subsidies did not stop, he and some 50,000 blacks would march on Washington, D.C. This threat was a factor in President Roosevelt's promulgation in June 1941 of **Executive Order 8802,** out of which grew the **Fair Employment Practices Committee.** President Harry S Truman established a similar committee in 1950. Randolph and Grant Reynolds of New York founded a movement against racism in the U.S. Army in 1947. Their movement influenced President Truman to give assurance in 1948 that segregation in the army would be abolished. Randolph was among the prominent leaders of the 1963 **March on Washington.** He remained active in the civil rights struggle until his death in 1979.

Selected Bibliography Jervis Anderson, *A. Philip Randolph: A Biographical Portrait* (1973); *Current Biography* (1951); Julius Jacobson, ed., *The Negro and the American Labor Movement* (1968); Thomas Palm, ed., *The Economics of Black America* (1972); Paula F. Pfeffer, *A. Philip Randolph: Pioneer of the Civil Rights Movement* (1990).

Amos J. Beyan

Randolph Institute, A. Philip　Founded in 1965 by **A. Philip Randolph** and **Bayard Rustin,** the Randolph Institute serves as a bridge between the African American community and organized labor. Part of the American Federation of Labor and Congress of Industrial Organizations, it seeks to represent the interests of each community to the other. In 1968 the institute established local affiliates; by the early twenty-first century there were more than 150 chapters in 36 states. There black union activists work on local civil rights, union, and community service issues including voter registration and get-out-the-vote drives, job training, union organizing, worker safety, food banks, health care, and winning community support for strikes or boycotts. The institute helped organize the Memphis, Tennessee, sanitation workers in 1968 and the Mississippi catfish workers in 1990. Its president, Norman Hall, has called the Institute's members "proud foot soldiers for freedom and democracy into the twenty-first century."

Selected Bibliography APR Institute, *A 'Freedom Budget' for All Americans: Budgeting Our Resources, 1966–1975 to Achieve 'Freedom from Want'* (1966); Norman Hill, "The APRI: Looking Back at 25 Years of Struggle," (Report, A. Philip Randolph Institute, 1990); Bayard Rustin, "The History of the A. Philip Randolph Institute," *Debate and Understanding* (Winter 1976), 29–35; Web site: www.apri.org.

Cheryl Greenberg

Rangel, Charles Bernard (11 June 1930, New York, N.Y.–). Born in Harlem, "Charlie" Rangel won a Purple Heart and a Bronze Star for service to his country during the Korean War. He graduated from New York University in 1957 and from St. John's Law School in 1960. He was first elected to Congress in 1970, and he has continued to hold the same seat in the House of Representatives for 15 terms. Rangel sponsored the bill that created the holiday honoring Martin Luther King, Jr., in 1983, and a bill to extend the life of the federal **Civil Rights Commission**. In 2003, he was considered the elder statesman among African Americans in Congress and was among the most powerful members of the House.

   Selected Bibliography John Hope Franklin and Alfred E. Moss, *From Slavery to Freedom: A History of African Americans*, 8th ed. (2000); Jessie Carney Smith, ed., *Notable Black American Men* (1999).

Thomas Adams Upchurch

Ransom, Freeman B. (7 July 1884, Grenada, Miss.–6 August 1947, Indianapolis, Ind.). Nationally known attorney, civic worker, and general manager of the **Madame C. J. Walker** Manufacturing Company, Ransom received a degree from the Law Department of Walden University in Nashville, Tennessee, and pursued further legal studies at Columbia University. He settled in Indianapolis in 1910 where he became one of its most respected residents. In 1940 he was voted Indianapolis's outstanding citizen. Eulogized as one "who served unselfishly the cause of progress for his race," Ransom was a member of the Legal Committee and the board of directors of the Indianapolis **NAACP.** He also served as vice president of the National Bar Association and of the **National Negro Business League.**

   Selected Bibliography *Chicago Defender,* 12 December 1936, 23 August 1947; *Crisis* 8 (September 1914), 237; Florence Murray, ed., *The Negro Handbook* (1949); John C. Smith, *Emancipation: The Making of the Black Lawyer* (1993); Thomas Yenser, ed., *Who's Who in Colored America* (1937).

Betty L. Plummer

Ransom, Reverdy Cassius (4 January 1861, Flushing, Ohio–22 April 1959, Wilberforce, Ohio). Ransom was the African Methodist Episcopal (A.M.E.) Church's earliest proponent of the social gospel and an outspoken opponent of accommodationism. His traditional ministries were infused with social and political programs; he founded the Institutional Church and Social Settlement in 1900 in Chicago. Ransom denounced **Booker T. Washington**'s tactics at the 1899 meeting of the **Afro-American Council** and gave a fiery address, "The Spirit of John Brown," at the **Niagara Movement**'s 1906 gathering at Harpers Ferry. His 1918 write-in campaign for the state legislature sponsored by the United Civic League was an effective protest against Republican racial policies in Harlem. An acerbic advocate of a more educated ministry, Ransom was a mentor to young A.M.E. scholars such as **R. R. Wright, Jr.,** Charles H. Wesley, and **Monroe Work.** Ransom was editor of the A.M.E. Church *Review* from 1912 to 1924 when he was elected 48th bishop of the African Methodist Episcopal Church in 1924.

Selected Bibliography Calvin Morris, *Reverdy C. Ransom* (1990); Anthony B. Pinn, ed., *Making the Gospel Plain: The Writings of Bishop Reverdy C. Ransom* (1999); The Reverdy Ransom Collection, Ohio Historical Society; Reverdy C. Ransom, *The Pilgrimage of Harriet Ransom's Son* (1949); Milton C. Sternett, *Bound for the Promised Land: African American Religion and the Great Migration* (1997); David Wills, "Reverdy Ransom, The Making of an A.M.E. Bishop," in *Black Apostles: Afro-American Clergy Confront the Twentieth Century* (1978).

Francille Rusan Wilson

Rauh, Joseph, Jr. (3 January 1911, Cincinnati, Ohio–3 September 1992, Washington, D.C.). Rauh, a lawyer noted for his tireless efforts behind the scenes of the civil rights movement, as well as for peace and union activism, worked with **A. Philip Randolph** in drafting **Executive Order 8802,** which created the **Fair Employment Practices Committee** in 1941. In 1947, Rauh helped lead the fight to adopt a civil rights plank in the Democratic party platform, which caused the southerners to bolt from the convention. After 1964, Rauh fell out of favor with more militant blacks, particularly because of his role in attempting a compromise between the **Mississippi Freedom Democratic Party** and the Lyndon B. Johnson camp at the 1964 Democratic convention. He was the founder and past president of the **Americans for Democratic Action** (ADA) and longtime attorney for the Leadership Conference on Civil Rights.

Selected Bibliography Thomas R. Brooks, *Walls Come Tumbling Down: A History of the Civil Rights Movement, 1940–1970* (1974); David J. Garrow, *Bearing the Cross: Martin Luther King, Jr., and the Southern Christian Leadership Conference* (1986); Kay Mills, *This Little Light of Mine: The Life of Fannie Lou Hamer* (1994); Obituary, *New York Times.* 5 September 1992; Milton Viorst, *Fire in the Streets: America in the 1960's* (1979).

Carol Wilson

Red Summer Black writer and civil rights leader **James Weldon Johnson** coined the phrase *Red Summer* to describe the wave of racial violence that swept through America between late spring and early fall of 1919. As many as 25 incidents have been identified; the major confrontations occurred in Charleston, South Carolina (see **Charleston race riot**); Longview, Texas (see **Longview race riot**); Washington, D.C.; Chicago, Illinois (see **Chicago race riot**), Knoxville, Tennessee; Omaha, Nebraska and Elaine, Arkansas (see **Elaine, Arkansas, race riot**). These episodes varied widely in nature and scale. The deadliest occurred in Chicago, where 38 died during nearly a week of urban warfare, and in Arkansas, where white planters, responding to rumors of black insurrection, massacred over 200 black sharecroppers. The racial violence of 1919 had precedents extending back to slavery days, but its particular intensity has been linked to the unrest of the immediate post–World War I years. The Red Summer coincided with the Red scare—the wave of antiradicalism and xenophobia that followed the 1918 Armistice—and analysts have seen in both a need to find an "inner enemy" to account for unsettling social change. White northerners feared the rapid increase in the black population resulting from wartime migration, while white southerners resented the growing assertiveness of a people they had long dominated. Whites initiated most of the violence in 1919, but blacks fought back, presaging the more militant mood of the 1920s.

Selected Bibliography Richard C. Cortner, *A Mob Intent on Death: The NAACP and the Arkansas Riot Cases* (1988); William M. Tuttle, Jr., *Race Riot: Chicago in the Red Summer 1919* (1970); Arthur I. Waskow, *From Race Riot to Sit-In, 1919 and the 1960's: A Study in the Connections between Conflict and Violence* (1966).

Allan H. Spear

Reeb, James J. (1 January 1927, Wichita, Kan.–10 March 1965, Selma, Ala.). Reeb, a white Unitarian minister, was murdered during civil rights activities in Selma, Alabama. Attacked by club-wielding whites on 8 March 1965, Reeb died from massive head injuries in a Birmingham hospital two days later. Whereas the nation scarcely noticed the murder of a black activist 18 days earlier, Reeb's death prompted a national outcry, including a presidential call to the bereaved family. Reeb's murder, among other such incidents in and around Selma, sparked a demand, particularly from the nation's religious leaders, for federal legislation against civil rights violence. Such legislation was passed in 1968 after the assassination of **Martin Luther King, Jr.**

Selected Bibliography Michael R. Belknap, *Federal Law and Southern Order: Racial Violence and Constitutional Conflict in the Post-Brown South* (1987); Henry Hampton and Steve Fayer, *Voices of Freedom: An Oral History of the Civil Rights Movement from the 1950s through the 1980s* (1990); Jack Mendelsohn, *The Martyrs: Sixteen Who Gave Their Lives for Racial Justice* (1966); *New York Times*, 11–13 March 1965.

Andrew M. Manis

Reid, Ira De A. (2 July 1901, Clifton Forge, Va.–16 August 1968, Haverford, Pa.). Scholar, teacher, writer, activist, and son of a Baptist minister, Reid was raised in both Philadelphia and Georgia. A 1922 graduate of Morehouse College, he studied sociology at the Universities of Chicago and Pittsburgh and in 1939 he received a Ph.D. from Columbia. Supported in his studies by a **National Urban League** (NUL) fellowship, Reid became industrial secretary of the New York Urban League in 1924 and later succeeded **Charles S. Johnson** as NUL director of research and editor of *Opportunity*. During the 1930s, Reid combined roles as sociologist, Urban League official, and race relations adviser to the Roosevelt administration. From 1934 until 1946, he taught sociology at **Atlanta University** and later headed the Department of Sociology and Anthropology at Haverford College. He also edited *Phylon* (1943–46) and wrote extensively on black economic and social life. His *Urban Negro Worker in the United States* (1938) was one of the first major studies on black labor conditions. Reid's expertise in black economics and his Urban League experience led to his appointment in the late 1930s and early war years as a race relations adviser to the Social Security Board and the War Manpower Commission in the Roosevelt administration. Like many black activists and professionals of his time, Reid sought to provide a scientific basis for analyzing and assessing black American racial and class circumstances while working within and outside government for meaningful social programs that responded to those conditions.

After World War II, he remained active both as a sociologist and public advocate for black rights and equal opportunity.

Selected Bibliography *American National Biography,* vol. 18 (1999); Harvard Sitkoff, *A New Deal for Blacks: The Emergence of Civil Rights as a National Issue* (1978); Nancy J. Weiss, *The National Urban League: 1910–1940* (1974); Raymond Wolters, *Negroes and the Great Depression* (1970).

John B. Kirby

***Reitman v. Mulkey,* 387 U.S. 369 (1967)**   This was one of several 1960s cases concerning the issue of housing discrimination. Voters in California supported Proposition 14, which resulted in an amendment to the state constitution prohibiting the state from interfering with the right of individuals to sell or lease property to whomever they chose. The California Supreme Court decided that the amendment violated the U.S. Constitution. The U.S. Supreme Court adjudicated two fair housing cases together: *Reitman v. Mulkey,* and *Prendergast v. Snyder.* The Mulkeys, husband and wife, charged that they had been prevented from renting an apartment because of their race. Another black couple, the Prendergasts, sued their landlord for attempting to evict them, again because of race. The Supreme Court upheld the decision of the California court, five to four. Justice Byron R. White wrote the majority opinion, arguing that the state was a neutral party in housing matters. It did not have an obligation to enforce fair housing practices, but it could not be prevented from doing so. The California amendment, he claimed, had, in effect, legalized discrimination.

Selected Bibliography Derrick A. Bell, Jr., *Race, Racism and American Law* (1980); Rowland L. Young, "Review of Recent Supreme Court Decisions," *American Bar Association Journal* 53 (1967), 753–54.

Carol Wilson

Reparations   Demands for reparations have generally taken two forms: direct compensation paid to individuals, to the former slaves or their descedents; and dollars paid to black communities, to enhance their infrastructure and institutions and to support black economic development. There is no clear dividing line between these approaches, but the passing of the generation born to slavery logically brought about an emphasis on community compensation. In early 1865, Union General William T. Sherman set aside abandoned lands on the Sea Islands off South Carolina and Georgia for former slaves, but in 1866 President Andrew Johnson negated the order. In 1915 an African American named Cornelius Jones filed a $68 million lawsuit against the U.S. Treasury Department, demanding restitution for surviving former slaves and their descendants. Jones argued that, for decades, the federal government had profited from taxes it imposed on cotton grown by uncompensated slave labor. The case was thrown out of court. In 1955, after discovering a passage in a Methodist encyclopedia that said "a captive people have one hundred years to state their judicial claims against their captors or international law will consider you satisfied with your condition," Queen Mother Audley Moore founded the Reparations Committee of Descendants of United States Slaves. Seven years later, a year before the 100th anniversary of the Emancipation Proclamation, the committee filed a claim in California for $500 million, but the case went nowhere. In May 1969, in New York City's Riverside Church, the former executive secretary of the **Student Nonviolent Coordination Committee** (SNCC), **James Forman,** read a manifesto demanding reparations. According to Forman's demands, white churches and synagogues should pay $500 million to black organizations, which would invest it in education and job training, businesses, a black owned media industry, and banks that would keep wealth in black communities. In 1991 economist David Swinton called for reparations of between $700 million and $1 trillion to be invested in African American communities, as compensation for the economic, social, and political inequalities imposed by slavery and a century of **Jim Crow.** Activists have also taken their demands and claims directly to the federal government. In 1989 and again in 1999, Representative John Conyers of Michigan introduced resolutions to the House of Representatives (H.R. 3745 and H.R. 40) calling for a commission to study reparations and a formal apology for slavery. Both times the resolution was voted down. In 1999 Representative Tony Hall proposed House Resolution 356, calling for the U.S. government to acknowledge its role in and apologize for slavery, but it too was rejected. In 1995, in the case of *Cato v. United States,* the Ninth Circuit Court of Appeals decided that reparations claims lacked "legal cognizable basis." Although final, this decision had to be considered in light of recent legal precedent in both the United States and abroad: the official apology and reparations paid to Japanese American citizens who were interred in American concentration camps during World War II; President Bill Clinton's 1993 apology to Hawaiians for American participation in a coup that overthrew the native government a century earlier; settlements made with Native Americans for past injustices; Florida's payment of $2.1 million to the survivors of the 1923 **Rosewood, Florida,** massacre; and the German government paying billions of dollars in reparations to Holocaust survivors. Building on these precedents, a group of African American lawyers, including Harvard Law Professor Charles Ogletree and Johnny Cochran, have organized with the specific purpose of filing a lawsuit against the U.S. government, seeking compensation for the injustices of slavery, and its sequel, **Jim Crow.**

Selected Bibliography Richard America, *Paying the Social Debt: What White America Owes Black America* (1993); Boris Bittker, *The Case for Black Reparations* (1973); "Making the Case for Racial Reparations: Does America Owe a Debt to the Descendants of its Slaves?" *Harper's Magazine* 301 (November 2000), 37–51; Randall Robinson, *The Debt: What America Owes to Blacks* (2001).

Eric Love

Republic of New Africa Brothers Milton Henry (Gaidi Obadele) and Richard Henry (Imari Abubakari Obadele) led the founding in March 1968 of the Republic of New Africa (RNA) with **Robert F. Williams**, who was living in exile in Cuba, as president. The RNA, which during the early 1970s claimed about 2,500 adherents, advocated African American separatism in an independent country that was to include Louisiana, Mississippi, Alabama, Georgia, and South Carolina. African American migration into these states was to provide a popular majority who would gain political control peacefully and then secede. If necessary, African Americans in northern cities would conduct an urban guerilla war. The RNA included a military arm, the Black Legion. In 1971 the RNA dedicated a Mississippi farm as its first sovereign territory. Significant RNA activity ended in August 1971 with a shoot-out between RNA members and FBI agents and local police in Jackson in which one policeman died. Eleven RNA members were imprisoned. The RNA began the modern **reparations** for slavery debate in the late 1960s and early 1970s. This issue has grown in visibility in the twenty-first century with the introduction of bills in the U.S. House of Representatives and frequent debate in the media.

Selected Bibliography Robert H. Brisbane, *Black Activism: Racial Revolution in the United States 1954–1970* (1974); Donald Cunninger, "Bringing the Revolution Down Home: The Republic of New Africa in Mississippi: *Sociological Spectrum* 19 (1999), 63–93; Raymond L. Hall, *Black Separatism in the United States* (1978); *Jackson(Mississippi) Clarion-Ledger,* 28 January 1990.

Lorenzo Crowell

Resurrection City   During the spring of 1968, Dr. **Martin Luther King, Jr.,** and his advisers mapped strategy for a **Poor People's March on Washington** to dramatize the need for the national government to better address the needs of the poor. After King's assassination in April, plans for the march continued under the direction of **Ralph David Abernathy.** Leaving Memphis, Tennessee, on 2 May, the marchers officially began the Poor People's Campaign on 12 May in Washington with a Mother's Day March and an address by **Coretta Scott King,** King's widow. Construction of a temporary town to house the demonstrators began on 11–12 May near the Lincoln Memorial, and was dubbed "Resurrection City" by the campaign's strategists. Consisting chiefly of plywood and tarpaper shacks, Resurrection City was designed to depict the real living conditions of many poor blacks. Bad weather during May turned the campsite into a quagmire, and tension increased between Resurrection City's inhabitants and District of Columbia authorities. On 24 June, District police moved in to clear the area, since the campaign's camping permit had expired. Abernathy and about three hundred others were arrested soon after when they marched on the Capitol to protest the razing of the city.

Selected Bibliography Peter M. Bergman, *The Chronological History of the Negro in America* (1969); Charles E. Fazer, *Uncertain Resurrection: The Poor People's Washington Campaign* (1969); David J. Garrow, *Bearing the Cross: Martin Luther King, Jr., and the Southern Christian Leadership Conference* (1986).

Allen Dennis

Reuther, Walter   (1 September 1907, Effengham, Ill.–9 May 1970, Pellston, Md.). A leader in the United Auto Workers (UAW) from 1936 until his death in a plane crash in 1970, Reuther became the union's president in 1947.

Trained as a tool and die maker, he moved to Detroit, Michigan, in 1927 and attended what is now Wayne State University as a prelaw student while working briefly at Briggs Manufacturing Company and Ford Motor Company from 1927 to 1932. From early 1933 to 1935 Reuther's activities included traveling in Europe and working as a tool and die maker at the Molotov Automobile Works in the Soviet Union. Soon after returning to Detroit in 1936, he was elected to the executive board of the UAW and became president of West Side Local 174. Leading the effort to organize automotive workers in Detroit, Reuther collided with Ford's infamous Service Bureau and he and others were severely beaten. This so-called Battle of the Overpass catapulted Reuther to national prominence. He was elected president of the UAW in 1946 and took control of the executive board in 1947. Reuther's power in the UAW was never seriously challenged, and he became the third president of the Congress of Industrial Organizations in 1952. A powerful figure in labor and politics, Reuther was active in the civil rights movement. He participated in both the **Selma to Montgomery March** and the **March on Washington.**

Selected Bibliography John Barnard, *Walter Reuther and the Rise of the Auto Worker* (1983); Frank Cormier and William J. Eaton, *Reuther* (1970); Jean Gould and Loren Hickok, *Walter Reuther: Labor's Rugged Individualist* (1972); Irving Howe and B. J. Widick, *The UAW and Walter Reuther* (1949); Nelson Lichtenstein, *The Most Dangerous Man in Detroit: Walter Reuther and the Fate of American Labor* (1995); Bruce Nelson, "The Triumph and 'Tragedy' of Walter Reuther," *Reviews in American History* 24 (1996), 488–94.

Clarence Hooker

Revels, Hiram R. (27 September 1827, Fayetteville, N.C.–16 January 1901, Aberdeen, Miss.). In 1870 Mississippi elected Hiram R. Revels, a free-born black Natchez resident, to Jefferson Davis's unexpired term in the U.S. Senate. Educated in Midwestern Quaker seminaries and at Knox College in Galesburg, Illinois, Revels was the first of his race to sit in the U.S. Senate. An African Methodist Episcopal minister, he had spent most of his adulthood tending the spiritual needs of his people, so little politically constructive action was expected of him as a senator. He refused to regard his election as a mere symbolic gesture, however. By nature unassuming and cautious, he supported amnesty for ex-Confederates and urged black moderation in the treatment of former slaveholders. He reminded white America of its debt to blacks for their loyalty during the Civil War and appealed eloquently to Republicans to protect black civil and political rights. Revels failed to convince colleagues that integrating the District of Columbia's schools would lessen racial prejudice, but he won white support and black acclaim for his efforts to integrate the work force in Baltimore's naval shipyard. He encouraged black elevation through education and, following his one year Senate term, he became president of Alcorn State University, in Lorman, Mississippi. Notwithstanding his controversial support for Mississippi Democrats after the overthrow of Republican rule, Revels remained for many late-nineteenth-century blacks a symbol of their hopes and aspirations for full American citizenship.

Hiram Rhoades Revels, African American senator. Photograph by Matthew Brady. © Library of Congress.

Selected Bibliography Robert L. Jenkins, "The Senate Careers of Hiram R. Revels and Blanche K. Bruce" (M.A. thesis, Mississippi State University, 1976); John R. Lynch, *Reminiscences of an Active Life: The Autobiography of John Roy Lynch* (1970); George Sewell and Margaret L. Dwight, *Mississippi Black History Makers* (1977); Julius E. Thompson, "Hiram Rhodes Revels, 1827–1901: A Reappraisal," *Journal of Negro History* 79 (1994), 297–303; Vernon L. Wharton, *The Negro in Mississippi* (1947).

Robert L. Jenkins

Revolutionary Action Movement This Marxist-Leninist revolutionary organization of about fifty dedicated individuals, organized in 1963 by American exile **Robert F. Williams,** intended to wage an urban guerilla war against the U.S. establishment in the cause of African American nationalism. Revolutionary Action Movement (RAM) adherents armed themselves heavily. After raids by the police in New York City and Philadelphia, RAM members were charged in 1967 with planning such terrorist acts as the assassinations of **Roy Wilkins** of the **NAACP** and **Whitney M. Young, Jr.,** of the **National Urban League** and the poisoning of the Philadelphia water supply. In 1968 the RAM collapsed under police pressure.

Selected Bibliography John H. Bracey, Jr., August Meir, and Elliott Rudwick, eds., *Black Nationalism in America* (1970); Robert H. Brisbane, *Black Activism: Racial Revolution in the United States 1954–1970* (1974).

Lorenzo Crowell

Rice v. Arnold, 340 U.S. 848 (1950)   Joseph Rice, a black resident of the city of Miami, sued H.H. Arnold, the superintendent of the Miami Springs Country Club, because his use of the public golf course was restricted to Mondays whereas whites had use of the facilities the other six days. Rice sought **Fourteenth Amendment** "equal protection under the law" compliance to use the golf course without day or hour restriction. The claim was denied. On appeal, the U.S. Supreme Court held, per curiam, that the judgment be vacated and remanded to the Supreme Court of Florida for reconsideration in light of the recent (1950) federal Supreme Court decisions of **Sweatt v. Painter** and **McLaurin v. Oklahoma State Regents.** The Florida Supreme Court concluded that neither case, involving glaring inequalities in segregated higher education, applied to the Rice appeal because the same public golf course facilities were used by both whites and blacks and because neither case voided the separate-but-equal doctrine of **Plessy v. Ferguson.** Because appellant Rice had not properly raised the issue that the regulations failed to grant equal facilities and because he was inappropriately seeking to invalidate legally upheld segregation laws, the Florida Supreme Court affirmed their earlier decision and rejected Rice's petition. On reappeal, the Supreme Court denied certiorari because the Florida case was based on nonfederal issues. Justices Black and Douglas dissented.

Selected Bibliography "Rice v. Arnold," *Minnesota Law Review* 35 (1951), 399–41; "Rice v. Arnold," *Notre Dame Lawyer* 27 (1952), 270–73.

William A. Paquette

Rice v. Elmore, 165 F.2d 387 (4th Cir., 1947)   After the Supreme Court in 1944 overturned the Texas **white primary** in **Smith v. Allwright,** South Carolina attempted to circumvent that decision. On 20 April 1944, the state legislature deleted all statutes relating to primaries on the assumption that without state sanction the Democratic primary became a private matter operating outside the scope of the **Fifteenth Amendment**'s ban against official suffrage discrimination. Represented by **Thurgood Marshall,** the chief counsel of **NAACP,** George Elmore challenged South Carolina's action. On 12 July 1947, Federal District Judge **J. Waties Waring**, an iconoclastic Charleston native who braved the enmity of his neighbors, ruled in favor of the plaintiff. He asserted that as long as the Democratic primary constituted the only real election in the state, blacks were entitled to participate in it. On appeal, Circuit Court Judge John J. Parker, whose nomination to the Supreme Court the NAACP had helped block in 1930, upheld the ruling. After the Supreme Court refused to grant review, further attempts to resurrect the white primary came to an end. In August 1948, 35,000 blacks voted in the South Carolina Democratic primary for the first time.

Selected Bibliography V. O. Key, *Southern Politics in State and Nation* (1949); Steven F. Lawson, *Black Ballots: Voting Rights in the South, 1944–1969* (1976); Henry Lee Moon, *Balance of Power* (1948); Tinsley E. Yarbrough, *A Passion for Justice: J. Waties Waring and Civil Rights* (1987).

Steven F. Lawson

Richmond Planet   See Mitchell, John R., Jr.

Rives, Richard Taylor (15 January 1895, Montgomery, Ala.–27 October 1982, Montgomery, Ala.). Educated in the public schools in Montgomery, Alabama, Rives attended Tulane University in New Orleans, Louisiana, for one year (1911–12) before financial considerations forced him to drop out of school and study law at a Montgomery law firm. Admitted to the Alabama bar in 1914, he rose in the esteem of fellow lawyers to become president of both the Montgomery and the Alabama Bar Associations. In 1941 he was appointed by President Harry S Truman to the **United States Court of Appeals for the Fifth Judicial Circuit,** where he served until his retirement in 1966. During the last six years of his tenure he was chief judge. He spoke with the accent but not the language of segregation. On the Fifth Circuit he was a powerful voice for equal rights and justice for blacks. Together with fellow Fifth Circuit judges **Elbert P. Tuttle, John Minor Wisdom,** and **John Robert Brown,** he helped to ensure the success of the civil rights movement by making the federal courts, and especially the Fifth, a powerful vehicle for social and political change. He was impatient with the delaying tactics employed by southern whites to postpone compliance with the decision in **Brown v. Board of Education,** and he continually reminded fellow southerners that they must obey the law whether they liked it or not. He played a key role in implementing in the lower South the *Brown* decision calling for the desegregation of public schools. He also helped to expand *Brown's* mandate for equality beyond education, joining in landmark decisions issued by the Fifth Circuit Court that swept away barriers of discrimination in jury selection, employment, and voting.

Selected Bibliography Jack Bass, *Unlikely Heroes* (1981); Harvey C. Couch, *A History of the Fifth Circuit, 1891* (1984); J. W. Peltason, *Fifty-eight Lonely Men: The Federal Judges and School Desegregation* (1961).

Charles D. Lowery

Robeson, Paul (9 April 1898, Princeton, N.J.–23 January 1976, New York, N.Y.). The son of William Drew Robeson and Maria Louisa Bustin, he received his elementary, secondary, and college education in the Garden State. In 1915 he won a scholarship to attend Rutgers University. While there, Robeson earned Phi Beta Kappa honors as a junior and was valedictorian of his class. In addition, he was the class debating champion, won 13 varsity letters in four sports, and was a member of the Cap and Skull Honorary Society as well as the Glee Club, the last of which had race restrictions that barred him from traveling with the club. In 1919 Robeson entered Columbia Law School. Following his graduation in 1923, he briefly practiced law in New York City. From 1924 through the 1950s Robeson exhibited remarkable talent on the stage and in film as a concert singer and actor. During this period he performed in concerts throughout the United States and Europe, including the Soviet Union, and starred in over 10 major musicals, movies, and plays, including *Porgy and Bess, Show Boat, Othello,* and *The Emperor Jones.* Robeson received the Donaldson Award for the best acting performance of the year and the Gold

Paul Robeson as Othello, 1944. © Library of Congress.

Medal Award granted by the American Academy of Arts and Sciences for the actor with the best diction.

Robeson was also a political activist. In 1946 he led a delegation of the "American Crusade to End Lynching" to see President Harry S Truman to demand that he sponsor antilynching legislation. In 1949 he called for African Americans, if drafted, to resist. During the midst of the Cold War and the Red Scare, Robeson's name became synonymous with anti-American rhetoric and Communism. During the House Committee on Un-American Activities hearings in 1947, for example, Richard M. Nixon asked Adolphe Menjou how the government could identify Communists. Menjou said it was anyone who attended a Robeson concert or who purchased his record albums. In 1958 the government lifted the ban it had earlier imposed prohibiting Robeson from leaving the United States. From this period until his death in 1976, he spent his time writing, traveling, and occasionally giving public lectures. By the end of the 1960s Robeson had become one of the most recognized Americans in the world. African leaders as well as European governments viewed and honored him as a great civil and human rights advocate. Robeson recorded his remarkable career in his autobiography entitled, *Here I Stand*.

Selected Bibliography Sheila T. Boyle and Andrew Buni, *Paul Robeson: The Years of Promise and Achievement* (2001); Martin Baunt Duberman, *Paul Robeson* (1988); Editors of *Freedomway*, *Paul Robeson: The Great Forerunner* (1985); Paul Robeson, Jr., *The Undiscovered Paul Robeson: An Artistic Journey, 1898–1939* (2001).

Vibert L. White

Robinson, Jackie (31 January 1919, Cairo, Ga.–24 October 1972, Stamford, Conn.). A football, baseball, basketball, and track star at UCLA, Robinson gained national prominence in 1947 when he smashed major league baseball's color bar. Although blacks like **Joe Louis** and **Jesse Owens** were outstanding in boxing and track, organized baseball had been segregated since the 1880s. In 1945 the Brooklyn Dodgers purchased Robinson's contract from the black Kansas City Monarchs. After his brilliant season with their Montreal farm team, the Dodgers promoted him to the majors in 1947 when he was rookie of the year. Robinson survived merciless taunts from players and fans to become the league's most valuable player in 1949, a favorite of blacks and whites, and the first black in baseball's Hall of Fame in 1962. Larry Doby, Leroy "Satchel" Paige and other talented blacks followed his path, and the signing of Elijah "Pumpsie" Green by the Boston Red Sox in 1959 marked the final integration of all major league teams. Subsequent

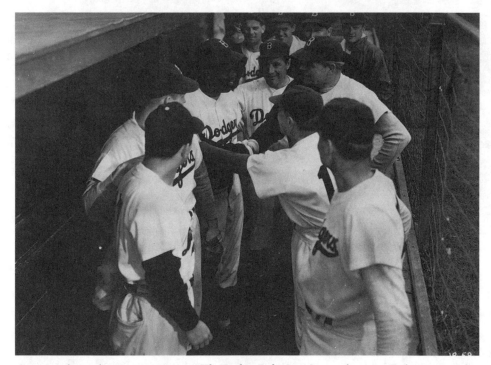

A scene from the motion picture *The Jackie Robinson Story*, showing Robinson in the dugout with fellow Brooklyn Dodgers. © Library of Congress.

participation of blacks in tennis, football, and basketball was a precursor of the later civil rights revolutions.

Selected Bibliography Jonathan Mercantini, "Coming Home: Jackie Robinson and the Dodgers Face the Crackers," *Atlanta History* 41 (No. 3, 1997), 5–18; Arnold Rampersad, *Jackie Robinson: A Biography* (1997); Jackie Robinson, *Baseball Has Done It* (1964); Jules Tygiel, *Baseball's Great Experiment: Jackie Robinson and His Legacy* (1983).

James B. Potts

Rochester, New York, Race Riot (1964)   Situated in Monroe County about 250 miles northwest of New York City, Rochester was considered to be a model city in terms of race relations. Out of a population of 318,611, African Americans numbered 35,000. City planners boasted of their efforts to improve the quality of housing and provide job opportunities for the black residents. Yet there were tensions, mostly centered on subtle forms of discrimination and police actions in the black community. One hot July evening, at a fund raising street dance in the heavily black Genesee Street–Joseph Avenue District, two police arrested a 17-year-old black male on charges of public drunkenness. Remembering the brutal beating of a black teenager the year before and the widely publicized refusal to serve **Richard Claxton (Dick) Gregory** and several black ministers at the Rochester airport in the spring, a crowd of 500 people began smashing windows. The police were reinforced and joined by fire men who turned high pressure hoses on the crowd. By morning the black commercial district (50 blocks) was in a shambles, and the city manager proclaimed a state of emergency. The next night rioting began again: some ten thousand people were in the streets as gangs of white youths joined blacks in smashing shops and stores. The National Guard was called to quell the disturbances. Calm was finally restored on 26 July. Four died, 350 were injured, including 35 policemen, and 800, three-fourths of whom were black, were arrested.

Selected Bibliography "Civil Rights: The White House Meeting," *Newsweek* (3 August 1964); "Crisis in Race Relations," *U.S. News and World Report* (10 August 1964); *Rochester Democrat and Chronicle*, 26, 27 July 1964.

Charles T. Pete Banner-Haley

Rodney King Riot   On 3 March 1991, African American Rodney Glenn King, a high school dropout, drug addict, and convicted felon, refused police orders to step out of his car during a routine traffic stop. The white policemen dragged him out of the car and beat him. A local citizen captured the affair on videotape, portions of which were soon broadcast to an angry Los Angeles television audience. The segment of the videotape that was repeatedly played on the television news seemed to show clear evidence of unnecessary police brutality, but the mostly white jury in Los Angeles surprisingly found the police officers not guilty. A riot in South Central Los Angeles ensued and lasted more than a day and was seen around the world via television. The national public was shocked at the rioters who burned and looted businesses, and attacked white and Asian motorists and innocent passersby. Fifty-two people died,

2,500 were injured, and there was property damage and related costs of nearly a billion dollars. The case against the police officers was appealed, and in the second trial in April 1993, two of the four defendants were convicted. Ironically, prosecutors used video evidence to arrest those responsible for the riots. Los Angeles mayor Tom Bradley had warned of the impending danger of such a riot in the event of a not-guilty verdict and had appealed to the George Bush administration for support, but the president responded slowly and inadequately to the crisis, which was partly responsible for his failed reelection bid in November 1992. This riot revealed the racial turmoil that still existed in the inner cities of the United States more than 20 years after the civil rights movement, as blacks still believed that the predominantly white justice system unfairly targeted and punished them.

Selected Bibliography Stacey Coon, *Presumed Guilty: The Tragedy of the Rodney King Affair* (1992); Robert Deity, *Willful Injustice: A Post–O. J. Look at Rodney King, American Justice, and Trial by Race* (1996); Jewelle Taylor Gibbs, *Race and Justice: Rodney King and O. J. Simpson in a House Divided* (1996); John Robert Greene, *The Presidency of George W. Bush* (2000); Tom Owens with Rod Browning, *Lying Eyes: The Truth behind the Corruption and Brutality of the LAPD and the Beating of Rodney King* (1994); Brenda Wall, *The Rodney King Rebellion: A Psychopolitical Analysis of Racial Despair and Hope* (1992).

Thomas Adams Upchurch and Able A. Bartley

Rogers v. Alabama, 192 U.S. 226 (1904)   Dan Rogers was an Alabama black who had been indicted for murder. In the state trial court, Rogers's attorney moved to quash the indictment on the ground that the juror list from which grand jurors were selected systematically excluded blacks, in violation of the equal protection clause of the **Fourteenth Amendment.** The motion also suggested that juror lists excluded nonvoters, among them blacks who had been wrongly disenfranchised by the Alabama Constitution. The trial court overruled the motion and was upheld by the Alabama Supreme Court, which held that Rogers's two-page motion was too long under Alabama's code of civil procedure. In a unanimous decision, the U.S. Supreme Court overturned the decision of the state court. Delivering the Supreme Court's opinion, Oliver Wendell Holmes dismissed the state's procedural objections, although he did seem to suggest that the claimed suffrage restrictions were irrelevant to Rogers's case. Nevertheless, Holmes noted that prior decisions of the court had barred racial discrimination in grand jury selection and that Rogers had raised a legitimate constitutional issue that the lower courts should have addressed. The case was returned to the Alabama courts for further hearings on Rogers's original motion. Despite Holmes's unambiguous language, the question of racial discrimination in grand jury selection would bedevil the Supreme Court for years to come.

Selected Bibliography Romualdo P. Eclavea, "Construction and Application of Provisions of Jury Selection and Service Act of 1968," in Henry C. Lind, ed., 17 *American Law Reports, Federal* 590 (1973); Marvin E. Frankel and Gary P. Naftalis, *The Grand Jury* (1975); Richard D. Younger, *The People's Panel: The Grand Jury in the United States, 1634–1941* (1963).

Jeff Broadwater

Roosevelt, Eleanor   (11 October 1884, New York, N.Y.–7 November 1962, New York, N.Y.). Wife of President Franklin D. Roosevelt, she became known as a strong defender of racial justice and black equal opportunity. In the late 1920s, she became acquainted with the black educator **Mary McLeod Bethune,** who remained her close friend and adviser on racial issues throughout her life. When the New Deal was launched in the early 1930s, Mrs. Roosevelt sought to link its social and economic programs to the special needs of black Americans. She was instrumental in the selection of Bethune to head the Negro Division of the National Youth Administration. Along with a handful of other racial liberals, Mrs. Roosevelt was a persistent advocate of greater black participation in the federal government and urged her husband and such powerful New Deal officials as Harry Hopkins and Frances Perkins to employ the powers of the federal government in their behalf. Frequently she used her ties to the president to gain Administration support for such concerns as federal antilynching laws. Mrs. Roosevelt was especially close to **NAACP** national secretary, **Walter Francis White,** and in 1934 she arranged a meeting between White and her husband to discuss proposed antilynching legislation. Although no law came out of their conference, Mrs. Roosevelt continued to lobby for such legislation.

Her identification with such prominent black figures as White and Bethune, her entertaining of black groups at the White House, her participation in pro–civil rights organizations such as the **Southern Conference for Human Welfare,** and, during the war, her advocacy of the rights of black workers, nurses, and servicemen, won her the applause of friends and the condemnation of white racists. Her best known championing of racial justice involved her resignation from the Daughters of the American Revolution in 1939 following their refusal to permit noted black singer, **Marian Anderson,** to perform in Constitution Hall. Her support for Anderson won her the coveted NAACP **Spingarn Medal** in 1939.

Although during the post World War II years she sometimes hesitated to fully embrace the civil rights struggles and refused to advocate fundamental changes in American institutions, she remained until her death a close friend and supporter of black Americans. As her long time friend, Walter White, wrote in 1945, Eleanor Roosevelt "gave to many Americans, particularly Negroes, hope and faith which enabled them to continue the struggle for full citizenship."

Selected Bibliography Blanche Wieson Cook, *Eleanor Roosevelt: A Life* (1992); John B. Kirby, *Black Americans in the Roosevelt Era* (1980); Joseph P. Lash, *Eleanor and Franklin* (1971); Nancy J. Weiss, *Farewell to the Party of Lincoln* (1983); Joanna Schneider Zangrando and Robert L. Zangrando, "ER and Black Civil Rights," in Joan Hoff-Wilson and Marjorie Lightman, eds., *Without Precedent* (1984).

John B. Kirby

Roots   In 1976 **Alex Haley** wrote *Roots: The Saga of an American Family,* an historical novel in which he traced six generations of his family lineage from eighteenth-century Africa. After 12 years of research based on family stories

Eleanor Roosevelt presenting a "My People" radio program, devoted to African Americans, in 1943. © Library of Congress.

he had heard while growing up in Tennessee, he discovered the name of his Gambian ancestor, Kunte Kinte. Haley's discovery of the tangible link between his family and its African ancestry recaptured and reaffirmed the African heritage of all African Americans and the richness of their African identity. In telling the personal history of his family, Haley brought to life the oppression and struggles of African Americans as well as their faith, hope, and triumphs. Transformed into the first television miniseries after its publication, *Roots* awakened the consciousness of the nation to the impact of racial discrimination in America. The later controversy over plagiarism accusations against Haley has not dimmed the impact of the book and television series.

Selected Bibliography A'Lelia Bundles, "Looking back at the *Roots* Phenomenon," *Black Issues Book Review* 3 (No. 4, 2001), 12–15; Alex Haley, *Roots: The Saga of an American Family* (1976).

Lillie Johnson Edwards

Rope and Faggot: A Biography of Judge Lynch Walter Francis White's 1929 investigative study of mob lynching centers on the psychological, economic, political, religious and sexual causes of the lynchings that occurred in the late nineteenth and early twentieth centuries. White explains that lynchings functioned as a solution to white America's "Negro problem" and helped to retain the status quo of antebellum race relations. Extralegal lynchings did not take place to protect white womanhood but to control African American social, economic and political progress. Mobocracy, he concludes, could only be checked by the federal government either as a law or as a constitutional amendment. White and other national antilynch law advocates used the study to change public opinion on extralegal lynchings.

Selected Bibliography Donald L. Grant, *The Anti-Lynching Movement: 1883–1932* (1975); Lynching Records, Tuskegee Institute Archives, Tuskegee, Alabama; George C. Rable, "The South and the Politics of Antilynching Legislation, 1929–1940," *Journal of Southern History* 51 (May 1985), 201–20; Walter White, *A Man Called White* (1948); Walter White, *Rope and Faggot: A Biography of Judge Lynch* (1929); Robert L. Zangrando, *The NAACP Crusade against Lynching, 1909–1950* (1980).

Thaddeus M. Smith

Rose McClendon Players Producer Dick Campbell and actress-singer Muriel Rahn founded this community theater group in the late 1930s. Campbell believed that Broadway would continue to reflect stereotypes of African American life and to mistreat black actors. The group's goal, therefore, was to provide a supportive base for black playwrights, producers, and actors. In 1938 the community group was invited to use the auditorium of the 135th Street branch of the New York City Public Library. There they formed the Rose McClendon Workshop Theater in 1939. Among the productions that year were George Norford's *Joy Exceeding Glory*, about Father Divine (see **George Baker**), Abram Hill's *On Striver's Row*, and William Ashley's *Booker T. Washington*. The players thrived until World War II, when the group was disbanded. It was never revived. Its alumni included such notables as Canada Lee, Dooley Wilson, Christola Williams, George Norford, Margerie Strickland Green, Ossie Davis, and Ruby Dee.

Selected Bibliography James Haskins, *Black Theater in America* (1982); Lofton Mitchell, *Black Drama: The Story of the American Negro in the Theater* (1967).

Judith N. Kerr

Rosenwald, Julius (12 August 1862, Springfield, Ill.–6 January 1932, Ravinia, Ill.). A businessman and philanthropist who amassed his fortune through the Sears, Roebuck and Company mail order firm, Rosenwald was a major contributor to African American educational and social institutions. His gifts led to the construction of 25 YMCA buildings for black youth and over 5,000 schools for black children in the rural South. A friend and supporter of **Booker T. Washington,** he shared his philosophy of self-help, and his contributions were usually contingent upon additional funds from the local community. The Julius **Rosenwald Fund,** established in 1917, carried on his philanthropic work until its dissolution in 1948.

Selected Bibliography Edwin Embree and Julia Waxman, *Investment in People: The Story of the Julius Rosenwald Fund* (1949); M. R. Werner, *Julius Rosenwald: The Life of a Practical Humanitarian* (1939).

Allan H. Spear

Rosenwald (Julius) Fund   One of the several philanthropic educational funds founded in the early decades of the twentieth century, the fund was created in 1917 by **Julius Rosenwald,** an Illinois native and president of Sears, Roebuck and Company. Until its demise in 1948, the Fund's program focused on enlarging opportunities for southern African Americans by making funds available for schoolhouse construction, educational programs at high schools and colleges, fellowships for career advancement, support for hospitals and health agencies, development of library services, and improvement of race relations. Rosenwald policy required matching funds from grant recipients for construction of "Rosenwald Schools" and resulted in African Americans contributing a significant portion of the total resources expended for southern schools.

Selected Bibliography James D. Anderson, *The Education of Blacks in the South, 1860–1935* (1988); Edwin R. Embree and Julia Waxman, *Investment in People: The Story of the Julius Rosenwald Fund* (1949); Mabel M. Smythe, ed., *The Black American Reference Book* (1976).

Janice M. Leone

Rosewood, Florida   This city was founded on 10 March 1845, nine miles east of Cedar Key. It had a voting district of 255 people with a post office, African American hotel, Masonic lodge, school, baseball team, and several large, two-story homes. On 1 January 1923 a white woman name Fannie Taylor accused an unidentified African American man of raping her. Police officers organized local whites into posses, numbering between 400 and 500 people, many in Klan uniforms, to find the assailant. Suspicion eventually fell on an escaped convict named Jessie Hunter. The mob attacked Rosewood under the auspices of looking for Hunter. From 1 through 8 January whites ravaged and burned Rosewood, forcing its residents to flee to other areas and thus destroying a once-prosperous African American community. In the mid-1990s, the State of Florida compensated the victims of the attack.

Selected Bibliography Michael D'Orso, *Like Judgment Day: The Ruin and Redemption of a Town Called Rosewood* (1996); Maxine Jones, et al., *The Rosewood Report: A Documented History of the Incident Which Occurred at Rosewood, Florida, in January 1923,* submitted to the Florida Board of Regents, 22 December 1993 (1993).

Able A. Bartley

Ruffin, Josephine St. Pierre   (31 August 1842, Boston, Mass.–13 March 1924, Boston, Mass.). Philanthropist, suffragist, and civil rights activist, Ruffin was educated in the public schools of Salem, Massachusetts and, after 1855, when Boston ended segregation in its schools, at Bowdoin School in Boston. Ruffin's life was one of tireless philanthropic work and social activism on issues relating to civil rights, women's suffrage, and local welfare. She is perhaps best known for her involvement in the women's club movement, founding the Woman's Era Club in 1894 and in 1895 organizing the first national conference of black women. Ruffin's aims were fourfold: to mobilize the energies and unlock the potential of black women, to press for social reforms, to facilitate black uplift, and to demonstrate to whites that blacks were worthy of equal rights. Under Ruffin's direction, women's groups played an important part in the civil rights movement by challenging all forms of social injustice to which women and blacks were subjected.

While never rejecting racial solidarity and self-help, Ruffin was a committed integrationist, as evidenced by her club's willingness to accept members regardless of race or gender, her membership in predominantly white women's clubs, and her opposition to segregated facilities, such as those at the Cotton States and International Exhibition in Atlanta in 1895. Through such positions she offered an alternative to the accommodationist philosophy of **Booker T. Washington** and helped set in motion a process of interracial cooperation that continued into the twentieth century.

Selected Bibliography E. Flexner, *Century of Struggle: The Women's Rights Movement in the US* (1959); E. T. James, ed., *Notable American Women 1607–1950* (1971); J. W. Leonard, ed., *Woman's Who's Who of America: A Biographical Dictionary of Contemporary Women of the U.S. and Canada* (1914); Rayford W. Logan and M. R. Winston, eds., *Dictionary of American Negro Biography* (1982); W. J. Moses, *The Golden Age of Black Nationalism, 1850–1925* (1978); A. H. Zophy and F. M. Karenik, eds., *Handbook of American Women's History* (1990).

Jeffrey Sainsbury

Russell, Daniel Lindsay, Jr. (7 August 1845, Winnabow Plantation, Brunswick County, N.C.–14 May 1908, Belville Plantation, Brunswick County, N.C.). Scion of two prominent Whig planter families in eastern North Carolina, Russell pursued a highly unorthodox political career from the Civil War into the twentieth century. After a brief stint at the University of North Carolina, an abortive career in the Confederate army, and two terms in the North Carolina General Assembly, 1864–66, Russell was admitted to the bar and elected as a Republican in 1868 to a six-year term as judge of the Superior Court of the Fourth Judicial Circuit. In that capacity he rendered an opinion in the 1873 Wilmington "opera house case" that anticipated *Plessy v. Ferguson* (1896). When a theater manager refused to seat a group of blacks, Judge Russell declared that no "public place" could deny a person admittance "only on account of color or race." Russell said the theater could "separate different classes of persons whose close association is not agreeable to each other," but the "accommodations given, the comfort, style, convenience" must be "the same as to all." Russell's political career culminated in his election to the governorship of North Carolina, 1897–1901, in a fusion campaign of Populists and Republicans. During his term the Democrats launched two furious white supremacy campaigns, incited the Wilmington race riot of 1898, enacted **Jim Crow** legislation, and passed a suffrage amendment in 1900 that disfranchised blacks and poor whites.

Selected Bibliography Jeffrey J. Crow and Robert F. Durden, *Maverick Republican in the Old North State: A Political Biography of Daniel L. Russell* (1977); Robert F. Durden, *Reconstruction Bonds and Twentieth-Century Politics: South Dakota v. North Carolina (1904)* (1962).

Jeffrey J. Crow

Rustin, Bayard (17 March 1912, West Chester, Pa.–24 August 1987, New York, N.Y.). Preeminent nonviolent strategist, Rustin helped shape and connect the civil rights and peace movements, before he turned to coalition politics in later life. After five years in the Young Communist League, Rustin became an organizer for the **Fellowship of Reconciliation** (1941) and simultaneously served as youth organizer for the **March on Washington Movement.** He was significant in founding the **Congress of Racial Equality,** served prison time as a conscientious objector (1942–45) and worked on a chain gang following arrest in the 1947 **Journey of Reconciliation.** In 1953 Rustin became Executive Secretary of the War Resisters League. Behind the scenes, he helped guide the **Montgomery bus boycott** and launch and develop tactics for the **Southern Christian Leadership Conference.** He spearheaded civil rights demonstrations at both national party conventions in 1960, was master planner for the 1963 **March on Washington,** was a principal strategist behind the 1964 New York City public schools boycott, and was a leading author of the "Freedom Budget" alternative to Lyndon B. Johnson's **War on Poverty.** After 1964, while executive director of the **A. Philip Randolph Institute,** Rustin advocated a change "From Protest to Politics" and broke with peace movement allies over U.S. foreign policy. A homosexual, he saw the emergence of the gay rights movement as an important extension of the civil rights movement. He declared shortly before his death: "The barometer of where one is on human rights questions is no longer the black community, it's the gay community. Because it is the community which is most easily mistreated."

Selected Bibliography Jervis Anderson, *Bayard Rustin: Trouble I've Seen* (1997); Taylor Branch, *Parting the Waters: America in the King Years, 1954–63* (1989); George Chauncey and Lisa Kennedy, "Time on Two Crosses: An Interview with Bayard Rustin," *The Village Voice* (30 June 1987), 28–29; David J. Garrow, *Bearing the Cross: Martin Luther King, Jr., and the Southern Christian Leadership Conference* (1986); Daniel Levine, *Bayard Rustin and the Civil Rights Movement* (2000); Bayard Rustin, *Down the Line* (1971); Bayard Rustin, *Strategies for Freedom* (1976).

Jo Ann O. Robinson

Bayard Rustin on the platform in 1965. © Library of Congress.